Creating a Business Letter

Use Word's built-in Letter Wizard to save time creating letters. See "Calling on the Letter Wizard First," page 156.

Enter your correspondent's name and address from your electronic address book. See "Using Your Address Books," page 159.

Let Word enter today's date for you automatically. See "Inserting the Date," page 162.

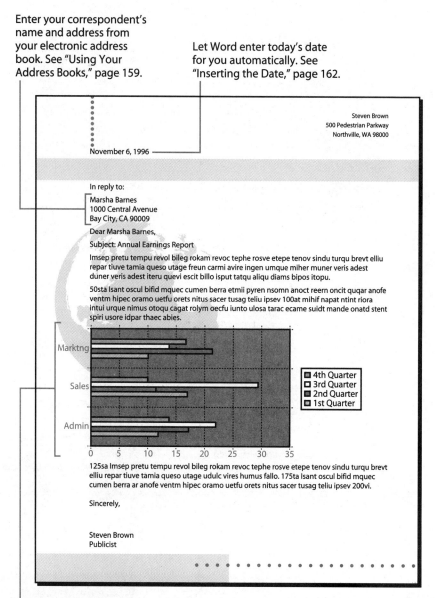

Steven Brown
500 Pedestrian Parkway
Northville, WA 98000

November 6, 1996

In reply to:

Marsha Barnes
1000 Central Avenue
Bay City, CA 90009

Dear Marsha Barnes,

Subject: Annual Earnings Report

Imsep pretu tempu revol bileg rokam revoc tephe rosve etepe tenov sindu turqu brevt elliu repar tiuve tamia queso utage freun carmi avire ingen umque miher muner veris adest duner veris adest iteru quevi escit billo isput tatqu aliqu diams bipos itopu.

50sta Isant oscul bifid mquec cumen berra etmii pyren nsomn anoct reern oncit quqar anofe ventm hipec oramo uetfu orets nitus sacer tusag teliu ipsev 100at mihif napat ntint riora intui urque nimus otoqu cagat rolym oecfu iunto ulosa tarac ecame suidt mande onatd stent spiri usore idpar thaec abies.

Marktng

Sales

Admin

0   5   10   15   20   25   30   35

- 4th Quarter
- 3rd Quarter
- 2nd Quarter
- 1st Quarter

125sa Imsep pretu tempu revol bileg rokam revoc tephe rosve etepe tenov sindu turqu brevt elliu repar tiuve tamia queso utage udulc vires humus fallo. 175ta Isant oscul bifid mquec cumen berra ar anofe ventm hipec oramo uetfu orets nitus sacer tusag teliu ipsev 200vi.

Sincerely,

Steven Brown
Publicist

Insert a chart created in Microsoft Excel. See "Inserting a Chart from Microsoft Excel," page 397.

Print envelopes of various sizes. See "Printing an Envelope," page 198.

About the Author

Russell Borland started as a technical writer for Microsoft Corporation in 1980 and rose to Manager of Technical Publications. In 1984, Bill Gates asked him to join a team to design and develop a new product, code-named Cashmere. This project evolved into Opus, the code name for Word for Windows version 1. Borland helped develop the product specification, the interface design, and the messages in version 1, and wrote the printed documentation.

In 1992, at the age of 46, Borland took up motorcycle riding. His first bike was a 1992 Harley-Davidson FXRS-Con Low-Rider Convertible.

Borland transferred to Microsoft Press in 1988 to write a book about Word for Windows version 1, titled *Working with Word for Windows*. He has since revised this book several times under the title *Running Microsoft Word for Windows*. Borland, now a Master Writer, is also the author of *Microsoft WordBasic Primer, Microsoft Word for Windows 2.0 Macros, Getting Started with Microsoft Windows 3.1, Running Microsoft Mail for Windows 3,* and *Microsoft Exchange in Business*. He is coauthor of *Windows 3.1 Companion* and *Windows for Workgroups Companion*. All of these books are published by Microsoft Press.

Borland earned a bachelor of arts degree from Whitworth College, a master of arts degree from Portland State University, and a Ph.D. from the University of Washington.

In 1992, at the age of 46, Borland took up motorcycle riding. His first bike was a 1992 Harley-Davidson FXRS-Con Low-Rider Convertible. He named this bike "Gloria" and its engine "Lore," the Evo Twin. In 1993, Borland traded Gloria for a blue 1993 Harley-Davidson FLHS Electra Glide Sport, which he named "Blake." Whenever possible, Borland rides Blake back and forth the 90 miles from his home at the base of Sauk Mountain to the Microsoft corporate campus.

RUNNING

Microsoft® Word 97

Russell Borland

Microsoft Press

PUBLISHED BY
Microsoft Press
A Division of Microsoft Corporation
One Microsoft Way
Redmond, Washington 98052-6399

Library of Congress Cataloging-in-Publication Data pending.

Printed and bound in the United States of America.

1 2 3 4 5 6 7 8 9 QMQM 2 1 0 9 8 7

Distributed to the book trade in Canada by Macmillan of Canada, a division of Canada Publishing
Corporation.

A CIP catalogue record for this book is available from the British Library.

Microsoft Press books are available through booksellers and distributors worldwide. For further
information about international editions, contact your local Microsoft Corporation office. Or
contact Microsoft Press International directly at fax (206) 936-7329.

Acquisitions Editor: Kim Fryer
Project Editors: Lucinda Rowley, Saul Candib

Chapters at a Glance

Table of Contents

For my mother, Dorotha Borland, who gave me life,
and for Retta, who daily brings me back to it.

Acknowledgments

I t is with deep gratitude that I acknowledge the contributions of my project editors, Lucinda Rowley, who started the project off; and Saul Candib, who carried it through to completion.

Thanks go to Lisa Labrecque and her staff: Tory McLearn for project management, Judith Brown for manuscript editing, Terry O'Donnell for technical editing, and to the others at Labrecque who performed proof-reading, composition, typography, and production.

And to all the members of the acquisitions, production, manufacturing, marketing, sales, and distribution groups at Microsoft Press, thank you for getting this book into the hands of the people for whom it is intended.

Lazaruss Acres, 1996

Introduction

Microsoft Word 97 is a powerful word processing program that you use primarily for letters, memos, and reports. From this basic usage, you can extend your word processing prowess to forms, form letters, résumés, presentations, and even books and World Wide Web pages.

How This Book Is Organized

This book guides you through a strategic selection of Word's features. At the beginning of this book, you'll find a summary of the new features in Word 97 and a guided tour, which briefly introduces most of Word's features. Then you'll find chapters for the various types of Word documents. Information about features appears in the chapters on the types of documents for which they are most useful; for example, the chapter on reports covers tables and charts. Finally, four appendixes describe the many ways that you can customize Word.

Who This Book Is For

This book is for beginners and intermediate users. It contains step-by-step instructions for setting up the various types of documents. This book also contains a CD-ROM, which provides instructions for examples to extend your knowledge of Word's powers. By the time you finish this book, most of your colleagues will think of you as some kind of "Word guru."

Conventions Used in This Book

Because Windows 95 is so very "mouse-centric," most of the instructions in this book are based on the mouse actions for using Word. In most cases, keyboard methods are omitted. Where keystrokes appear, the name for the key usually appears with an initial capital letter (the Move key). Shortcut keys are indicated with plus signs: Alt+Ctrl+1, for instance, means that you should press all three keys at the same time. Filenames are shown in mixed case because Windows 95 lets you use any combination of uppercase and lowercase letters in your filenames.

Wherever you see the "See Also" icon, you'll find references to sections of the book or files on the CD that provide more information.

Using the Companion CD

Bound into the back of this book is a CD-ROM disc. The companion CD contains an on-line, HTML version of this book; Microsoft Internet Explorer; and the book's sample files.

Installing Microsoft Internet Explorer 3.0

While you can use most Web browsers to view the online version of this book, the text is best viewed in Microsoft Internet Explorer 3.0. For this reason, a copy of Internet Explorer 3.0 is included on the CD. When you run the installation program, you will be able to add some extras to your browser, such as NetMeeting, Comic Chat, Microsoft Internet Mail & News, and ActiveMovie.

To install Internet Explorer from the CD, choose Run from the Start menu, and then type *d:\IE30\setup.exe* in the Run dialog box (where *d* is the drive letter of your CD-ROM drive.) Then follow the instructions for installation as they appear.

When you run Internet Explorer after installing it, you will see the Internet Connection Wizard. This wizard helps you set up an account with an Internet service provider or establish a connection to your current service provider. (You do not have to be connected to a service provider to use the files on the CD.)

Viewing the Online Version of the Book

The online version of *Running Microsoft Word 97* provides easy access to every part of the book, and the powerful search feature will help you find the information you're looking for in record time.

You can use Internet Explorer (or another browser if you prefer) to view the book on line. Access the CD's home page by choosing Run from the Start menu and entering *d:\contents.htm* in the Run dialog box (where *d* is the drive letter of your CD-ROM drive). This will display the *Running Microsoft Word 97* home page in your default browser, from which you can choose to view the book on line.

Accessing the Book's Sample Files

You can use the book's sample files for hands-on exploration or as templates for your own work. Many of the sample files are examples with step-by-step instructions to help you accomplish complex or interesting tasks with Word. You can either install the sample files on your hard disk or access them directly from the companion CD.

To install the sample files on your hard disk, be sure the companion CD is in your CD-ROM drive. Choose Run from the Start menu, and then type *d:\samples\setup.exe* (where *d* is the letter of your CD-ROM drive). Then follow the instructions for installation as they appear.

If you prefer, you can use the sample files directly from the CD without installing them on your hard disk. Note, however, that you cannot update any of the sample files directly on the CD. If you want to make changes to the data, use the Setup program to copy the samples onto your hard disk.

Note that you can also access the sample files from the CD's home page. (See the instructions on the previous page.)

Additional Information

In addition to access to the online version of this book and to the book's sample files, the CD's home page offers access to the Microsoft Knowledge Base, the Microsoft Press home page, and e-mail links to the authors.

If you have comments, questions, or ideas regarding this book or the companion disc, please write to Microsoft Press at the following address:

> Microsoft Press
> Attn: Running Series Editor
> One Microsoft Way
> Redmond, WA 98052-6399

You can also send feedback to Microsoft Press via electronic mail at mspinput@microsoft.com. Please note that product support is not offered through this e-mail address.

PART I

Getting Started

What's New in 97

Microsoft Word 97 contains some new features and many changes to features in previous versions. The list on the following pages summarizes what's new for Word 97 and gives the chapters where you'll find details.

Editing Features and Tools

These Word 97 features help to simplify the editing process as you develop your documents.

- **Grammar checking as you type.** Word can check your grammar as you type, just as it checks spelling as you type. See Chapters 2 and 3.

- **AutoText enhancements.** AutoText contains many of the common entries you need to complete a specific type of document.

  One feature of AutoText is AutoComplete. As you type, Word can display tags at the insertion point that suggest a probable completion of a word you've started typing. For example, if you type *Jan*, Word proposes January. AutoComplete uses all the entries in AutoText and AutoCorrect to propose completions. So, where you once had to type an abbreviation for AutoText and press F3 to insert it, you now simply start typing the AutoText name. Word proposes the complete name, you press Enter, Word inserts the AutoText, and you continue typing. You can also ignore the suggestions and simply keep typing, and you can turn them off. See Chapters 2, 3, and 19.

- **Table drawing.** The new drawing tools make it possible to draw a table to the size and cell arrangement you want. The table drawing tool lets you add cell borders, color them, change their line width, and erase cell borders to merge cells. You can now also merge cells down columns. See Chapter 8.

- **New drawing tools.** Word shares in the enhanced drawing tools that are part of the Office 97 package. See Chapter 10.

- **Comment tags.** When you're reviewing a document and see a comment reference mark (formerly called annotation reference mark), simply position the mouse pointer over the comment reference mark, and Word displays a tag that shows you who added the comment and the text of the comment. See Chapter 13.

Formatting Features and Tools

These Word 97 features make it even easier for you to enhance your documents.

- **Visual styles.** The Styles box on the Formatting toolbar shows the name of the style in the font and size in which the text will appear. Word contains a number of new styles, including four styles for hypertext and hyperlinks—two of these styles show that the link has not been traveled (read) and two show that the link has been read. You can also give a style an outline level as part of its style definition, which makes it easier to collect titles and headings that aren't heading styles in a table of contents. See Chapters 2 and 22.

- **Borders and shading for words.** Now you can give any selection a border and shading, not only paragraphs. (You can still apply borders to paragraphs, too.) See Chapters 2 and 10.

- **Page borders.** Word gives you a simple way to add a page border, using either lines or supplied images. See Chapter 3.

- **Text boxes.** Frames have been replaced with text boxes. Text boxes are based on the new drawing tools. (Text boxes have been brought into the mainstream of document work from the drawing arena where you used text boxes to add text or pictures to a drawing.) Text boxes can be linked to flow text from one box to the next. With this linking, you can set up articles and sidebars that continue on a different page and not have to worry about cutting and pasting to get it just right. See Chapters 8, 9, and 10.

- **Text direction.** In table cells and text boxes, you can set the text direction to horizontal or vertical. For vertical, you have two choices—to read from the right side or to read from the left side. See Chapters 8 and 10.

- **Enhanced shading.** Shading is no longer simply colors and patterns. For shading you can now also choose gradient colors (one color gradually changes to another) in a variety of directions across the shaded area, texture (wallpaper patterns), and even a picture. See Chapter 10.

■ **Floating toolbars.** These are submenus for certain commands or buttons that you can "tear off" and drag into the Word window as floating toolbars. This gives you immediate access to the submenu's options when you are using them repeatedly. See Chapters 2, 3, and 10.

■ **List lead-in emphasis.** If you start a bulleted or numbered list with a special font style (bold, italic, and so on) to emphasize the beginning of each list item (like this list you're reading), Word automatically applies the same font style to the beginning of the next item in the list as you start typing it and turns it off at the appropriate place. See Chapter 13.

■ **Online view.** With this new view, you can see how your document will appear online as a Web page. In this view, you can see a Background, a new feature that lets you add any of the shading choices to your Web page or other online document. See Chapter 21.

■ **Online and Web documents.** Word benefits from the Microsoft Internet strategy. Not only can you save documents in HTML format, but AutoFormat now recognizes and converts Internet addresses and document pathnames to hyperlinks. Thus, you and your readers simply click a hyperlink to jump to another Web page or document. See Chapters 21 and 22.

Other Helpful Tools

Whether you need helpful information or convenient access to a tool, these Word 97 features can help you streamline your work.

■ **Office Assistant.** A new Office Assistant, a cartoon character, serves as a guide to help you set up documents and find helpful information when you're stuck. The Office Assistant gives you a box to type in a question in your own words, and then compiles a list of help topics related to your inquiry. See Chapter 2.

■ **Floating Toolbars.** Various menu commands and toolbar buttons have submenus that you can "tear off" and drag into the Word window as floating toolbars. When you're using a command or several commands from the same submenu repeatedly, you can drag the submenu out as a floating toolbar to make the commands quickly accessible to your work. See Chapters 2 and 10.

- **New wizards.** Word's wizards have been enhanced, especially the Letter Wizard, which not only helps you set up various types of letters, but also helps you with setting up envelopes and mailing labels. See Chapters 2, 3, 6, 7, 15, 17, and 21.

- **New macro language.** WordBasic is replaced by Visual Basic for Applications. Now all the Microsoft Office programs use the same programming language. Visual Basic for Applications is not covered in this book. See *Microsoft Word 97/Visual Basic Step by Step*, by Michael Halvorson and Chris Kinata (Redmond: Microsoft Press, 1997).

Document and File Management Features

These Word 97 features help you manage your documents and find the information you want faster.

- **Background saving.** When you save a document after the initial save, Word saves the document in the background. This means that you can just keep working, and Word writes your changes to the disk file without interrupting your work. See Chapter 2.

- **Select Browse Object button.** This new button on the vertical scroll bar gives you 10 ways to browse and scroll through your document. Clicking this button displays a menu of buttons for browsing by Go To, Find, edits, headings, graphics, tables, fields, endnotes, footnotes, comments (formerly called annotations), sections, and pages. See Chapter 2.

- **Version control.** Word gives you an enhanced way to save various versions of a document. Because you can set up a Word document for several people to work on at once, Word can keep track of who made what changes and when in a list of versions. See Chapter 13.

- **AutoSummarize.** With the new AutoSummarize command, you can have Word create a summary of the key points of a document. This feature should be handy for creating executive summaries. See Chapter 14.

■ **Document map.** A document map shows you the various headings and parts of a document. It's similar to an outline, but Word sets it up automatically. You can use the document map to navigate to the various parts of a document to see what's there without tediously scrolling a page at a time. See Chapter 21.

CHAPTER 2

Guided Tour: Eight Stations of a Document

This chapter attempts to give you some sense of the stages you take a document through to complete it. Along the way, as you read about each stage—called "stations" here—you'll see a brief introduction to a variety of tools and powers you can call on in Word to help with your work. Of course, at each end of the line, you have to start and quit Word.

The eight stations I've identified and used to structure this chapter are by no means rigid, sequential steps. After you start a document, you'll probably save it many times before you complete it. (In fact, you're well advised to save your documents often, rather than wait until you've done all the work.) Likewise, you will probably format the document as you type, or let Word do that for you, as well as proofread it (check the spelling and grammar). You might produce a printed copy of the document at some intermediate stage. Such is the topsy-turvy nature of document preparation, but presenting the stations in spaghetti fashion doesn't help you learn or see what you need to know.

Like eight strands of spaghetti dropped onto a plate, the processes in the eight stations described in this chapter can crisscross, overlap, intertwine, and jumble. All I've done in this chapter is separate the eight strands so that you can see more easily what they are and how they relate to Word 97.

Start Microsoft Word

Obviously, before you can produce documents with Word, you have to start it up. You can start Word using any of the following methods:

- Clicking the Windows 95 Start button

- Clicking an icon on the Office shortcut bar

- Opening a My Computer or Explorer window

- Starting Word automatically when you start Windows 95

Start Button

The Start button on the Windows 95 taskbar contains four commands that you can use to start Word: Programs, Documents, New Office Document, and Open Office Document.

Programs Command

To start Word the most direct way, simply select Microsoft Word on the Programs submenu. Word starts and creates a blank document based on the Normal template.

Documents Command

The Documents submenu contains the names of the documents you have worked on recently. The submenu can contain both Word documents and Word templates (if you had a template open to work on it), as well as files for any other Windows-based program. To start Word and open a particular document or template, choose the document or template name from the Documents submenu.

New Office Document

When you choose the New Office Document command from the Windows 95 Start button, you see the New Office Document dialog box, which looks something like the one shown on the next page.

1 Select the tab for the category of document you want to create.

2 Select a template for the type of document you want to create.

3 Click OK.

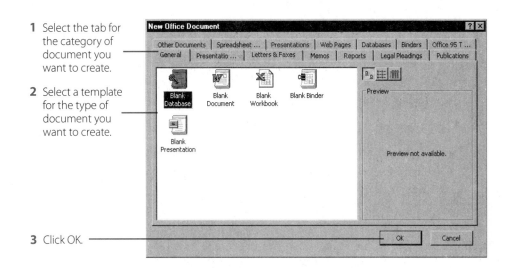

You can use the New Office Document command to start any Office 97 program and create the type of document you want. All you do is select the template you want to use. Office opens the correct program for working on the document and creates a document based on the template you chose.

Open Office Document

When you choose the Open Office Document command from the Windows 95 Start button, you see the Open Office Document dialog box, which looks something like the one shown here:

1 If necessary, select the disk and folder that contain the document you want to open.

2 Select the document or template you want to work on.

3 Click Open.

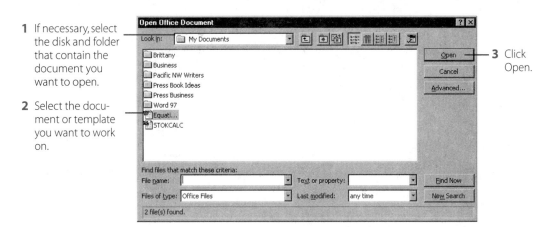

You can use the Open Office Document command to start any Office 97 program and open the document you select in the Open Office Document dialog box. All you do is select the document you want to open. Office opens the correct program for working on the document.

Desktop Shortcut

If you set up a shortcut to a Word document or template on your Windows desktop, simply double-click the shortcut icon to start Word, and open the document or create a document from the template.

> If you installed a stand-alone version of Word (as opposed to installing Word as part of Office 97), the New Office Document command, Open Office Document command, and Office Shortcut Bar methods will not be available to you.

Office Shortcut Bar

When you install Office 97, the Setup program adds the Office shortcut bar to your Windows 95 startup sequence. The Office shortcut bar can have several panels. At the very least, it has an Office panel, which looks pretty much like the one shown here:

Click here to create a new Word or other Office document (same as selecting the New Office Document command).

Click here to open a Word (or other Office) document (same as selecting the Open Office Document comand).

You can also turn on a Favorites panel on the Office shortcut bar. Onto the Favorites panel, you can add a folder or a document. If you add a document and then click its icon, you start Word and open the document associated with the icon. If you add a document template and then click its icon, you start Word and create a document based on that template. If you click a folder, Windows opens the folder, where you can double-click a document icon to start Word and open that document.

To add the Favorites panel to the Office shortcut bar, take these steps:

1 Right-click the Office shortcut bar.

2 Select Favorites from the shortcut menu.

To add a folder to the Favorites panel of the Office shortcut bar, take these steps:

1 Click the Favorites icon on the Office shortcut bar to display the Favorites panel.

2 Right-click the Favorites panel, and then select Customize from the shortcut menu.

3 Click the Buttons tab.

4 Click the Add Folder button.

5 Switch to the folder you want to add, and then click the Add button.

6 Click OK.

 TIP

> If you want to add more than one folder, more than one document, or both folders and documents to the Favorites panel, simply click the Add File or Add Folder button again rather than clicking OK after you add each folder or document.

To add a document to the Favorites panel of the Office shortcut bar, take these steps:

1 Click the Favorites icon on the Office shortcut bar to display the Favorites panel.

2 Right-click the Favorites panel, and then select Customize from the shortcut menu.

3 Click the Buttons tab.

4 Click the Add File button.

5 Switch to the disk and folder that contain the document you want to add.

6 Select the document you want to add, and then click the Add button.

7 Click OK.

My Computer or Explorer Window

To start Word with a specific document, double-click the My Computer icon on the Windows desktop or open Windows Explorer, switch to the folder that contains the document you want to open, and then double-click the document's icon in the window.

When You Start Windows 95

If you use Word almost every day, consider setting up Word to start whenever you start Windows 95. It takes a little longer to start Windows 95 with this method, but you won't have to start Word separately.

To start Word each time Windows 95 starts, do the following:

1 Click the Start button, select Settings, and then click Taskbar.

2 Click the Start Menu Programs tab.

3 Click the Add button.

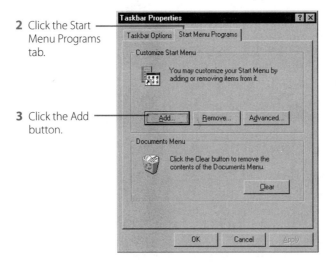

4 In the Create Shortcut dialog box, click the Browse button.

5 Find and select the Word program (Winword.exe), and then click the Open button. Windows 95 inserts the proper command line for you in the Command Line box of the Create Shortcut dialog box, as shown next.

TIP

If you put Word where Setup suggested, you'll find your Word program in the Office folder inside the Microsoft Office folder inside the Program Files folder on drive C.

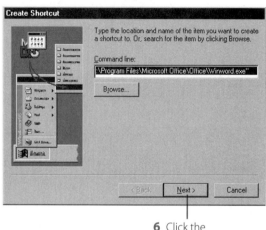

6 Click the
Next button.

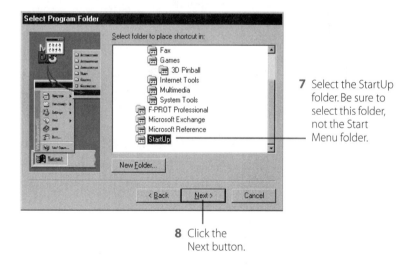

7 Select the StartUp
folder. Be sure to
select this folder,
not the Start
Menu folder.

8 Click the
Next button.

Getting Started

9 Either accept the proposed title or type a new title.

10 Click the Finish button.

11 Click OK in the Taskbar Properties dialog box.

Now if you click the Start button, select Programs, and then select StartUp, you'll see the title you gave Word 97 listed, and Word will automatically start the next time you start Windows 95.

What You See in the Word Window

When Word starts, you see a window, toolbars, ruler, and document—something like Figure 2-1.

FIGURE 2-1.
This Word window displays a blank document in Page Layout view.

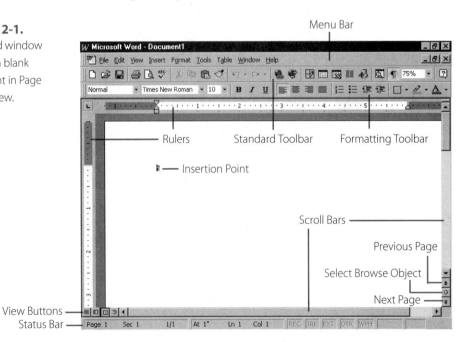

If you start Word with a particular document or from a particular template, you'll see that document or a new document based on that template. If you start Word without specifying a document or template, you'll see a blank document, as shown in Figure 2-1.

Station 1: Set Up

Aller Anfang ist schwer. "The first step is the hardest." So goes the German proverb. Setting up a document can be time-consuming and even very difficult, especially when you're staring at a blank page. "What do I want to put on these pages?" "What do I put where?" "How do I get my pearls to shine?" These and other similar questions can plague your creativity at the start. Word provides three tools that can help you get past these hurdles and make the first step easier:

■ Office Assistant

■ Wizards

■ Document templates

Office Assistant

Word shares the new helper called Office Assistant, which displays an animated character and a text balloon. Office Assistant provides two kinds of help. First, it can provide steps for completing a task. You'll see this kind of help with the Letter Wizard.

Second, Office Assistant can provide a list of topics in response to a question you type. To get this second kind of help, either press F1 or click the Office Assistant button on the Standard toolbar.

Office
Assistant

When you turn on Office Assistant, you see the character and a balloon, something like the one in the graphic on the next page.

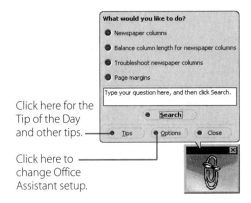

Click here for the Tip of the Day and other tips.

Click here to change Office Assistant setup.

When you click the Options button in the Office Assistant balloon, you see the Office Assistant dialog box with one of the two tabs—Options or Gallery—showing:

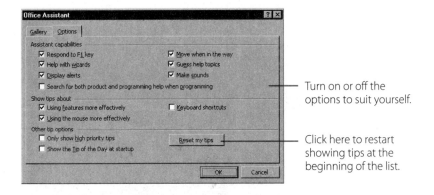

Turn on or off the options to suit yourself.

Click here to restart showing tips at the beginning of the list.

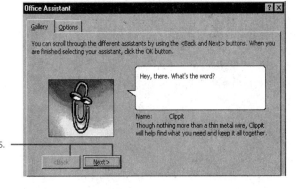

Click Next or Back to see the nine Assistant characters.

Wizards

Word comes with a number of wizards, which display panels that ask you questions. Your job is to answer the questions. The wizard then creates an appropriate document based on your answers. After the wizard creates the document, you simply fill in the necessary text and art to complete the document. You'll find discussions of the wizards in Chapters 3, 6, 7, and 17.

Document Templates

A template is a pattern, model, or plan for creating a new product. A tailor's pattern for a jacket is a template. At the simplest level, tracing around the end of a soup can to draw a circle can be considered to be using a template. In Microsoft Word, templates are used for creating documents.

If you simply start Word, Word opens a new blank document, based on the Normal template. When you create a document, however, you can instead select a special template that works together with the Normal template to help you create and work on a document. Special document templates (templates other than the Normal template) give Word its ability to adapt to specific work.

A special template sets up common text and adjusts the menus, toolbars, and keys to turn Word into a specialized word processor for a particular type of document. A typical special document template contains some common text and fonts, which means that every document you create from that special template contains the same basic text, formatted and positioned in the same way. For example, by creating all your memos from a memo document template, you ensure that your memos match your memo standard.

Document templates can also supply special styles and AutoText and document-specific macros, menus, shortcut keys, and toolbars. A template can run any macros you want before you begin working.

A special template's true power becomes obvious when you work on a variety of documents at the same time. For example, suppose that you're working on a letter in one window, a memo in another, and a report in a third. As you switch to each window in turn, the AutoText, styles, menus, shortcut keys, macros, and toolbars can change for each document. The special document template makes each window a construction zone specially set up for working on the active document.

You can change the special template attached to a document. You'll do this to supply tools and materials that you want to use on the document but that the current special template does not contain. If you change the special template to Normal, you in effect make no special template available for your work on the document.

One more note about special templates: you can add any special template to your supply of tools and materials for your work on any document. You add these special templates as global templates so that you can use their AutoText entries, styles, macros, menus, shortcut keys, and toolbar changes.

With all these templates supplying so much material and tools, what should you use where? In part, of course, that's a personal decision. You, as document project manager, decide when and where to use which materials and tools. At the same time, Word gives you some help in this task. Word is set up to prefer some areas of the warehouse (some templates) over others. Knowing where and when a template affects your work allows you to use templates powerfully. That's the topic of "Understanding Where and When Templates Work," page 24.

You'll find information about document templates in almost every chapter of this book. In particular, see Chapter 19, "Using Word's Blank Document Template," and Chapter 20, "Using Other General Templates and Add-Ins."

Fabricating Your Own Templates

Before long, you'll probably find good reasons to fabricate your own templates. If you find yourself opening an old document and making changes to build a new document, you're ready to fabricate a template.

You can fabricate document templates three ways:

- By building or changing a document and saving it as a template. You typically use this method when you've built a document and want to use its setup (that is, its styles and fonts, its AutoText entries, and some of its text) to build more documents. This method is the simplest of the three.

■ By transforming an existing template and saving it. You can save the changed template with the same name to make the template yours. This is the method you use to make Word's templates fit your work. Or you can save the changed template with a new name to have a new template. Use this method when the existing template's setup is similar to what you need and requires few alterations. Also use this method when you want to keep the old template as it is.

■ By building a new template based on an existing template. The new template inherits the setup of the original template. You then change the template to suit your document needs. This is the method that you'll use most often throughout this book.

The following sections and example show you the basic steps for fabricating a template.

Analyze

Analyze typical examples of the type of document you want to create from your template. Answer the following questions:

■ What text is common to all the examples?

■ Can any text of a similar type be spawned by fields?

■ What layout and fonts do the documents have? Is there a style sequence in most documents of this type—for example, Normal text following headings; extra space following tables; citations following quotations; or a byline, an abstract paragraph, and Normal text following a title?

■ Which commands will you use often? Which commands will you never use? And which commands will you use occasionally?

■ What macros would be useful? Would any of these macros be handier if assigned to a menu, shortcut keys, or a toolbar?

Plan

Plan the AutoText, styles, and macros you need. Jot down their text, fonts, and actions.

Build

You want Word to store all this work in your new template, so if a dialog box gives you a choice of templates, select your new one. To build the new template, do the following:

1 Choose the File New command, select the Blank Document icon (which is the Normal template) as your base template from the list in the General tab in the New dialog box, select the Template option, and click OK.

2 Add the text that will be the same in every document.

3 Insert fields for text that is similar in type but unique to each document (for example, the date).

4 Set up AutoText.

5 Build styles. Choose the Format Style command, and for places in the document where you can predict the sequence of styles, select a style for next paragraphs in the New Style or Modify Style dialog box.

6 Record or write macros. Assign to menus, shortcut keys, or toolbars any macros and commands that you'll use often.

Save

Save the template, give it a name, and add a description. To do so, perform these steps:

1 Choose the File Properties command, and then select the Summary tab.

2 Type a description of the template's purpose in the Title box, turn on the Save Preview Picture check box, and then click OK.

3 Choose the File Save As command.

4 Type a name in the File Name box of the Save As dialog box that indicates the type of documents you will create from this template, and click OK.

Things Templates Can Contain

A document template is a document building plan: you tell Word to build a new document from a document blueprint—the template—and the template lays out, inserts, and formats the standard building materials for documents that you create. Here is a list of the building materials and tools a document template can provide:

- Page setup—paper settings, margins, section layout

- Standard contents—text and artwork that appear on pages and in headers and footers of every document of the type you are creating a template for

- AutoText—standard text or art that you need to insert in various places in a document

- AutoCorrections—text or art you want to insert as you type, either to correct typing mistakes or simply to transform a small word or abbreviation into something longer

- Fonts—formatting choices for text characters

- Language—the primary language setting for a document; for example, you can set the language for a letter that goes to a correspondent in a country where the language is different from yours

- Styles—formatting and layout of paragraphs and special phrases

- Toolbars—modified versions of the toolbars built into Word and custom toolbars you create yourself to present the buttons most useful to you while working on a particular type of document

- Menus—changes to the menus, including renaming them, changing their order, adding new menus, removing unnecessary or unwanted menus, and changing the commands, their names, and their positions on the menus

- Key assignments—changes to the actions a key or key combination performs

- Macro project items—macros that perform actions suited to a particular type of document

Understanding Where and When Templates Work

To understand and use templates most effectively, you need to understand where and when the materials and tools can work. Materials and tools can belong to a document, a template, or the global village, as listed here and shown in Figure 2-2.

- Document—materials and tools for a single document only

- Template—materials and tools for documents that use a particular template only; a template can also shut off tools in documents that use the template

- Global—the materials and tools for all documents

FIGURE 2-2.
The where and when of building materials and tools in Word.

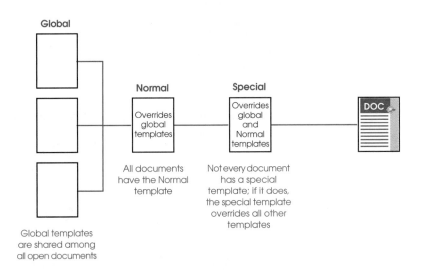

When you set up text, AutoText, styles, macros, menus, shortcut keys, and toolbars, you can set them up in a document, a special template, or a global template. For example, you usually add text to a document. You can, however, add text to a special template so that it appears automatically in any new documents you create from the template. Likewise, you usually build a style in a specific document, but it's much more powerful to build a style in a template so that you can use the style in many documents.

Word has preferences. When the building materials stored in a document differ from the document's special template or global template, Word favors the document. Word favors documents over special

Getting Started

templates, and special templates over global templates. Tools used in a special template block global tools.

Word favors the macros, menus, and shortcut keys stored in a special template over those in the Normal template and other global templates. The tools used in the special template override the same tools in the global templates. If the special template contains no overriding tools, Word supplies tools from the global templates.

Toolbars

A toolbar is a strip that contains buttons. When you click a button, Word performs an action. Word provides a great many toolbars to help you with your work.

To display or hide a toolbar, take these steps:

1 Right-click any visible toolbar or the menu bar.

2 On the Toolbars shortcut menu, click the name of the toolbar you want to display or hide. If the toolbar you want to display isn't listed on the shortcut menu, use the steps for displaying or hiding several toolbars at once.

To display or hide several toolbars at once, take these steps:

1 Choose the View Toolbars command, and select Customize from the submenu.

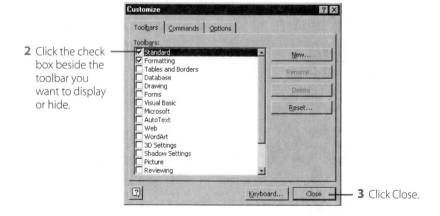

2 Click the check box beside the toolbar you want to display or hide.

3 Click Close.

TIP

Instead of choosing the View Toolbars command, you can right-click any visible toolbar, and then select Customize from the shortcut menu.

Floating Toolbars

Some of the buttons on toolbars display menus. Some of these menus have a thin stripe across the top border. When you see this stripe, you can display the toolbar button menu as a floating toolbar. Some of the commands on a toolbar button menu also display a submenu. In many cases, you can also display these submenus as floating toolbars. A floating toolbar looks like and acts like a toolbar.

To display a toolbar button menu as a floating toolbar, take these steps:

1 Click the toolbar button to display its menu. If you want to display a submenu of a toolbar button menu command as a floating toolbar, open the submenu.

2 Drag the top stripe into the Word window. Word displays the menu as a floating toolbar. The floating toolbar displays buttons in place of the text names on the toolbar button menu.

Here is an example of a toolbar button with a menu that can appear as a floating toolbar and a submenu that can appear as a floating toolbar:

Two sample floating toolbars taken from the preceding menus are shown next.

Station 2: Flesh Out

You have several ways to pour words into a document: you can type them using the keyboard and get Word to complete some of the words for you; place them from AutoText entries (a Word feature that allows you to store words and later insert them into a document); or use retyping, repeated actions, and overtyping. And you can, of course, erase words and undo the actions you take with words.

Typing Tips: Word AutoComplete

In Word 97, AutoComplete can perform more completion actions when you type. You type the first three letters of some words, and if the word contains at least three more letters (it's at least six letters long), Word can complete the word for you, correctly spelled. AutoComplete displays a tip at the insertion point. The tip appears when AutoComplete displays what you are typing, in the following order:

- A date

- An AutoText name

- A word in one of your custom spelling dictionaries

② SEE ALSO

To add AutoText entries, see "AutoText," page 167. To add words to a custom dictionary, see "Dictionaries for Other Languages," page 412.

To accept Word's AutoComplete tip, press Enter. To reject Word's AutoComplete tip, just keep typing or press Escape.

To turn AutoComplete on or off, take these steps:

1 Choose the Tools AutoCorrect command, and then click the AutoText tab.

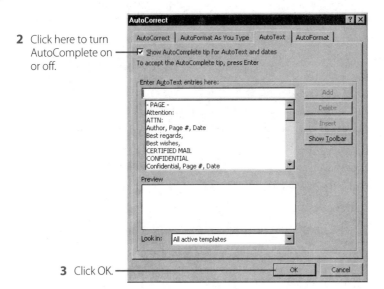

2 Click here to turn AutoComplete on or off.

3 Click OK.

Erasing Mistakes

? SEE ALSO

For another way to erase actions you've taken, see "Reversing Your Course: Undo," page 30.

As one pundit has written, "A word processor is a great eraser." This statement refers to the fact that one of the great advantages a word processor has over a typewriter is the ability to erase and correct mistakes without leaving a smudge on the paper. In Word, the usual ways to erase while typing are to delete characters with the Backspace key, delete characters with the Delete key, and type over existing characters.

■ Press the Backspace key to erase back over any typing mistakes.

■ Press the Delete key to erase over typing mistakes ahead of the insertion point.

Both keys erase all the selected text.

Repeat Typing, Retyping, and Overtyping

Most of your editing will probably involve typing beside or over existing text. Word provides three forms of typing for editing: simply typing new text, repeating what you just typed but in a new place, and for the brave, overtyping some existing text.

Repeat Typing

Sometimes you need to type the same text repeatedly in a document. That's when repeat typing fits the bill. You can use repeat typing either at an insertion point or over a selection of text you want to replace. To use repeat typing, do the following:

1 Type the text you want to repeat.

2 Position the insertion point or select the text where you want to use repeat typing.

3 Press the Repeat shortcut key (F4).

You can also use the Edit Repeat command or the Ctrl+Y Repeat shortcut key.

> The Edit Repeat command and Repeat shortcut keys (F4 and Ctrl+Y) repeat your last action, if possible. (Some actions can't be repeated.) To use repeat typing, typing must have been the last thing you did before you started using Edit Repeat. You can, however, use Edit Repeat any number of times to repeat the same action. To be sure that typing was your last action, look on the Edit menu. You should see *Repeat Typing*. If the Edit menu shows *Repeat* with any other action, Repeat won't repeat your typing.

Retyping

Retyping is a matter of selecting the text you want to replace and then typing the new text. As you start to type, Word removes the text you selected and inserts the new text as you type it. If the selected text is not deleted when you type, you'll need to turn on the Typing Replaces Selection option by choosing the Tools Options command, selecting the Edit tab in the Options dialog box, and turning on the Typing Replaces Selection check box.

Overtyping

With Overtype turned on, whatever you type replaces something in the document. Overtyping changes when you have Typing Replaces Selection turned on or off.

To turn on overtyping, double-click the OVR label in the status bar. If you want to turn off overtyping, double-click the OVR label in the status bar again. To turn off Typing Replaces Selection, choose the Tools Option command, select the Edit tab, and turn off the Typing Replaces Selection check box.

With both Typing Replaces Selection and Overtype turned on, typing replaces as follows:

- If you select text and start typing, Word replaces the selection with the first character you type.

- If you have an insertion point, Word replaces the character to the right of the insertion point with the character you type. This also happens when you start with a selection: the second character you type replaces the first character to the right of the selection and then continues to the right.

With Overtype turned on and Typing Replaces Selection turned off, typing replaces as follows:

- If you select text and start typing, Word replaces the first character of the selection and then positions the insertion point after the character you type.

- If you have an insertion point, Word replaces the character to the right of the insertion point with the character you type.

Reversing Your Course: Undo

Most of the actions you take with words (and indeed most of the actions you take anywhere in Word) can be reversed with the Edit Undo command. Until Word 6 for Windows, you could undo 3 actions. In Word 6 and Word 95, you could undo 100 actions. In Word 97, you can save the actions (called "Saved Undos"—see sidebar, page 32).

Undo

To undo the last action you took, click the Undo button on the Standard toolbar or press Ctrl+Z.

To undo several actions (up to all actions taken since you opened the document), take these steps:

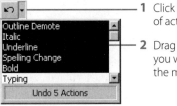

1 Click the down arrow to see the list of actions.

2 Drag down to select all the actions you want to undo, and then release the mouse button.

Reusing Words: AutoText

AutoText stores material so that you can reuse it easily. You can use AutoText entries to store bunches of words and lots of other things that you don't want to reconstruct every time you need them. When you store words as AutoText entries, you give them a simple name, even an abbreviation. When you want to add words from an AutoText entry to your document, you can simply type the AutoText name, and then ask Word to replace the name with the words from the AutoText entry.

Of course, before you can use an AutoText entry, you have to create it. For information about using an AutoText entry after you create it, see "AutoText," page 167.

Built-In AutoText

To assist you with typing, Word contains a fairly large number of built-in AutoText entries. To make using them easy, Word provides the AutoText toolbar.

1 Click here to see the list of AutoText categories.

2 Select a category.

3 Click a name to insert the AutoText.

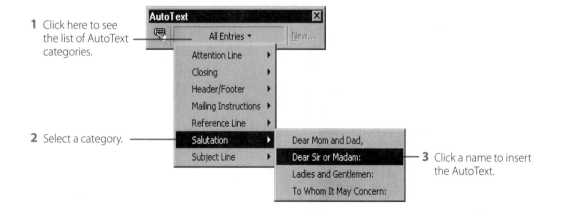

Depending on what part of a document you are working on, the AutoText toolbar may show the name of one category instead of All Entries. Word tries to show the category that applies to your current work. If you want to see all the categories in the list, hold down Shift as you click.

> ### Saved Undos
>
> Word can keep a history of all the changes you've made to a document, even after you save the document. For Word to save all your actions, you must save at least one version with the File Versions command—for details, see "Tracking Versions of Your Document," page 630.
>
> The newer version shows in the undo list attached to the Undo button all the changes you've made since saving the version. The older version doesn't show the changes in the undo list. Instead, the list attached to the Redo button shows the list of changes you made after saving this older version. This setup means that you can work back from the newer version toward the older version, and you can work forward from the older version toward the newer version.
>
> To open an older version, choose the File Versions command, select the version you want to open, and then click the Open button. For this older version, the title bar shows the name of the document, the date and time the version was saved, and the version number.

Automatic Corrections: AutoCorrect

As you type, you might notice that Word automatically corrects some common typing mistakes. For example, if you capitalize the first two letters of the word at the beginning of a sentence instead of only the first letter, or if you type *teh* instead of *the*, Word corrects the mistake for you. Word calls this AutoCorrect. You can add to or customize the list of mistakes Word looks for by choosing the Tools AutoCorrect command and changing the settings in the AutoCorrect dialog box.

> NOTE

> When you press the quotation mark key, Word by default inserts curly quotes (" ", opening and closing quotation marks) instead of straight quotes (" ", also called inch marks). Word also inserts curly single quotes (' ', opening and closing single quotation marks) when you press the apostrophe key. These quotation marks are called Smart Quotes in Word because Word automatically determines whether the quotes that you insert should be opening or closing marks.
>
> If you would rather use straight quote marks, choose the Tools AutoCorrect command and select the AutoFormat tab. Then turn off the "Straight Quotes" With "Smart Quotes" check box by clicking it.

Built-In Corrections

Word comes to you with a large number of automatic corrections already set up. The list is too large to give here (over 480 entries). The list includes many common typing and spelling errors. (Besides replacing *teh* with *the*, Word fixes typing errors such as *don;t* for *don't* and *could of had* for *could have had*).

These corrections are set up and turned on when you first set up Word. If you don't want some of these corrections, you can delete or change them (see "Changing an Automatic Correction," page 816). If you don't want any automatic corrections, you can turn off AutoCorrect.

You can, of course, add your own favorite automatic corrections. You probably have "favorite" typing mistakes, which Word can automatically fix so you don't have to go back and fix them yourself. For details about adding your own automatic corrections to AutoCorrect, see "Setting Up Your Own Automatic Corrections," page 813.

Exempting Mistakes from Corrections

Even though you might want AutoCorrect to fix many of your typing and spelling mistakes, there can be exceptions. Word gives you a way to set up exceptions to the AutoCorrect rules. To set up exceptions, take these steps:

1 Choose the Tools AutoCorrect command, and then click the AutoCorrect tab.

2 Click the Exceptions button.

3 To add an abbreviation, type it here.

4 Click the Add button. Repeat step 3 and step 4 for each new abbreviation.

5 Click OK to close the dialog box, or to add words with unusual initial capitalization, click the INitial CAps tab.

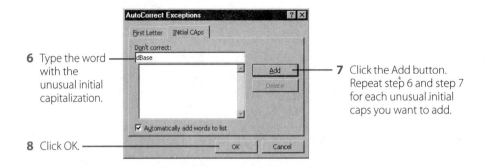

6 Type the word with the unusual initial capitalization.

7 Click the Add button. Repeat step 6 and step 7 for each unusual initial caps you want to add.

8 Click OK.

9 Click OK in the AutoCorrect dialog box.

Turning Off AutoCorrect

When you don't want Word to make any automatic corrections in your typing, you can turn off AutoCorrect. To do so, take these steps:

1 Choose the Tools AutoCorrect command, and then click the AutoCorrect tab.

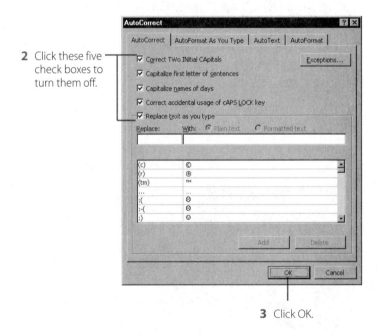

2 Click these five check boxes to turn them off.

3 Click OK.

Station 3: Format

Formatting is primarily the look of characters (letters, numbers, and symbols)—their font, size, and style—and the arrangement and layout of paragraphs—line spacing, indention, and spacing between. To help you apply formatting consistently to text and paragraphs, you can rely on styles—combinations of formatting that you apply all at once by choosing style names. Formatting also includes the look and layout of pages—columns, headers and footers, and borders.

Hiring a Decorator: AutoFormat

Automatic formatting, called AutoFormat, is an easy way to have Word format and polish your work. With AutoFormat, you can focus on your document's content while Word takes care of your document's looks. You don't have to know much about how the formatting gets done; you just look at the results and decide whether or not you like them. If you do like them, you accept them; if you don't, you reject them. And there are no costly decorating bills.

There are three ways to use Word's AutoFormat feature: as you type (without reviewing the results—"Trust me"); after the fact without review; or after the fact with a chance to accept or reject each change ("I want to inspect when you're done"). After the fact, you can hire AutoFormat for an entire document or for only part of it—like decorating one room at a time or the whole house at once.

- To format an entire document as you type, turn on the AutoFormat As You Type options.

- To format an entire document after the fact, set an insertion point anywhere in the document before you turn AutoFormat loose.

- To format only part of a document after the fact, select that part before you turn AutoFormat loose.

AutoFormat as You Type

Imagine that you're redoing the walls in a room. As you put up each new wall panel, your decorator comes along behind you and paints the wall. As you finish putting up the wall panels, the decorator finishes painting. You didn't have to do the decorating yourself, and it's done as soon as you are. That's what AutoFormat As You Type is like.

To try automatic formatting as you type, type some text, such as the text shown here:

My Wild Ride
¶
The story of my first ride through the woods has three parts:
1. Riding on the back roads
2. Stopping to enjoy the scenery
3. Leaving before the storm
¶
The serenity of the woods surprised me. As I stopped, I felt the solitude of the forest closing in around me. The stillness was quickly broken by the sound of a small creature moving through the underbrush. I stood there and watched in silence.
I soon realized I was not alone, and during my trip I saw
* Raccoons
* Deer
* Squirrels
¶
I hated to leave, but the clouds were building. I found the road to the main highway and soon felt the first raindrops fall.

> NOTE

If the text does not automatically format, you may have turned off some of the AutoFormat As You Type options. See "AutoFormat Options," page 991, for information on setting your AutoFormat As You Type options.

As you type text, you're providing some clues to help Word pick the right formatting. For example, when you type *1.*, some text, and then press Enter, you're telling Word that you are creating a numbered list. AutoFormat replaces the number you typed with special paragraph numbering and, when you press Enter, adds the special numbering to the next paragraph—*2* automatically appears at the beginning of your new paragraph.

- Add an extra paragraph after the last numbered item to resume normal paragraphs.

- Type an asterisk as your bullet character and a space in front of the first bulleted item. When you press Enter, AutoFormat replaces the bullet you typed with a bullet character that is part of the paragraph formatting. The special bulleted list paragraph formatting is also applied to the new paragraph. Type an extra paragraph after the last bulleted item.

Figure 2-3 shows the results of using AutoFormat As You Type.

Getting Started

FIGURE 2-3.

Document with font formatting applied by AutoFormat As You Type.

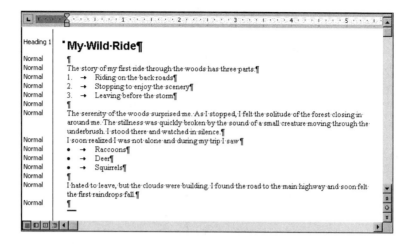

AutoFormat As You Type has several other options that you can choose. To see what they are, turn to "Reviewing AutoFormat Changes," page 40.

> **NOTE**
>
> Unless you know that you want a particular style for a paragraph, leave the style set to Normal. AutoFormat usually works only on paragraphs that use the Normal and Body Text styles. Also, AutoFormat does not automatically apply formats to tables; you must choose the Table AutoFormat command from the Table menu. See "Hiring Table AutoFormat," page 327, for information about automatically formatting tables.

AutoFormat Without Review

To simply have Word apply a format to your document quickly after you're done adding text, set an insertion point in the document (or select a portion of the document if you want to decorate only that portion), and then follow these steps:

1 Choose the Tools AutoCorrect command, click the AutoFormat As You Type tab, turn off all the options, and click OK.

2 Choose the Format AutoFormat command, select AutoFormat Now, and then click OK.

In just a few moments, your document looks like Figure 2-4, next page.

FIGURE 2-4.
Document with formatting applied using the AutoFormat button. The Style area is displayed to show applied paragraph styles.

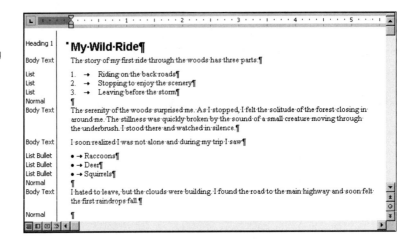

There are several differences between the results shown in Figure 2-4 and those shown in Figure 2-3.

- In the numbered paragraphs of Figure 2-4, the paragraphs use the List style. In Figure 2-3, the paragraphs are Normal style with special formatting added to the style.

- In the bulleted paragraphs in Figure 2-4, the paragraphs use the List Bullet style. In Figure 2-3, the paragraphs are Normal style with special formatting added to the style.

- The regular paragraphs in Figure 2-4 use the Body Text style instead of the Normal style used in Figure 2-3.

AutoFormat has several other options that you can choose. To see what they are, turn to "Reviewing AutoFormat Changes," page 40.

 NOTE

Remember, AutoFormat usually formats only paragraphs with the Normal or Body Text style. If you have already given a paragraph a different style but you want AutoFormat to change that style, choose the Tools AutoCorrect command, select the AutoFormat tab, and then turn off the Styles check box in the Preserve section of the AutoFormat tab.

AutoFormat with Review

If you want a chance to review and possibly reject the formatting AutoFormat applies to your document or if you want to change the formatting AutoFormat applies, choose the Format AutoFormat command.

To use the Format AutoFormat command, do the following:

1 Choose the Format AutoFormat command. Word first displays a dialog box, shown here, that gives you a chance to back out of automatic formatting:

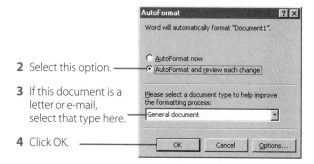

2 Select this option.

3 If this document is a letter or e-mail, select that type here.

4 Click OK.

It is at this point that you select the AutoFormat options if you need to reset them for the document you're working on. See "Reviewing AutoFormat Changes" on the next page.

Word applies formatting to the document, and then displays the dialog box shown here:

Following is an explanation of the buttons in the dialog box.

Button Name	Action
Accept All	Accepts the formatting that Word applied. (Typically, you'll click Accept All only after you have reviewed the changes.)
Reject All	Cancels all formatting that Word applied.
Review Changes	Reviews each formatting change that Word applied.
Style Gallery	Gives you the option of using styles from a different document template.

When you click the Review Changes button, Word displays the Review AutoFormat Changes dialog box, which appears over your document.

Reviewing AutoFormat Changes

When you review AutoFormat changes, Word highlights the changes in the following ways:

■ Deleted items appear in red or with red strikethroughs.

■ Inserted items appear in blue or with blue underlining.

■ A change bar appears in the left margin for both insertions and deletions.

To start your review, click the →Find button. Word highlights the first change that appears after the insertion point in the document and provides a description in the Review AutoFormat Changes dialog box.

If you don't like the change, click the Reject button. If you choose Reject, Word reverses the change. After you decide whether to reject or keep a change, click the →Find button again to review the next change.

You can replace one of AutoFormat's changes with a change of your own by doing the following:

1 Click in the document, outside the dialog box.

2 Move to any part of the document, and make any change you want. When you switch to the document, the Review AutoFormat Changes dialog box remains open, on top of the document, but inactive. If the dialog box covers up text that you want to see or change, move the dialog box out of the way by clicking and dragging its title bar.

3 Make your changes to the document.

4 Click anywhere on the dialog box to activate it and continue your review.

To see the document as it will look after the changes, click the Hide Marks button. Word removes the deleted items, the underlining, and the change bars. The Hide Marks button then becomes the Show Marks button. The Reject button becomes unavailable (dimmed) because there are no visible changes to reject.

If you want to review more changes, click the Show Marks button to display the changes and their revision marks again, or click one of the Find buttons.

As you examine the formatting changes, you might want to return to an earlier change. To jump back to a previous change, click the ←Find button. This button will take you back only to a change you accepted, because rejected changes are no longer a part of the document.

To undo a rejection (if you decide you want the change after all), click the Undo button. Each time you click this button, Word jumps back to your last rejection and reverses it—that is, Word reinstates the change that AutoFormat made.

After you conclude your review, click the Cancel button. Word returns to the AutoFormat dialog box. At this point, click the Accept All button to keep the changes you accepted during your review.

 TIP

Experimenting a Little with Different Fonts

To experiment with different fonts, click the Style Gallery button in the AutoFormat dialog box. The Style Gallery dialog box displays a preview of your document with the automatic formatting applied. You can choose different document templates to see the other formats that are available. For information about the Style Gallery, see "Visiting the Style Gallery," page 60.

AutoFormat Options

When you use AutoFormat—either as you type or after you have completed your document—Word applies specific types of formatting. You can customize the way AutoFormat works by changing its options. AutoFormat usually uses special formatting for bulleted lists, replaces straight quotes with Smart Quotes (curly), replaces some fractions with a true fraction character, replaces symbol characters with true symbols, and puts the letters that go with ordinal numbers in superscript.

Some options apply only if you use AutoFormat As You Type, while others apply only when you use the AutoFormat button or command. For example, AutoFormat As You Type formats all numbered lists in the same way, but when you use the AutoFormat button, AutoFormat can apply different types of formats to different types of lists.

For details on all the AutoFormat options, see the "AutoFormat Options" section in Appendix A, page 987.

Text Looks

Improving the looks of characters means adding decorative touches to the basic appearance of words—selecting the font name, style, size, and colors; setting superscripts and subscripts; and setting spacing between characters. You can use the mouse, the keyboard, or the Format Font command to improve the looks of characters.

When you use the mouse or the keyboard to "accessorize," you change only one part of the character looks at a time. For example, to make letters and words boldface and underlined, you change them to boldface, and then in a second effort, you add underlining. When you use the Format Font command, however, you can make almost all the formatting changes at one time in the Font dialog box. The Font tab of the Font dialog box, shown in Figure 2-5, also gives you more options for changing the looks of characters than the mouse or the keyboard does.

Adding and Removing Font Styles

The basic steps you follow to add or remove font styles are the same; you toggle between the on and off settings.

To change the font style of text, follow these steps:

1 Select the text you want to change.

2 Apply the new font style in one of the following ways:

B
Bold

- Click the Bold button on the Formatting toolbar.

- Press Ctrl+B for boldface.

I
Italic

- Click the Italic button on the Formatting toolbar.

- Press Ctrl+I for italic.

- Choose the Format Font command, click the Font tab, select Regular (to remove font styles) Bold, Italic, or Bold Italic from the Font Style list, and then click OK.

FIGURE 2-5.
The Font tab in the Font dialog box.

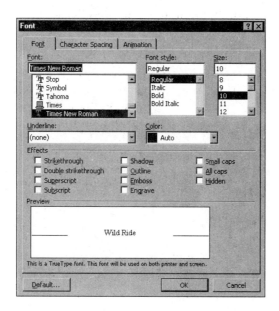

You can open the Font dialog box by clicking the right mouse button on the selection and then choosing the Font command from the shortcut menu, shown here.

Any time you add one character look to another with the toolbar buttons or the shortcut keys, the new and the existing looks combine. When you use the Format Font dialog box for boldface and italic, you must choose the combined look (Bold Italic); choosing one does not add the new choice to the existing one. The other looks in the Format Font dialog box can be added to an existing look, however.

> To remove all at once the character formatting you added, select the text and press Ctrl+Spacebar.

Underlining Your Words

Word 97 gives you nine underlining choices. (In Word 95, you have four choices, and in Word 6, you have three choices.) Only the single underline of words and spaces has a button on the Formatting toolbar. Only the single underline of words and spaces, double underline of words and spaces, and the single underline of words only (but not spaces) have shortcut keys (see Table 2-1). All of the underlining styles are available on the Font tab of the Font dialog box. The following table lists the names and shows a sample of each underlining choice.

Underlining Name	Sample
Single	Wild Ride
Words Only	Wild Ride
Double	Wild Ride
Dotted	Wild Ride
Thick	Wild Ride
Dash	Wild Ride
Dot Dash	Wild Ride
Dot Dot Dash	Wild Ride
Wave[1]	Wild Ride

1 Note that if you set the color of the selected characters to red or blue, you won't be able to tell the difference between a wave underline and a spelling or grammar error.

TABLE 2-1. **Shortcut Keys for Formatting Characters.**

Shortcut	Action
Ctrl+B	Toggles boldface.
Ctrl+I	Toggles italic.
Ctrl+U	Toggles continuous underlining. (Does not break between words.)
Ctrl+Shift+W	Toggles word underlining. (Breaks between words.)
Ctrl+Shift+D	Toggles double underlining. (Does not break between words.)
Ctrl++	Toggles subscript.
Ctrl+Shift+=	Toggles superscript.
Ctrl+Shift+A	Toggles all capital letters.
Ctrl+Shift+K	Toggles small capital letters.
Ctrl+Shift+F	Activates the Font list box on the Formatting toolbar, where you select a font name. When the Formatting toolbar is turned off, pressing Ctrl+Shift+F once displays the Font dialog box.
Ctrl+Shift+P	Activates the Font Size list box on the Formatting toolbar, where you select or type a number. When the Formatting toolbar is turned off, pressing Ctrl+Shift+P once displays the Font dialog box.
Ctrl+Shift+H	Toggles hidden-text format.
Ctrl+> (Ctrl+Shift+.)	Increases the font size to the next larger available size on the current printer.
Ctrl+< (Ctrl+Shift+,)	Decreases the font size to the next smaller available size on the current printer.
Ctrl+]	Increases the font size by 1 point.
Ctrl+[	Decreases the font size by 1 point.
Shift+F3	Changes the case of selected letters from lowercase to initial caps, from initial caps to uppercase, and from uppercase to lowercase. Words with strange combinations of uppercase and lowercase first change to either lowercase or initial caps and then follow the changes listed above.
Ctrl+Spacebar or Ctrl+Shift+Z	Removes all the added text formatting; the text format is set only by the paragraph style.
Ctrl+Shift+Q	Switches selected text to Symbol font.
Ctrl+D	Displays the Font dialog box.

Shortcut Keys for Fonts

You can use the keyboard to add formatting to characters. Table 2-1 lists the shortcut keys you can use. Note that the shortcut keys for applying formatting to characters are designed to let you spice up your text without removing your fingers from the keyboard. As you are typing, you toggle on your formatting choice, type the text, and then toggle off the formatting choice. For example, to add boldface, press Ctrl+B, type the text, press Ctrl+B again, and continue typing.

Adding Color to Your Words

Font Color

The Font Color button on Word 97's Formatting toolbar applies the color shown in the color stripe on the button below the letter *A*. (If you're familiar with Microsoft Excel 95 and version 5.0, this button is similar to the Text Color button on the Formatting toolbar in Microsoft Excel. Word's Drawing toolbar contains a duplicate Font Color button.)

You can change the color of any amount of text—a character, a word, a sentence, a paragraph, and so on. And you can use all 16 colors in a single document. If you have a color printer, Word prints your text in the colors you apply. If you don't have a color printer, Word prints your text using the printer's single color. Some printers will substitute grayscale images for colors; on other printers the printing will appear in black only.

To apply color to your words with the Font Color button, do the following:

1 Select some words.

2 If the color you want to apply is showing in the color stripe on the Font Color button, simply click the button—you're done. If you want to apply a different color, go to the next step.

3 If you want to apply a different color from the one in the color stripe, click the down arrow along the right side of the Font Color button.

Drag this strip into the window for a Color floating toolbar.

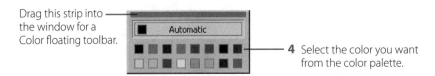

4 Select the color you want from the color palette.

You can also use the Font tab on the Font dialog box to apply color to your words. To apply color to your words with the Font dialog box, do the following:

1 Select some words.

2 Choose the Format Font command, and select the Font tab in the Font dialog box.

3 From the Color palette, select one of the colors, and then click OK.

The Auto color setting tells Word to use whatever Window Text color you've set on the Appearance tab in the Display Properties dialog box of the Windows Control Panel.

> **NOTE**

Font color does not affect pictures or other objects. To color pictures or objects, you have to edit them in their source programs. (You can color pictures and objects with Word's drawing tools. For more information see "Drawing Pictures," page 458.)

> **NOTE**

Word has a Highlight button on the Standard toolbar. The highlight actually adds color over text, just as a Hiliter® pen does. Because the major use for the highlighter feature is for documents built and refined by a workgroup, you'll find information about the Highlight button in "Spotlighting Your Concerns with Word's Highlight Feature," page 624.

Font Effects

The following table lists the font effects you can apply and shows you a sample of each.

Font Effect	Sample	Description
All Caps	WILD RIDE	Displays all letters as uppercase. This is a font effect; the letters retain their original case. To change letter case, use the Change Case command or press Shift+F3 to switch from lowercase, to initial letter uppercase, to all uppercase, and back to lowercase.
Double Strikethrough	Wild Ride	Draws two parallel lines through the characters. Word uses the font color to draw the lines.

(continued)

Font Effect	Sample	Description
Emboss	Wild Ride	Creates the effect of the characters being raised up from the page. Word uses an outline along the right and bottom sides of the characters. If the color is Auto when you select Emboss, Word changes the font color to white. If you have selected any other color already, Word uses a different color for the embossing outline.
Engrave	Wild Ride	Creates the effect of the characters being pressed down into the page. Word uses an outline along the left and top sides of the characters. If the color is Auto when you select Engrave, Word changes the font color to white. If you have selected any other color already, Word uses a different color for the engraving outline.
Hidden	Wild·Ride	Shows the dotted underline for hidden text when you have Show/Hide ¶ turned on. When you turn off Show/Hide, Word makes the selected characters disappear and closes up the space between the visible characters on either side of the hidden characters.
Outline	Wild Ride	Fills the insides of the characters with white. If you choose White for the color, the characters disappear.
Shadow	Wild Ride	Adds a copy of the characters in a lighter color slightly below and to the right of the shadowed characters.
Small Caps	WILD RIDE	Displays all letters as uppercase in a smaller font size. This is a font effect; the letters retain their original case. To change letter case, use the Change Case command or press Shift+F3 to switch from lowercase, to initial letter uppercase, to all uppercase, and back to lowercase.
Strikethrough	Wild Ride	Draws a horizontal line through the characters. Word uses the font color to draw the lines.
Subscript	W$_{ild}$ Ride	Lowers the characters 3 points below the baseline and displays them in a smaller font size.
Superscript	W^{ild} Ride	Raises the characters 3 points above the baseline and displays them in a smaller font size.

To apply any of the font effects, take these steps:

1 Select the words.

2 Choose the Font Format command, or right-click the selection and select Font from the shortcut menu.

3 Click the check boxes for the font effects you want to apply, and then click OK.

Choosing some font effects turns off others, as follows:

Choosing This Effect	Turns Off This Effect
Strikethrough	Double Strikethrough
Double Strikethrough	Strikethrough
Superscript	Subscript
Subscript	Superscript
Shadow	Emboss, Engrave
Outline	Emboss, Engrave
Emboss	Shadow, Outline, Engrave
Engrave	Shadow, Outline, Emboss
Small Caps	All Caps
All Caps	Small Caps

? SEE ALSO
You can change the look of words by adding more or less space between characters. For details, see "Stretching and Shrinking Words," page 447. With a new font feature in Word 97, you can animate words. For details, see "Dancing: Animated Text," page 876.

Copying Formatting Within or Between Documents

Sometimes you'll want to reuse some of your font and paragraph formats to save yourself time and effort. In Word, you can copy character and paragraph formatting from one place to another within a document or between documents.

To copy font formats with the mouse, follow these steps:

1 Select a word (or character) that has the font formats you want to copy.

Format
Painter

2 Click the Format Painter button on the Standard toolbar. When you move the mouse pointer into the document window, it displays a paintbrush beside the I-beam pointer, as shown here:

3 Drag the paintbrush across the words to which you want to apply the font formatting.

4 When you release the mouse button, Word formats the words so that the formatting matches the original selection.

⚙ **SEE ALSO**

You can also add borders and shading to other parts of a document. To add borders and shading to tables, see "Changing Borders and Shading," page 340. To add borders and shading to art and text boxes, see "Adding a Border," page 515. To add borders to a page, see "Page Borders," page 175, and "Adding Page Border Lines," page 192.

Borders and Shading

You can add a border or shading to any letters or words, even a selection that crosses a paragraph mark, whether or not it includes an entire paragraph. To add borders and shading to words (or any selection of characters including entire paragraphs), take these steps:

1 Select the text you want to give a border and shading.

2 Choose the Format Borders And Shading command.

3 For borders, click the Borders tab and set up the borders you want. For descriptions of your choices, see "Page Borders," page 175, and "Adding Page Border Lines," page 192.

4 For shading, click the Shading tab and set up the shading you want. For descriptions of your choices, see "Changing Borders and Shading," page 339.

5 In the Apply To box, indicate whether you want the border or shading to apply only to the selected text, or to the entire paragraph or paragraphs.

6 Click OK.

Paragraphs

Perhaps the most common changes you'll make to paragraphs are changing the indention (labeled "indentation" in the Paragraph dialog box), changing the line spacing, changing the paragraph alignment, and setting up numbered and bulleted lists.

Indents

Every paragraph can have three kinds of indention: left side, right side, and first line. You can change the indent to push the edge of the paragraph toward the center of the page or to pull it out toward the margin (sometimes referred to as "outdent").

Increase
Indent

- To set a left indent at the next tab stop in a paragraph (normally set every 0.5 inch), select the paragraphs you want to indent, and then click the Increase Indent button on the Formatting toolbar, or press Ctrl+M.

Decrease
Indent

- To decrease the left indent by one tab stop (normally set every 0.5 inch), select the paragraphs you want to indent, and then click the Decrease Indent button on the Formatting toolbar, or press Ctrl+Shift+M.

- To set a hanging indent (the first line sticks out to the left of the rest of the lines) at the next tab stop in a paragraph (normally set every 0.5 inch), press Ctrl+T.

- To decrease a hanging indent by one tab stop (normally set every 0.5 inch), press Ctrl+Shift+T.

To set a right indent for a paragraph, or to set a left, first-line, or hanging indent at a distance other than at the tab stops, you use the Format Paragraph command. To set indents with the Format Paragraph command, take these steps:

1 Select the paragraphs you want to indent.

2 Choose the Format Paragraph command.

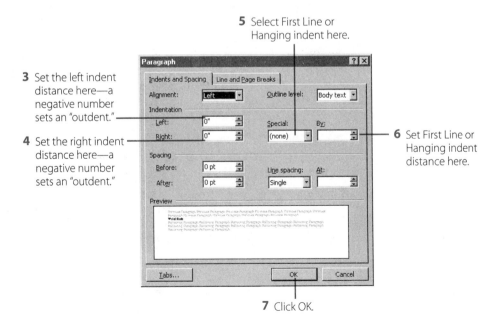

5 Select First Line or Hanging indent here.

3 Set the left indent distance here—a negative number sets an "outdent."

4 Set the right indent distance here—a negative number sets an "outdent."

6 Set First Line or Hanging indent distance here.

7 Click OK.

Getting Started

I

To set paragraphs with a first-line indent of 0.5 inch, select the paragraphs, press Ctrl+M to indent the entire paragraph 0.5 inch, and then press Ctrl+Shift+T to leave the first line indented and move the rest of the lines to the left by 0.5 inch.

To apply a hanging indent that puts the beginning of the first line in the left margin, select Hanging in the Special box, set the hanging distance in the By box, and then set that same distance as a negative number in the Left box.

Line Spacing

Nowadays, most documents have single-line spacing. From time to time, however, you might want double-spaced lines or lines spaced one-and-one-half lines apart.

- To set paragraph lines to double space, press Ctrl+2.

- To set paragraph lines to one-and-one-half space, press Ctrl+5.

- To return paragraph lines to single space, press Ctrl+1.

For other line spacing choices, use the Line Spacing and At boxes on the Indents And Spacing tab of the Format Paragraph dialog box. The Line Spacing box contains six line spacing choices, shown in the following table.

Line Spacing Choice	Effect on Lines
Single	Lines are single-spaced at a height set by the font for printing. Each line expands its line spacing to fit the tallest font size in the line.
1.5 Lines	Lines are single-spaced at a height set by the font for printing. Each line expands its line spacing 1.5 times the tallest font size in the line.
Double Space	Lines are double-spaced at a height twice as tall as the height set by the font for printing a single-spaced line. Each line expands its line spacing to twice the tallest font size in the line.
At Least	Lines are spaced at least as tall as the height set in the At box. Each line expands its line spacing to fit the tallest font size in the line.

Line Spacing Choice	Effect on Lines
Exactly	Lines are spaced exactly as tall as the height set in the At box. Fonts taller than the line height are chopped off at the top.
Multiple	Lines are spaced at a multiple of the height set by the font for printing a single-spaced line. Each line expands its line spacing to the multiple set in the At box of the tallest font size in the line.

Paragraph Alignment

Most documents rely on left-aligned paragraphs; that is, the left edges of the paragraphs are flush with the left margin, and the right edges are uneven along the right margin. The second most common paragraph alignment is probably justified; that is, left edges of the paragraphs are flush with the left margin and the right edges of the paragraphs are flush with the right margin. Centered paragraphs are popular for titles and title pages; that is, the paragraphs are centered between the left and right margins. In rare and special cases, people set up a paragraph with right alignment; that is, the right edges of the paragraphs are flush with the right margin, and the left edges are uneven along the left margin.

To change paragraph alignment, take these steps:

1 Select the paragraphs you want to align.

2 Use one of the following methods to set paragraph alignment:

- For justified alignment, click the Justify button on the Formatting toolbar, or press Ctrl+J.

- For centered paragraphs, click the Center button on the Formatting toolbar, or press Ctrl+E.

- For right alignment, click the Align Right button on the Formatting toolbar, or press Ctrl+R.

- To return to left alignment, click the Align Left button on the Formatting toolbar, or press Ctrl+L.

You can also select the paragraph alignment in the Alignment box on the Indents And Spacing tab of the Format Paragraph dialog box.

Numbered and Bulleted Lists

The Formatting toolbar contains a button for bulleted lists and a button for numbered lists. To number or bullet paragraphs for a list, take these steps:

1 Select the paragraphs you want to number or bullet for a list.

Numbering   Bullets

2 Click the Numbering or the Bullets button on the Formatting toolbar.

> You can also bullet a paragraph by pressing Ctrl+Shift+L.

Also remember that if you type a number followed by a period and space or by a tab character to start your list, AutoFormat turns each succeeding paragraph into a numbered paragraph. If you type an asterisk or a lowercase *o* followed by a tab character to start your list, AutoFormat changes the character into a bullet character on each succeeding paragraph. If you type a hyphen followed by a tab character, AutoFormat makes the paragraph a bulleted item with the hyphen as the bullet character on each succeeding paragraph. If you number or bullet a paragraph and then start a new paragraph, the new paragraph also shows a number or bullet.

In all of these methods for setting up a bulleted list, the bulleted item also gets the List Bullet style. To stop a numbered or bulleted list, press Enter twice at the end of the last paragraph in the list. Then press Backspace to erase the extra paragraph mark. For another way to set up numbered or bulleted lists—the Format Bullets And Numbering command—see "Creating Lists," page 587.

Using Different Styles

Using styles to set the look of text gives you additional design power with minimum effort. Word starts every new document with 5 basic styles at the ready: Normal, Heading 1, Heading 2, Heading 3, and the character style Default Paragraph Font. These styles are among the most frequently used of the 91 built-in styles Word provides. The names of these 5 styles appear in the Style box on the Formatting toolbar. In the Styles list in the Style dialog box, you see only Normal and Default Paragraph Font.

In addition to these 5 ready-to-wear styles, Word includes 86 more built-in styles. Nine of the built-in styles are character styles; the others are paragraph styles. Word uses many of these built-in styles automatically at special places in a document. Word also uses its built-in styles when you use the AutoFormat command and when you use one of the document wizards to create a special document, such as a letter. For information on how to print a list of all Word's styles and their descriptions, see "Choosing What to Print," page 127.

After you insert text that uses a built-in style, that style's name appears in the Style box on the Formatting toolbar and in the Style dialog box. The built-in styles (except for Normal, Heading 1, Heading 2, Heading 3, and Default Paragraph Font) do not appear in the list until you use them in a document.

> To see all the built-in styles in the Style box on the Formatting toolbar, hold down the Shift key and click the down arrow at the right side of the Style box. To see all the built-in styles in the Style dialog box, choose the Format Style command to display the dialog box, and select All Styles in the List box.

After you insert text that uses a built-in style, you can select any different style you want to use instead. Doing this, however, forfeits the convenience of using a built-in style. A better alternative is to change the built-in style if you don't like the way it looks.

To use a different style for a paragraph, do the following:

1 Select the paragraph. You can select a portion of a paragraph, select the entire paragraph, or simply position the insertion point anywhere in the paragraph.

2 Use one of the methods described in the following sections to select the style you want to use.

Selecting Styles from the Formatting Toolbar

The Formatting toolbar contains the Style box. You use the Style box to directly select a style. The Style box on the Formatting toolbar shows

? SEE ALSO

You can select heading styles and Normal style in Outline view with the Outline toolbar and with key combinations. For information about this, see "Selecting Styles in Outline View," page 566.

the styles with the font formatting for each style. You can use the Format Painter button on the Standard toolbar to copy a style.

To select a style from the Style box, do the following:

1 On the Formatting toolbar, click the down arrow at the right side of the Style box to see a list of styles currently in use in the document, like the one that's shown here:

2 Click the style you want to apply. —————

Style names show font formats and alignment for each style.

  TIP

To have the Style box list include all styles, hold down the Shift key as you click the down arrow.

Using a Character Style

The only major difference between using a paragraph style and using a character style is a matter of selection. As noted earlier, when you want to use a paragraph style you "select" a paragraph one of three ways: by positioning the insertion point in the paragraph, by selecting some part of the paragraph, or by selecting the entire paragraph. For character styles, you select exactly the text to which you want to give the character style. Word uses the character style only for the selected text and nothing else. As with paragraph styles, to select a character style for the selected text, you use the Formatting toolbar's Style box or the Format Painter button, or you use the Format Style command. See "Copying Formatting Within or Between Documents," page 49, for information about using the Format Painter button.

NOTE

> If you change any formatting in a paragraph and then reapply the same style to the paragraph, Word asks whether you want to reapply the style as it is or to change the style definition to include the formatting changes you made. Select the action you want Word to take, and then click OK.

To copy a style from one paragraph to another, do the following:

1 With the mouse, select the paragraph that uses the style you want to copy. Make certain that you select the entire paragraph, including the paragraph mark if it is visible—triple-click inside the paragraph or double-click in the paragraph's selection bar. (See "Clicking, Double-Clicking, and Triple-Clicking," page 85, and "Using the Mouse in the Selection Bar," page 87.)

Format
Painter

2 Click the Format Painter button, or press Ctrl+Shift+C.

3 Click the paragraph you want to format.

 TIP

> If you want to use the Format Painter button to copy a style to several paragraphs, double-click the Format Painter button in step 2. When you're done copying the style to all the paragraphs you want, click the Format Painter button again to stop copying.

Selecting Styles with Commands

Word provides several commands to work with styles, as described here:

- The Format AutoFormat command to automatically apply paragraph styles to your text. (See "Hiring a Decorator: AutoFormat," page 35.)

- The Format Style command to define and apply paragraph and character styles. (See "Shopping in the Style Boutique: The Format Style Command," page 59.)

- The Format Style Gallery command to see the effects of different styles on your document. (See "Visiting the Style Gallery," page 60.)

- The Edit Replace command to replace one style with another. (See "Replacing Styles," page 62.)

There are also several commands and actions that cause Word to assign styles for you. For the commands you use or the actions you take, and the styles Word uses, see Table 2-2.

Using Word's Built-In Styles

You can use many styles without having to worry about selecting them yourself. You simply insert text, and Word uses the appropriate style. Word automatically uses a style for text you insert with the commands shown in Table 2-2.

Word has 91 built-in styles; see "Choosing What to Print," page 127, for information on how to print out a complete listing and description of Word's built-in styles.

TABLE 2-2. Built-In Styles That Word Uses Automatically.

Built-In Style	When Word Uses It	Command
Comment Reference	When you insert a comment reference	Insert Comment
Comment Text	When you insert a comment	Insert Comment
Caption	When you insert a caption	Insert Caption
Endnote Reference	When you insert an endnote reference	Insert Footnote
Endnote Text	When you insert an endnote	Insert Footnote
Envelope Address	When you set up an envelope with the Tools Envelopes And Labels command	Tools Envelopes And Labels
Envelope Return	When you set up an envelope with the Tools Envelopes And Labels command	Tools Envelopes And Labels
Footer	When you insert text in a footer	View Header And Footer
Footnote Reference	When you insert a footnote reference	Insert Footnote
Footnote Text	When you insert a footnote	Insert Footnote

(continued)

Table 2-2. *continued*

Built-In Style	When Word Uses It	Command
Header	When you insert text in a header	View Header And Footer
Heading 1	When you switch a new document (one that has no content) to Outline view, Word uses Heading 1 instead of Normal for the first paragraph	View Outline
Hyperlink	When you insert a hyperlink	Insert Hyperlink
Index 1–Index 9	When you insert an index	Insert Index And Tables
Index Heading	When you insert an index	Insert Index And Tables
Line Number	When you turn on line numbering	File Page Setup
Page Number	When you insert a page number in a header or footer	Insert Page Numbers
Table of Authorities	When you insert a table of authorities	Insert Index And Tables
Table of Figures	When you insert a table of figures	Insert Index And Tables
TOA Head	When you insert a table of authorities	Insert Index And Tables
TOC 1–TOC 9	When you insert a table of contents	Insert Index And Tables

Shopping in the Style Boutique: The Format Style Command

The Format Style command displays the Style dialog box, where you can see a list of all the styles Word uses. Usually, Word lists Styles In Use in the document, which means that only Normal and Default Paragraph Font styles plus any other styles you have already used in the document appear in the list. You have two other choices of what styles are displayed: All Styles, which lists all of Word's built-in styles as well as any you have built, and User-Defined Styles, which lists only the styles you have built.

To apply a style using the Format Style command, do the following:

1 Select the paragraph, paragraphs, or text to which you want to apply the style.

2 Choose the Format Style command.

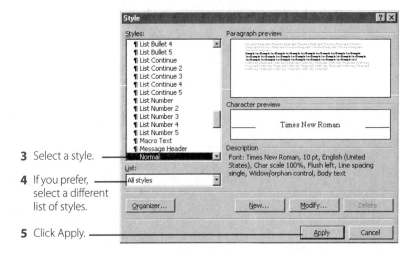

3 Select a style.

4 If you prefer, select a different list of styles.

5 Click Apply.

Visiting the Style Gallery

If you want to experiment a little with the looks of all the text at once, you can visit the Style Gallery. The Style Gallery provides a preview of your current document as it would look with different styles applied. You also see a list of all the available document templates.

 NOTE

> The Style Gallery does not use character styles.

To visit and use the Style Gallery, take these steps:

1 Choose the Format Style Gallery command. You can also reach the Style Gallery after you use the Format AutoFormat command by clicking the Style Gallery button in the AutoFormat dialog box that appears after you've applied an AutoFormat. The Format AutoFormat command is discussed in "Hiring a Decorator: AutoFormat," page 35.

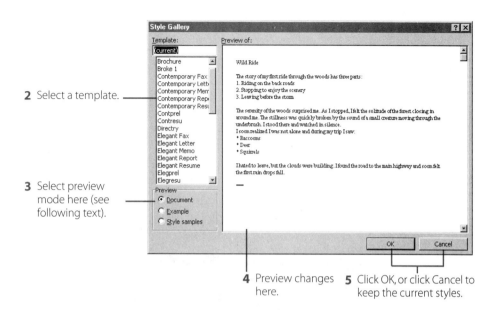

2 Select a template.

3 Select preview mode here (see following text).

4 Preview changes here.

5 Click OK, or click Cancel to keep the current styles.

Most often, you'll want to select the Document option in the Preview section of the Style Gallery dialog box. This option displays your document with the template styles applied in either Normal or Page Layout view, depending on the view displayed when you chose the Format Style Gallery command.

The usefulness of the other two options, Example and Style Samples, depends on the template you select in the Template list. If the document template has an accompanying sample document, you can select the Example option to display text that demonstrates the styles in the selected template. The Style Samples option shows all the styles of the selected template used for sample text. The Normal template does not supply samples, but many other templates do.

Replacing Styles

To replace a style with another style, do the following:

1 Choose the Edit Replace command, and click the More button.

2 Delete any text in the Find what box.

3 Click the Format button, and select Style.

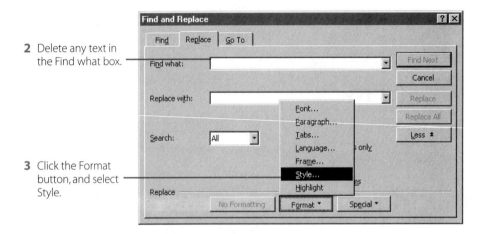

4 Select the style you want to replace.

5 Click OK.

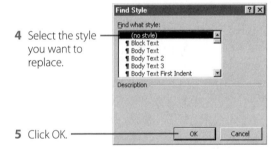

6 In the Find and Replace dialog box, click in the Replace With box and delete any text in the box.

7 Repeat step 3, step 4, and step 5 for the Replace With box.

8 Use the Replace command as you do for replacing text. To replace all occurrences of the style, click the Replace All button in the dialog box. To replace some occurrences of the style, click the Find Next button, and then click either the Replace button to replace the style or the Find Next button to leave the style as it is.

TIP

Replacing Formatted Text

Step 2 and step 6 direct you to delete any text in the Find What and Replace With boxes. These steps are necessary if you want to find all occurrences of the style in your document. You certainly can, however, put text into the Find What and Replace With boxes when you want to replace a style for particular text. For example, you might have used the same style (say, Note) for both notes and tips, but now you want to use a separate Tip style for tips. If you started every tip in your document with the word TIP, you could type *tip* in the Find What box and select Note as the style to find, and then type *tip* in the Replace With box and select Tip as the replacement style.

Selecting Styles with the Keyboard

You don't have to lift your fingers from the keyboard to select a style. Word provides the following shortcut keys for selecting a style:

- Ctrl+Shift+S

- Ctrl+Y or F4

- Alt+Shift+→, Alt+Shift+←, Tab, and Shift+Tab

- Alt+Ctrl+number

- Ctrl+Shift+letter

- Ctrl+Q

- Ctrl+Spacebar

The following sections discuss the purpose for each shortcut key.

 TIP

You can also assign shortcut keys to a style name so that you can directly select the style by pressing that key combination. For details about assigning styles to shortcut keys, see "Creating Key Assignments," page 1025.

Select Style Keys: Ctrl+Shift+S

The Ctrl+Shift+S shortcut key either activates the Style box on the Formatting toolbar or displays the Style dialog box. If the Formatting toolbar is visible when you press Ctrl+Shift+S, the Style box becomes active. If the Formatting toolbar is not visible when you press Ctrl+Shift+S, Word displays the Style dialog box.

Getting Started

To select a style with the Ctrl+Shift+S shortcut key, do the following:

1 Press Ctrl+Shift+S.

2 Press the ↓ key or the ↑ key to select the style. You can press Alt+↓ or Alt+↑ to open the list.

3 Press Enter.

> You can type a few letters of the style's name and then press ↓ to select the first name that begins with the letters you typed. This is a handy way to quickly select a name or to quickly move near the name of the style you want to select.

Repeat Keys: Ctrl+Y or F4

Immediately after you apply a style, you can apply that same style to another paragraph. To repeat the same style after you select a style for a paragraph, do the following:

1 Select the next paragraph for which you want to use the same style.

2 Press Ctrl+Y or press F4.

> If you've done anything else since you applied a style, Word repeats that action instead of repeating the style.

Promote and Demote Keys: Alt+Shift+→, Alt+Shift+←, Tab, and Shift+Tab

In any view of a document, you can press one of two shortcut keys to promote or demote a heading by changing the style for the heading:

- Press Alt+Shift+← to select the next higher heading style (Heading 1 through Heading 9 styles).

- Press Alt+Shift+→ to select the next lower heading style.

In Outline view only, you also have the following choices:

- Press Shift+Tab to select the next higher heading style (Heading 1 through Heading 9 styles).

- Press Tab to select the next lower heading style.

TIP

> To insert a tab character while you're working in Outline view, press Ctrl+Tab.

Heading Style Keys: Alt+Ctrl+Number

In any view of the document, you can press one of the following shortcut keys to apply one of the heading styles:

- Press Alt+Ctrl+1 to apply the Heading 1 style.

- Press Alt+Ctrl+2 to apply the Heading 2 style.

- Press Alt+Ctrl+3 to apply the Heading 3 style.

 NOTE

> Word doesn't continue the progression below heading level 3. That is, Alt+Ctrl+4 does not apply the Heading 4 style. If you want to make these key assignments, see Appendix D, "Playing the Keyboard."

Other Style Keys: Ctrl+Shift+Letter

Word has a couple of other shortcut keys for selecting styles:

- Press Ctrl+Shift+L to select the List Bullet style.

- Press Ctrl+Shift+N to select the Normal body text style.

Two other shortcut keys affect the style Word selects for a paragraph when you choose the Format AutoFormat command. These keys don't select the styles themselves; they merely set up the paragraphs so that Word selects the appropriate styles.

- Press Ctrl+M to increase paragraph indention. When you indent a paragraph, Word selects a style for indented paragraphs that sets the correct indention. For example, if you indent a bulleted list under a numbered list item, Word selects List Bullet 2 style rather than List Bullet style to properly indent the bulleted list under the numbered list item.

Getting Started

- Press Ctrl+Shift+M to decrease paragraph indention. This shortcut key decreases the amount of paragraph indention, which directs Word to select a higher level of style for these paragraphs. Compare the effect of this shortcut key with the effect of the previous shortcut key (Ctrl+M).

Reset Style Keys: Ctrl+Q

At times we all get lazy. Well, at least I do. Rather than creating a style, I'll add some paragraph formatting to change the look of a paragraph. Later I might decide that I don't want that particular look anymore—I just want the look given by the style.

To remove a paragraph look and return to the "pure" style, select the paragraph and then press Ctrl+Q. This shortcut key resets the paragraph to the pure style.

Remove Formatting Keys: Ctrl+Spacebar

Another time I get lazy is when I want to apply a font attribute to some text in a paragraph to set it off from the rest of the paragraph. For example, I might italicize a word or two. Later I come to my senses and decide to remove the italics.

To remove font attributes from text in a paragraph, select the text and press Ctrl+Spacebar. In effect, pressing Ctrl+Spacebar applies the Default Paragraph Font character style to the selected text. Doing this removes any additional font attributes that you've added to the text.

NOTE

Ctrl+Spacebar also replaces any other character style with the Default Paragraph Font character style.

Margins

Word sets up all documents in the United States with 1.25-inch side margins and 1-inch top and bottom margins. If you want different margins, take these steps:

1 Choose the File Page Setup command.

2 Click the Margins tab.

3 Set the margins you want in these boxes.

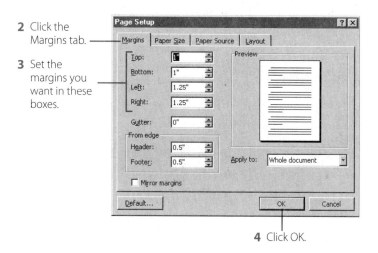

4 Click OK.

Margins are only one part of page setup, as you'll notice when you look into the Page Setup dialog box. For information about your options for page setup, see "Set Up Pages in the Page Setup Dialog Box," page 788.

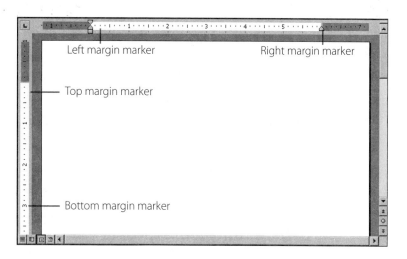

Left margin marker

Right margin marker

Top margin marker

Bottom margin marker

Changing Margins on the Ruler
To change the margins on the ruler, display the ruler (choose the View Ruler command) in Page Layout view. To set new side margins, drag the margin markers on the horizontal ruler. Over the horizontal margin markers, the mouse pointer becomes a two-headed horizontal arrow. To set new top and bottom margins, drag the margin markers on the vertical ruler. Over the vertical margin markers, the mouse pointer becomes a two-headed vertical arrow.

Page Numbers

For any document longer than one page, you're likely to want to add page numbers. Doing so is a simple process. Take these steps:

1 Choose the Insert Page Numbers command.

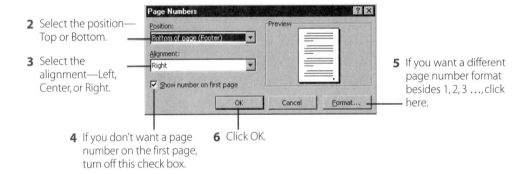

2 Select the position—Top or Bottom.

3 Select the alignment—Left, Center, or Right.

4 If you don't want a page number on the first page, turn off this check box.

5 If you want a different page number format besides 1, 2, 3 …, click here.

6 Click OK.

Page Borders

Word gives you tools for setting up very sophisticated headers and footers. For details on headers and footers, see "Setting Up Headers and Footers," page 288.

In Word 97, page borders have finally become an integral part of Word. (In earlier versions of Word, you had to install the add-in called Word Assistant.) You can add border lines to a page, and you can add decorative artwork as a border. For details about page borders, see "Page Borders," page 175, and "Adding Page Border Lines," page 192.

With the inclusion of tools for creating online documents for the Web, Word allows you to give an online page a background shading. For details about page backgrounds, see "Setting the Background," page 873.

Station 4: Proofread

For information about
Word's ability to check
spelling and grammar
as you type, see "Proof-
reading for Spelling
and Grammar," page
186.

Before you send out a document for others to read, you might want to let Word proofread it for you—check the spelling and grammar. Word can automatically check your spelling and grammar by comparing words in your document against Word's spelling dictionaries and grammar rules.

Spelling and grammar are strongly linked in Word 97. While spell checking alone often overlooks correctly spelled words that aren't correct for the sentence, grammar checking catches these "misses" of the word so that your document has very few, if any, "spelling" errors after checking. For example, if you type *form* when you want *from,* or *to* instead of *too* or *two,* grammar checking can catch that, advise you, and give you a chance to correct this "misspelling." Word also checks for repeated words and for words that seem to be incorrectly capitalized. Word's grammar checking also does style checking by finding awkward, long, or difficult sentences. You then have a chance to change the sentences to something a little more pleasing.

Word can only check spelling or grammar if you have the checking instructions and dictionaries installed. If you have only the spelling instructions and dictionary installed, Word won't check grammar, and you'll see only a Spelling command on the Tools menu. Also, if you have only the grammar instructions and dictionary installed, Word won't check spelling, and you'll see only a Grammar command on the Tools menu. If you have neither spelling nor grammar installed, you see neither command on the Tools menu. This section is based on a Word installation that has both spelling and grammar installed. If you have only one of these two proofreading tools installed, simply ignore discussion of the other tool as you read.

For each word not found in a dictionary and each sentence that "breaks" a grammar rule, Word gives you a way to do any of the following:

- Provide the correct spelling of the word.

- Use a suggested spelling or an AutoCorrect entry.

- Leave the word as it is.

- Leave the word as it is and add it to a dictionary.

- Correct the spelling and add the word to the AutoCorrect list so that the next time you type the word incorrectly, Word will automatically fix the spelling. (For more information about the AutoCorrect list, see "Adding Words to AutoCorrect During Proofreading," page 79, and "Setting Up Your Own Automatic Corrections," page 813.)

- Correct the grammar of a sentence.

- Leave the grammar as it is.

- Ignore a grammar rule for an instance, as in a sentence, or the entire document.

Word can also check the spelling and grammar of words and sentences in other languages.

? SEE ALSO

For information about proofreading options, see "Spelling & Grammar Tab," page 972.

After Word finishes proofreading, you see a summary of readability ratings and statistics about your document, such as word and character counts, the average number of sentences per paragraph, and reading-ease ratings, as shown in Figure 2-6.

FIGURE 2-6.
The Readability Statistics dialog box.

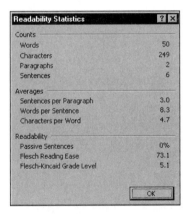

Even though Word is set up to check spelling and grammar as you type, you might prefer to proofread after you finish a batch of work. In this case, you'll want to turn off full-time as-you-type proofreading.

You can also turn off as-you-type spelling checking and as-you-type grammar checking separately. Here's how:

1 Choose the Tools Options command, and then click the Spelling & Grammar tab.

2 Click here to turn off as-you-type spell checking.

3 Click here to turn off as-you-type grammar checking.

4 Click OK.

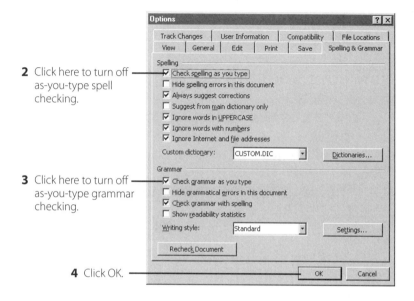

Spelling and Grammar

To proofread your entire document (whether as-you-type checking is turned on or off), click the Spelling And Grammar button on the Standard toolbar.

⭐ TIP

Instead of clicking the Spelling And Grammar button on the Standard toolbar, you can press the shortcut key, F7. You can, of course, also choose the Tools Spelling And Grammar command.

Word starts proofreading your document, beginning with the first word after the insertion point. The following message appears in the status bar: *Word is checking the spelling and grammar in the document....* First Word checks the spelling of each word in the sentence. Then Word checks the grammar. Word repeats this process for each sentence in the document.

If Word finds no problems in the entire document, it displays the Readability Statistics dialog box, as shown in Figure 2-6. Click OK to resume work on your document.

If Word finds a problem, it displays the Spelling And Grammar dialog box. The look of the dialog box changes slightly for spelling errors and grammatical errors, as you can see in Figure 2-7 (below) and in Figure 2-8 (on page 74).

Handling Spelling Errors

When Word finds a word in a document that is not found in any of the active dictionaries, Word displays the Spelling dialog box, shown in Figure 2-7. The word appears in red boldface. The dialog box offers a variety of options to solve your spelling dilemma.

FIGURE 2-7.
The Spelling And Grammar dialog box for a spelling error.

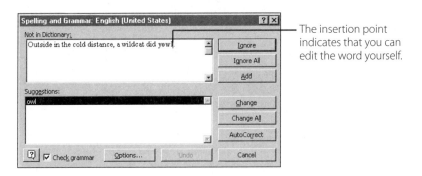

The insertion point indicates that you can edit the word yourself.

If Word has any suggested spellings, they automatically appear in the Spelling dialog box if the Always Suggest check box is selected on the Spelling & Grammar tab of the Options dialog box. (If you have turned off this check box, you are on your own to come up with a correction. You can, of course, turn on suggestions at any time: click the Options button, click the Always Suggest check box, and then click OK.)

> **NOTE**
>
> To make valid suggestions, Word generally relies on you to type the first letter or first two letters of a word correctly.

Hand-Correcting Spelling Errors

If none of the suggestions is useful, you can edit the word in the Not In Dictionary box. The Undo Edit, Change, and Options buttons become the only active buttons when you change the spelling of the red, highlighted word. If you don't like the change you've made, click the Undo Edit button to return the word in the Not In Dictionary box to the way the word is in the document. You can then again change the word yourself, or click one of the buttons to change, ignore, or add the word, as you see fit.

Click Change to correct the misspelling to match the way you changed the red, boldface word in the Not In Dictionary box. After you click Change, Word moves to the next misspelling (or unknown word) in the sentence, if there are any more. After you correct all the misspellings in a sentence, Word checks the grammar.

Taking a Suggestion

If you see a suggestion in the Spelling And Grammar dialog box that you want to use, click it, and then click the Change button. After you click Change, Word moves to the next misspelling (or unknown word) in the sentence, if there are any more. After you correct all the misspellings in a sentence, Word checks the grammar.

Adding Words to a Custom Dictionary

? SEE ALSO

For more information about custom dictionaries, see "Custom Dictionaries Dialog Box," page 975.

When Word finds a special or unusual word in your document that isn't contained in any of the dictionaries, you'll probably want to add this name to a custom dictionary so that the spelling checker won't stop at the word in future passes (unless it is spelled incorrectly). To add a word to a dictionary, click the Add button.

Ignoring a Misspelling

If Word stops on a word you want to leave as is, click the Ignore button. Word skips that instance of the word and searches for another unknown word. If Word finds another instance of a word you ignored, you see that word in the Spelling And Grammar dialog box. (The Ignore All button skips all instances of an unknown word throughout the rest of the document.)

The Ignore button is handy if you have a word you want spelled one way in one instance and another way in a later instance. For example, suppose your document contains a quotation that includes a misspelled word. You want to repeat the quotation as it was written, but you don't want to misspell the word in your own writing. In this case, you click the Ignore button for the misspelled word in the quotation, but you correct any misspellings in your own writing.

Getting Spelling to Ignore Words from the Start

You can save yourself time and aggravation during spell checking by getting Word to ignore peculiar words and phrases. How? Simple. Select the word or phrase, choose the Tools Language command, select (No Proofing) from the Mark Selected Text As box, and then click OK. When you check spelling, Word ignores text marked as (No Proofing).

If you realize that you have incorrectly changed or ignored a word, you can choose the Undo Last button to undo the change. By repeatedly clicking the Undo button, you can undo as many of your changes as you want, all the way back to the first change you made during this spelling check.

Handling Grammatical Errors

Word first checks spelling in each sentence and then checks grammar and style. If Word finds a potential grammar or style problem, the Spelling And Grammar dialog box appears, as shown in Figure 2-8.

FIGURE 2-8.
The Spelling And Grammar dialog box for a grammatical error.

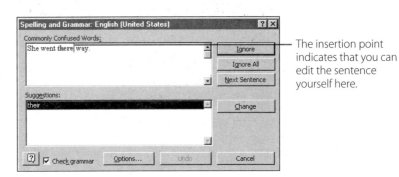

The insertion point indicates that you can edit the sentence yourself here.

In the top box of the Spelling And Grammar dialog box, Word displays the potential problem and highlights it in green boldface. This top box changes its label to tell you what kind of error Word has detected.

Getting an Explanation

Assistant

In the Suggestions box, Word displays suggested ways to correct or improve the sentence. If you want an explanation of the grammar or style rules that apply to the problem before you change the grammatical error, click the Assistant button in the lower left corner of the dialog box to display a grammar explanation (see Figure 2-8).

For instance, for the problem reported in Figure 2-8 the following explanation appears when you click the Assistant button:

Click anywhere or press the Escape key to close the Assistant balloon.

Taking a Suggestion

To correct the grammatical problem with one of the suggested changes, click the suggestion you want to use, and then click the Change button. Word moves on to the next grammatical error in the sentence, if there are any more. If the sentence is now grammatically acceptable, Word moves on to the next sentence to check the spelling of the words before checking the grammar.

Hand-Correcting a Grammatical Error

If you don't like any of the suggestions Word gives you but you do want to change the problem Word found, change the sentence in the top box, and then click the Change button. Word moves on to the next grammatical error in the sentence, if there are any more. If the sentence is now grammatically acceptable, Word moves on to the next sentence to check the spelling of the words before checking the grammar.

Ignoring a Grammatical Problem

To ignore a grammatical problem, click the Ignore button. Sometimes Word finds two or more problems in one sentence. If, after reviewing the sentence, you decide not to change the sentence at all, click the Next Sentence button. Word ignores all problems in the sentence and moves on to check the next one.

To ignore a problem throughout a document, click the Ignore All button. Word turns off the grammar or style rule that applies to that particular problem. To turn off a rule permanently, take the following steps.

1 Click the Options button to display the Spelling & Grammar tab in the Options dialog box.

2 Click the Settings button.

3 Turn off the check box for the applicable rule.

4 Click OK.

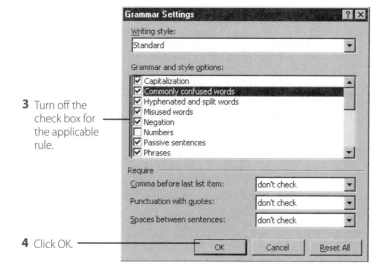

Selecting Grammatical Sensitivity

On some occasions, you'll write very formal documents, which must adhere to the strictest grammatical rules. Most of the time, you'll write business or personal documents in which the grammar may be more informal. For each document, you can select the level of grammatical strictness you want to observe. Word contains five built-in settings for grammatical strictness. Four of these settings have names that indicate proposed uses. The Custom setting allows you to design your own level of strictness without disturbing the other built-in settings. (Explore the list as directed in step 3 in the following list.) You can, however, adjust any of the settings to your liking by turning off selected grammar and style rules, as described in "Ignoring a Grammatical Problem" on the previous page.

To select the setting for grammatical strictness, take these steps:

1 Click the Options button to display the Spelling & Grammar tab in the Options dialog box.

2 Click the Settings button.

3 In the Writing Style box, select the level of strictness you want to use, and then click OK.

4 Click OK on the Spelling & Grammar tab.

 TIP

Correcting Proofreading Errors Directly

At any time, you can edit the document directly rather than in the Spelling And Grammar dialog box. To do so, click in the document window to activate it, and then make the changes you wish. (You might need to move the Spelling And Grammar dialog box out of the way first—to do this, drag the title bar of the dialog box.) When you've finished making changes, either click the Resume button (which replaces the Ignore button temporarily) in the Spelling And Grammar dialog box, press F7, double-click the Spelling and Grammar Status icon, or choose the Tools Spelling And Grammar command again to continue proofreading.

After the grammar check is complete, Word can display the Readability Statistics dialog box (see Figure 2-6 on page 70).

When you've finished reviewing the statistics, click OK.

To have Spelling And Grammar display readability statistics, take these steps:

1 Choose the Tools Options command and click the Spelling & Grammar tab, or click the Options button in the Spelling And Grammar dialog box.

2 Turn on the Show Readability Statistics check box.

3 Click OK.

4 Perform a spelling and grammar check.

You can get the readability statistics at any time after a document has been checked for spelling and grammar errors. Simply click the Spelling And Grammar button on the Standard toolbar. However, if the document contains possible errors, then clicking this button displays the Spelling And Grammar dialog box.

Resetting Ignore All

After you ignore words and grammar rules, you might need to proofread a document in which you want those words checked and those rules applied. Word holds on to the list until you quit Word. However, you might want to switch to another document before you quit Word, and you might want Word to catch words and grammar errors in the new document that you ignored in another document. Fortunately, Word lets you clear the Ignore All list.

To clear the Ignore All list, do the following:

1 Choose the Tools Options command, and click the Spelling & Grammar tab.

2 Click the Recheck Document button. (If you haven't yet proofread the document, the button label is Check Document.) Word displays the following warning message:

Click Yes to reset Word to catch all the words and grammar rules for which you previously clicked Ignore All.

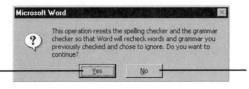

Click No to keep the Ignore All list.

3 Click OK to close the Options dialog box.

Now proofread your document as you usually do—automatically or manually.

 TIP

> If you click Ignore All during the current proofing check and later realize you made a mistake, click the Undo button until you return to the word or sentence, perform the correct action, and then continue forward with proofreading.

Adding Words to AutoCorrect During Proofreading

Adding words to AutoCorrect during proofreading is extremely easy and is possibly the best way to set up corrections for typing mistakes. Word gives you two ways to add a word to AutoCorrect during proofreading: during automatic proofreading and during manual proofreading.

To add a word to AutoCorrect during automatic proofreading, take these steps:

1 Click the right mouse button on a word with a red sawtooth underline that you want to add to AutoCorrect.

2 Click AutoCorrect on the Spelling shortcut menu, and select the correct spelling of the word from the AutoCorrect submenu.

 NOTE

> If the correct spelling of the word is not listed on the AutoCorrect submenu, you will need to use the steps for adding a word to AutoCorrect during manual proofreading.

To add a word to AutoCorrect during manual proofreading, take these steps:

1 Display the Spelling dialog box. If you're running as-you-type spell checking, use the right mouse button to click a marked word, and choose Spelling from the shortcut menu. If you're running a regular spelling check, Word displays the Spelling dialog box when it encounters a misspelled or unknown word.

2 Select the correction for the mistyped word.

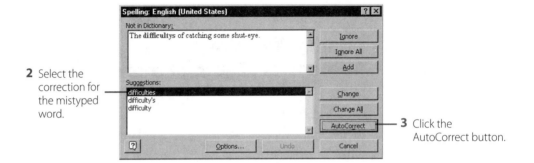

3 Click the AutoCorrect button.

Word corrects the word in the document, adds your mistyping of the word and its correction to the AutoCorrect list, and continues with the spelling check.

Station 5: Review

Now that you've got a document, how do you work on it? You need to know how to find and select text anywhere in the document.

- To see text that's out of sight, use the scroll bar in the window.

- To add text, position the insertion point, which appears as a blinking vertical bar, at the place where you want Microsoft Word to insert the new text or art.

- To make changes—for example, to edit, format, or copy—you first select the text or art you want to change. Selecting text is discussed in detail in "Selecting Text," page 85.

Moving Through a Document

You move through a document to see text and art that's out of sight, to set the insertion point at a new place, or to select text and art for changes. In most cases, as you move through a document, you also move the insertion point as you go. To move the insertion point in your document, you can use the mouse, the keyboard, or several commands, most notably the Edit Go To command.

The following keys and commands move the insertion point:

- Cursor keys (the keys on the numeric keypad on the right side of your keyboard, described in Table 5-1, page 235)

- Repeat Find shortcut key (Shift+F4)

- Next Field shortcut key (F11)

- Previous Field shortcut key (Shift+F11)

- Go Back shortcut key (Shift+F5)

- Edit Go To command

- Edit Find command

The following sections explain all the ways you can move through a document and position the insertion point.

Moving with the Mouse

Scrolling with the mouse in Normal view is the same as scrolling in any Windows-based application—that is, you click the up, down, left, and right scroll arrows; click the scroll bar itself, between the scroll box and a scroll arrow; or drag the scroll box.

⭐ TIP

> **Scrolling Outside the Left Margin in Normal View**
> If you are in Normal view and your document has text outside the left margin, don't worry. Even though the scroll box appears to be at its left limit when you reach the left margin, you can scroll the window past the margin by clicking the left scroll arrow of the horizontal scroll bar with the left mouse button. To realign the left margin with the left edge of the window, click the horizontal scroll bar to the right of the scroll box, and then click again to the left of the scroll box.

Four Views to a Word Document

Sometimes you can simplify the process of moving through a document by changing your view. At the left end of the horizontal scroll bar you see four view buttons, as shown here:

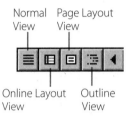

Normal View   Page Layout View
Online Layout View   Outline View

Each button displays the document you're working on in a different way. The first button displays a document in Normal view. In Normal view (what you're probably looking at now and use most of the time in Word), you work on the text and its appearance.

The second button, for Online Layout view, displays the pages of your document as readers will view them as Web pages. For more about Online view, see Chapter 21, "Creating Online Documents."

The third button, for Page Layout view, displays the pages of your document as Word will print them; that is, as they will emerge from the printer. In Page Layout view, you work on the look of pages, including inserting and working on art, drawn tables, and text boxes. For more about art, drawn tables, and text boxes, see Chapter 8, "Filing Your Report," and Chapter 10, "Brocading a Brochure."

The fourth button displays a document in Outline view. In Outline view, you can set up headings for the various parts of a document, rearrange the order of paragraphs, and hide or show as many or as few levels of headings as you want. For more about Outline view, see "Understanding Master Documents and Subdocuments," page 558.

In addition to each of these four views, you can turn on the document map beside each view. The document map shows you a list of the important points (usually headings) in your document. For more about the Document Map feature, see "Document Map," page 870.

? SEE ALSO

For more information about the Select Browse Object button, see "Finding Your Way with the Select Browse Object button," page 109.

? SEE ALSO

You can also use the Go To command, the Find command, and the Select Browse Object button on the vertical scroll bar to move to specific places in a document. For information about these methods, see, "Finding Your Place with Find," page 97.

★ TIP

Word provides three extra controls on the vertical scroll bar: the Previous Page button, the Select Browse Object button, and the Next Page button.

If you scroll through your document with the mouse, the insertion point does not move. Mouse scrolling is handy if you want to see something elsewhere in your document and then continue typing where you were. However, if you start scrolling with the mouse and then press a key or choose a command that moves the insertion point, the insertion point shifts from its current position.

Getting Back Home

Suppose you move the insertion point to another part of your document and then want to return to the insertion point's previous location. Press the Go Back shortcut key (Shift+F5) to quickly return to the previous location. Word remembers the last three places where you made a change. By repeatedly pressing the Go Back shortcut key, you can move the insertion point among the last three places and the current place. If one of the places is in a different document that's still open, Word switches to that document.

> **Getting to the Insertion Point or the Last Save Point**
>
> If you scroll the window with the mouse but then want to return the current insertion point to view, press the Go Back shortcut key (Shift+F5). Also note that when you open a document, pressing the Go Back shortcut key jumps the insertion point to the position it was in when you last saved the document.

Moving with the Cursor Keys

When you press keys to move through a document, you're simply moving the insertion point. To move the insertion point, press the cursor keys on the numeric keypad (while the Num Lock key is turned on) or the cursor keys located between the numeric keypad and the typing keys. Table 2-3 on the next page lists the cursor keys and their corresponding actions.

TABLE 2-3.   The Cursor Keys and Their Actions.

Cursor Keys	Action
→	Moves to the next character or to the end of the selection
←	Moves to the previous character or to the beginning of the selection
↓	Moves down one line (same column)
↑	Moves up one line (same column)
Home	Moves to the beginning of the line
End	Moves to the end of the line
Page Down	Moves down the height of the window
Page Up	Moves up the height of the window
Ctrl+→	Moves to the next word or the end of the selection
Ctrl+←	Moves to the previous word or to the beginning of the selection
Ctrl+PgUp	Moves to the previous browse object
Ctrl+PgDn	Moves to the next browse object
Ctrl+↑	Moves to the beginning of the current paragraph and then to the beginning of each preceding paragraph thereafter
Ctrl+↓	Moves to the beginning of the next paragraph
Alt+Ctrl+PgUp	Moves to the beginning of the first visible line of the window
Alt+Ctrl+PgDn	Moves to the end of the last visible line of the window
Alt+↑	Moves to the previous frame or object
Alt+↓	Moves to the next frame or object
Ctrl+Home	Moves to the beginning of the document
Ctrl+End	Moves to the end of the document

Selecting Text

You select text when you want to perform an action on it—for example, edit it, format it, or copy it. To select text means to expand a highlight from the insertion point across all the text you want to select. When you select text, the insertion point still sits at one end of the selection, even though you can't see it blinking. If you select from left to right, the insertion point is located at the right end of the selection. If you select from right to left, the insertion point is located at the left end of the selection.

To use the mouse to select, you click, double-click, triple-click, or drag, with or without pressing the Shift key, the Alt key, or the Ctrl key. These options are explained in the following sections.

To use the keyboard to select, hold down the Shift key or press the Extend Selection shortcut key (F8) while you move the insertion point. For a list of keys that move the insertion point, see Table 2-3.

Selecting with the Mouse

Perhaps the greatest benefit of having a mouse is using it to select text. You can use the mouse alone to select by clicking, double-clicking, triple-clicking, or dragging. You can also use the mouse along with the Shift key, the Alt key, or the Ctrl key to select text in special ways. You can use these mouse methods in document text and in the selection bar. (The following sections explain all of these methods.)

Clicking, Double-Clicking, and Triple-Clicking

Microsoft set up Word to make selecting specific pieces of text quick and easy. What you select depends on how many times you click the left mouse button, as follows:

Mouse Action	Use
Click	To position the insertion point or to select a picture or object
Double-click	To select a word
Triple-click anywhere in a paragraph	To select the entire paragraph
Hold down the Ctrl key and click anywhere in the sentence	To select a sentence

You can also use mouse clicks and the Shift key to select any block of text by doing the following:

1 Click at the beginning of the block you want to select.

2 Hold down the Shift key.

3 Click at the end of the block.

Dragging

Dragging is holding down the left mouse button as you move the mouse. Dragging selects text. To select by dragging, follow these steps:

1 Move the mouse pointer to the beginning of the text that you want to select.

2 Hold down the left mouse button.

3 Move the mouse to expand the selection in any direction you want. When you move the mouse left or right, the selection expands character by character. When you move the mouse up or down, the selection expands line by line.

If you double-click and drag, you can select by words. In this case, when you double-click, you click, release, and then click and hold down the second click. The time between clicks must be as short as when you double-click to select a word. You can triple-click or hold down the Ctrl key and drag to select by paragraphs or by sentences.

To select by words, do the following:

1 Double-click a word and hold down the mouse button on the second click.

2 Drag to expand the selection by words.

You can't use the double-click and drag method if you start your selection on a picture or an object. Double-clicking a picture or an object starts the picture editor or the application that created the object.

To select by sentences, do the following:

1 Hold down the Ctrl key, click in a sentence, and hold down the mouse button when you click.

2 Drag to expand the selection by sentences.

To select by paragraphs, do the following:

1 Triple-click in a paragraph and hold down the mouse button on the third click.

2 Drag to expand the selection by paragraphs.

Using the Mouse in the Selection Bar

The selection bar is an invisible column along the left edge of the document window. While in the selection bar, the mouse pointer changes to an arrow that points northeast, as shown here:

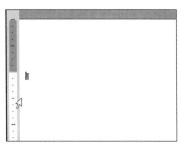

Various clicks in the selection bar select various amounts of text, as follows:

Mouse Action	Use
Click	To select one line
Double-click	To select one paragraph
Triple-click	To select the entire document

You can also drag in the selection bar to select the text you want. When you drag in the selection bar, the way in which the selection expands depends on your original selection, as follows:

Mouse Action	Use
Click and drag	To expand selection by lines
Double-click and drag	To expand selection by paragraphs

Using the Mouse to Select by Columns

To select by columns, do the following:

1 Position the insertion point at any corner of the column you want to select.

2 Hold down the Alt key and drag to the diagonally opposite corner of the column, as shown in the following illustration. You can select up or down and right or left.

Alt+click at one corner (any corner).

Drag to the opposite corner.

3 Release the Alt key and mouse button after you have completed your selection.

Selecting with the Keyboard

To select text with the keyboard, hold down the Shift key while pressing the cursor keys that move the insertion point. When the highlight includes all the text that you want to select, release the Shift key. (For a review of which keys move the insertion point, see Table 2-3 on page 84.)

You can also use the Extend Selection shortcut key (F8), the Shrink Selection shortcut key (Shift+F8), and the Column Selection shortcut key (Ctrl+Shift+F8) to select text.

If you're selecting to a faraway spot in a document, use the Extend Selection shortcut key (F8), or double-click the label *EXT* in the status bar. With Extend Selection turned on, you can extend the selection with cursor keys or the mouse without holding down the Shift key. You can also select by pressing any character key; the selection extends to the next character that matches the one you type, and even jumps to the next paragraph mark when you press the Enter key.

To select text that Word recognizes as a text unit (a word, a sentence, and so on), press F8 again. Each time you press F8, the selection expands to the next larger unit of text. For example, if you press F8 to select a word, pressing F8 again selects the sentence.

You cancel Extend Selection by double-clicking *EXT* in the status bar, pressing the Escape key, or choosing a command that affects the selection. Pressing Escape, however, does not change the selection.

The counterpart of the Extend Selection shortcut key (F8) is the Shrink Selection shortcut key (Shift+F8). When you press Shift+F8, the selection shrinks to the next smaller unit of text. If you extend the selection by using the Extend Selection shortcut key, the Shrink Selection shortcut key shrinks the selection back through the same selections the Extend Selection shortcut key made. If you do not use the Extend Selection shortcut key, Word shrinks to the first unit in the selection that is the next smaller size. For example, if you select a paragraph and then press Shift+F8, the selection shrinks to the first sentence in the paragraph.

Figure 2-9 illustrates the effects of using F8 and Shift+F8 to extend and then shrink selections.

FIGURE 2-9.

Using the Extend Selection shortcut key and the Shrink Selection shortcut key.

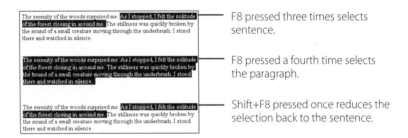

F8 pressed three times selects sentence.

F8 pressed a fourth time selects the paragraph.

Shift+F8 pressed once reduces the selection back to the sentence.

To select by columns, use the Column Selection shortcut key (Ctrl+Shift+F8) and the cursor keys:

1 Position the insertion point at any corner of the column you want to select.

2 Press Ctrl+Shift+F8. The *COL* label appears in the status bar.

3 Use the cursor keys to select the columns you want; you can select up or down and right or left.

4 Turn off Column Selection by double-clicking *COL* in the status bar, by pressing the Escape key, or by choosing a command that changes the selection.

Finding Your Place with Go To

You might want to go to page 13, or you might want to find a specific heading or table. You might just want to look at all the pictures. To move the insertion point to a specific place in a single bound, display the Go To tab of the Find And Replace dialog box (shown in Figure 2-10). To display this tab, use one of the following methods:

- Choose the Edit Go To command.

- Press the Go To shortcut key (Ctrl+G or F5).

- Double-click in the page number section or the location section of the status bar.

FIGURE 2-10.
The Go To tab of the Find And Replace dialog box.

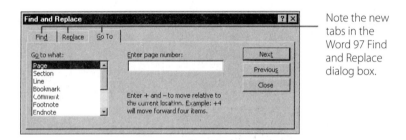

Note the new tabs in the Word 97 Find and Replace dialog box.

On the Go To tab you must specify a place. A place can be one of the following:

- A specific place, such as a page or a line

- A place relative to the insertion point

- A percentage of the way through the document

Specific Destinations

When you select a specific type of place, Word jumps to a point in the document measured from the beginning of the document. To select a destination, do the following on the Go To tab.

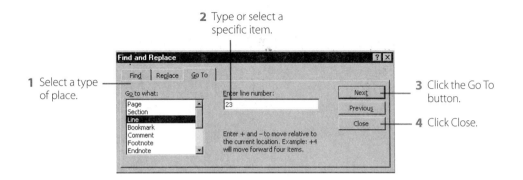

2 Type or select a specific item.

1 Select a type of place.

3 Click the Go To button.

4 Click Close.

The insertion point moves to the beginning of the specific destination.

Relative Destinations

The Go To command lets you jump to the next or previous instance of a place. The Go To command can jump the insertion point relative distances, as well. A relative distance is some distance away from a specific place.

To move the insertion point to the next place or to a previous place, follow these steps:

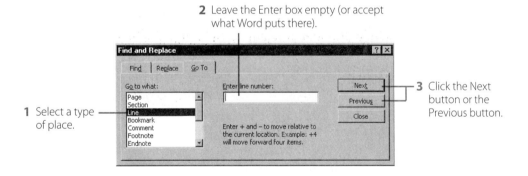

2 Leave the Enter box empty (or accept what Word puts there).

1 Select a type of place.

3 Click the Next button or the Previous button.

To move a relative distance from a specific place, use a plus or minus sign and a number in the Enter box. The plus sign moves the insertion point forward in the document; the minus sign moves the insertion point backward. For example, if you select Page in the Go To What list and then type -*10* in the Enter box, Word moves the insertion point back 10 pages from its current position. If you choose Line and type +*100*, Word moves the insertion point forward 100 lines.

Table 2-4 on the next page lists the places and the possible contents of the Enter box for each destination type.

Percentage Distances

The Edit Go To command also lets you move a percentage of the way through your document. To do so, follow these steps:

1 Open the Go To dialog box.

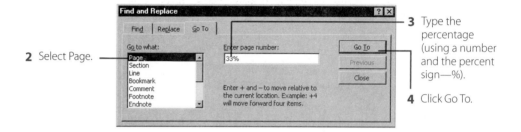

2 Select Page.

3 Type the percentage (using a number and the percent sign—%).

4 Click Go To.

Word moves the insertion point into the document the distance specified, measuring from the beginning of the document. For example, type *33%* to move about one third of the way into a document. If you type a percentage greater than 100, Word moves the insertion point to the document's end.

Bookmark Destinations

A bookmark is a name you assign to a particular place in a document that lets you quickly jump to that place again or refer to the text at that place—with a cross-reference, for example. A bookmark can mark either an insertion point or a selection of any size.

You can jump to specific text by using a bookmark name as the Go To destination:

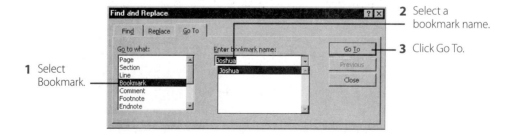

1 Select Bookmark.

2 Select a bookmark name.

3 Click Go To.

Word jumps to the location and selects the text that is marked by the bookmark.

TABLE 2-4.   Places and Values Used with the Edit Go To Command.

Go To What	In Enter Box, Type or Select
Page	Number, +number, or –number
Section	Number, +number, or –number
Line	Number, +number, or –number
Bookmark	A name from the list of bookmarks
Comment	"Any Reviewer" or the name of a specific reviewer optionally followed by number, +number or –number
Footnote	Number, +number, or –number
Endnote	Number, +number, or –number
Field	"Any Field" or a specific field name optionally followed by number, +number or –number
Table	Number, +number, or –number
Graphic	Number, +number, or –number
Equation	Number, +number, or –number
Object	"Any Object" or a specific object type optionally followed by number, +number, or –number
Heading	Number, +number, or –number (headings don't need heading numbers)

Setting and Changing Bookmarks

Follow these steps to set a new bookmark:

1 Select the text you want to mark, or position the insertion point to create a bookmark that does not contain text.

2 Choose the Insert Bookmark command to display the Bookmark dialog box, shown in Figure 2-11 on the next page.

FIGURE 2-11.

The Bookmark dialog box.

3 Type a new name (a name not already in the Bookmark Name list).

4 Click the Add button to create a new bookmark.

To change the position of a bookmark, you create a new bookmark using the same bookmark name by doing the following:

1 Select the text you want to mark, or position the insertion point at the location you want to mark.

2 Choose the Insert Bookmark command to display the Bookmark dialog box.

3 Select a name from the list of bookmarks.

4 Click the Add button.

You can use the Insert Bookmark command to jump to a bookmark:

1 Choose the Insert Bookmark command.

2 In the Bookmark dialog box, click Sort By Name to see an alphabetical list, or click Sort By Location to see the names in the order that occur in the document.

3 Select a bookmark name.

4 Click the Go To button.

5 Click the Close button.

Deleting a Bookmark

When you no longer need or want a bookmark, you can delete it by doing the following:

1 Choose the Insert Bookmark command to display the Bookmark dialog box.

2 Select the name of the bookmark you want to delete from the list of bookmarks.

3 Click the Delete button.

Listing Hidden Bookmarks

Word has several uses for hidden bookmarks and several ways to add them to a document. You can insert a Set or Ask field (used in mail merge), and you can insert cross-references. You can't see these bookmarks, and in previous versions of Word, you couldn't delete them, at least not without destroying a bunch of text.

The Bookmark dialog box in Word 97 gives you a way to see the names of hidden bookmarks. This way, you can select the name of a hidden bookmark and perform any bookmark action on it. To see hidden bookmarks, choose the Insert Bookmark command.

Hidden Bookmarks

Turn on this check box to see hidden bookmarks. Turn it off to hide them. If the hidden bookmarks don't appear with this check box turned on, turn it off, and then turn it on again.

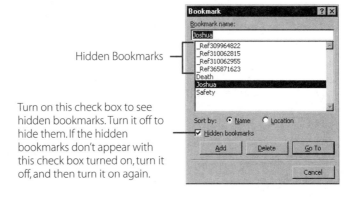

As you can see, hidden bookmarks have strange names that don't tell you what they mark. To see what a hidden bookmark marks, click Go To.

Viewing Bookmarks

Sometimes it's hard to know where a bookmark starts and ends in your document. There is an easy way to display bookmarks in your text, plain as day.

To display bookmarks in text, do the following:

1 Choose the Tools Options command, and select the View tab.

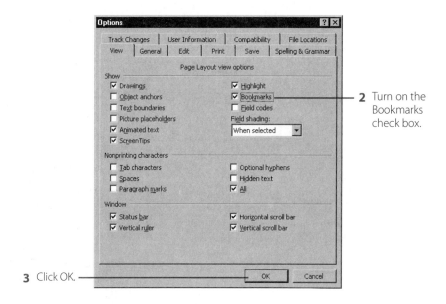

2 Turn on the Bookmarks check box.

3 Click OK.

Bookmarks for a selection appear as square brackets surrounding the selection. A bookmark for an insertion point appears as an I-beam. (It's the two square brackets overlapping.) Both are shown in Figure 2-12.

FIGURE 2-12.
The insertion point bookmark and a selection bookmark.

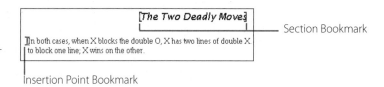

Section Bookmark

Insertion Point Bookmark

Word doesn't display bookmark brackets for hidden bookmarks.

Bookmarks can overlap other bookmarks (the beginning of a bookmark can be inside a second bookmark, while the end is outside the second bookmark). You can also nest bookmarks (set a bookmark inside another bookmark). Word doesn't distinguish between overlapping bookmarks and nested bookmarks. The text shown in Figure 2-13, for example, contains three bookmarks; the numbers in the figure indicate matching pairs of brackets and don't appear in your Word document.

FIGURE 2-13.
Overlapping and nested bookmarks.

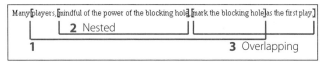

Editing Around Bookmarks

Within a bookmark, you can revise text as you please and as you normally do in any text that doesn't have a bookmark. When you revise bookmarked text at the bookmark brackets, however, you need to be aware of what will happen. If you type or insert text in front of the first bookmarked character (just to the right of the beginning bookmark bracket), what you type gets added to the bookmarked text. If you don't want this change, move to the left of the beginning bookmark bracket, and then type or insert the new text. If you type or insert text after the last bookmarked character, the new text is *not* added to the bookmark. If you want the new text as part of the bookmarked text, position the insertion point to the left of the last bookmarked character, type the last character, and then type the new text. After you type the new text at the end of the bookmark, delete the character that was previously at the end of the bookmark.

Finding Your Place with Find

Sometimes you just need to find the right words, to copy them, to move them, or to change them. You might want to change the words themselves, or you might want to change the way they look (their formatting). Maybe, after all, all you want to do is read them. Word's Find command gives you several ways to locate words so that you can do whatever you want to them.

The Find command can find specific words, regardless of how they look. The Find command can find all the various forms of a word, such as *format, formatting, formatted,* and *formats.* The Find command can find specific types of formatting, regardless of what the words are. Or, the Find command can find specific words with specific formatting. And finally, the Find command can find phrases with specific characters or words in them.

Text Finds

To direct Word to find specific text only, regardless of its formatting, do the following:

1 Choose the Edit Find command to display the Find dialog box.

 TIP

> The keyboard shortcut to the Find tab of the Find And Replace dialog box is Ctrl+F.

2 Type or select the text you want to find. Find What here is linked with Find What on the Replace tab.

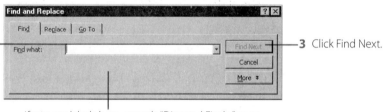

3 Click Find Next.

If you see labels here, consult "Directed Finds," page 100, "All Word Form Finds," page 101 and "Format Finds," page 101, for steps to take to turn them off.

 NOTE

> If you have a selection in the document when you choose the Find command, Word looks only within the selection. After Word finishes looking at the selection, you'll see a message asking if you want to continue looking in the rest of the document. Click Yes to look through the entire document. Click No to look only within the selection. (For information about using this trick for a limited find, see the sidebar "Limited Find and Replace," page 110.) If you select a direction (Up or Down instead of All), Word looks from the insertion point toward one end of the document (see "Directed Finds," page 100). When Word reaches that end of the document, you see a message asking if you want to continue from the other end of the document. Click Yes to look from the other end of the document back to the insertion point from which Word started. Click No to stop searching.

Finding Whole Words and Matched Cases

Some longer words contain within them shorter words. For example, *if* is the middle word in *life*. Some words can simply be the names of things (for example, *windows*), and at other times, they are the proper names of things (for example, *Windows*); or they might be the first word in a sentence. In these latter two cases, the word is capitalized. When you want to find only short words that are words unto themselves (and not part of a longer word), you'll want to direct Word to find whole words only. Also, if you want to find words that have a specific uppercase and lowercase arrangement, you'll want to direct Word to match the case exactly. If you don't direct Word to do this, Word finds all matches without regard to the arrangement of uppercase and lowercase letters.

NOTE

You can find whole words and match cases for replacements, too.

To direct Word to find whole words or match cases, take these steps:

1 Choose the Edit Find command.

2 Click the More button.

3 Type the text you want to find here.

4 Turn on this check box to exactly match the use of uppercase and lowercase letters. Turn off this check box to find all instances of the Find What text, regardless of uppercase or lowercase.

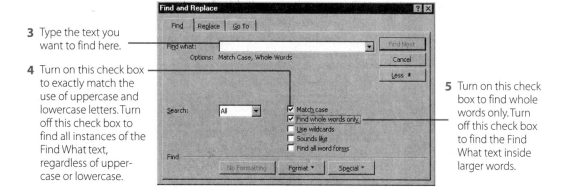

5 Turn on this check box to find whole words only. Turn off this check box to find the Find What text inside larger words.

Repeated Finds

After you use the Find dialog box to find an instance of what you're looking for, you have a couple of choices:

■ Click in the document. The document becomes active, and the Find dialog box becomes inactive but remains visible. When you're ready to find the next instance, click the Find Next button in the Find dialog box.

■ Close the Find dialog box, make your changes, and then press Shift+F4 to find the next instance.

> The Find What box also contains a list of your seven previous finds. You can click the down arrow at the right end of the Find What box, and then select a Find What item you used before.

Directed Finds

Word is set up originally to look through the entire document to find matches for the Find What text and formatting. You can, however, change this. You can direct Word to look up or down in a document. The Up direction means look from the insertion point toward the beginning of the document. The Down direction means look from the insertion point toward the end of the document.

But why would you choose to look Up or Down instead of throughout All? Here's one situation that might call for this approach. You start reviewing at the beginning of the document and see something you want to change. You change it, and then you realize that there might be other instances like the one you changed later in the document. Rather than straining your eyes to find them, you want to let Word find them for you. You set up a Find, but to save time, you decide you only need to look from the insertion point where you just changed the document toward the end. In this case, you might choose the Down direction. Or, in another case, you're working near the end of a document and realize you need to change something you've done several times earlier in the document. In this case, you might choose the Up direction.

You can also choose a direction for replacements. Your choice affects the Find part of Replace.

To direct Word to look up or down through a document instead of throughout the whole document, take these steps:

1 Choose the Edit Find command.

2 Click the More button.

3 Type the text or select the formatting for the material you want to find in the Find What box.

4 Select any of the check box options to control the Find operation.

5 Select Up or Down from the Search list.

6 Click the Find Next button.

When Word reaches the beginning or end of the document, you see a message asking if you want to continue from the other end of the document. Click Yes to look from the other end of the document back to the insertion point from which Word started. Click No to stop searching.

To direct Word to look through the whole document again, choose All from the Search list the next time you set up another Find or Replace.

All Word Form Finds

In English, many verbs have irregular forms for the past tense and past perfect tense. For example, *say*, *says*, and *said*; or *do*, *does*, *did*, and *done*. When you want to find all the forms of a verb, take these steps:

1 Choose the Edit Find command.

2 Type or select the base verb you want to find. The base verb is the simplest form of the verb (the infinitive without *to*). For example, *do* is a base verb.

3 Click the More button to expand the Find tab.

4 Turn on the Find All Word Forms check box in the Find dialog box.

5 Click the Find Next button.

> **NOTE**

For Find All Word Forms, Word uses a special dictionary. If you installed Word on a laptop, you might not have this dictionary. Word will let you know. To add the dictionary Word needs, rerun Setup and add this component.

Format Finds

When you need to find all the boldface words or all the paragraphs with a particular style, you can use Find without text to find only the formatting.

To direct Word to find a specific format only, do the following:

1 Choose the Edit Find command.

2 Leave the Find What box blank. (Delete any text in the box, if necessary.)

3 Click the More button to expand the Find tab.

4 Click the Format button to display the list of the types of formats, shown here:

5 Select the type of format you want to find. Word displays the dialog box for the type of format you select.

6 Select only the settings that specify the formatting you want to find, and then click OK in the dialog box to return to the Find tab.

Your formatting selections are listed beneath the Find what box.

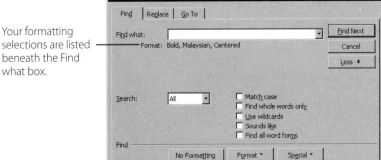

7 Click the Find Next button.

Formatted Text Finds

To find formatted text, do the following:

1 Choose the Edit Find command.

2 Type or select the text you want to find in the Find What box.

3 Click the More button to expand the Format tab.

4 Click the Format button to display the list.

5 Select the type of format you want to find, and in the dialog box that appears, select only the settings that specify the formatting you want to find.

6 Click OK to return to the Find and Replace dialog box.

7 Click the Find Next button.

Special Finds

Sometimes you might want to find a variety of words. At other times you might want to find words that sound like other words. And at still other times you might want to find special characters or special parts of a document. That's where the Sounds Like check box, the Use Wildcards check box, and the Special button come into play.

Sounds Like Finds

Turn on the Sounds Like check box to find words that sound the same as the Find What text but are spelled differently, such as "prise" and "prize" and "colour" and "color."

> **NOTE**

Be aware that what sounds alike to Word might strike you a bit strangely. For example, if you type *to*, *two*, and *too* in your document, and then type either *to* or *too* in the Find What box, Word finds "to" and "too," but not "two." Why not? (Shrug.) Or, type *rode* in the Find What box, and Word finds "right," "read," "red," "writ," and "wrote," as well as "road" and "rode."

Special Element Finds

A Word document can contain many elements that are not part of the text, such as paragraph marks, tables, and page breaks. There are also some characters that require special handling, such as the caret character and the em dash. Clicking the Special button displays a list of the special elements you can search for in a document, as shown in Figure 2-14.

FIGURE 2-14.

The Special button list when the Use Wildcards check box is turned off.

Paragraph Mark
Tab Character
Comment Mark
Any Character
Any Digit
Any Letter
Caret Character
Column Break
Em Dash
En Dash
Endnote Mark
Field
Footnote Mark
Graphic
Manual Line Break
Manual Page Break
Nonbreaking Hyphen
Nonbreaking Space
Optional Hyphen
Section Break
White Space

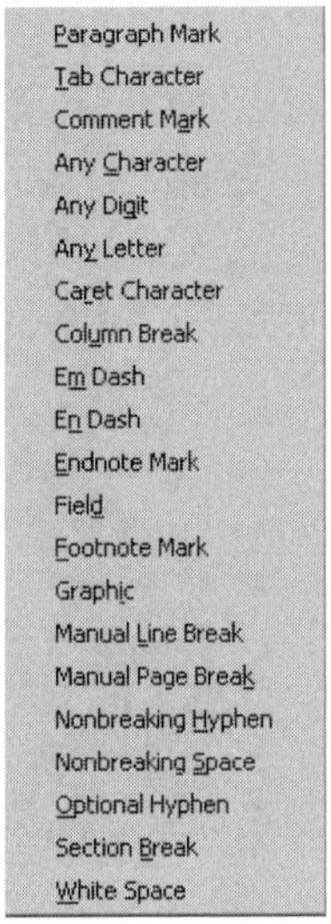

> **NOTE**
>
> The list in Figure 2-14 appears when the Use Wildcards box is turned off. With the Use Wildcards box turned on, you see the list shown in Figure 2-15, page 106.

Table 2-5 lists the other special elements you can find and the special characters you use to find them. Word inserts the appropriate special characters in the Find What box when you select a special element from the Special button list. You can also type the special characters.

TABLE 2-5. Special Elements You Can Find and the Special Characters That Find Them When the Use Wildcards Check Box Is Turned Off.

Special Element	Special Characters
Paragraph mark	^p
Tab character	^t
Comment mark	^a
Any character	^?
Any digit	^#

(continued)

Table 2-5. *continued*

Special Element	Special Characters
Any letter	^$
Caret character	^^
Column break	^n
Em dash	^+
En dash	^=
Endnote mark	^e
Field	^d
Footnote mark	^f
Graphic	^g
Manual line break	^l
Manual page break	^m
Nonbreaking hyphen	^~
Nonbreaking space	^s
Optional hyphen	^-
Section break	^b
White space	^w

Use Wildcards

It's possible to find several different words (or pieces of text) with the same find. By adding special symbols to letters and numbers, you can direct Word to find different words with similar patterns of letters and numbers.

With the Use Wildcards check box turned on, click the Special button in the Find dialog box to insert the special symbols from the list shown in Figure 2-15.

FIGURE 2-15.
The Special button list
of special elements
when the Use
Wildcards check box is
turned on.

Any Character	?
Character in Range	[-]
Beginning of Word	<
End of Word	>
Expression	( )
Not	[!]
Num Occurrences	{ , }
Previous 1 or More	@
0 or More Characters	*
Tab Character	
Comment Mark	
Caret Character	
Column Break	
Em Dash	
En Dash	
Graphic	
Manual Line Break	
Page / Section Break	
Nonbreaking Hyphen	
Nonbreaking Space	
Optional Hyphen	

Table 2-6 lists the names, special symbols, and examples for the additional items (top nine) in the Special button list when you turn on the Use Wildcards box. (The rest of the elements you see listed in Figure 2-15 are the same items that are on the list in Table 2-5.)

TABLE 2-6. **Additional Special Symbols You Use to Find a Variety of Text When the Use Wildcards Check Box Is Turned On.**

Option	Use	Examples
Any Character ?	Substitute for any single letter, number, or symbol	*h?m* finds "ham," "him," and "hum"
Character In Range [-]	This special symbol can take two forms:	
	[ ] Find any text that contains one of the characters in the brackets	*h[ai]m* finds "ham" and "him"
	[-] Find any text that contains one of the characters in the series of characters in the brackets; the characters in brackets must be in alphabetical order	*[b-p]ike* finds "bike," "dike," "hike," "like," "mike," and "pike"
Beginning Of Word <	Find text that contains the characters listed after the symbol if the characters occur at the beginning of a word	*<dog* finds "dog" and "dogged," but not "hotdog"

(continued)

Table 2-6. *continued*

Option	Use	Examples
End Of Word >	Find text that contains the characters listed before the symbol if the characters occur at the end of a word	*dog>* finds "dog" and "hotdog," but not "dogged"
Expression ( )	Group special symbols together	*<(d[io]g)* finds "dog," "dogged," "dig," and "digging," but not "dug" or "hotdog"
Not [!]	Find any single character with the exception of the characters in the brackets	*L[!au]ck* finds "Lick" and "Lock," but not "Lack" or "Luck"
Num Occurrences {,}	This special symbol can take three forms:	
	{*n*} Find text with exactly *n* instances of the preceding character or special symbols	*bo{2}st* finds "boost" but not "boast"
	{*n*,} Find text with at least *n* instances of the preceding character or special symbols	*be9{3,}am* finds "be999am," "be9999am," and so on, but not "be9am" or "be99am"
	{*n,m*} Find text with from *n* to *m* instances of the preceding character or special symbols	*be9{1,3}am* finds "be9am," "be99am," and "be999am," but not "be9999am," "be99999am," and so on
Previous 1 or More @	Find text with one or more instances of the preceding character or special symbols	*be9@am* finds "be9am," "be99am," "be999am," "be9999am," and so on
0 or More Characters *	Substitute for any group of letters, numbers, and symbols	*h*m* finds any series of characters starting with "h" and ending with "m," such as "harm," "helm," and "hokum"

> **NOTE**
>
> You can choose either the Use Wildcards check box or the Sounds Like check box, but not both. If you turn on one of these check boxes and then turn on the other one, Word turns off the first check box.

To use wildcards, do the following:

1 Choose the Edit Find command, and then click the More button.

2 Turn on the Use Wildcards check box.

3 Think of the pattern that will match the words you want to find. Type in the Find What box the letters and numbers that are common to all the words you want to find.

> **NOTE**
>
> Type the letters in the case (uppercase and lowercase) you want to find. With the Use Wildcards check box turned on, Word automatically turns on the Match Case check box, even though it doesn't appear turned on. Note also that the Match Case check box is dimmed so that you can't change it.

4 In the Find What box, position the insertion point where you want to insert the wildcard special symbols.

5 Click the Special button, and click the types of special symbols that suit your find.

6 As needed, fill in the letters, numbers, and symbols for the different words you want to find.

7 Set any options you want for finding formatting.

8 Click the Find Next button.

> **TIP**
>
> **Finding Wildcard Symbols as Regular Characters**
> If, while you have the Use Wildcards check box turned on, you want to search the document for a special symbol itself—@, for example—precede the special symbol with a backslash (\). To search for a backslash, type a double backslash (\\). With the Use Wildcards check box turned off, don't type the backslash in front of the special characters.

Finding Your Way with the Select Browse Object Button

Near the bottom of the vertical scroll bar you'll find the Select Browse Object button, sandwiched between the Previous Page and Next Page buttons.

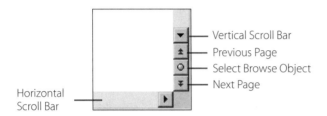

Vertical Scroll Bar
Previous Page
Select Browse Object
Next Page

Horizontal Scroll Bar

When you click this button, a grid of buttons appears that you can use to browse the document. You can also use this button to quickly find specific types of places in your document. To find a specific type of place in your document, take these steps:

1 Click the Select Browse Object button.

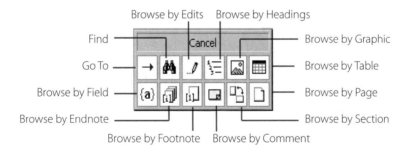

Browse by Edits   Browse by Headings

Find
Go To
Browse by Field
Browse by Endnote

Browse by Graphic
Browse by Table
Browse by Page
Browse by Section

Browse by Footnote   Browse by Comment

2 Click the button for the type of object you want to browse. Word jumps to the next instance of the object in the document.

3 Repeat step 1 and step 2 to jump to the next object in the document.

For details about the Go To, Headings, Graphic, Table, Field, Endnote, Footnote, Comment, Section, and Page buttons, see "Finding Your Place with Go To," page 90. For details about the Find button, see "Finding Your Place with Find," page 97.

Limited Find and Replace

There will be times when you want Word to look only in part of a document to find or replace words or formatting. When you want to limit the range of find or replace, take these steps:

1 Select only the part of the document where you want Word to look for words or formatting to find or replace.

2 Set up the find or replace according to the steps for the type of find or replace you want Word to perform.

3 Click Find Next to find or to decide to replace.

For replace, click the Replace button, and then click the Find Next button again. Or, to replace all instances, click the Replace All button at any time.

When Word has finished looking through the selection, you see a message asking if you want to look in the rest of the document. Click No to limit the find or replace to the selection. Click Yes if you want Word to look through the rest of the document, too.

Station 6: Revise

When you're ready to revise a document, you have several tactics at your disposal. First, you can type new text anywhere in the document. Simply position the insertion point where you want the new text, and then type it. You can replace text by typing: select the text you want to replace, and then type the new text. (See the Tip "Editing Around Bookmarks," page 97, for an exception to this simple technique.) You can also select and then press Delete or Backspace to erase text. Or, you can position the insertion point, and then press Delete to delete characters to the right of the insertion point or press Backspace to delete characters to the left of the insertion point.

In addition to these simple typing techniques for revising text, you can copy and move text, and you can have Word perform wholesale replacements of one piece of text with another.

Copy and Move with Copy, Cut, and Paste

You can copy words by copying and pasting. This means copying some words and inserting them in another place. To copy and paste, do the following:

1 Select the words you want to copy.

2 Choose the Edit Copy command to put a copy of the words on the Clipboard.

3 Position the insertion point where you want to insert the words.

4 Choose the Edit Paste command to insert the words.

 TIP

> You can set up the Insert key to act as a Paste key (just like Ctrl+V, the shortcut key for Paste). To do so, choose the Tools Options command, select the Edit tab, turn on the Use The INS Key For Paste check box, and then click OK.

You can move words by cutting and pasting. This means removing the words from one place and inserting them in another. To cut and paste, do the following:

1 Select the words you want to move.

2 Choose the Edit Cut command to move the words to the Clipboard.

3 Position the insertion point where you want to insert the words.

4 Choose the Edit Paste command to insert the words.

NOTE

> Word is set up to cut and paste spaces as needed. This is called Smart Cut And Paste. When you cut words from your document, Word also removes any extra spaces. When you paste, Word adds a space, if needed, between the words you are pasting and the words that are in your document to prevent the words from running together (as long as you paste whole words or sentences). If you don't want Word to remove or add spaces for you, turn off the Use Smart Cut And Paste check box on the Edit tab of the Tools Options dialog box.

Moving and Copying Contents with Special Keys

You can also use special keys to move or copy words to a new location without using the Clipboard. To do so, use the Move key (F2) or the Copy shortcut key (Shift+F2).

To move words, do the following:

1 Select the words you want to move.

2 Press F2 to see the question *Move to where?* displayed in the status bar.

3 Set a new insertion point with either the mouse or the keyboard.

4 Press Enter to move the selection to the new insertion point, or press Escape instead of Enter to cancel the move.

The steps are similar for the Copy shortcut key (Shift+F2). To copy words, do the following:

1 Select the words you want to copy.

2 Press Shift+F2 to see the question *Copy to where?* displayed in the status bar.

3 Set a new insertion point with either the mouse or the keyboard.

Press Enter to insert a copy of the selection at the new location, or press Escape instead of Enter to cancel the copy.

Copy and Move with Drag and Drop

The cut-and-paste and copy-and-paste methods are straightforward, but whenever you use them to put words on the Clipboard, you erase whatever words you stored on there the last time. You might find that you prefer using the drag-and-drop method with the mouse for moving and copying, because drag and drop doesn't require moving any words to the Clipboard. You'll find drag and drop really handy when you have stored on the Clipboard other words that you want to keep there. Using the mouse to drag and drop is also much faster than cutting and pasting or copying and pasting.

Moving Words with the Left Mouse Button

To move words with the mouse, take these steps:

1 Select the words you want to move.

2 Position the mouse pointer anywhere in the selection, and then press and hold down the left mouse button. The mouse pointer changes, as shown here:

3 Drag the selection until a dotted insertion point sits just before the words where you want to move the selection.

4 Release the left mouse button.

Copying Words with the Left Mouse Button

To copy words with the mouse, take these steps:

1 Select the words you want to copy.

2 Position the mouse pointer anywhere in the selection, hold down the Ctrl key, and press and hold down the left mouse button. The mouse pointer changes, as shown here:

3 Drag the selection so that the dotted insertion point sits to the left of the words where you want to copy the selection.

4 Release the left mouse button.

 TIP

The drag-and-drop method is best for moving or copying a selection to a relatively close part of the same document. For moving or copying over long distances, consider using cut and paste or copy and paste, or the Move key or Copy key combination, as described in the sidebar "Moving and Copying Contents with Special Keys," opposite.

Moving and Copying Words with the Right Mouse Button

If you click the right mouse button, Word displays the shortcut menu you see here:

However, if you hold down one or two keys as you click the right mouse button, Word moves or copies the selection.

To move the selection with the right mouse button, take these steps:

1 Select the words you want to move.

2 Position the insertion point where you want to move the selection.

3 Hold down the Ctrl key as you click the place where you want to move the words.

To copy the selection with the right mouse button, take these steps:

1 Select the words you want to copy.

2 Position the insertion point where you want to copy the selection.

3 Hold down Ctrl+Shift as you click the place where you want to move the words.

Move Here, Copy Here, and Link Here with the "Third" Mouse Button

If your mouse has a third button (a "middle" button), you can use it to move, copy, or link the selection, but you'll have to program it to do what it is you want it to do. To program the mouse's third button for a Word operation, use the program that is supplied with your mouse.

> **NOTE**

If you have a two-button mouse, click both mouse buttons at the same time to imitate a middle mouse button.

(?) SEE ALSO

The Link Here and Create Hypertext Here commands reach their full usefulness when you link between documents. For information about links between documents, see Chapter 21, "Creating Online Documents."

To use the middle mouse button and the commands on its shortcut menu, do the following:

1 Select the words you want to move, copy, or link.

2 Position the mouse pointer on the selection.

3 Hold down the middle mouse button (or hold down both mouse buttons at the same time on a two-button mouse).

4 Drag in the document where you want to put the words or link, and then release the mouse button. (You can drag to another Word document or to a document in another Office 97 application.) Word displays the shortcut menu shown here:

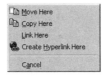

5 Select the command you want to use. (See Table 2-7 for more information about each command.)

**TABLE 2-7. Commands on the Shortcut Menu
When Using the Middle Mouse Button.**

Command	Action
Move Here	Moves the selection to a new location.
Copy Here	Copies the selection to a new location.
Link Here	Sets up a link to the selection at a new location. When you change the words at the source of the link, the linked words automatically change, too.
Create Hyperlink Here	Sets up a jump to the selection from a new location.

The Mysterious, Hidden Spike

One tool in Word that seems to escape the notice of everyone is called Spike. Spike is a special form of AutoText that acts like the Clipboard, with one important difference. In Spike, you can collect text and art from various places in a document and then insert them all at one time in a new location in the document. Spike is an electronic version of a spindle file, which looks like a large pin mounted on a stand.

You create Spike AutoText one of several ways:

- Press the Spike shortcut key (Ctrl+F3).

- Create AutoText named Spike on the AutoText tab of the Tools AutoCorrect dialog box or with the New button on the AutoText floating toolbar.

You can insert Spike AutoText in several ways:

- Press the Unspike shortcut key (Ctrl+Shift+F3).

- Type *Spike* (or *spike*) in your document, and then press Enter. (This is the AutoComplete typing method.)

- Select Spike from the list on the AutoText floating toolbar.

The method you use to create and insert entries from the Spike has a different effect on Spike and on your document, as shown in the following table.

Method	Actions
Create with Spike key (Ctrl+F3)	Deletes the selection from the document and adds it to text already stored in Spike AutoText
Create on AutoText tab or floating toolbar	Replaces Spike's contents with selection from document and does not delete the selection from the document
Insert with Unspike key (Ctrl+Shift+F3)	Empties Spike's contents and inserts them in document at the insertion point
Insert with Auto-Complete or AutoText floating toolbar	Inserts Spike's contents in the document at the insertion point and does not empty Spike

Replace

Let's say that you've been using the term "text" throughout a document. Your boss comes in and says, "New policy: instead of using 'text,' we're now going to use 'words' when referring to document contents." You've got to find all the instances of "text" in your document and change them to "words." Your boss adds that the company has decided to change all instances of boldface italic type to italic only. And your team decides that every appearance of the term "Bozo Bit" must be formatted a special way, to make it look like the Bozo Bit logo.

Jobs like these call for Word's Replace command. The Replace command can send in replacements for text only, for formatting only, and for specific text with specific formatting. You'll learn about text and formatting replacements in the following sections.

> **NOTE**
> The following sections concentrate on the replacement function of the Replace dialog box. For details about the find function, see "Finding Your Place with Find," page 97.

Text Replacements

So you need to replace "text" with "words." Here's what you do:

1 Choose the Edit Replace command to display the Replace dialog box.

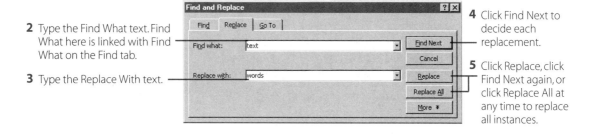

2 Type the Find What text. Find What here is linked with Find What on the Find tab.

3 Type the Replace With text.

4 Click Find Next to decide each replacement.

5 Click Replace, click Find Next again, or click Replace All at any time to replace all instances.

> **TIP**
> The keyboard shortcut to the Replace tab of the Find And Replace dialog box is Ctrl+H.

> If you have a selection in the document when you choose the Replace command, Word looks only within the selection. After Word finishes looking at the selection, you'll see a message asking whether you want to continue looking in the rest of the document. Click Yes to look through the entire document. Click No to look only within the selection. (For information about using this trick for a limited replace, see the sidebar "Limited Find and Replace," page 110.) If you select a direction (Up or Down instead of All), Word looks from the insertion point toward one end of the document (see "Directed Finds," page 100). When Word reaches that end of the document, you see a message asking whether you want to continue from the other end of the document. Click Yes to look from the other end of the document back to the insertion point from which Word started. Click No to stop searching.

Repeated Replacements

Let's say you want to perform a replacement in one document that you've already performed in another document. Pressing the Repeat shortcut keys (F4 and Ctrl+Y) or choosing the Edit Repeat command doesn't directly repeat the Replace command. The Repeat command displays the Replace tab of the Find And Replace dialog box. If the Find What and Replace With boxes contain the words you want to find and replace, click Find Next or Replace All. If the words you want are not shown—but you know you've entered them in the Replace dialog box before—you can click the down arrow at the right side of the Find What or Replace With box. A list of up to seven previous finds appears next to the Find What box, and a list of previous replacements appears next to the Replace With box. You can then select the Find What and Replace With items you want to use again.

All Word Form Replacements

Many English verbs have irregular forms—*see, sees, saw, seen,* for example. Replacing irregular verbs can cause problems during replacement. For example, if you decide to replace "see" with "observe," you'll find that "see" becomes "observe," "sees" becomes "observes," "saw" remains "saw," and "seen" becomes "observen." The problems here are obvious. Luckily, you can direct Word to replace all forms of the Find What text by turning on the Find All Word Forms box. With this box on, "see" becomes "observe," "sees" becomes "observes," "saw" becomes "observed," and "seen" becomes "observed."

> For Find All Word Forms, Word uses a special dictionary. If you installed Word on a laptop, you might not have this dictionary. Word will let you know. To add what Word needs, rerun Word Setup and add this dictionary.

Getting Started

Special Replacements

At times you might want to have Word perform special replacements, such as these:

- Find and replace a variety of words

- Find words that sound like other words and replace them with a different word

- Find special characters or special parts of a document and replace them with different special characters

- Find regular words and add special characters in or around them

In cases such as these, the Sounds Like and Use Wildcards check boxes and the Special button come into play.

Sounds Like Replacements

The Sounds Like check box turns on sound-alike finds, as described in "Sounds Like Finds," page 103, but does not create sound-alike replacement words. So a Sounds Like replacement means you replace all words that sound alike with the same replacement text.

Special Element Replacements

As noted in "Formatted Text Finds," page 103, a Word document can contain many elements that are not words, such as paragraph marks, column breaks, and page breaks. Clicking the Special button displays a list of the special elements you can use as replacements, as shown in Figure 2-16 on the next page.

Table 2-8 lists the names of the other special elements and the special characters Word inserts in the Replace With box when you select a special element from the Special button list.

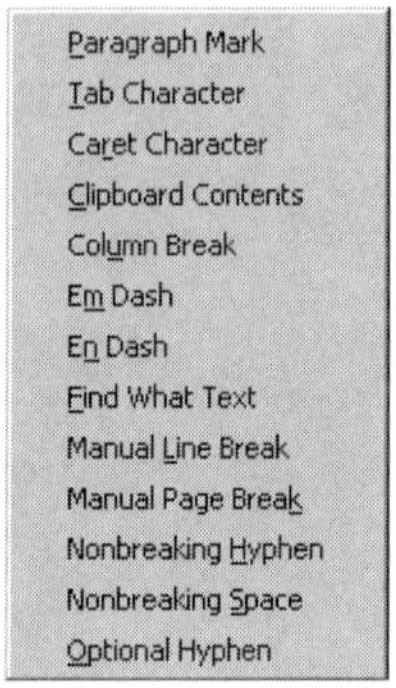

FIGURE 2-16.

The Special button list of special symbols for Replace With.

Paragraph Mark
Tab Character
Caret Character
Clipboard Contents
Column Break
Em Dash
En Dash
Find What Text
Manual Line Break
Manual Page Break
Nonbreaking Hyphen
Nonbreaking Space
Optional Hyphen

TABLE 2-8. **The Special Elements You Can Replace Find What Entries with and the Special Characters That Represent Them.**

Special Element	Special Characters
Paragraph mark	^p
Tab character	^t
Caret character	^^
Clipboard contents	^c
Column break	^n
Em dash	^+
En dash	^=
Find what text	^&
Manual line break	^l
Manual page break	^m
Nonbreaking hyphen	^~
Nonbreaking space	^s
Optional hyphen	^-

You can also type the special characters yourself.

Wildcard Replacements

Earlier in this chapter, you saw a description of the Use Wildcards check box for finding text (page 105). The information there applies directly to the Replace With box for wildcard replacements. For details, see Figure 2-15, page 106, and Table 2-6, page 106.

When the Use Wildcards check box is turned on, the Special button list for the Replace With box appears, as shown in Figure 2-17.

FIGURE 2-17.
The Special button list for the Replace With box when the Use Wildcards box is turned on.

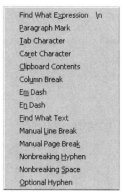

This list contains a single different wildcard choice: Find What Expression $\backslash n$. When you type a number after the backslash, Word inserts the specified group from the Find What box (you define groups by enclosing them in parentheses, and Word then numbers the groups sequentially). You can use this technique to rearrange the text in the Find What box by listing a different order for the groups in the Replace With box. For example, if the Find What box contains *(Suddenly) (Seymour)* and the Replace With box contains $\backslash 2\backslash 1$, Word changes the text "Suddenly Seymour" to "Seymour Suddenly." The other choices in the list are the same whether the Use Wildcards check box is turned on or off. See Table 2-8, opposite, for explanations of the other items in the list.

You can also type the special characters yourself.

 NOTE

You can turn on either the Use Wildcards check box or the Sounds Like check box, but not both. If you turn on one of these check boxes and then turn on the other one, Word turns off the first check box.

Replacing Formatting in a Document

You can use Word's Replace command to find specific formatting and replace it with different formatting. Or you can find specific text with specific formatting and replace the text, the formatting, or both.

Replacing Formatting Only

Now, at last, you decide that all the text in boldface italic really should be just italic. You probably can't remember every word or phrase in boldface italic, so you need to replace formatting only. To replace the formatting only, follow these steps:

1 Choose the Edit Replace command.

2 Click the More button.

3 Delete any text.

4 Click Format.

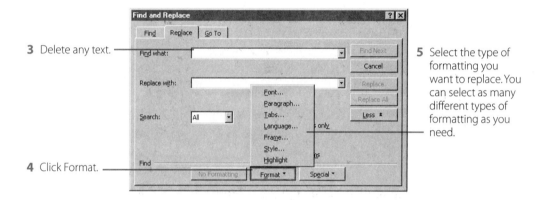

5 Select the type of formatting you want to replace. You can select as many different types of formatting as you need.

6 In each formatting dialog box, select the formatting you want to find, and click OK.

7 Delete any text.

8 Click Format.

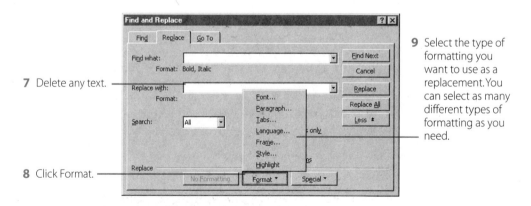

9 Select the type of formatting you want to use as a replacement. You can select as many different types of formatting as you need.

10 In each formatting dialog box, select the formatting you want to use as a replacement, and click OK.

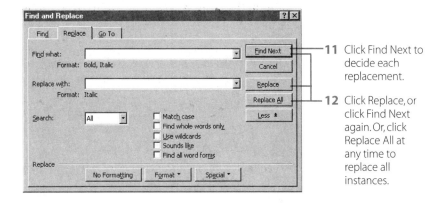

11 Click Find Next to decide each replacement.

12 Click Replace, or click Find Next again. Or, click Replace All at any time to replace all instances.

Replacing Formatted Text

Your team has reached a new style decision. From now on, every instance of "Bozo Bit" must appear in 16-point, boldface Matura MT Script Capitals, colored red. Here's how you do that:

1 Choose the Edit Replace command.

2 Click the Find What box, and type *Bozo Bit*. If any formatting is listed for the Find What box, click the No Formatting button.

3 In the Replace With box, delete all text and remove any formatting.

4 Click the Format button and select Font.

5 On the Font tab of the Font dialog box, select Matura MT Script Capitals, Bold, 16, and Red, and then click OK.

6 Turn on the Match Case box.

7 Click Find Next to decide each replacement.

8 Click Replace, Find Next again, or Replace All.

9 When a message tells you how many replacements Word made, click OK.

10 Click the Close button to close the Find And Replace dialog box.

Station 7: Print

Printing a Word document is an easy task when your printer is ready to use. You can print parts of a document and additional special information—such as summary information—either along with or instead of the document text.

Checking Your Printer Setup

Your printer software was probably set up when you ran the Setup program for Windows. If you didn't set up your printer during installation or if you've added or changed printers since you ran the Windows Setup program, you need to set up your printer in Windows. To do this, select Settings on the Start menu, select Printers from the submenu that appears, double-click the Add Printer icon in the Printers window, and work your way through the Add Printer Wizard.

After you've set up your printer in Windows, you are ready to print in Word. If you use more than one printer, you might want to choose the printer you need for the current document: see "Choosing Your Printer," below. You might also want to check your printer setup before starting printing: see "Setting Your Printer's Options," page 130.

Choosing Your Printer

To choose the printer you want Word to print to, do the following:

1 Choose the File Print command.

2 Click here and select the printer you want to use.

3 For details, see "Setting Your Printer's Options," page 130.

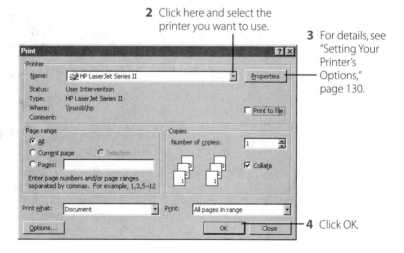

4 Click OK.

Print

How to Print a Document

To print one copy of an entire document, click the Print button on the Standard toolbar.

Using the Print Dialog Box for Special Printing Tasks

Printing one complete copy of a document might be the most common printing job you'll run, but from time to time you might want to print only part of a document or special information about a document or about Word itself. Various printing options are available to you in the Print dialog box.

To print a document or part of a document, follow these steps:

1 Choose the File Print command.

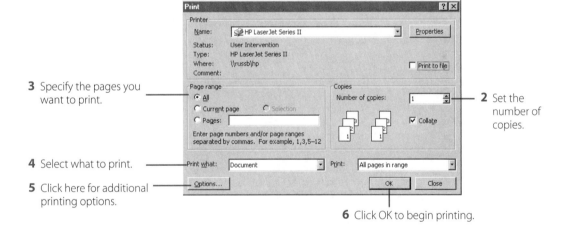

3 Specify the pages you want to print.

4 Select what to print.

5 Click here for additional printing options.

2 Set the number of copies.

6 Click OK to begin printing.

Collating Copies

Word usually prints multiple copies one copy at a time—that is, Word prints one complete copy, then a second complete copy, and so on. This is indicated by the Collate check box and the pictures of the pages in the Copies section of the Print dialog box.

If you turn off the Collate check box, Word prints the first page for however many copies you selected, and then prints the second page, and so on, as indicated by the pictures of the pages that appear when you turn off the Collate check box.

NOTE

> After Word finishes printing, it resets Number Of Copies to 1 so that the next time you print you don't accidentally get multiple copies when you wanted only one.

Printing Only Part of a Document

You don't have to print the entire document every time. You can print only part of it, if you prefer. You can print the current page, individual pages, a series of pages, only the odd-numbered pages, or only the even-numbered pages. You can even print just the selected text. The following sections explain all the choices that you can make in the Print dialog box.

Printing the Current Page

To print the current page, click the Current Page option.

 NOTE

> Word prints the page that contains the insertion point. If you have a selection that spans a page break, Word prints only the first page of the selection.

Printing Individual Pages

To print individual (or nonconsecutive) pages, type the page numbers, separated by commas, in the Pages box—for example *1,4,7,9*. When you start typing, the Pages option is automatically selected.

 TIP

> You can combine ranges and individual pages; for example, you could type *3,4, 8-10,13-14,18*. See "Printing from Page to Page," below.

Printing from Page to Page

You can print a group of consecutive pages, starting and ending at any page you want. To do so, type in the Pages box the first page number, a hyphen, and the ending page number—for example, *2-9*.

If a document contains sections and you want to print a range of pages, be sure to include the section numbers. For documents with sections, type *p*, the page number, *s*, and the section number—for example, type *p4s2* to print the fourth page of section 2. You can type the section and page number combination as part of a page range as well as for individual pages—for example, *3, p4s2-p5s3, 10-29, 69.*

Printing Odds or Evens

To print only the odd-numbered pages of a document, select Odd Pages in the Print drop-down list near the lower right corner of the Print dialog box. To print only the even-numbered pages of a document, select Even Pages in the list.

The standard choice is to print all of the odd or even pages. You can also choose to print only the odd pages or only the even pages within a range of pages. For example, if you type in a page range of 10-20 and select Even Pages, Word prints pages 10, 12, 14, 16, 18, and 20.

Printing a Selection from a Document

You can print a selection from a document by doing the following:

1 Select the part of the document you want to print.

2 Choose the File Print command.

3 Click the Selection option.

4 Click OK.

> When you print a selection, Word does *not* print the headers and footers. Also, the printing starts at the top of the paper rather than where the text is positioned on the page in the document.

Choosing What to Print

Word lets you print more than just your document. From Word's Print What drop-down list, you can choose what helpful information related to the document you'll print, as shown in Table 2-9 on the next page.

Printing to a File

On rare occasions you might need to print your work to a file so that you can print from a computer that does not have Word for Windows installed, print to a printer other than the one you were using when you originally created the document, or send an electronic printing file to a printer.

TABLE 2-9.   Options in the Print What Box.

Print What?	What's Printed
Document	The document
Document Properties	Information from the file's Properties dialog box (to print document properties along with your document, see "Setting Word's Printing Options," page 129)
Comments	The comments only (to print comments along with your document, see "Setting Word's Printing Options," page 129)
Styles	Style names and their descriptions
AutoText Entries	AutoText names and their contents
Key Assignments	Key combinations and their actions

To print to a file, do the following:

1 Choose the File Print command.

2 In the Print dialog box, set up printing the way you want it. If you are going to send the file to a different printer from the one you usually use, be sure to select the correct printer.

3 Turn on the Print To File check box, and click OK. Word displays the Print To File dialog box, shown here:

6 Click OK.

4 Select the disk and folder where you want to store the print file.

5 Type a name for the print file.

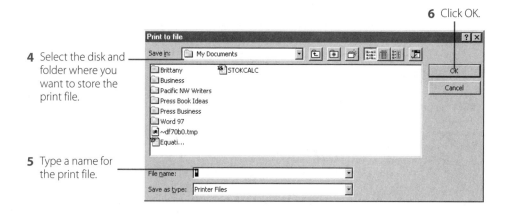

Just the Outline

If you want to print only an outline of your document, do the following:

1 Click the Outline View button at the lower left corner of the window to switch the document to Outline view.

2 Turn on and then turn off the All button on the Outlining toolbar to hide body text and leave only the outline headings showing. If you want to print only a certain number of levels of the outline (for example, only the first three levels), click the Number button on the Outlining toolbar that corresponds to the lowest level of head you want to print.

 TIP

If you want to print part of the body text from the document, click the All button to display all paragraphs. You can then use the Collapse button on the Outlining toolbar to collapse the headings for sections whose body text you don't want to print.

Show Formatting

3 If you want to print the outline in a draft font, turn off the Show Formatting button on the Outlining toolbar.

Word prints the outline as you see it in Outline view. With the Show Formatting button turned on, Word prints all the text formatting.

4 Print the document as you do in Normal or Page Layout view. Word prints only the paragraphs that you see in Outline view, nothing more.

 NOTE

Any manual page breaks that are placed immediately before headings cause page breaks in the printed outline.

Setting Word's Printing Options

To set or change Word's additional printing options, do the following:

1 Choose the File Print command, and then click the Options button to display the Options dialog box. When you click the Options button in the Print dialog box, Word selects the Print tab. As an alternative, you can display the print options, as shown in Figure 2-18,

by choosing the Tools Options command to display the Options dialog box and then selecting the Print tab.

2 Turn on or change any printing options you want to use, and then click OK.

If you used the Options button in the Print dialog box, Word returns you to that dialog box so that you can proceed to printing.

FIGURE 2-18.
The Print tab in the Options dialog box.

 SEE ALSO

For more information about the other options on the Print tab, see "Print Tab," page 969.

Setting Your Printer's Options

Most printers have a number of options that you can set, such as resolution, default number of copies, and default paper size. Some fancier printers also have duplex printing (printing on both sides of the paper) and color capabilities. You can select and adjust special options for your printer in its Properties dialog box.

NOTE

As you might expect, the Properties dialog box fits the printer you're using. When you switch printers, the Properties dialog box changes. Even the title changes. For example, one of my Properties dialog box titles is *HP LaserJet II Series on FILE: Properties.* The part of the title after "on" tells you where your printing output is directed—to a file (FILE), a parallel port (LPT), or a communications port (COM).

To select options in your Properties dialog box, do the following:

1 Choose the File Print command.

2 In the Print dialog box, click the Properties button to display the Properties dialog box.

3 Select each tab, and change any printer settings.

4 Click OK in the Properties dialog box.

Printing from Windows 95

When you print a Word document directly from Windows 95, you specify the printer but you cannot make any other printing choices.

To print a Word document from Windows 95, do the following:

1 Open a My Computer or Explorer window, and open the folder that contains the document you want to print.

2 Click the Start button, select Settings, and select Printers to open the Printers window. If the Printers window is already open, you don't have to use (or repeat) this step.

3 Drag the icon for the document you want to print onto the icon for the printer you want to use. You can select more than one document icon at a time and drag them all to the printer icon at the same time. Windows starts Word, opens the document, prints it, and then closes Word.

★ TIP

As an alternative to dragging the document icon onto the printer icon, you can select in the My Computer or Explorer window the documents you want to print, and then select the File Print command or right-click the document icon and choose Print from the shortcut menu.

When you use Windows to print, Word must use the default printer. If you have dragged the document icon to a printer other than the default printer, Windows asks you if you want to make the second printer the default printer. If you do not, the document will not be printed. If you do make it the default printer, it will remain the default printer until you change it.

Station 8: Store and Locate

After you start a document, and many times while you're working on it, you'll want to save your work.

Saving Your Work

After you've done some initial work on your document, save it before you go on.

To save a document, take these steps:

Save

1 Click the Save button on the Standard toolbar. If the document has been saved previously, the updated version will be saved, replacing the previous version you last saved. If the document has not yet been saved, the Save As dialog box appears.

3 To create a new folder, click here (see "Creating a New Folder," next page).

5 Click Save.

2 Select the disk and folder for the document.

4 Accept the name or type a new name.

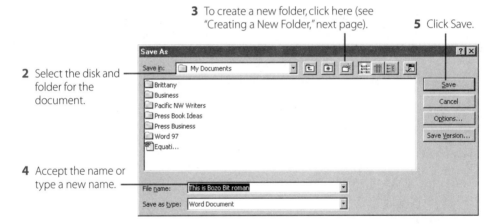

A document name can be up to 255 characters long, including the DOC extension. Don't worry about typing the extension, though, because Word will add it for you. The DOC extension identifies the document as a Word document.

After you've saved your work once, click the Save button on the Standard toolbar to save your additional work. After you've saved the document the first time, Word doesn't display the Save As dialog box with each subsequent save.

TIP

Print and Save One Last Time

After you finish printing, save your work before closing the document or exiting Word. After you save the document, you can be sure that it exactly matches the printed document. You might be saving only the new page breaks or the newest field results (dates, for example), but saving this information could become important later if you want to make changes based on your printed copy.

Creating a New Folder

To create a new folder in the folder that you have open, take these steps:

1 Click the Create New Folder button in the Save As dialog box.

2 Type a name for the folder.

3 Click OK.

Changing the Name and Storage Place of a Document

For various reasons, you might want to change the name or the storage place of a saved document. For example, you might edit a document and want the edited version to have a new name. Or you might decide to store a copy of a document in another folder or on another disk.

To change a document's name or storage place, do the following:

1 Choose the File Save As command.

2 If you want, select a different disk or a different folder to store the document.

3 If you want, type a different name for the document.

4 Click Save.

 NOTE

If you do not want to keep the old copy of the document, you can delete it in Windows; Word will not delete it for you.

Getting Started

TIP

When you change a document's name, you might also want to change the document's properties to fit the revised document.

Fill Out the Paperwork!

Before you save a Word document, it's a good idea to fill out the Properties dialog box as completely as you can to store descriptive information about the file. The more information you supply, the easier it is to find your document later if you can't immediately locate it with the File Open command. Also, you can use the properties you enter in the Properties dialog box to find files that have something in common but are stored in different folders or on different disks. To fill out the Properties dialog box, do the following:

1 Choose the File Properties command. Word displays the Properties dialog box, shown here:

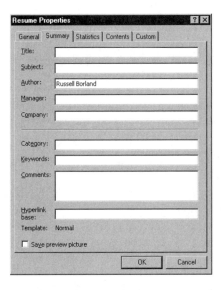

2 Fill in as much information on the Summary tab in the Properties dialog box as you wish, and then click OK.

One way to assure yourself that you'll remember to fill in the Summary tab is to turn on the Prompt For Document Properties check box on the Save tab in the Options dialog box. With this check box turned on, Word displays the Properties dialog box the first time you save a document. For information on changing settings on the Save tab, see "Save Tab," page 971.

Controlling Automatic Saves

Word is set up to save your work every 10 minutes or less automatically. (The time is less if you perform lots of editing or formatting.) You can adjust how often Word performs automatic saves, or you can turn off the automatic saving option.

To change the time between automatic saves, do the following:

1   Choose the Tools Options command, and click the Save tab.

2   In the Minutes box, set the number of minutes between saves, and then click OK.

You can set the Minutes box from 0 minutes to 120 minutes. As a rule of thumb, set the time between saves to the maximum amount of work you're willing to lose (and would have to reconstruct). If the power fails or a program stops working, Word attempts to recover the document when you restart Word.

Even though you can continue to type, edit, or format your work while Word is in the process of automatically saving your document, the screen won't show the results of your efforts until Word has finished saving. For this reason, you probably won't want to set the save interval to a very short time period.

To turn off automatic saves, do the following:

1   Choose the Tools Options command, and in the Options dialog box, select the Save tab.

2   Turn off the Save AutoRecover Info Every check box (or in the Minutes box, scroll below 1 so no number is displayed), and then click OK.

Using Your Other Savings Plans

(?) SEE ALSO

For a complete description of Word's save options, see "Save Tab," page 971.

Besides saving a document with a different name or in a different place, Word gives you several other options for saving that you might want to use regularly. Among the more interesting save options are deciding whether or not Word makes "fast saves," saving documents in a different file format, and setting up protection to guard your masterpiece from prying eyes or prying fingers.

TIP

You can get to the save options in two ways: choose the Tools Options command, and select the Save tab in the Options dialog box; or click the Options button in the Save As dialog box. (Word automatically selects the Save tab in the Options dialog box.)

The Race Isn't Always to the Fastest Save

Microsoft set up Word with a "fast save." This ability to save your work very quickly means that you can return to work sooner; however, Word's ability to save quickly is the result of a trick, and this trick ultimately costs you disk space and computer memory. If you keep fast saving, it eventually will cost you speed in Word's responses to your commands.

 TIP

Use Background Save Instead of Fast Saves

Now that Word has a background save feature, fast saves are no longer really necessary. Background saving means that Word writes your changes to the disk file as you continue to work. Using background save is the fastest way to return to work.

With Word's Allow Fast Saves box turned on, every time Word saves your document it actually builds a list of all your changes and saves the list rather than making the actual changes to your stored work. That's the trick. When the list of changes grows very long, Word lets you know that it can no longer perform a fast save but must instead perform a regular save (called a full save). A full save works through the list of changes and saves your work with the changes in place. The list of changes is then empty, and Word can again perform its fast-save trick.

You might prefer to turn off fast saving, for several reasons:

- To conserve computer memory and, eventually, computer speed.

- To conserve disk space. (Your work plus the list of changes usually create a larger file than a full-save file.)

- To get the full benefit of the Find File tool.

Regarding the benefit of the Find File tool: when you fast-save your work, the saved file still contains all the text you deleted, and the new text isn't yet incorporated into the file. One of the ways you can search for documents is by specific text in the files. If you use Find File to locate specific text, the list of documents might contain some documents from which you deleted the text you want to find, and Find File might miss some documents to which you added the text. For an absolutely accurate result from Find File, all the documents you're going to search should be saved with a full save rather than a fast save. For more information on finding files based on text, see "Using the Advanced Button for Hard-to-Locate Files," page 146.

To turn off fast saving, do the following:

1 Choose the Tools Options command, and click the Save tab box.

2 Turn off the Allow Fast Saves box, and then click OK.

 TIP

> Fast save gives you the greatest benefit when your work contains pictures, tables, columns, or OLE objects. In these cases, I use fast save for saving my work every 5 or 10 minutes. I then switch to full save (by turning off the Allow Fast Saves box) every half hour or so to save a major portion of my work.

Sure, Buddy, I Can Save in Your File Format

Because of the variety of programs that people use to work on documents, you might need to save a document in a different file format before you pass your work to someone else. The Save As dialog box also gives you choices for storing your work in different file formats.

Word can save your work in the following file formats in addition to Word's standard format (the list in your Save As dialog box depends on the formats you installed):

■ Word's document template

■ Text only

■ Text only with line breaks

■ MS-DOS text (for MS-DOS applications that use the extended ASCII character set)

■ MS-DOS text with line breaks

- Rich Text Format (a descriptive format for file conversion)

- Unicode Text (characters are saved with two bytes instead of one, for easier translations to Asian languages)

- Text with layout (text with the headers and footers and other paragraph formatting intact)

- MS-DOS text with layout (for MS-DOS applications that include the extended ASCII character set), with the headers and footers and other paragraph formatting intact

- (Microsoft) Works for MS-DOS 3.0

- (Microsoft) Works for Windows 3.0, 4.0

- Word for Windows 2.x (Microsoft Word 2 for Windows), 6.0/95

- Windows Write (Microsoft Write for Windows) 3.0, 3.1

- WordPerfect 5.0, 5.1 for MS-DOS, 5.x for Windows, 5.0, 5.1 or 5.2 Secondary File

- (Microsoft) Word for MS-DOS 3.x–5.x, 6.0

- Microsoft Word for the Macintosh 4.0, 5.0, 5.1, 6.0

- RFT-DCA

- HTML Document

To save your work in a different file format, do the following:

1 Choose the File Save As command.

2 From the Save As Type list, select the file format you want. Word automatically inserts the correct filename extension at the end of your document name.

3 If you prefer, select a different disk or folder in which to save your work.

4 If you prefer, change the filename (but not the filename extension).

5 Click Save.

Safeguarding Your Masterpiece

When you save your document, Word offers several ways for you to protect your work from prying eyes and fingers: Password To Open, Password To Modify, and Read-Only Recommended.

A document set to read only has the words *(Read-Only)* in the title bar after the document name; you can save changes to the document only by giving it a different name. The following sections explain each of these options.

> **NOTE**

> It's also possible to make a file read-only through Windows. In this case, use My Computer or the Windows Explorer to open the folder that contains the file, right-click the file's icon, click the Properties command to open the Properties dialog box for the file, turn on the Read-Only check box in the Attributes section of the General tab in the dialog box, and then click OK. There is no password in this case, but neither you nor anyone else can save changes to the file unless you again change the file's read-only status in the Properties dialog box.

Tell Me More About Read-Only

Read-only is designed to protect documents from unauthorized changes. When you open a document as read only, you can't change anything in the document. Well, actually, to be more accurate, you can't save any changes you make to the document. Word prevents you from saving the changes to the same document name. This means, however, that you can give the altered document a different name. Your original read-only document remains safe and unchanged.

Hiding from Prying Eyes: Password To Open

You can save your document so that only those people who know the password you gave for the document can open the document. As long as you or anyone else knows the password, you and they have free rein in the document. That is, you can make any changes you want and save them.

To give a document a password to open, do the following:

1 Choose the File Save As command.

2 Click the Options button.

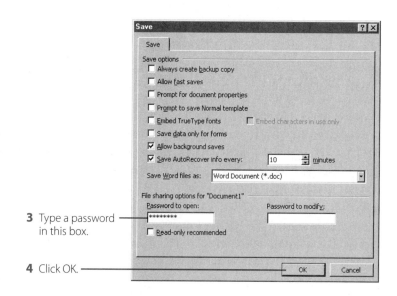

3 Type a password in this box.

4 Click OK.

Word displays the Confirm Password dialog box, shown here:

5 Type the same password again, *exactly* as you typed it the first time.

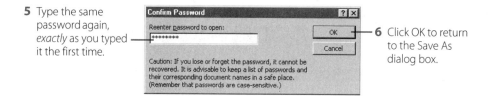

6 Click OK to return to the Save As dialog box.

7 If you haven't given the document a name yet, type a name for the document in the Save As dialog box.

8 Click Save in the Save As dialog box.

The next time you or anyone else tries to open the document, you'll see the Password dialog box. You must type the password correctly to open the document. For more information about the Password dialog box, see "What's This Pesky Password Box?" page 142.

Protecting from Prying Fingers: Password To Modify

Password To Modify is a fancy term for read-only. Read-only is designed to protect documents from prying fingers (unauthorized changes). The Save tab in the Options dialog box contains a box labeled Password To Modify. This label means that others can open the document to read it, but they can't save changes to the document.

To keep out all prying fingers except those with your permission, do the following:

1 Choose the File Save As command to display the Save As dialog box.

2 Click the Options button.

3 Type a password in the Password To Modify box, and then click OK. Word displays the Confirm Password dialog box.

4 Type the same password again, exactly as you typed it the first time, and then click OK to return to the Save As dialog box.

5 If you haven't given the document a name yet, type a name for the document in the Save As dialog box.

6 Click Save in the Save As dialog box.

The next time you or anyone else tries to open the document, you'll see the Password dialog box. You must type the password correctly to open the document so that you can save changes. For more information about the Password dialog box, see "What's This Pesky Password Box?" page 142.

Recommending Safety

If you want, you can direct Word to display a dialog box that recommends opening the document as read-only, but remember, this is only what Word recommends. Anyone can either open the document as read-only or open it and make and save all kinds of changes. This form of "safety" is really only a reminder that you might want to keep the document as it is.

To recommend safety (read-only), do the following:

1 Choose the File Save As command to display the Save As dialog box.

2 Click the Options button.

3 Turn on the Read-Only Recommended check box, and then click OK. Word returns you to the Save As dialog box.

4 If you haven't given the document a name yet, type a name for the document in the Save As dialog box.

5 Click Save in the Save As dialog box.

When you or anyone else tries to open the document next time, you'll see a dialog box that recommends opening the document as read-only. For more information about this dialog box, see "What's This Pesky Password Box?" below.

Choosing a Protection Type

One rule of thumb when you're deciding how to safeguard your document is to give a document the minimum protection necessary. Why? Because the inconvenience to you and others who need to open the document can make you reluctant to use any protection at all.

The following table lists the forms of protection, where you set them, whether or not they use a password, whether or not the protection is enforced, and when you use each form of protection.

Type	Where to Set It?	Password?	Enforced?	Use?
Password To Open	Word	Yes	Not applicable	To keep out prying eyes
Password to Modify	Word	Yes	Yes	To keep out prying fingers; eyes OK
Read-Only Recommended	Word	No	No	To remind you to open as read-only
Read-Only	Windows	No	Yes	For eyes only

What's This Pesky Password Box?

If you or the person who last saved a document protected it with a password (see "Safeguarding Your Masterpiece," page 139), Word displays one or more dialog boxes, depending on the type of protection.

Password to the Entire Kingdom

If someone saved a document with Password To Open, Word displays the dialog box shown here when you try to open the document:

To open the document, you must type its password exactly. If you mis-type the password, Word prevents you from opening the document and displays a message similar to the one shown here:

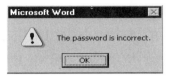

You'll have to click OK and then try to open the document again, this time *correctly* typing the password.

Password to the Scriptorium

If someone saved a document with Password To Modify (you can save changes only if you know the password), Word displays the dialog box shown here when you try to open the document:

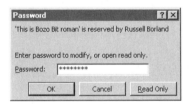

To open the document so that you can save any changes you make, you must type its password exactly. If you don't, Word displays a mes-sage that the password is incorrect. When you click OK, Word returns you to the Password dialog box so that you can either try to type the password again or open the document as read-only by clicking the Read Only button.

On Your Honor to Make the Right Choice

If someone saved a document with the Read-Only Recommended option, Word displays the dialog box shown here:

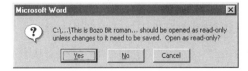

In this case, you click the button you prefer. Click Yes to open the document as read-only. Click No to open the document for full editing. Click Cancel if you don't want to open the document.

Finding a Document

When you want to open a document, you first go looking in the Open dialog box. You see a list of documents in the current folder. If the document you seek is not in that folder, you head out on a walkabout through other folders. You might click folders in the window to look in them, or you might click the One Level Up button to look in other folders and even on other disks. But if you have a very large disk with lots of folders and documents, searching randomly can be time-consuming, frustrating, and even unfruitful.

If you cannot find a document quickly in the Open dialog box, you can use the Find Files That Match These Criteria section at the bottom of the Open dialog box to send Word on a walkabout for you. You can become an armchair traveler through the roots and branches of your computer's outback—disks and folders.

Finding Your Work

The Open, Insert File, Insert Picture, and Open Data Source dialog boxes all contain a Find Files That Match These Criteria section and an Advanced button, which you can use to find files. All of these steps apply to all four dialog boxes.

To search for lost files, follow these steps:

1 Choose the appropriate command to display the dialog box. For example, choose File Open and the Open dialog box appears.

2 In the File Name box, type a name, or type part of a name, or type a filename pattern. Word recognizes two special characters for filename patterns:

- An asterisk (*) takes the place of any number of letters in a filename. For example, to find all Word files, type *.doc*.

- A question mark (?) takes the place of one letter in a filename. For example, to find all the chapters of a book whose files are named chap01.doc, chap02.doc, and so on, type *chap??.doc* in the File Name box.

You can also search without using either of these special characters by typing part of a name—any series of characters in a filename. For example, typing *Amp* might yield Sample1.doc, Sample2.doc, and Ampere.doc.

You can also click the down arrow at the right end of the File Name box to select from a list of names and filename patterns you've used before.

3 You can use the Files Of Type box to search for patterns based on the different kinds of file formats Word can open, such as *.dot for Word templates, *.txt for text files, and *.* for all files. The exact list depends on the text and graphics conversion files you have installed with Word.

4 If you want to find all the files in the folder that contain specific text, including any text in their Properties dialog boxes, type that text in the Text Or Property box.

5 If you want to find files you last modified before, on, or after a specific date, select a date range in the Last Modified box. Your choices are Yesterday, Today, Last Week, This Week, Last Month, This Month, and Any Time.

6 Click the Find Now button to start the search.

When Word's search is done, Word displays the list of files you wanted. Figure 2-19 shows the results of a search for Word documents with the word *Letter* in them. The search looked in a folder that contains 117 files.

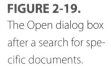

FIGURE 2-19.
The Open dialog box after a search for specific documents.

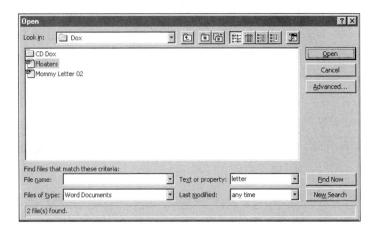

If, after a search, you want to see all the files again, click the New Search button, which resets the Find boxes.

The Find boxes are just the beginning of your Find options. The Advanced button in the Open dialog box opens the Advanced Find dialog box, which is chock-full of tools for advancing your searches for files.

Using the Advanced Button for Hard-to-Locate Files

The Open dialog box (as well as the Insert File, Insert Picture, and Open Data Source dialog boxes) gives you some tools to find files on the various disks you have available—disks in your computer as well as disks on a network. These tools will probably be enough to find most of the files you work on regularly. But sometimes you have only a faint memory of work you've done before that you'd like to reuse—if only you could find the file it's in. To find files by searching for some of their properties, you need to use Word's Advanced Find dialog box.

To use the Advanced Find dialog box, do the following:

1 Choose the File Open command.

2 Move to the drive and the folder where you want to start looking.

3 Complete as much information as possible in the Find Files That Match These Criteria section of the Open dialog box.

4 Click the Advanced button.

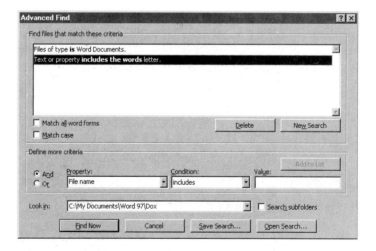

5 Inspect the list of properties in the Find Files That Match These Criteria box. If a criterion is already listed in this box that you don't want to use for this search, select it and click the Delete button. If you delete all the criteria, Word will display *[Find all files]* in the Find Files That Match These Criteria box.

6 In the Property box, select the property you want to use to find files. The properties are listed below:

Application Name	Last Printed	Number of Paragraphs
Author	Last Saved By	
Category	Manager	Number of Slides
Comments	Number of Characters	Number of Words
Company		Revision
Contents	Number of Characters + Spaces	Size
Creation Date	Number of Hidden Slides	Subject
File Name		Template
File of Type	Number of Lines	Text or Property
Format	Number of Multimedia Clips	Title
Hyperlink Base		Total Editing Time
Keywords	Number of Notes	
Last Modified	Number of Pages	

These properties all appear in the Properties dialog box. For an explanation of each property, choose the File Properties command, select the tab with the properties you want to learn about, click the Help button at the top of the dialog box, and then click the property to see the explanation.

7 In the Condition box, select the test you want to use with the property. What is listed in the Condition box depends on the property selected. For example, you might use "Include Phrase" for the Contents property or "On Or Before" for the Creation Date property.

8 In the Value box, type the value of the property you want Word to find. The value depends on the property you are using. For example, you'd enter a date if the property was Creation Date and a name if the property was Last Author.

9 Select either the And option or the Or option. The And option tells Word to find files that match this criterion and all others that you marked with And. The Or option tells Word to find files that match this criterion or that match other criteria you have set up.

10 Click the Add To List button to add the property to the Find Files That Match These Criteria list.

11 Repeat steps 6 through 10 until you have set up all the properties you want to use to find files.

12 If you also want to look in folders inside the current folder, turn on the Search Subfolders box.

13 Click Find Now to find the files that fit the properties you have set up. Word displays the list of files in the Open dialog box.

Word's Advanced Find dialog box gives you several more options to use in your file search. You can tell Word that the property values must match exactly what you type in the Value box, or you can tell Word to find all the variations of what you type in the Value box. You can also save the criteria you've created so that you can use them again.

Finding the Variations

Turn on the Match All Word Forms check box if the values you're searching for might be in different word forms in your documents. For example, if you're conducting a search based on the keyword *motorcycle,* Word can also find documents with the keyword *motorcycles.*

Match Cases

To make sure that Word finds properties with values that exactly match what you type in the Value box, turn on the Match Case check box. When this check box is turned on, Word finds only those files with property values that exactly match the combination of uppercase and lowercase letters that you type in the Value box. When you turn off this check box, Word ignores case.

Saving Your Search Criteria

After you set up the criteria for finding a particular set of files, you might want to save that specific search so that you can use it another time without having to set up all the criteria again. To save your criteria:

1 Click the Save Search button. The Save Search dialog box appears, as shown here:

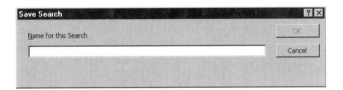

2 Type a name for the criteria—a name that reminds you what properties the criteria find, and then click OK.

To change the properties of a saved search, click the Open Search button in the Advanced Find dialog box, select the search's name, and click the Open button. Add or delete criteria, click the Save Search button, type the same name, click OK, and then click Yes to replace the existing saved search with the new one.

Open Search

If you've been kind to yourself and saved your searches, do the following to reuse a search:

1 Choose the File Open command, and in the Open dialog box, click the Advanced button.

2 Click the Open Search button.

3 Click the search you want to reuse.

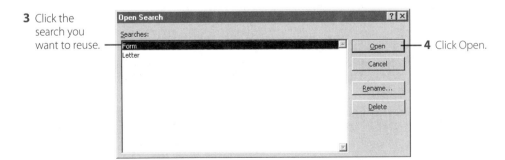

4 Click Open.

The criteria of the search are displayed in the Advanced Find dialog box.

5 Click the Find Now button to conduct the search.

Exit Word

You can exit Word in several ways, as described in the following list.

- Click the Close button (marked with an X) at the right end of Word's title bar. This is the easiest way to exit Word.

- Choose the File Exit command.

- Click Word's Control menu icon at the left end of Word's title bar, and choose the Close command from the drop-down menu.

- Click the right mouse button on Word's title bar, and choose the Close command from the drop-down menu.

- Press Alt+F4.

When you exit Word using any of these methods, Word checks all open documents and templates. If you have not saved your changes to any of these documents or templates, Word gives you a chance to do so, as shown here:

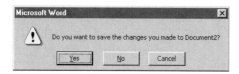

PART II

Correspondence

CHAPTER 3

Enlisting the Letter Wizard

Word 97 makes it easier than ever to write letters. Not only does Word provide a Letter Wizard to help you assemble the structure and basic parts of a letter, but Word is also set up from the get-go to turn any general document into a letter. This chapter shows how this works.

Jump-Starting a Letter

Word's AutoComplete feature comes to your aid when you begin typing in a document, as follows:

1 Start typing the date, for example, *Jan*. Word's AutoComplete typing feature displays a tip that suggests the month you're typing, in this case, *January:*

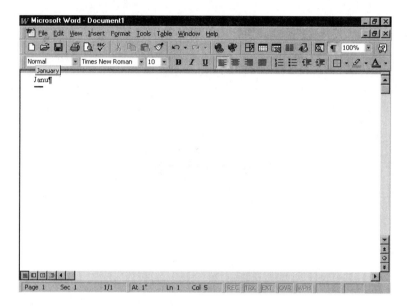

2 Simply press Enter to insert the full name of the month into your letter.

3 Press the Spacebar. AutoComplete proposes today's date, as shown in the example on the next page.

4 Press Enter to insert the rest of today's date.

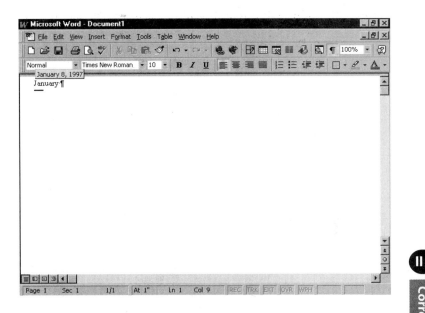

5 Now press Enter a couple of times, type *Dear Mother,* and then press Enter a couple more times. The Assistant comes up on the screen, like this:

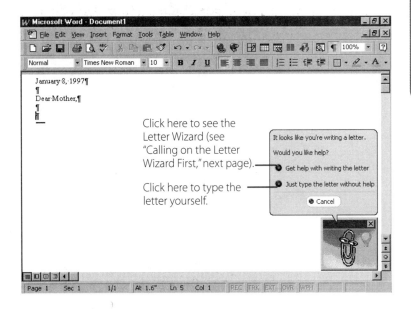

Click here to see the Letter Wizard (see "Calling on the Letter Wizard First," next page).

Click here to type the letter yourself.

It looks like you're writing a letter.

Would you like help?

Get help with writing the letter

Just type the letter without help

Cancel

Correspondence

Rather than jump-starting a letter and then switching to the Letter Wizard, you can start with the Letter Wizard. You'll find how in the next section.

Calling on the Letter Wizard First

You can plan all the elements of your letters before you start writing them by using the Letter Wizard. The tabs in the Letter Wizard dialog box let you set up basic information that you can reuse in other letters. To start the Letter Wizard, take these steps:

1 Choose the Tools Letter Wizard command. The Letter Wizard dialog box opens to the Letter Format tab, shown in Figure 3-1.

FIGURE 3-1.

Letter Wizard dialog box with the Letter Format tab selected.

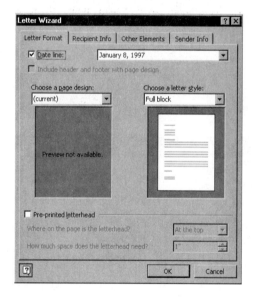

2 Fill in the Letter Format tab, and then click the Recipient Info tab, shown in Figure 3-2. (If you're using the Letter Wizard from a jump start, you can click Next instead.)

3 Fill in the Recipient Info tab, and then click the Other Elements tab, shown in Figure 3-3. (If you're using the Letter Wizard from a jump start, you can click Next instead.)

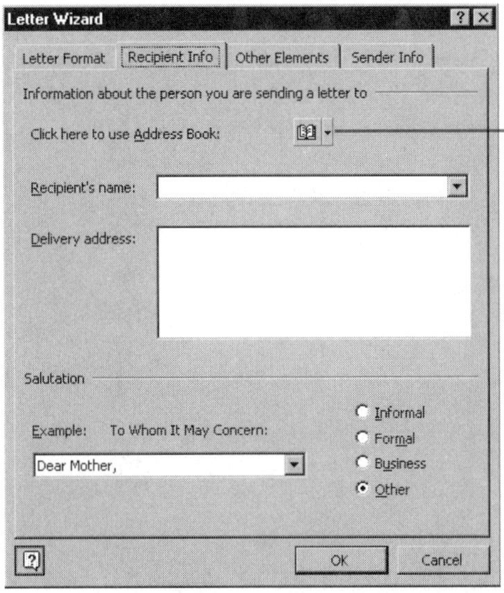

FIGURE 3-2.
Letter Wizard dialog
box with the Recipient
Info tab selected.

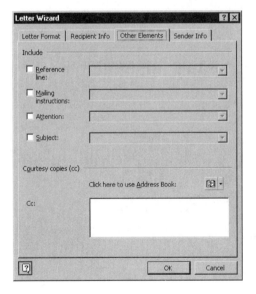

Click here to use
address books
(see "Using Your
Address Books,"
page 159).

FIGURE 3-3.
Letter Wizard dialog
box with the Other
Elements tab selected.

Correspondence

4 If any of the options on the Other Elements tab apply to your
letter, fill in the tab as appropriate, and then click the Sender Info
tab. (If you're using the Letter Wizard from a jump start, you can
click Next instead.) Figure 3-4 shows the Sender Info tab.

FIGURE 3-4.

Letter Wizard dialog box with the Sender Info tab selected.

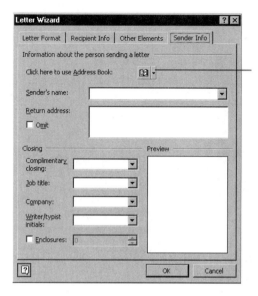

Click here to use address books (see "Using Your Address Books," next page).

5 Fill in the Sender Info tab, and then click OK. (If you're using the Letter Wizard from a jump start, click Finish instead of OK.)

If you're using the Letter Wizard from a jump start, the Letter Wizard asks whether you want help with setting up an envelope or if you want to rerun Letter Wizard. Click the button that suits your purposes.

Click here to set up an envelope (see "Printing an Envelope," page 198).

Click here to set up a mailing label (see "Licking Labels," page 202).

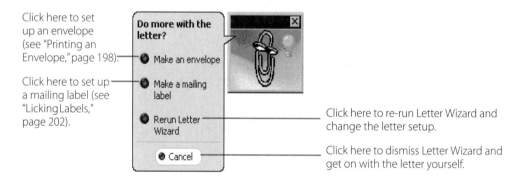

Click here to re-run Letter Wizard and change the letter setup.

Click here to dismiss Letter Wizard and get on with the letter yourself.

After you're done with the Letter Wizard, you see a letter that is set up according to your specification. The letter on the next page was set up with an envelope. It's shown in Page Layout view.

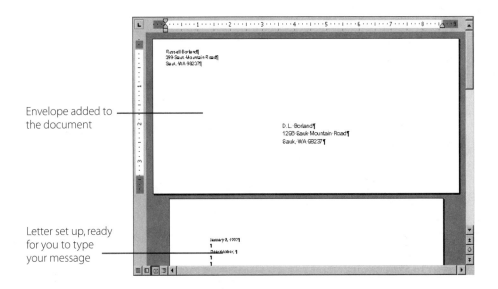

Envelope added to the document

Letter set up, ready for you to type your message

Now all you have to do is type the letter and add art, charts, tables, and anything else you want. Then format the words and paragraphs as you see fit. It's done! All that's left to do is print and mail the letter or send the letter through Microsoft Exchange. When you've done that, save the letter for future reference.

 TIP

Save a Letter as a Template for Future Use

After you run the Letter Wizard and set up a letter, but before you add the contents to the specific recipient, you might want to save the letter setup as a template. That way, the next time you need to send a letter to this recipient, you simply create a new document with this template. That makes the entire process faster and easier for you. For details, see "Storing Your Personal Letter as a Template," page 176, or "Storing Your Business Letter as a Template," page 194.

Using Your Address Books

You can easily add names and addresses to your documents by using your address books. Which address books you use depends on what e-mail systems you are connected to, how they are configured, and whether you have Microsoft Schedule+ or Microsoft Outlook installed. To use any of the address books, you must have Microsoft Exchange

Correspondence

installed on your computer. When you click the Insert Address button, Microsoft Exchange will start, if it is not already running. Table 3-1 lists the most common address books.

TABLE 3-1. Common Address Books and Their Descriptions.

Address Book	Description
Microsoft Exchange Address Book	Part of your network e-mail system.
Personal Address Book	An address book in Exchange with names and addresses that you have copied from messages sent to you, copied from other address books, or typed.
Schedule+ Contact List	Part of Schedule+ 7.0. You enter the names, addresses, and telephone numbers of people you contact regularly (or even irregularly).

Insert Address

To use the address book for letters, envelopes, and address labels, click the Insert Address button.

You'll find an Insert Address button on both the Recipient Info and Sender Info tabs of the Letter Wizard and on both the Envelopes tab and the Labels tab of the Envelopes And Labels dialog box. Clicking this button displays the Select Name dialog box. Follow the steps you see here to insert an address:

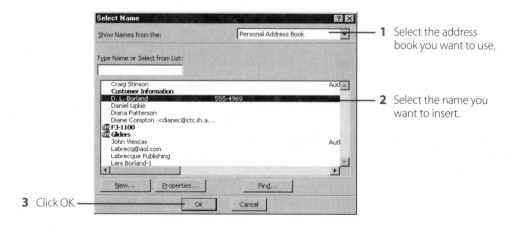

1 Select the address book you want to use.

2 Select the name you want to insert.

3 Click OK.

You see the name and address added, like this:

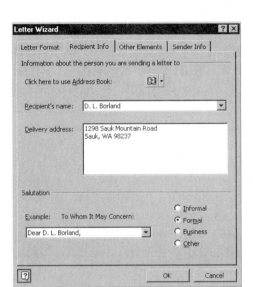

After you use the Insert Address button, Word adds the name to the list under the Insert Address button, like this:

When you want to use an address you've used before, click the down arrow beside the Insert Address button and select the name.

Getting Personal:
Elements of a Personal Letter

A personal letter is usually informal, both in content and structure. Most personal letters I've read contain the date, a greeting, page numbers, a closing, and a signature, along with a message of one or more paragraphs and possibly pictures. That's about it. To create a personal letter template, we'll jump-start the letter and then call the Letter Wizard to add a few structural items and special touches. After you create a personal letter template and save it, you can start a personal letter from the template to quickly set up the letter. You can then concentrate on adding the message.

Setting Up Pages in a Personal Letter

You can do the basic page setup in the Letter Wizard on the Letter Format tab (see Figure 3-1, page 156), but you might also need to make some changes using the Page Setup dialog box. The following sections describe how to set up your pages using both methods.

Inserting the Date

SEE ALSO

For details of the Include Header And Footer With Page Design box, see "Setting Up Headers and Footers," next page.

With the Date Line check box turned on, the Letter Wizard inserts the date into the letter. After you turn it on, Word automatically selects the long date format (for example, January 30, 1997). You can choose a different date format from the list. All of the date formats appear as examples, which use the current date to illustrate the format.

Choosing a Page Design

SEE ALSO

For details of the Choose A Letter Style box, see "Paragraphs," page 172.

You see a list of possible page designs in the Choose A Page Design list box. Choose one for your letter. When you select a page design, you see a preview of it below the list box.

Setting the Paper Size

If you want to print your personal letter on unusual size paper, you need to set the paper size on the Paper Size tab in the Page Setup dialog box. On the Paper Size tab, set the height and width of the paper you'll use to print your letter.

Adjusting the Margins

If you're printing a letter on an unusual size paper, such as a note sheet, you'll want to adjust the margins. To do this, choose the File Page Setup command and enter a measurement for the width of that margin in the appropriate box on the Margins tab of the Page Setup dialog box.

TIP

If you're going to print your letter onto a greeting card, set the paper size to the size of the card when it's unfolded. Then set the left margin width as the distance from the left edge of the open card to the point where you want the left edge of the text to print, which is to the right of the card's fold.

Setting Up Headers and Footers

Even personal letters usually have the page number on the sheets after the first page. Some people also like to add the date to the headers on every page. To set up a header with the date on every page and the page number on the pages after the first page, follow these steps:

1 Start your letter with the date, press Enter to insert another paragraph, and then press Ctrl+Enter to insert a page break. (You'll remove this page break later.)

2 Choose the View Header And Footer command. The Header and Footer toolbar appears, as shown here:

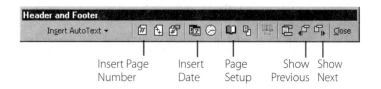

3 Click the Page Setup button on the Header and Footer toolbar.

4 Click the Layout tab, turn on the Different First Page check box, and then click OK.

5 If necessary, click the Show Previous button until the header space shows First Page Header.

Align Right

6 Click the Align Right button on the Formatting toolbar.

7 Click the Insert Date button on the Header And Footer toolbar.

8 Click the Show Next button on the Header And Footer toolbar.

9 Click the Insert Date button on the Header And Footer toolbar.

10 Press the End key to move to the end of the header line, and then press the Enter key to start a new paragraph in the header.

11 Click the Insert Page Number button on the Header And Footer toolbar.

12 Click the Close button on the Header And Footer toolbar.

13 Select the page break you inserted in step 2, and then press Delete to remove the page break. (To learn about selecting, see Chapter 2, "Guided Tour: Eight Stations of a Document.")

Fleshing Out the Message in Your Personal Letter

For most personal letters, you'll probably start with a blank sheet and simply type your message. If, however, you want to set up a letter template for specific people to whom you write regularly, you can add some text, such as the salutation (*Dear Mom,* for example), and you could add your standard closing for this person (*Your loving child,* for example).

Adding standard letter text is unlikely to be very useful to you, but you can set up automatic corrections and AutoText entries that will help you complete the letter with less typing.

AutoCorrect

Word can fix your typing mistakes. If you mistype a name or other word that you sometimes have difficulty typing, Word fixes the word to its correct spelling. Word can also expand personal abbreviations to their full text. If you want to use personal abbreviations, you can set them up in Word's AutoCorrect. After you do, you simply type the abbreviation, and Word expands it to its full text.

Deciding Between AutoCorrect and AutoText

As you read these two sections ("AutoCorrect" and "AutoText"), you might wonder (and well you should) how to decide between setting up an AutoCorrect entry and an AutoText entry. Here's the rule of thumb: if you want the correction to take place automatically every time you type the word a particular way, set up an AutoCorrect entry. If you want the correction or expansion to happen only when you want it to, set up an AutoText entry. AutoText gives you the power to decide whether to accept or ignore the correction or expansion. AutoCorrect simply makes the change, whether or not you want it.

 NOTE

If you select a mistyped or misspelled word and you have both the Check Spelling As You Type and Always Suggest Corrections check boxes turned on (Tools Options Spelling & Grammar) in your document, Word puts the selected word in the Replace box.

To set up AutoCorrect for a mistyped word or a misspelling, follow these steps:

1   Make sure the Check Spelling As You Type check box and the Always Suggest Corrections check box are turned on. These options are on the Spelling & Grammar tab of the Options dialog box (Tools Options Spelling & Grammar).

2   In a document, type the incorrect or misspelled version of the word. (You can also use a word that is already in the document.)

3   Select the word that you mistyped or misspelled.

4   Choose the Tools AutoCorrect command, and then click the AutoCorrect tab. You'll see this dialog box:

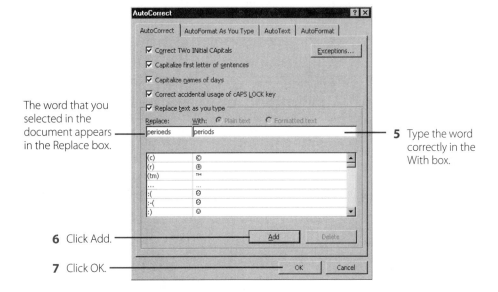

The word that you selected in the document appears in the Replace box.

5   Type the word correctly in the With box.

6   Click Add.

7   Click OK.

? SEE ALSO

To learn about selecting, see Chapter 2, "Guided Tour: Eight Stations of a Document."

To set up AutoCorrect for a personal abbreviation, follow these steps:

1   In a document, type the entire word or phrase for which you want to use an abbreviation.

2   Select the phrase.

3   Choose the Tools AutoCorrect command, and then click the AutoCorrect tab.

4 Type the abbreviation in the Replace box. See the example on the following page.

5 If you want the replacement to retain its original formatting, click Formatted Text.

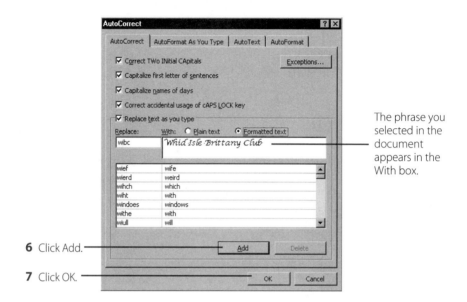

The phrase you selected in the document appears in the With box.

6 Click Add.

7 Click OK.

SEE ALSO
For more information about AutoCorrect, see "AutoCorrect," page 164.

Adding an Unusual Word to AutoCorrect

If you select a mistyped or misspelled word, Word puts that word in the Replace box. If you select a correctly typed word, Word puts that word in the With box. Word assumes, probably correctly in most cases, that you want to set up a correction for a mistyped or misspelled word and that you want to set up an abbreviation for a correctly spelled word. If Word marks a word as incorrect but it's a word for which you want to create an abbreviation, first mark the word as correct (right-click the word, and then select either Ignore All or Add from the Spelling shortcut menu) before you choose the AutoCorrect command.

AutoText

AutoText is a handy place to store pieces of text or pictures that you want to retrieve quickly and easily. When you create an AutoText entry, all you have to do when you're typing is to start typing the abbreviation (the AutoText name), and the complete AutoText entry pops up. When you see the pop-up message, all you do is press Enter to insert the phrase into your document, like this:

Whid Isle Brittany Club

I'm glad I joined wibc

Here are the steps to create an AutoText entry:

1 Type a word or phrase you want to store for easy retrieval.

2 Select the phrase you've just typed. (To learn about selecting, see Chapter 2, "Guided Tour: Eight Stations of a Document.")

3 Choose the Tools AutoCorrect command, and then click the AutoText tab. Word uses part of the phrase you selected as the proposed name, as shown here:

4 Edit the name Word proposes, or type a new name for the AutoText.

5 Click Add to create the AutoText.

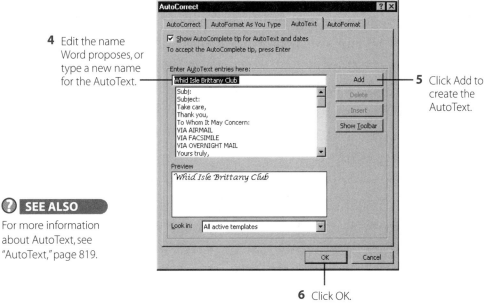

6 Click OK.

? SEE ALSO

For more information about AutoText, see "AutoText," page 819.

Correspondence

Formatting a Personal Letter

Besides the simple joy of writing down your thoughts and feelings and sending them to a personal correspondent, you might want to decorate your letter in several ways to add spice and to make reading it more visually interesting. Of course, you can format your letter in hundreds of ways, and you can add all kinds of art, tables, and other objects. Most personal letters aren't that complicated. Still, the following sections suggest several ways you can decorate your letters. You'll find out how to change the fonts, change the paragraph formatting, and add a page border.

Fonts

Most people I know who use a computer to write personal letters prefer to select a font that seems more personal to them than Word's standard Times New Roman font. Times New Roman is a very readable font and probably a safe choice for Microsoft to make the standard font. Nonetheless, it doesn't have much personality; it's corporate, serious, and conservative. If that's your personality and the image you want to give your personal correspondents, that's fine. You need make no change to the standard font in Word.

If, on the other hand, you want to show your personal correspondents a different image, you'll want to change the standard font. To do so, you need to perform two actions: first you need to save the letter setup as a template, and then you need to set a different standard font.

Setting a New Standard Font

To save your personal letter setup as a template, take these steps:

1 Choose the File Save As command.

2 Select Document Template (*.dot) in the Save As Type box.

3 Switch to the Letters & Faxes folder.

4 In the File Name box, type a name for your template.

5 Click the Save button.

To change the standard font for your personal letter template, follow these steps:

1 Choose the Format Font command. The following Font dialog box will open:

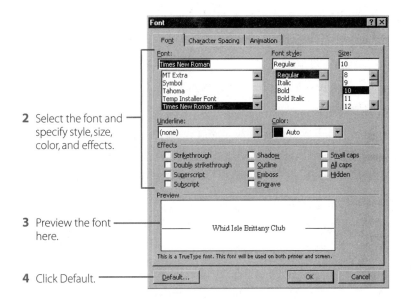

2 Select the font and specify style, size, color, and effects.

3 Preview the font here.

4 Click Default.

5 When Word asks if you want to change the default font for this template, click Yes.

Changing Fonts Within the Letter

If you like to add flair and flamboyance or emphasis and variety to your personal letters, you'll want to make font changes at various places. In these cases, rather than use your standard font, you'll want to select some distinctively different fonts, font styles, or font effects. To change the font in some part of your letter, take these steps:

1 Select the words you want to change.

2 Use one of the following methods to apply the changes you want to make:

- Use the Font dialog box. To display it, either choose the Format Font command, press Ctrl+D, or click the right mouse button on the selection and then select Font from the shortcut menu that appears, shown on the next page.

Correspondence

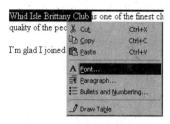

- Click the appropriate buttons on the Formatting toolbar.

- Press the appropriate Font shortcut keys.

Any time you add one character look (that is, a font, a font style, or a font effect) to another, the new and the existing looks combine. The exception to this rule occurs when you use the Font dialog box for boldface and italic. Then you must choose the combined look (Bold Italic); choosing one does not add the new choice to the existing one. The other looks in the Font dialog box can be added to an existing look, although conflicting font effects, such as small caps and all caps, don't combine.

Table 3-2 lists the most common font changes and how to make them using the Font dialog box, the Formatting toolbar, and shortcut keys.

TABLE 3-2. Font Change Options.

Formatting Action	Font Dialog Box	Formatting Toolbar	Shortcut Keys
Boldface	Font Style: Bold	Bold (toggles)	Ctrl+B (toggles)
Italic	Font Style: Italic	Italic (toggles)	Ctrl+I (toggles)
Toggle continuous underlining (does not break between words)	Underline: Single	Underline (toggles)	Ctrl+U (toggles)
Word underlining (breaks between words)	Underline: Words Only		Ctrl+Shift+W (toggles)
Double underlining (does not break between words)	Underline: Double		Ctrl+Shift+D (toggles)

(continued)

Table 3-2. *continued*

Formatting Action	Font Dialog Box	Formatting Toolbar	Shortcut Keys
Font name	Font: select or type a name	Font: select or type a name	Ctrl+Shift+F: when the Formatting toolbar is turned on, activates the Font box on the Formatting toolbar where you select a font name; when the Formatting toolbar is turned off, displays the Font dialog box
Font size	Size: select or type a number	Font Size: select or type a number	Ctrl+Shift+P: when the Formatting toolbar is turned on, activates the Font Size box on the Formatting toolbar where you select or type a number; when the Formatting toolbar is turned off, displays the Font dialog box
Increase the font size by one point	Size: select or type a number one point size larger	Font Size: select or type a number one point size larger	Ctrl+]
Decrease the font size by one point	Size: select or type a number one point size smaller	Font Size: select or type a number one point size smaller	Ctrl+[
Color	Color: select a color	Font Color: click button to use current color setting; click down arrow to select and apply new color	
Remove all the added text formatting			Ctrl+Spacebar or Ctrl+Shift+Z

Paragraphs

Most personal letters use one of two main paragraph styles—full block (all paragraphs flush with the left margin) and semi-block (all paragraphs have an indented first line). If you want to use one of these two paragraph styles, you can set up the style on the Letter Format tab of the Letter Wizard dialog box.

However, you might like to use a variety of paragraph formats, or a similar style in every paragraph, but one that is different from the two styles in the Letter Wizard. Either way, you can adjust paragraph formatting with the Format Paragraph command, the Formatting toolbar, or shortcut keys.

Formatting Paragraphs with the Letter Wizard

In the Choose A Letter Style box, choose a style for the paragraphs and the placement of the date, salutation, and closing. Table 3-3 lists your choices. When you select a letter style, you see a preview of it below the list box.

TABLE 3-3.   Choices in the Choose A Letter Style Box.

Letter Style Choices	Effect on the Letter
Full Block	The date, inside address, salutation, body paragraphs, and closing are flush with the left margin.
Modified Block	The date and closing are shifted to the right. All other paragraphs are flush with the left margin.
Semi-Block	The date and closing are shifted to the right. Body paragraphs are indented on their first lines by one-half inch. The inside address and salutation are flush with the left margin.

Customizing Paragraph Formats

You can also change paragraph formatting with the Format Paragraph command, the Formatting toolbar, or shortcut keys, as shown in Table 3-4.

TABLE 3-4. **Options for Changing Paragraph Formatting.**

Formatting Action	Paragraph Dialog Box	Formatting Toolbar	Shortcut Keys
Left-align	Alignment: Left	Align Left	Ctrl+L
Center	Alignment: Centered	Center	Ctrl+E
Right-align	Alignment: Right	Align Right	Ctrl+R
Justify	Alignment: Justify	Justify	Ctrl+J
Single-space	Line Spacing: Single		Ctrl+1 (above the letter keys only)
Double-space	Line Spacing: Double		Ctrl+2 (above the letter keys only)
One-and-a-half-line spacing	Line Spacing: 1.5 Lines		Ctrl+5 (above the letter keys only)
Line space above (toggles)	Spacing Before: 12 pt or 0 pt		Ctrl+0 (zero) (above the letter keys only)
Indent to the next tab stop; first line indents by the same amount	Indentation Left: 0.5" (or increase by 0.5"); Indentation Special: (None)	Increase Indent	Ctrl+M
Decrease left indent to the previous tab stop (default is 0.5"); first line indents by the same amount	Indentation Left: 0" (or decrease by 0.5"); Indentation Special: (None)	Decrease Indent	Ctrl+Shift+M
Hanging indent: indent to the next tab stop (the default is 0.5"); first line remains at its current position	Indentation Special: Hanging; By: 0.5" (or increase by 0.5")		Ctrl+T
Decrease hanging indent to the previous tab stop (default is 0.5"); first line remains at its current position	Indentation Special: (None); or Indentation Special: Hanging; By: decrease by 0.5"		Ctrl+Shift+T
Remove any paragraph formatting	Alignment: Left; Line Spacing: Single; Spacing Before: 0 pt		Ctrl+Q

II

Correspondence

Setting a New Standard Paragraph

If you want most of the paragraphs in your letters to have a particular format, you'll want to change the standard paragraph format. To do so, you need to perform two actions: first you save the letter setup as a template (if you haven't already done so), and then you set a different standard paragraph format.

To save your personal letter setup as a template, follow these steps:

1 Choose the File Save As command.

2 Select Document Template (*.dot) in the Save As Type box.

3 Switch to the Letters & Faxes folder.

4 In the File Name box, type a name for your template.

5 Click the Save button.

To change the standard paragraph format for your personal letter template, take these steps:

1 Choose the Format Style command. You will see the Style dialog box:

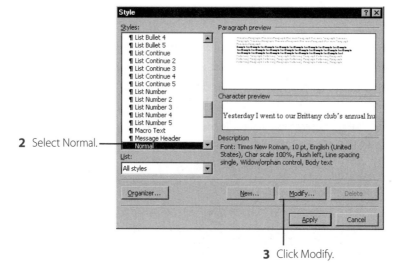

2 Select Normal.

3 Click Modify.

The Modify Style dialog box will open.

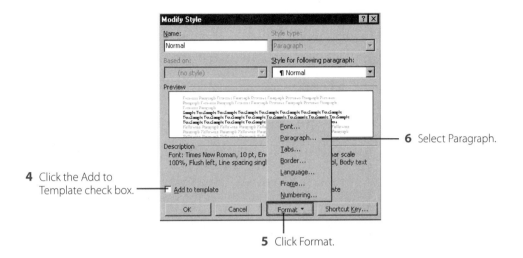

4 Click the Add to Template check box.

6 Select Paragraph.

5 Click Format.

You will see the Paragraph dialog box:

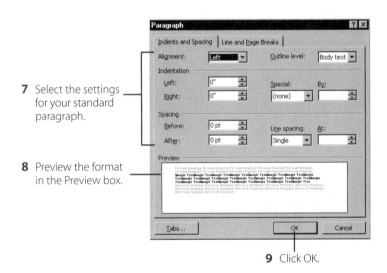

7 Select the settings for your standard paragraph.

8 Preview the format in the Preview box.

9 Click OK.

10 Click OK in the Modify Style dialog box.

11 Click Apply in the Style dialog box.

Page Borders

While most people concentrate on writing the words in their letters, there are some brave souls who like to add decorations. Sometimes these decorations are doodles, sometimes they are pictures, and sometimes they are border decorations. One correspondent I know likes to

Correspondence

add trees to her page borders because she lives in a rural setting, surrounded by trees, and wants to give her correspondents a sense of her environment.

(?) SEE ALSO

For more information about page borders, see "Changing Borders and Shading," page 340.

In Word 97 you can add borders to your pages as either lines or decorative objects. To add a page border to your letter, choose the Format Borders And Shading command, and then click the Page Border tab. You will see the Borders And Shading dialog box, where you can take the steps shown.

1 Select the type of border (see "Setting," page 193.

2 Select the line style or No Border.

3 Select a color for line borders.

4 Select a line width for line borders.

5 If you want art instead of lines, select the art object here.

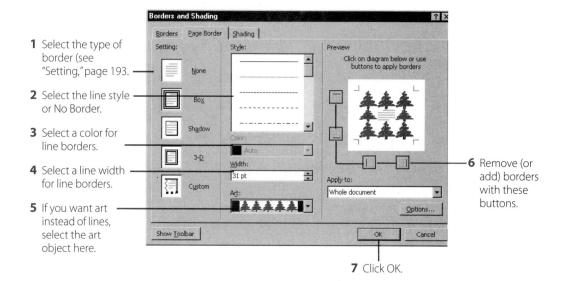

6 Remove (or add) borders with these buttons.

7 Click OK.

Storing Your Personal Letter as a Template

When the personal letter template is complete, store it so that you can use the template to create other letters to the same person. To store the personal letter template, follow these steps:

1 Choose the File Save As command.

2 Select Document Template (*.dot) in the Save As Type box.

3 Switch to the Letters & Faxes folder.

4 In the File Name box, type a name for your template, such as *Momleter.*

5 Click the Save button.

To use your personal letter template to send another letter to your mother, follow these steps:

1 Choose the File New command.

2 Click the Letters & Faxes tab.

3 Select the template for your personal letter to your mother, and then click OK.

4 Position the insertion point in the second empty paragraph below the greeting.

5 Type your letter.

6 Add an envelope. For directions, see "Add to Document Button," page 199.

7 Print your envelope and letter.

8 Save your letter.

9 Mail your letter.

Getting Down to Business: Elements of a Business Letter

A typical business letter contains a return address, the date, an inside address, a formal greeting, a formal closing, and a signature. Most business letters also contain the sender's and the typist's initials, and some business letters contain a list of people who receive courtesy copies and a list of enclosures. In reality, these options suggest four business letter templates:

- One without courtesy copy and enclosure lists

- One with a courtesy copy list but no enclosures

- One with enclosures but no courtesy copy list

- One with both lists

To illustrate the issues and the possibilities for suiting the business letter template to your situation, we'll set up a business letter template with both a courtesy copy list and an enclosure list.

Setting Up Pages in a Business Letter

The Letter Wizard provides a handy way to set up the pages of a business letter, just as it does for personal letters. For details of page setup for a letter, see "Setting Up Pages in a Personal Letter," page 162.

For a business letter, several other page elements can be very important. The following sections describe how to set up a letter for printing on pre-printed letterhead; how to set up your own logo on letterhead; and how to add a reference line, attention line, subject line, complimentary closing, your title, your organization's name, the number of enclosures, and a list of the names of those who receive courtesy copies. You'll also learn how to set up headers for the pages of a business letter after the first page.

Using Letterhead

If your organization uses pre-printed letterhead, you'll want to set up your business letter template to fit onto the letterhead for the first page of a business letter. For additional pages, you'll want to set up the pages to fit on blank second sheets. With the Letter Wizard, this setup is easy.

To set up your business letter to print on letterhead, follow these steps:

1 Choose the Tools Letter Wizard.

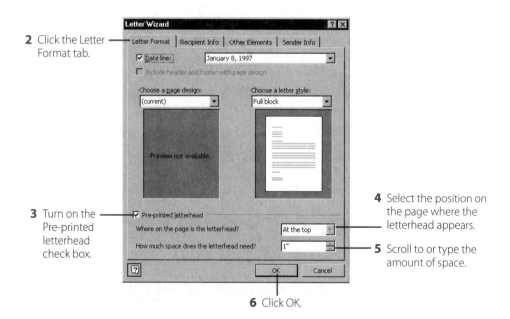

2 Click the Letter Format tab.

3 Turn on the Pre-printed letterhead check box.

4 Select the position on the page where the letterhead appears.

5 Scroll to or type the amount of space.

6 Click OK.

Creating Your Own Letterhead

If you're not using pre-printed letterhead, you might want to create your own letterhead in Word. That way, whenever you create a business letter, your letterhead appears as part of the letter. Setting up a letterhead as a part of your business letter template means that you have the benefits of pre-printed paper without the expense of printing it ahead of time.

To create a letterhead, follow these steps:

1 Choose the View Header And Footer command.

2 Click the Page Setup button, and then click the Layout tab.

3 Turn on the Different First Page check box, and then click OK. This step isolates your letterhead to the first page of the letter.

4 Insert the text of the letterhead and set the font.

5 Set the paragraph formatting (such as right alignment and line spacing).

6 Set borders and shading if desired.

7 Insert clip art, art from a file that contains your organization's logo, or draw art with Word's Drawing toolbar. (For information about inserting and drawing art, see Chapter 10, "Brocading a Brochure.)

8 When you've finished creating your letterhead, click Close on the Header And Footer toolbar.

Here is a sample letterhead created with Word. The text color is green. The banner behind the text is turquoise (or cyan).

 TIP

If you have a color printer, you can set up the artwork and logo type in your organization's colors. Doing so will make your created letterhead look more like letterhead you'd get from a stationer.

Adding Other Elements to Your Business Letter

On the Sender Info tab (see Figure 3-4, page 158) and on the Other Elements tab (see Figure 3-3, page 157) of the Letter Wizard, you'll find several boxes handy for adding other elements to your business letters. Figure 3-5 shows you where these elements are placed in a letter document automatically when you turn on their respective options.

FIGURE 3-5.
The locations for added letter elements.

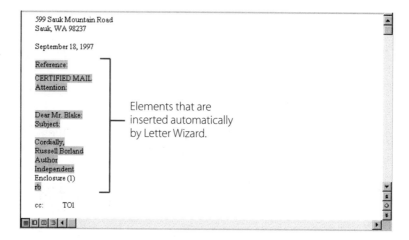

Elements that are inserted automatically by Letter Wizard.

Reference Line

When you're answering a letter or other inquiry, you might want to include a line at the top of the letter referring to the date and type of correspondence to which you're responding. A reference line also makes it easier to file copies of the letter in the appropriate place.

To add a reference line to your letter, turn on the Reference Line check box, and then select or type the reference line tag. You can also type the reference itself in the Reference Line list. After you insert a reference line into a letter, Word keeps that name in the list for use in future letters. Letter Wizard places the reference line just below the date line.

Attention Line

While the common practice nowadays is to address a letter directly to the recipient, there are times when you might prefer the older style of sending the letter to an organization and then adding an attention line. Letter Wizard places the attention line between the inside address and the greeting.

To add an attention line to your letter, turn on the Attention check box, and then select or type the attention tag. You can also type the name of the recipient in the Attention list. After you insert an attention line into a letter, Word keeps that tag in the list for use in future letters.

Subject Line

If you want to include a subject line in your letter as a short summary of your letter's contents, turn on the Subject check box, and then select or type the subject tag line you want to use. The original list contains only the tag line *Subject:*. After you type and use a different tag line, Word adds that tag line to the list in the Letter Wizard. Letter Wizard places the subject line just below the greeting.

Complimentary Closing

To have the Letter Wizard add and set up a complimentary closing, select the closing you want to use from the Complimentary Closing list. You can also type your own preferred complimentary closing, which Word then adds to the list for use in future letters.

Your Title

Type your job title in the Job Title box to add it after your name at the end of the letter. After you insert this job title into a letter, Word keeps that title in the list for use in future letters.

Your Organization's Name

Type your organization's name in the Company box to add it after your name (or after your job title) at the end of the letter. After you insert this company name into a letter, Word keeps that name in the list for use in future letters.

Enclosures

When you're sending enclosures with your letter, you can have the Letter Wizard add the label *Enclosures* and the number of enclosures in parentheses after the label. To add this label and the number to your letter, turn on the Enclosures check box, and then type or scroll to the number of enclosures you're sending (if you're sending more than one). The maximum number of enclosures is 32,767. If you scroll down to zero or type a zero for the number of enclosures, Word automatically turns off the Enclosures check box. Letter Wizard adds the enclosures line below your name, title, and company.

II

Correspondence

NOTE

> If you want to include a list of the names of the enclosures, you'll have to type the list yourself below the *Enclosures* label.

Courtesy Copies

Business letter writers often send courtesy copies (they used to be called carbon copies in the days of typewriters and carbon paper). Including a list of the people who receive courtesy copies is a common, ethical, and polite practice. If you're sending courtesy copies of a letter, the Letter Wizard makes it easy to add a list of the people who are receiving them.

To add to your letter a list of people who will receive courtesy copies, you can add the names in one of these ways:

- Type the names in the Cc box on the Other Elements tab. You can type the names all on one line, separated by commas, or you can put the names on separate lines. To start a new line in the Cc box, press Enter.

- Click the Insert Address button on the Other Elements tab, and select a name from an address book. To select more than one name, hold down the Ctrl key as you click each name. After you select all the names, click the Cc button in the address book, and then click OK. The names appear in the Cc box on the Other Elements tab on one line, separated by commas.

- Click the down arrow part of the Insert Address button, and then select the name of the person who is to receive a courtesy copy. With this method, you can add only one name. If you select another name, the new name replaces the previous name you selected.

- If you want the names to appear on separate lines, select the comma and the space between two names in the Cc box, and then press Enter.

After you click OK in the Letter Wizard, Word adds to the bottom of your letter *cc:* followed by a tab character and the names.

Sender's and Typist's Initials

It is customary for a typist preparing a letter to add the sender's initials and the typist's initials at the foot of the letter. Adding these initials is easy with the Letter Wizard.

To add the sender's and typist's initials to a business letter, follow these steps:

1 Choose the Tools Letter Wizard command, and then click the Sender Info tab.

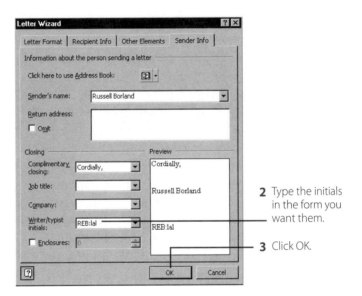

2 Type the initials in the form you want them.

3 Click OK.

Setting Up Headers for Additional Pages

It is common practice in business letters to include the recipient's name, the date, and the page number on the pages after the first page. Using a combination of the Letter Wizard and AutoText, you can set this up easily.

To set up headers for additional pages of a business letter, follow the steps on the next page.

Correspondence

II

1 Choose the Tools Letter Wizard command, and then click the Recipient Info tab.

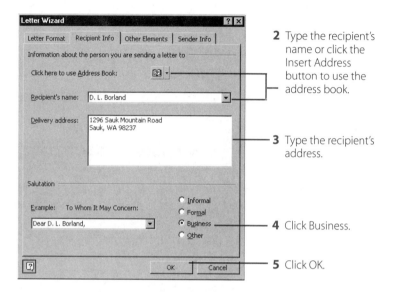

2 Type the recipient's name or click the Insert Address button to use the address book.

3 Type the recipient's address.

4 Click Business.

5 Click OK.

6 Press Ctrl+End to move to the end of the letter, and then press Ctrl+Enter to insert a page break. (You can remove this page break later—in step 18.)

7 Choose the View Header And Footer command.

8 Click the Page Setup button on the Header And Footer toolbar, and then click the Layout tab. You will see the dialog box:

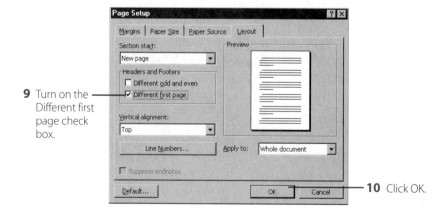

9 Turn on the Different first page check box.

10 Click OK.

11 Click the Align Right button on the Formatting toolbar.

12 Press and hold Shift, click the Insert AutoText button on the Header And Footer toolbar, and select the name of the recipient (Inside Address Name) from the list.

13 Press Enter to start a new paragraph.

14 Click the Insert Date button on the Header And Footer toolbar.

15 Press Enter to start another new paragraph.

16 Click the Insert Page Number button on the Header And Footer toolbar.

17 Click the Close button on the Header And Footer toolbar.

18 Select the page break you inserted, and press Delete.

Now when your letter runs to more than one page, the additional pages will print with the recipient's name, the date of the letter, and the page number.

Fleshing Out the Message in Your Business Letter

After you run the Letter Wizard, you'll see the sentence *Type your text here.* inserted into the letter after the greeting. Word selects this text and you simply start typing your letter's message. If you have taken other actions since using the Letter Wizard, however, this sentence might not be selected any longer. In this case, select the sentence (hold down Ctrl and click the sentence), and then type your message.

In business letters, as in personal letters, you will probably use terms, names, and phrases that you'd like to insert with a minimum of effort. That's where Word's AutoCorrect and AutoText come in handy. For more information on using these two tools, see "AutoCorrect," page 164, and "AutoText," page 167. To create the other text in your letter, simply type it, paste it, or insert files, objects, art, tables, or other objects as appropriate.

II

Correspondence

For a business letter template, add only the text and other items that belong in all your business letters.

Proofreading for Spelling and Grammar

So you're a lousy typist. Me too. Luckily for us, Word can automatically check spelling and grammar as we create a document. While Word proofreads your document automatically, the Spelling And Grammar Status icon in the status bar shows a moving pencil and a flipping page, like the following, although here it appears frozen during its animation:

The moving pencil indicates Word is proofreading the document.

Word shows you when it detects a spelling or grammar error in the following ways:

■ In the status bar, the Spelling And Grammar Status icon has an X on it, as shown here:

Double-click on this icon to jump to the next error and display a shortcut menu

■ When the icon has a check mark on it, as shown here, no errors are detected:

■ Word marks spelling and grammar errors with a sawtooth underline in your text, as shown here:

A red, sawtooth underline indicates a spelling error.

A green, sawtooth underline indicates a gramatical error.

What to Do About Sawtooth Underlines

When you see sawtooth underlines, you have several options, depending on whether you want to deal with each one individually as you go, or later in a separate spelling and grammar check of the entire document. You can do one of the following:

- Correct the word or sentence yourself.

- Point to an underlined word with the mouse, and click the right mouse button to display the Spelling or Grammar shortcut menu, like the ones shown in Figure 3-6 and Figure 3-7.

FIGURE 3-6.
A sample Spelling shortcut menu.

FIGURE 3-7.
A sample Grammar shortcut menu.

- Double-click the Spelling And Grammar Status icon in the status bar to jump to the next sawtooth underline and display the Spelling or Grammar shortcut menu; each double click jumps to the next sawtooth underline.

 TIP

> Instead of double-clicking on the Spelling and Grammar Status icon, you can press the keyboard shortcut, Alt+F7.

Spelling and Grammar

- Click the Spelling And Grammar button on the Standard toolbar or press F7 to display the Spelling And Grammar dialog box. (See "Station 4: Proofread," page 69, for more information on spelling and grammar checking using this dialog box.)

 **TIP**

Hiding the Red and Green Sawtooth Underlines

If you want Word to check spelling and grammar as you type but you don't really want to see those red and green sawtooth underlines until you're done, you can tell Word to hide your mistakes for the time being. To do so, follow these steps:

1   Choose the Tools Options command.

2   Click the Spelling & Grammar tab. (See Figure 3-8.)

3   Turn on the Hide Spelling Errors In This Document check box to hide spelling errors.

4   Turn on the Hide Grammatical Errors In This Document check box to hide grammatical errors.

FIGURE 3-8.

The Spelling & Grammar tab in the Options dialog box.

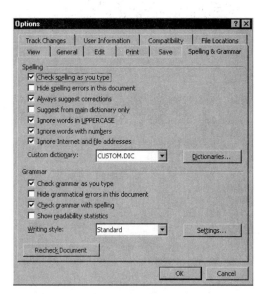

Using the Shortcut Menus

Notice that both the Spelling and Grammar shortcut menus (see Figure 3-6 and Figure 3-7) include a list of some suggestions for correcting the marked problem, an Ignore All command, and a Spelling command or Grammar command. The Spelling shortcut menu also displays an Add command and an AutoCorrect command. You can do any of the following in the shortcut menus.

- To change the marked word in your document to one of the words on the shortcut menu, click the word on the menu.

- To tell Word that you like the word as it is, click Ignore All— Word won't mark that word as wrong until you restart Word. (If you mistakenly click Ignore All, see "Resetting Ignore All," page 78, to set things right again.)

- To add a word marked with a red sawtooth underline to a custom dictionary, click Add—Word won't ever mark that word as wrong again. (If you mistakenly click Add, see "Adding Words to a Custom Dictionary," page 73.)

- If you want more choices for a word, click Spelling on the shortcut menu. In the Spelling dialog box, you can add the word to the custom dictionary of your choice or to your AutoCorrect list (see "Adding Words to AutoCorrect During Proofreading," page 79).

Correspondence

When Grammar Checking Is Too Uptight

Word's grammar checking can be set to different levels of strictness. Originally, Word's grammar checking is set up to a level named Standard, meant for checking grammar for business letters. For personal letters, you probably want a less strict check of your grammar. For this reason, Word offers a setting named Casual.

To change the grammar checking level to Casual Communication, take these steps:

1 Choose the Tools Options command, and then click the Spelling & Grammar tab.

2 In the Writing Style drop-down list box, select Casual, and then click OK.

Also note on the Spelling & Grammar tab that you can turn off grammar checking by turning off the Check Grammar As You Type check box.

For more details about the Spelling & Grammar tab, see "Spelling & Grammar Tab," page 972.

Formatting a Business Letter

Like personal letters, business letters can be set up to use special fonts and special paragraph formatting. For details about adding these elements to your business letter, see "Formatting a Personal Letter," page 168.

Many organizations regularly conduct business in other countries. Some of these organizations even conduct some of their business correspondence in a language other than the language of their home country. In Word, you can set up your business letters for another language, either for the entire letter or for certain words, phrases, or parts of a letter.

Also, some business letters include a page border. You are most likely to see page borders on pre-printed letterhead. But if you're setting up your logo and letterhead in Word, you might want to set up special borders, too.

The following sections describe using various languages in your letters and adding page borders.

Using Words in Various Languages

For the most part, words in a business letter or any other type of document are in the primary language you use on your computer. When you set up Windows, the standard language is the primary language of your country. From time to time, however, you might use a few words from another language, or you might compose an entire business letter in another language for colleagues or associates in another country, particularly if your organization conducts business outside your home country.

There are also times when you might want to turn off the spelling checker and hyphenation for some words or elements in a document. You can mark words in a different language so that Word checks their spelling and sets their hyphenation properly for that language (provided you have the related language dictionaries installed—see "Dictionaries for Other Languages," next page). You can mark words and elements you want the spelling checker and hyphenation to skip as having no language.

To mark a word as belonging to a different language, follow these steps:

1 Select the word you want to mark as belonging to a different language.

2 Choose the Tools Language command, and then select Set Language from the submenu.

3 Select the language for the selected word in the Language dialog box, shown here:

4 Click OK.

If you haven't installed the dictionary for the language you select installed, you see a message that tells you that Word cannot find the dictionary. Simply click OK.

To mark a word as having no language so that the spelling checker and hyphenation skip it, follow these steps:

1 Select the word or element you want to mark as having no language.

2 Choose the Tools Language command, and then select Set Language from the submenu.

3 Select (No Proofing).

4 Click OK.

Dictionaries for Other Languages

Before you can check the spelling and set the hyphenation of words in a different language, you need to add a dictionary for that language to your Word or Office setup. Copy the language dictionary to the Proof folder inside the Microsoft Shared folder inside the Common Files folder inside the Program Files folder on your computer's hard disk.

Now you need to activate the dictionary in Word. To do so, take these steps:

1 Choose the Tools Options command, and then click the Spelling & Grammar tab.

2 Click the Dictionaries button, and then click the Add button.

3 In the Add Custom Dictionary dialog box, select the language dictionary, and click OK.

4 Click OK in the Custom Dictionaries dialog box, and then click OK in the Options dialog box.

> The steps for adding dictionaries for other languages also apply to adding specialty dictionaries, such as medical and law dictionaries.

Keyboards for Other Languages

With Windows 95, you can switch keyboards "on the fly." This means that you can disconnect the keyboard you are using, plug in a keyboard for a different language, and keep typing without having to change settings in the Control Panel and then stop and restart Windows.

When you switch keyboards and start typing, Word automatically sets the language of your typing to the keyboard you are using.

Adding Page Border Lines

Some organizations have sheets of letterhead that include a borderline. Sometimes the border is a line down the left side or up the right side. Some letterheads have borderlines at the top or at the bottom; some have borderlines all around the sheet.

To add a page borderline to your business letter template, choose the Format Borders And Shading command, click the Page Border tab, and then follow the steps on the next page.

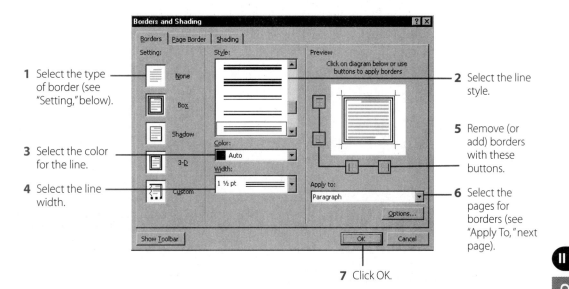

1 Select the type of border (see "Setting," below).

2 Select the line style.

3 Select the color for the line.

4 Select the line width.

5 Remove (or add) borders with these buttons.

6 Select the pages for borders (see "Apply To," next page).

7 Click OK.

Correspondence

Setting

The first four Setting choices are easy to understand. The icon on the button illustrates the type of border the button adds to the page. The fifth Setting button—Custom—lets you choose which borders you want. The Custom button also lets you put a different border along each edge of the page, if you want. For example, if you want a fat, blue line at the top of the page and a thin, black line down the left side of the page, take these steps:

1 Click the Custom button.

2 Select the solid line from the Style list.

3 Select Blue in the Color box.

4 Select ¼ pt in the Width box.

5 Check the example in the Preview box. If the blue border appears along any edges besides the top, click those lines or click the button for those edges to turn off the blue border for all edges except the top. If no borders appear, click the top edge of the Preview page or the Top Border button.

6 Select Black in the Color box.

7 Select ¾ pt in the Width box.

8 In the Preview box, click the left edge of the Preview page or the Left Border button.

Apply To

You can apply a page border to all the pages, the first page only, or all pages except the first page. If you're creating a letterhead, you'll probably want the border only on the first page.

Storing Your Business Letter as a Template

When the business letter template is complete, store it so that you can use the template to create other business letters. Here's how to store the business letter template:

1 Choose the File Save As command.

2 Select Document Template (*.dot) in the Save As Type box.

3 Switch to the Letters & Faxes folder.

4 In the File Name box, type a name for your template.

5 Click the Save button.

To use your business letter template, follow these steps:

1 Choose the File New command.

2 Click the Letters & Faxes tab.

3 Select the template for your business letter, and then click OK.

4 Position the insertion point in the second empty paragraph below the date.

5 Choose the Tools Letter Wizard command, and then click the Recipient Info tab.

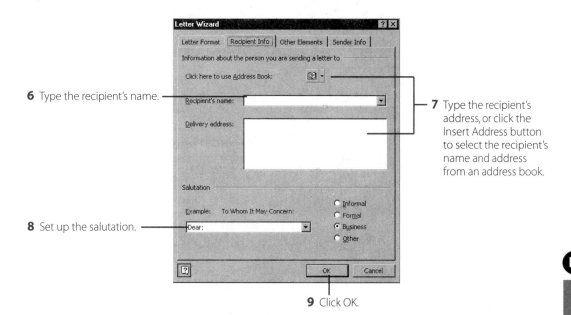

6 Type the recipient's name.

7 Type the recipient's address, or click the Insert Address button to select the recipient's name and address from an address book.

8 Set up the salutation.

9 Click OK.

10 Fill in the list for courtesy copies, if any, in the Other Elements tab. Press Enter at the end of each name of a recipient of a courtesy copy.

11 Fill in the closing information in the Sender Info tab. Then click OK to close the Letter Wizard dialog box.

12 Type your letter.

13 Add an envelope. For directions, see "Add To Document Button," page 199.

14 Print your envelope and letter.

15 Save your letter.

16 Mail your letter.

Correspondence

CHAPTER 4

Setting Up and Printing Envelopes and Labels

One of my big gripes about using a computer to print letters has been envelopes. In the past either I had to write in long hand on the envelope (now doesn't *that* look professional), or I had to hunt up a typewriter. But Word makes printing envelopes and mailing labels pretty easy. As long as your printer has a manual feed slot, Word can print your envelopes and labels for you. If your printer has a special envelope feeder or tray, you're a lucky duck because you don't have to stand in front of the printer and feed the envelopes one at a time.

Printing an Envelope

Word gives you two ways to print an envelope: you can print the envelope separately, or you can add the envelope to the top of your document and then print the envelope and the document at the same time. Word lets you choose the size of envelope you're printing on, whether you want postal bar codes (in the United States only), and which fonts you want for the delivery and return addresses. Depending on your requirements, you might need to select the correct envelope options before printing the envelope. (See "Envelope Options," page 200.)

Both methods of printing an envelope are the same until the last step, as follows:

1 If the delivery address is already in the letter, select the address. If not, start with step 2.

2 Choose the Tools Envelopes And Labels command, and then click the Envelopes tab.

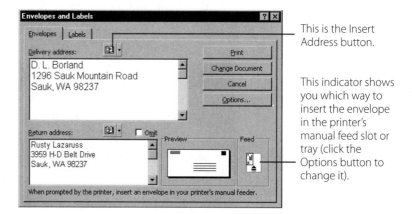

This is the Insert Address button.

This indicator shows you which way to insert the envelope in the printer's manual feed slot or tray (click the Options button to change it).

3 Type or change the delivery address. As an alternative, click the Insert Address button, and choose a name and address from one of your address books (see "Using Your Address Books," page 209).

4 If necessary, change the address in the Return Address box. As an alternative, click the Insert Address button, and choose a name and address from your address books.

5 Click the Print button to print the envelope immediately. As an alternative, click the Add To Document button to add the envelope to your letter.

If you changed the address in the Return Address box, Word asks if you want to make this your standard (default) return address. If you click Yes, Word puts the new return address on the User Info tab of the Options dialog box. If you click No, Word uses the new return address for this one printing only.

Return Address

Word uses the address it finds on the User Information tab of the Options dialog box for the return address. For information about this tab, see "User Information Tab," page 982. You can also click the Insert Address button and choose a name and address from your address books for the return address.

Envelope Orientation

See "Oh, No! My Envelope's Disoriented!" on page 201, for more information.

Add To Document Button

If you click the Add To Document button, your document will look something like the one shown in Page Layout view in Figure 4-1. To print the envelope in this case, print the letter. Word will print the envelope first and then print the letter on the correct paper size and in the correct direction.

FIGURE 4-1.
A letter with the envelope added, shown in Page Layout view at 50 percent zoom.

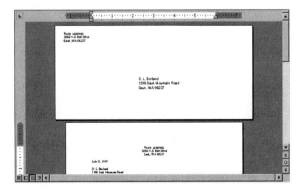

Envelope Options

In the United States, Word starts out with a standard size 10 (business) envelope. Also, Word doesn't print a postal bar code. Word uses the built-in Envelope Return and Envelope Address styles for the addresses on the envelope. These styles define the fonts used to print the return and delivery addresses. You can change any or all of these settings on the Envelope Options tab in the Envelope Options dialog box. To change the setup for an envelope, use the following steps:

1 On the Envelopes tab of the Envelopes And Labels dialog box, click the Options button.

2 Click the Envelope Options tab.

3 Select the size here.

4 Turn this on to add a postal bar code (U.S. only).

5 Click here to select the font.

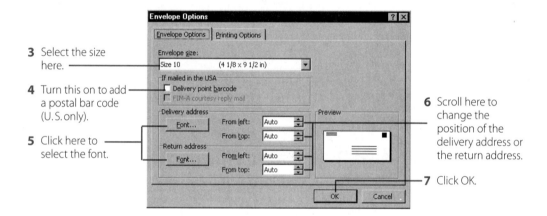

6 Scroll here to change the position of the delivery address or the return address.

7 Click OK.

Custom Size

If the Envelope Size list doesn't contain the size of the envelope you're using, select Custom Size in the Envelope Size list box. Word displays the Envelope Size dialog box you see here. Then use the following steps to set a custom size:

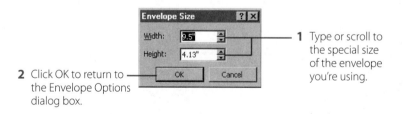

1 Type or scroll to the special size of the envelope you're using.

2 Click OK to return to the Envelope Options dialog box.

From Left and From Top Boxes

The positions in the From Left and From Top boxes start at Auto, which is the standard position set by the Envelope Address and Envelope Return styles. For the Envelope Address style, the bottom line of the delivery address is centered on the bottom margin, which is 0.5 inch; for Envelope Return, the first line of the return address is at the corner of the top margin (0.25 inch) and left margin (0.4 inch). When you use a position other than Auto, the distances you set for Top and Left are the distances from the top and left edges (not from the margins) of the envelope to the first line of the delivery or return address. The range of positions you can choose depends on the size of envelope you select. To see the various positions, scroll the measurement boxes, and watch the address position in the Preview box change as you scroll.

Oh, No! My Envelope's Disoriented!

Did you ever receive an envelope that was printed upside down? Pretty funny, wasn't it? But you probably don't think it's funny when you do it, do you? Me neither. Word does a pretty good job of showing you the right way to put an envelope into a printer, but there's always the chance that the method Word suggests won't work for your specific printer. If your envelope prints upside down or if only part of the address lands on the envelope, you can select a different way to feed the envelope so that Word gets it right. Also, if your envelope address prints on the wrong paper (for example, a sheet instead of an envelope), you can choose the right source for your printer by doing the following:

1 In the Envelopes And Labels dialog box, click the Options button on the Envelopes tab.

2 Select the Printing Options tab.

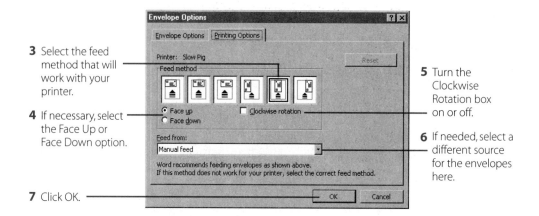

3 Select the feed method that will work with your printer.

4 If necessary, select the Face Up or Face Down option.

7 Click OK.

5 Turn the Clockwise Rotation box on or off.

6 If needed, select a different source for the envelopes here.

8 Test your choices. If the envelope still doesn't print correctly, make more changes until it does.

Clockwise Rotation

The three pictures on the right in the Feed Method section change when you turn on the Clockwise Rotation check box. These methods change the orientation of the envelope's delivery and return addresses as the envelope is fed into the printer. Not all printers support these rotated feed methods; however, you can use the Clockwise Rotation option if your particular printer happens to print the addresses in an orientation that matches one of these methods.

Licking Labels

If printing envelopes using a printer connected to a computer has been bad news for a long time, the news was even worse for large envelopes—the kind you usually paste a mailing label onto. But now, just as Word makes printing envelopes pretty easy, Word also makes printing mailing labels pretty easy, too. Word gives you two printing choices: you can print the labels immediately, or you can set up a label document and then print that. The label document makes it easy to print more of the labels if you need them again later.

Before you start printing labels, you need to select the right label options. (See "Label Options," next page.) Here are the steps to set up and print labels:

1 If the delivery address is already in a letter, select the address. If not, start with step 2. If you select the delivery address in a letter before choosing the command, the address appears in the Address box.

2 Choose the Tools Envelopes And Labels command, and select the Labels tab.

3 If necessary, type or change the address here.

Or, click the Insert Address button, and choose a name and address from one of your address books.

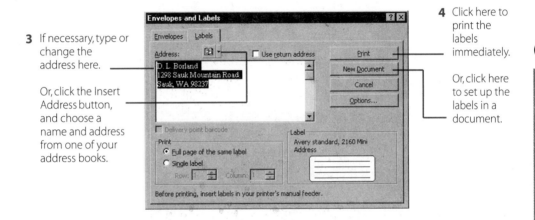

4 Click here to print the labels immediately.

Or, click here to set up the labels in a document.

New Document Button

When you click the New Document button, the new label document will look something like the one shown in Figure 4-2. To print the labels in this case, print the label document.

FIGURE 4-2.
A new document of labels, ready to print onto a label sheet.

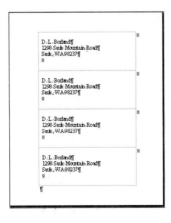

SEE ALSO

For information about printing labels for a mass mailing (mail merge), see "Creating Mass Mail Address Labels," page 206.

The steps in this section show you how to print multiple copies of the same label, but you can trick Word into printing different addresses on different labels on a sheet. For that, see the sidebar "Trickery: Printing a Single Label on a Sheet," opposite.

Label Options

In the United States, Word is initially set up to use Avery Standard labels. You might be using quite different label stock. The Options button on the Labels tab in the Envelopes And Labels dialog box gives you a long list of label choices. If none of these choices suits your fancy, you can set up custom labels—that is, set up Word to print on the labels you want to use, as described in the "Details Button" section below. To change the setup for labels, first open the Envelopes And Labels dialog box, click the Labels tab, click the Options button, and follow the steps you see here:

1 Select the type of printer here.

2 Select a label product line here.

3 Select the product number that matches the number on your package of labels here.

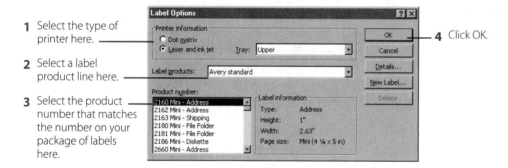

4 Click OK.

You're now ready to print labels as described in "Licking Labels," page 202.

Details Button

To check your product number selection or to set up Custom labels, click the Details button. You'll see a graphic description and measurements for the selected label, similar to the details for the Avery Standard label, shown on the next page. To set up Custom labels, select an Avery Standard label that is close to the size you need, and then follow the steps in the next graphic.

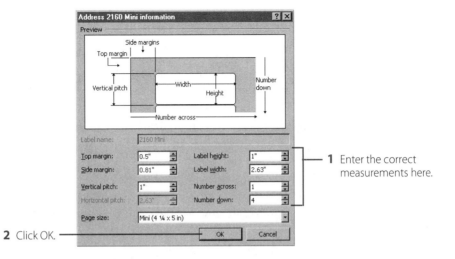

1 Enter the correct measurements here.

2 Click OK.

Trickery: Printing a Single Label on a Sheet

As you saw in Figure 4-2, page 203, Word usually prints an entire sheet of labels with the same address. This is handy for return address labels or if you send a lot of things to the same person or organization, but it's not handy if you need only one label with that address. In this case, you can use some of Word's trickery to print a single label on a sheet and then later print another single label, as you need it. To do this, follow these steps:

1 Set up the label as you want it to print.

2 Turn on the Single Label option on the Labels tab of the Envelopes And Labels dialog box.

3 Select the row number and column number of the label you want to print.

4 Click the Print button.

Note that you can't send the label to a new document, only directly to the printer.

Correspondence

Creating Mass Mail Address Labels

? SEE ALSO

If you are unfamiliar with mail merging in Word, see Chapter 5, "Mass Mail Letters."

Mail merging address labels makes it easy to create an up-to-date mailing list. You can maintain one master data document that contains many types of information. Then you can pull only the names and addresses for the labels you need for a mailing, rather than creating a special data document for address labels and a second, separate data document for another use.

To assist you in trying out the following steps, you can use the data document MAILLIST.DOC on the CD in this book. Here are the general steps you take to create and print mass mail address labels:

1 Get the data document.

2 Set up labels.

3 Add merge fields to the labels.

4 Merge the labels.

Getting the Data Document

The steps for getting the data document are as follows:

1 Choose the Tools Mail Merge command.

2 Click the Create button, and select Mailing Labels from the list.

3 In the message box, click either the Active Window button or the New Main Document button.

4 Click the Get Data button, and select Open Data Source from the list.

5 In the Open Data Source dialog box, select the name of the data document that contains the names and addresses you want to use, and then click Open. Word displays a message telling you that it needs to set up your main document.

6 Click the Set Up Main Document button. The Label Options dialog box appears. Use the steps in the next section to set up labels.

Setting Up Labels

Now you're ready to set up labels, using these steps:

1 If the Label Options dialog box is not open, click the Mail Merge Helper button, and click the Setup button. Word displays the Label Options dialog box, shown on page 204.

2 Set the appropriate choices in the Printer Information section.

3 In the Label Products box, select the product name for the labels you are using.

4 From the Product Number list, select the product number that matches the number on your package of labels. To check your product number selection, click the Details button to see the Information dialog box, which contains a graphic description and measurements for the selected label, as shown on page 205.

5 When the Label Options dialog box is properly set, click OK. Word displays the Create Labels dialog box, shown here:

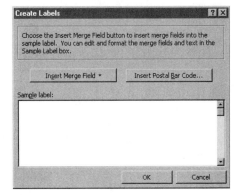

Adding Merge Fields to Labels

The steps for adding merge fields to labels are as follows:

1 Click the Insert Merge Field button to see a list of the merge fields available from the data document.

2 Insert the fields, setting them up as you want them to appear on the address labels—be sure to include spaces and punctuation.

II

Corespondence

Press Enter to start a new line. A sample of a label setup is shown here:

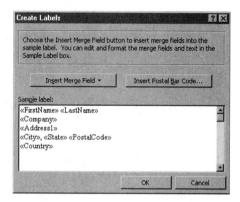

3 If you want Word to print the postal bar code on your labels, click the Insert Postal Bar Code button, which displays the dialog box shown here:

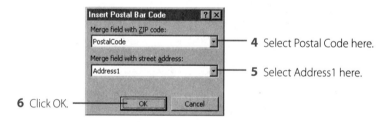

4 Select Postal Code here.

5 Select Address1 here.

6 Click OK.

7 When you have finished setting the Create Labels dialog box, click OK.

Repositioning the Postal Bar Code

When you insert a postal bar code, Word puts it above the address. To put the bar code beneath the address, insert the bar code first, put the insertion point at the left end of the bar code field, press Enter to start a new paragraph, move up to the empty paragraph, and insert the fields as described in step 2.

Merging the Labels

The final part of your mass mailing is to merge the labels. Here are the steps:

1 In the Mail Merge Helper dialog box, click the Merge button.

2 In the Merge dialog box, select New Document in the Merge To box.

3 Select the option that does not print blank lines when data fields are empty, and then click the Merge button. Word merges the data into a Labels document, which might take several minutes.

When Word finishes the merge, you see a Labels document, like the one in Figure 4-3, ready for you to print the mailing labels. You can also look at the main document, like the one in Figure 4-4.

FIGURE 4-3.
The result of the mail merge for labels is stored in a document.

FIGURE 4-4.
The main document for creating labels.

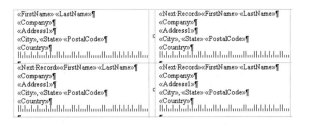

Using Your Address Books

You can easily add names and addresses to your documents by using your address books. Which address books you use depends on what e-mail systems you are connected to, how they are configured, and if you have Microsoft Schedule+ or Microsoft Outlook installed. To use any of the address books, you must have Microsoft Exchange installed on your computer. When you click the Insert Address button in the Envelopes and Labels dialog box or the Letter Wizard dialog box,

Microsoft Exchange will start if it is not already running. The following are the most common address books.

- Microsoft Exchange Address Book is part of your network e-mail system.

- Personal Address Book is an address book in Exchange and Outlook containing names and addresses that you have copied from messages sent to you or from other address books, or that you have typed in.

- Schedule+ Contact List is part of Schedule+ 7.0. You enter the names, addresses, and telephone numbers of people you contact regularly (or even irregularly). Outlook's contact list is more or less the same.

 NOTE

To add the Insert Address button to one of the toolbars, choose the Tools Customize command. Click the Commands tab and select Insert from the Categories list; select Address Book from the Commands List, and then drag Address Book onto the toolbar where you want it.

To use an address book for letters, envelopes, and address labels, follow these steps:

Insert
Address

1 Click the Insert Address button.

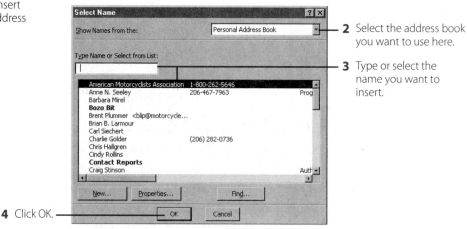

2 Select the address book you want to use here.

3 Type or select the name you want to insert.

4 Click OK.

You will see the name and address added to the document.

After you use the Insert Address button, Word adds the name to the list under the button, like this:

When you want to use an address you've used before, click the down arrow beside the Insert Address button and select the name.

Adding a Name and an Address

If your address books don't contain the name and address you want for the current letter, you can add them. You add a name to your Personal Address Book when the person has an e-mail address. You add a name to your Schedule+ or Outlook Contact List when the person doesn't have e-mail.

> When you create a new entry in your Personal Address Book or your Schedule+ or Outlook Contact List from Word, Word inserts the new name and address into your document when you finish setting up the new entry.

To add a name to your Personal Address Book, follow these steps:

1 Click the Insert Address button.

2 Select Personal Address Book in the Show Names From The box.

3 Click the New button, and the New Entry dialog box opens:

4 Select Other Address here.

5 Click OK.

7 Click the Business tab.

6 Fill in the Display name, E-mail address, and E-mail type boxes.

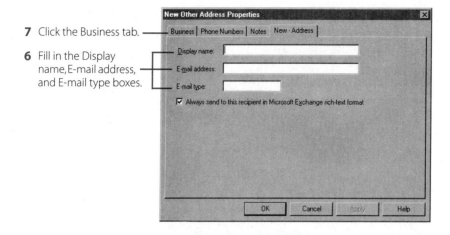

8 Cut the last name from the First Name box.

9 Paste the last name into the Last Name box.

10 Fill in the remaining boxes, as necessary.

11 Fill in other tabs as suits you.

12 Click OK.

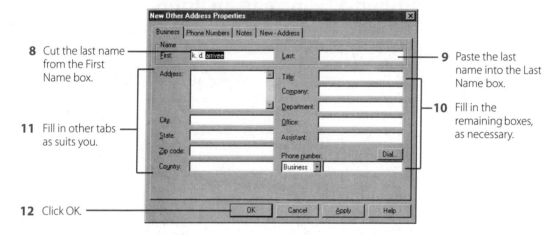

To add a name to your Schedule+ or Outlook Contact List, follow these steps:

1 Click the Insert Address button.

2 Select Contacts or Outlook Contact List in the Show Names From The box.

3 Click the New button to see the New Contact Properties dialog box.

4 Fill in the First and Last boxes in the Name section and the Address, City, State, and Zip Code boxes. You must fill in at least the First and Last boxes in the Name section.

5 Fill in other information on the Business and other tabs as suits you, and then click OK.

CHAPTER 5

Mass Mail Letters

To create and send a mass mailing, you use Word's mail merging feature. Mail merging is combining two documents to produce a series of different documents. One document, called the main document, contains subject matter that is the same for every document you create. If the final result is a form letter, for example, the main document contains the letterhead, message, and closing, which are the same in every form letter. The main document also contains fields for subject matter that is unique in each letter, such as name and address.

The second document, called the data document, contains a table of the subject matter that is different for every document you merge. Again, if the final result is a form letter, the data document contains the names and addresses for the letters and any other subject matter you want to send to each person.

Microsoft Word provides a Mail Merge Helper that guides you through the entire mail merge process. This chapter describes the steps that you follow to build a data document and a main document, to check the validity of the two documents, and then to merge them and print the combination.

Building a Main Document

To mail merge, you build a main document, either build or add on a data document, add the unique text to the main document, and then merge the two documents.

To build a main document, follow these steps:

1 Create or open a document. If the kind of document you want to use for the mail merge is already open, you can start with step 2.

> If you want to build a main document from a template other than Normal, start the document before you start mail merge.

You can create a new document from any template. If you're building form letters, you might want to create a new document using the Letter Wizard. If a document is already built and you want to use it for a mail merge, open it now.

> You must have a document open before you can start mail merge.

2 Choose the Tools Mail Merge command. The Mail Merge Helper dialog box appears, as shown here. The dialog box also illustrates the basic mail merge process.

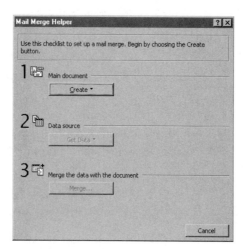

3 Click the Create button in the Mail Merge Helper dialog box. Word displays the list of choices shown here:

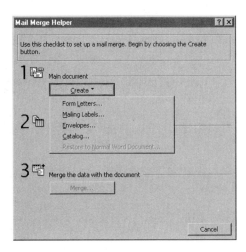

4 From the list, select the type of merge you want. To merge form letters, for example, select Form Letters. (For mailing labels, see "Creating Mass Mail Address Labels," page 206.) For all types, Word displays a message, shown here, asking whether you want to use the active document window or open a new one.

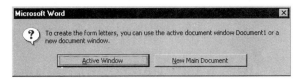

5 Click the Active Window or New Main Document button. Click New Main Document when the active document is not the one you want to use for mail merging. Click Active Window if you created the document from a special template.

The New Main Document button opens a document using the Normal template only. If you want to open a document using a different template, click Cancel in the message box, click Cancel in the Mail Merge Helper dialog box, open a new document using the template you want to use, and then perform step 2 again.

Correspondence

II

Word adds an Edit button beside the Create button in the Mail Merge Helper dialog box and activates the Get Data button, as shown here:

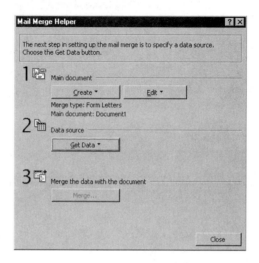

Word displays the document type and the name of the active main document below the Create button. If the type is wrong, click the Create button again, and then select the correct type of main document from the Edit button's list. In the next dialog box, click the Change Document Type button to confirm the change. If the document name that appears under the Edit button is wrong, you can create a new, blank document by clicking the Create button, selecting the same document type, and then clicking the New Main Document button in the message box. To use a different existing main document, you must close the Mail Merge Helper dialog box, open or activate the correct main document, and choose Tools Mail Merge again.

After you create the main document, you have a choice: you can add the common text to the main document first, or you can get the data. Let the purpose and the situation guide your choice.

- If your main document already exists, click the Get Data button so that you can select an existing data document or create a new one that fits the main document.

- If neither kind of document exists, the choice might be a toss-up. But you can use this guideline: if your main document is a form letter or a catalog, you might prefer to insert the common text in the main document and then get (attach or create) the data document. You'll need to leave blank paragraphs and empty spaces where you want the merge data to appear, and then later, after you get the data document, you'll insert the merge fields in the appropriate spots.

- If you prefer to create your main document in one fell swoop or if the main document consists of mailing labels or envelopes, you might as well get the data document. Because your main document consists entirely (or almost entirely) of merged data, you'll need the data document to set up your main document.

6 Click the Edit button. Word displays the document type and the name of the document in the list below the Edit button:

7 Click the document type and the name in the Edit button list. Word displays the main document and the Mail Merge toolbar, shown on the next page.

NOTE

If you decide at this point to get the data document instead, click the Mail Merge Helper button on the Mail Merge toolbar, and then click the Get Data button.

Mail Merge toolbar ———

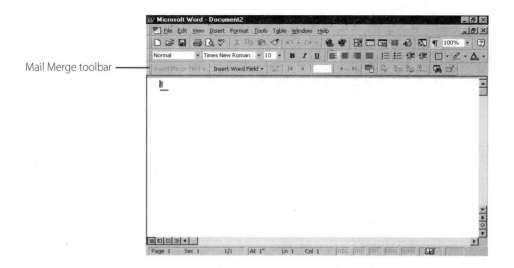

8 Add the common text to the main document.

Be sure to leave blank paragraphs and enough empty spaces to properly set off merge fields from common text where you want the unique text (the information that will be added during the mail merge) to appear. Figure 5-1 shows a sample main document with common text and blank paragraphs and spaces for merge fields.

FIGURE 5-1.
A main document containing common text with empty paragraphs and extra spaces for merge fields.

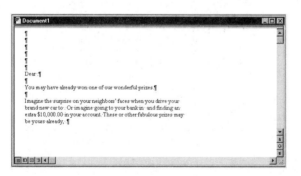

9 Check your spelling, and then save the document.

Building a Data Document

To build a data document, you get the data document in the Mail Merge Helper. Here's what you do:

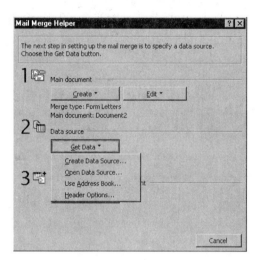

Mail Merge Helper

1 Click the Mail Merge Helper button on the Mail Merge toolbar.

2 When the Mail Merge Helper dialog box reappears, click the Get Data button to have Word display a list of choices, as shown here:

3 Select Create Data Source, and you will see the following dialog box:

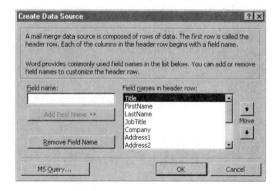

If you want to use an existing data document, select Open Data Source instead of Create Data Source. Select Header Options if your data document does not provide header information (the names of the data fields). For the form letter in Figure 5-1, on page 218, you need the fields FirstName, LastName, Address1, City, State, and PostalCode; you need to remove the fields you won't be using.

4 In the Create Data Source dialog box, select one of the field names you won't be using, such as Title, in the Field Names In Header Row list, and then click the Remove Field Name button. Word removes that name from the list and places it in the Field Name box in case you change your mind and want to return the name to the list. (You can think of this as an "Undo Remove" feature.)

To change the name of a field, move the field name to the Field Name box, where you can edit it. After you change the name, click the Add Field Name button to add the changed name to the list.

NOTE

> The names in the Field Names In Header Row list make up the header record, or header row, of your data document. They identify the columns of unique text you want to merge.

5 Repeat step 4 to remove any other unwanted field names from the list.

The Create Data Source dialog box should now look something like this:

> Spaces are not valid characters in field names. Notice that the field names listed in the Field Names In Header Row box of the Create Data Source dialog box do not contain spaces. For example, "CustomerNumber" or "Customer_Number" is a valid field name; "Customer Number" is not.

6 Click OK. The Save As dialog box appears:

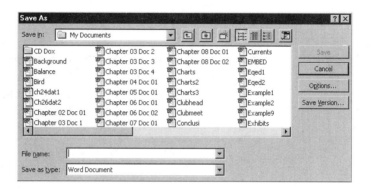

7 Type a name for your data document, and then click Save. Word displays a message that allows you to edit either the data document or the main document. If your data document already exists and needs no editing, click the Edit Main Document button to return to your document; if your data document needs editing, you should move on to step 8.

8 Click the Edit Data Source button. Word displays the Data Form dialog box, in which you'll enter the data for the various fields. The Data Form dialog box contains one data field for each field name you included in the header row in the Create Data Source dialog box, as you can see here:

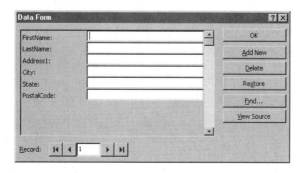

9 Fill out one data form for each data record. A data record is all the information you need for each form letter.

10 After you fill out a data form, click the Add New button. Word displays a blank form so that you can add another record.

11 Fill out a data form for each additional record.

12 After you fill out a data form for the last record, click the View Source button. You see your entire data document, like the document shown in Figure 5-2.

FIGURE 5-2.
A sample data document.

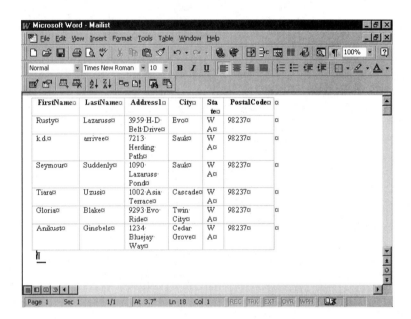

FirstName	LastName	Address1	City	State	PostalCode	
Rusty	Lazaruss	3959 H-D Belt Drive	Evo	WA	98237	
k.d.	arrivee	7213 Herding Path	Sauk	WA	98237	
Seymour	Suddenly	1090 Lazaruss Pond	Sauk	WA	98237	
Tiara	Uzusi	1002 Asia Terrace	Cascade	WA	98237	
Gloria	Blake	9293 Evo Ride	Twin City	WA	98237	
Anikust	Ginsbels	1234 Bluejay Way	Cedar Grove	WA	98237	

TIP

If you have Word set to check spelling automatically, Word marks the field names and people's names as misspelled. To hide the red sawtooth underlines, choose the Tools Options command, click the Spelling & Grammar tab, turn on the Hide Spelling Errors In This Document check box, and then click OK.

Getting Your Document Back

At any time, you can select the Restore To Normal Word Document option from the Create button list in the Mail Merge Helper dialog box. When you do, Word displays a message warning you that your choice means the document is no longer a mail merge main document and asking whether you want to continue:

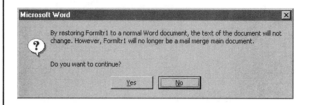

If you want to back out of mail merging, or if you want to select a different type of merge document, click Yes to make your document "normal" again. Click No if you still want to use the document for mail merge.

Viewing the Data Document

SEE ALSO

You'll find the sample data document MAILLIST.DOC on the CD included with this book.

As you can see in Figure 5-2, Word sets up your data in a table. To set column widths, Word uses the width of the field names in the header record. If some of the text is cramped in the column (as it is in the Address1 and City columns in Figure 5-2), you can select the table, choose the Table Cell Height And Width command, select the Column tab, and click the AutoFit button. Your data document will now look like the table shown in Figure 5-3.

FIGURE 5-3.
The data document table adjusted with the AutoFit button.

FirstName¤	LastName¤	Address1¤	City¤	State¤	PostalCode¤	¤
Rusty¤	Lazaruss¤	3959·H-D·Belt·Drive¤	Evo¤	WA¤	98237¤	¤
k.·d.¤	arrivee¤	7213·Herding·Path¤	Sauk¤	WA¤	98237¤	¤
Zoe¤	Society¤	1894·Sauk·Parkway¤	Sauk¤	WA¤	98237¤	¤
Seymour¤	Suddenly¤	1090·Lazaruss·Pond¤	Sauk¤	WA¤	98237¤	¤
Tiara¤	Uzusi¤	1002·Asia·Terrace¤	Cascade¤	WA¤	98237¤	¤
Gloria¤	Blake¤	9293·Evo·Ride¤	Twin·City¤	WA¤	98237¤	¤
Anikust¤	Ginsbels¤	1234·Bluejay·Way¤	Cedar·Grove¤	WA¤	98237¤	¤

When you view the data document, Word displays the Database toolbar, which contains buttons that help you work on the data document table. Using these buttons, you can rename fields, add or delete fields or records, sort records, update fields, or switch to the main document. The Database toolbar buttons are identified in Figure 5-4.

FIGURE 5-4.
The Database toolbar.

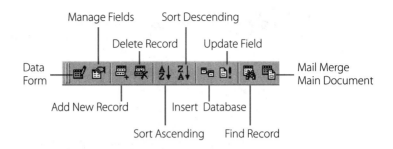

You can use the AutoFit button on the Columns tab in the Cell Height And Width dialog box to see the entire table within the window. To have fewer wrapped lines in the cells, you can also choose File Page Setup, select the Paper Size tab, set the Apply To box to Whole Document, and select the Landscape option.

Adding Data Fields

After you set up a data document, you might need to add more columns (fields) for new types of information. For example, you might want to add columns for a person's job title, company name, and P.O. box. To add data fields, perform these steps:

1 Click the Edit button in the Data Source section of the Mail Merge Helper dialog box, and click the name of your data document in the list below the Edit button.

2 In the Data Form dialog box that appears, click the View Source button to view your data document.

Activating a Mail Merge Document

You can always activate any open mail merge document (data document or main document) by choosing its name from the Window menu. As a shortcut, click the Edit Data Source button on the Mail Merge toolbar, which you can display by clicking the Mail Merge Main Document button on the Database toolbar.

Manage
Fields

3 Click the Manage Fields button on the Database toolbar to display the Manage Fields dialog box.

4 In the Field Name box, type the name of the field you want to add, and then click the Add button.

5 Repeat step 4 for other fields you want to add, and then click OK.

Adding Data to New Fields

To add data to the new fields, do the following steps:

Data
Form

1 Click the Data Form button on the Database toolbar to display the Data Form dialog box again.

2 Starting with Record 1, add data for the new fields. Click the Next Record button (the button to the right of the record number at the bottom of the dialog box) to move to the next record, and complete each new record until you've added data to all the records.

3 After you fill in data forms for all applicable records, click OK.

 TIP

You can use these steps to edit records. After you edit a data record, you can click the Restore button to undo your editing changes. See the sidebar "Tools for Working with Data Records," page 227, for help with finding specific records.

Adding Merge Fields

Now let's move on to work on your main document. The process of adding merge fields to the main document is the same whether you have followed the steps in this chapter to this point or are adding merge fields as you create your main document.

II

Correspondence

Mail Merge
Main Document

1 Click the Mail Merge Main Document button on the Database toolbar. Word displays the Mail Merge toolbar, shown in Figure 5-5.

FIGURE 5-5.
The Mail Merge toolbar.

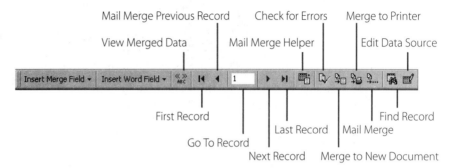

2 Position the insertion point in the first blank paragraph, and use the Insert Date And Time command to insert the date as a field.

3 Position the insertion point in the third blank paragraph in your main document (where the letter recipient's name and address will go), and click the Insert Merge Field button on the Mail Merge toolbar to display a list of the merge fields available from the data source.

4 Click FirstName to insert this field in the main document at the insertion point.

5 Type a space, and then click LastName on the Insert Merge Field list to insert this field.

6 In the second paragraph, insert the Address1 merge field.

7 In the third paragraph, insert the City, State, and PostalCode fields, with appropriate spacing and punctuation.

8 Insert the appropriate merge fields in the rest of the document, as shown in Figure 5-6.

FIGURE 5-6.
The main document with merge fields added.

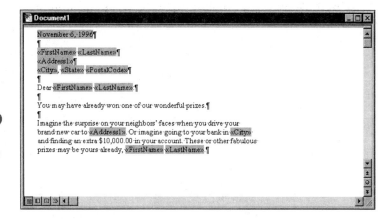

 SEE ALSO

To see a sample main document with merge fields added, open CONTEST.DOC on the CD in this book.

 TIP

The fields in Figure 5-6 appear shaded in gray. To get this result, choose Tools Options, click the View tab, set Field Shading to Always, and then click OK.

Tools for Working with Data Records

If you need to return to a record to check it or edit it while you are working in the Data Form dialog box, click the Previous Record button or type the record number in the Record Number box at the bottom of the dialog box and press Enter. If your data document is long, you can find a record by clicking the Find button to display the Find In Field dialog box, shown here:

1 Type the data you want to find.

2 Select a field name.

3 Click Find First.

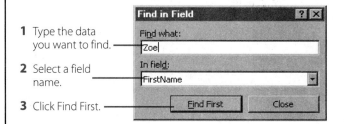

If more than one record contains the same information for the selected field, the Find First button changes to Find Next; click it to jump to the next record that contains the information. When you have found the record you want, click Close.

II

Correspondence

Testing the Merge Operation

Now that you have created both the main document and the data document, you are ready to test how well the two documents merge.

To test the merge operation, follow these steps:

Check For
Errors

1 Activate the main document, and click the Check For Errors button on the Mail Merge toolbar. Word displays the Checking And Reporting Errors dialog box:

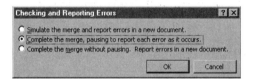

This dialog box gives you three options for checking and reporting errors. To simply test the merge (without merging), select the first option, which simulates the merge and reports errors in a new document. To test and perform the merge, select either the second option, which completes the merge and reports each error as it occurs, or the third option, which completes the merge without pausing and reports errors in a new document.

 NOTE

Data missing from a merge field in the main document is not a mail merge error. If data is missing, Word simply leaves a blank space in the merged document.

2 Select the first option, and then click OK. If Word finds no mail merge errors, a message appears, indicating that no errors have been found. If, on the other hand, Word does find an error, a dialog box reports the nature of the error and provides you with some options for correcting it, for example:

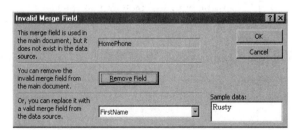

3 When an error occurs, take one of the following three actions:

- Click the Remove Field button to remove the invalid field from the main document.

- Replace the invalid field in the main document with a valid field from the data document. To do so, select a valid field name in the box at the bottom left of the dialog box, and then click OK. The Sample Data box shows data for the field from the first record that contains data for the field.

- Click the Cancel button. Word reports the error in the main document but leaves the invalid field in place.

After you take an action, Word continues to check the merge, pausing at each error to allow you to take the appropriate action. After checking the entire merge, Word displays a Mail Merge Errors document that lists the errors.

If you clicked the Cancel button for any error, use the Mail Merge Errors document to help you find and edit the data document or the main document to solve the problem.

TIP

Viewing the Data in the Main Document

You can view the data instead of the merge fields in the main document by clicking the View Merged Data button on the Mail Merge toolbar. Then when you click the Next Record, Previous Record, or Go To Record button to move to another record, the results of the fields in the document change to display the data from the appropriate record. You cannot edit these results, however. To edit the results of the fields, you must make the changes in the data document. Clicking the View Merged Data button again displays the merge fields instead of the field results.

Correspondence

Printing Form Letters

When your main and data documents contain no errors, you are ready to merge the documents. You can either merge to a new file or send merged documents to a printer.

Merging to a New Document

Merge To New Document

To merge to a new file and see on the screen the effect of merging, click the Merge To New Document button on the Mail Merge toolbar. Word merges the documents to a file called Form Letters1. Word separates merged documents in the file with a Next Page Section break, as shown in Figure 5-7.

The advantage of merging documents to a file is that you can preview the resulting document before you send it to a printer. You can then change the document before printing, without having to merge the documents again. Also, you can transport the file to another computer to print it, if necessary.

FIGURE 5-7.

Word displays the merged documents as Form Letters1.

```
November·6,·1996¶
¶
Rusty·Lazaruss¶
3959·H-D·Belt·Drive¶
Evo,·WA·98237¶
¶
Dear·Rusty·Lazaruss:¶
¶
You·may·have·already·won·one·of·our·wonderful·prizes.¶
¶
Imagine·the·surprise·on·your·neighbors'·faces·when·you·drive·your·brand-new·car·to·
3959·H-D·Belt·Drive.·Or·imagine·going·to·your·bank·in·Evo·and·finding·an·extra·
$10,000.00·in·your·account.·These·or·other·fabulous·prizes·may·be·yours·already,·Rusty·
Lazaruss.¶
·····················································Section Break (Next Page)·····················
November·6,·1996¶
¶
k.d.·arrivee¶
7213·Herding·Path¶
Sauk,·WA·98237¶
¶
Dear·k.d.·arrivee:¶
¶
You·may·have·already·won·one·of·our·wonderful·prizes.¶
¶
Imagine·the·surprise·on·your·neighbors'·faces·when·you·drive·your·brand-new·car·to·
7213·Herding·Path.·Or·imagine·going·to·your·bank·in·Sauk·and·finding·an·extra·
$10,000.00·in·your·account.·These·or·other·fabulous·prizes·may·be·yours·already,·k.d.·
arrivee.¶
·····················································Section Break (Next Page)·····················
November·6,·1996¶
```

Merging to the Printer

Merge To
Printer

To print the merged documents directly, click the Merge To Printer button on the Mail Merge toolbar. Word merges and prints a document for every data record in the data file without displaying a dialog box.

Printing Another Way

You can also use the Mail Merge Helper button to merge and print, as follows:

1 Click the Mail Merge Helper button on the Mail Merge toolbar. You'll see the Mail Merge Helper dialog box.

2 Click the Merge button. Word displays the Merge dialog box, shown in Figure 5-8. "Setting Mail Merge Options," next page, explains the various options available in the Merge dialog box.

FIGURE 5-8.
The Merge dialog box.

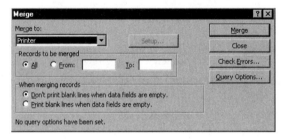

3 Select Printer in the Merge To box, and click the Merge button. The Print dialog box appears.

4 Click OK.

> You don't need to open the data document before carrying out a mail merge. Word automatically (but invisibly) "opens" the data document for merging and then "closes" it again (invisibly) when the mail merge is finished.

Merging to a Fax or an Electronic Mail System

If your computer is attached to an electronic mail system, you can send a mail merge over that system. Your data document should have a data field that contains the fax or electronic mail address for each document.

When the main document and data document are ready for merging, use the following steps to merge to a fax or electronic mail system.

1 Click the Mail Merge Helper button to display the Mail Merge Helper dialog box.

2 Click the Merge button.

3 Select Electronic Fax or Electronic Mail in the Merge To box. The name of the system appears only if it is available on your computer.

4 Click the Setup button.

5 Select the merge field name that contains the electronic fax or mail address in the Data Field With Mail/Fax Address box.

6 If you want, type a subject line for electronic mail in the Mail Message Subject Line box.

7 Turn on or off the Send Document As An Attachment check box. Turn on this check box to preserve the looks of the merged document. Remember that your recipients must be able to open a Word document attached to an e-mail or a fax message for them to be able to view your letter. Turn off this box to send the document as plain text.

8 Click OK to close the Setup dialog box.

9 Click the Merge button in the Merge dialog box. Word sends out the merged documents electronically.

Setting Mail Merge Options

The Merge dialog box, shown in Figure 5-8, on the previous page, contains some of the most important and most frequently used mail merge options.

Two choices in the Merge To box correspond to two buttons on the Mail Merge toolbar: New Document and Printer. The Merge To box might also list choices for electronic mail and fax, depending on your system's configuration.

In the Records To Be Merged option box, you can choose to print a merged document for every data record or for a specific range of data records. The numbers you type in the From and To boxes refer only to data records; the header record is not counted in the numbering.

The When Merging Records options deal with the pesky problem of the blank lines that often appear in merged documents. For example, if some addresses in a data document contain four lines and some contain three lines, you might end up with a blank line in a merged document. Suppose, for example, that you have the following inside-address setup for a main document:

```
<FirstName> <LastName>
<Title>
<Company>
<POB>
<Street>
<City> <State> <PostalCode>
```

Some people listed in the data document won't have a post office box. Some people might not be associated with a company, and others might not have a title. In these cases, the blank cells in the data document would leave blanks in a merged document.

You can, however, tell Word how to deal with the blank lines. Select the second When Merging Records option to print the blank lines wherever blank fields appear; select the first option to omit the blank lines for blank fields. The following examples show how addresses handled with these various options will appear.

Full Address	Partial Address, Blank Lines Omitted	Partial Address, Blank Lines Printed
Yllek Kcek¶	McKenzie Heimweh¶	McKenzie Heimweh¶
Manager¶	8212 Telegraph Hill¶	¶
Tours & Beyond¶	Cape Watch, NC 43000¶	¶
P.O. Box 1234¶		¶
2121 Camino Real¶		8212 Telegraph Hill¶
Weed, OR 97000¶		Cape Watch, NC 43000¶

The Check Errors button performs the same actions as the Check For Errors button on the Mail Merge toolbar (see Figure 5-5, page 226). For details about using the Query Options button, see "Querying the Options," on the next page.

Creating Target Mailings

On occasion, you might want Word to select or exclude data records when you merge. In such cases, you can ask Word to mail merge to a target group—for example, to all customers with a specific postal code. You can also ask Word to exclude a group from a merge. For example, you could exclude from a mailing all customers who didn't buy anything from your last catalog. On other occasions, you might want to know which data record number was used in a specific merged document. The following sections include examples of these mail merge options.

Querying the Options

The Filter Records tab in the Query Options dialog box provides very powerful record selection. You reach the Query Options dialog box, shown in Figure 5-9, by clicking on the Query Options button in the Mail Merge Helper dialog box. To use the Query Options dialog box to its full potential, you must understand how its elements work. The Field box and the Compare To box are easy to understand, but the Comparison box and the And/Or boxes (the unmarked boxes lining the left side of the dialog box) require some explanation.

FIGURE 5-9.

The Query Options dialog box with the first And/Or box's drop-down list displayed.

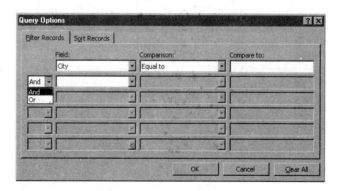

The Comparison box lists all the available ways to compare the data item for a field name to a value that you type in the Compare To box. Table 5-1 lists the choices in the Comparison box and gives examples of their use.

Along the left side of the Query Options dialog box is a column of boxes. Each box can contain And or Or. For each selection rule you add, a new And/Or box becomes active, until you have set up a maximum of six selection rules. As you add selection rules, the And/Or box for the next row becomes active. Until a row displays a rule, the box beside the next row is inactive.

For record selection, the And option narrows the selection, and the Or option broadens the selection. Each And rule adds another requirement to the record selection rules. Each Or rule sets up an additional option. Suppose that your record selection rules are the following:

"*City* is equal to *New York*" And "*PostalCode* is not equal to *10001*"

TABLE 5-1. **Comparison Box Choices in the Query Options Dialog Box.**

Comparison Item	Example Rule	Explanation
Equal To	*City* is equal to *New York*	Merges documents only for addresses in New York City
Not Equal To	*State* is not equal to West Virginia	Merges documents for all states except West Virginia
Less Than	*PostalCode* is less than 20000	Merges documents for all postal codes from 00000 through 19999
Greater Than	*Amount* is greater than $100.00	Merges documents only for data records with values larger than $100.00 in the Amount field
Less Than Or Equal	*PostalCode* is less than or equal to 20000	Merges documents for all postal codes from 00000 through 20000
Greater Than Or Equal	*Service* is greater than or equal to 5	Merges documents for all employees who have worked five years or longer
Is Blank	*New_Customer* is blank	Merges documents only for data records that have a blank (no value) in their New_Customer field
Is Not Blank	*Number_of_Purchases* is not blank	Merges documents only for those data records that have some value in their Number_of_Purchases field

According to these rules, each data record Word selects must contain New York in its City field and must also contain a postal code that is not 10001. Used alone, the rule for the PostalCode field would merge records with any postal code other than 10001. The rule for the City field, however, further restricts postal codes to those in New York (10001 through 10999). Together, these selection rules restrict the records to those that have a postal code of 10002 through 10999. For this case, the settings in the Query Options dialog box look like this:

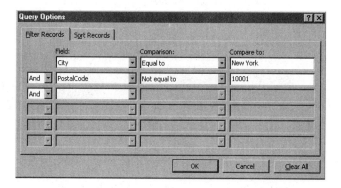

Let's look at another example. If your selection rules are

"*City* is equal to *New York*" Or "*City* is equal to *Los Angeles*"

each data record Word selects must contain either New York or Los Angeles in its City field, as shown here:

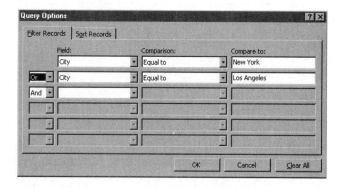

In brief, selecting the Or option means that a data record needs to contain only one of the values listed in the two rules (either this or that, or both). Selecting the And option means that a data record must contain both values listed in the two rules (both this and that).

To add a selection rule, follow these steps:

1 On the first empty line, select a field.

2 Select a choice in the Comparison box.

3 Type a value in the Compare To box.

4 Select the And or Or option.

To change a single selection rule, use these steps:

1 Select a new field.

2 Select a new choice in the Comparison box.

3 Type a new value in the Compare To box.

4 Select the And or Or option.

To remove all selection rules, click the Clear All button. You'll want to clear all rules when your mail merge no longer requires any selection rules or when you want to radically change the selection rules.

Keeping Track of Records

Word keeps track of data records by invisibly assigning each one a record number. The first data record following the header record is record 1. Other records are numbered consecutively to the end of the data document, although you see no visible evidence of the numbers in the documents.

 TIP

> You can see the record number in the Data Form dialog box and on the Mail Merge toolbar when you are viewing the main document. To see the data for a record in the main document, click the View Merged Data button on the Mail Merge toolbar.

At times, you might want to know which data record Word used for a particular merged document. For example, if the document printed incorrectly or if you want to change some information in a record, having the record number helps you identify the erroneous record so that you can change it. Or if you're printing part of a data document (only a range of record numbers), you might want to know where you started and finished printing.

Correspondence

By inserting a MERGEREC field in your main document, you tell Word to print the record number on each merged document. For instance, you might put a MERGEREC field in a header or footer, where it would not distract the reader but would allow easy identification.

To insert a MERGEREC field in a main document footer, do the following steps:

1 Activate the main document.

2 Choose the View Header And Footer command.

Switch Between
Header and Footer

3 Click the Switch Between Header And Footer button on the Header And Footer toolbar to move to the footer area.

4 Click the Insert Word Field button on the Mail Merge toolbar, and select Merge Record # from the list.

5 Click the Close button on the Header And Footer toolbar.

View Merged Data

The result of a MERGEREC field is the data record number from the data document. You won't see a result until after you merge the document or click the View Merged Data button on the Mail Merge toolbar. Figure 5-10 shows the MERGEREC field in a footer as well as the record numbers in the footers of two resulting documents.

FIGURE 5-10.
A MERGEREC field in a footer and record numbers in two resulting documents.

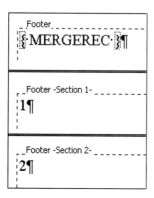

 NOTE

The MERGEREC field appears in the main document as Merge Record # and not as MERGEREC. To see the inserted field as MERGEREC, move the insertion point into the field and press the Toggle Field key (Shift+F9).

> ### Getting Consecutive Record Numbers for a Selective Mail Merge
>
> When you use selection rules to include only certain records, the results of MERGEREC fields might not be consecutive. You might, however, want to consecutively number the merged documents regardless of the record numbers used in the merge. For example, you could use the numbering to monitor the progress of the printing or to see how many merged documents you printed.
>
> To number merged documents consecutively, you can insert a MERGESEQ field:
>
> **1** In your main document (or in its header or footer), click the Insert Word Field button on the Mail Merge toolbar.
>
> **2** Select Merge Sequence # from the list.
>
> The result of a MERGESEQ field is the number of the current merged document. The first merged document is 1, the second is 2, and so on. The Merge Sequence # field is totally independent of the Merge Record # field. Thus, if your first merged document uses data record number 39, the merged document is still merge sequence number 1.
>
> The MERGESEQ field can be used in the footer of a document to produce a unique reference number for the specific document. For example, you could insert PRINTDATE and MERGESEQ fields to form a reference number that combines the date you print the merged document and the number of the merged document.

II

Correspondence

Altering Contents While Merging

> **? SEE ALSO**
>
> Look for the file HOWPRIZE.DOC on the CD in this book for an example that uses these two fields for a prize contest.

You can use the fields described here in any document, whether or not a mail merge is involved. But keep in mind that these fields are especially useful in helping you to create snazzy merged documents.

The INCLUDETEXT field inserts one document in another document. In a mail merge, you can set up a main document to insert a whole document or part of a document in each printed copy. You can also set up the main document to insert a whole document or only part of a document, depending on where or to whom the form letter is being sent.

You can use the IF field to compare a data item with a guideline and then let merge actions depend on the outcome of that comparison. A comparison might verify whether a data item matches a guideline or whether it is larger or smaller than a guideline. For example, you might want to know whether a house number ends in an odd or an even number. When you get the answer, you can tell Word to create the document according to specific guidelines—for instance, inserting one list of prizes if the house number is odd, and inserting another list of prizes if the house number is not odd (that is, even).

Using Microsoft Excel in a Mail Merge

You can also use a Microsoft Excel worksheet file as a data document for a Word main document. A Microsoft Excel worksheet file works the same way as a Word data document set up as a table. You must be sure the first row of the worksheet contains column labels that match the appropriate fields. Alternatively, you can create a separate header file for the column labels and attach the header file to the main document.

> **NOTE**
>
> After you open a Microsoft Excel worksheet as a data document, you can edit it—that is, you can add the header record to the worksheet instead of creating a separate header file. If you use a database file as your data document, you will most likely need to create a separate header file. The steps for creating a header file for any data document—created in Word, Microsoft Excel, Lotus 1-2-3, Microsoft Access, SQL, dBASE, and so on—are exactly the same.

To set up a separate header file for a data document after you have already set up your main document, use these steps:

1 Choose the Tools Mail Merge command to display the Mail Merge Helper dialog box.

2 Click the Get Data button, and select Open Data Source. In the Open Data Source dialog box, select the name of the data document you want to use, and then click Open.

3 In the Mail Merge Helper dialog box click the Get Data button again, and this time select Header Options. The Header Options dialog box appears, as shown on the next page.

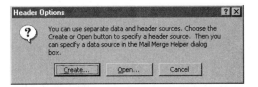

4 If you already have an appropriate header file set up, click the Open button. In this example, click the Create button to have Word display the Create Header Source dialog box.

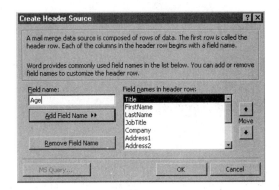

This dialog box is the same as the Create Data Source dialog box you saw on page 219; the only difference is the title in the title bar. Add and remove field names as you did in the Create Data Source dialog box. Be sure to move the field names in the list so that their order exactly matches the order of columns in your data document. When you have finished adding, removing, and reordering field names, click Save.

5 Word displays the Save As dialog box. Type a name for the header file, and then click Save.

6 Word returns you to the Mail Merge Helper dialog box. The header document name now appears in the dialog box, below the name of the data document, as shown on the next page.

7 Now proceed to edit the main document and the data document if necessary. Be sure to check the validity of the main, header, and data documents by using the Check For Errors button on the

Correspondence

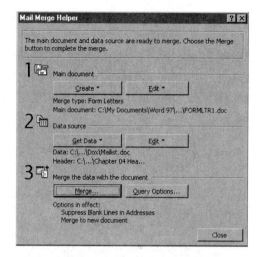

SEE ALSO

For information about using Excel worksheets within Word, see "Exchanging Information with Excel," page 364.

Mail Merge toolbar or the Check Errors button in the Merge dialog box.

CHAPTER 6

Investigating the Fax

Word provides a bevy of tools and options for using your computer to create and send fax documents. You set up a fax document in Word, and then either send the fax through your computer's modem or print the fax and send it through a standard fax machine.

Word supplies three fax templates and a Fax Wizard for creating a fax on the spot. You can also use the Fax Wizard to set up a "one off" fax—a fax that you send only one time. While the basic elements of the fax templates in Word might serve your purposes in the main, you will want to tweak them to better fit your style or your organization.

The next several sections walk you through a variety of ways to add material to faxes and to remodel the fax templates. Before you get into remodeling and using the fax templates, however, you need to take some important preliminary steps: you need to create a template that you can remodel.

To create a fax template you can remodel, you have two choices:

■ Create a fax template with the Fax Wizard, and then save it.

■ Create a new fax template from one of the fax templates supplied by Microsoft.

For the first method, follow the directions in "Summoning the Wizard," next page. For the second method, follow the directions below.

1 Choose the File New command.

2 Click the Letters & Faxes tab.

3 Click the icon for the fax template you want to use. See Figures 6-1, 6-2, and 6-3 for some examples.

4 Click Template.

5 Click OK.

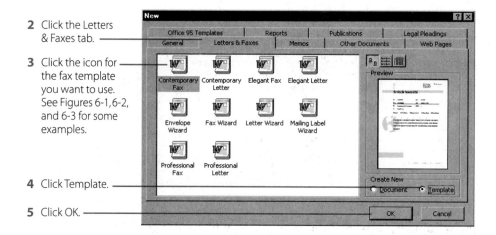

6 Follow the directions starting with "Adding More Common Text," page 252, and the sections that follow to the end of this chapter.

FIGURE 6-1.
Preview of the Contemporary Fax cover page.

FIGURE 6-2.
Preview of the Elegant
Fax cover page.

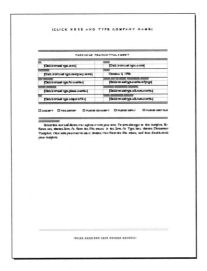

FIGURE 6-3.
Preview of the Profes-
sional Fax cover page.

Summoning the Wizard

You can summon the Fax Wizard to create a fax template or simply to create and send a fax. To summon the Fax Wizard, first choose the File New command, and then take the steps shown in the figure on the next page.

II

Correspondence

1 Click the Letters & Faxes tab.

2 Click the Fax Wizard icon.

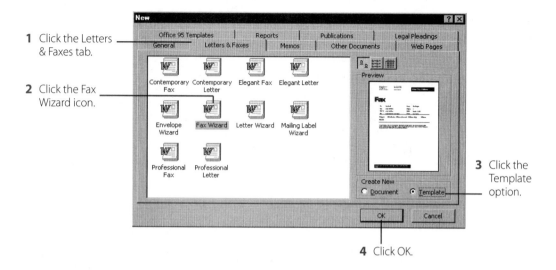

3 Click the Template option.

4 Click OK.

Click the Document option if you simply want to create a fax rather than a template.

The Start panel of the Fax Wizard will open:

Notice the outline along the left side of the Start panel. This outline lists the steps you take with the Fax Wizard to create a fax or fax template. These steps match the next five sections.

> If you want to jump to any particular panel of the Fax Wizard, click that panel's name in the outline. You can jump forward or backward to any panel.

Click the Next button of the Fax Wizard to move on to the Document To Fax panel.

Setting the Fax Foundation

On the Document To Fax panel, you select the page structure of your fax.

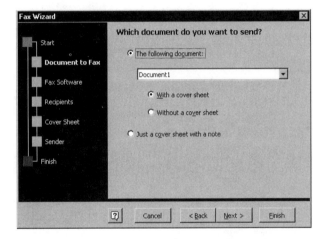

You can either set up the current document as a fax, with or without a cover sheet, or set up only a fax cover sheet on which you can add your message.

> If you want to use a special document template to create a fax or if you want to send a non-fax document by fax, start with that document open, and then use the steps in the preceding section to start the Fax Wizard. If you start the Fax Wizard before you open or set up a special document you want to fax, click Cancel to stop the Fax Wizard.

- To send a document with a separate cover sheet, click The Following Document and With A Cover Sheet options.

- To send a document without a cover sheet, click The Following Document and Without A Cover Sheet options.

- To send a fax that is a cover sheet on which you can type a message (which can extend to several pages if you want), click Just A Cover Sheet With A Note.

After you select the fax structure on the Document To Fax panel, click Next.

Choosing the Medium for the Message

On the Fax Software panel, you select the method you want to use to send your fax.

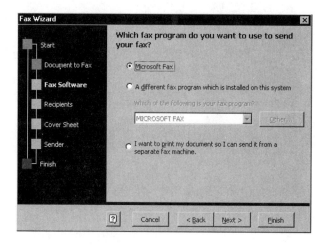

- To send a fax with Microsoft Fax (which is linked with Microsoft Outlook or Exchange), click Microsoft Fax.

- If you have other fax software installed (perhaps software supplied with your fax modem), click A Different Fax Program Which Is Installed On This System, and then select the program from the list. If you have another fax program installed and it's not listed, click Other, select the system from the Print Setup dialog box, and then click Set As Default Printer.

■ If you don't have a fax modem installed on your computer, click I Want To Print My Document So I Can Send It From A Separate Fax Machine. You can select this option even if you have a fax modem but would rather use a separate fax machine.

After you select the medium for sending your fax on the Fax Software panel, click Next.

Who Gets This Fax?

On the Recipients panel, you set up the names of the people who will receive the fax.

If you're setting up a template, you won't want to add recipient information, because this will change each time you use it. You can simply click Next to move to the Sender panel of the Fax Wizard.

If, however, you're simply creating a fax to send without creating a template, add the recipients' names and fax numbers on the Recipients panel. To help you add the names and numbers, you can click the Address Book button, which displays the Select Name dialog box in Microsoft Outlook or Exchange. You can select an address book from the Show Names From The list box, and then select the recipients, as shown here:

1 Select the address book you want to use.

2 Select the name(s) of the recipients.

3 Click OK.

The Fax Wizard puts the names and fax numbers into the boxes on the Recipients panel. When you're done with the Recipients panel, click Next.

Fax Wizard Keeps a History List of Your Recipients

After you add a name and fax number to the Recipients panel, the Fax Wizard keeps a record of the names and numbers you've used. The next time you use the Fax Wizard to create and send a fax, the names appear in the list under each Name box, and the numbers appear in the list under each Fax Number box. To select a name or number you've used previously, click the down arrow at the right end of the box, and select the name or number from the list that drops down.

Covering the Fax Style

On the Cover Sheet panel, select the style of fax you want to use.

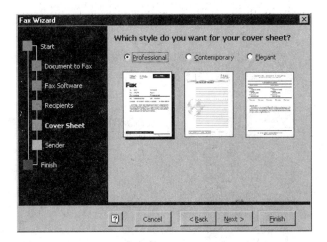

After you select the cover sheet style you want to use, click Next.

Who Are You?

Whether you're creating a fax template or simply creating a fax to send, fill out the Sender panel with all the information you want to appear on the fax.

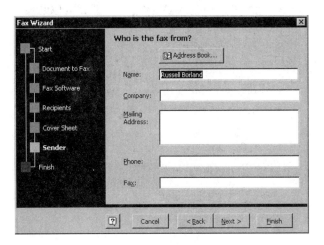

If your own sender information appears in an address book or if you're sending a fax for someone else whose name appears in an address book, you can click the Address Book button to select sender information. When you're done with the Sender panel, click Next. The Finish panel opens:

Click Finish, and you are now ready to remodel your fax template or to go forward to "Sending a Fax," page 257.

Adding More Common Text

Do you have a message you want to print on every cover page of every fax you send? If so, type it either as part of the Comments or Notes section on the cover page or as a separate paragraph above the Comments or Notes section.

To add common text to the Comments or Notes section, follow these steps:

1 Click the text *Click here and type any comments*.

2 Type the common text.

To add common text as a separate paragraph above the Comments section, take these steps:

1 Click at the beginning of the Comments or Notes line.

2 Press Enter to insert a paragraph above the Comments or Notes line.

3 Press the Up arrow key, and then type the common text.

Flexing the Fonts

The message of a fax is set up with the Body Text style. Each fax style has a different font for the Body Text style, as shown in this list:

■ Contemporary—Times New Roman, 10-point

■ Elegant—Garamond, 12-point

■ Professional—Arial, 10-point

If you'd like to use a different font for your fax messages, follow these steps:

1 Click after the] (the closing bracket) in the Comments or Notes section.

2 Choose the Format Style command.

3 Click the Modify button.

4 Click the Format button, and select Font.

5 Select the font settings you want to apply to the Body Text style, and then click OK.

6 Click OK in the Modify Style dialog box.

7 Click Apply in the Style dialog box.

If you want to change the font for the header or other parts of the fax form, click the part you want to change, and then use steps 2 through 7 to change the font of the style.

Creating a Header

For faxes with more than one page (one or more pages beyond the cover page), you might want to add a header on the other pages with the name of the recipient, the date of the fax, the page number, and the number of pages in the fax.

To set up a header for the other pages, you'll need to set up the document, set up the header layout, and then set up the header text.

Set Up the Document

1 Click the name of the recipient.

2 Press Ctrl+Shift+S, type *Recipient,* and then press Enter.

3 If your fax will have more than one page but you haven't yet put in the message, position the insertion point at the end of the Comments or Notes line, press Enter to insert another paragraph, and then press Ctrl+Enter to insert a page break and start a second page.

Set Up the Header Layout

1 Choose the View Header And Footer command.

Page Setup

2 Click the Page Setup button on the Header And Footer toolbar.

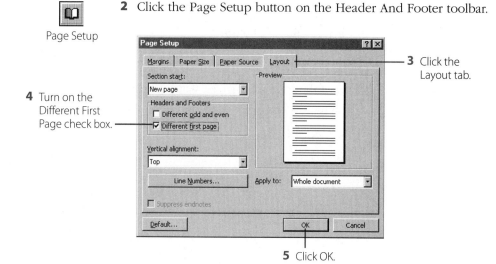

3 Click the Layout tab.

4 Turn on the Different First Page check box.

5 Click OK.

6 If the header label shows First Page Header, click the Show Next button on the Header And Footer toolbar.

7 To place the header at the right margin of the other pages, press Ctrl+R to set the header alignment to Right.

Set Up the Header Text

1 Choose the Insert Field command to see the dialog box shown here:

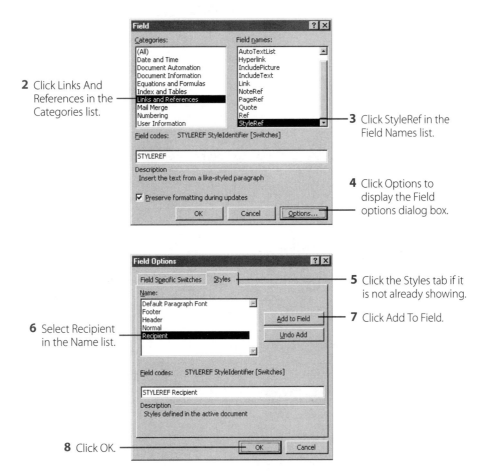

2 Click Links And References in the Categories list.

3 Click StyleRef in the Field Names list.

4 Click Options to display the Field options dialog box.

5 Click the Styles tab if it is not already showing.

7 Click Add To Field.

6 Select Recipient in the Name list.

8 Click OK.

Enter the Header Information

1 Click OK in the Field dialog box.

2 Press Shift+Enter to start a new line.

Insert Date

3 Click the Insert Date button.

4 Press Shift+Enter to start a new line.

5 Type *Page* and a space.

Insert Page Number

6 Click the Insert Page Number button.

7 Type a space, *of*, and a space.

Insert Number of Pages

8 Click the Insert Number Of Pages button.

9 Click Close on the Header And Footer toolbar.

Saving Your Template

After you have set up your fax template, save it so that you can use the template to build and send faxes. To save your fax template, take these steps:

1 Choose the File Properties command, and click the Summary tab.

2 Turn on the Save Preview Picture check box, and then click OK.

3 Choose the File Save command.

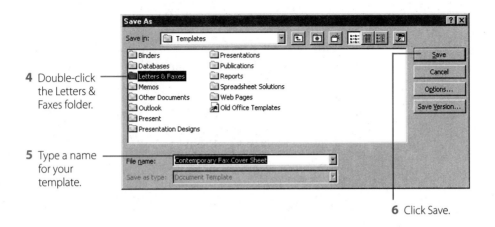

4 Double-click the Letters & Faxes folder.

5 Type a name for your template.

6 Click Save.

If you also want to send faxes in another style, rerun the Fax Wizard, choose the other fax style you want to set up, set up the fax format, and then save the setup as a template.

Sending a Fax

Now that you have a fax template set up, you're ready to create a fax and send it.

To send a fax using a fax template, follow these steps:

1 Choose the File New command, and select the Letters & Faxes tab.

2 Click the icon for the fax template you want to use.

> You can check the appearance of your fax template selection in the Preview box. If you want to use a different fax template, click the icon for that template, and recheck the preview.

3 Click OK.

4 Add recipient information (name and fax number) to the fax header.

5 Add your message to the fax.

6 Choose the File Send To command, and select Fax Recipient from the submenu. Or click the Send Fax Now button on the floating Fax Wizard toolbar.

To send a fax using the Fax Wizard, follow these steps:

1 Follow the steps for creating a fax given at the beginning of this chapter, "Summoning the Wizard," page 245, through "Covering the Fax Style," page 251.

2 Add your message to the fax.

3 When your fax is ready to send, simply click the Send Fax Now button on the Fax Wizard toolbar.

4 When Word notifies you that the fax has been sent, click OK.

CHAPTER 7

Committing Your Thoughts to Memo

Word lets you create memos quickly and easily. You can either use Word's three built-in memo templates or create your own memos and templates using the Memo Wizard. You can also customize Word's memo templates to suit your personal or company style.

In the next few sections, you'll see how easy it is to create a memo template; add a title, heading, address, and closing to a memo; and customize a memo template.

To create a memo template you can then change to suit your style, you
can do one of the following:

- Create a memo template using the Memo Wizard, and then save
  that template. For this method, follow the directions starting with
  "Summoning the Wizard," page 262.

- Create a new memo template from one of Word's built-in memo
  templates. For this method, follow the directions below.

1 Choose the File New command.

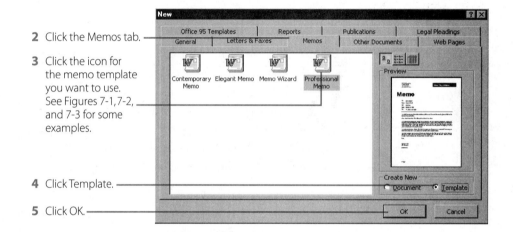

2 Click the Memos tab.

3 Click the icon for
the memo template
you want to use.
See Figures 7-1, 7-2,
and 7-3 for some
examples.

4 Click Template.

5 Click OK.

6 Follow the directions starting with "Dealing with the Memo Message," page 271, and the following sections to the end of this
chapter.

 NOTE

Click the Document option in the New dialog box if you simply want to create a
memo rather than a template.

FIGURE 7-1.
Preview of the Contemporary Memo.

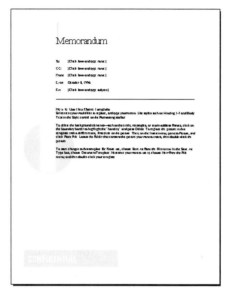

FIGURE 7-2.
Preview of the Elegant Memo.

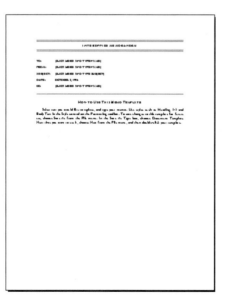

Correspondence

FIGURE 7-3.
Preview of the Professional Memo.

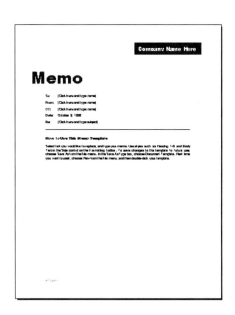

Summoning the Wizard

You can use Word's Memo Wizard to create memos and memo templates. To summon the Memo Wizard, choose the File New command and then proceed as follows:

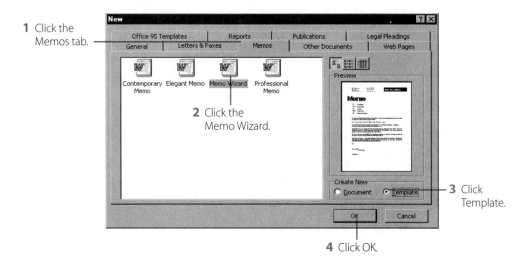

1 Click the Memos tab.

2 Click the Memo Wizard.

3 Click Template.

4 Click OK.

NOTE

> Click the Document option if you simply want to create a memo rather than a template.

Along the left side of the Memo Wizard's Start panel is an outline showing the Memo Wizard panels you use to create a memo or memo template. These panels are described in the next six sections.

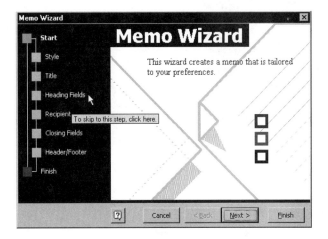

TIP

If you want to jump to any particular panel of the Memo Wizard, click that panel's name in the outline. You can jump forward or backward to any panel.

Click the Next button of the Memo Wizard to display the Style panel.

Styling the Memo

On the Style panel, select the style of memo you want to use.

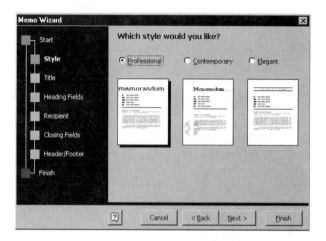

After you select the cover sheet style you want to use, click Next.

Giving Your Memo a Title

On the Title panel, you can set up a memo either with or without a title, as shown here:

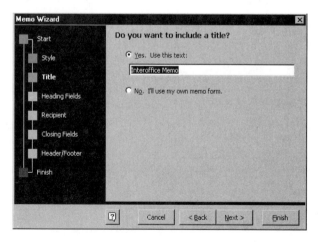

- If you plan to print your memo on plain paper, click Yes. Use This Text. Then type the title you want to use. (If you don't want a title, simply delete the text in the box.) The title text you type in the box appears at the top of the memo page in the positions you see in Figures 7-1, 7-2, and 7-3.

- If you want to print your memo on a pre-printed memo form, click No. I'll Use My Own Memo Form. When you turn on this option, Memo Wizard adds the following choices for specifying the size and placement of the heading on the pre-printed memo form.

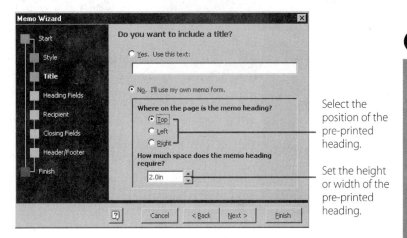

Select the position of the pre-printed heading.

Set the height or width of the pre-printed heading.

When you have made your choice for the memo title, click Next.

Heading Up Your Memo

On the Heading Fields panel, you select and set up the lines you want to head up your memo.

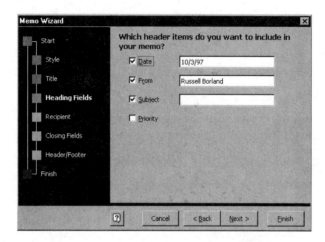

To include any of the four lines on the panel in your memo, turn on the check box to the left of the label. Then type the information you want on that line in the box to the right of the label.

- **Date**—The Memo Wizard uses a short form for the date. If you want the date in a different form (such as July 21, 1997), type the date the way you want it. Also, if you want your memo to show a date other than the day on which you create it, type the date you want to use.

- **From**—The Memo Wizard uses the name that appears on the User Information tab of the Options dialog box for the From line. If you're creating a memo for someone else, type that person's name in the From box.

- **Subject**—If you're creating a memo template, leave the Subject box blank. If you're creating this memo for one time only, type the subject of the memo.

- **Priority**—Turn on this check box to have the Memo Wizard place *Priority* in the memo heading under the Subject line.

When you have made your choices and filled in the boxes you want to fill, click Next.

Who Gets This Memo?

On the Recipient panel, you enter the names of the people who will receive the memo.

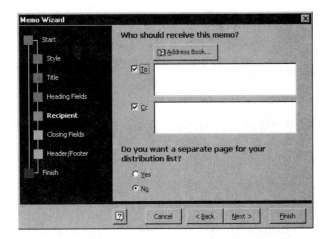

You won't want to add recipient information to a template. If you're Creating a Template, click Next to move to the Closing Fields panel of the Memo Wizard.

If, however, you're not creating a template, but simply a memo to be sent one time only, add the recipients' names to the To and Cc boxes on the Recipient panel. Clicking the Address Book button displays the Select Names dialog box, shown on the following page, which lets you select from a list of names to add.

You can print the names of the recipients in the heading of your memo or on a separate sheet. If your distribution list contains many names, you'll probably prefer to set up a separate page. To set up a separate page for the names, click Yes on the Recipient panel.

When you're done with the Recipient panel, click Next.

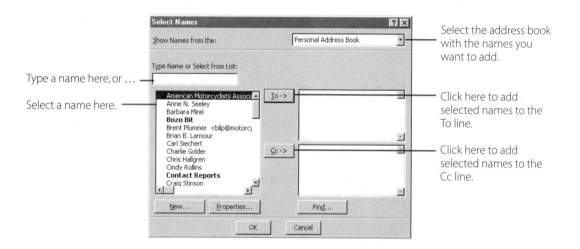

Type a name here, or ...

Select a name here.

Select the address book with the names you want to add.

Click here to add selected names to the To line.

Click here to add selected names to the Cc line.

Closing Out Your Memo

On the Closing Fields panel, you set up information that appears at the end of a memo.

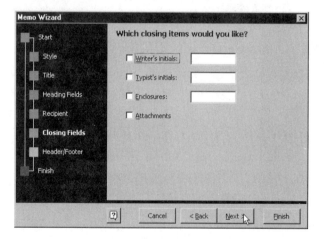

For memos that you create for someone else, you'll want to add the writer's initials and the typist's initials (probably your initials). If you're sending other documents with the memo, you'll want to add an Enclosures line and the number of enclosures or the names. To let your recipients know that you have attached other documents as part of the memo, you might want to turn on the Attachments check box.

To add any of the pieces of information from the Closing Fields panel, turn on the check box to the left of the label, and then type the information in the box to the right of the label.

- **Writer's Initials**—Type the initials of the person sending the memo. For a template, turn on the check box to the left of the Writer's Initials label, but leave the box to the right of the label empty.

- **Typist's Initials**—Type the initials of the person typing the memo. For a template, turn on the check box to the left of the Typist's Initials label, but leave the box to the right of the label empty.

- **Enclosures**—When you're sending enclosures with your memo, you can enter the number of enclosures in this box, or instead, you can type the names of the enclosures. All the names will appear on the same line, so you'll probably want to separate them with commas or semicolons.

- **Attachments**—If you're adding attachments to your memo, turn on the Attachments check box to add an *Attachments* label to the end of your memo.

When you're done with the Closing Fields panel, click Next.

Creating a Memo's Header and Footer

On the Header/Footer panel, you set up headers for the second and subsequent pages of your memo and footers for all pages.

As you can see on the Header/Footer panel on the next page, the Memo Wizard is set up to put only the memo's title in the header. If you also want the date and page number in headers after the first page, turn on the Date and Page Number check boxes. In the footer, the Memo Wizard puts the date of the memo, a Confidential label, and the page number.

- **Topic**—the Memo Wizard inserts the title you set up on the Title panel. If you want a different title to appear in the header on pages after the first page, type that title in the box to the right of

Correspondence

the Topic label. Changing the text in the Topic box doesn't change the title you set up on the Title panel.

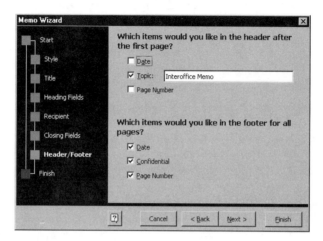

When you're done with the Header/Footer panel, click Next. The Finish panel opens, as shown here:

Click Finish, and you are now ready to remodel your memo template or to put your message into a memo and send it.

Dealing with the Memo Message

When you create a memo or a memo template from the memo templates supplied with Word, you'll see the text "How to Use This Memo Template" along with a note when the memo document opens.

- When you're creating a memo, select all this text, and then type your message.

- When you're creating a new memo template, select all this text and delete it.

Flexing the Fonts

The message of a memo uses the Body Text style. Each memo style uses a different font for the Body Text style, as follows:

- Contemporary—Times New Roman, 10-point

- Elegant—Garamond, 11-point

- Professional—Arial, 10-point

If you'd like to use a different font for your memo messages, follow these steps:

1 Click in the last paragraph of the memo text.

2 Choose the Format Style command.

3 Click the Modify button.

4 Click the Format button, and select Font.

5 Select the font settings you want to apply to the Body Text style, and then click OK.

6 Click OK in the Modify Style dialog box.

7 Click Close in the Style dialog box.

If you want to change the font for the header, footer, or other parts of the memo, click the part you want to change, and then use steps 2 through 7 to change the font of the style.

Saving Your Template

After you have set up your memo template, you should save it so that you can use the template to build memos. To save your memo template, take the following steps:

1 Choose the File Properties command, and click the Summary tab.

2 Turn on the Save Preview Picture check box, and then click OK.

3 Choose the File Save command.

6 Click Save.

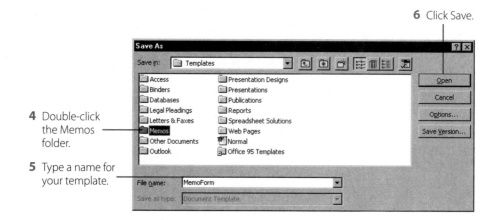

4 Double-click the Memos folder.

5 Type a name for your template.

If you also want to send memos in another style, rerun the Memo Wizard, choose the other memo style you want to set up, set up the memo format, and then save the setup as a template.

Creating a Memo

Now that you have a memo template set up, you're ready to create a memo.

To use a memo template to create a memo, take these steps:

1 Choose the File New command, and select the Memos tab.

2 Click the icon for the memo template you want to use.

> You can check the appearance of your memo template selection in the Preview box. If you want to use a different memo template, click the icon for that template, and recheck the preview.

3 Click OK.

4 Add recipient information (To and Cc names) to the memo header.

5 If necessary, add the sender's name to the From line.

6 Type the subject of the memo in the Re line.

7 Select all the text from the heading, "How to Use This Memo Template" to the end of the document, and then type your message.

To use the Memo Wizard to send a memo, take these steps:

1 Follow the steps for creating a memo given at the beginning of this chapter, "Summoning the Wizard," page 262, through "Flexing the Fonts," page 271.

2 Add your message to the memo.

Sending a Memo Through Your Computer

While the most common practice is probably to print a memo and then send copies to the recipients, Word contains commands on the File menu for sending a memo through your computer. To send your memo electronically, take these steps:

1 Choose the File Send To command. You will see this submenu:

2 From the submenu, select the command for the method you want to use to send your memo. (See the following sections for details and additional steps.)

To send a memo electronically, you must be connected to a network, or you must be running an e-mail program compatible with the Messaging Application Programming Interface (MAPI), or both. For more information, see the topic "Sending and Routing E-mail Documents" in the Word online help file.

Mail Recipient

When you choose Mail Recipient from the File Send To submenu, Word inserts your memo as an attachment to a Microsoft Exchange (or Outlook) message, as shown here:

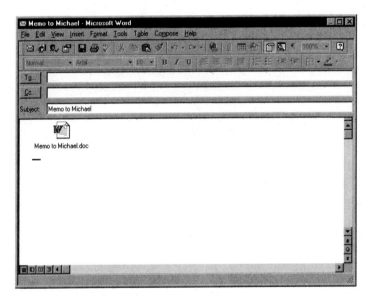

Notice that if you save your memo document before you choose the Mail Recipient command, the document name appears in the Subject line.

To send your memo, fill in the To line (and the Cc line, if appropriate). Also, you can type a cover message for your memo, if you wish. When the message is ready to send, click the Send button.

Routing Recipient

The Routing Recipient command lets you send your memo to a list of recipients, either one at a time or all at once. You'll want to choose the Routing Recipient command (instead of the Mail Recipient command)

PART III

Publications

CHAPTER 8

Filing Your Report

Word supplies three report templates: a "contemporary" report, an "elegant" report, and a "professional" report. Figures 8-1, 8-2, and 8-3 on the following pages give you a two-page preview of each style of report.

Like other Word templates, report templates contain a sample page and instructions on using and customizing templates. You should customize report templates so they better suit the particular needs and style of your organization or company. For example, you can save yourself a lot of repetitive work in the future by adding to a template any names, titles, text, or logos that will show up repeatedly in reports you produce.

The first few sections of this chapter show you how to rework a report template so that it is better suited to your needs—a process I call remodeling. Start by creating a new template based on one of Word's existing report templates.

FIGURE 8-1.
Preview of the Contemporary Report template.

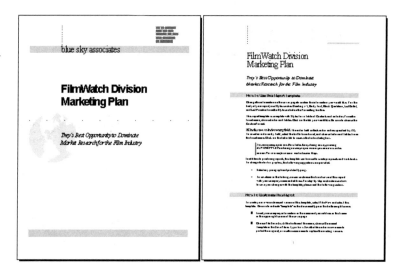

FIGURE 8-2.
Preview of the Elegant Report template.

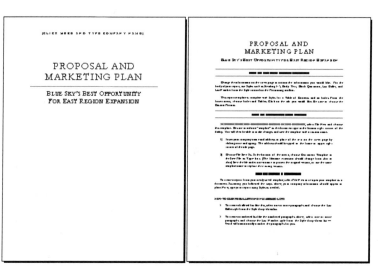

⭐ **TIP**

Before you start remodeling a template, print a copy of the report template you're going to remodel. You can follow the instructions in the report template as the preliminary guide toward transforming the template.

FIGURE 8-3.
Preview of the Professional Report template.

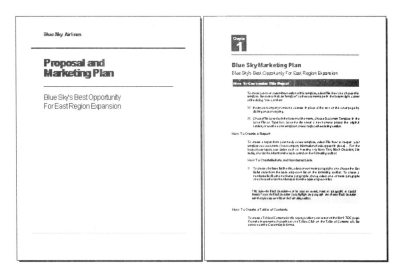

To create a report template you can remodel, take these steps:

1 Choose the File New command.

2 Click the Reports tab.

4 Click the Template option.

3 Click the style of report you want to remodel (see Figures 8-1 through 8-3).

5 Click OK.

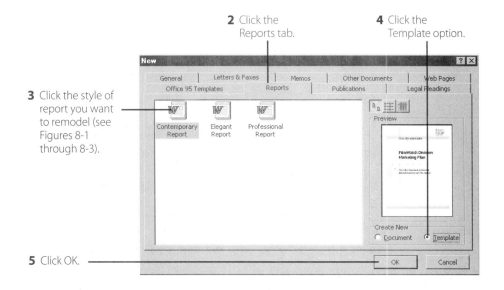

Remodeling the Text in a Report Template

The report templates all contain text with instructions for using them. You can follow the directions in the template. Here are the steps I use to remodel a report template.

III

Publications

Remodeling the Cover

To remodel the cover, take these steps:

1 If you don't see a hatched border around the return address in the upper part of the cover, click the return address; if you do see it, go on to step 2.

2 Hold down the Ctrl key as you click the organization name.

3 Type your organization's name.

4 Press Enter and type each line of the return address.

5 Select the large organization name ("blue sky associates").

6 Type your organization's name.

7 Hold down the Ctrl key as you click the report title, which begins with the name "FilmWatch" in the contemporary template.

8 Type a new title for the report's cover, based on how you want to use this report template.

- If you're simply creating a report document, type the report title.

- If you're setting up a report template for a report you submit repeatedly, type the report title.

- If you're setting up a report template for a variety of reports, take the steps in the sidebar "Setting Up a Title and Subtitle for a Variety of Reports," page 283.

9 Hold down the Ctrl key as you click the report subtitle, which appears below the title.

10 Type a new subtitle for the report's cover, based on how you want to use this report template.

- If you're simply creating a report document, type the report subtitle, if you want one. If not, press the Delete key.

- If you're setting up a report template for a report you submit repeatedly, type the report subtitle, if you want one. If not, press the Delete key.

- If you're setting up a report template for a variety of reports, take the steps in the sidebar "Setting Up a Title and Subtitle for a Variety of Reports" below.

Centering the Cover Page Vertically

More often than not, you'll want Word to print most of the pages of a report starting at the top margin and ending somewhere on the last page of the section. On the cover page, you might want the text to expand vertically to fill all the space between the top and bottom margins. This vertical alignment is called justified. Or you might want the text centered between the top and bottom margins.

For these cases, you can set the vertical alignment of the cover-page section. In vertical alignment, Word aligns the paragraphs on the cover page relative to the top and bottom margins.

Setting Up a Title and Subtitle for a Variety of Reports

If you're going to use a report template for a variety of reports, you'll want to set up the cover page and the top of the second page in the template to accept the title and subtitle you need for each report. There are many ways to do this in Word; here's a fairly simple way:

1 Hold down the Ctrl key as you click the cover page title, and then press Delete.

2 Choose the Insert Field command.

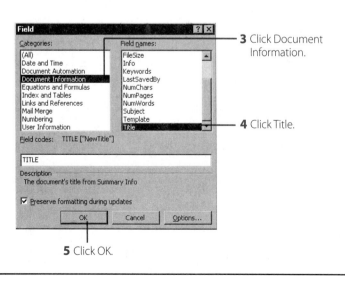

3 Click Document Information.

4 Click Title.

5 Click OK.

Setting Up a Title and Subtitle for a Variety of Reports *continued*

6 Select the cover's title paragraph, and then press Shift+F9 to reveal the field code.

7 Position the insertion point between the two spaces following *TITLE*, and then choose the Insert Field command.

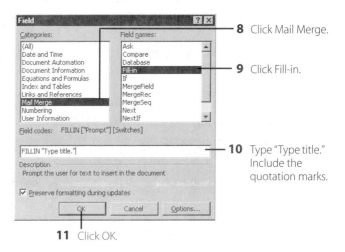

8 Click Mail Merge.

9 Click Fill-in.

10 Type "Type title." Include the quotation marks.

11 Click OK.

12 Leave the Microsoft Word dialog box that appears blank by clicking OK.

13 Press Shift+F9 to hide the field code.

14 Hold down the Ctrl key as you click the cover's subtitle, and then press Delete.

15 If you want to set up a subtitle, repeat steps 2 through 13 for the cover's subtitle—in step 4 select Subject instead of Title, in step 7 position the insertion point between the two spaces following SUBJECT, and in step 10 type *"Type subtitle."*

16 Hold down the Ctrl key as you click the title on the second page, and then press Delete.

17 Repeat steps 2 through 5.

18 Hold down the Ctrl key as you click the subtitle on the second page, and then press Delete.

19 If you want to set up a subtitle on the second page, repeat steps 2 through 5—in step 4 select Subject instead of Title.

Setting Up a Title and Subtitle for a Variety of Reports *continued*

With this setup, when you create a report from this template, take these steps:

1 Press Ctrl+A to select the entire document, and then press F9.

2 Type the title in the Microsoft Word dialog box, and then click OK.

3 Type the subtitle in the next Microsoft Word dialog box, and then click OK.

Filling in these fields also fills in the Title and Subject boxes on the Summary tab of the Properties dialog box.

Here's a summary of the different vertical alignment options and their effects.

Vertical Alignment	**Effect on a Page**
Top	Places the top line of the first paragraph on a page at the top margin
Center	Places all the text in the center of a page between the top and bottom margins
Justified	Expands the space between paragraphs to place the top line of the first paragraph on a page at the top margin and the bottom line of the last paragraph at the bottom margin

For vertical alignment to work, you must observe these two rules:

■ The section you are aligning vertically must start on a new page. Also, the section following the vertically aligned section must start on a new page.

■ The contents of the section should be less than a full page. If not, you will likely see little or no effect from selecting a vertical alignment other than Top. If the section covers several pages, you might see some effect on some of the pages and a negligible effect on others.

III

Publications

To center or justify the contents of the cover page of a report, take these steps:

1 Switch to Normal view.

2 Locate and delete the page break character between the cover page and the second page.

3 Position the insertion point on the second page.

4 Choose the File Page Setup command.

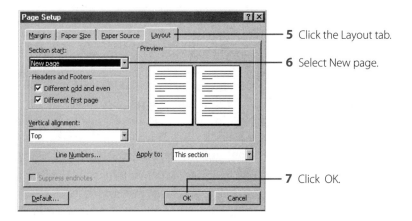

5 Click the Layout tab.

6 Select New page.

7 Click OK.

8 Position the insertion point on the cover page.

9 Choose the File Page Setup command.

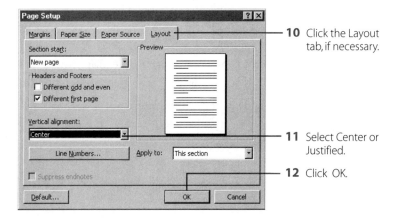

10 Click the Layout tab, if necessary.

11 Select Center or Justified.

12 Click OK.

Remodeling the Other Pages

You'll want to remove the text from the rest of the report template, as well as from a report document. To remodel the other pages, take these steps:

1 Position the insertion point at the beginning of the first paragraph after the "How To Use This Report Template" paragraph.

2 Press Ctrl+Shift+End to select the rest of the text.

3 Press Delete to remove the selected text.

4 Hold down the Ctrl key as you click the "How To Use This Report Template" heading.

5 Press Delete to remove the heading text.

Dealing with the Art in Reports

If you are in Page Layout view, you'll see a column of dots as a decorative touch at the top of the pages. (This decoration also appears on the third page before you delete from the template the remaining text following the heading on the second page.) These decorations are text boxes filled with periods and set to vertical direction. (You'll learn about text boxes later in this chapter—see "Wrapping Up Text Boxes," page 399.) Because these decorations were placed directly on each page, when you add pages you won't see these decorations unless you put them there yourself. To do this, copy the decoration to the Clipboard, and then paste it into the headers for the other pages (for directions, see "Setting Up Headers and Footers," page 288).

Adding More Art to Your Report

The types of art most often used in reports are charts and tables. All the same, pictures find their ways into reports, too—product pictures, people pictures, and sometimes even decorative art. Chapter 10, "Brocading a Brochure," contains directions for adding various types of art to a document. To insert clip art and art from other files, see "Adding Art from Files," page 455. To draw pictures yourself, see "Drawing Pictures," page 458. To add WordArt, see "Bending Text—WordArt," page

III

Publications

507. To change the size of art and add a border, see "Formatting Art, WordArt, and Other Objects," page 515.

Collecting a List of Figures

Word can collect a list of figures that includes each figure's caption and the page number on which each figure appears. Only figures that have captions will be included in the list.

> Before you can collect a list of figures, you must give each figure a caption. To add captions to figures, use the steps in "Adding Captions," page 396.

To collect a list of figures, use the steps listed in "Collecting a List of Tables," page 349. In those steps, simply substitute "Figures" for "Tables."

Setting Up Headers and Footers

You add information to headers and footers in exactly the same way you add information—text and artwork—to the body of your report. To add text, you simply type it. You can also use fields to automatically add information to a header or footer—see "Fields," page 291. For information about adding artwork, see the art topics in Chapter 10, "Brocading a Brochure." Use the steps and directions you find there to add art to your headers and footers.

Whenever you set up a header or footer in a document, Word automatically applies the Header style to headers and the Footer style to footers. These two styles are based on the Normal style but add two tab stops—one centered tab stop at 3 inches and a right flush tab stop at 6 inches. These styles give you a quick setup for placing header or footer information at the right margin, at the center of the page, and at the left margin.

This standard setup might not suit your report. Also, Word provides some tricks for putting information into headers and footers. The following sections guide you in changing some elements of header and footer setup.

Laying Out Headers and Footers

The report templates are set up with a different first page header and footer and different headers and footers for odd and even pages. Because you changed the section break at the end of the cover page to Next Page, you'll need to change the header and footer layout for the other pages. You might also want to change the different headers and footers for odd-numbered and even-numbered pages.

To change the layout of your headers and footers, take these steps:

1 Position the insertion point on the second page of the template (after the section break at the end of the first page).

The report template opens in Page Layout view with nonprinting characters (paragraph marks, spaces, page breaks, and section breaks) visible. If you want to hide these nonprinting characters, click the Show/Hide ¶ button on the Standard toolbar or press Ctrl+*. Click the Show/Hide ¶ button again when you want to see the nonprinting characters.

2 Choose the File Page Setup command, and then click the Layout tab.

3 Turn off this check box for headers and footers to be the same on all pages.

4 Turn off this check box.

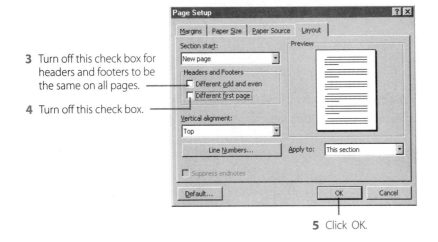

5 Click OK.

Alignment

With the standard setup for header and footer styles, you simply insert a tab character to align the information at the center position and another tab character to align the information at the right margin. So, for example, if you want to place the document title at the left margin, the page number in the center, and the date in the right margin, you take these steps:

1 Choose the View Header And Footer command.

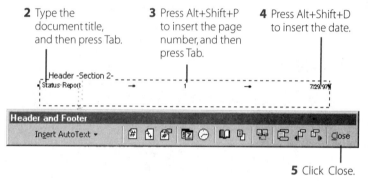

2 Type the document title, and then press Tab.

3 Press Alt+Shift+P to insert the page number, and then press Tab.

4 Press Alt+Shift+D to insert the date.

5 Click Close.

This alignment of elements might not suit your report, however. For example, you might want all the header or footer information to appear at the right margin. (Or, you might want the tab stops at different positions—see the next section, "Tabs.") To change the standard alignment of the header or footer, take these steps:

1 Choose the Format Style command.

2 If you don't see Header and Footer in the Styles list, select All Styles in the List box.

3 Select Header (or Footer) in the Styles list, and then click the Modify button.

4 Click the Format button, and then select Paragraph.

5 In the Alignment box, select Right, and then click OK.

6 Click OK in the Modify Style dialog box, and click the Apply button in the Style dialog box.

Tabs

The standard tab stop settings for headers and footers are centered at 3 inches and right flush at 6 inches. To change these tab stop settings, take these steps:

1 Choose the Format Style command.

2 If you don't see Header and Footer in the Styles list, select All Styles in the List box.

3 Select Header (or Footer) in the Styles list, and then click the Modify button.

4 Click the Format button, and then select Tabs.

5 Delete the tab stops you don't want to keep—select the setting from the Tab Stop Position list, and then click Clear.

6 Set the tab stops you want to add to the Header (or Footer) style—type a position measurement, select the alignment you want, and then click Set—repeat this step for each tab stop you want to set.

7 Click OK in the Tabs dialog box, click OK in the Modify Style dialog box, and then click the Apply button in the Style dialog box.

Fields

The joy of fields in headers and footers (as well as in other parts of a document) is that Word puts the correct information in place for you. This way, you know that the information is always current and correct. You can add any of Word's many fields to a header or footer. Table 8-1 on the next page lists some of the more likely fields for headers and footers, along with the type of information the fields insert and the major options you can set for the fields. The list in Table 8-1 comes from the Document Information and Links and References categories in the Field dialog box.

III

Publications

To insert a field into a header or footer, take these steps:

1 Choose the View Header And Footer command.

2 Choose the Insert Field command.

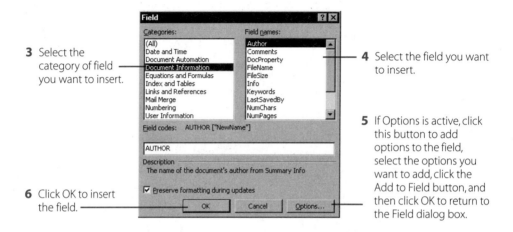

3 Select the category of field you want to insert.

4 Select the field you want to insert.

5 If Options is active, click this button to add options to the field, select the options you want to add, click the Add to Field button, and then click OK to return to the Field dialog box.

6 Click OK to insert the field.

7 Click the Close button on the Header And Footer toolbar.

TABLE 8-1. Table of Fields Especially Useful in Headers and Footers.

Field Name	Use	Options
Document Information		
Author	Add author's name	
NumPages	Add number of pages*	
NumWords	Add number of words	
Title	Add report title	
Subject	Add report subtitle	
Links and References		
AutoText	Add AutoText entry	Names of AutoText entries
Ref	Add bookmark text from report text—mark report text with a bookmark before inserting this field	Bookmark names
StyleRef	Add text with a particular style—such as a heading—mark report text with a style before inserting this field	Style names \l switch—locates text with style nearest the bottom of the page instead of the top

*You can insert this field by clicking the Insert Number Of Pages button on the Header And Footer toolbar.

Saving Your Template

Now that you have remodeled a report template, you need to save it so that you can create reports from it. To save your template, take these steps:

1 Choose the File Properties command, and then click the Summary tab.

2 Turn on the Save Preview Picture box, and then click OK.

3 Click the Save button on the Standard toolbar. You will see the Save As dialog box as shown here:

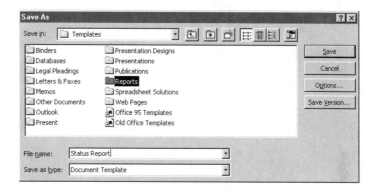

4 Double-click the Reports foldera.

5 Type a name for your template file in the File Name box.

6 Click Save.

You can now create reports from your report template.

Creating a Report

1 Choose the File New command.

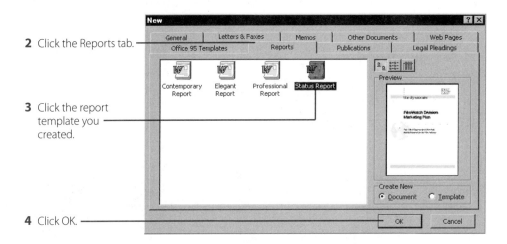

2 Click the Reports tab.

3 Click the report template you created.

4 Click OK.

5 Type a title, or accept the one that is shown, and click OK in the Microsoft Word dialog box.

6 Type the report subtitle (if any) in the subtitle dialog box, and then click OK.

7 Press Ctrl+A to select the entire report, and then press F9 to update the fields you inserted.

8 Type the report title in the Microsoft Word dialog box, click OK, type the report subtitle (if any) in the next Microsoft Word dialog box, and then click OK.

9 Position the insertion point in the heading paragraph on the second page, and then type the first heading.

10 Press Enter and type text.

11 Consult the remaining sections in this chapter for directions on inserting information in other reports.

Setting Tables in Your Report

If you want to set a table in a report, you can either craft the structure of the table and then fill in the text or insert the text first and then convert it to a table. Word offers these methods for crafting a table:

- The Insert Table button on the Standard toolbar

- The Table Insert Table command

- The table drawing tool

The Insert Table button and the Table Insert Table command insert standard tables—tables with the same number of columns in every row and the same number of rows in every column. You can change the number of columns in any row, and you can change the number of rows in a column.

With the table drawing tool, you can draw complex tables—tables with any number of rows in any column and any number of columns in any row. You can also use the table drawing tool to change a standard table, but not to insert one.

You also have a choice of methods for crafting a table from text that is already in a document:

- The Table Convert Text To Table command

- The Insert Table button on the Standard toolbar

- The Table Insert Table command

> **NOTE**

You cannot use the table drawing tool to craft a table from text that is already in a document.

Crafting a Table with the Toolbar

Insert
Table

You can use the Insert Table button on the Standard toolbar to quickly insert an unformatted table in a document.

III

Publications

To craft a table with the toolbar, take these steps:

1 Position the insertion point in a document, and click the Insert Table button. A grid with four rows and five columns drops down below the button, as shown here:

2 Drag across and down the grid to select the number of rows and columns you want your table to have, and release the mouse button to insert the table. To lengthen the grid, drag downward, past the fourth row. To widen the grid, drag to the right. As you drag, Word displays the size of the grid as rows by columns. For example, the notation *6 x 7 Table* means a table with six rows and seven columns.

If you click the Insert Table button, select cells in the grid, and then decide not to insert a table, you can cancel by dragging the mouse pointer outside the grid or back to the toolbar button and then releasing the mouse button. If you haven't yet selected in the grid, you can cancel by clicking the toolbar button, the Cancel box in the grid, or anywhere outside the grid.

A table can have as many as 63 columns and 32,767 rows. When you use the Insert Table button, the size of the table you create is limited by the size of the grid that can be displayed on your screen. For very large tables, you must use the Table Insert Table command.

Crafting a Table on Command

You can choose the Table Insert Table command to craft a table. To craft a table on command, take these steps:

1 Position the insertion point where you want a table, and then choose the Table Insert Table command.

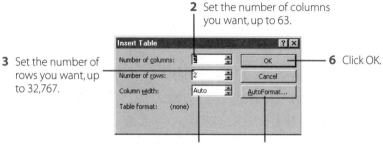

2 Set the number of columns you want, up to 63.

3 Set the number of rows you want, up to 32,767.

6 Click OK.

4 Set the width you want for all columns. Auto divides the width between margins evenly among columns.

5 Click here to add a preset table format (see "Hiring Table AutoFormat," page 327).

Drawing a Table

The new table drawing tool in Word 97 lets you set up tables with all kinds of unusual cell arrangements. To draw a table, you activate the table drawing tool by doing one of the following:

■ Choose the Table Draw Table command.

■ Click the Tables And Borders button on the Standard toolbar.

Tables and Borders

Word turns on the Tables And Borders toolbar, activates the table drawing tool, and the Assistant appears. When the table drawing tool is active, the mouse pointer changes to a pencil.

With the table drawing tool active, take these steps to draw a table:

1 Position the table drawing tool at one corner of the space where you want to draw the table.

2 Drag the table drawing tool to the opposite corner of the table space, to the height and width you want the table, and then release the mouse button.

View the Text Boundaries of Your Table
When you're drawing a table, you might want to see the width of the text column where you're drawing. You can turn on the text boundaries. To do so, choose the Tools Options command, click the View tab, turn on the Text Boundaries check box, and then click OK. If you do this while in the midst of drawing a table, click the Draw Table button on the Tables And Borders toolbar to change the mouse pointer back to a pencil.

3 Draw the columns and rows you want in the table:

- Draw from one side to the other to draw a row.

- Draw from top to bottom (or bottom to top) to draw a column.

- To draw a partial row, draw from one side of a column to the other side of the column(s) where you want the partial row.

- To draw a partial column, draw from the top of a row to the bottom of the row(s) where you want the partial column.

4 When you're done drawing the table, click the Draw Table button on the Tables And Borders toolbar.

Draw
Table

Eraser

If you decide that you want to move a column line, erase it and draw a new line at the new position. You can also move a column or row line by setting the row height or column width using the Table Cell Height And Width command or the Distribute Rows Evenly and the Distribute Columns Evenly buttons on the Tables And Borders toolbar—see "Formatting a Table," page 326.

To remove a row or column line, take these steps:

1　Click the Eraser button on the Tables And Borders toolbar.

2　Drag the eraser tool along the column or row border you want to erase.

> You use the same steps to fill, format, and change a drawn table as you do for a standard table.

Filling Table Cells

To fill a cell, you can use all the steps you use to add text to a document. To move from cell to cell, you press the Tab key. To move backward to the previous cell, press Shift+Tab.

> If you draw a table with cells that are more than one row high beside columns that have two or more rows, pressing the Tab and Shift+Tab keys works slightly differently in this part of a table, as shown below. The numbers here represent the order in which each cell becomes active each time the Tab key is pressed.
>
> | 1 | 2 | 3 | 4 | 5 |
> |---|---|---|---|---|
> | 6 | 7 | 8 | 9 | 10 |
> | 11 | 12 | 13 | 14 | 15 |

Cutting and pasting and copying and pasting differ a bit in some cases; see "Working with Table Text," page 305, for details.

Formatting a Cell's Contents

You can format a cell's contents just as you can format other text. Word lets you set both paragraph and font formatting in each cell. The paragraph formats you set apply only to the paragraphs in one cell. The cells are independent of one another, so you must select all the cells for which you want to set paragraph or font formatting.

A table appears on the screen with borders that outline each cell. To change the borders around each cell, choose the Format Borders And Shading command or select the border style you want from the

Outside
Border

Outside Border button's list. This list appears when you click the button's drop-down arrow on the Tables And Borders toolbar. If you turn off borders, you see gridlines along the sides of cells without borders. Word does not print these gridlines; they're for display only, and you can turn them off by choosing the Table Hide Gridlines command. To turn on gridlines again, choose the Table Show Gridlines command.

If you turned on the Text Boundaries check box on the View tab of the Options dialog box, you'll see dotted lines around cells even with borders removed and gridlines turned off. To hide this dotted outline, turn off the Text Boundaries check box.

Sending Table Text in a New Direction

Particularly in drawn tables, you can have cells that are taller than they are wide. In these cells, you might want some of the text to run vertically instead of horizontally. Here's an example:

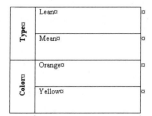

To change the direction of text, take these steps:

1 Select the text you want to send in a new direction.

2 Choose the Format Text Direction command. You will see this dialog box:

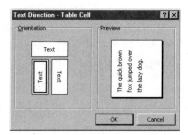

3 Click the direction you want the text to run in the Orientation box.

4 Check the Preview box to see text running in the new direction.

5 Click OK.

When the text direction is vertical, several changes occur in Word:

- The insertion point is horizontal when it is in vertical text.

- The paragraph alignment buttons on the Formatting toolbar show vertical alignment rather than horizontal alignment. Click these buttons to adjust vertical alignment of vertical text.

- The Align Top button on the Tables And Borders toolbar becomes an Align Left button; the Center Vertically button becomes a Center Horizontally button; and the Align Bottom button becomes an Align Right button. Click these buttons to adjust horizontal alignment of vertical text.

- Paragraph space before and after settings become horizontal spacing between the left and right borders of the cell.

 TIP

Change
Text
Direction

Shortcut to Change Text Direction

As a shortcut, select the text you want to redirect, and then click the Change Text Direction button on the Tables And Borders toolbar. Each time you click the Change Text Direction button, the text switches to the next direction—vertical down, vertical up, horizontal. The button image shows the new direction for the text the next time you click the button.

Converting Existing Text to a Table

Word gives you several ways to convert existing text to a table. Sometimes you might prefer to add text to your document first and then put it in a table later. Or perhaps your document contains text arranged in columns, separated by tab stops. Each method requires that you first select the text that you want to put in a table.

Using the Insert Table Toolbar Button

To convert text to a table with the Insert Table button on the Standard toolbar, take these steps:

1 Select the text.

2 Click the Insert Table button.

Word calculates the number of rows and columns needed and crafts the table for you.

Using the Table Insert Table Command

To convert text to a table with the Table Insert Table command, take these steps:

1 Select the text.

2 Choose the Table Insert Table command.

Word calculates the number of rows and columns needed and crafts the table for you.

Using the Table Convert Text To Table Command

Use the Table Convert Text To Table command to craft a table from existing text when you need to select the column-separator character or you want to change the number of columns from what Word calculates for the table.

How Word Counts Rows and Columns

When you convert existing text into table format, Word sets up one table row for each paragraph in the text. Word sets the number of columns in the table to match the maximum number of column-separator characters in any one line of the text. Word recognizes only tabs, commas, and paragraph marks as column-separator characters. If any line in your selection contains neither tab characters nor commas, Word inserts a one-column table. If a selection contains both tab characters and commas, use the Table Convert Text To Table command so that you can select the column-separator character you want to use.

To use the Table Convert Text To Table command, take these steps:

1 Select the text you want to convert to a table.

2 Choose the Table Convert Text To Table command to display the Convert Text To Table dialog box.

3 If you wish, change the number of columns. Word changes the number of rows.

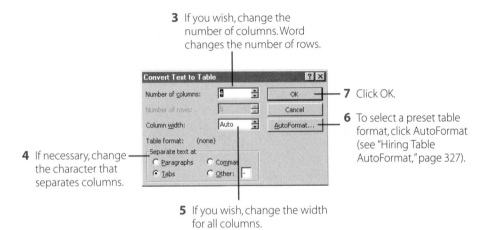

7 Click OK.

6 To select a preset table format, click AutoFormat (see "Hiring Table AutoFormat," page 327).

4 If necessary, change the character that separates columns.

5 If you wish, change the width for all columns.

Moving and Selecting Parts in a Table

Before you begin changing cell contents, reshaping the table, or setting fonts for a table, you need to know how to move around and select text within a table using the mouse, the keyboard, the Table menu, and the Table shortcut menu.

Within a cell, you move and select in the same way you do in text that is outside a table. You use a different approach, however, to select an entire cell (all the contents and the cell marker), more than one cell, a row, a column, or an entire table. But before you can understand the steps involved, you might want to know more about the parts of a table (see the sidebar "The Parts of a Table" on the next page).

Using the Mouse to Select Text

You can use the mouse to position the insertion point and to select text within a cell in the same way you select text outside tables. If you select by dragging, the selection grows by whole cells after you cross a cell boundary. The mouse also provides shortcuts for selecting cell contents, rows, and columns, as pointed out in Table 8-2.

III

Publications

TABLE 8-2. Mouse Shortcuts for Selecting in a Table.

To Select	Do This
Cell contents	Click in the cell selection bar (along the inner left side of a cell).
An entire row	Click in the row selection bar (just outside the left border of the table), or double-click in any cell selection bar. The mouse pointer becomes a white arrow pointing up and slightly to the right when it is over the row selection bar.
An entire column	Click in the column selection bar (along the top border of the top cell in a column). The mouse pointer becomes a downward-pointing black arrow when it is over the column selection bar.
All the cells in rows with a cell that crosses two or more rows	Drag from the row selection bar (just outside the left border of the table) to the cell that is in the opposite corner (farthest down and to the right) in the block of cells to be selected.
All the cells in columns with a cell that crosses two or more columns	Drag along the column selection bar (along the top border of the top cell in a column) until you select all the columns and rows you want.

The Parts of a Table

A table is made up of rows and columns. The block of space formed where a row and a column cross is called a cell. So, a table that contains four rows by five columns contains 20 cells. Each cell can hold anything you can add to a Word document except another table, a frame, a column break, or a section break. (If you insert a section break, column break, or page break while the insertion point is in a cell, Word inserts the break above the row of the cell that contains the insertion point.)

The height of a row is set by the height of the tallest cell in that row. The tallest cell is the one that contains the tallest text. A row can be as short as 1 point, which is 1/72 of an inch. If a row contains more text than can be printed on one page, Word splits the row with the page break unless you turn off the Allow Row To Break Across Pages check box in the Cell Height And Width dialog box. If you turn off this check box, Word prints only as much of the cell's contents as fits on the current page. To turn off this check box, choose the Table Cell Height And Width command and select the Row tab. The check box is at the bottom of the dialog box.

If your table is wider than the window, you can scroll the table horizontally by clicking or dragging in the horizontal scroll bar. (If the horizontal scroll bar is not turned on, you can choose Tools Options, click the View tab, turn on the Horizontal Scroll Bar check box, and then click OK.) If the cells you want to select include more than those visible, begin selecting by dragging across the cells. When the mouse pointer reaches the edge of the window, hold it there. Word will automatically scroll the table for you.

Selecting with Keys

The ↑, ↓, ←, and → keys, the Ctrl+← shortcut key, the Ctrl+→ shortcut key, and the Home and End keys perform the same actions within a single cell that they perform in text outside a table. When the insertion point reaches the top, bottom, left, or right edge of a cell, however, the ↑, ↓, ←, and → keys act differently, as Table 8-3 explains.

If your table is wider than the window, press Alt+End to jump to the final column; Word scrolls the window to show the right end of the table. To scroll the window back to the left, press Alt+Home. The Tab key and the Shift+Tab shortcut keys scroll the table horizontally if the selection jumps to a cell that is outside the window.

Selecting from the Table Menu

The Table menu contains three commands for selecting in a table: Select Row, Select Column, and Select Table. Each command selects the portion of the table that its name describes. The Table Select Row and Table Select Column commands select the row or the column that contains the insertion point or the selection. If you have already selected cells in more than one row, the Table Select Row command selects all the cells in all the rows that contain selected cells. Likewise, if you have already selected cells in more than one column, the Table Select Column command selects all the cells in all the columns that contain selected cells.

Working with Table Text

Within each cell, you can change text the same way you do outside a table. But when you cross cell boundaries or want to insert a tab

TABLE 8-3.   Keys Used for Moving and Selecting Within a Table.

Key	Action
↑	Moves the insertion point up one cell in the same column (or out of the table from the top row) when the insertion point is located in the top line of a cell.
↓	Moves the insertion point down one cell in the same column (or out of the table from the bottom row) when the insertion point is located in the bottom line of a cell.
←	Moves the insertion point left one cell in the same row when the insertion point is located at the beginning of the text in a cell. If the cell is the first cell in the row, pressing ← moves the insertion point to the preceding row's row marker (or out of the table from the upper left cell).
→	Moves the insertion point right one cell in the same row when the insertion point is located at the end of the text in a cell. If the insertion point is at the row marker, pressing → moves the insertion point to the first cell in the next row (or out of the table from the last row marker).
Tab	Selects the contents of the next cell. At the end of the row, pressing Tab selects the contents of the first cell of the next row. At the end of the last row, pressing Tab adds a new row to the bottom of the table.
Shift+Tab	Selects the contents of the preceding cell. At the beginning of a row, pressing Shift+Tab selects the contents of the last cell of the preceding row. If you press Shift+Tab in the first cell of the table, Word beeps to let you know that you cannot back up any farther.
Home	Moves the insertion point to the beginning of the current line in the cell.
End	Moves the insertion point to the end of the current line in the cell.
Alt+Home	Moves the insertion point to the beginning of the first cell in the current row.
Alt+End	Moves the insertion point to the beginning of the last cell in the current row.
Alt+Page Up	Moves the insertion point to the beginning of the top cell in the current column.
Alt+Page Down	Moves the insertion point to the beginning of the bottom cell in the current column.
Alt+5*	Selects the entire table.
Shift+↑, Shift+↓, Shift+←, Shift+→	Selects text or content within a cell. When the selection crosses a cell boundary, pressing one of these shortcut keys selects a whole cell.
F8	When pressed once, F8 turns on Extend mode so that the arrow keys can be used to select text or content from the insertion point position, as it does in regular text. Pressing F8 twice selects the current word; pressing it three times selects the current line or the entire sentence; pressing it four times selects the entire cell; and pressing it five times selects the entire section or document.

* Located on the numeric keypad, pressed with Num Lock turned off.

character in a cell, some things change. The following sections explain those changes for inserting a tab character in a cell, deleting cell contents, pasting contents into cells, or copying and moving cell contents.

Inserting a Tab Character

As you work with text in a cell, you might want to set up some of the text as columns or tabular material within a single cell. In most such cases, you'll find that the best solution is to draw another column in the table. However, if you do need to insert a tab character in a cell, you don't simply press the Tab key. Remember that the Tab key is used for moving and selecting within a table. To insert a tab character in a cell, press Ctrl+Tab.

Removing Text from Cells

? SEE ALSO

For more information about removing or rearranging cells, see "Reshaping a Table," page 307.

To remove text from cells, you use the same steps you use for regular text: select the text, and then use the Cut or Clear command. When you select an entire row, the Cut command removes both the cells and their contents. Using the Clear command when your selection is completely within a table removes the text from the cells but does not remove the cells themselves; the empty cells remain in the table. Pressing Delete also does this. Note, however, that if your selection includes part or all of a table as well as text outside the table, the Clear command does delete both the cells and their text, as well as the selected text outside the table. When you cut a selection that contains cells, Word places both the cells and their text on the Clipboard.

Pasting Cells and Their Contents

Using the Paste command, you can paste cells that you have put on the Clipboard to the current insertion point position, either outside or inside a table. If the insertion point is located outside a table, your pasting inserts a table of the same size, shape, and format as the cells on the Clipboard. If the insertion point is located in a table cell, your pasting inserts the cell contents from the Clipboard into the existing table.

When you paste cells (not entire rows or columns) into an existing table, the contents of the cells on the Clipboard replace the contents of existing cells in a corresponding number and shape, beginning at the insertion point. For selections on the Clipboard that require more columns than the table has, Word adds columns as needed—to the end of the row in a standard table or within the row in a complex table. If pasting the Clipboard contents creates more rows than the existing table has, Word adds the rows of cells from the Clipboard to the table below the row that contains the insertion point.

The Table Shortcut Menu

When you position the mouse pointer within a table and click the right mouse button, Word displays a Table shortcut menu. This shortcut menu contains some of the handiest commands for working in tables. The commands that appear on the Table shortcut menu change depending on what, if anything, you've selected in the table. The following shows the commands offered by this menu, depending on what is selected in the table.

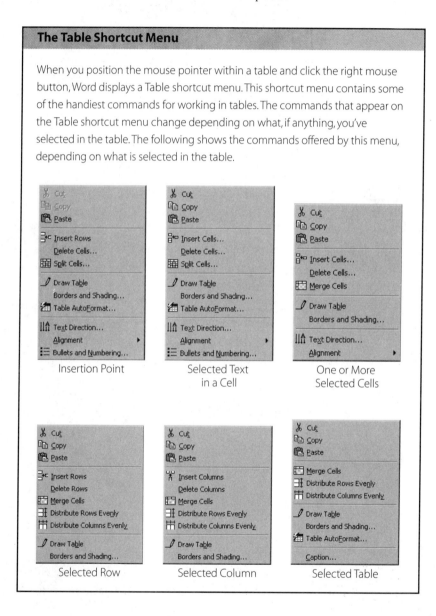

When the Clipboard contains table cells—individual cells, whole rows, whole columns, or an entire table—the Paste command on the Edit menu usually changes its name to Paste Cells. However, if the insertion point is anywhere in the first column of a table or if you select rows (or an entire table) and the Clipboard contains rows (or an entire table), the command becomes Paste Rows. If the insertion point is anywhere in the first row or if you select columns and the Clipboard contains columns, the command becomes Paste Columns. If you choose Paste Rows, Word adds rows to the table; if you choose Paste Columns, Word adds columns.

You can select cells in a table and then paste cells from the Clipboard into the selection, but you must be certain that the selection in the table is exactly the same size and shape as the cells on the Clipboard. If your selection is a different shape or size, the following message appears:

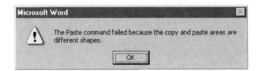

It's usually better to position the insertion point in the cell where the pasting should begin rather than selecting a group of cells in the table. The insertion point method always works because Word can determine the correct size and shape of the group of cells it needs. (If you accidentally replace cell contents that you want to keep, click the Undo button on the Standard toolbar or choose the Edit Undo command to undo the pasting.)

If the Clipboard contains only text taken from outside a table, you can paste the contents into a single table cell. But if the Clipboard contains a mixture of text from both inside and outside a table, you cannot paste the Clipboard's contents into a table. If you try, Word displays a message telling you that this won't work.

To paste cells into an existing table when the Clipboard contains a mixture of cells and regular text, first paste the contents of the Clipboard outside the table. Then select only the table portion of the newly pasted text, choose the Edit Cut command, and paste the cells into the table.

TABLE 8-4.　The Various Cell-Pasting Possibilities.

Contents of Clipboard	Position of Insertion Point	Result
Individual cells	Anywhere in a table	Replaces cell contents; adds rows and columns as needed
Entire row(s)	In the first column or in a selected row	Inserts the row(s) above the row containing the insertion point
Entire row(s)	Anywhere except in the first column	Replaces cell contents; adds rows and columns as needed
Entire column(s)	In the first row or in a selected column	Inserts the column(s) to the left of the column containing the insertion point
Entire column(s)	Anywhere except in the first row	Replaces cell contents; adds rows and columns as needed

Copying and Moving Cell Contents

The commands and shortcut keys for copying and moving work for cell contents just as they do for regular text outside tables—with a few restrictions.

When you use the Copy (Shift+F2) and Move (F2) shortcut keys, select within only one cell at a time. If you select any cell markers and press one of these keys, the message *This is not a valid selection* appears. When you see this message, click OK, select contents (but not the cell marker) within only one cell, and then try the Copy or the Move shortcut key again. If you want to copy or move entire cells, including their contents and fonts, select the cell marker as well as the contents, and then use any copy or move method except the Copy and Move shortcut keys.

When you want to copy contents from multiple cells, select the contents, choose the Edit Copy command or click the Copy button, position the insertion point where the copy is to appear, and then choose the Edit Paste command or click the Paste button. Word also lets you copy and move contents from a cell to outside a table, from outside a table into a cell, and from a cell in one table into another cell in the same table or into a cell in another table.

You can also copy and move contents in a table by the drag-and-drop method. To do so, select the cells, and drag to move, or hold down Ctrl and drag to copy cell contents to a new cell location.

Reshaping a Table

You can make many changes to the number of cells in a table. You can insert or delete cells, rows, or columns, and you can merge and split cells.

Adding Rows and Columns

You can insert rows and columns anywhere in a table. When you do, Word inserts new rows above the row that contains the insertion point and new columns to the left of the column that contains the insertion point. Therefore, adding new rows to the bottom of a table or new columns to the right side of a table requires special steps, as outlined in "Adding a Row at the Bottom of a Table" and "Adding a Column on the Right Side of a Table."

New rows inserted in a table with the Table Insert Rows command have the same cell and text format as the cells in the row below them, but a new row added at the bottom of the table has the same cell and text format as the cells in the row above it. Likewise, new columns inserted in the table with the Table Insert Columns command have the same cell and text format as cells in the column to the right of the new columns, but a new column added to the right side of a table has the same cell and text format as the cells in the column to the left.

Inserting a Row Above a Row

Insert
Rows

To insert a row anywhere in a table other than at the bottom, you use the Insert Rows button on the Standard toolbar or the Table Insert Rows command. The Insert Table button becomes the Insert Rows button when the insertion point is in a table or when you have selected one or more rows in a table.

To add a row above a row, take these steps:

1 Select the row immediately below where you want a new row. If you select more than one row, Word inserts that number of new rows above the top row of the selection.

2 Click the Insert Rows button on the Standard toolbar, or choose the Table Insert Rows command.

In the new rows, each cell has the same size and formatting as the cell immediately below it.

Adding a Row at the Bottom of a Table

When you need to make a table longer, it's a simple matter to add a row to the bottom of the table.

1 Position the insertion point in the last row's last cell.

2 Press the Tab key. Word adds a new row to the bottom of the table.

Inserting a Column to the Left of a Column

Insert
Columns

To insert a column anywhere in a table other than at the right side of the table, you use the Insert Columns button on the Standard toolbar or the Table Insert Columns command. The Insert Table button becomes the Insert Columns button when you have selected one or more columns in a table.

To insert a column to the left of a column, take these steps:

1 Select the column to the right of where you want the new column. If you select more than one column, Word inserts that number of new columns to the left of the selection.

2 Click the Insert Columns button on the Standard toolbar, or choose the Table Insert Columns command.

In the new columns, each cell is the same width as the cell beside it in the first column of the selection.

Adding a Column on the Right Side of a Table

Occasionally, you might want to insert another column at the right side of a table, a process that is similar to inserting a new column at the left side of an existing cell or column. When you insert a column at a table's right side, however, you must select the row markers outside the last cell in each row. To insert a new column at the right side of a table, take these steps:

1 Select the row markers in the table by positioning the mouse pointer above the markers and clicking the left mouse button.

2 Click the Insert Columns button on the Standard toolbar, or choose the Table Insert Columns command.

Notice that each cell in the new column is the same width as the cell to its left.

Inserting a Cell

You can add a cell or a group of cells anywhere in the table.

1 Select a cell or a group of cells. To insert a single cell, select the cell to the right of where you want the new cell. To insert a group of cells, select the group of cells that occupies the area where you want the new cells to appear, as shown in Figure 8-4. Word will insert the same number of cells as you have selected.

FIGURE 8-4.
Select where you want Word to insert the new group of cells.

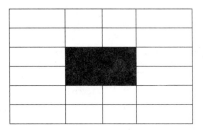

Insert
Cells

2 Click the Insert Cells button on the Standard toolbar, or choose the Table Insert Cells command. The Insert Table button becomes the Insert Cells button when you have selected one or more cells (but not entire rows or columns).

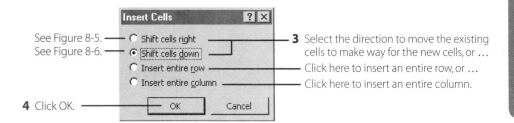

See Figure 8-5. — Shift cells right
See Figure 8-6. — Shift cells down

3 Select the direction to move the existing cells to make way for the new cells, or …

Insert entire row — Click here to insert an entire row, or …

Insert entire column — Click here to insert an entire column.

4 Click OK. — OK   Cancel

Publications

Figure 8-5 and Figure 8-6 show examples of how Word inserts groups of cells.

FIGURE 8-5.
How Word inserts a group of cells when you select Shift Cells Right.

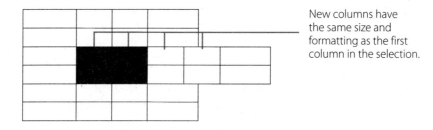

New columns have the same size and formatting as the first column in the selection.

FIGURE 8-6.
How Word inserts a group of cells when you select Shift Cells Down.

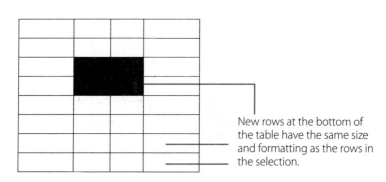

New rows at the bottom of the table have the same size and formatting as the rows in the selection.

Removing Cells, Rows, and Columns

When you select entire rows, you can use the Table Delete Rows command or the Cut command to delete any number of rows in a table. When you select cells but not entire rows, using the Cut command deletes the cell contents but not the cells themselves. Pressing the Delete key deletes the contents of selected cells—even if you selected rows rather than cells. Deleting cells has no effect on the formatting of empty cells or on the contents or formatting of the rest of the table.

Removing Cells

You can remove one cell or a group of cells from multiple rows and columns by following these steps:

1 Select the cells you want to remove.

2 Choose the Table Delete Cells command.

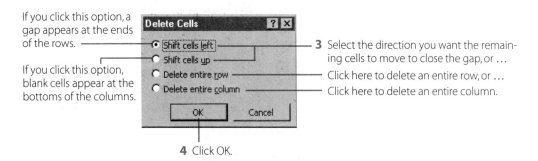

If you click this option, a gap appears at the ends of the rows. ──────

If you click this option, blank cells appear at the bottoms of the columns.

3 Select the direction you want the remaining cells to move to close the gap, or …

Click here to delete an entire row, or …

Click here to delete an entire column.

4 Click OK.

Removing Rows

To remove rows from a table, select the rows, and then choose the Table Delete Rows command or use the Cut command.

Removing Columns

To remove columns from a table, select the columns, and then choose the Table Delete Columns command or use the Cut command.

Merging Cells

Word lets you merge cells, which combines cell contents in the merged cells. (You can also split cells, as described in the following section.)

Take these steps to merge cells:

1 Select any group of cells, for example cells F, G, J, and K, as shown.

A¤	B¤	C¤	D¤	¤
E¤	F¤	G¤	H¤	¤
I¤	J¤	K¤	L¤	¤
M¤	N¤	O¤	P¤	¤

2 Choose the Table Merge Cells command.

Publications

Merged cells look like this:

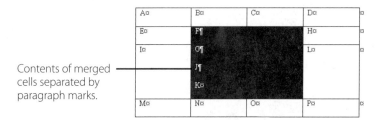

Contents of merged cells separated by paragraph marks.

Splitting Cells

As you set up a table, you might find that you need additional columns or rows in part of a table, but not for entire rows or columns. When this situation arises, it's time to split some cells.

To split cells, take these steps:

1 Select the cells you want to split.

2 Choose the Table Split Cells command.

3 Set the number of columns for each selected cell.

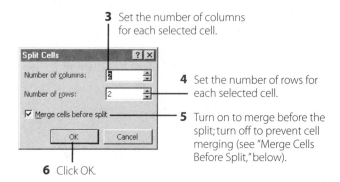

4 Set the number of rows for each selected cell.

5 Turn on to merge before the split; turn off to prevent cell merging (see "Merge Cells Before Split," below).

6 Click OK.

Merge Cells Before Split

With the Merge Cells Before Split check box turned on, Word combines all the selected cells into one cell, and then splits the cells into the number of columns and rows you set. The contents of the selected cells split as outlined in the sidebar "How Many Split Cells?" on the next page. With the Merge Cells Before Split check box turned off, Word splits the cells into the number of columns and rows you set and simply splits the contents of the selected cells as described in the following section.

How Many Split Cells?

There are restrictions on the number of splits you can select. For columns, remember that a table can have a total of only 63 columns. The number you set in the Split Cells dialog box (to indicate how many cells you want each split cell to yield) must be between 2 and 63. But 63 might produce too many columns. Word shows you a message if that will be the case.

The maximum number of columns you can set for a split is 63 minus the number of unsplit columns there will be after the split. Stated another way, the total number of columns is equal to the number of cells in a row that are left unsplit, plus the number of cells that are split.

For example, suppose you have a 21-column table. You select a row of cells across 10 columns to split. The maximum number you can set in the Split Cells dialog box is 52. Because there will be 11 unsplit cells, and the maximum number of columns is 63, you can set 63–11, or 52 cells. If you were to set 53 in the Split Cells dialog box, that would make 53+11, or 64 columns, which is over the limit of 63.

The fewer columns in a row and the fewer cells you select to split, the more splits you can set.

For rows, there are more restrictions on the number of splits you can select.

- If the selected cells are all in one row and the Merge Cells Before Split box is turned on, the maximum number of rows you can set depends on the number of cells you have selected.

  - If you select one cell, the maximum number of rows you can set 11.

  - If you select two cells, the maximum number of rows you can set is 22.

  - If you select three cells, the maximum number of rows you can set is 33.

  - If you select four or more cells, the maximum number of rows you can set is 45.

- If the selected cells are all in one row and the Merge Cells Before Split box is turned off, the maximum number of rows you can set is 11.

- If the selected cells are in more than one row and the Merge Cells Before Split box is turned on, the maximum number of rows you can set is the number of rows you have selected.

- If the selected cells are in more than one row and the Merge Cells Before Split box is turned off, Word sets the number of rows to 1 and deactivates the Number Of Rows box so that you can't change the number of rows.

III

Publications

How Cell Contents Split

When you split a cell, Word divides the cell into the number of cells you specify and divides any text by placing one paragraph in each column. If the selected cell contains more paragraphs than columns after splitting, Word distributes the paragraphs so that the first one appears in the first column and the last one appears in the last column, with the rest distributed evenly among the columns. For example, look at this cell containing multiple paragraphs:

A¤	B¤	C¤	D¤	¤
E¤	F¶ Z¶ Y¶ X¶ W¤	G¤	H¤	¤
I¤	J¤	K¤	L¤	¤
M¤	N¤	O¤	P¤	¤

If you split this cell into two columns, here is the result:

A¤	B¤		C¤	D¤	¤
E¤	F¶ Z¶ Y¤	X¶ W¤	G¤	H¤	¤
I¤	J¤		K¤	L¤	¤
M¤	N¤		O¤	P¤	¤

If you choose Edit Undo Split Cells and then split the cell into four columns, this is the result:

A¤	B¤				C¤	D¤	¤
E¤	F¶ Z¤	Y¤	X¤	W¤	G¤	H¤	¤
I¤	J¤				K¤	L¤	¤
M¤	N¤				O¤	P¤	¤

Sorting Inside and Outside of Tables

After you squeeze content into table cells, you might find that the order of rows in a table isn't quite the best for your purposes. You need to sort the table. Or you might want to sort the table several different ways to emphasize a point about the content for a particular column or row. For these situations, you use the Table Sort command.

You can sort a table or text in either ascending or descending order. (For more information about ascending vs. descending order, see the sidebar "What Ascending and Descending Mean," page 323.) In addition, you can sort a table or text with one, two, or three "sorting keys." A sorting key is the column of the table or text you want Word to sort. A single key sort sorts all the rows based on one column. A multiple key sort sorts all the rows based on two or three columns.

You can also use the Table Sort command to sort text that's not in a table. When you select text outside a table, the command becomes Table Sort Text. You'll find more about that in "Sorting Text," page 324.

Single Key Table Sorts

To sort all table rows with a single sort key (based on one column), take these steps:

1 Position the insertion point anywhere in the table. Word sorts the entire table unless you turn on a special option—for more on this, see "Table Sorting Options," page 321.

2 Choose the Table Sort command.

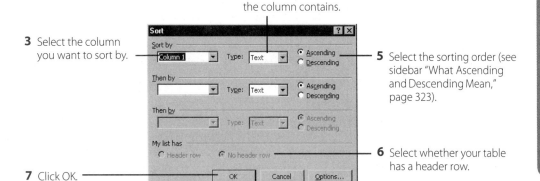

4 Select the type of information the column contains.

3 Select the column you want to sort by.

5 Select the sorting order (see sidebar "What Ascending and Descending Mean," page 323).

6 Select whether your table has a header row.

7 Click OK.

III

Publications

Sort By

The Sort By box lists the columns you have selected. If you select only one column, the Sort By box lists only one column. If you select three columns, the Sort By box lists them by their numbers (for example, column 1, column 2, and column 3). If you select the entire table, the Sort By box lists all the columns.

If you turn on the Header Row option, the Sort By box lists the names of the columns. The names come from the contents of the cells in the first row of the table—up to three words for each column. If you turn on the No Header Row option, Word lists the columns as Column 1, Column 2, and so on.

My List Has

If you want the top row of a table to stay at the top, turn on the Header Row option. If you want the top row of a table sorted into its proper place in the sorting order, turn on the No Header Row option.

NOTE

> If you turn on the Headings setting for the top row of a table (Table Headings command), Word automatically turns on the Header Row option, and then deactivates the My List Has choices so that you can't change the choice. For sorting purposes, only the top row of a table is considered a heading row, with one exception: if you turn on the Headings setting for more than one row at the top of a table, sorting recognizes all those rows as part of the headings of columns. Remember, though, that the Headings setting *must* include the topmost row.

Multiple Key Table Sorts

Most of the time you'll sort only one column at a time, but you might have a table that you want to sort several ways.

For example, suppose you have a table that lists dates in column 1, names in column 2, and dollar amounts in column 3. Now suppose that you want to sort the dates in ascending order (earliest to latest), the names in ascending order (alphabetical order), and the dollar amounts in descending order (largest to smallest). For a case like this, you can direct Word to perform a multiple sort, as shown on the next page.

1 Select the table. It's important to select all the columns you want Word to sort.

2 Choose the Table Sort command.

3 Select the most important column here.   **4** Select its type here.

6 Select the next most important column here.

9 Select the third most important column here.

12 If you have column headings, turn on the Header Row option.

13 Click OK.

5 Select the sort order for this column.

7 Select its type here.

8 Select the sort order for this column.

10 Select its type here.

11 Select the sort order for this column.

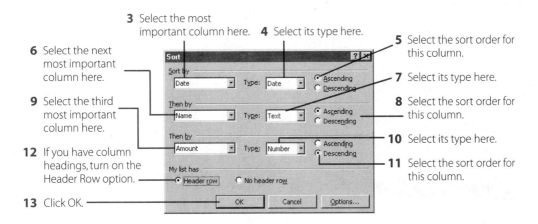

Sort By, Then By, Then By

The guideline for selecting columns in the Sort By and Then By boxes in the Sort dialog box is to select the most important column first, then the next most important, and then the third most important. Word then sorts identical items in any column in the order you set for the items in the next most important column.

Table Sorting Options

The Options button in the Sort dialog box gives you additional options for sorting. When you click the Options button with the entire table selected, you see the Sort Options dialog box shown here:

When you select an entire table, you can't sort by column only.

If you select one column, several columns, all the columns, or some cells, but not the entire table, you see the Sort Options dialog box shown here:

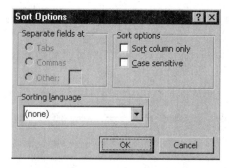

Here's what the options do for your sorting.

Sort Column Only

If you want to sort only some columns or cells and leave all the other columns in their current order, turn on the Sort Column Only check box. Word then sorts only the selected columns or cells. With this check box turned off, Word sorts the entire table. This check box is inactive when you have selected an entire table.

 NOTE

> Be aware that when you sort a column only, any connection between the content in the various columns is broken.

Case Sensitive

As pointed out in the sidebar "What Ascending and Descending Mean," Word usually ignores the case of letters for sorting. If, however, it's important that lowercase precede uppercase when sorting in ascending order, turn on the Case Sensitive check box. When you turn on the Case Sensitive check box, "after" comes before "After." With the Case Sensitive check box turned off, Word sorts "After" and "after" in their relative order in the table. For example, if "After" appears near the top of the table and "after" appears near the bottom, an ascending sort puts "After" before "after."

There's a little more to this, too. Word looks at each letter to sort words. If similar words have various combinations of uppercase and lowercase letters—for example, "After," "after," "aFter," and "AFter"—an ascending sort rearranges the words into this order: "after," "aFter," "After," "AFter," when the Case Sensitive check box is turned on.

Sorting Language

If the table contains text or dates in the format of a language other than the language for which Windows is set up, you can select that language so that Word sorts the table properly for that language. Note, however, that you must have the proper language dictionary installed before Word can sort words in that language. For more information, see "Writing Your Report in Another Language," page 411.

What Ascending and Descending Mean

What do "ascending" and "descending" mean in sorting? Basically, ascending means from lowest to highest, and descending means from highest to lowest—just like ascending or descending in an elevator. For numbers, this is pretty easy to understand. For letters, it's not too much more difficult to grasp. For dates, it can be a little more of a challenge. There are also a couple of tricky steps along the way.

First, the basics. The following table gives some examples of ascending vs. descending for each of the three types of content—numbers, letters, and dates.

Type	Ascending	Descending
Numbers	0, 1, 2, 3, 4, 5, 6, 7, 8, 9	9, 8, 7, 6, 5, 4, 3, 2, 1, 0
Text (letters)	A, B, C ... X, Y, Z	Z, Y, X ... C, B, A
	After before *Zebra*	*Zebra* before *After*
	Bath before *Young*	*Young* before *Bath*
	Cat before *Xylophone*	*Xylophone* before *Cat*
Dates	Earlier date to later date	Later date to earlier date
	March 3, 1996, before January 8, 1997	January 8, 1997, before March 3, 1996

For letters, Word is usually set up to ignore case. That is, Word sees no difference between a capital letter and a lowercase letter. You can change this, however; see "Text Sorting Options," page 325.

Publications III

Sorting Text

While it's more common to sort tables than to sort regular text, you might have occasion to sort outside a table. You can sort paragraphs, and you can sort tabular text separated by tab characters, commas, or some other character you choose.

To sort text outside a table, take these steps:

1 Select the text you want to sort.

2 Choose the Table Sort command.

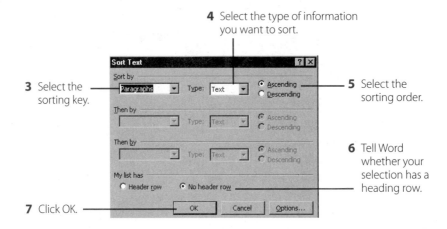

4 Select the type of information you want to sort.

3 Select the sorting key.

5 Select the sorting order.

6 Tell Word whether your selection has a heading row.

7 Click OK.

Sort By and Then By

When you select tabular text, Word lists Paragraphs and either Field numbers or column headings in the Sort By and Then By boxes. You see *Field* when you turn on the No Header Row option. You see the column headings for the tabular text when you turn on the Header Row option. *Field* means tabular text separated by tab characters, commas, or some other character you choose in the Sort Options dialog box. (See the next section, "Text Sorting Options," for details.)

Note that if you select Paragraphs in the Sort By box, you can't perform multiple key sorts on text outside a table. If, however, you select a field in Sort By, you can then set up a multiple key sort. For information about multiple key sorting, see "Multiple Key Table Sorts," page 320.

Text Sorting Options

The Options button in the Sort Text dialog box gives you some additional options for sorting text. When you click the Options button with text selected, you see the Sort Options dialog box, shown here:

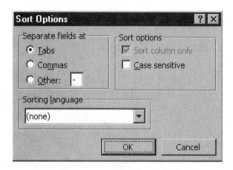

In addition to the Case Sensitive check box (see "Table Sorting Options," page 321, for details), you can choose the character that separates the fields of tabular text.

To select columns in text set up with tab characters, position the insertion point at one corner of the column, hold down the Alt key, and then drag with the left mouse button to the opposite corner of the column. With tabular text selected this way, the Sort Column Only check box in the Sort Options dialog box will be active.

Separate Fields At

Most people who don't use Word's tables use tab characters to separate columns in tabular text, but you might also separate columns with commas or with another character, including any letter, number, or symbol. To tell Word that your tabular text uses a character other than tab to separate columns, either turn on the Commas option or turn on the Other option. If you turn on the Other option, type the character in the box to the right of the Other label.

Word tries to determine the field separators and automatically selects either the Tabs or Commas option. Word cannot detect other types of field separators and won't select the Other option.

Numbering Cells

There are times when it becomes necessary to number rows or columns or even, I suppose, an entire table. Numbering cells is relatively easy.

In tables, there are a couple of points you need to keep in mind:

- Word numbers every selected cell.

- Word numbers a table across rows.

- Word numbers every paragraph in every selected cell.

To number cells in a table, take these steps:

1 Select all the cells that you want to number.

2 Click the Numbering button on the Formatting toolbar.

Different Table Numbering Schemes

Numbering

The Numbering button on the Formatting toolbar uses the numbering scheme you last used in the Bullets And Numbering dialog box. Most of the time, the numbers will be Arabic numerals followed by a period (1.). If you want a different numbering scheme—for example, no period or a different number form such as alphabetic or Roman numerals—number your table cells with the Format Bullets And Numbering command rather than with the Numbering button on the Formatting toolbar.

For more complete details on the Format Bullets And Numbering command, see "Bulleted Lists," page 588, "Numbered Lists," page 592, and "Lists Within Lists," page 599.

Formatting a Table

Formatting a table includes adjusting the column widths, adjusting the row heights, spacing the columns, indenting rows, aligning rows, and setting cell borders and shading. For all table adjustments and formatting, you can use the Table AutoFormat command. Or you can choose separate commands for each of these formatting tasks. In addition, you can use the rulers to fit rows and columns.

Hiring Table AutoFormat

The Table menu and the Table shortcut menu contain the Table AutoFormat command. In a table, choose this command to see the Table AutoFormat dialog box, shown here:

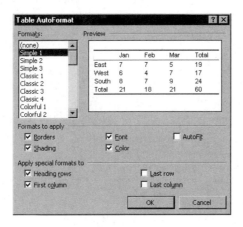

You use the Table menu's Table AutoFormat command and its dialog box to select a preset table setup. To preview the choices, select each one in the Formats list and study its effect in the Preview box. Select (None) in the Formats list and click OK when you want to remove an existing table setup, regardless of whether the setup was one you crafted or was crafted by Table AutoFormat.

The one dialog box option that continues to affect your table's formatting even if you select (None) is the AutoFit check box. When you turn on this check box, Word makes each column of the table as wide as the widest cell contents in that column. If you have already set column widths as you want them but you want to use Table AutoFormat for borders, shading, and other table formatting, turn off the AutoFit check box. For more details on the AutoFit check box, see "Adjusting Column Width to the Best Fit," page 329.

You can change the preset schemes by changing the Formats To Apply check boxes. If you turn off all these check boxes, your table has no formatting. If you turn on one or more of the check boxes, Word adds formatting set for the preset setup you selected in the Formats list. You can add borders, shading, fonts, and color to your tables.

Note that some of the Formats To Apply check boxes depend on others. If you have the Shading check box and the Borders check box turned on, the Color check box replaces gray shading and borders with colored shading and borders. The effect of the Font box depends on the options you select in the Apply Special Formats To check boxes. The Font check box controls what special font settings are used by the choices in the Apply Special Formats To check boxes. When you turn off the Font check box, all content in the table appears with the font settings you apply directly or with styles.

The Apply Special Formats To check boxes let you choose which parts of the table should have special formatting. The formatting for those parts depends on the design of the preset setup and the Formats To Apply check boxes you turn on.

The best way to get a feel for what the Table AutoFormat dialog box offers is to explore the different combinations of options. The Preview box lets you see the result without closing the dialog box. When you are satisfied with your selections, click OK.

If you prefer table formatting that is different from the choices in the Formats list, you can create your own table formatting. First format your table, and then save it as AutoText. For information about storing a special table as AutoText, see "Storing Table Setups," page 358.

Fitting Columns

As you create tables, you can adjust column width. When you initially craft an empty table, all its columns are equally wide. Their width is either one that Word calculated or one that you set in the Column Width box in the Insert Table dialog box.

You can quickly change the column width to the best fit for the cell contents. To separately adjust the width of a cell, column, row, or table, you can use the mouse and column border lines, the mouse and the ruler, or the Table menu commands.

Adjusting Column Width to the Best Fit

Rather than struggle to make column widths just right for the width of their contents, you can use the mouse, use the AutoFit button in the Cell Height And Width dialog box, or turn on the AutoFit check box in the Table AutoFormat dialog box. To see how AutoFit works, look at this example:

One	Two	Three	Four
Five	Six	Seven	Eight
Nine	Ten	Eleven	Twelve
Thirteen	Fourteen	Fifteen	Sixteen

To adjust the columns with the mouse, double-click the table's leftmost vertical gridline. The table now looks like this:

One	Two	Three	Four
Five	Six	Seven	Eight
Nine	Ten	Eleven	Twelve
Thirteen	Fourteen	Fifteen	Sixteen

To adjust the columns to fit the cell contents, take these steps:

1 Select the entire table.

2 Choose the Table Cell Height And Width command.

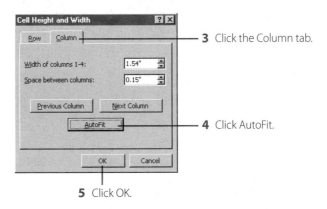

3 Click the Column tab.

4 Click AutoFit.

5 Click OK.

In the Table AutoFormat dialog box, turn on the AutoFit check box to have Word adjust column width as part of the process of formatting the table. For more information about the Table AutoFormat command, see "Hiring Table AutoFormat," page 327.

Adjusting Individual Columns and Cells
To adjust a single column to its best fit, select the column, and then double-click the vertical gridline on either side of the column. To adjust a single cell, select the entire cell (including the cell marker), and then double-click the vertical gridline on either side of the cell. To adjust a selection of cells, double-click a vertical gridline of one of the selected cells.

Using the Mouse and Column Borders to Set Column Width

The mouse gives you the power to set the width of columns visually. You can adjust column width in three ways:

- By changing the width of one column and the column to its right

- By changing the width of one column and all columns to its right

- By changing the width of one column only, without changing the width of the column to its right

The first two methods leave the total height of the rows at their current total height. The third method changes the total height of the rows in which you change column widths.

Before you start setting column widths with the mouse, turn on the ruler by choosing the View Ruler command.

To adjust the width of one column and the column to its right, take these steps:

1 Position the mouse pointer on the right border of the column you want to adjust. The mouse pointer changes to a vertical bar with two horizontal arrowheads:

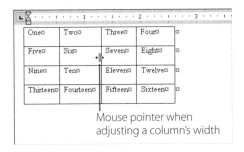

Mouse pointer when adjusting a column's width

2 Drag the column border left or right to the width you want. Notice that the column to the right of the border you drag widens or narrows so that the other columns and the table retain their original widths.

To adjust the width of one column and all columns to its right, take these steps:

1 Position the mouse pointer on the right border of the column you want to adjust.

2 Hold down the Ctrl key while you drag the right column border.

The columns to the right of the moved border move along with it, making the width of the columns expand or contract accordingly.

To adjust the width of one column only, without changing the width of the columns to its right, take these steps:

1 Position the mouse pointer on the right border of the column you want to adjust.

2 Hold down Shift as you drag the column border left or right to the width you want.

The widths of the other columns stay the same, but the table becomes narrower or wider.

III

Publications

Using the Mouse and the Ruler to Set Column Width

To set column width with the mouse and the ruler, take these steps:

1 Position the insertion point in a cell in the column you want to adjust.

2 Turn on the View Ruler command if it is not already turned on. When the insertion point or a selection is in a table, column markers appear on the ruler, as shown here:

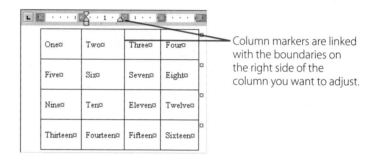

Column markers are linked with the boundaries on the right side of the column you want to adjust.

3 Drag column markers on the ruler. You get the same results with dragging, dragging with the Shift key, and dragging with the Ctrl key as you do when you drag column borders in a table. (For details, see "Using the Mouse and Column Borders to Set Column Width," page 330.)

Using the Table Cell Height And Width Command to Set Column Width

Although the mouse allows you to adjust column width visually, the Cell Height And Width command on the Table menu gives you both more precision and more flexibility. You can set all selected columns to the same width or set each column to a different width. To use the Cell Height And Width command to set column width, you click the Column tab in the Cell Height And Width dialog box.

To set the same width for all selected columns, take these steps:

1 Position the insertion point in the one column whose width you want to adjust, select one or more columns whose width you want to make the same, or select the entire table to make all the columns the same width. (For another way to make columns the same width, see "Setting Columns to Auto Width," page 334.)

2 Choose the Table Cell Height And Width command.

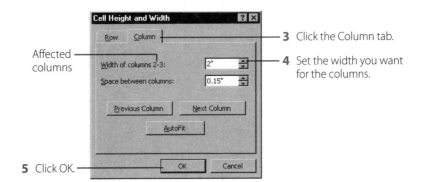

Affected columns

3 Click the Column tab.

4 Set the width you want for the columns.

5 Click OK.

To adjust several columns to different widths, take these steps:

1 Position the insertion point in the first column you want to adjust.

2 Choose the Table Cell Height And Width command, and click the Column tab.

3 Set a width in the Width Of Columns box, and then click the Next Column button.

4 For the second column you want to set, set a width in the Width Of Columns box.

5 Click the Previous Column button or the Next Column button, and set a width for each column as needed. Then click OK.

Displaying Column Widths and Row Heights on the Ruler

If you hold down the Alt key as you drag column or row borders in a table or drag column or row markers on the ruler, Word displays column-width measurements or row-height measurements on the ruler. This illustration shows column widths on the ruler:

To turn off the display of measurements, release the Alt key as you drag.

Setting Columns to Auto Width

After you adjust column widths, your table might end up either narrower or wider than the margins of the page. You can use an "Auto" width setting for some or all columns to fit the table into the width of the margins. If you select only some of the columns, Word sets the selected columns to widths that equally divide the width left over between the margins after you subtract the widths of the columns you haven't selected. For example, suppose you have a four-column table and select two columns. Suppose also that the two columns you haven't selected are each 2 inches wide and the width between the margins is 6 inches. This leaves 2 inches for the two selected columns. When you set Auto width for the two selected columns, each will be about 1 inch wide. (The columns will actually be slightly less than 1 inch because of the width between columns—see "Spacing the Columns.")

To use Auto width, take these steps:

1 Select the columns you want to set with Auto width.

2 Choose the Table Cell Height And Width command, and click the Column tab.

3 Select or type *Auto* in the Width Of Columns box. If the Width Of Columns box shows a width, you can type a zero, and then click the down arrow on the box to select Auto.

4 Click OK.

Distributing Columns Evenly

You can quickly set any number of columns to the same width. To do so, take these steps:

1 Select the columns you want to set to the same width.

2 Choose the Distribute Columns Evenly command either from the Table menu or from the Table shortcut menu.

Word divides the width of all the selected columns equally among the selected columns. The other columns you don't select keep their current width, and the table remains its current width.

Spacing the Columns

The Space Between Columns measurement on the Column tab in the Cell Height And Width dialog box sets the minimum amount of blank space that Word leaves between neighboring columns. This measurement affects all cells in the selected rows. Although the table gridlines and cell borders do not show this space, Word inserts the space when you print the table. You'll seldom change this measurement unless you have a special requirement for space between columns.

To adjust the space between columns, take these steps:

1 Select the rows you want to adjust.

2 Choose the Table Cell Height And Width command, and click the Column tab.

3 Set a width in the Space Between Columns box, and then click OK.

 NOTE

The width of the column markers on the ruler shows the width of the space between columns.

Fitting Rows

Each row in a table adjusts its height for the tallest cell in the row. A cell adjusts its height to fit all the text it contains. In some cases, you might want to set a minimum row height, even if none of the cells in the row are as tall as that height. Or you might want to set a specific cell height, no matter what fills a cell.

Using the Mouse and Row Borders to Set Row Height

The mouse gives you the power to set the height of rows visually. To adjust the height of one row only, without changing the height of the other rows, take these steps:

1 Switch to Page Layout view. (This method only works in Page Layout view.)

2 Position the mouse pointer on the bottom border of the row you want to adjust.

3 Drag the row border up or down to the height you want.

III

Publications

The widths of the other rows stay the same, but the table becomes shorter or taller.

Using the Table Cell Height And Width Command to Set Row Height

You might want some rows of a table to have a minimum height. That way these rows will always be at least the height you set but can also grow taller if you insert lots of text or a tall graphic.

To set a row to a minimum height, take these steps:

1 Position the insertion point in the cell or row you want set to a specific height.

2 Choose the Table Cell Height And Width command.

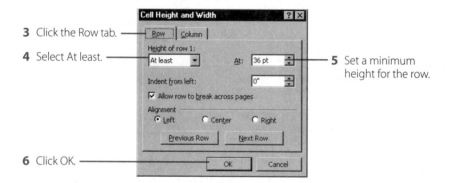

3 Click the Row tab.

4 Select At least.

5 Set a minimum height for the row.

6 Click OK.

In forms and other special tables, you might want to set a row to a specific, nonadjusting height. To freeze the row height, take these steps:

1 Select the row whose height you want to freeze.

2 Choose the Table Cell Height And Width command, and click the Row tab.

3 Select Exactly in the Height Of Row box on the Row tab.

4 Set a height in the At box.

5 Click OK.

If the cell contents are taller than the row height you set, Word displays and prints only the top portion that fits in the cell. Word keeps all of the contents in the cell, although you can't see it. You cannot scroll cell

contents. To see the complete cell contents in this case, increase the cell's height, or select Auto or At Least in the Height Of Row box on the Row tab.

> **Let Word Set the Row Height**
> To make a row fit the height of its contents, select the row, choose the Table Cell Height And Width command, click the Row tab, select Auto in the Height Of Rows box, and then click OK. Word sets the row height to fit the tallest cell in the row. This setting is the same as the setting for a new table.

Distributing Rows Evenly

After you set row heights, you might decide that you want all the table rows to have the same height, but that you also want the table to keep its current overall height. You might get into this situation, for example, by stretching the bottom row of a table to make the table fit a specific height requirement in your report. In another case, you might want several rows of a table to have equal heights, while keeping the height of the other rows unchanged.

To distribute the entire height of rows evenly among the selected rows, take these steps:

1 Select the rows you want to set with equal heights, or select the entire table to make the height of all rows equal.

2 Choose the Distribute Rows Evenly command, either from the Table menu or from the Table shortcut menu.

Word makes the heights of the selected rows equal, based on the tallest row in the selection.

Setting Row Height from the Vertical Ruler

In Page Layout view, Word displays a vertical ruler in addition to the horizontal ruler you see in Normal view.

> The vertical ruler appears only if the page in the window is the page that contains the insertion point or selection. Remember that you can scroll the document to see other pages without moving the insertion point. If you're in Page Layout view but the vertical ruler doesn't show, click somewhere on the page.

III

Publications

When the insertion point or selection is in a table, the vertical ruler shows row markers for that table:

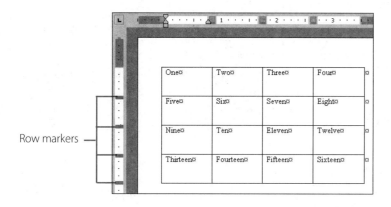

Row markers —

Each row marker is connected to the bottom boundary of a row. To increase the height of a row, drag its row marker downward on the vertical ruler. To decrease the row height, drag the row marker upward on the vertical ruler.

Dragging a row marker on the vertical ruler sets a minimum height for the row—the Height Of Rows box in the Cell Height And Width dialog box shows At Least, if you select the adjusted row.

Aligning Cell Content Vertically

If you set the row height to be taller than the content of its cells, you have three choices for vertical alignment within the cells—top, center, and bottom. To set the alignment of cells, take these steps:

Tables and Borders

1 Display the Tables And Borders toolbar—click the Tables And Borders button on the Standard toolbar.

2 Select the cells in which you want to set the vertical alignment.

3 Click the Align Top, Center Vertically, or Align Bottom button on the Tables And Borders toolbar—see Figure 8-7.

FIGURE 8-7.
The alignment buttons on the Tables And Borders toolbar.

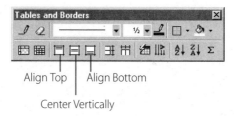

Align Top   Align Bottom

Center Vertically

Indenting Rows

You might occasionally want to indent a single row or a group of rows in a table—for example, to set it off from text. Word provides a way of indenting rows that's similar to the way you indent paragraphs. (Indenting rows does not affect cell contents. The cell contents have their own indention set with the Format Paragraph command.)

Because you can indent each row individually, you can set every row to a different indent. To indent only one row, select a cell in that row only. To indent several rows the same amount, select a cell in each row you want to indent. If you want to set the entire table to the same indent, select an entire column.

To indent a table from the left margin, take these steps:

1 Select at least one cell in each row you want to indent. To indent the entire table, select at least one column.

2 Choose the Table Cell Height And Width command, and then click the Row tab.

3 In the Indent From Left box, set a measurement to indent the table that distance from the left margin. Set a positive measurement to push the selected rows to the right. Set a negative measurement to pull the selected rows to the left.

4 Click OK.

Positioning Rows Between the Margins

For tables that are narrower than the page margins, you can set the position of a row between the document's margins. Word provides three positions for rows on the Row tab in the Cell Height And Width dialog box:

- Left: the left edge of the row lines up with the left margin.

- Right: the right edge of the row lines up with the right margin.

- Center: the row is centered between the margins.

Because you can position each row individually, you can position every row differently. To position only one row, select a cell in that row only. To place several rows in the same between-margins position, select a cell in each row you want to position. To position the entire

III

Publications

table, select an entire column. You can use the Indent From Left setting to vary the location used for the left margin when calculating alignment.

To align a table, take these steps:

1 Select at least one cell in each row for which you want to change the alignment. To align the entire table, select at least one column.

2 Choose the Table Cell Height And Width command, and then click the Row tab.

3 Click the alignment you want for the rows—Left, Center, or Right.

4 Click OK.

Row positioning does not affect cell contents. Within cells, use the Format Paragraph command or the alignment buttons on the Formatting toolbar to align text.

If you select an entire row, you can click the alignment buttons on the Formatting toolbar to align the text within the selected cells left, center, or right.

Changing Borders and Shading

When you insert a table, Word gives the table ½-point black borders around every cell. You can change the thickness, style, color, and arrangement of borders around individual cells, around a group of cells, or around the entire table, and you can add borders to cell contents, too. You can also choose colors and patterns for shading cells and their contents.

The steps for changing borders and adding shading also apply to document contents outside tables.

Changing Borders

The Borders tab in the Table Borders And Shading dialog box, shown below, gives you lots of choices for border styles and for colors, plus some preset border designs.

To change a table border, take these steps:

1 Select the text or cells for which you want to change the borders.

2 Choose the Format Borders And Shading command.

3 Click the Borders tab.

4 Click a border setting.

5 Select a line style.

6 Select a line color.

7 Select a line width.

10 To apply shading now, click the Shading tab.

9 For custom borders, click lines or button.

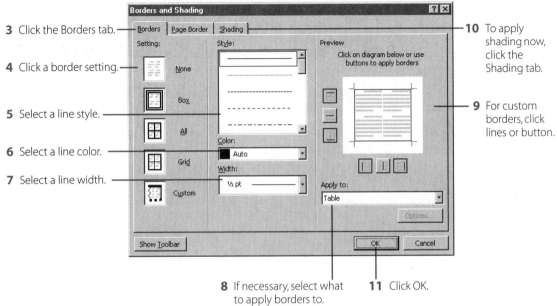

8 If necessary, select what to apply borders to.

11 Click OK.

Border Setting

You see five choices for border setting in the Borders And Shading dialog box. There are, however, two sets of five choices. Which set of five choices you see depends on your choice in the Apply To box.

- If you select Table in the Apply To box, you have the choices None, Box, All, Grid, and Custom.

- If you select Text or Paragraph in the Apply To box, Shadow replaces All, and Three-D replaces Grid.

- If you select Cell in the Apply To box, the set of border setting buttons you see depends on your selection in the table. If you select two or more cells, you see the five choices you have for Table. If you select one cell, select some or all of the contents of a cell, or position the insertion point in a cell, you see the five choices you have for Text and Paragraph.

III

Publications

Table 8-5 lists all the choices and their effects on the selection. All of the border setting choices affect the portion of the selection you choose in the Apply To box.

TABLE 8-5. **Border Setting Choices and Their Effects on the Selection.**

Border Choice	Effect on Selection
None	Removes all borders from the part of the selection you chose in the Apply To box.
Box	Sets border lines around the outside of the selection you chose in the Apply To box.
All	Sets border lines along every side of every cell in the selection.
Grid	Sets border lines along every side of every cell in the selection, like the All setting, except that the inside lines are thinner than the outside lines. For line styles smaller than 1½ points, the outside and inside lines will look the same. For line styles 1½ points and larger, you'll see that the outside lines are thicker than the inside lines.
Shadow	Sets a box border around the text or paragraphs of the selection, according to your choice in the Apply To box.
Three-D	Sets a box border with a three-dimensional look around the text or paragraphs of the selection, according to your choice in the Apply To box. The Three-D setting has an effect only if you select an asymmetric line style (thin-thick, thick-thin, embossed, or engraved).
Custom	See "Custom Borders," below.

Custom Borders

Clicking the Custom button has no immediate effect. To set up a custom border (borders only on some sides or different border style, color, or width on various sides), you must click the border buttons or border lines in the Preview. When you click a border button or border line in the Preview, Word automatically selects the Custom Setting button.

Using the Apply To Choices for Borders and Shading

Except for placing an insertion point within a table, any other selection you set in a table before you choose the Format Borders And Shading command, you always have the same four choices in the Apply To box on both the Borders and the Shading tabs—Text, Paragraph, Cell, and Table. (If your selection is outside a table, you have only the two choices Text and Paragraph. If you set an insertion point outside a table, you have only the Paragraph choice.) The four choices in the Apply To box and what each choice does are listed below. Note that you can select different Apply To choices for borders and for shading.

Apply To Choice	What Each Choice Does
Text	Applies choices to the selected text. If a selection includes any paragraph marks, the border and shading choices apply to the paragraphs, including a paragraph that contains partially selected text, which follows the last paragraph mark in the selection.
Paragraph	Applies choices to the selected paragraphs. If a table cell has no paragraph marks, Word applies the border and shading to the cell.
Cell	Applies choices to the selected cells.
Table	Applies choices to the entire table.

The border buttons you see in the Preview depend on your choice in the Apply To box and your selection.

■ When you choose Text in the Apply To box, you'll see four border buttons—top, bottom, left, and right.

■ When you choose Paragraph in the Apply To box, you'll see either four or five buttons. If the selection includes only one paragraph (or part of one paragraph), you'll see the same four buttons you see when you choose Text. If the selection includes two or more paragraphs, you'll see a fifth button for a horizontal border between the paragraphs. For five buttons, you'll also see a horizontal gap between the paragraphs in the Preview.

- When you choose Cell in the Apply To box, you'll see four, five, or six buttons. If the selection includes only one cell (or part of one cell), you'll see the same four buttons you see when you choose Text. If the selection includes two or more cells in one column, you'll see a fifth button for a horizontal border between cells. If the selection includes two or more cells in one row, you'll see the fifth button for a vertical border between cells. If the selection includes cells in two or more rows and columns (at least four cells in a two-by-two arrangement), you'll see six buttons—top, bottom, left, right, vertical gap between cells, and horizontal between cells. For five buttons, you'll also see either a horizontal or a vertical gap between the cells in the Preview. For six buttons you'll see both a horizontal and a vertical gap between the cells.

- When you choose Table in the Apply To box, you'll usually see all six buttons. If the table contains only one row or one column, you'll see only five buttons. For a one-column table, you'll see the horizontal between cells button, as well as the four outside buttons. For a one-row table, you'll see the vertical between cells button, as well as the four outside buttons. For six buttons, you'll see both a horizontal and a vertical gap between the cells. For five buttons, you'll also see either a horizontal or a vertical gap between the cells in the Preview.

Shading with Color and Patterns

The Borders And Shading dialog box also contains a Shading tab. On the Shading tab, shown on the next page, you can add color in various shades and patterns to any text, paragraph, cell, or table.

Shading can be solid color, a shading percentage of a color, or a two-tone pattern of dots or lines in a foreground color, with a background color in the spaces between the dots or lines.

To shade text or a cell, use these steps:

1 Select the text or cells you want to shade.

2 Choose the Format Borders And Shading command.

4 Click a fill color to apply or None to remove shading.

5 For a pattern, select a style and color for lines or dots.

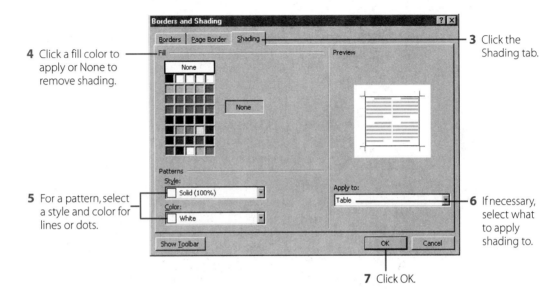

3 Click the Shading tab.

6 If necessary, select what to apply shading to.

7 Click OK.

Pattern Style and Color

The Style box under Patterns contains the choices Clear, Solid (100%), various percentages, and 12 patterns. The Clear choice sets the Fill color choice and turns off the Color box under Patterns. The Solid (100%) choice applies only the Color choice under Patterns and ignores the Fill color choice. The percentage and pattern choices in the Style box use the Fill color for the selection and the Color choice under Patterns for dots (when a percentage is set in the Style box) or lines (when a pattern is set in the Style box).

 NOTE

If you select the same color for the Fill color and Patterns color, every choice in the Style box has the same effect—shading with a single color.

III

Publications

Using the Tables And Borders Toolbar for Borders and Shading

A convenient way to apply borders and shading to cells is with the Tables And Borders toolbar. To display this toolbar, use any one of the methods listed here:

- Click the Tables And Borders button on the Formatting toolbar.

- Click the right mouse button while pointing to a visible toolbar, and choose Tables And Borders from the Toolbars shortcut menu.

- Choose the View Toolbars command, and choose Tables And Borders from the submenu.

- Choose the Format Borders And Shading command, and click the Show Toolbar button.

Word adds the Tables And Borders toolbar, shown in Figure 8-8, to the window.

FIGURE 8-8.

The Tables And Borders toolbar.

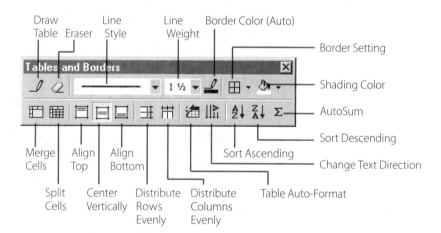

To paint borders and shading with the Tables And Borders toolbar, take these steps:

1 In the Line Style box, select the line style you want.

2 In the Line Weight box, select the line width you want.

3 Click the Border Color button, and select the border color you want.

4 Click the Border Setting button, and select the border you want. As an alternative, you can use the drawing tool to apply borders—see the next section, "Drawing Borders."

5 Click the Shading Color button, and select the shading Fill color you want. The Shading Color button includes gray percentage choices, but no patterns. The Shading Color button always uses Black as the Patterns Color choice. Even if you select a pattern style and color on the Shading tab of the Borders And Shading dialog box, any choice you make with the Shading Color button on the Tables And Borders toolbar resets the pattern color to Black and replaces any pattern with a solid color or a percentage of gray.

Drawing Borders

Instead of selecting a border setting using the Border Setting button on the Tables And Borders toolbar, you can draw the borders you want around cells. To draw borders, take these steps:

1 In the Line Style box, select the line style you want.

2 In the Line Weight box, select the line width you want.

3 Click the Border Color button, and select the border color you want.

Clicking any of the three buttons in steps 1, 2, or 3 turns on the Draw Table button.

4 If the Draw Table button isn't on, click it.

5 Drag the drawing tool (mouse pointer in the shape of a pencil) along the border you want to add or change.

To erase a border but keep the cells intact, click the Border Color button and select white, and then drag the drawing tool along the border you want to erase.

III

Publications

> If you drag the drawing tool in the table and you don't drag along a cell border, you insert a new cell border, which splits the cells you draw through. To see the cell borders when they aren't colored, turn on the Show Gridlines command on the Table menu.

Doing More with Your Tables

You can perform the following special actions in tables:

- Set up column headings to print at the top of each page when a table is longer than one page

- Add a caption that identifies the table and explains its purpose

- Number your tables, and then collect a list of tables (similar to a table of contents), including the page numbers on which the tables appear in the document

- Divide a table in two, between any two rows

- Position page breaks in a table that is longer than one page

- Convert a table, a group of rows, or a single row to regular text

Column Headings for Long Tables

Word prints lengthy tables on consecutive pages. When this happens, you usually want the column headings to repeat at the top of each new page.

To set up column headings for a long table, take these steps:

1 Select the first table row (plus any additional rows that you want to repeat).

2 Choose the Table Headings command.

Although nothing appears to happen in Normal view, you can see the effect, shown in Figure 8-9, when you switch to Page Layout view and select a Zoom Control setting that allows you to see more than one page. You can also see this effect if you choose Print Preview or print the document.

FIGURE 8-9.
Column headings can be repeated when a table crosses a page break.

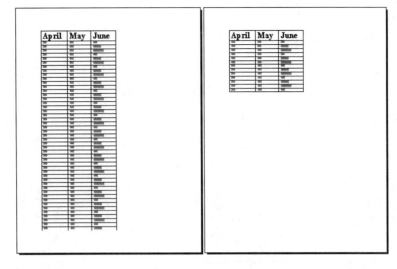

Table Headings is a toggle command. If you previously chose the command, the Table menu shows a check mark next to the command when the insertion point or selection is in the row or rows that you set up as column headings.

To remove the column headings from subsequent pages, follow these steps:

1 Select the heading row or rows at the top of the table.

2 Choose the Table Headings command again.

> Word repeats the column headings you specify only if you let Word insert page breaks (soft page breaks). If you insert a page break yourself (a hard page break), Word does not repeat the column headings.

Collecting a List of Tables

Well, now you've done it. You've gone and built an amazing document full of very wonderful tables. And you just know for sure that your readers will want to look up this or that table. So what you need is a list of tables, right? Right!

Word can collect a list of tables that includes each table's caption and the page number on which each table appears. Only tables that have captions will be included in the list.

Before you can collect a list of tables, you must give each table a caption. To add captions to tables, see "Adding Captions," page 396.

To collect a list of tables, take these steps.

1 Position the insertion point where you want the list of tables to appear.

2 Choose the Insert Index And Tables command.

3 Click the Table of Figures tab.

4 Select Table.

5 Select a format.

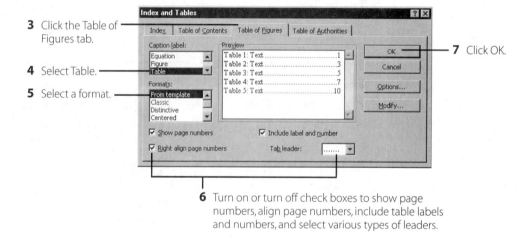

7 Click OK.

6 Turn on or turn off check boxes to show page numbers, align page numbers, include table labels and numbers, and select various types of leaders.

A list of tables might look something like this:

Table of Figures

Table 1. First Quarter Results. 2
Table 2. Second Quarter Results. 3
Table 3. Third Quarter Results. 6
Table 4. Fourth Quarter Results. 9
Table 5. Year End Results. 13

Page Breaks in Wide or Long Tables

When you craft a table, you might expect all of it to print on one page. Some tables, however, are too wide for one page. Others are too long for one page or begin near the bottom of a page and finish on the next page.

Don't Split the Rows

Word is set up to split a row by using a page break if necessary. You can stop Word from splitting a row. You can also insert your own page breaks. If you prefer that Word not split a row by using a page break, take these steps:

1 Position the insertion point anywhere in the table.

2 Choose the Table Cell Height And Width command, and click the Row tab.

3 Turn off the Allow Row To Break Across Pages box, and then click OK.

When you turn off this check box, Word no longer splits any row by using a page break. This means that the contents of each cell within every row must fit on a single page. If a cell's contents are longer than a page, Word moves the row containing the cell to the start of the next page. If the cell's contents are still too long for the page, Word prints only as much as will fit on the page (printing to the bottom edge of the page rather than stopping at the bottom margin).

Breaking Table Pages Yourself

If you don't like where Word breaks a table, you can insert a page break yourself. To do so, take these steps:

1 Position the insertion point in the row immediately below where you want a page break.

2 Use one of these methods:

• Choose the Insert Break command, click the Page Break option, and then click OK.

• Press Ctrl+Enter.

In both cases, Word first inserts a paragraph mark above the row containing the insertion point, and then inserts a page break above the paragraph mark. In Normal view, Word displays a manually inserted page break (a hard page break) as a closely spaced dotted line across the width of the window, with the label *Page Break*.

III

Publications

⭐ **TIP**

Have Your Page Break and Column Headings Too

Remember that Word does not automatically repeat column headings when you insert a manual page break. Suppose, however, that you don't like where Word broke a paragraph when it set a page break. As an alternative to inserting a manual page break, you can choose the Table Cell Height And Width command and turn off the Allow Row To Break Across Pages check box on the Row tab. This way, the paragraphs in a cell cannot be broken with a page break, but Word can still repeat column headings. See "Don't Split the Rows," page 350, for more information about preventing page breaks inside a row.

Splitting a Table

If you find that you need to split a single table into smaller tables, you can do so by splitting the table between rows. You can split any table that contains two or more rows.

1 Position the insertion point in the row immediately below where you want the split.

2 Split the table using one of these methods:

   • Choose the Table Split Table command.

   • Press Ctrl+Shift+Enter.

In both cases, Word splits the table above the row that contains the insertion point by inserting a paragraph mark between the two parts of the table. Word now sees the rows as parts of two tables rather than as parts of one table.

Converting Rows to Regular Text

After you insert a table, you might realize that the text is better suited to standard paragraphs than to a table. Or you might need more than 63 columns, which is the limit for a table, and you might want to convert a table to tabular text using tab stops and tab characters.

To take text out of a table and convert it to regular or tabular text, take these steps:

1 Select the table or the rows you want to take out of the table.

2 Choose the Table Convert Table To Text command.

3 Select the separator character.

4 Click OK.

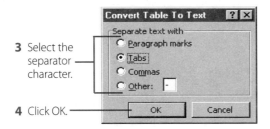

Word separates the cells by replacing the cell markers with the character you select in the Convert Table To Text dialog box: a paragraph mark, a tab, a comma, or the character you type in the Other box. Word replaces row markers with paragraph marks.

If a cell contains more than one paragraph, the paragraph mark is kept intact after the conversion even if you did not turn on the Paragraph Marks check box. Because the paragraph mark is kept intact, a conversion separated by tabs, commas, or other characters can look different from the table setup.

Calculating Tables

? SEE ALSO

For other ways to set up calculation tables, see Chapter 15, "Doing Business: Word's Other Documents," which describes the invoice, purchase order, and time sheet templates. These templates use form fields for calculations. For more information about setting up forms in Word, see Chapter 18, "Creating Your Own Business Forms."

One common use for tables in documents is to display numbers, calculate their sums, and display the totals. You might use tables in this way, for example, in letters that describe bids on projects, in business activity reports, or in invoices. To satisfy the need for these sorts of calculations, Word provides a Table Formula command.

Electronic worksheet programs such as Microsoft Excel and Lotus 1-2-3 are designed to calculate numbers for business reports and invoices—and to perform much more complicated calculations as well. Although you can easily import part or all of a Microsoft Excel or a Lotus 1-2-3 worksheet into a Word document, it's a bonus to be able to perform some calculations using Word. You can perform calculations even if you don't own a worksheet program.

III

Publications

In Word, you can set up a table anywhere in your document and use the Table Formula command to insert Formula fields that will perform calculations and display the results. The following sections show you how to perform three types of calculations in a table:

- Calculations that are limited to a single cell

- Calculations that refer to another cell in the same table

- Calculations that refer to a cell in another table

Before you set up a table to perform calculations, you should review the use of the Formula field, which is the backbone of performing calculations in Word tables. The next section provides this review.

Calculating Within a Cell

To calculate numbers within a single cell, you insert and update a Formula field to perform the calculation. For example, to calculate an 8.1 percent sales tax on $123.45, you insert a Formula field like this:

{ =$123.45*8.1% }

To insert this field, take these steps:

1 Position the insertion point in a table cell.

2 Choose the Table Formula command.

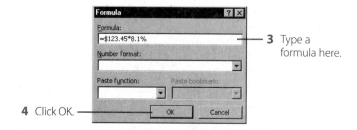

3 Type a formula here.

4 Click OK.

 TIP

If a cell above or to the left of the cell containing the formula has numbers, you'll see =SUM() with ABOVE or LEFT between the parentheses. Simply delete everything except the equal sign.

This example shows a simple calculation, but the Formula field can perform much more complicated calculations, including calculations that use numbers from other cells.

 TIP

> You can use the Table Formula command to insert Formula fields anywhere in a document, not only in tables.

Calculating Numbers from Other Cells

Calculations that use numbers in other table cells are the rudiments of a worksheet. Within one table cell, you can refer to one or more other cells as part of a formula that calculates numbers.

Each cell in a table has an "address," which is counted from the top left cell of the table. Columns are lettered (A, B, C, ...), and rows are numbered (1, 2, 3, ...). Each cell's address is the combination of its column letter and row number. For example, the address of the top left cell is A1, meaning column A, row 1. (In fields, you can use the lowercase form a1.) Figure 8-10 shows the cell addresses for a four-row-by-four-column table.

FIGURE 8-10.
Cell addresses
in a table.

A1	B1	C1	D1
A2	B2	C2	D2
A3	B3	C3	D3
A4	B4	C4	D4

A cell reference consists of one or more cell addresses. In a Formula field, you can use any of the forms of cell reference shown in Table 8-6.

To simplify some of the calculations that use a cell reference, you can use one of Word's built-in mathematical functions. In the Formula dialog box, select the function you want to use from the Paste Function box. Some functions you might use regularly are listed in Table 8-7. All of these functions operate on a list of numbers inside parentheses. A number can either come from a cell reference or be typed directly into the list. When using a cell reference, place it between brackets ([ ]). Use commas to separate items (numbers and cell references) in the list.

TABLE 8-6. **Cell References That Can Be Used in a Formula Field.**

Cell Reference	Meaning
n:n	Refers to all cells in row n, where n represents the row number. For example, 2:2 means all cells in the second row of the table. If a cell reference refers to its own row, the cell reference also refers to the cell that contains the reference.
L:L	Refers to all cells in column L, where L represents the column letter. For example, A:A means all cells in the first column of the table. If a cell reference refers to its own column, the cell reference also refers to the cell that contains the reference.
Ln	Refers to a cell in column L and row n. L represents the letter of the column, and n represents the number of the row. For example, B3 refers to the cell that's in the second column of the table's third row.
Ln:Tv	Refers to all cells inside a square that has the two cell addresses at opposite corners. L represents the column of the first corner cell, n represents the row of the first corner cell, T represents the column of the opposite corner cell, and v represents the row of the opposite corner cell. For example, A1:D4 refers to all the cells in Figure 8-10.

TABLE 8-7. **Formula Functions You Might Use Regularly.**

Function Name	Operation
AVERAGE	AVERAGE calculates the average of the numbers in a list by summing all the numbers and then dividing this result by the number of numbers.
MAX	MAX finds the highest number in the list.
MIN	MIN finds the lowest number in the list.
PRODUCT	PRODUCT multiplies the numbers in the list. For example, { =PRODUCT([A1:C1],[C2],10%) } multiplies [A1]*[B1]*[C1]*[C2]*10%.
SUM	SUM adds the numbers in the list.

Doing Your Sums

When you need a total for a column or a row, you can quickly insert a formula to give you a sum. You can insert a formula for a sum either with the Table Formula command or with the AutoSum button on the Tables And Borders toolbar. To do your sums, take these steps:

1 Position the insertion point in the cell where you want a sum.

2 Insert a Sum formula field in one of the following ways:

- Choose the Table Formula command, and then click OK.

- Click the AutoSum button on the Tables And Borders toolbar.

All of the functions in Table 8-7 can also use special cell references: ABOVE, BELOW, LEFT, and RIGHT. You usually use these cell references in the columns and rows along the outside edges of tables, but you don't have to. Table 8-8 shows you what each of these cell references mean.

TABLE 8-8. **Special Cell References for Formula Functions.**

Special Cell Reference	Meaning
ABOVE	All the cells in this column above the cell that contains this cell reference
BELOW	All the cells in this column below the cell that contains this cell reference
LEFT	All the cells in this row to the left of the cell that contains this cell reference
RIGHT	All the cells in this row to the right of the cell that contains this cell reference

Calculating Outside a Table Using Numbers in a Table

In a Formula field, you can refer to a number in any cell of any table. The field that refers to a cell in a table can be anywhere in a document, either outside or inside a table. You refer to a table by first inserting a bookmark anywhere in that table and then adding the name of the bookmark to the formula. To refer to specific cells in that table, you follow the bookmark's name with cell references.

To insert in text outside of the table a Formula field that uses numbers in a table, take these steps:

1 Position the insertion point anywhere in the table.

? SEE ALSO

For more information about creating and using bookmarks, see "Bookmark Destinations," page 92.

2 Choose the Insert Bookmark command, type a name for the bookmark, and click the Add button to put the bookmark in the table. The bookmark's name is not visible on the screen, but you can turn on indicators to show the locations of bookmarks: choose the Tools Options command, click the View tab, turn on the Bookmarks check box, and click OK.

3 Outside the table, position the insertion point where you want to insert the Formula field.

4 Choose the Table Formula command. Notice that the Paste Bookmark box is now available.

5 In the Paste Bookmark box, select the bookmark for the table.

6 After the bookmark name in the Formula box, type the cell reference(s) inside square brackets (such as [A5:D8]).

7 Complete the formula, which can include additional references to cells in any table. You can also insert references to bookmarks on numbers in regular text outside tables.

8 When the formula is complete, click OK.

If you change the numbers in the table (or in bookmarked numbers in regular text outside tables), select the Formula field, and press the Update Field key (F9) to update the Formula field result.

Storing Table Setups

Some of the reports that you will be creating may be quite similar; in particular, tables often reappear in regular, periodic reports. Many of the tables you create are straightforward, containing several columns and several rows all the same width and height, with no special border formatting. But if you create an unusual or complex table, you can spend a lot of time setting up a table structure. For example, you might want a table whose column headings have special formatting, or that includes adding special borders and split cells, or whose columns have different widths. A table might contain calculations that you want to reuse. If you store the table as AutoText, you'll have a ready-made table for your next report without having to set it up again. Even if you habitually use Table AutoFormat to set up a table, having a one-step method for inserting a table can be very handy.

Importing Worksheet Cells with the Insert File Command

If, during Word setup, you installed the Excel and Lotus 1-2-3 file conversions, you can also import worksheet cells through the Insert File command. To do so, take the following steps:

1   Choose the Insert File command.

2   In the Files Of Type box, select All Files.

3   If necessary, switch to the disk and folder that contain the file you want to open.

4   Select the file.

5   If you want to set up a link between the worksheet file and your Word document, turn on the Link To File check box.

6   If you want to insert only part of the worksheet, move to the Range text box, and either type a range name (a name you applied to a selection of cells) or type the cell references for the range of cells.

7   Click the OK button to insert the cells.

8   If you left the Range text box blank in step 6, Word will prompt you for the worksheet and range to insert. Make the appropriate selections, and then click OK.

If you turned on the Link To File check box, Word inserts an INCLUDETEXT field. If you left the Link To File check box turned off, Word inserts the cell contents as text in a Word table.

Turn on the Confirm Conversion At Open check box on the General tab in the Options dialog box if you want to confirm the file format of the original file. For information about the General tab, see "General Tab," page 963.

? SEE ALSO

For information about using a Microsoft Excel worksheet file with a Word document file, see "Inserting Worksheets (Spreadsheets)," page 361.

III

Publications

To store a table as AutoText, take these steps:

1 Select the cells containing the contents that change from one report to the next and you don't want to keep, and then press the Delete key. Keep any cells that are referenced by formulas and calculations that you want to use again.

2 Select the entire table or the portion of the table you want to reuse.

3 Choose the Insert AutoText command.

4 Select New from the submenu.

5 Type an AutoText name.

6 Click OK.

If you insert a table from AutoText and then add contents that are too wide for a cell, you can quickly reset the column widths to fit the width of the contents, by taking these steps:

1 Select the table.

2 Choose the Table Cell Height And Width command, and click the Column tab.

3 Click the AutoFit button.

Deciding How Many Rows to Store

Before you store a table as AutoText, decide how many rows to store. As a general rule, store as few rows as possible to save disk space. More specifically, if the table uses the same cell and contents formatting in every row, save only one row as AutoText. You can add rows to the table later by pressing the Tab key at the end of the last row. The added row gets the cell and contents formatting of the row above it. If the table has column headings that differ from the rest of the table's rows, however, save the heading row plus one regular row.

Save the entire table as AutoText when the table has any unique rows or columns, particularly if one of the unique rows is located below the table's first row. Otherwise, you'll need to manually change the rows after you insert the AutoText, which defeats the purpose of saving the table as AutoText.

Inserting Worksheets (Spreadsheets)

Microsoft Excel is a powerful data analysis tool that helps you create worksheets, charts, and other information. Microsoft Word is a powerful communications tool that lets you create state-of-the-art documents. Now, you'll learn how Word and Excel can work together.

Importing a Worksheet

You can open an Excel file directly in Word, just as you open a Word document. To do so, take these steps:

1 Click the Open button on the Standard toolbar.

2 In the Files Of Type box, select Microsoft Excel Worksheet.

3 If necessary, switch to the disk and folder that contain the Excel worksheet you want to open.

4 Select the icon for the worksheet file, and click the Open button.

5 Select the worksheet name or number that you want to see. ———

6 Select Entire Worksheet, select a range name, or type the cell addresses.

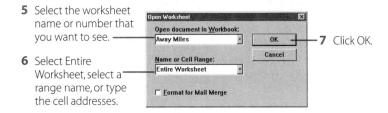

7 Click OK.

The contents of the worksheet appear in a Word table, as shown here:

Home	I-5	Oak Harbor	Ferry	Ferry	101	Shelton	Hwy 8	Montesano
0	36	25	13	0	13	63	30	28
	36	61	74	0	13	76	108	134
						310		
Seaside	Tillamook	Tillamook	Lincoln City	Lincoln City	Waldport	Waldport	Reedsport	Reedsport
0	44	0	39	0	42	0	55	0
			83		125			
						446		
Eureka	Garberville	Garberville	Ukiah	Ukiah	Santa Rosa	Santa Rosa	Vallejo	Vallejo
0	66	0	102	0	67	0	29	0
			168				96	
						365		

III

Publications

You can make any changes you want to the imported worksheet information and then save the document, either as a Word document or as a worksheet file.

Inserting a Worksheet Object

You can insert a worksheet object into a Word document. When you activate a worksheet for editing, you can set up calculations just as you do in Microsoft Excel. To insert a worksheet object, take these steps:

1 Choose the Insert Object command.

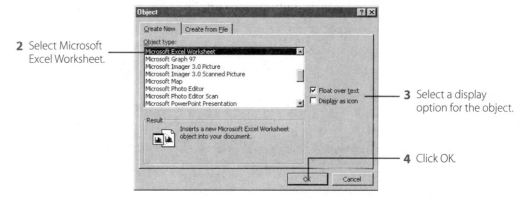

2 Select Microsoft Excel Worksheet.

3 Select a display option for the object.

4 Click OK.

5 Now set up the worksheet to perform the calculations.

6 To return to Word, take the step that applies to the type of object you inserted:

- For a Float-Over-Text object, as you can see in Figure 8-11, click anywhere outside the worksheet object to return to Word.

- For a Display-As-Icon object, as you can see in Figure 8-12, close the Microsoft Excel window. You can see an icon in the document (see Figure 8-13, page 364).

To edit any worksheet object, double-click it.

FIGURE 8-11.
The Word window with a Float-Over-Text Excel object.

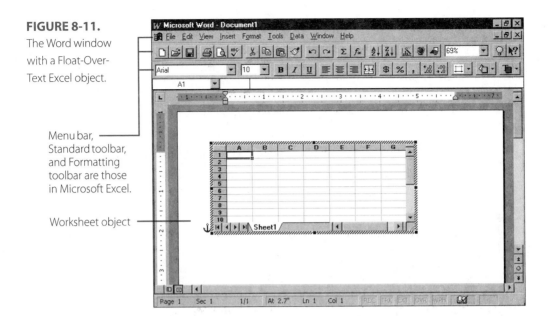

Menu bar, Standard toolbar, and Formatting toolbar are those in Microsoft Excel.

Worksheet object

FIGURE 8-12.
The Word window with an Excel window for Display-As-Icon Excel object.

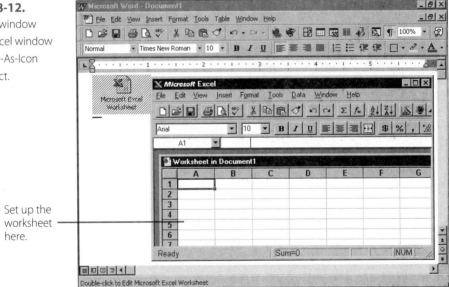

Set up the worksheet here.

FIGURE 8-13.
Microsoft Excel object icon in a Word document.

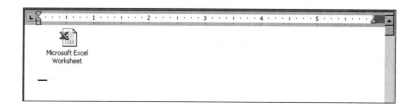

Using the Microsoft Excel Buttons

Word provides two Excel buttons—one on the Standard toolbar (at left) and one on the Microsoft toolbar (below).

Insert
Microsoft
Excel
Worksheet

Microsoft Excel

To display the Microsoft toolbar, choose the View Toolbars command, choose Customize from the submenu, turn on the Microsoft check box in the Customize dialog box, and click Close.

When do you click which button? Use these guidelines:

- The Insert Microsoft Excel Worksheet button on the Standard toolbar embeds a worksheet in your Word document—you'll be able to see part of your Word document around the worksheet while you edit it.

- The Microsoft Excel button on the Microsoft toolbar links a worksheet or inserts a database from Excel; clicking the button starts or switches to Excel in a separate window.

Exchanging Information with Excel

Information from an Excel workbook can be copied, embedded, linked, or extracted, depending on the current needs and future use of the Word document and the Excel information. Use the following guidelines to decide which method is most suitable for your work.

- Copy the information from an existing Excel workbook and paste it in a Word document if you do not plan to change the information in the workbook or if you do not want or need the information in the Word document to reflect any future changes in the Excel workbook. The information is copied to the Word document as a Word table or as a Word drawing.

■ Embed the information if the Excel worksheet relates to only one document and will not be used outside Word or by other Word documents and if the information might need to be changed. You can embed either an existing worksheet or a newly created worksheet. The information in the worksheet is stored in the Word document.

■ Link the information if the original Excel workbook will be used outside Word (for example, in Excel without Word running) or if it will be used by different documents or by different applications. Any changes you make to the original workbook also change the linked information in the Word document. The Excel workbook must already exist (you must name and save it) before you can link it to a Word document. The information in the workbook is stored in an Excel file.

■ Extract the information if you want only information from an existing workbook that meets specific criteria. Insert the extracted information as a field if you want changes in the Excel workbook to appear in the Word document whenever you update the field in Excel. Extracted information is stored in the Word document, and the Excel workbook information remains in an Excel file. See "Extracting Data: Specifying Query Options," page 369, for more information about extracting information from Excel.

Pasting Cells

To paste cells from an Excel worksheet, take these steps:

1 Click the Microsoft Excel button on the Microsoft toolbar to start Excel.

2 Either open an existing workbook or set up a new worksheet.

3 Select the cells containing the material you want to paste into your Word document, and then choose the Edit Copy command.

4 Switch to your Word document, position the insertion point where you want to paste the cells, and then choose the Edit Paste command.

III

Publications

After the paste is complete, the cell contents appear in a Word table and have no connection to Excel or to an Excel file.

Embedding Cells

To embed Excel cells in a Word document, take these steps:

1 Click the Microsoft Excel button on the Microsoft toolbar to start Excel.

2 Either open an existing Excel workbook or type the contents of a new worksheet. If you create a new worksheet, be sure to save it.

3 Select the cells containing the information you want to embed in your Word document, and then choose the Edit Copy command.

4 Switch to your Word document, and position the insertion point where you want to add the embedded worksheet cells.

5 Choose the Edit Paste Special command.

6 In the Paste Special dialog box, leave the selection set to Formatted Text (RTF). Make sure the Paste Link option is off, and click OK.

As an alternative, you can choose Word's Insert Object command—see "Inserting a Worksheet Object," page 362.

Linking Cells

To link cells from an Excel workbook to a Word document, take these steps:

Before you can link cells into a Word document, the worksheet *must* be saved in an Excel file.

1 Click the Microsoft Excel button on the Microsoft toolbar to start Excel.

2 Either open an existing Excel workbook or type the contents of a new worksheet. If you create a new worksheet, be sure to save it.

3 Select the cells containing the information you want to link to your Word document, and then choose the Edit Copy command.

4 Switch to your Word document, and position the insertion point where you want to add the linked worksheet cells.

5 Choose the Edit Paste Special command.

6 In the Paste Special dialog box, leave the selection set to Formatted Text (RTF). Turn on the Paste Link option, and click OK.

The cell contents retain a connection to Excel and are stored in the original Excel file.

> To quickly link the entire first worksheet in an Excel file to a Word document, choose the Insert Object command and click the Create From File tab in the Object dialog box. Type or select the name of the workbook containing the worksheet you want to link, turn on the Link To File check box, and click OK.

Pulling Data from Excel

Because a worksheet can contain many kinds of information, there may be times when you might want to pull only certain types of information from a worksheet into a Word document. In this section, you'll learn how to extract and connect information from an Excel worksheet to Word using Word's Insert Database button on the Database toolbar, shown in Figure 8-14.

FIGURE 8-14.
The Database toolbar.

Insert Database button

To display the Database toolbar, click the right mouse button on any toolbar, and then choose Database from the Toolbars shortcut menu. If you're working without any toolbars, choose the View Toolbar command, and choose Database from the submenu.

Preparing a Worksheet

The first step in connecting Word and Excel is to establish a source from which Word can draw information. You can use any data. Whatever worksheet you use must have at least one named range. Naming ranges on a worksheet lets you specify certain parts of the worksheet to examine, rather than the entire worksheet. You can have several named ranges on a worksheet, each referring to a different area of interest.

III

Publications

Word uses the names in the top row of a worksheet or a range to name its data fields. If the names in the worksheet are located in a different row, (with blank rows above, for example), you must define the range to start in the row that contains the names. Take these steps to define a range on a worksheet:

1   Start Excel, and open the workbook. Select the worksheet you want to work with.

2   Select all of the column headings and the data you want included in a named range.

3   Define a range by choosing the Insert Name command. Choose Define from the submenu, type a name in the Names In Workbook box of the Define Name dialog box, and then click OK.

4   Choose the File Save command to save the change.

Now, when you pull in information from the worksheet, you can tell Word to look at only the section of the worksheet you named.

 **TIP**

If you plan to extract data from an entire worksheet, place the field names in the first row of the worksheet so that you will not need to define a range before using the data. To define names for the data fields when you are extracting data from only part of the worksheet, either include or insert a row containing the names at the top of the range.

Pulling Information into Word

To extract information from a worksheet into Word, take these steps:

1   Click the Insert Database button on the Database toolbar.

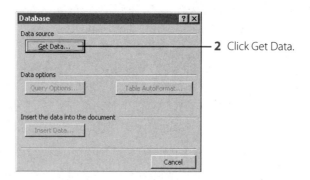

2   Click Get Data.

3 When the Open Data Source dialog box appears, switch to the disk and the folder that contain the worksheet you want to use.

4 In the Files Of Type box, select MS Excel Worksheets.

5 Select the icon for the worksheet you want to use, and then click the Open button.

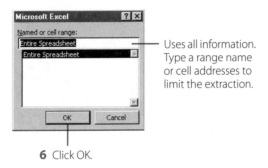

Uses all information. Type a range name or cell addresses to limit the extraction.

6 Click OK.

The Database dialog box remains open. Go on to the next section to read about its other options.

Extracting Data: Specifying Query Options

If you want to pull in all the information from a worksheet or range, you don't set query options. On the other hand, from all the information on the worksheet (or even from the range you specified), you might want to extract only specific information. If so, you'll need to extract a subset of the data from the worksheet by setting specific criteria.

When you work with database information, you deal with two kinds of fields: comparison fields and extract fields. Comparison fields are used to find records that match your criteria, and extract fields contain the information you want to pull from those records into your Word document.

III

Publications

To extract only specific information from a worksheet, take these steps:

1 In the Database dialog box, click the Query Options button.

3 Select the field you want to search.

4 Select the type of comparison.

2 Click the Filter Records tab to define which type of records you want to find.

For additional records, select AND or OR (see step 6).

5 Type a name or number to compare fields with.

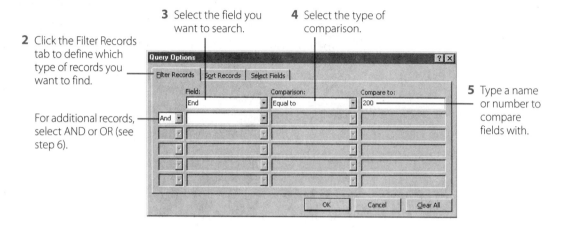

6 Repeat steps 3 through 5 for additional comparisons, and select AND to make the criteria narrower (fewer records found), or select OR to make the criteria broader (more records found).

7 Click the Select Fields tab.

This box displays all the fields in the database.

8 Remove the fields you don't want to use.

This box displays the fields from which Word will draw data.

9 Click the Sort Records tab.

10 Select the field you want to use to sort the information.

11 Select the sorting order.

12 Click OK.

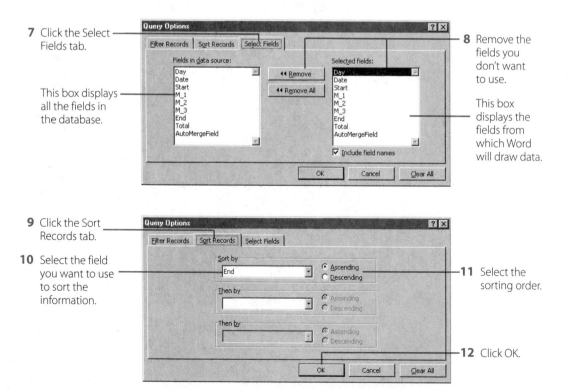

Inserting the Records

Now that you have set up the extraction process, you're ready to insert the records. To do so, take these steps:

1 In the Database dialog box, click the Insert Data button to display the Insert Data dialog box.

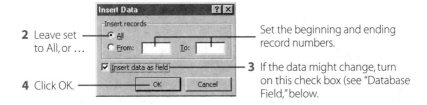

2 Leave set to All, or …

Set the beginning and ending record numbers.

3 If the data might change, turn on this check box (see "Database Field," below.

4 Click OK.

The information now appears in Word in a table.

Database Field

You can insert the database information as a Database field. Then, when the worksheet changes, you simply position the insertion point in the information and press F9 to update the extracted information in Word.

Collecting a List of Worksheets

Word can collect a list of worksheets that includes each worksheet's caption and the page number on which each worksheet appears. Only worksheets that have captions will be included in the list.

 NOTE

Before you can collect a list of worksheets, you must give each worksheet a caption. To add captions to worksheets, first set up a special caption label for worksheets—see "Creating a Special Caption Label," page 397. Then add the captions with the steps in "Adding Captions," page 396.

To collect a list of worksheets, take the steps listed in "Collecting a List of Tables," page 349. In those steps, simply substitute "Worksheets" for "Tables."

III

Publications

Inserting Charts

Business communications that must present and interpret numbers (quantitative information) often require visual displays such as charts and graphs to clarify data. Microsoft Graph is an application that you can use within Microsoft Word to create a wide variety of charts—from bar graphs to plotted lines to pie charts, many of them in 3-D—for many kinds of data.

Essentially, Microsoft Graph provides the same charting features found in Microsoft Excel. In fact, if you know how to create and edit charts in Excel, you already know how to create and edit charts in Graph.

Microsoft Excel offers many additional features for working with numbers—perhaps more features than you need if your primary purpose is simply creating visual displays in documents. If Excel is available to you, you can also create a chart in Excel and then link or embed the chart in your Word document. If Excel chart files are available to you, you can import a chart into Graph, edit the chart, and then embed the chart in a Word document (see "Inserting a Chart from Microsoft Excel," page 386).

If Excel is not available to you, you can use Microsoft Graph to create and embed charts in your Word documents. Microsoft Graph has two parts: the datasheet and the chart. In the datasheet, you type the labels and numbers for the chart you want to create. The chart reflects the labels and numbers in the datasheet, in the chart style and variation you select. The chart appears in your Word document, but the datasheet doesn't.

You can change the size of the chart and datasheet to see more of them. To create a different chart to present the same information, you edit the datasheet and select a different chart style.

Creating a Chart

If you're creating a new chart or graph, Graph always displays a sample chart and its related datasheet, as shown in Figure 8-15.

FIGURE 8-15.
The Microsoft Graph sample chart, datasheet, and Standard toolbar.

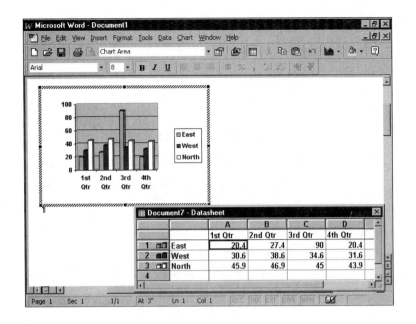

To add a chart to a Word document, take these steps:

1 Position the insertion point where you want the chart to appear.

2 Choose the Insert Picture command, and select Chart from the submenu.

3 Change, add, and remove the labels and numbers in the sample datasheet to set up the chart you need.

4 Click the chart area.

5 Click the down arrow next to the Chart Type button on the toolbar, and select the chart style you want from the list that appears.

6 Click outside the graph and datasheet in your Word document to return to Word.

Changing an Existing Chart

If your Microsoft Word document already contains a chart that was created in Graph, double-click the chart to start Graph. Or you can select the chart, choose the Edit Chart Object command, and choose Edit or Open from the submenu. The Edit command sets up Word for chart editing in place. The Open command opens a separate Microsoft Graph window for editing the chart.

III

Publications

SEE ALSO

For more information about setting a picture editor option, see "Edit Tab," page 965.

If you have a Microsoft Excel chart embedded or linked directly from Excel, double-clicking the chart starts Excel for editing. If you use the Paste Special command to insert an Excel chart as a picture, double-clicking it starts Picture Editor for editing. You can set which picture editor to use in the Edit tab in the Options dialog box.

Understanding the Datasheet, Chart, and Toolbars

Because controlling the final chart depends on your ability to control the datasheet as well as the chart itself, you should understand the structure of the datasheet and the chart and how the toolbars work.

The Datasheet

Microsoft Graph's datasheet, like a worksheet in Microsoft Excel, contains a grid of cells. Each cell can contain either text or numbers. To create a chart, Graph uses the datasheet rows and columns of cells. Usually, each row represents a category. For example, the sample datasheet that Graph initially displays contains three categories: East, West, and North. The columns represent the data points for each category. All the data points for one category make up a data series.

 NOTE

You can alter the relationship between the datasheet and the chart. You can tell Graph to use the columns for categories and the rows of cells for data points. To do so, choose the Data Series In Columns command.

As shown in Figure 8-15, on the previous page, small images of the chart that appear in the left or top border of the Datasheet window mean that Graph is using the cells in the row or column for the chart. The small chart images appear beside rows when the categories are in the first column (Series In Columns). The small chart images appear above columns when the categories are in the first row (Series In Rows). Rows and columns of cells that are not being used show nothing at the border of the datasheet.

If you scroll through the datasheet, you'll notice that the first column and the first row of the datasheet always remain in view, so that you can always see the column headings.

The Chart

A chart consists of numerous elements: a chart area, a plot area, axes, a data series, walls (for 3-D charts), a legend, labels, and various objects you can add, such as text boxes and arrows. You can select each element in a chart individually, or you can select an element type as a whole.

■ To select an element type in a chart, click the element or select its name from the Chart Objects box on the Standard toolbar—see "The Toolbars," below.

■ To select a single data item or other individual part of an element type in a chart, select the element type first (as noted in the preceding bulleted point), and then click the part of the element type you want to select. Note that you can select the individual part only after you select the element type.

Figure 8-16 shows a chart with the East data series selected and the same chart with a single data point of the series selected.

FIGURE 8-16.
The left chart shows an entire data series selected; the right chart shows only one data point selected.

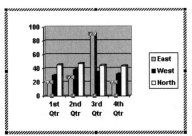 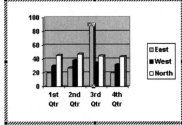

🌟 **TIP**

To quickly display the dialog box for changing an element type, double-click the element. To display the dialog box for a part of an element type, select the part and then double-click it.

The Toolbars

Graph starts with one toolbar visible—its Standard toolbar. Graph has two other toolbars—Formatting and Drawing. You can turn the display of toolbars on and off as you do in Word: choose the View Toolbars command, or click the right mouse button on a toolbar. The Standard toolbar in Graph is shown in Figure 8-17; the Drawing toolbar in

III

Publications

Graph is shown in Figure 8-18; and the Formatting toolbar in Graph is shown in Figure 8-19.

FIGURE 8-17.
The Standard toolbar in Microsoft Graph.

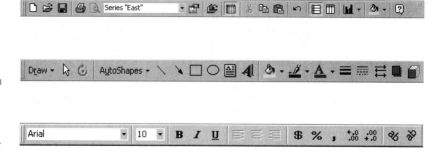

FIGURE 8-18.
The Drawing toolbar in Microsoft Graph.

FIGURE 8-19.
The Formatting toolbar in Microsoft Graph.

Changing the Look of a Chart

You can change a chart by changing the labels and numbers on the datasheet. When you change the row or column headings, you change the labels on the chart. When you change the numbers in the cells, you change the data points on the chart.

To change the datasheet, select a cell, type the new label or number, and press Enter. Graph then redraws the chart. To move from the current cell to another cell, click the next cell you want to change. You can also press an arrow key or the Tab key.

If you want to change a series of cells—for example, one row—select all the cells you want to change, type the new information for the first cell, and then press Enter or Tab. The information appears in the first cell, and the cell highlight moves to the second selected cell. Provided that you press Enter or Tab to move to the next cell, the highlight will move from cell to cell through the selection.

Formatting Cells

For each cell, you can set formatting for text, numbers, dates, and times. For text, you can set the font, font size, alignment in the cell, color, and style (bold, italic, underline, strikeout, superscript, or subscript). For numbers, you can select a display format, such as decimal points, number of decimal places, currency format, percentage, and commas for thousands. You can also create your own display format for numbers. For dates and times, you can select a format such as 10/19/97 or 19-Oct-97 for dates and 1:29 PM or 13:29 for times.

 NOTE

Graph has no menu command for setting cell alignment.

To change text formatting, do this:

1 On the Formatting toolbar, click the Font button to select a font.

2 Click the Font Size button to select a font size.

3 Click the Bold, Italic, or Underline button to add these font settings; and click the Align Left, Center, or Align Right button to align the cell contents.

Or, choose the Format Font command.

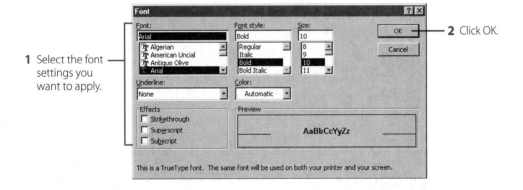

1 Select the font settings you want to apply.

2 Click OK.

 NOTE

Font changes affect all cells in the datasheet. You can't make one cell different from other cells. Also, font changes on the datasheet are not sent to the chart. You change the font formatting of the chart labels on the chart itself. For details, see "Formatting Chart Objects," page 384.

Publications

To format numbers, dates, or times, use these steps:

1 Select the cells that contain the numbers, dates, or times you want to format.

2 Choose the Format Number command.

3 Select a category of format.

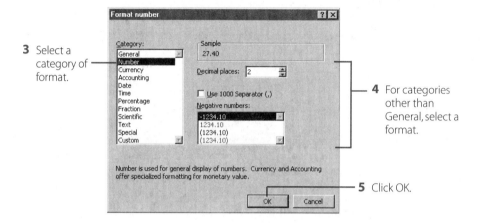

4 For categories other than General, select a format.

5 Click OK.

If you select Custom from the Category list, you can select from a wide variety of number formats. You can also create your own special number formats. Graph adds to the Type list any new formats that you type or edit, so you can easily select the format again. If you later find that you don't need a format that you added to the list, you can select the format and click the Delete button to remove the format from the list.

To apply some number formats, you can click the number buttons on the Formatting toolbar. At the right end of the Formatting toolbar you'll find the buttons Currency Style, Percent Style, Comma Style, Increase Decimal, and Decrease Decimal. These buttons are shown in Figure 8-19, page 376.

To create or edit a number format, use the characters shown in Table 8-9.

TABLE 8-9.   Number Formatting Characters Used in Microsoft Graph.

Character	Effect on Number Format
0 (zero)	Holds a place and inserts 0 if the number has no digit for the place
#	Holds a place, but doesn't insert anything if the number has no digit for the place
$	Inserts a dollar sign
,	Inserts a comma
(...)	Displays the numbers in parentheses
[color]	Displays numbers in the color named inside the brackets
+	Inserts a plus sign
–	Inserts a minus sign
"text"	Displays text contained inside the quotes
\	Displays the character that follows the backslash
*	Fills the empty space of the cell with the character that follows the asterisk
;	Separates sections of a number format into formats for positive and negative numbers or into formats for positive, negative, and zero
%	Displays a number as a percentage
E+	Displays a number in scientific notation
m	Displays the month as a single digit if less than 10
mm	In a date, displays the month as a double digit; in a time, displays minutes
mmm	Displays the month as a three-letter abbreviation
mmmm	Displays the full month name
- (hyphen)	Separates parts of a date (optional)
d	Displays the day as a single digit if less than 10
dd	Displays the day as a double digit
ddd	Displays the day name as a three-letter abbreviation
dddd	Displays the full day name

III

Publications

(continued)

TABLE 8-9. *continued*

Character	Effect on Number Format
yy	Displays the last two digits of the year
yyyy	Displays the full year, including the century
h	Displays the hour as a single digit if less than 10
hh	Displays the hour as a double digit
AM/PM	Displays AM or PM and sets hours to be displayed on a 12-hour clock; uses uppercase letters (AM/PM), lowercase letters (am/pm), a combination (Am/Pm), or the single letter pairs A/P or a/p
:	Identifies a time format and separates hours, minutes, and seconds
ss	Displays seconds

Selecting a Different Type of Chart

In Microsoft Graph you can select from many different built-in chart types and their subtypes. You have two ways to select a chart type: select the Chart Type button on the Standard toolbar and choose a chart type; or, choose the Chart menu's Chart Type command. The Chart Type button sets only the basic chart type. The Chart Type command can set the basic chart type and show you subtypes, too. After you choose a chart type and subtype, you then set chart options and change individual parts of a chart to suit you.

To select one of the basic chart types, take these steps:

1 Activate Microsoft Graph by double-clicking the chart.

2 Click the Chart Type button on the Standard toolbar—see Figure 8-17, page 376. It drops down to show you the chart types at the left.

3 Select the basic type you want for your chart.

To give yourself more choices for the chart form, take these steps:

1 Activate Microsoft Graph by double-clicking the chart.

2 Choose the Chart Type command on the Chart menu.

3 Click the Standard Types tab.

4 Select a chart type.

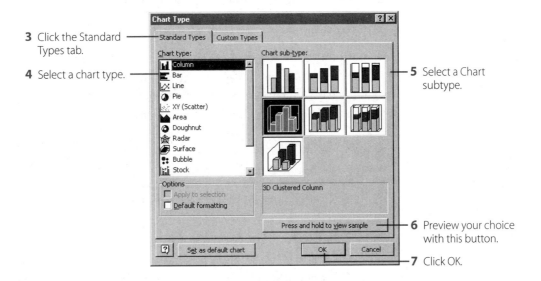

5 Select a Chart subtype.

6 Preview your choice with this button.

7 Click OK.

Alternative Chart Types

Instead of selecting a chart type from the Chart Type button or the Standard Types tab of the Chart Type dialog box, you can select a custom chart type. To do so, click the Custom Types tab in step 3 in the preceding illustration. Custom chart types don't have subtypes, so skip step 5. Also, the preview is automatic, so you can skip step 6 as well.

You'll also notice that the Custom Types tab contains a User-Defined option. For information about this option and its use, see "Adding Your Own Chart Types," page 385.

If you set chart options or changed the formatting of chart elements (see the next two sections), you can return the chart to its original form by clicking the Default Formatting check box, and then clicking OK.

Choosing a Different Proposed Chart Type

Microsoft set up Graph to always propose a 3-D clustered column chart. Your reports, however, might call for a different chart type. You can change the proposed chart type and save yourself some steps during chart creation.

To set a different proposed chart type, take these steps:

1 Activate Microsoft Graph by double-clicking the chart.

2 Choose the Chart Type command on the Chart menu.

3 Click the tab that contains the chart you want to use most often— Standard Types tab or Custom Types tab. If you want to set a custom chart you created (see "Adding Your Own Chart Types," page 385), click the User-Defined option.

4 Select the chart type (and subtype on the Standard Types tab).

5 Click the Set As Default Chart button.

6 Click Yes in the message box that appears.

7 Click OK.

Setting Chart Options

For each chart type and subtype, you can set a variety of options. To see the options for the selected chart type and subtype, take these steps:

View
Datasheet

1 Activate the chart by clicking either the chart itself or the View Datasheet button on the Standard toolbar. If the datasheet hides part or all of the chart, click the View Datasheet button to hide the datasheet. This button is a toggle; click it again to display the datasheet.

2 Choose the Chart Options command on the Chart menu.

3 In the chart Options dialog box, set the options you want for titles, axes, gridlines, legend, data labels, and data table on the six tabs.

4 Click OK.

Changing the Third Dimension

When you're setting up a three-dimensional chart, you can adjust the 3-D view in a variety of ways. To do so, take the steps on the following page.

1 Activate the chart by clicking either the chart itself or the View Datasheet button on the Standard toolbar.

2 If the current chart is not a 3-D chart type, click the Chart Type button's down arrow, and select a 3-D chart type option.

3 Choose the Chart 3-D View command.

4 Click to see the chart more straight on or from above.

5 Click to see the chart more from below.

6 Click to see the chart more from right-side viewpoint.

7 Click to see the chart more from left-side viewpoint.

8 Click to turn off this option, which displays the Perspective options you see below.

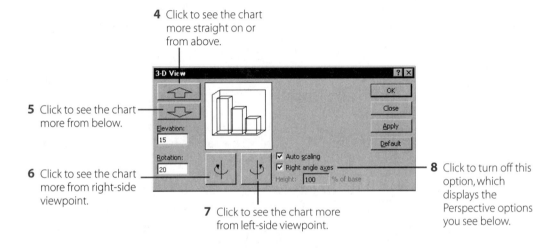

9 Click to see the chart from a closer viewpoint.

10 Click to see the chart from a farther viewpoint.

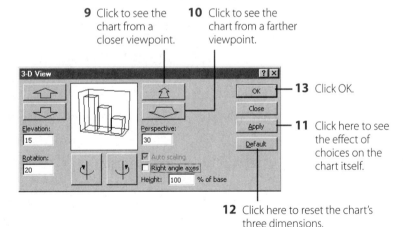

13 Click OK.

11 Click here to see the effect of choices on the chart itself.

12 Click here to reset the chart's three dimensions.

> **NOTE**
>
> Depending on the chart type you have selected, the 3-D View command may not be available. Change it to a 3-D type to activate the command.

III

Publications

Formatting Chart Objects

In addition to selecting a chart type and subtype and setting chart options, you can format any chart object with these steps:

1 Activate Microsoft Graph by double-clicking the chart.

2 Activate the chart by clicking either the chart itself or the View Datasheet button on the Standard toolbar.

3 Select the chart object you want to change. To do so, use one of these methods:

- Select the object from the Chart Objects list on the Standard toolbar.

- Click the object in the chart. To be sure you are selecting the object you want, pause the mouse pointer over the object until a ScreenTip appears with the name of the object in it.

4 If you want to format a specific element within an object (such as one data point in a series or one label in a legend), click the specific element you want to format differently.

5 Choose the Format Selected command. (The command name changes depending on the chart element you select.) For labels, you can also choose the Format Font command.

TIP

The fastest way to select the Format Selected command is to press Ctrl+1.

6 In the dialog box that appears, make your choices. Note that the dialog box changes to match the part of the chart you selected. Also, the dialog box usually contains more than one tab, letting you select various ways to change that part of the chart.

7 Click OK to make the change on the chart.

TIP

You can add the chart form you devise with chart options and object formatting to the Custom tab of Graph's Chart Type dialog box. For details, see "Adding Your Own Chart Types," next.

Adding Your Own Chart Types

Whether you spend a lot of time or just a few moments setting up a chart, you might want to have your special chart form readily at hand for the next chart you add to a report. After you set up a special chart, you can add it to Graph's Custom Types. Here's how:

1 Set up your special chart the way you want it.

2 Choose the Chart Type command on the Chart menu.

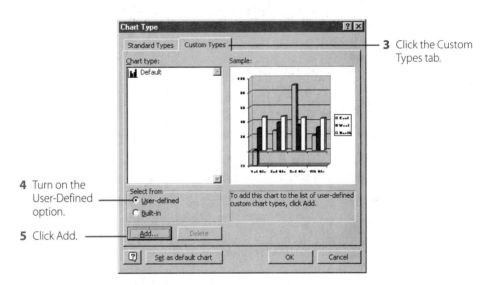

3 Click the Custom Types tab.

4 Turn on the User-Defined option.

5 Click Add.

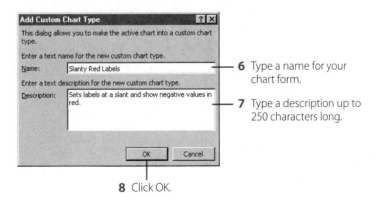

6 Type a name for your chart form.

7 Type a description up to 250 characters long.

8 Click OK.

9 If you want to use your custom chart as the proposed chart for all new charts in your reports, click the Set As Default Chart button, and then click Yes in the message box that appears.

III

Publications

10 Click the OK button in the Chart Type dialog box.

The next time you choose the Chart Type command on the Chart menu, click the Custom Types tab, and click the User-Defined option. Your special chart form appears in the Chart Type list.

? **SEE ALSO**

On the CD in this book, you'll find the file QTRCHART.DOC, which provides a procedure for modifying the sample Microsoft Graph chart.

If you no longer want to use a special chart you set up as a user-defined custom type, you can remove it from Graph as follows:

1 Choose the Chart Type command on the Chart menu, and click the Custom Types tab.

2 Turn on the User-Defined option.

3 Select the custom chart type.

4 Click the Delete button.

5 Click OK in the message box that asks you to confirm, and then click OK in the Chart Type dialog box.

Drawing on Your Chart

You can add arrows, notes, and callouts to your charts. For these elements, you use the tools on the Drawing toolbar (shown in Figure 8-18, page 376). For details about using the Drawing toolbar, see "Drawing Pictures," page 458.

You can also place WordArt on a chart. For details about WordArt, see "Bending Text—Word Art," page 507.

Inserting a Chart from Microsoft Excel

Inserting an Excel chart in a Word document involves the same methods you use for inserting worksheet cells. You can use a regular paste from the Clipboard, you can embed a Microsoft Excel chart, or you can insert a linked chart.

? **SEE ALSO**

For help with choosing between pasting, embedding, and linking a chart, see the guidelines for worksheets in "Exchanging Information with Excel," page 364.

Pasting a Chart

To paste a chart from Excel, take these steps:

1 Click the Microsoft Excel button on the Microsoft toolbar to start Excel.

2 Open an existing Excel file that contains a chart, or create a new chart, either as a chart sheet or as an embedded chart in a worksheet.

3 Select the chart, and choose the Edit Copy command to copy the chart to the Clipboard.

4 Switch to your Word document, position the insertion point where you want to paste the chart, and then choose the Edit Paste Special command.

5 In the Paste Special dialog box (shown in Figure 8-20), select Picture from the list.

6 Turn on the Paste option, and then click OK to perform a regular paste.

After the paste is complete, the chart appears but has no connection to Excel or to an Excel file.

When you paste a chart in this way, you can double-click the chart or select the chart and choose the Edit Picture command. Word loads the chart into a picture editing window. You can now use Word's drawing tools to edit the chart. (See "Drawing Tools," page XXX, for information on Word's drawing tools.)

FIGURE 8-20.
The Paste Special dialog box.

Click here to embed.

Click here to link.

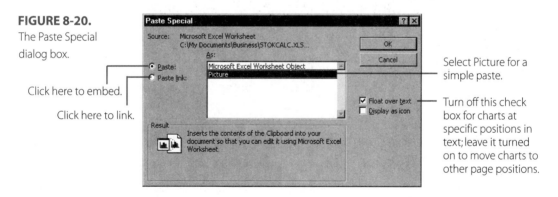

Select Picture for a simple paste.

Turn off this check box for charts at specific positions in text; leave it turned on to move charts to other page positions.

Embedding a Chart

To embed an Excel chart in a Word document, take these steps:

1 Click the Insert Microsoft Excel Worksheet button on the Standard toolbar, and drag on the grid to create a large enough number of cells to set up the data for the chart.

2 Type the labels and numbers for the chart in the worksheet cells.

3 Select the cells that contain the labels and numbers.

Publications

4 Choose the Insert Chart command to start the Chart Wizard. The Chart Wizard displays four dialog boxes from which you can choose the chart's type—standard or custom—and subtype, source data selection, options, and location. If you choose the As New Sheet option in the Chart Wizard's fourth dialog box, the chart will be placed on its own sheet; if you select the As Object In option, you will be able to see the chart and its source data on the same sheet.

5 Click the Finish button when you are through selecting options in the Chart Wizard. Then click in your Word document outside the chart object.

6 Size the chart object so that the chart looks good on your Word document page.

 TIP

Other Ways to Embed a Chart

If you've already created the chart in Excel, the easiest way to embed the chart in a Word document is to copy the chart from Excel to the Clipboard, switch to your Word document, and then choose the Edit Paste command. The chart appears in Word but retains a connection to Excel, although not to a separate Excel file.

As an alternative to the Insert Microsoft Excel Worksheet button on the Standard toolbar, you can start Excel, create or open a chart, copy the Excel chart to the Clipboard, and then in Word choose the Edit Paste Special command. From the list in the Paste Special dialog box, select Microsoft Excel Chart Object, turn on the Paste option, and then click OK.

Word's Insert Object command also allows you to embed an Excel chart—either a new chart you set up or a chart from an existing file.

Linking a Chart

 CAUTION

Before you can link a chart into a Word document, the chart *must* be saved in an Excel file.

Linking a chart to a Word document involves these steps:

1 In Excel, open an existing Excel file or create a chart, either as a chart sheet or as an embedded chart in a worksheet. If you create a new chart, save the Excel workbook.

2 Choose the Edit Copy command to copy the chart to the Clipboard, leave Excel running, switch to Word, and then in Word choose the Edit Paste Special command.

3 From the list in the Paste Special dialog box, select Microsoft Excel Chart Object. Then select the Paste Link option and click OK.

The chart appears in Word, retains a connection to Excel, and is stored in a separate Excel file.

Collecting a List of Charts

Word can collect a list of charts that includes each chart's caption and the page number on which each chart appears. Only charts that have captions will be included in the list.

> Before you can collect a list of charts, you must give each chart a caption. To add captions to charts, first set up a special caption label for charts—see "Creating a Special Caption Label," page 397. Then add the captions with the steps in "Adding Captions," page 396.

To collect a list of charts, take the steps listed in "Collecting a List of Tables," page 349. In those steps, simply substitute "Charts" for "Tables."

Inserting Equations

Many mathematical and scientific research papers present proofs and results in mathematical form. Mathematical formulas typically include symbols and arrangements of characters that are unusual in documents outside the scientific realm.

Microsoft Word for Windows includes Equation Editor, which lets you position numbers, symbols, and text to set up mathematical formulas on the screen and print them.

Equation Editor is a visual editing tool that provides a structure of formula parts into which you can type and paste numbers, letters, symbols, and additional structural parts. You can edit an Equation Editor formula that appears in a Word document by double-clicking it or by selecting the formula, choosing the Edit Equation Object command,

III

Publications

and then choosing Edit from the submenu. Word starts Equation Editor, with the formula parts ready for editing.

To add an equation to your report, take these general steps:

1 Position the insertion point where you want the equation to appear.

2 Choose the Insert Object command, click the Create New tab, and select Microsoft Equation 3.0 from the Object Type list. If you want the equation to float over or behind text anywhere on the page, leave the Float Over Text check box turned on. To put the equation among text and keep it next to specific text, turn off the Float Over Text check box.

3 Click OK to start Equation Editor. The Equation Editor menu bar, the Equation toolbar, and an Equation frame appear, as shown in Figure 8-21.

4 Use the palettes and buttons on the Equation toolbar to set up a formula.

5 When you're finished setting up the formula, click in the document outside the Equation frame.

FIGURE 8-21.

The Equation Editor menu bar, Equation toolbar, and Equation frame.

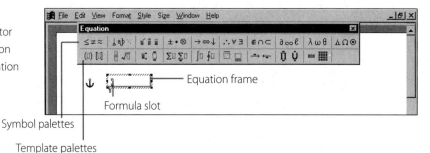

In the top row of the Equation toolbar (symbol palettes), you select mathematical and formula symbols. In the bottom row of the Equation toolbar (template palettes), you select formula structures.

You insert all elements of a formula—including letters, numbers, and symbols you type and symbols you select from the symbol palettes—in formula slots. Most templates contain an empty formula slot, along with the symbols shown fical bar and underline. The blinking vertical bar and underline represent the insertion point.

🕐 **SEE ALSO**

On the CD in this book, you'll find the file EQUAZONS.DOC, which provides three sample equations and steps for creating them.

To give you a better feel for the kinds of particulars you face when taking these steps to add an equation to your report, the rest of the sections on Equation Editor give you practice building a sample formula.

Practice Building a Formula

Building a formula is like building a three-dimensional puzzle: you add one interlocking piece at a time to form a completed shape, such as a ball or a cube. If you misplace a piece, you can't produce the correct result. The step-by-step directions for building the formula shown in Figure 8-22 give you an introduction to how Equation Editor works.

FIGURE 8-22.

The sample formula.

$$z^3 = \sqrt[3]{\left(\dfrac{1}{\sqrt{x^2 + y^2}}\right)^2}$$

To build the formula shown in Figure 8-22, you must divide it into parts. You then insert the formula one part at a time, as shown here:

Step	Description
$z^3 =$	z cubed equals
$\sqrt[3]{\Box}$	Cube root
$\left(\Box\right)$	Parentheses that apply the exponent to the whole fraction
$\dfrac{1}{\sqrt{\Box}}$	Fraction that contains a square root in the denominator
$x^2 + y^2$	Binomial expression that includes two separate superscript slots

III

Publications

Building the Left Side of the Equation

To build the left side of the equation in Figure 8-22, take these steps:

1 Type z. Equation Editor automatically displays the letter in the slot. The letter appears in italics because all variables appear in italics in the Math style.

2 Click the third button in the second row of the Equation toolbar to display the available exponent templates. To select a power of z, select the superscript template (which appears in the first row and column), as shown in Figure 8-23. Equation Editor inserts a superscript slot, which is raised above the z and is smaller in size.

3 Type 3, and then press the Tab key to move out of the superscript slot and back into the main slot of the formula. The Tab key advances the insertion point between the different parts of a formula, such as between the exponent and the variable.

4 Now type an equal sign. You've finished the first part of the equation shown in Figure 8-22.

FIGURE 8-23.

The superscript template.

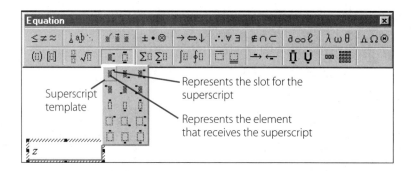

Superscript template

Represents the slot for the superscript

Represents the element that receives the superscript

 TIP

You can change the size of any element in an equation by choosing the Size Define command. In the Sizes dialog box, you can specify new sizes for regular characters, subscripts and superscripts, symbols, and any element that you have defined.

Building the Cube Root Part of the Formula

To build the cube root part of the formula, take these steps:

1 Click the second button in the second row of the Equation toolbar to display the available radicals. Select the multiple-root radical from the fractions and radicals palette, shown in Figure 8-24. Equation Editor puts the insertion point under the radical.

2 Press the Tab key to move to the multiple-root slot, and type *3*.

FIGURE 8-24.
The template for a multiple-root radical.

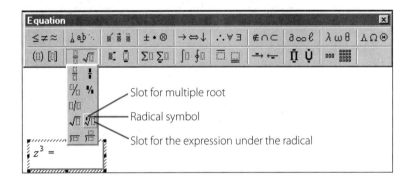

Creating the Formula Inside the Radical

To type the formula inside the radical, you press the Tab key to move between different positions in the equation, as follows:

1 Press Shift+Tab to move back under the radical. The Shift+Tab shortcut key moves the insertion point backward through the slots of a formula.

2 In the slot under the radical, insert the parentheses by selecting the parentheses template from the template palette, as shown in Figure 8-25 on the next page.

3 In the parentheses slot, insert a fraction from the template shown in Figure 8-26 on the next page.

4 In the numerator slot, type *1*.

III

Publications

FIGURE 8-25.
The parentheses template.

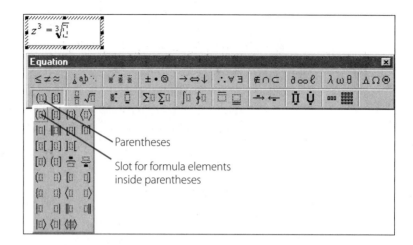

Parentheses

Slot for formula elements inside parentheses

FIGURE 8-26.
The fraction template.

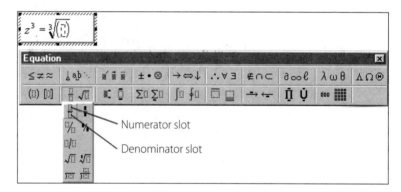

Numerator slot

Denominator slot

> **NOTE**

Instead of inserting parentheses in a formula by using the parentheses template, you can type them in yourself. Typing in the parentheses works fine as long as the element inside the parentheses is one character tall; for example, (x). If an element is more than one line high, however, you need to insert parentheses from the template because the template parentheses will grow vertically to surround everything you insert in their slot.

Adding the Denominator's Formula

The last step in creating the formula is creating the denominator's formula. Again, you use the Tab key—in this case, to move between the variable and the exponent—as follows:

1 Press the Tab key to move to the denominator slot.

2 Insert a square-root radical by selecting the square-root radical template, shown in Figure 8-27.

3 In the square-root slot, type *x*.

4 Insert a superscript slot and type *2*.

5 Press the Tab key, and then type +*y*.

6 Insert another superscript slot, and then type *2*.

FIGURE 8-27.
The square-root radical template.

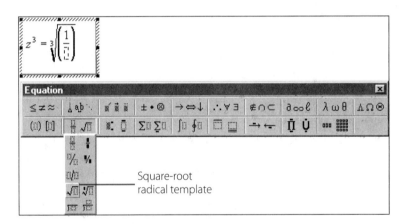

Square-root radical template

Finishing the Formula

The last step in building the formula is adding the exponent on the outside of the parentheses, as follows:

1 Press the Tab key four times to move the insertion point outside the parentheses.

2 Now insert a superscript slot, and type *2*. The formula is finished.

3 Click anywhere outside the equation's frame in the document window. Word turns off the Equation toolbar and reinstates Word's standard menus.

III

Publications

Collecting a List of Equations

Word can collect a list of equations that includes each equation's caption and the page number on which each equation appears. Only equations that have captions will be included in the list.

> **NOTE**
>
> Before you can collect a list of equations, you must give each equation a caption. To add captions to equations, see "Adding Captions," next.

To collect a list of equations, take the steps listed in "Collecting a List of Tables," page 349. In all the steps, simply substitute "Equations" for "Tables."

Adding Captions

Figures, tables, and equations often appear with captions that number them and explain what they show. To add a caption to any of these objects, take these steps:

1 Select the object.

2 Choose the Insert Caption command.

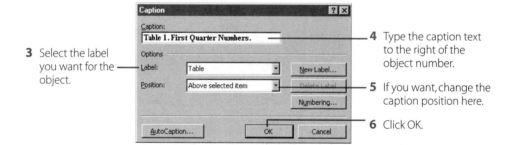

3 Select the label you want for the object.

4 Type the caption text to the right of the object number.

5 If you want, change the caption position here.

6 Click OK.

The caption will look something like this:

Table 1. First Quarter Numbers.

April	May	June
234	567	890
234	345	$9.999
246	357	$899.999

If you later insert or delete an object with a caption (for example, a table) that appears earlier in the document, Word automatically renumbers the captions for the remaining objects of that type (that is, the remaining objects with the same label).

Working with Labels and Numbers

Word has the built-in caption labels Figure, Table, and Equation ready for you to use. With these labels Word can collect tables of contents, lists of figures, lists of tables, and lists of equations. If you insert worksheets or charts into your report, you might want to add captions to these objects and, perhaps, collect a list of them. You might also want to label other types of objects in a document and collect a list of them. For these cases, you will want to create a special caption label. You can later delete from the list in the Caption dialog box any label you create (but you cannot delete Word's built-in labels from the list). And you can change the number format for caption numbering.

Creating a Special Caption Label

To set up a special caption label, take these steps:

1 Choose the Insert Caption command.

2 Click the New Label button in the Caption dialog box.

3 Type the new label in the New Label dialog box and click OK.

Word adds the new label to the Label box in the Caption dialog box.

Getting Rid of Your Old Labels

To delete a special caption label you created, take these steps:

1 Choose the Insert Caption command.

2 Select the label in the Label box.

3 Click the Delete Label button.

Changing the Caption Numbering Scheme

You can also change the number format in each type of caption by taking the steps on the following page.

III

Publications

1 Choose the Insert Caption command.

2 Click the Numbering button in the Caption dialog box.

3 Select a number format.

4 If your document has chapters, turn on this check box to include chapter numbers in the table number (see Note below).

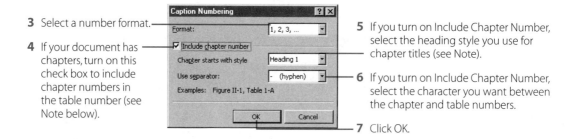

5 If you turn on Include Chapter Number, select the heading style you use for chapter titles (see Note).

6 If you turn on Include Chapter Number, select the character you want between the chapter and table numbers.

7 Click OK.

 NOTE

To include chapter numbers in a table number, you must use one of the heading styles (Heading 1 through Heading 9) for the chapter title. Then you must use the Customize Outline Numbered List dialog box, which you get to by clicking the Customize button on the Outlined Numbered tab in the Format Bullets And Numbering dialog box to number the heading style that you use for the chapter title. For details, see "Setting Up Legal Numbering," page 732.

Inserting Captions Automatically

If you want every table you craft to have a caption, you can turn on AutoCaption. To automatically add table captions, take these steps:

1 Choose the Insert Caption command.

2 Click the AutoCaption button.

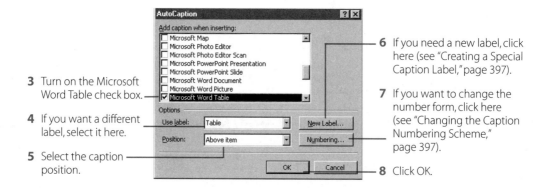

3 Turn on the Microsoft Word Table check box.

4 If you want a different label, select it here.

5 Select the caption position.

6 If you need a new label, click here (see "Creating a Special Caption Label," page 397).

7 If you want to change the number form, click here (see "Changing the Caption Numbering Scheme," page 397).

8 Click OK.

After you set up AutoCaption for tables, Word automatically adds the caption whenever you craft a table. You must simply type the caption text in the document to complete the caption.

Turning Off AutoCaptions

To turn off AutoCaptions for an item, take these steps:

1 Choose the Insert Caption command.

2 Click the AutoCaption button.

3 Turn off the check box for the item in the Add Caption When Inserting list.

4 Click OK.

Wrapping Up Text Boxes

A text box is a rectangle, like a picture frame, that you position and size at some particular place on a page. Into a text box you can insert text, tables, worksheets, or other objects. When a text box is in place, you can set internal spacing, select how Word should wrap text around the text box, and change its border and shading.

In some cases, you might want to change the direction of text in a text box. You can change the direction to vertical so that it reads either from the left side or the right side. And, as an added bonus, you can link text boxes so that long text can flow from one text box to the next; this is a useful feature for setting up sidebars or articles that you want to continue on a later page.

Inserting a Text Box

Word gives you two ways to insert a text box: with the Insert Text Box command and with the Text Box button on the Drawing toolbar. For both methods, you draw a text box on the page where you want it to appear. It's then ready to format (size, border, shading, wrapping, text direction, and internal spacing) and to fill with whatever you want to put into a text box.

III

Publications

To insert a text box, take these steps:

1 Display the page where you want to insert a text box. If the current view of the document is not Page Layout view, Word switches to Page Layout view for you when you take step 2.

Drawing   Text Box

2 Activate the text box drawing tool with one of the following methods:

- Choose the Insert Text Box command.

- Click the Drawing button on the Standard toolbar to display the Drawing toolbar, and click the Text Box button on the Drawing toolbar.

3 Position the drawing pointer (mouse pointer in the shape of a crosshair) where you want one corner of the text box to sit on the page.

4 Drag the drawing pointer toward the opposite corner of the text box to the size you want it. Remember that you can later change the size.

? SEE ALSO

After you insert a text box, you might want to change its position. For directions on how to do this, see "Positioning Objects on a Page," page 409. You might also want to change the size of a text box. For this you use the same steps you take for sizing a graphic (see "Sizing— Scaling and Cropping," page 516).

When you release the mouse button after dragging out a text box, you see an empty box on the page with a hatched border, as shown here:

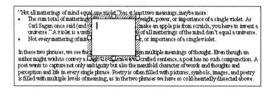

The hatched border means that the text box is active and ready for formatting, filling, or editing.

Changing Text Box Borders and Shading

When you insert a text box, Word automatically gives it a ¾-point single-line border and no shading. You can change the text box border lines and add shading with two different tools: the Format Text Box command and the Drawing toolbar. The Drawing toolbar (discussed in the next section) gives you additional choices for borders, namely, 3-D effect and shadows.

SEE ALSO

For details about your choices on the Colors And Lines tab, see "Filling the Text with Color," page 513.

To change text box borders with the Format Text Box command, take these steps:

1 Click the text box to activate it.

2 Choose the Format Text Box command.

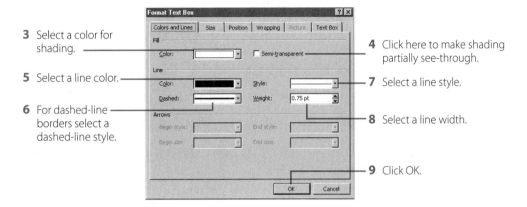

3 Select a color for shading.

5 Select a line color.

6 For dashed-line borders select a dashed-line style.

4 Click here to make shading partially see-through.

7 Select a line style.

8 Select a line width.

9 Click OK.

Changing Text Box Borders and Shading with the Drawing Toolbar

 SEE ALSO

For full details of the Drawing toolbar and of these buttons, see "The Drawing Toolbar," page 459. Also see "Using the Picture Toolbar," page 523, for tools you can use with text boxes as well as with pictures.

Several buttons on the Drawing toolbar give you access to text box border and shading choices. The Drawing toolbar also gives you special borders effects—3-D effect and shadows—which you can't get in the Format Text Box dialog box.

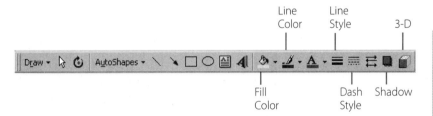

Line Color

Line Style

3-D

Fill Color

Dash Style

Shadow

Adding a Shadow

When you want to add a shadow to a text box, take these steps:

1 Click the text box.

2 Click the Shadow button on the Drawing toolbar. A palette drops down to give you many shadow options, shown on the next page.

III

Publications

3 Select a shadow style.

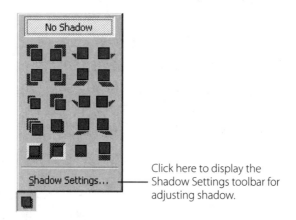

Click here to display the
Shadow Settings toolbar for
adjusting shadow.

Adjusting a Shadow

After you add a shadow to a text box, you might want to adjust the
shadow. Here are the steps:

1 Click the text box with a shadow.

2 Click the Shadow button on the Drawing toolbar.

3 Click the Shadow Settings button to display the toolbar shown here:

Shadow On/Off

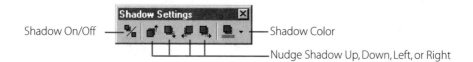

Shadow Color

Nudge Shadow Up, Down, Left, or Right

4 Click the buttons to adjust the shadow.

Expanding into 3-D

You can give a text box a 3-D look. With a 3-D look, a text box looks
like a cube, with the text on the front surface. To expand a text box
into the third dimension, take these steps:

1 Click the text box.

2 Click the 3-D button on the Drawing toolbar, and the drop-down
menu on the next page opens.

3 Select a 3-D style.

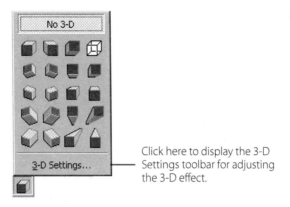

Click here to display the 3-D Settings toolbar for adjusting the 3-D effect.

Adjusting 3-D

After you add a 3-D effect to a text box, you might want to adjust the 3-D effect. Here are the steps:

1 Click the text box with a 3-D effect.

2 Click the 3-D button on the Drawing toolbar.

3 Click the 3-D Settings button to display the following toolbar:

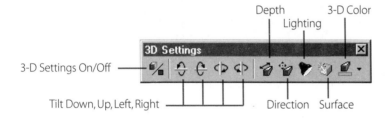

4 Click the buttons to adjust the 3-D effect.

Wrapping Document Text Around Text Boxes

After you insert a text box, you can set the kind of text wrapping you want around the text box. (You can use these same steps to set text wrapping around any floating object on a page.) Initially, Word sets text wrapping to none. This setting means that the object obscures the text on the page. If the object is see-through, you can still see the text behind it, more or less. You can also move the object behind the text so that the text prints over the top of the object (see "Grouping Parts of

① SEE ALSO

For details about your wrapping style choices, see "Wrapping Style," page 520. For details about the sides for wrapping, see "Wrap To," page 521. For details about the distance from the text, see "Distance From Text," page 522. Also, you can change your wrapping style with the Picture toolbar. For details, see "Adjusting the Wrap," page 522.

Your Drawing," page 479). While there may be occasions when you want these two effects, it's more likely that you'll want the document text to wrap around the object, rather than appear either on top or beneath the object.

To change the text wrapping around a floating object, take these steps:

1 Click the object. When you do, Word gives the object a hatched border to show that you have selected it.

2 Choose the Format (Object) command. This command changes its name for text boxes, tables, and pictures.

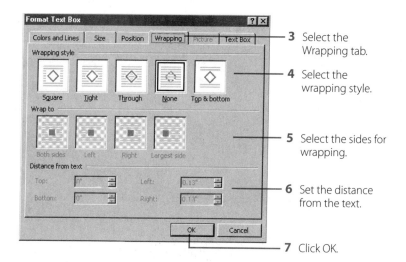

3 Select the Wrapping tab.

4 Select the wrapping style.

5 Select the sides for wrapping.

6 Set the distance from the text.

7 Click OK.

Filling a Text Box

① SEE ALSO

A pull quote is text in the report that you want to highlight by setting it apart in a special box on the page. For details, see "Are You Pulling My Quote?" page 439.

Inside a text box, you can insert anything that you can insert into a Word document. You can then format the text, art, table, or other object in all the ways you format them in Word text outside text boxes. In fact, think of a text box as a miniature document (except you can't insert a page break, column break, or section break, and you can't format a text box with multiple columns).

You can put as much text, art, and tables as you want into a text box, but remember that only the portion that fits within the text box size will be visible. You can't scroll a text box, but you can link text boxes so that long text can continue in the next text box—see "Continued on Another Page: Linking Text Boxes," page 407.

Check out the document TOPXREF.DOC on the CD in this book for the steps you use to insert a topical cross-reference into text.

Sending Text Box Text in a New Direction

You can make text in text boxes run vertically instead of horizontally. To change the direction of text, take these steps:

1 Click in the text box text.

2 Choose the Format Text Direction command to see this dialog box:

3 Click the direction you want the text to run.

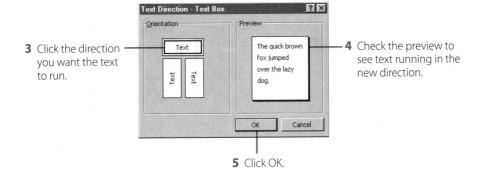

4 Check the preview to see text running in the new direction.

5 Click OK.

When the text direction is vertical, several changes occur in Word:

- The insertion point is horizontal in vertical text.

- The paragraph alignment buttons on the Formatting toolbar show vertical alignment rather than horizontal alignment. Click these buttons to adjust vertical alignment of vertical text.

- Paragraph space before and after settings become horizontal spacing between the left and right borders of the text box.

Change
Text
Direction

Shortcut for Changing Text Direction

As a shortcut, click in the text box, and then click the Change Text Direction button on the Text Box toolbar. Each time you click the Change Text Direction button, the text switches to the next direction—vertical down, vertical up, and horizontal. The button image shows the new direction for the text the next time you click the button.

III

Publications

Controlling Internal Spacing in a Text Box

When you insert a text box, Word sets up internal margins for space between the contents of the text box and its borders. The standard space is 0.1 inches on the sides and 0.005 inches top and bottom. When you insert text, art, a table, or another type of object into a text box, you might want more or less room for the internal margins.

NOTE

If you set the internal margins too wide, you might not leave enough internal space to display the entire contents of your text box. In this case, you can either make the text box larger, the text a smaller point size, reduce the internal margins, or set up a link to another text box to show the remainder of the text box contents. Remember that pictures and objects won't flow from one text box to another, but text in tables and worksheets will.

To change the internal margins of a text box, take these steps:

1 Click the text box to activate it.

2 Place the mouse pointer over a border of the text box, so that the mouse pointer changes to four arrows.

3 Right-click the text box border, and then select Format Text Box from the shortcut menu.

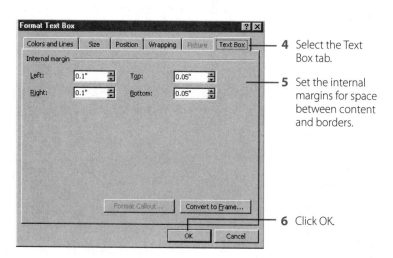

4 Select the Text Box tab.

5 Set the internal margins for space between content and borders.

6 Click OK.

Continued on Another Page: Linking Text Boxes

One of the great aggravations readers face is the continued article—you know, you read down a column or page and then read something like "Continued on page 69." You too can join in creating reports that serve up this kind of aggravation—you use linked text boxes to do it.

When you link text boxes, the text flows from one box to the next box in the chain of links. You can link any one text box to any other text box in any order anywhere in a document. You can skip over intervening text boxes when you link. And you can have text flow past other streams of text in other text box chains. For example, you can continue text from page 10 to page 23. Then with other text boxes, you can continue text from page 18 to page 14 to page 5; or the other way around.

To link text boxes, take these steps:

1 Insert two or more text boxes anywhere in the document. They can be on the same page, they can overlap or stack one over the other, and they can be pages apart.

2 Choose the View Toolbars command, and select Text Box from the submenu to display the Text Box toolbar, shown here:

Create Text Box Link

3 Click the text box from which you want the text to flow to another text box.

4 Click the Create Text Box Link button on the Text Box toolbar. The mouse pointer becomes a coffee cup. When the mouse pointer is over an *empty* text box, the coffee cup tilts and shows letters spilling out. When the mouse pointer is over document text or a text box that has content, the coffee cup is upright—to show that you can't link to the place where the mouse pointer sits.

5 Click the text box where you want the text to flow from the pre-ceding text box in the chain.

6 Repeat steps 4 and 5 to add more text box links to the chain of text boxes.

Jumping the Links from One Text Box to Another

After you set up a chain of text box links, you might want to move quickly along the chain to edit or format various parts of the text that flows from one box to another. After you set up a link between text boxes, the jump buttons on the Text Box toolbar come alive, and you can use them to jump from text box to text box.

Previous Text Box—inactive at the head of the chain

Next Text Box—inactive at the end of the chain

Converting a Text Box to a Frame

If you have used an earlier version of Word, you might be familiar with frames. You can convert a text box to a frame if you prefer frames. Note that you can't directly insert a frame in Word 97. To insert a frame, you have to insert a text box, and then convert it to a frame. Also, the text box you want to convert cannot be linked to another text box.

To convert a text box to a frame, take these steps:

1 Click the text box.

2 Choose the Format Text Box command, and then select the Text Box tab.

3 Click the Convert To Frame button.

4 When Word asks if you're sure you want to convert, click OK.

When you convert a text box to a frame, Word changes border and shading colors, if necessary, to one of the 16 basic colors. Any special border effects are flattened. You can no longer use the Drawing toolbar to add special effects to the frame. A text box gives you many more formatting options than a frame. Also, a text box avoids all the quirks that frame users came to know and expect but hate.

Breaking Links

If you no longer want text to flow to a text box, you can break the link with these steps:

1 Click the text box you want removed from the chain of links.

2 Click the Previous Check Box button on the Text Box toolbar.

3 Click the Break Forward Link button on the Text Box toolbar.

Positioning Objects on a Page

All of the objects you learn about in this chapter—art, WordArt, tables, worksheets, charts, equations, and text boxes—can be set anywhere on a page. Once the object is in the position you want, you can wrap the text around the object in several clever ways. Text boxes, art, WordArt, charts, and equations (as well as any other object you insert with the Insert Object command) are originally set up to float above the page. (For information about the various layers on a Word page, see the sidebar "The Drawing Layers on a Page," page 459.) You can also move these floating objects around on a page or even move them to some other page entirely.

 NOTE

You must insert tables and worksheets inside a text box to be able to position them freely on a page and wrap text around them.

To position an object on its page, Word gives you two methods:

- Drag the object into position.
- Set the position with the Format (Object) command.

Dragging an Object into Position

To position an object by dragging it, take these steps:

1 Position the mouse pointer on the object border so that the mouse pointer becomes a four-headed arrow.

2 Drag the object to the new position you want it to occupy on the page.

III

Publications

Positioning an Object by Command

To position an object by command, take these steps:

 SEE ALSO

For more details of the Position tab, see "Positioning," page 518.

1 Click the object. When you do, Word gives the object a hatched border to show that you have selected it.

2 Choose the Format Object command. This command changes its name for text boxes, tables, and pictures.

3 Select the Position tab.

4 Set the horizontal distance.

6 Set the vertical distance.

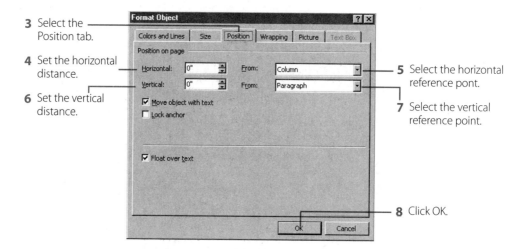

5 Select the horizontal reference pont.

7 Select the vertical reference point.

8 Click OK.

Moving an Object to Another Page

While it is easy to move an object around on its own page, moving an object to another page takes an additional step—you use Print Preview.

To move an object from one page to another, take these steps:

Print Preview

1 Click the Print Preview button on the Standard toolbar.

2 Set the display to the number of pages you need with the Multiple Pages button on the Print Preview toolbar.

Multiple Pages

Set up enough pages so that you can see at the same time the page where the object is now and the page where you want to move the object.

3 If necessary, click the Magnifier button to turn it off; otherwise, you will not be able to select an object on a page in the Print Preview window.

4 Position the mouse pointer on the object border so that the mouse pointer becomes a four-headed arrow.

5 Drag the object to the new page and to the position you want it to occupy on that new page.

Remember that you can use the Format (Object, Text Box, Picture) command to position the object precisely on its new page, as well as to set borders, shading, wrapping, and other traits.

Writing Your Report in Another Language

For the most part, words in business letters and reports or any other type of document are in the primary language you use on your computer. When you set up Windows, the standard language is the primary language of your country. From time to time, however, you might use a few words from another language, or you might compose an entire document in another language for colleagues or associates in another country, particularly if your organization conducts business outside your home country.

There are also times when you might want to turn off the spelling checker and hyphenation for some words or elements in a document. For words in a different language, you can mark them so that Word checks their spelling and sets their hyphenation properly for that language (providing you have the related language dictionaries installed—see "Dictionaries for Other Languages," page 412). For words and elements you want the spelling checker and hyphenation to skip, you can mark them as having no language.

To mark a word as belonging to a different language, take these steps:

1 Select the word you want to mark as belonging to a different language.

2 Choose the Tools Language command, and then choose Set Language from the submenu.

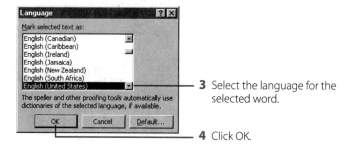

3 Select the language for the selected word.

4 Click OK.

If the dictionary for the language you select is not installed, you see a message telling you that Word cannot find the dictionary. Simply click OK.

To mark a word as "no language" so that the spelling checker and hyphenation skip them, take these steps:

1 Select the word or element you want to mark as "no language."

2 Choose the Tools Language command, and then select Set Language from the submenu.

3 Select (No Proofing) at the top of the Mark Selected Text As list.

Dictionaries for Other Languages

Before you can check the spelling and set the hyphenation of words in a different language, you need to add a dictionary for that language to your Word or Office setup. Copy the language dictionary to the Proof folder inside the Microsoft Shared folder inside the Common Files folder inside the Program Files folder on your computer's hard disk. Now, you need to activate the dictionary in Word. To do so, take these steps:

1 Choose the Tools Options command, and then click the Spelling & Grammar tab.

2 Click the Dictionaries button, and then click the Add button.

3 In the Add Custom Dictionary dialog box, select the language dictionary, and click OK.

4 Click OK in the Custom Dictionaries dialog box, and then click OK in the Options dialog box.

These same steps apply to specialty dictionaries, such as medical or law dictionaries.

Keyboards for Other Languages

With Windows 95, you can switch keyboards "on the fly." This means that you can disconnect the keyboard you are using, plug in a keyboard for a different language, and keep typing, without having to change settings in the Control Panel and then stop and restart Windows.

When you switch keyboards and start typing, Word automatically sets the language of your typing to the keyboard you are using.

III

Publications

CHAPTER 9

Publishing
a Newsletter

Word supplies you with a Newsletter Wizard that performs some of the basic setup work you'd have to do on your own. By using the Newsletter Wizard to create the basics of your newsletter template, you have a good foundation you can remodel and build on to create your own newsletter style.

To create a newsletter template you can remodel, take these steps:

1 Choose the File New command.

2 Click the
Publications tab.

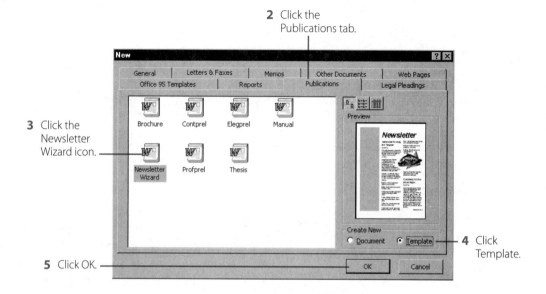

3 Click the
Newsletter
Wizard icon.

4 Click
Template.

5 Click OK.

The Newsletter Wizard displays five panels on which you make choices about the style of newsletter (its general look) and the number of columns you want, you type the newsletter title, and you choose items to put in the masthead. When you finish with the Newsletter Wizard, it sets up a newsletter template based on your choices.

Save your new template before you begin beating it into its final shape. That's what the rest of this chapter is about.

Wrestling Paper Tigers

Perhaps you always print your newsletter on standard letter-size paper. Perhaps you always print your newsletter on some other size paper. Perhaps sometimes you print special pages sideways or print inserts on special-size paper. You can set up your newsletter pages for all these situations on the Paper Size and Paper Source tabs of the Page Setup dialog box. The next several sections provide descriptions of your choices.

Changing the Paper Size

Word, like most word processors, lets you select various paper sizes. Many printers have different paper trays, allowing you to use them either one at a time or more than one at a time. Some printers also provide a way for you to manually feed various sizes of paper. Some printers even provide a means of feeding envelopes to the printer.

For all of these cases, you need to be able to set the paper size. You set the paper size on the Paper Size tab in the Page Setup dialog box.

> **NOTE**

The Print dialog box contains a Properties button. You can click this button to set the paper size, orientation, and paper source for the entire document. You cannot set custom paper sizes in the Printer Properties dialog box. To set custom paper sizes and to set paper size, orientation, and source for only part of a document, you must use the File Page Setup command. Page Setup affects sections of a document. Printer Properties affects the entire document.

You can also manually set up different paper sizes for different pages of a document. To do so, you set up a separate section, and then adjust the paper size for that section only.

> **NOTE**

When you set up a different paper size for a section, that section must print on a separate page. This seems obvious because a printer can't print on different sizes of paper on a single page. If you don't set the section to start on a new page, Word makes that change itself. If you want the section to print narrower than the paper size for a section in the middle of a page, change the margins for the section rather than changing the paper size.

When you select the Paper Size tab in the Page Setup dialog box, you see the tab shown in Figure 9-1 on the next page. The Paper Size list contains standard paper sizes for the country for which Windows is set up, plus a Custom option.

III

Publications

FIGURE 9-1.
The Paper Size tab of the Page Setup dialog box.

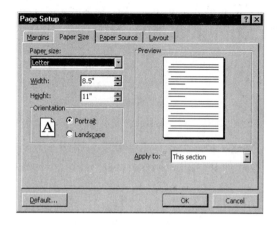

Setting a Custom Paper Size

The Custom option lets you set the paper size to any measurement from 0.1 inch to 22 inches. Note, however, that in practice, the minimum width is 0.5 inch because Word requires that columns be at least 0.5 inch wide. Also, if you set a very small paper size, Word will warn you that the margins, column spacing, or paragraph indents are too large. For example, if you set a paper width of less than 3 inches and leave the Left and Right margins at 1.25 inches, Word warns you that the column width cannot be less than 0.5 inch.

One more bugaboo: many printers cannot print closer to the edge of the paper than 0.5 inch because the printer needs the space to grab the paper and pull it through the printer. If your side margins are narrower than your printer's dead zone, Word displays the warning shown here:

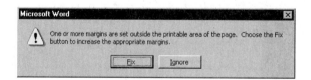

Click the Fix button to set the margins to the minimum required by the printer. Click the Ignore button to tell Word to ignore the minimum and set the margins to the width you specified.

> **NOTE**

Any time you change the Width or Height measurement to something other than one of the standard paper sizes on the Paper Size list, Word automatically selects the Custom Paper Size option.

Setting Page Orientation

On occasion, you might have an extra-wide table or picture that fits better on a page if printed sideways. That is, instead of looking at the page with the shorter sides at the top and bottom, you look at the page with the longer sides at the top and bottom. Printers call such pages "turn pages," because you turn the page sideways to see its contents. In Word, a sideways page is called a "landscape page," because a photograph or painting of a landscape is typically set up to be wider than it is tall. (The other printing option is called "portrait," because a portrait of a person or object is typically taller than it is wide.)

> **NOTE**

When you set up a different page orientation for a section, that section must print on a separate page. If you don't set the section to start on a new page, Word makes that change itself. Word can't set up a page to print different directions on a single page. You can, however, use WordArt to create text that prints with different orientations on the same page. See Chapter 10, "Brocading a Brochure."

The two Orientation choices in the Page Setup dialog box swap the measurements for Height and Width. For the standard U.S. letter-size paper, the Landscape option sets Width to 11 inches and Height to 8.5 inches. Similarly, if you set a custom paper size that is taller than it is wide, the Landscape option swaps the Height measurement for the Width measurement.

> **NOTE**

If you set up a paper size that is wider than it is tall, Word doesn't automatically turn on the Landscape option. Because of this, the first time you click the Landscape option, you see no change in the Preview box. If you then click the Portrait option, you see a change. Click the Landscape option again, and the Preview box returns to the paper size you set in the Width and Height boxes.

III

Publications

Specifying the Paper Source

The Paper Source tab in the Page Setup dialog box gives you a means of changing the paper feed on your printer. Select the Paper Source tab in the Page Setup dialog box, shown here:

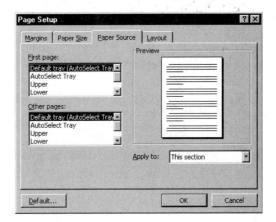

? SEE ALSO

Consult the file
BOOKDOT.DOC on the
CD in this book for
directions on printing
sideways when you
want smaller "pages"
to print on standard
letter-size paper. You
can see an example
of a turn page in
SIDEWAYS.DOC on the
CD in this book.

The Paper Source tab gives you two choices: the source of the first page and the source of all the other pages. When would you exercise these choices? Many organizations use a letterhead sheet for the first page of a letter and "second sheets" (sheets without letterhead) for all the other pages. In this case, you select the letterhead source for First Page and the second sheet source for Other Pages.

The exact list of sources depends on your printer. Some printers use only one paper tray at a time and have a slot for manual feeding. Some printers have two trays. In this case, the list will show two trays. For printers that have an envelope feeder, the Paper Source tab lists that option.

 NOTE

You don't have to add sections to your document to print the first page on paper from a different source from the rest of the pages. But remember: if you set up a document with multiple sections, Word prints the first page of each section on paper from the First Page source. In this case, then, set a different paper source for the first page of the first section only. Change all the other sections to a single paper source.

Word gives you the benefit of the two paper sources automatically when you use the Tools Envelopes And Labels command. If you set up an envelope and ask Word to print the envelope, Word sets the First Page option to Manual Feed or Envelope Feeder, as appropriate. If you tell Word to add the envelope to your document, Word inserts the envelope in a separate section and sets the First Page source for that section to Manual Feed or Envelope Feeder, as appropriate.

Automating Parts of the Masthead

As you probably know if you've ever worked on newsletters or newspapers, the masthead is the part of the front page that contains the name of the publication, the date of publication, and the volume and issue numbers. (A masthead can contain other information as well.) In the newsletter templates Word creates, the sample dates and volume and issue numbers are simply typed text. You can set up these elements so that Word inserts the correct information for you when you create a new newsletter document. The next two sections explain how you do this.

Automating the Publication Date

 SEE ALSO

For a list of additional date formats you can use, see Table 18-2, page 767.

 SEE ALSO

On the CD in this book, the file DATETIME.DOC, lists and explains all the elements of date and time instructions (called Date-and-Time Switches). When you understand how the elements of the date and time instructions work, you can easily set up the date in the format you prefer.

To automate the insertion of the publication date, you insert a Date field with the appropriate instructions for formatting the date as you want it to appear: a full date for a daily newsletter; a month and year for a monthly newsletter; or only the year for a quarterly, semiannual, or annual newsletter. Table 9-1 on the next page shows the field instructions you insert for each case.

To set up a field to automatically insert the date, take these steps:

1 Select the date that appears in the newsletter template, and press Delete.

2 Position the insertion point where you want the date to appear.

3 Press Ctrl+F9 to insert the field characters ({ }).

4 Type *DATE* \@ followed by a space and the appropriate instructions from Table 9-1. Be sure to type a space between the field name "DATE" and the backslash (\) character.

5 Press F9 to generate the date.

III

Publications

TABLE 9-1. Field Instructions and Examples for Various Types of Dates.

Type of Date	Field Instructions	Example Date Result
Daily—full date	"MMMM d, yyyy" "MMM-d-yy" "M/d/yy"	March 15, 1997 Aug-13-97 11-24-97
Monthly—month and year	"MMMM yyyy" "MMM-yy" "M/yy"	March 1997 Aug-97 11/97
Quarterly, semi-annual, or annual—year only	"yyyy" "yy"	1997 97

Automating Volume and Issue Numbers

Some publications show only a publication date. Some publications show only volume and issue numbers. Some publications show both. If your publication shows volume and issue numbers, you can get Word to insert the correct numbers for you. This way you don't have to try to remember these numbers.

To calculate the volume number, you'll insert a calculation field that subtracts the year *before* the year of volume 1 from the current year. To calculate the issue number, you'll insert a calculation field that uses the current month as the basis for calculating the issue number. (Most daily publications I've seen don't use volume and issue numbers.)

To insert a field to calculate the volume number, take these steps:

1 Select the volume number that appears in the newsletter template, and press Delete.

2 Position the insertion point where you want the volume number to appear.

3 Press Ctrl+F9 to insert the field characters ({ }).

4 Type an equal sign (=) and a space, and then press Ctrl+F9 again.

5 Inside the second set of field characters (the insertion point is already where you want it), type *DATE \@ yyyy*.

6 Move the insertion point between the two ending field characters (as shown by the vertical line in the following:

{ = { DATE \@ yyyy }| }

7 Type a space, a minus sign (-), another space, and then the year *before* the year of volume 1; for example, if volume 1 appeared in 1984, you type the year 1983. The set of fields would look like this:

{ = { DATE \@ yyyy } - 1983 }

8 Press F9 to generate the volume number.

> If you want the volume number in Roman numerals, add the formatting switch * Roman to the end of the field, like this:
>
> { = { DATE \@ yyyy } - 1983 * Roman }

To insert a field to calculate the issue number, take these steps:

1 Select the issue number that appears in the newsletter template, and press Delete.

2 Position the insertion point where the issue number is to appear.

3 Insert the appropriate field instructions from Table 9-2.

4 Press F9 to generate the issue number.

TABLE 9-2. **Field Instructions and Examples for Various Frequencies of Issues.**

Issue Frequency	Field Instructions	Date Example	Result Example
Monthly	{ DATE \@ M }	9/23/97	9
Bimonthly (even-numbered months)	{ = { DATE \@ M } / 2 }	10/3/97	5
Bimonthly (odd-numbered months)	{ = ROUND({ DATE \@ M } / 2, 0) }	7/13/97	4
Quarterly (Jan-Mar, Apr-Jun, Jul-Sep, Oct-Dec)	{ = INT({DATE \@ M } / 3.1) + 1 }	5/30/97	2
Semiannual (Jan–Jun, Jul–Dec)	{ = INT({DATE \@ M } / 6.1) + 1 }	8/12/97	2

Dressing Up Columns

Most documents start their life (when you create them) with one column of text that spans the page between the left and right margins. The width of a single column is the width between the two side margins. (For more about this, see the sidebar "Figuring Margin Settings," page 799.) Newsletters typically have more than one column—the Newsletter Wizard and the newsletter template are set up with three columns. You don't have to worry about sections if your entire document is formatted in more than one column and the number of columns doesn't change. If you want the entire document in three columns, you simply set the number of columns to three for the entire document.

> **NOTE**
>
> In Word, the term *column* is used in two senses. In one sense, column refers to a part of a table—a table column. In another sense, the sense used here, column refers to the type of columns you see in a newspaper or a magazine. In fact, some people call these columns *newspaper columns* to distinguish them from table columns. Other people like to call them *snaking columns* because you read them top to bottom and then jump back to the top of the page and read the next column down, and so on. The resulting pattern of reading looks like the path of a sidewinder snake.

If, however, you want part of a document in one column and other parts in more than one column, you have to deal with sections. Let's say, for example, that you want the newsletter's masthead (title, volume and series number, and date) to print in one column, but you want the rest of the document to print in three columns. You set up two sections. In the first section, you leave the number of columns set to 1, but in the second section, you change the number of columns to 3. (This is what the Newsletter Wizard and the newsletter template set up for you.)

You can also set up different numbers of columns within a single page. For example, you want a list of items to appear in two columns, but you want the rest of the text to appear in three columns. In this case, you set off the text for the three columns in a separate section with the number of columns set to 3. You leave sections before and after the three-column list set to 2 columns.

Using the Columns Button

Columns

Using the Columns button on the Standard toolbar, you can change the number of columns for the selected sections.

Because the Columns button always inserts equal-width columns with the standard 0.5-inch spacing between them, the only thing you can change with the Columns button is the number of columns. To remodel columns in other ways, use the Format Columns command.

Using the Format Columns Command

With the Format Columns command, you can change the number of columns, you can change their widths, you can put a line between columns, and you can start a new column section. To set up columns with the Format Columns command, take these steps:

1 Choose the Format Columns command.

2 For quick setup, select a preset column setup or go to step 3.

3 Set the number of columns.

4 Turn off this check box to set up custom unequal columns.

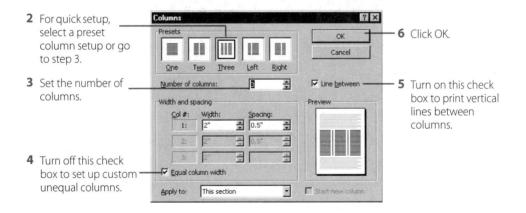

6 Click OK.

5 Turn on this check box to print vertical lines between columns.

 TIP

If you type in values, the preview may not be accurate until you move to a different part of the dialog box. If you see that the preview doesn't seem to show you the changes you made, press the Tab key to move to a different box or option, and Word will update the preview.

III

Publications

Number Of Columns Box

You can enter any number in the Number Of Columns box, but Word resets the number to fit within the margins of the paper width. On standard U.S. letter-size paper (8.5 inches wide) with standard margins (1.25 inches on each side), Word lets you set up to 12 columns. This gives you 12 half-inch columns with no space between them—not very practical, but you can do it if you want each column to run into the neighboring columns.

Equal Column Width Box

When you turn off the Equal Column Width check box, you can set the column width of each column individually. With this check box turned off, all the boxes in the Width And Spacing area of the dialog box become active. With the Equal Column Width check box turned on, only the Col # 1 boxes are active. In this latter case, you adjust the column width and spacing between columns for all the columns at the same time.

Should You Use Columns or Tables?

Many times you'll find that setting up a table for items is easier and gives you more control than setting up more than one column. How do you decide which to use?

If your items are static, you can use a table, if you find that easier. Also, if your items need to appear in tabular form (that is, some items need to appear beside certain other items), a table is the only realistic (and sane) way to set this up.

If, however, your material is changeable (you add or remove items from time to time) and you don't need to line up some items with other items, setting up columns might be a better choice.

Most times, the choice is pretty clear. You want the page to print in a number of columns for certain kinds of subject matter—that's columns. Or you want items to match up for comparison or reference—that's tables.

Note that you can insert tables into a column of any width, just as you do in a document with one column.

Starting a New Column

In normal cases, when you select text and set the number of columns, Word inserts Continuous section breaks at the beginning and ending of the selection. If you prefer a section with Column section breaks instead of Continuous section breaks, turn on the Start New Column check box. Turning on this check box places the first column of the new section at the top of a column and places the first column of the following section at the top of a column. In most cases, this means that the section breaks act like the New Page setting in the Section Start box on the Layout tab in the Page Setup dialog box. The columns will appear on the same page only under all the following special circumstances:

- You have set up three or more columns for at least the section you selected and the sections before and after the selection.

- The preceding section doesn't end in the last column on the page.

- The selected section doesn't end in the last column on the page.

Adding the Articles

? SEE ALSO

"Adding Chapters from Separate Files," page 652, contains the steps you take to insert text from other files. Chapter 10, "Brocading a Brochure," has extensive directions and descriptions about adding art and drawing art.

For the most part, adding articles to your newsletter is a simple matter of typing the text, pasting text you've copied from another document, or inserting a file that contains the article. Likewise for artwork, it's a simple matter of inserting art from a file or drawing a picture. These actions are fully described elsewhere in this book.

There are a few points to understand about newsletters you create from Word's newsletter templates. First, you'll want to understand how to set up a headline for an article. Second, you may want to preserve the initial drop capital at the beginning of articles. Third, you need to understand how to deal with artwork so that you can insert captions properly.

Editing Around Bookmarks

You may see several sets of bookmark brackets on parts of the newsletter. If you need to edit the text within a bookmark, you can revise text as you please and as you normally do in any text that doesn't have a bookmark. When you revise bookmarked text at the bookmark brackets, however, you should be aware of some precautions you need to take.

If you type or insert text in front of the first bookmarked character (just to the right of the beginning bookmark bracket), what you type is added to the bookmarked text. If you don't want this change, move to the left of the character just to the left of the beginning bookmark bracket, and then type or insert the new text. If you type or insert text after the last bookmarked character, the new text is not added to the bookmark. If you want the new text as part of the bookmarked text, position the insertion point to the left of the last bookmarked character, type the last character, and then type the new text. After you type the new text at the end of the bookmark, delete the character that was previously at the end of the bookmark.

Formatting Headlines

Depending on the newsletter style you select, the newsletter template uses the Heading 1 (followed by the name of the style, such as Professional) style for article titles. While you can use any style you want, including one you create yourself, you'll want to format all the article titles with the same style. Not only does this make the headlines look the same throughout your newsletter, but it also means that you can more easily build a table of contents for your newsletter from the article titles.

Dropping Caps

For details of drop capitals, see "Creating Drop Capital Letters," page 450.

Sometimes articles begin with a drop capital letter. The easiest way to deal with these drop capitals is simply to select the letter, and then type a letter you want in its place.

Dealing in Art

In Chapter 10, "Brocading a Brochure," you'll find extensive directions and descriptions about adding art and drawing art. You'll also find complete directions for scaling and cropping art ("Sizing—Scaling and Cropping," page 516). At this point, it's useful to cover cropping art for one important reason: picture captions. Word provides the Insert Caption command to label pictures, tables, equations, and any other object you want to give a caption. These captions give the object a label and a number (such as "Figure 3"). But in a newsletter (and in some other types of documents you can think of) captions usually don't have labels and numbers; captions are simply text.

You can trick Word into using a label that is blank, but you can't get rid of the number. So what do you do instead? Simple: you "crop" the picture to give it extra space below the image, and then you place a text box where you want to place the caption. When you make a picture larger by cropping, it's called a "negative crop." Here are the steps:

1 If the art isn't inserted already, insert it, and then select it. (See Chapter 10, "Brocading a Brochure," for details of inserting art.)

Crop

2 Click the Crop button on the Picture toolbar.

3 Drag the bottom border down enough to provide space to hold your caption.

4 Click outside the picture so that it's not selected.

5 Choose the Insert Text Box command.

6 Draw a text box in the empty space below the picture.

7 Type your caption.

You get a picture with a caption, something like what you see in Figure 9-2.

III

Publications

FIGURE 9-2.
A text box with a caption over a picture with a negative crop.

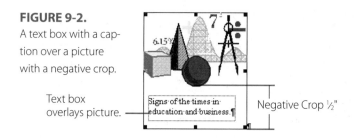

Text box
overlays picture.

Signs of the times in education and business.¶

Negative Crop ½"

Handling Hyphenation

Regular one-column documents, such as letters and memos, rarely require hyphenation. If you set up a document in more columns or if you set up paragraphs as justified (flush with both the left and right margins), you might find some pretty ugly patches in your document. In sections with multiple columns, you might find long blank spaces at the ends of lines. And if you justify the paragraphs, you might find large gaps down the middle of the text (called "rivers," because they look like water or ink could just pour down the page).

You can lessen this ugliness by using hyphenation in your document. Word's Tools Language Hyphenation command gives you two choices: automatic hyphenation and manual hyphenation. When you select automatic hyphenation, Word inserts the hyphens for you, following the guidelines you set for hyphenation. Manual hyphenation means that you decide where to insert each hyphen.

In both cases, you start by choosing the Hyphenation command from the Tools Language submenu to display the Hyphenation dialog box.

Asking Word to Hyphenate for You

If you don't have the time or patience to make every hyphenation decision yourself, you can have Word hyphenate for you. You retain control over the width of the hyphenation zone and the number of consecutive hyphens. Besides speed and the fact that Word keeps hyphenation current as you edit, automatic hyphenation lets you see hyphenation quickly, so you can delete or add hyphens yourself in places where you see a better hyphenation choice.

To automatically hyphenate a document, take these steps:

1 Choose the Tools Language command, and then select Hyphenation from the submenu.

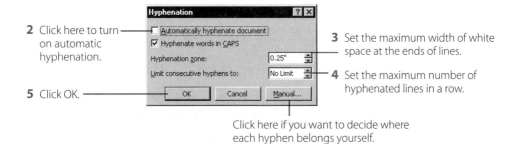

2 Click here to turn on automatic hyphenation.

5 Click OK.

3 Set the maximum width of white space at the ends of lines.

4 Set the maximum number of hyphenated lines in a row.

Click here if you want to decide where each hyphen belongs yourself.

Traveling in the Hyphenation Zone

The Hyphenation Zone distance is the maximum width of blank space that Word leaves at the end of a left-justified line. The narrower the distance, the more hyphens Word will try to insert. The wider the distance, the fewer hyphens Word will need to insert.

Limiting Consecutive Hyphens

If you don't like to see lots of hyphens in a row at the ends of consecutive lines, set a maximum number in the Limit Consecutive Hyphens To box. The number you enter in this box is the maximum number of consecutive hyphens you'll allow per document page. The No Limit option directs Word to hyphenate every line, if necessary. The maximum number in the Limit Consecutive Hyphens To box is 32,767. But because most standard U.S. documents, even single-spaced ones, have no more than about 54 lines per page, entering any number larger than 54 is essentially the same as selecting No Limit.

Hyphenating a Document Yourself

To manually hyphenate your document, take these steps:

1 Choose the Tools Language command, and then select Hyphenation from the submenu.

2 If necessary, change the Hyphenation Zone distance.

III

Publications

3 If you don't like to see lots of hyphens in a row at the ends of consecutive lines, set a maximum number in the Limit Consecutive Hyphens To check box.

4 Click the Manual button.

The initial position indicates the legal hyphen placement, according to the dictionary.

This line indicates the end of the text line—if you try to hyphenate to the right of it, the word will not be hyphenated.

5 Click between the letters where you want to change the hyphen's position.

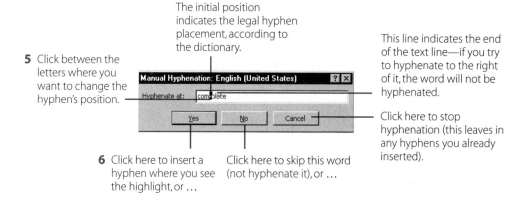

Click here to stop hyphenation (this leaves in any hyphens you already inserted).

6 Click here to insert a hyphen where you see the highlight, or ...

Click here to skip this word (not hyphenate it), or ...

 NOTE

The Manual Hyphenation dialog box displays the language for hyphenation; that is, the language of the hyphenation dictionary Word is using. If you have text in another language and Word has that language dictionary installed, Word shows that language when it's hyphenating words in that language.

Preventing Hyphens in Paragraphs

Both manual and automatic hyphenation look at every line of a document, unless you set a limit on the number of consecutive hyphens. In that case, Word ignores a line after inserting the maximum number of consecutive hyphens. But you might want to prevent hyphenation, for example, in headings and headlines. Word lets you prevent hyphenation on a paragraph-by-paragraph basis.

Here's how to prevent hyphenation in a single paragraph:

1 Select the paragraph, and choose the Format Paragraph command.

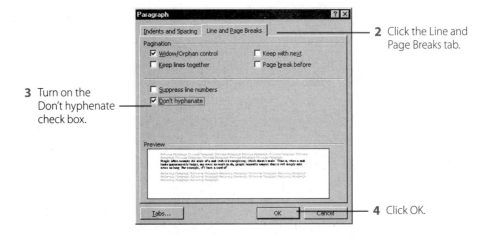

2 Click the Line and Page Breaks tab.

3 Turn on the Don't hyphenate check box.

4 Click OK.

Inserting Hyphens with Keys

Word's Hyphenation command inserts *optional hyphens*. Optional hyphens appear when needed but are normally invisible when their position is not at the end of a line. Regular hyphens, which are always visible, are inserted by pressing the hyphen key (-).

You can insert optional hyphens yourself by pressing Ctrl+- (hyphen).

Word provides one other kind of hyphen, a *nonbreaking hyphen*. A nonbreaking hyphen prevents Word from starting a new line between the hyphen and the word that follows the hyphen. For example, you might type a hyphenated name, such as *Eoj-Enaj*. You might want Word to keep this name all on one line, rather than breaking it so that the first part of the name is at the end of one line and the second part is at the beginning of the next line. In this case, insert a nonbreaking hyphen by pressing Ctrl+Shift+-.

If you turn on Show/Hide ¶, you can see that the three types of hyphens have different looks, as shown in the following table, even though they all print as regular hyphens.

Hyphen Type	Key(s)	Nonprinting Appearance	Description
Regular	-	-	Regular hyphen
Optional	Ctrl+-	¬	Logical NOT symbol
Nonbreaking	Ctrl+Shift+-	–	Elongated hyphen, between the lengths of an en dash and an em dash

If you have certain types of paragraphs that you regularly don't want hyphenated, you can set the styles of those paragraphs to prevent hyphenation. In the newsletter template, the only style you'll want to hyphenate is the Body Text style, which the template uses for the text of news items. The easiest way to take care of the problem is to set the Normal style to Don't Hyphenate, and then set the Body Text style to Hyphenate. To set up the newsletter styles with the proper hyphenation and hyphenation prevention, take these steps:

1 Choose the Format Style command.

2 Select Normal from the Styles box, and then click Modify.

3 In the Modify Style dialog box, click the Format button and select Paragraph.

4 In the Paragraph dialog box, click the Line And Page Breaks tab.

5 Turn on the Don't Hyphenate check box, and then click OK.

6 Click OK in the Modify Style dialog box.

7 In the Style dialog box, select Body Text from the Styles box, and then click Modify.

8 In the Modify Style dialog box, click the Format button and select Paragraph.

9 In the Paragraph dialog box, click the Line And Page Breaks tab.

10 Turn off the Don't Hyphenate check box, and then click OK.

SEE ALSO

For more information about changing paragraph styles, see "Changing a Paragraph Style," page 834.

11 Click OK in the Modify Style dialog box, and then click Apply in the Style dialog box.

Word will now automatically hyphenate (or manually hyphenate) the text of your news items but won't hyphenate your headlines or other text items in your newsletter.

Using Text Boxes

A text box is an area you set aside for placing text at a special position on a page. Text boxes can be linked so that text that is too long for one text box flows into the next text box in the chain of linked text boxes. In a newsletter, you'll use text boxes in the following ways (and in any other ways you can think up):

- To contain and place a sidebar article at a specific place on a specific page

- To continue a long article on another page

- To place a pull quote on a page

The following sections describe how to use a text box for these purposes.

Placing a Text Box

A very common use of text boxes in newsletters is to place a sidebar article on a page. To set up a sidebar, you insert a text box, and then simply add the sidebar text inside the text box.

To insert a text box, take these steps:

1 Display the page where you want to insert a text box. If the current view of the document is not Page Layout view, Word switches to this view for you when you take step 2.

2 Choose the Insert Text Box command.

3 Position the drawing pointer (the mouse pointer in the shape of a crosshair) where you want one corner of the text box to sit on the page.

4 Drag the drawing pointer toward the opposite corner of the text box to make the box the size you want it. You can change the size later.

When you release the mouse button after dragging out a text box, you see an empty box on the page with a hatched border, as shown here:

"Not all matterings of mind equal one violet," has at least two meanings, maybe more:
- The sum total of matterings weight, power, or importance of a single violet. As Carl Sagan once said (and make an apple pie from scratch, you have to invent a universe." A violet is a uni of all matterings of the mind don't equal a universe.
- Not every mattering of mir, or importance of a single violet.

In these two phrases, we see the multiple meanings of thought. Even though an author might wish to convey a crafted sentence, a poet has no such compunction. A poet wants to capture not only ambiguity but also the manifold character of words and thoughts and perception and life in every single phrase. Poetry is often filled with pictures, symbols, images, and poetry is filled with multiple levels of meaning, as in the two phrases we have so cold-heartedly dissected above.

SEE ALSO

For information about formatting text boxes and performing other wonderful feats with them, see "Wrapping Up Text Boxes," page 399, and "Formatting Art, WordArt, and Other Objects," page 515.

The hatched border means that the text box is active and ready for formatting, filling, or editing.

If you're using the text box for a sidebar, simply type, paste, or otherwise insert the text you want in the text box. Be aware that a text box can contain only one column. If you want two or three columns in a text box, you'll need to set up a text box for each column, and then link the text boxes, as described in the next section.

Continued on Another Page

Newsletters are notorious for containing continued articles. You know what I mean—you start reading an article and at the end of a column or page you see some text that reads something like "Continued on page 69." You can set up continued articles in Word by placing text boxes and linking them. You can link any text box with any other text box, even one that already has a forward link into it. The links can jump around the document in any order—forward or backward.

When you link text boxes and then insert text into one that has a following link (the link goes to another text box), the text flows into the second text box when the first one is full. If there's another text box linked from the second text box, the text flows to that one after the second text box is full, and so on.

To link text boxes, take these steps:

1 Insert at least two text boxes of any size at any location. You decide the locations and the sizes yourself.

2 Click the text box you want to be the first in the chain of linked text boxes. If the Text Box toolbar doesn't appear, and if it's not already visible, display it by choosing the View Toolbars command and selecting Text Box to turn it on.

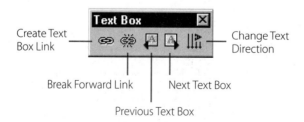

Create Text Box Link — Break Forward Link — Previous Text Box — Next Text Box — Change Text Direction

3 Click the Create Text Box Link button. The mouse pointer changes to a coffee cup.

4 Click the second text box (the one you want the text to flow into next). This text box can be any other empty text box anywhere in the document, even a text box that already has a forward link into it.

5 Repeat step 3 and step 4 to extend the chain of text box links.

 TIP

Recognizing Linked Text Boxes

If you set a link into a text box that already has a link into it, the new link replaces the previous link. When text boxes are linked, only the first text box shows a paragraph mark until the text begins to flow into the next text box in the chain. If you try to click in an empty text box that's part of a chain, nothing happens. One way to know if a text box containing text has a link into it is to click the text box and see whether the Previous Text Box button becomes active.

Jumping from One Text Box to Another

When you link text boxes, the Previous Text Box and Next Text Box buttons can become active. If you're in the text box at the head of a chain of text box links, only the Next Text Box button is active. If you're in the text box at the end of a chain of text box links, only the Previous Text Box button is active. If you're in a text box that has at least one text box ahead of it in the chain and at least one text box after it in the chain, then both the Previous Text Box and Next Text Box buttons become active.

- To jump to the next text box in the chain, click the Next Text Box button on the Text Box toolbar.

- To jump to the preceding text box in the chain, click the Previous Text Box button on the Text Box toolbar.

Changing the Text Box Text Direction

While you might seldom use this feature in a newsletter, you might want to know that you can change the direction of the text in a text box. The Change Text Direction button on the Text Box toolbar switches the direction of the text in a text box to the direction shown on the button. When you change the text direction, the button shows

III

Publications

the next direction the text will change to when you click the button. The button shows three directions, as shown in Table 9-3.

 **NOTE**

> When you're working with a chain of linked text boxes, the Change Text Direction button on the Text Box toolbar is active only in the first text box in the chain. When you change the text direction in the first box in a chain of linked text boxes, that text direction applies to all the text boxes in the chain.

TABLE 9-3. **The Ways You Can Change Text Direction in a Text Box.**

Button Face	New Direction	Example
	Text points down— Turn the page counterclockwise to read the text.	The quick red fox jumped over the lazy brown dog.
	Text points up— Turn the page clockwise to read the text.	The quick red fox jumped over the lazy brown dog.
	Text is horizontal— Text reads normally, from left to right.	The quick red fox jumped over the lazy brown dog.

Are You Pulling My Quote?

A pull quote is text in a newsletter or other document that you want to highlight by setting it apart in a special box on the page.

To insert the pull quote, take these steps:

1 Select the text you want to pull for quotation.

2 Choose the Insert Bookmark command.

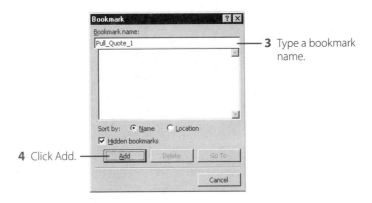

3 Type a bookmark name.

4 Click Add.

5 Insert a text box where you want to place the pull quote—for directions see "Placing a Text Box," page 435.

6 Choose the Insert Cross-Reference command.

7 Select Bookmark.

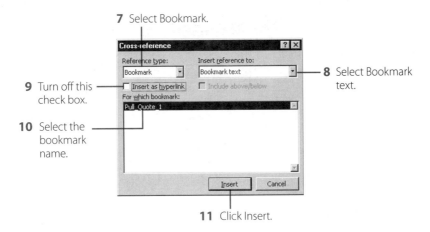

8 Select Bookmark text.

9 Turn off this check box.

10 Select the bookmark name.

11 Click Insert.

III

Publications

12 Click the Close button. (The Cancel button changes to the Close button after you click the Insert button.)

After you click the Close button and add some formatting (boldface, 16-point font size, and paragraph centering), your text box might look something like this:

? SEE ALSO

Check out the document TOPXREF.DOC on the CD in this book for an example of a pull quote in a text box.

Format the pull quote as you wish. If you want to keep the pull quote as it is regardless of any editing changes made to the original quotation, click the pull quote and press Ctrl+Shift+F9 to convert the cross-reference field to regular text. Whether you convert the field to regular text or leave it as a field, you can edit the pull quote as you wish. If you choose to leave the pull quote as a field, you might want to lock the field so that it won't change during printing. To lock the cross-reference field, click the pull quote, and then press Ctrl+F11.

Setting Up the Table of Contents

Most newsletters include a table of contents. Usually, the table of contents lists article titles. The Newsletter Wizard and template insert a sample table of contents that's purely text. This isn't unfortunate—your table of contents will end up as pure text, too. But before you get to that point, you'll direct Word to collect the table of contents. Then you'll manipulate it to make it look the way you want.

The following steps tell you how to build the table of contents for your newsletter and one way you can format it. The result of taking these steps appears in Figure 9-3, page 442.

1　If the newsletter document shows a table of contents, select it and delete it. If the table of contents appears in a table, you'll have to delete the table with the Table Delete Rows command.

2　Insert a text box of the right size in the space where you want the table of contents to appear.

3　Choose Format Text Box, click the Text Box tab, and click the Convert To Frame button. Click OK in the message box that appears.

4　Choose the Insert Index And Tables command, click the Table Of Contents tab, set Show Levels to 1, and then click the Options button.

5　In the Table Of Contents Options dialog box, type *1* in the box beside the name of the style you used for the headlines in your newsletter. Remove the number 1 from the Heading 1 style, unless that is the style you use for headlines.

6　Click OK in the Table Of Contents Options dialog box, and then click OK in the Index And Tables dialog box.

7　Click the table of contents, and press Ctrl+Shift+F9 to turn the TOC field into regular text.

8　Choose the Table Convert Text To Table command, select Separate Text At Tabs, and then click OK.

9　If Word inserts a table caption, delete it.

10　Select the second column (position the mouse pointer at the top of the second column, where it turns into a downward pointing arrow, and then click). If the frame's top edge prevents you from seeing the arrow, select the Table Select Column command instead.

11　Drag the second column to the left of the first letter in the top cell of the first column. This action swaps the positions of the columns.

12　Select the first column, choose the Table Cell Height And Width command, click the Column tab, and then click the AutoFit button.

13 Select the second column, choose the Table Cell Height And Width command, click the Column tab, set Width Of Column 2 to Auto, and then click OK.

14 Select the entire table, click the down arrow on the Borders button, and select No Border.

15 Click the down arrow on the Borders button again, and select Inside Horizontal Border.

Your table of contents should look something like the one shown in Figure 9-3.

FIGURE 9-3.

A sample table of contents for a newsletter.

1	Author News
2	Latest Mysteries
4	Latest Romances
7	Hot New Tech Books
8	Staff News

Brocading a Brochure

W e've all seen a wide variety of brochures—from simple, typewritten sheets that are hand-folded to glossy booklets with lots of color and graphics. Word provides a brochure template as a starting point for you to brocade your own brochure.

Figure 10-1 on the next page shows the two pages of the brochure template that comes with Word. Note that the brochure template sets up pages in landscape orientation with three columns. This arrangement gives you a bifold brochure—two folds that give you three panels on each side of the paper. As you can see, there's lots of text and some art.

For a fuller look at the structure of the brochure template, click the Show/Hide ¶ button on the Standard toolbar. After you do this, you'll see many empty paragraph marks, a column break character, and a continuous section break character on the first page. These special characters contribute to the layout of the brochure and are important elements for you to work with when you're setting up your own brochure.

FIGURE 10-1.

The two pages of Word's brochure template.

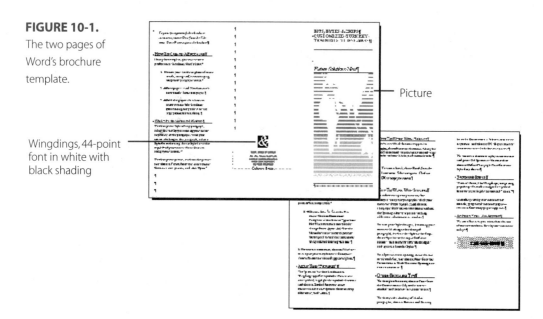

Picture

Wingdings, 44-point font in white with black shading

Setting Up a Brochure

Because the brochure template that comes with Word is full of text and art, you'll want to create your own brochure template, which you can then use to create a variety of brochures. To create your first brochure template, you can clone the brochure template supplied with Word, modify it, and then save your new template.

To create a brochure template, take these steps:

1 Choose the File New command.

2 Click the Publications tab.

3 Select Brochure.

4 Click Template.

5 Click OK.

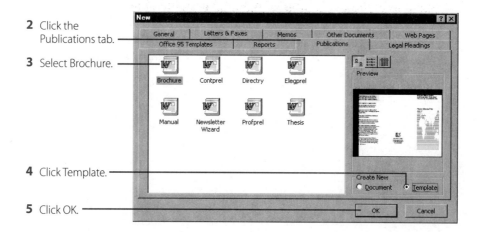

Print Word's brochure and read the instructions included on it for tips about customizing the brochure.

Clearing Out the Template

Your first task is to clear out the text that's part of the template so you can add your own text and art. As you'll notice in Figure 10-1, there are several paragraphs of text and some empty paragraph marks. The first thing you should do is clear out the text but leave all the paragraph marks. To do this, triple-click a single paragraph, press Shift+←, and then press Delete. Repeat these steps for all the paragraphs in the left column on the first page and all the columns on the second page that have text. Later in this chapter, you will deal with the picture on the third panel of the first page. Next, we'll discuss the middle panel on the first page.

Dealing with the Logo Panel

At the bottom of the middle column on the first page of the brochure template, you'll see the organization's logo (an ampersand) and some other information about the organization. This effect was set up with the "quick and dirty" method (also known as the lazy method). The creator of this template simply typed a bunch of paragraph marks until the logo ended up at the bottom of the column. Although this method works, the result is by no means stable. Any change to the length of the text in the left-hand column on the first page will shift the position of the logo up the column or down to the next column.

SEE ALSO

For more information about text boxes, see "Wrapping Up Text Boxes," page 399. For more information about wrapping text around text boxes and other objects, see "Wrapping Brochure Text Around Objects," page 520.

If you want to assure that the logo appears at the bottom of the middle panel on the first page, put the entire logo inside a text box that fits the space of the middle panel, and set the wrapping to Top And Bottom. Then set the top internal margin in the text box to push the logo to the bottom of the text box. Here are the steps you take to accomplish this setup:

1 Select the logo paragraphs.

2 Choose the Format Insert Text Box command. Word inserts a text box.

III

Publications

3 If necessary, drag the text box to the top of the middle panel, then drag the bottom right corner sizing handle down and to the right to take up all the space of the middle panel.

4 Choose the Format Text Box command, and click the Colors And Lines tab.

5 Select No Line in the Line area's Color box, and then click the Text Box tab.

6 Set the Top box to 5.85 inches, and then click OK.

7 Position the insertion point at the left end of the Column Break character that now appears on the third panel, and then press Backspace until the Column Break character appears at the bottom of the first panel.

The first page of the brochure should now look something like this:

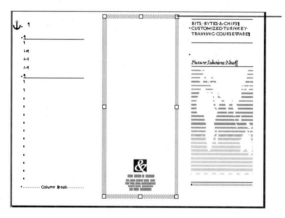

Text box with its border removed and a top internal margin of 5.85 inches.

Saving Your Template

Now that you have remodeled the brochure template, you need to save it so that you can create brochures from it. To save your template, take these steps:

1 Choose the File Properties command, and then click the Summary tab.

2 Turn on the Save Preview Picture check box, and then click OK.

3 Click the Save button on the Standard toolbar.

4 Double-click the Publications folder.

5 Type a name for your template file.

6 Click Save.

You can now create brochures from your brochure template.

Flexing the Fonts

? SEE ALSO

For information about setting fonts, see "Flexing the Fonts," page 253 or page 271. For details about a dramatic way to flex fonts, see "Bending Text—WordArt," page 507.

Brochures often use decorative initial letters at the beginning of paragraphs or sections and wording that has unusual spacing. In the next two sections, you can read about how to stretch and shrink words, how to set letter spacing (called *kerning*), and how to set up decorative initial letters called *drop capitals*.

Stretching and Shrinking Words

Perhaps you've seen a brochure with a title or organization name stretched across the top of a page, something like this:

Words stretched by 14 points

M i c r o s o f t   P r e s s

Microsoft Press

Regular (normal) spacing

At other times, you might see a word jammed up on itself, compressed into a small space, something like this:

Walrus —— Regular (normal) spacing

Walrus —— Words compressed by 12 points

To create either of these effects, you use the Character Spacing tab in the Font dialog box. To stretch or compress words, take these steps:

1 Select the words you want to stretch or compress.

2 Choose the Format Font command.

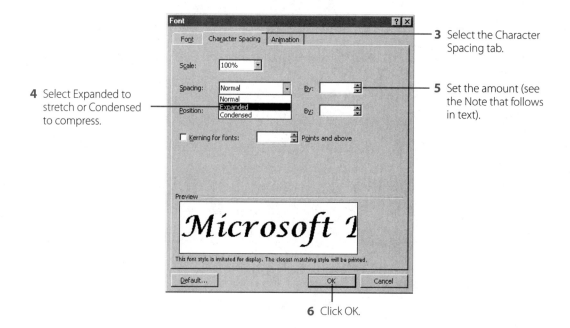

3 Select the Character Spacing tab.

4 Select Expanded to stretch or Condensed to compress.

5 Set the amount (see the Note that follows in text).

6 Click OK.

> **NOTE**
>
> Stretching letter spacing adds the amount of space specified in the Spacing By box to the right side of the selected letters. Compressing letter spacing subtracts the amount of space specified in the Spacing By box from the right side of letters. You can set the Spacing By box to stretch or compress by 1,584 points (22 inches). Unless you're using super-gigantic fonts, however, the maximum effective compression is about 1.25 points. Also remember that Word can handle a page up to 22 inches wide. For this reason, stretching up to 22 inches is well beyond a useful measurement. Generally, the maximum stretching you'll use is probably around 14 points.

> **Scaling Instead of Expanding or Condensing**
>
> Instead of selecting Expanded or Condensed and setting the amount, you can set a Scale percentage. Set a percentage larger than 100% (from 101% up to 600%) to stretch the selected characters. Set a percentage smaller than 100% (from 99% down to 1%) to compress the selected characters.

Setting Letter Spacing (Kerning)

When you use large fonts, and more especially when you use italic lettering, the spaces between letters can start to look very strange. For these situations, you'll want to adjust the spacing between pairs of characters to make the entire word look as if it truly hangs together as one word, not as several bunches of letters. These adjustments between pairs of letters is called *kerning*.

You have two ways to adjust the letter spacing between pairs of letters. You can select the first letter of a pair, and then condense the space following the first letter to give the two letters the proper spacing—to do this, use the steps in the preceding section. Adjusting the spacing yourself is the most accurate way to accomplish proper letter spacing, but it's extremely tedious, partly because you may have to manually adjust many pairs of letters, and partly because you may have to adjust a pair of letters several times to get the spacing just right.

Instead of "hand kerning," as it's called, you can have Word automatically adjust kerning for letters that are larger than a particular size. Then, if the result is not entirely satisfactory in all cases, you can resort to hand kerning as needed.

> Word can automatically kern only TrueType or Adobe Type Manager fonts.

To automatically adjust kerning, take these steps:

1 Select the text you want to kern automatically. If you want to kern the entire document, select the entire document.

2 Choose the Format Font command, and click the Character Spacing tab.

III

Publications

3 Click the Kerning For Fonts check box to turn it on (if it's off).

4 Select the minimum point size you want Word to kern automatically, and then click OK.

> **The Best Way to Handle Automatic Kerning for an Entire Document**
>
> To use automatic kerning for an entire document, set the kerning for the Normal style. To do this, take these steps:
>
> **1** Choose the Format Style command.
>
> **2** From the Styles list in the Style dialog box, select Normal, and then click the Modify button.
>
> **3** In the Modify Style dialog box, click the Format button, and select Font from the button's list.
>
> **4** Click the Character Spacing tab, set the kerning, and then click OK.
>
> **5** Click OK in the Modify Style dialog box, and then click Close in the Style dialog box.

Creating Drop Capital Letters

You might want to start a topic with a large or fancy letter, a style adapted from illuminated medieval manuscripts. You can, of course, simply format the letter with a fancy font and larger font size. Word will still treat it as a single character, allowing you to type text on the same line. Figure 10-2 shows you the difference between a drop capital letter (or drop cap) and a large, fancy first letter.

If you just change the looks of the first letter, Word lets you type only one line next to the large character. To allow text to flow along the entire height of a tall character, you need to enclose the character in a text box or frame and position the text box or frame next to the text that will flow beside the character. The Format Drop Cap command sets up the necessary text box and size for you.

FIGURE 10-2.
A drop cap (in the top example) and a large, fancy first letter (in the bottom example).

You'll probably want to customize all your templates when you discover how editing and re-saving your templates would make creating future documents easier.

You'll probably want to customize all your templates when you discover how editing and re-saving your templates would make creating future documents easier.

To set up a drop capital, take these steps:

1 Position the insertion point anywhere in the paragraph whose first character you want to set up as a drop capital.

2 Choose the Format Drop Cap command.

3 Select the position for the drop cap.

Removes drop cap

Keeps drop cap inside the margin and indents lines next to it

Puts drop cap outside the margin without indenting the lines

5 Set the number of lines to drop.

4 Select a font.

6 Set space between drop cap and the lines beside it.

7 Click OK.

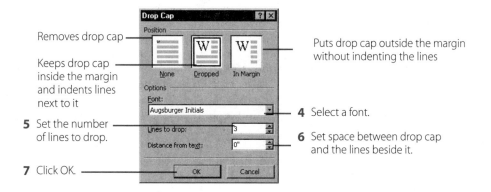

Word switches to Page Layout view (if you're in Normal view) and converts the first character of the paragraph into a drop capital by adding and positioning a borderless frame that contains the first character.

After you insert a drop capital, you can change the font, font style, size, color, and any other font settings of the character.

III

Publications

> **Raising Drop Capitals**
>
> If you want the drop capital to appear beside a couple of lines but also extend above the first line, do this:
>
> **1** Select the letter's frame by clicking the frame's border.
>
> **2** Drag the frame up to the position where you want it.

Creating Drop Cap Words

Instead of just the first letter of a paragraph, you can select several characters at the beginning of a paragraph and change all the selected characters to a "drop capital." Figure 10-3 shows an example of a word treated as a drop capital.

FIGURE 10-3.
A word treated as a drop capital.

To set up a drop cap word, select as much of the first word of a paragraph as you want to drop cap, and then use steps 2 through 7 in the preceding section, "Creating Drop Capital Letters."

> Be sure the first character is included in your selection. If it's not, Word sets up only the first letter of the paragraph as a drop capital. Also, if you select more than the first word of a paragraph, Word sets up only the first letter of the paragraph as a drop capital.

Controlling Brochure Text Vertically on the Page

In some cases, such as on a title page of a brochure, you might want the subject matter to expand vertically to fill all the space between the top and bottom margins, or you might want the text centered between the top and bottom margins. For example, on a title page, you might want the title, author's name, and the organization's name or logo to spread vertically down the page—the title at the top margin, the author's name in the middle, and the organization's name or logo at the bottom. This vertical alignment is called justified.

For these cases, you can set the vertical alignment of a section. Vertical alignment is like paragraph alignment. Paragraph alignment lets you place the left edge of a paragraph against the left margin (left), center a paragraph between the margins (centered), place the right edge of a paragraph against the right margin (right), or make it even with both the left and right margins (justified). In vertical alignment, instead of the lines of a paragraph being aligned with the side margins, the paragraphs on a page are aligned with top and bottom margins. Top, Center, and Justified alignments are shown in Figure 10-4.

FIGURE 10-4.
Three sections with Top, Center, and Justified vertical alignment.

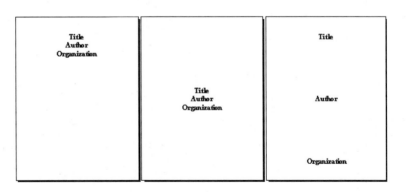

To change the vertical alignment, follow these steps:

1 Choose the File Page Setup command.

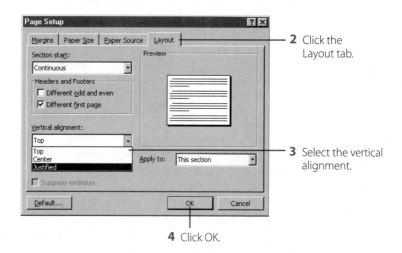

2 Click the Layout tab.

3 Select the vertical alignment.

4 Click OK.

The following table lists the different vertical alignment options and their effects.

Vertical Alignment	Effect on a Page
Top	Places the top line of the first paragraph on a page at the top margin
Center	Places all the subject matter in the center of a page between the top and bottom margins
Justified	Expands the space between paragraphs to place the top line of the first paragraph on a page at the top margin and the bottom line of the last paragraph at the bottom margin

For vertical alignment to work, you must observe these two rules:

■ The section you are aligning vertically must start on a new page. Also, the section following the vertically aligned section must start on a new page.

■ The contents of the section should be less than a full page. If not, you will likely see little or no effect from selecting a vertical alignment other than Top. If the section covers several pages, you might see some effect on some of the pages and a negligible effect on others.

Dealing with the Picture in the Brochure

Figure 10-1 on page 444 gives you a clear view of the picture that's on the third panel of the first page. If you like this picture and want to use it for your own brochures, you don't have to do a thing with this picture. If, however, you want some other piece of art on the brochure or you want the art at a different place, you'll have to deal with this picture. Here are some ways you might deal with the existing picture:

- You can edit the existing picture. To edit the existing picture, simply double-click it, and then use Word's drawing tools to make the changes you want. For details on using the drawing tools, see "The Drawing Toolbar" and the sections that explain its buttons and tools, starting on page 459.

? SEE ALSO

If you simply want to move the picture to a different position on the first page or to a position on the second page, see "Positioning," page 518, and "Positioning Objects on a Page," page 409.

- You can draw a new piece of art. To do this, click the existing picture, delete it, and then draw a new picture in its place with Word's drawing tools. For details of the drawing tools, see "The Drawing Toolbar" and the sections that explain its buttons and tools, starting on page 459.

- You can substitute any picture from an art file. To do this, click the picture, and then follow the steps in the next section, "Adding Art from Files."

- You can replace the existing picture with WordArt. To do this, click the picture, and then create and insert the WordArt. For details on WordArt, see "Bending Text—WordArt," page 507.

Adding Art from Files

The Office and Word packages include a large number of art files. Windows includes a number of art files for wallpaper. In addition, you may have any number of art files stored on your computer's hard disk from a variety of other sources. And you may have created art files of your own with one of the many graphics programs available.

Word provides graphics filters (programs that translate graphics files into the proper format for inclusion in a Word document). With these graphics filters, you can add art from files in the following formats:

- AutoCAD Format 2-D (DFX)

- Computer Graphics Metafile (CGM)

- Corel Draw (CDR)

- Encapsulated PostScript (EPS)

- GIF

- Hewlett-Packard Graphics Language (HGL)

- JPEG File Interchange Format

- Kodak Photo CD

- Micrografx Designer/Draw (DRW)

- Macintosh PICT (PCT)

- PC Paintbrush (PCX)

- Portable Network Graphics

- Tag Image File Format—TIFF (TIF)

- Targa (TGA)

- Windows Bitmap (BMP)

- Windows Enhanced Metafile

- Windows Metafile

- WordPerfect Graphics (WPG)

If you have an art file in a different graphics format, you can't insert it directly into Word, but you have two choices for inserting it using other programs. First, if you have the program that created the art and that source program is able to save it in one of the preceding file formats, you can open it in that program, and then save it in one of the graphics file formats Word accepts. If you don't have the source program available to you, you need to find someone who does and get her or him to save the art in one of the file formats Word accepts. Second, if you have the program that created the art but that source program is not able to save it in one of the compatible file formats, you can open the art file in the source program, copy the image to the Clipboard, and then paste the image into your Word document.

To help you insert art from art files in these graphics formats, Word contains an Insert Picture command and an Insert Picture button on the Picture toolbar.

To insert art from an art file in a valid format, take these steps:

1 Choose the Insert Picture command, and then choose the submenu command that corresponds to the type of art you want to insert from the submenu.

- For Clip Art, see Figure 10-5 and its steps.

- For From File, see Figure 10-6 on the next page and its steps.

- For AutoShapes, see "Drawing Pictures," on the next page.

- For WordArt see "Bending Text—WordArt," page 507.

- For Chart, see "Inserting Charts," page 372.

FIGURE 10-5.
The Clip Gallery.

2 Select a clip art category here.

3 Select the clip art you want to use.

4 Click Insert.

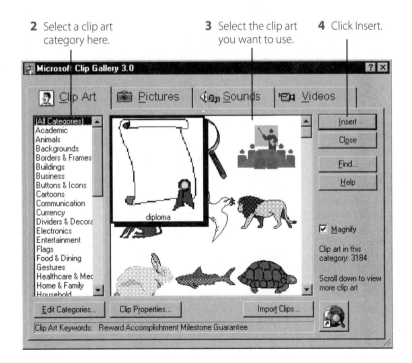

III

Publications

 **TIP**

As a shortcut to the Insert Picture From File command, you can click the Insert Picture button on the Picture toolbar—see Figure 10-11, page 523.

FIGURE 10-6.
The Insert Picture dialog box.

1 Locate the folder of the art file you want to use.

3 Click Insert.

2 Click the file that contains the art.

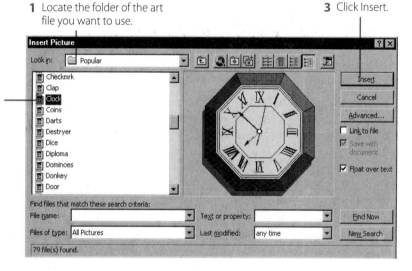

Drawing Pictures

Word provides a Drawing toolbar with a variety of drawing tools you can use to create your own drawing directly in a Word document. The following sections explain each of the drawing tools. But first, a few words about the nature of a drawing program.

The Nature of Drawing Programs

? SEE ALSO

You can, of course, add art from files to your brochure. For directions on doing this, see "Adding Art from Files," page 455.

You might already know that a painting program provides a single-layer tray of lights, with each pixel, or dot, on the screen representing a light that you can turn on and off. (In a color painting program, you can turn on the pixels in one of the available colors.) A drawing program, however, has many layers. In a drawing, each line, box, curve, circle, or piece of text you add floats in its own layer, with its own tray of lights. A complete drawing consists of various pieces that are layered to give the appearance of a single drawn object.

Because a drawing consists of various pieces, editing a part of a drawing is easy. You select the part of the drawing you want to change, and then make the change. The rest of the drawing is left undisturbed. (In a painting program, however, you must be careful during editing not to alter neighboring parts of the painting.) This ease of editing requires that you think of a drawing as a composite of pieces rather than as a single unified object.

To begin a drawing, first separate the image into shapes that the drawing tools can draw. Then draw each part of the drawing and position each part to create the complete image.

The Drawing Toolbar

In Word, a "picture" is a graphic (such as the sample art files) that you import with the Insert Picture command or create in a separate window called the Picture Editing window. A "drawing" is a graphic that you create using the drawing tools in Page Layout view in the same window as your main document.

The Drawing Layers on a Page

Like a drawing, a Word document contains layers. Word's four layers are Foreground, Text, Background, and Header/Footer. You can use them to create a layered effect on the printed page. For example, you might want to add a drawing behind some text in a letter. To do so, you create the drawing in the Foreground layer, and then move it to the Background layer so that it doesn't obscure the text, as shown in Figure 10-7 on the next page.

As you can see in Figure 10-8, also on the next page, the Header/Footer layer is the bottom layer of a Word document. Above this is the Background layer, then the Text layer, and finally the Foreground layer. Any contents in a lower layer are obscured by the contents of a higher layer. But the contents of lower layers will "show through" the empty portions of the upper layers.

Use the Header/Footer layer for headers and footers and for watermarks, which are drawings that appear on every page. (Drawings in all of these layers are items that must be created using Word's drawing tools—but you can include graphics, imported pictures, and text in such an item.) Use the Background layer to add a drawing behind text. Word places text you type, drawings in frames, and pictures from graphics files in the Text layer. By default, Word places drawings in the Foreground layer so that they obscure the contents of the other three layers. Use this layer only if you want your drawing to hide the contents underneath it.

(?) SEE ALSO

See WATERMRK.DOC on the CD included with this book for information about how to insert a watermark in the Header/Footer layer.

III

Publications

FIGURE 10-7.
Sample of a layered
Word document.

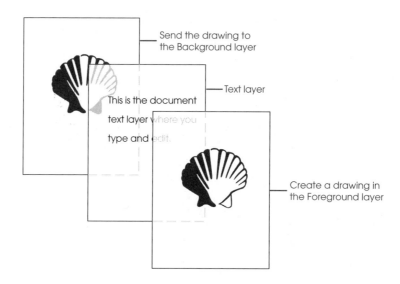

Send the drawing to
the Background layer

Text layer

Create a drawing in
the Foreground layer

FIGURE 10-8.
The four layers of a
Word document.

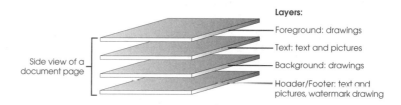

Side view of a
document page

Layers:

Foreground: drawings

Text: text and pictures

Background: drawings

Header/Footer: text and
pictures, watermark drawing

Drawing

When you want to add a drawing to your document, position the insertion point where you want the drawing to appear. Then click the Drawing button on the Standard toolbar.

The Drawing toolbar, shown in Figure 10-9, appears, and Word automatically switches to Page Layout view. The Drawing toolbar provides the tools you need to create or edit your drawings and pictures. To select a tool, simply click its button. Many of the buttons also have menus from which you can select a category of the tool. And in some cases the menu items have their own submenus from which you select a special variation of the category of tool. When you draw a picture, it can lie directly on the page, float above or below the page, or lie on one of the other layers of a Word page (see the sidebar "The Drawing Layers on a Page," page 459). You use the same drawing tools wherever you decide to draw.

FIGURE 10-9.
The Drawing toolbar.

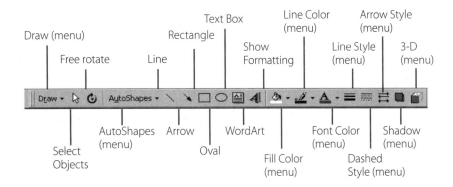

TIP

Setting Up AutoShape Floating Toolbars

The menus for the AutoShapes and the AutoShapes submenu commands, and for the Fill Color, Line Color, and Font Color buttons are floating toolbars (similar in looks and action to a toolbar). At the top of these menus you see a colored stripe. This stripe means that you can drag the menu into the window to display the menu as a floating toolbar. If you'll be drawing many different shapes and adding fills or line colors to them, you might find it extremely handy to set up these menus as floating toolbars to make it easier to select the shape, fill color, or line color you want to use.

The following sections explain the drawing tools on the Drawing toolbar. When you use the Line or Arrow button to draw a line or an arrow, you can change the length and angle of the line or arrow by clicking the object and then dragging one of its ends (shown by sizing handles) in the direction you want it to change. Similarly, when you draw a shape—such as a rectangle, square, oval, or circle—you can change its size and shape by clicking the object and then dragging one of the sizing handles in the direction you want the object to change.

You can also change the line style for any of these objects with the Line Style button (see page 499) and the Dash Style button (see page 500). The ends of lines and arrows can be changed with the Arrow Style button (see page 500), or you can change all traits of an object by clicking the object and then choosing the Format AutoShape command (or by double-clicking the object) to display the Format AutoShape dialog box.

The Line Button

Use the Line tool to draw straight lines. Begin by clicking the Line button. Position the pointer where you want the line to start, and then drag in any direction to draw the line. Release the mouse button to complete the line. To draw a line that snaps to a vertical, horizontal, or one of several diagonal positions (15-degree increments between horizontal and vertical), hold down the Shift key as you drag.

 TIP

> The AutoShapes button menu contains a Lines command. If you want to draw shapes with curving lines or straight lines or if you want to draw free-form lines, choose those line styles from the Lines submenu.

If you hold down the Ctrl key as you drag, the line expands from the point where you begin dragging an equal distance both in the direction you drag and in the opposite direction. When you release the mouse button, the line is twice as long as the distance you dragged.

The Arrow Button

SEE ALSO

To learn how to change an arrow's line style, see "The Line Style Button," page 499, and "The Dash Style Button," page 500. To learn how to change an arrow's line ends, see "The Arrow Style Button," page 500.

Use the Arrow tool to draw straight arrows. Begin by clicking the Arrow button. Position the pointer where you want the arrow to start, and then drag in any direction to draw the arrow. Release the mouse button to complete the arrow. To draw an arrow that snaps to a vertical, horizontal, or one of several diagonal positions (15-degree increments between horizontal and vertical), hold down the Shift key as you drag.

If you hold down the Ctrl key as you drag, the arrow expands from the point where you begin dragging an equal distance both in the direction you drag and in the opposite direction. When you release the mouse button, the arrow is twice as long as the distance you dragged.

If you want to change all the traits of an arrow, click the arrow, and then choose the Format AutoShape command (or double-click the arrow) to display the Format AutoShape dialog box.

TIP

Drawing More Than One Line or Arrow at a Time
If you click the Line or Arrow button once, the button turns off after you draw the line or arrow. You can double-click the Line or Arrow button to keep the button turned on. To turn off the button, click it or click another button.

The Rectangle Button

Use the Rectangle tool to draw rectangles and squares. Click the Rectangle button, and position the pointer where you want one corner of the rectangle to appear. Drag to draw the rectangle in the shape and size you want, and then release the mouse button to complete it.

- To draw a rectangle from its center rather than from a corner, hold down the Ctrl key as you drag.

- To draw a square, hold down the Shift key as you drag.

- To draw a square from its center, hold down both the Ctrl and Shift keys as you drag.

If you double-click in the document, Word automatically draws a 1-inch by 1-inch square, and then displays the Format AutoShape dialog box.

 TIP

Double-click the Rectangle button to draw several rectangles or squares one after another.

 SEE ALSO

To learn how to change a rectangle's line style, see "The Line Style Button," page 499, and "The Dash Style Button," page 500.

After you draw a rectangle or square, you can change its size and shape by clicking the object and then dragging one of the sizing handles in the direction you want the object to change.

If you want to change all the traits of a rectangle, click the rectangle, and then choose the Format AutoShape command (or double-click the rectangle) to display the Format AutoShape dialog box.

III

Publications

⭐ TIP

Labeling Rectangles

To label a rectangle, right-click the rectangle, choose Add Text from the shortcut menu, and type and format the label in the text box. Adjust and format the text box as necessary to fit the label where you want it. (For details about text boxes, see "The Text Box Button," page 476, and "Wrapping Up Text Boxes," page 399.)

The Oval Button

Use the Oval tool to draw ovals (also known as ellipses) and circles. Click the Oval button, and position the pointer at one corner of an imaginary rectangle that surrounds the oval you want to draw. Then drag to draw the oval in the direction, size, and shape you want, and release the mouse button to complete it.

- To draw an oval from its center, hold down the Ctrl key as you drag.

- To draw a circle, hold down the Shift key as you drag.

- To draw a circle from its center, hold down both the Ctrl and Shift keys as you drag.

If you double-click in the document, Word automatically draws a 1-inch by 1-inch circle, and then displays the Format AutoShape dialog box.

⭐ TIP

If you want to draw several ovals or circles, one after another, double-click the Oval button to keep the button turned on.

❓ SEE ALSO

To learn how to change an oval's line style, see "The Line Style Button," page 499, and "The Dash Style Button," page 500.

After you draw an oval or circle, you can change its size and shape by clicking the object and then dragging one of the sizing handles in the direction you want the object to change.

If you want to change all the traits of an oval, click it, and then choose the Format AutoShape command (or double-click it) to display the Format AutoShape dialog box.

TIP

> **Labeling Ovals**
>
> To label an oval, right-click the oval, select Add Text from the shortcut menu, and type and format the label in the text box. Adjust and format the text box as necessary to fit the label where you want it. (For details about text boxes, see "The Text Box Button," page 476, and "Wrapping Up Text Boxes," page 399.)

The AutoShapes Button

The AutoShapes button contains all the drawing shapes you're ever likely to need (and tools for other shapes). The shapes and tools are set up in six categories, represented by the six commands on the AutoShapes menu, shown here:

To draw one of the AutoShapes or to use one of the drawing tools, click the AutoShapes button, choose the category of shape you want to draw, and then choose the specific shape or tool from the submenu that appears for each category.

 TIP

> The AutoShapes menu and all of the submenus for the commands are floating toolbars (similar in look and action to a toolbar), which you can drag into the window to keep the tools handy when you'll be drawing many different shapes.

The following six sections describe each command on the AutoShapes menu and how to draw the shapes or use the tools that appear on the submenus.

Lines

Even though the Drawing toolbar contains a Line button and an Arrow button, you have many more options than merely drawing straight lines, with or without an arrowhead. You can draw curving lines and multiple-sided irregular shapes; and in the recent style of New York street trash decorations, you can draw all kinds of squiggly lines. The Lines command on the AutoShapes menu displays a menu of line style choices, shown here:

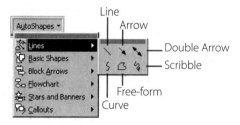

To draw a line, select the style of line you want to use from the Lines menu, and then use one of the two following sets of steps that fit the style of line you selected.

> As with the other command bars mentioned previously, you can drag the Lines menu into the window to display the menu as a floating toolbar. You will find this useful if you'll be drawing many lines.

To draw a straight line, arrow, double arrow, or scribble, take these steps:

1 Position the pointer where you want the line to start.

2 Drag away from that point in the direction you want the line to run.

3 Release the mouse button.

To draw a curve or free-form line, take these steps:

1 Position the pointer where you want the line to start.

2 Drag away from that point in the direction you want the line to run.

3 Click where you want the line to turn, and drag in the new direction.

4 Repeat step 3 until you have drawn the shape you want.

5 When you are finished with the shape, double-click to stop drawing a curve or free-form line.

Both the curve and free-form line can be either an open shape or a closed shape. To close the shape, drag back to the starting point of the line. If you miss, right-click the shape, and choose Close Curve from the shortcut menu. If the closure Word gives you isn't satisfactory (because it's jagged instead of smooth), use the Edit Points command on the Draw button menu or right-click the shape and choose Edit Points from the shortcut menu. For details about the Edit Points command, see "Editing Points of a Shape," page 488.

If you accidentally closed a curve or free-form shape and want it open, right-click the shape, and choose Open Curve from the shortcut menu.

> You can change curved lines in all the same ways you can change straight lines or arrows, including adding arrowheads to any open line shape you draw. For details, see "The Line Button," page 462, and "The Arrow Button," page 462.

Basic Shapes

A drawing can contain many different types of shapes. Some of these are familiar shapes, such as rectangles, ovals, parallelograms, trapezoids, octagons, hexagons, and triangles—the basic shapes of geometry that artists use regularly. These basic shapes appear on the Basic Shapes menu, shown here:

> You can drag the Basic Shapes menu into the window to display the menu as a floating toolbar, when you'll be drawing many basic shapes.

SEE ALSO

To learn how to change a basic shape's line style, see "The Line Style Button," page 499, and "The Dash Style Button," page 500. To learn how to change a basic shape's fill, see "The Fill Color Button," page 491.

To draw one of the basic shapes, take these steps:

1 Select the basic shape you want to use from the Basic Shapes menu.

2 Position the pointer where you want the shape.

3 Drag away from that point in the direction you want the shape to appear.

- To draw a shape from its center rather than from a corner, hold down the Ctrl key as you drag.

- To draw a regular (symmetrical) shape, hold down the Shift key as you drag.

- To draw a regular (symmetrical) shape from its center, hold down both the Ctrl and Shift keys as you drag.

4 Release the mouse button when the shape is the size you want it.

If you double-click in the document after selecting a basic shape, Word automatically draws a basic shape in a box 1-inch high by a proportional width—Word places the upper left corner of this box at the point where you double-click—and then displays the Format AutoShape dialog box.

TIP

Labeling Basic Shapes

To label a basic shape, right-click the basic shape, select Add Text from the shortcut menu, and type and format the label in the text box. Adjust and format the text box as necessary to fit the label where you want it. (For details about text boxes, see "The Text Box Button," page 476, and "Wrapping Up Text Boxes," page 399.

After you draw a basic shape, you can change its size and shape by clicking the object and then dragging one of the sizing handles in the direction you want the object to change.

You can change all the traits of the object by clicking it and then choosing the Format AutoShape command; by right-clicking the shape and choosing the Format AutoShape command; or by double-clicking the shape to display the Format AutoShape dialog box.

Using the Yellow Diamonds to Distort Shapes

After you draw some of the basic shapes, you'll see a yellow diamond. You use this yellow diamond to distort the basic shape by changing its width, height, and depth. To distort a basic shape, take these steps:

1 Position the mouse pointer on the yellow diamond. The mouse pointer changes to a special arrowhead.

2 Drag the arrowhead pointer around for the amount of distortion you want.

Block Arrows

The Lines menu and the Arrow button give you single-line straight arrows. In some cases, you might prefer an arrow that has width and open space inside it. That's when you'll open the Block Arrows menu, shown here:

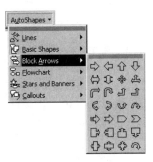

When you'll be drawing many block arrows, drag the Block Arrows menu into the window to display the menu as a floating toolbar.

To draw one of the block arrows, take these steps:

1 Select the block arrow you want to use from the Block Arrows menu.

2 Position the pointer where you want the block arrow.

3 Drag away from that point in the direction you want the block arrow to appear.

III

Publications

- To draw a block arrow from its center rather than from a corner, hold down the Ctrl key as you drag.

- To draw a regular (symmetrical) block arrow, hold down the Shift key as you drag.

- To draw a regular (symmetrical) block arrow from its center, hold down both the Ctrl and Shift keys as you drag.

4 Release the mouse button when the block arrow is the size you want it.

If you double-click in the document after selecting a block arrow, Word automatically draws a block arrow in a box about 1-inch high or wide by a proportional width or height—Word places the upper left corner of this box at the point where you double-click—and then displays the Format AutoShape dialog box.

(?) SEE ALSO

To learn how to change a block arrow's line style, see "The Line Style Button," page 499, and "The Dash Style Button," page 500.

After you draw a block arrow, you can change its size and shape by clicking the object and then dragging one of the sizing handles in the direction you want the object to change.

As with basic shapes, you can also fill the shape (see "The Fill Color Button," page 491). And you can change all the traits of the object by clicking it and then choosing the Format AutoShape command; by right-clicking the shape and choosing the Format AutoShape command; or by double-clicking the shape. In each case you display the Format AutoShape dialog box.

★ TIP

Using the Yellow Diamonds to Distort Arrows

After you draw a block arrow, you'll see one or more yellow diamonds, which you can use to distort the block arrow by changing the width of the arrow shaft and the length and width of the arrowhead. To distort a block arrow, first position the mouse pointer on a yellow diamond. The mouse pointer changes to a special arrowhead. Then drag the arrowhead pointer around for the amount of distortion you want.

Flow Charts

System designers (whether for computer systems or paper systems) often create flow charts to show the steps and types of processes that information and papers go through. Flow charts have their own standard symbols for various stations in the process the flow chart describes. When you need to create a flow chart, you'll want to open the Flowchart menu, shown here:

 TIP

Drag the Flowchart menu into the window to display the menu as a floating toolbar. When you're drawing a flow chart, this will keep the flow chart symbols handy.

To draw one of the flow chart symbols, take these steps:

1 Select the flow chart symbol you want to use from the Flowchart menu.

2 Position the pointer where you want the flow chart symbol.

3 Drag away from that point in the direction you want the flow chart symbol to appear.

- To draw a flow chart symbol from its center rather than from a corner, hold down the Ctrl key as you drag.

- To draw a regular (symmetrical) flow chart symbol, hold down the Shift key as you drag.

- To draw a regular (symmetrical) flow chart symbol from its center, hold down both the Ctrl and Shift keys as you drag.

4 Release the mouse button when the flow chart symbol is the size you want it.

III

Publications

TIP

Labeling Flow Chart Symbols

To label a flow chart symbol, right-click the symbol, select Add Text from the shortcut menu, and type and format the label in the text box. Adjust and format the text box as necessary to fit the label where you want it. (For details about text boxes, see "The Text Box Button," page 476, and "Wrapping Up Text Boxes," page 399.

 SEE ALSO

To learn how to change a flow chart symbol's line style, see "The Line Style Button," page 499, and "The Dash Style Button," page 500. To learn how to change a flow chart symbol's fill, see "The Fill Color Button," page 491.

If you double-click in the document after selecting a flow chart symbol, Word automatically draws a flow chart symbol in a box about 1-inch high or wide by a proportional width or height—Word places the upper left corner of this box at the point where you double-click—and then displays the Format AutoShape dialog box.

After you draw a flow chart symbol, you can change its size and shape by clicking the object and then dragging one of the sizing handles in the direction you want the object to change.

To change all the traits of a flow chart symbol, display the Format AutoShape dialog box in one of these ways:

- Click the symbol, and then choose the Format AutoShape command.

- Right-click the symbol, and then choose the format AutoShape command.

- Double-click the symbol.

 TIP

Connecting Flow Chart Symbols

To connect the flow chart symbols, draw arrows, either with the Arrow button or with the Arrow or Double Arrow choices on the Lines menu. To draw an arrow that turns a right-angle corner, double-click the Line button, hold down the Shift key as you draw the first leg of the arrow, release the mouse button, hold down the Shift key as you draw the second leg of the arrow, and then release the mouse button and Shift key. Now select the arrowhead you want from the Arrow Style button, or select the End Style and End Size for the arrowhead on the Colors And Lines tab of the Format AutoShape dialog box. Click the Line button again to turn it off.

Stars and Banners

When you're creating a certificate or award, you might want to include stars (for seals, for example) or banners. The Stars And Banners menu contains a variety of stars and banners, as shown here:

 TIP

If you'll be drawing many stars or banners, drag the Stars And Banners menu into the window to display the menu as a command bar.

To draw one of the stars or banners, take these steps:

1 Select the star or banner you want to use from the Stars And Banners menu.

 NOTE

The numbers that appear in the stars show you the number of points the star has. The numbers don't appear in the star shapes you draw.

2 Position the pointer where you want the star or banner.

3 Drag away from that point in the direction you want the star or banner to appear.

- To draw a star or banner from its center rather than from a corner, hold down the Ctrl key as you drag.

- To draw a regular (symmetrical) star or banner, hold down the Shift key as you drag.

- To draw a regular (symmetrical) star or banner from its center, hold down both the Ctrl and Shift keys as you drag.

4 Release the mouse button when the star or banner is the size you want it.

Labeling Banners and Stars

To label a banner or star, right-click the banner or star, select Add Text from the shortcut menu, and type and format the label in the text box. Adjust and format the text box as necessary to fit the label where you want it. (For details about text boxes, see "The Text Box Button," page 476, and "Wrapping Up Text Boxes," page 399.

SEE ALSO

To learn how to change a star or banner's line style, see "The Line Style Button," page 499, and "The Dash Style Button," page 500. To learn how to change a star or banner's fill, see "The Fill Color Button," page 491.

If you double-click in the document after selecting a star or banner, Word automatically draws the star or banner in a box about 1-inch high or wide by a proportional width or height—Word places the upper left corner of this box at the point where you double-click—and then displays the Format AutoShape dialog box.

As with the other AutoShapes that you draw, after you draw a star and banner, you can change its size and shape by clicking the object and then dragging one of the sizing handles in the direction you want the object to change.

Change all the traits of a star or banner, if you like, by clicking it and then choosing the Format AutoShape command; by right-clicking it and choosing the Format AutoShape command; or by double-clicking it. In each case you display the Format AutoShape dialog box.

As with the block arrows, you'll see one or more yellow diamonds after you draw a star or banner shape. Use the mouse to drag any yellow diamond to distort the widths and lengths of a star's points and a banner's curves.

Callouts

Many drawings include labels that point out and explain (call out) parts of the drawing, such as the labels that appear on many of the illustrations in this book. A callout includes a space for the text (a callout frame in the shape of a box, oval, or other shape) and a leader line (a line from the callout frame to a point on the drawing). The Callouts command on the AutoShapes menu displays a submenu with the available callout shapes. You use the Callouts command to add a label to a specific point on a drawing.

Select the style of callout you want to use from the Callouts menu, shown here:

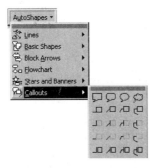

If you'll be drawing many callouts, drag the Callouts menu into the window to display the menu as a floating toolbar.

Position the pointer where you want the callout's leader line to point to, drag away from that point in the direction you want the callout to appear, and then release the mouse button.

If you double-click in the document after selecting a callout style, Word automatically draws a callout with a text box that fits in a 1-inch by 1-inch square—Word places the upper left corner of this square at the point where you double-click.

After you draw a callout, type the text you want inside the box. You can also insert a picture from a file, draw a picture, or put WordArt inside a callout. You can then format the text or art inside the callout.

Callouts are a special form of text box. For information about text boxes, see "The Text Box Button," below, and "Wrapping Up Text Boxes," page 399. If the text or art you place in a callout is larger than the callout, only the upper left portion of the contents appears. To see more of the contents, change the size of the callout, or draw another callout, or draw a text box and link the first callout to a second callout or to a text box to which the extra text can flow. (This works only for text.)

You can change the size and shape of a callout by clicking it and then dragging one of the sizing handles in the direction you want the callout to change.

? SEE ALSO

To learn how to change a callout's line style, see "The Line Style Button," page 499, and "The Dash Style Button," page 500. To learn how to change a callout's fill, see "The Fill Color Button," page 491.

You can change all the traits of a callout in the Format AutoShape dialog box. To display this dialog box, you can click the callout, and then choose the Format AutoShape command; right-click the callout, and then choose the Format AutoShape command; or double-click the callout.

You can also change the place where the leader line points. To move the leader line, click the tip of the line (where the leader line points). A yellow diamond appears at the tip of the line, and the mouse pointer becomes a special arrowhead over the diamond. Drag the yellow diamond to the new position where you want the leader line to point.

The Text Box Button

You use the Text Box drawing tool to add text to a drawing. Click the Text Box button, and position the pointer where you want one corner of the Text Box to appear. Drag to draw the text box in the shape and size you want, and then release the mouse button to complete it.

- To draw a rectangular text box from its center rather than from a corner, hold down the Ctrl key as you drag.

- To draw a square text box, hold down the Shift key as you drag.

- To draw a square text box from its center, hold down both the Ctrl and Shift keys as you drag.

If you double-click in the document, Word automatically draws a 1-inch by 1-inch square text box, and then displays the Format Text Box dialog box.

After you draw a text box, type the text you want inside the box. You can also insert a picture from a file, draw a picture, or put WordArt inside a text box. You can then format the text or art inside the text box.

NOTE

If the text or art you place in a text box is larger than the text box, only the upper left portion of the contents appears. To see more of the contents, change the size of the text box, or draw another text box, or draw a callout and link the first text box to a second text box or to a callout to which the extra text can flow. (This works only for text.)

? SEE ALSO

To learn how to change the line style of a text box, see "The Line Style Button," page 499, and "The Dash Style Button," page 500. For more information about Text Boxes, see "Wrapping Up Text Boxes," page 399.

You can change the size and shape of a text box by clicking it and then dragging one of the sizing handles in the direction you want the text box to change.

To change all the traits of a text box, display the Format Text Box dialog box. To do so, click the text box and then choose the Format Text Box command; right-click the text box and choose the Format Text Box command; or double-click the text box.

The WordArt Button

You can insert WordArt into your artwork or anywhere on a document page by clicking the WordArt button. For information about WordArt, see "Bending Text—WordArt," page 507.

The Select Objects Button

Click the Select Objects button to select more than one shape at a time. After you turn on the Select Objects button, you drag a selection box around all the shapes you want to select. This way you can change a trait of all the selected shapes at once, or move them all at once, or delete them all at once. You also use this selection method when you want to group several shapes into a single, combined shape.

When you're done selecting shapes and want to turn off the Select Objects button, click the button again, or click another Drawing toolbar button.

III

Publications

> **Selecting More Than One Shape at a Time**
>
> To select a single shape, you don't need to use the Select Objects button; simply click the shape. When you want to select more than one shape and the shapes are not next to each other (but are separated by other shapes you don't want to select), click the first shape you want to select, and then hold down the Shift key as you click each of the other shapes. You can do this with the Select Objects button turned on or turned off.

The Draw Button

The Draw button contains commands for changing how shapes fit into a total drawing. You use the Draw button commands after you have already drawn a shape. (To draw a shape, see "The AutoShapes Button," page 465.)

To manipulate the parts of a drawing in relation to the entire drawing, take these steps:

1 Select the shape or set of shapes you want to work with. To learn how to select more than one shape, see "The Select Objects Button," page 477.

2 Click the Draw button to see the menu shown here:

3 Choose the command you want to use from the Draw button menu (or from the submenu of one of the Draw menu commands).

The following sections explain the commands (and their submenu commands, if any) on the Draw button menu.

Moving and Copying Shapes

With the mouse, you can easily move or copy a shape you have drawn.

- To move a shape, click the shape to select it, and then drag the shape to the new position.

- To move a shape in a straight line, hold down the Shift key while you drag the shape to the new position. This technique keeps the shape in the same line, either vertically or horizontally. The direction you first drag the shape determines the line of the move. To move in the other direction, release the mouse button and Shift key, and then repeat these steps for a straight-line move in the new direction. If you don't release Shift while moving the shape and you switch directions, the shape will move in the new direction; however, it jumps so that it is in a straight line from its *original* location.

- To copy a shape, click the shape to select it, and then hold down the Ctrl key while you drag the copy of the shape to the new position. The original remains in its position, and the copy is set at the position you put it.

- To copy a shape in a straight line, hold down the Ctrl+Shift keys while you drag the shape to the new position. This technique keeps the copy of the shape in the same line, either vertically or horizontally, with the original shape. The direction you first drag the copy of the shape determines the line of the copy; however, if you switch directions without releasing Shift, the copy jumps so that it is in a straight line from the original in the opposite direction.

- To copy in the other direction, release the mouse button and Ctrl+Shift keys, and then repeat these steps for a straight-line copy in the new direction.

As you can learn from "Gridding Your Drawing," page 483, these moves and copies follow the drawing grid. To release a move or copy from the grid, hold down the Alt key as you move or copy the shape.

Grouping Parts of Your Drawing

Suppose that you are creating a drawing of a house, which requires using several different shapes positioned together. You will most likely draw the walls, doors, windows, and roof separately. If you now want to move, size, or format the entire house, you have to select each shape and move it, size it correctly, and format it. But Word provides an easier way: you can group the objects. You can easily group and ungroup shapes.

Group

To group shapes, take these steps:

1 Select all the shapes you want to group. Use the Select Objects button—for details, see "The Select Objects Button," page 477.

2 Click the Draw button on the Drawing toolbar.

3 Select the Group command from the Draw button menu.

Word combines all the selected shapes to create a group or single shape that you can move, size, or format any way you want.

Ungroup

If you later want to work with one particular shape within a group, you can break up the group (ungroup it). To ungroup a shape that you previously grouped, take these steps:

1 Select the group.

2 Click the Draw button on the Drawing toolbar.

3 Select the Ungroup command from the Draw button menu.

NOTE

The Ungroup command works only if you have selected a shape that you previously grouped from separate shapes.

Regroup

After you change a shape within a grouped shape, you may well want to group the objects together again. Instead of having to select all the separate shapes and choose the Group command again, you can simply regroup the shapes. To regroup shapes that were previously grouped and then ungrouped, take these steps:

1 Click any of the shapes that were previously a part of the group.

2 Click the Draw button on the Drawing toolbar.

3 Select the Regroup command from the Draw button menu.

You can later use the Ungroup command again to work on one shape within the grouped shape.

> The Regroup command works only if you have selected a shape that was part of a group you previously grouped from separate shapes.

Ordering Drawing Layers

Drawings you create with Word's drawing tools can be made up of layered shapes. Each shape you draw is in a layer of its own in the drawing. For example, if you draw a circle and then draw a square directly on top of it, the square is in the layer in front of the circle's layer. The contents of the front layers obscure the contents of the back layers unless you set their fill to Semitransparent or set them to No Fill.

The Draw button menu contains the Order command, which shows a menu with commands to change the order of layers in a drawing, as shown here:

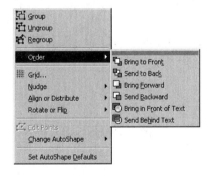

Setting Up the Order Floating Toolbar

The Order menu is a floating toolbar. At the top of this menu you see a horizontal stripe. This stripe means that you can drag the menu into the window to display it as a floating toolbar. If you'll be reordering many shapes, you might find it handy to set up the Order menu as a floating toolbar to make it easier to select the ordering command you want.

III

Publications

Bring To Front

To put a shape in the top (front) layer, select the shape, click the Draw button, and then choose the Bring To Front command.

Send To Back

To put a shape in the bottom (back) layer, select the shape, click the Draw button, and then choose the Send To Back command.

Bring Forward

In some cases, a shape needs to move forward (up a layer or two) from its current layer but not all the way to the front (top) layer. In these cases, select the shape, click the Draw button, and then choose the Bring Forward command. Each time you choose the Bring Forward command, the shape moves forward (up) one layer in the drawing.

Send Backward

In some cases, a shape needs to move backward (down a layer or two) from its current layer but not all the way to the back (bottom) layer. In these cases, select the shape, click the Draw button, and then choose the Send Backward command. Each time you choose the Send Backward command, the shape moves back (down) one layer in the drawing.

Bring In Front Of Text and Send Behind Text

SEE ALSO

See WATERMRK.DOC on the CD in this book for details about creating a watermark.

As mentioned in the sidebar "The Drawing Layers on a Page," page 459, each Word document contains four layers: the Foreground layer, the Text layer, the Background layer, and the Header/Footer layer. The top layer is the Foreground layer, and the bottom layer is the Header/Footer layer. Any drawing in an upper layer obscures text and drawings in the layers below it. Drawings you create in the Header/Footer layer appear on each page as a "watermark." Drawings you create on your document's page are contained in the Foreground layer.

If you prefer to position a shape or drawing in the Background layer, which is behind the Text layer (the layer that contains the text of your document), you use the Send Behind Text command. If you want to move a shape or drawing in front of text, you use the Bring In Front Of Text command.

To put a shape or drawing behind document text, take these steps:

1 Select the shape or drawing.

2 Click the Draw button on the Drawing toolbar.

3 Choose the Send Behind Text command from the Draw button menu.

To reposition the shape or drawing in the front of the document text, take these steps:

1 Click the Draw button on the Drawing toolbar.

2 Choose the Bring In Front Of Text command from the Draw button menu.

Gridding Your Drawing

Word is set up with a grid that positions the shapes you draw. This grid makes it easier for you to place objects in a row or in a column. The grid also comes into play when you move a shape or change its size. The shape moves to the next grid point, and it becomes larger or smaller by the amount of space between gridlines. You can disable the grid or change its size using the Grid command on the Draw button menu.

To turn off the grid or to change its size, take these steps:

1 Click the Draw button on the Drawing toolbar.

2 Choose the Grid command from the Draw button menu.

3 Turn off this check box to disable the grid.

4 Change the grid size in these boxes—set size from 0.01" to 22".

5 Turn off this check box to draw new shapes between gridlines.

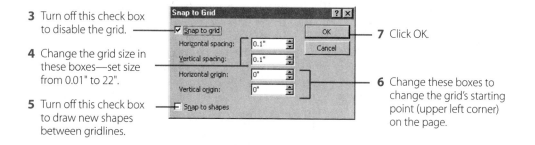

7 Click OK.

6 Change these boxes to change the grid's starting point (upper left corner) on the page.

Publications

TIP

Hold down the Alt key as you draw, move, or copy a shape to release it from the grid.

Nudging Parts of a Drawing

While it is easy to drag a shape into the position you want it, it can be difficult to get it exactly in the right place. You might find that when you release the mouse button, the shape isn't quite in the right position. For the last little nudge into the proper position, you can use the four Nudge commands on the Draw button menu.

 **NOTE**

The Nudge commands use the grid spacing as long as either the Snap To Grid or Snap To Shapes check box is turned on. To nudge a pixel at a time, turn off these two check boxes.

To nudge a shape, take these steps:

1 Select the shape you want to nudge.

2 Click the Draw button on the Drawing toolbar.

3 Select the Nudge command from the Draw button menu shown below.

4 Select the command for the direction you want to nudge the shape.

5 Repeat steps 2 through 4 for each nudge.

III

Publications

TIP

Setting Up the Nudge Floating Toolbar
The Nudge menu is a floating toolbar. If you'll be using a lot of nudges, you might find it handy to set up the Nudge menu as a floating toolbar to make it easier to nudge several times in various directions instead of repeatedly selecting the command from the submenu.

Aligning and Distributing Shapes in a Drawing

After you draw several shapes, you might want to align or distribute them horizontally or vertically, relative either to the page or to each other. Word makes it easy to align and distribute shapes you've drawn.

You can align objects relative to each other only if you have selected more than one object. You can distribute items only relative to the page.

To align or distribute shapes, take these steps:

1 Select the shapes you want to align or distribute.

2 Click the Draw button on the Drawing toolbar.

3 Click the Align Or Distribute command shown below.

4 To align or distribute shapes on the page, select the Relative To Page command to turn it on. To align shapes with each other, turn off the Relative To Page command.

5 To align shapes, repeat step 2 and step 3, and then choose the alignment command for the way you want to align the shapes:

- To align shapes horizontally, choose Align Left, Align Center, or Align Right.

- To align shapes vertically, choose Align Top, Align Middle, or Align Bottom.

6 To distribute shapes, repeat step 2 and step 3, and then choose the distribution command for the way you want to distribute the shapes:

- To distribute shapes horizontally, choose Distribute Horizontally.

- To distribute shapes vertically, choose Distribute Vertically.

> Drag the Align Or Distribute menu into the window to display the menu as a floating toolbar, especially if you'll be aligning and distributing many shapes.

Rotating and Flipping Shapes

If you need to turn a shape 90 degrees or 180 degrees from its current orientation, you can use the Rotate Left and Rotate Right commands on the Rotate Or Flip menu. For rotations between these 90-degree rotations, use the Free Rotate button on the Drawing toolbar—see "The Free Rotate Button," page 490.

Sometimes you draw a shape with the wrong orientation: backwards or upside down. If you draw a shape and then want its mirror opposite, you can copy the shape and then reverse it, either horizontally or vertically.

> Drag the Rotate Or Flip menu into the window to display the menu as a floating toolbar, when you'll be rotating or flipping many shapes or the same shape many times.

Free Rotate

This command duplicates the Free Rotate button on the Drawing toolbar. For details, see "The Free Rotate Button," page 490.

Rotate Left and Rotate Right

To rotate a shape, take these steps:

1 Select the shape. You can select several shapes or the entire drawing if you like.

2 Click the Draw button on the Drawing toolbar.

3 Click the Rotate Or Flip command on the Draw button menu.

4 Choose either the Rotate Left or Rotate Right command.

Each time you choose the Rotate Right command, Word rotates the selected shapes clockwise 90 degrees. Each time you choose the Rotate Left command, Word rotates the selected shapes counterclockwise (also called anti-clockwise) 90 degrees.

You can't rotate or flip text boxes. Also note that when you rotate or flip a shape, any shadow or 3-D effect keeps the same position relative to the shape. Neither the shadow nor the 3-D effect rotates or flips, but they do change shape to reflect the new orientation of the shape after flipping or rotating.

Flip Horizontal and Flip Vertical

The Flip Horizontal command flips, or reverses, the shape so that what was on the left side of the shape is moved to the right side. The Flip

Vertical button flips the shape so that what was on the top is moved to the bottom.

To flip a shape, take these steps:

1 Select the shape. You can select the entire drawing if you like.

2 Click the Draw button on the Drawing toolbar.

3 Choose either the Flip Horizontal or Flip Vertical command on the Draw button menu.

Editing Points of a Shape

If you have drawn any line shape with the Line button, Arrow button, or the commands on the Lines menu of the AutoShapes button, you can change its appearance with the Edit Points command on the Draw button menu.

To edit the points of a line shape, take these steps:

1 Click the line shape.

2 Click the Draw button on the Drawing toolbar.

3 Click the Edit Points command. Word adds point boxes to the shape wherever the line turns.

4 Use one of the following techniques to change the shape:

- To move a point, position the mouse pointer over one of the point boxes, and then drag the point to the new position. The mouse pointer becomes a box with a black dot in the middle and an arrowhead on each side. (The mouse pointer looks like a compass symbol.)

- To delete a point on a free-form shape, hold down the Ctrl key as you click the point. You'll notice that the mouse pointer becomes an X shape.

- To add another point on a free-form shape, position the mouse pointer on a line between two other points, and then drag in the direction you want the new point to take the line. The mouse pointer becomes a solid black box with a crosshair over it.

5 When you've finished reshaping, click the Edit Points command again, or click anywhere outside the shape.

Changing an AutoShape

After you draw an AutoShape, you might decide that you really need a different shape as your starting point. Rather than try to manipulate the current shape into the new shape (which you can't do in many cases), you can select a different AutoShape for a shape in the drawing.

To change an AutoShape to a different AutoShape, take these steps:

1 Select the AutoShape you want to change.

2 Click the Draw button.

3 Select the Change AutoShape command.

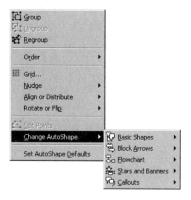

4 Select the AutoShape category you want to use.

5 Select the specific AutoShape you want to substitute for the current AutoShape.

The new AutoShape keeps the size, position, and other traits (other than shape) of the AutoShape you replace.

The Change AutoShape menu contains only five categories of shapes, as opposed to the AutoShapes button, which contains six categories. The Change AutoShape menu omits the Lines command you find on the AutoShapes button menu because you can't change a shape into a line. Also note that if you select a line on the drawing, all of the choices on the submenus of the Change AutoShape menu are unavailable because you can't change a line into a shape.

Setting AutoShape Defaults

SEE ALSO

For information about the AutoShapes you can select, see "The AutoShapes Button," page 465.

If your drawing will contain a variety of shapes that have some common traits—line width and color, fill, or shadow or 3-D effect—you can set AutoShapes to take only these traits when you draw new AutoShapes.

To set up AutoShapes with specific standard traits, take these steps:

1 Insert any AutoShape.

2 Select the AutoShape, and then choose the Format AutoShape command.

3 Change settings on the Colors And Lines tab, and then click OK.

NOTE

Instead of the Format AutoShape command, you can use the buttons on the Draw toolbar to set the line, fill, shadow, and 3-D effects.

4 Click the Draw button, and then select Set AutoShape Defaults.

The next new AutoShape you draw will have the traits you set on the Colors And Lines tab.

The Free Rotate Button

You can turn any shape completely around in a circle, spinning it around its position like a top, using the Free Rotate button. To rotate a shape visually to any angle, take these steps:

1 Click the shape you want to rotate. To rotate several shapes at the same time, select all the shapes you want to rotate the same amount. (For information about selecting several shapes at once, see "The Select Objects Button," page 477.)

2 Click the Free Rotate button.

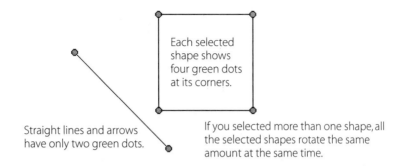

Each selected shape shows four green dots at its corners.

Straight lines and arrows have only two green dots.

If you selected more than one shape, all the selected shapes rotate the same amount at the same time.

3 Drag any one green dot to rotate the shape to the angle you want.

4 To rotate another separate shape, click it, and then repeat step 3. To rotate several other shapes at the same time, click one of them, and then hold down the Shift key while you click the other shapes you want to rotate at the same time.

5 When you're done rotating the shape, click the Free Rotate button again to turn it off.

To rotate a shape or several shapes 90 degrees, click the Draw button, choose the Rotate Or Flip command, and then choose Rotate Left or Rotate Right from the submenu. Also note that you can set the degree of rotation by choosing the Format AutoShape command, clicking the Size tab, entering a degree measurement in the Rotation box, and then clicking OK.

The Fill Color Button

Word doesn't automatically fill the shapes you draw with color. To fill the shapes you draw with an interior color, use the Fill Color button. The Fill button shows the currently selected fill color on its color stripe. To fill a shape with the currently selected color, click the shape, and then click the Fill button. To select a different fill color, click the down arrow along the right side of the Fill Color button. Then choose a color from the box that Word displays, shown on the next page.

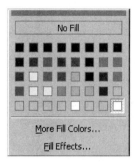

The color you choose from the Fill Color menu becomes the new color for the stripe on the Fill button.

The Fill button fills your shapes with one of the solid colors available on the Fill button menu. The menu also contains two commands: More Fill Colors and Fill Effects.

If you'll be filling many different shapes, drag the Fill Color menu into the window to display the menu as a floating toolbar.

Checking Out More Colors

To give yourself more fill-color choices, take these steps:

1 Click the down arrow along the right side of the Fill Color button.

2 Choose the More Fill Colors command from the menu:

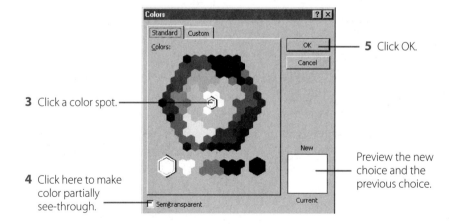

3 Click a color spot.

4 Click here to make color partially see-through.

5 Click OK.

Preview the new choice and the previous choice.

The color you select becomes the current color on the Fill button color stripe. The color also appears in its own color block on the Fill button menu in a row above the More Fill Colors command. Each time you select a new color with the More Fill Colors command, Word adds another color block to the row until it's full—the row holds eight blocks. After you've set up eight blocks, Word replaces the first color block with the next color you select, and then replaces each color block in turn along the row as you select new colors.

If you feel like mixing your own special color, click the Custom tab in the Colors dialog box.

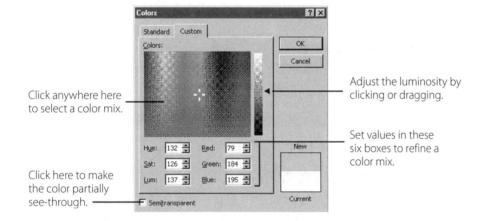

Click anywhere here to select a color mix.

Click here to make the color partially see-through.

Adjust the luminosity by clicking or dragging.

Set values in these six boxes to refine a color mix.

When you click OK, the color you mix becomes the current color on the Fill button color stripe. The color also appears in its own color block on the Fill button menu in a row above the More Fill Colors command in the same way as when you select a color on the Standard tab of the Colors dialog box with the More Fill Colors command.

Tumbling to the Fill Effects

Instead of a solid color, you can choose one of four categories of fill effects—gradient, texture, pattern, and picture—each of which offers you a number of choices.

Publications

To fill a shape with one of the fill effects, take these steps:

1 Click the shape you want to fill with a special effect.

 **TIP**

> The fill effects will be based on the current fill color of the shape. Be sure to select the fill color you want for the fill effect before you set it up.

2 Click the down arrow along the right side of the Fill Color button, and then choose the Fill Effects command.

3 Click the tab for the type of fill effect you want, and select the choices for that effect—see the following descriptions of each tab. You'll see a preview of the effect in the Sample box.

4 Click OK.

Gradient

A gradient fill gradually changes from one color to another across a shape. You have choices for the two colors and for the direction of the gradient change.

Select the colors to see different versions of the Colors section (see following text).

Select the shading style.

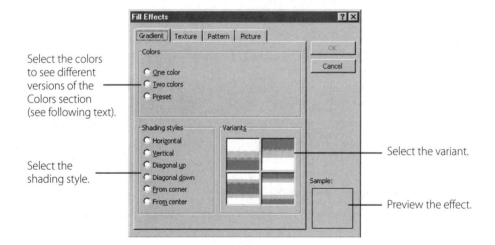

Select the variant.

Preview the effect.

When you click the One Color option, you see this version of the Colors section of the Gradient tab:

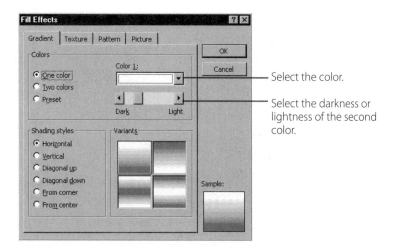

Select the color.

Select the darkness or lightness of the second color.

When you click the Two Colors option, you see this version of the Colors section of the Gradient tab:

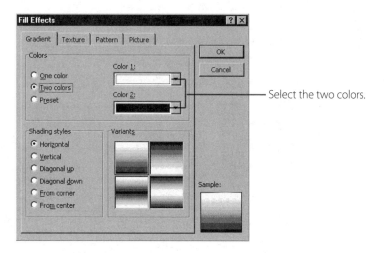

Select the two colors.

III

Publications

When you click the Preset option, you see the version of the Colors section of the Gradient tab:

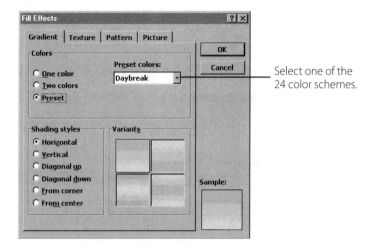

Select one of the 24 color schemes.

Texture

On the Texture tab, you have a choice of 24 fill textures. Textures are like wallpaper on the Windows desktop.

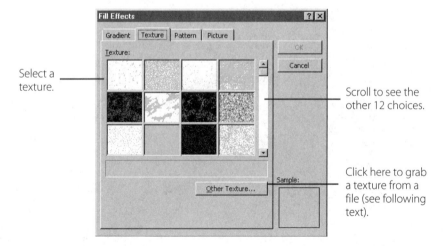

Select a texture.

Scroll to see the other 12 choices.

Click here to grab a texture from a file (see following text).

When you click the Other Textures button, Word displays the Select Texture dialog box, which is a File Open dialog box. When you find a picture file you want to use for texture and open it, the new texture appears in a new twenty-fifth square. Any other texture file you open replaces the texture in this twenty-fifth square.

> **Locating Wallpaper Files for More Texture Choices**
> You can find the wallpaper files in the Win95 folder. You can also use some of the picture files in the Clipart folder inside the Microsoft Office folder inside the Program Files folder. If the picture file you select is too large, Word displays a message telling you to edit the picture to a smaller size. Either edit the picture to a smaller size, or use the Picture tab.

Pattern

The Pattern tab displays 48 patterns that you can use to fill a shape or use for lines (through the Pattern Fill command on the Line Color button menu). Click a pattern square to apply the pattern to a selected shape.

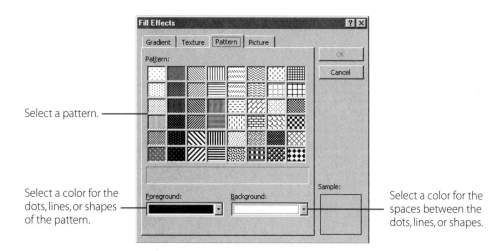

Select a pattern.

Select a color for the dots, lines, or shapes of the pattern.

Select a color for the spaces between the dots, lines, or shapes.

Picture

On the Picture tab, you can select a picture as the fill for a shape. The picture can be any picture file—picture size isn't restricted. See the figure on the next page. The Select Picture button opens the Select Picture dialog box from where you can choose a picture for the selected shape's fill.

Publications

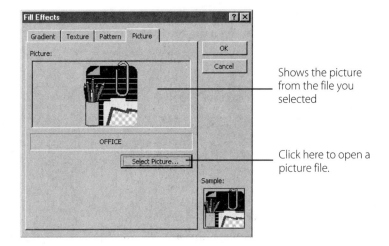

Shows the picture from the file you selected

Click here to open a picture file.

The Line Color Button

Word draws new shapes using the line color on the color stripe of the Line Color button. To select a different line color, click the down arrow along the right side of the Line Color button. Then choose a color from the box that Word displays:

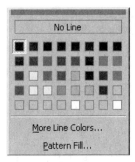

The color you choose from the Line Color menu becomes the new color for the stripe on the Line Color button and for the selected shape.

The Line Color button menu shows solid colors. The menu also contains two commands: More Line Colors and Pattern Fill. For information about the More Line Colors command, see "Checking Out More Colors," page 492. For information about the Pattern Fill command, see "Pattern," page 497.

TIP

> Drag the Line Color menu into the window to display the menu as a floating toolbar. You'll find this especially useful if you'll be coloring many lines.

The Font Color Button

The Font Color button on the Drawing toolbar and the Font Color button on the Formatting toolbar perform the same function—they change the color of text, whether the text is in the document or in a picture.

 TIP

> You can drag the Font Color button menus into the window to display them as floating toolbars.

The Line Style Button

You use the Line Style button to change the width and style of lines in a drawing. You can change any line and the outline of any shape. To change the line style, take these steps:

1 Click the line or shape.

2 Click the Line Style button.

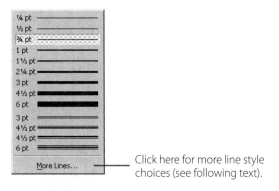

Click here for more line style choices (see following text).

3 Select the line width and style you want to use.

When you choose the More Lines command, Word displays the Colors And Lines tab of the Format AutoShape or the Format Text Box dialog box. (You can use any of the other tabs in the dialog box, too.) For information about the Format AutoShape dialog box that appears when you select More Lines from the Line Style submenu, see "Formatting Art, WordArt, and Other Objects," page 515.

The Dash Style button contains more line style choices. These choices are also available in the Dashed box on the Colors And Lines tab of the Format AutoShape and Format Text Box dialog boxes.

The Dash Style Button

You use the Dash Style button to select a dashed style for lines in a drawing. You can change any line and the outline of any shape. To change the line style to a dashed line, take these steps:

1 Click the line or shape.

2 Click the Dash Style button.

3 Select the dashed line style you want to use.

The dashed line styles are also available in the Format AutoShape and Format Text Box dialog boxes.

The Arrow Style Button

You use the Arrow Style button to select an arrow style for lines in a drawing. You can change any line, whether the line is currently an arrow or not. To change the arrow style, take these steps:

1 Click the line.

2 Click the Arrow Style button.

SEE ALSO

You can use any of the other tabs in the Format AutoShape dialog box, too. For information about the other choices in the dialog box, which appears when you select More Arrows from the Arrow Style submenu, see "Formatting Art, Word-Art, and Other Objects," page 515.

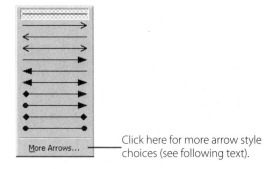

Click here for more arrow style choices (see following text).

3 Select the arrow style you want to use.

When you choose the More Arrows command, Word displays the Colors And Lines tab of the Format AutoShape dialog box.

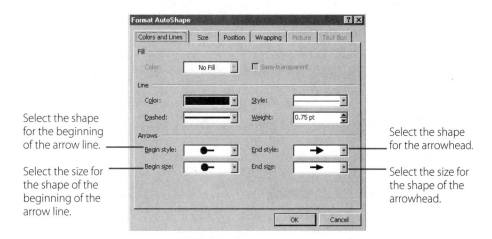

Select the shape for the beginning of the arrow line.

Select the size for the shape of the beginning of the arrow line.

Select the shape for the arrowhead.

Select the size for the shape of the arrowhead.

 TIP

To change the direction an arrow points, select an arrowhead shape in the Begin Style box, and select a begin shape in the End Style box.

The Shadow Button

With the Shadow button, you can add a shadow to any shape, including lines. To add a shadow to a shape, take these steps:

1 Click the shape.

2 Click the Shadow button on the Drawing toolbar.

Click here to display the
Shadow Settings toolbar
for adjusting a shadow.

3 Select a shadow style.

If you add a shadow to a shape that already has a 3-D effect, the shadow replaces the 3-D effect.

The Shadow Settings Toolbar

After you add a shadow to a shape, you might want to adjust the shadow. To adjust a shadow, take these steps:

1 Click the shape that has a shadow.

2 Click the Shadow button on the Drawing toolbar.

3 Click the Shadow Settings button.

Shadow On/Off ——

—— Shadow Color (menu)

Nudge Shadow Up, Down, Left, Right

4 Click the buttons to adjust a shadow.

Shadow On/Off

You'll use the Shadow On/Off button primarily to remove a shadow from a shape. If you remove a shadow by mistake, you can restore the same shadow to the shape by clicking this button. For new shapes that have not yet had a shadow, click this button to add a standard 50% gray shadow to the bottom and right sides of the shape.

Nudge Shadow Up, Down, Left, Right

The four Nudge Shadow buttons move the shadow either closer to the shape or farther away. Each click of a Nudge Shadow button moves the shadow one dot on the screen (one pixel).

Shadow Color

Word uses 50% Gray as its standard shadow color, which appears on the color stripe on the Shadow Color button. To select a different shadow color, click the down arrow along the right side of the Shadow Color button. Then choose a color from the box that Word displays:

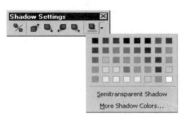

The color you choose from the Shadow Color menu becomes the new color for the stripe on the Shadow Color Button and for the selected shape.

The Shadow Color button menu shows solid colors. The menu also contains the command More Shadow Colors. For information about the More Shadow Colors command, see "Checking Out More Colors," page 492.

The 3-D Button

You can give any shape, including a line, a 3-D look. To expand a shape into the third dimension, take these steps:

1 Click the shape.

2 Click the 3-D button on the Drawing toolbar, shown on the next page.

3 Select a 3-D style.

III

Publications

Click here to display the
3-D Settings toolbar for
adjusting the 3-D effect.

 NOTE

If you add a 3-D effect to a shape that already has a shadow, the 3-D effect
replaces the shadow.

The 3-D Settings Toolbar

After you add a 3-D effect to a shape, you might want to adjust it. To
do so, take these steps:

1 Click the shape that has a 3-D effect.

2 Click the 3-D button on the Drawing toolbar.

3 Click the 3-D Settings button.

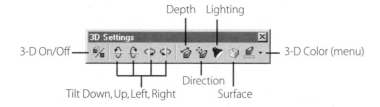

4 Click the buttons to adjust the 3-D effect.

3-D On/Off

You'll use the 3-D On/Off button primarily to remove a 3-D effect from
a shape. If you remove a 3-D effect by mistake, you can restore the
same effect to the shape by clicking this button. For new shapes that
have not yet had a 3-D effect, click this button to add a standard 50%
gray 3-D effect to the bottom and right sides of the shape.

Some AutoShapes turn off some of the 3-D toolbar buttons when you draw or select them. The shapes that are already 3-D in nature—some of the basic shapes, block arrows, and banners—must retain their 3-D look in order to maintain their shape. So for these shapes, you can't turn off or adjust the 3-D effect.

Tilt Down, Up, Left, Right

The four Tilt buttons change the angle of the 3-D effect.

Depth

The Depth button displays a menu of choices for setting the length of the 3-D effect.

Select 0 pt. to turn the 3-D effect into a flat effect. If the 3-D effect skews the face of the shape to make it appear that the 3-D shape is turned, setting 0 pt. leaves the face skewed but without depth.

For a depth other than the six listed choices, type the depth in points in the Custom box.

Direction

The Direction button displays a menu of choices for the direction in which the 3-D effect should extend.

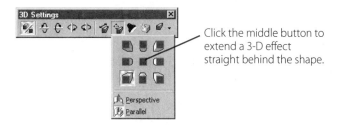

Click the middle button to extend a 3-D effect straight behind the shape.

III

Publications

When you add a 3-D effect to a shape, Word gives the 3-D shape a perspective effect. This means that it looks as if the shape extends into the distance because it gets smaller toward the far end of the 3-D effect. If you prefer a parallel 3-D effect—an effect that keeps the sides parallel to each other—select Parallel from the Direction button menu. If you have a shape with a parallel 3-D effect and want a perspective effect, select Perspective from the Direction button menu.

Lighting

An important part of any 3-D effect is the way light falls on the shape. With the Lighting button menu, you can select the direction you want light to shine on the 3-D shape, and you can select how brightly or dimly you want the light to shine.

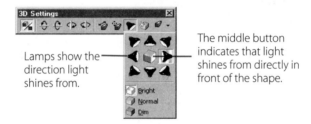

Lamps show the direction light shines from.

The middle button indicates that light shines from directly in front of the shape.

Surface

The way light plays on a shape and the way the colors look depend on the surface material of a shape. On the Surface button menu, you can select one of four surface materials.

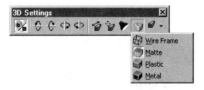

Wire Frame removes all the sides and shows only an outline of the shape. Matte gives the shape a dull surface that doesn't reflect. Plastic and Metal make the surface look as if the shape were made from those materials.

3-D Color

Word uses 50% Gray as its standard 3-D color, which appears on the color stripe on the 3-D Color button. To select a different 3-D color, click the down arrow along the right side of the 3-D Color button. Then choose a color from the box that Word displays:

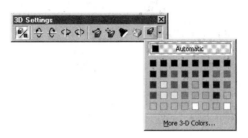

The color you choose from the 3-D Color menu becomes the new color for the stripe on the 3-D Color button and for the selected shape.

The 3-D Color button menu shows solid colors. The menu also contains the command More 3-D Colors. For information about this command, see "Checking Out More Colors," page 492.

Bending Text—WordArt

You've seen lots of brochures that are all text or text with a few pictures stuck in. Once in a while, you see a brochure with a fancy bit of text that looks like a piece of art. That's where WordArt comes into play. With WordArt, you can create your own arty text.

To add WordArt to your brochure, take these steps:

1 Position the insertion point where you want to insert the Word-Art. (You can easily change its position on the page later—see "Positioning," page 518.)

2 Choose the Insert Picture command, and then choose WordArt from the submenu.

III

Publications

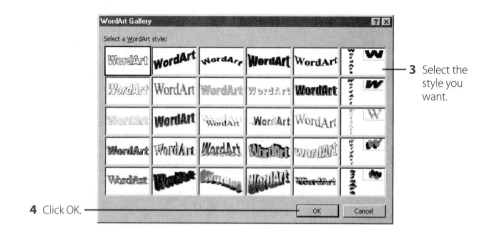

3 Select the style you want.

4 Click OK.

6 Select a font. **7** Select a font size.

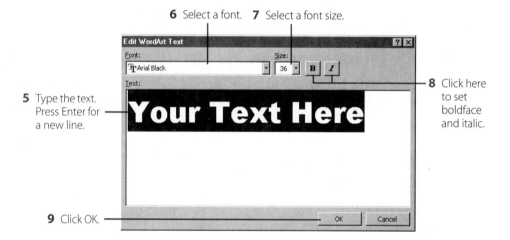

5 Type the text. Press Enter for a new line.

8 Click here to set boldface and italic.

9 Click OK.

Word inserts the WordArt into your document, adds a WordArt command to the Format menu, and displays the WordArt toolbar, shown here:

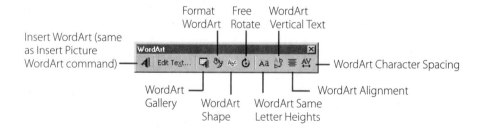

Format WordArt

Free Rotate

WordArt Vertical Text

Insert WordArt (same as Insert Picture WordArt command)

WordArt Gallery

WordArt Shape

WordArt Same Letter Heights

WordArt Alignment

WordArt Character Spacing

You can add special effects, described later in this chapter, using the Format WordArt command and the WordArt toolbar buttons.

When you have finished your WordArt, click anywhere on the screen outside the WordArt to turn off the WordArt toolbar.

Editing Existing WordArt

To change a piece of WordArt in a Word document, click it. Then click Edit Text on the WordArt toolbar. Alternatively, double-click the Word-Art to display the Edit WordArt Text dialog box.

Choosing a Shape for Your WordArt

When you click the WordArt Shape button on the WordArt toolbar, a list of available shapes drops down.

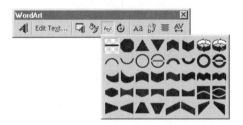

Select a shape from this list based on its visual outline.

Setting WordArt Letters to the Same Heights

The WordArt Same Letter Heights button on the WordArt toolbar makes uppercase and lowercase letters all the same height but does not change the case of the characters, as shown here:

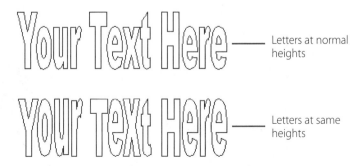

Letters at normal heights

Letters at same heights

Clicking the WordArt Same Letter Heights button again returns the characters to their original distinctive heights.

Spacing WordArt Characters

Click the WordArt Character Spacing button to display a list of character spacing choices:

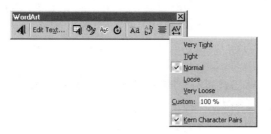

With this list, you can change the way your text fits inside the WordArt by moving the characters closer together or by spreading them out. You'll often want to adjust the character spacing when you change the font or the point size of your WordArt text.

The following picture shows text with character spacing set to Normal and to Very Loose.

Normal character spacing

Very loose character spacing

When you choose one of the preset spacing options, WordArt changes the percentage shown in the Custom setting. If you choose Custom, you can set any percentage from 0% to 500%. To set a custom percentage, type the percentage in the Custom box.

Turn on Kern Character Pairs to adjust individual characters to uniform spacing throughout the text.

Aligning Your WordArt

Click the WordArt Alignment button to choose an alignment for the text. The Center option centers each line of text within its area. The Left option aligns the text at the left edge of the area, and the Right option aligns the text at the right edge.

WordArt provides three options for justifying text—that is, having text align on both the left and right edges. To space the words in the text evenly between the left and the right edges of the area, select Word Justify. Word Justify doesn't affect character spacing. Select Letter Justify to space the characters in the text evenly between the left and the right edges of the area. (Blank spaces in the text are treated the same as letters, numbers, and symbols.) You can select Stretch Justify to stretch the characters laterally so that the text fills the area from left to right.

Switching WordArt Text to Vertical

Click the WordArt Vertical Text button to switch text from horizontal to vertical, as shown here:

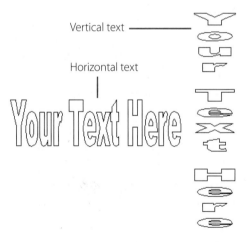

To restore the text to horizontal, click the WordArt Vertical Text button again.

III

Publications

Rotating WordArt

You can rotate your WordArt to any angle, even completely around. To rotate your WordArt text, take these steps:

1 Click the Free Rotate button on the WordArt toolbar. The mouse pointer changes to the rotation icon you see on the Free Rotate button.

2 Position the mouse pointer around one of the four green buttons at the corners of the WordArt.

3 Drag the green button to rotate the WordArt to the angle you want it.

4 When you've rotated the WordArt the way you want it, click again on the Free Rotate button.

You can also change the rotation with the Format WordArt command. To do so, take these steps:

1 Click the WordArt.

2 Click the Format WordArt button on the WordArt toolbar, or choose the Format WordArt command.

3 In the Format WordArt dialog box, click the Size tab (see more about using the Size tab in the section, "Scaling and Cropping with the Format Command," page 517).

4 Set the degree of rotation in the Rotation box.

5 Click OK.

Distorting Your WordArt

Somewhere on the WordArt text, you'll see a yellow diamond. You use this yellow diamond to distort your WordArt text by angling the letters to the left or right, as shown here:

To distort your WordArt, take these steps:

1 Position the mouse pointer on the yellow diamond. The mouse pointer changes to an arrowhead.

2 Drag the arrowhead pointer to the left or right for the amount of distortion you want.

Filling the Text with Color

You can change the color of the WordArt text. To do so, take these steps:

1 Click the WordArt.

2 Click the Format WordArt button on the WordArt toolbar, or choose the Format WordArt command.

3 In the Format WordArt dialog box, click the Colors And Lines tab (see Figure 10-10 on the next page).

4 In the Color box, select the color you want for the WordArt text from the list, which is shown here:

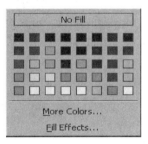

For more colors, select the More Colors command (see "Checking Out More Colors," page 492). For a special fill effect, select the Fill Effects command (see "Tumbling to the Fill Effects," page 493).

5 If you want the color to appear partially transparent, turn on the Semi-Transparent check box.

III

Publications

Semi-Transparent means half of the screen dots are "clear"—they let the color behind the WordArt text show through—while the other half of the dots are the selected color. The Semi-Transparent check box is unavailable if you select a gradient, texture, pattern, or fill effect for the WordArt text (see "Tumbling to the Fill Effects," page 493).

6 Click OK.

FIGURE 10-10.
The Colors And Lines tab of the Format WordArt dialog box.

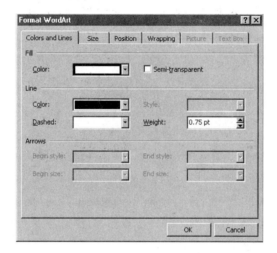

Changing the Text Outline

Each character of the WordArt text is surrounded by a border. You can change the way this text outline looks. To do so, take these steps:

1 Click the WordArt.

2 Click the Format WordArt button on the WordArt toolbar, or choose the Format WordArt command.

3 In the Format WordArt dialog box, click the Colors And Lines tab (see Figure 10-10).

4 In the Color box, select from the list the color you want for the outline. For more colors, select the More Colors command (see "Checking Out More Colors," page 492). For a special fill effect, select the Fill Effects command (see "Tumbling to the Fill Effects," page 493).

5 In the Weight box, set the thickness you want for the outline. The maximum thickness is 1,584 points (a thickness of 22 inches—the largest page size Word can handle, which makes this thickness unusable). Except for very large pieces of WordArt, a thickness of more than 3 points is usually uncalled for.

6 Click OK.

> To make the WordArt text appear without an outline, set the text and the outline to the same color.

Formatting Art, WordArt, and Other Objects

All of the graphic shapes and objects you can add to a document can have borders and shading. You can change the size of any piece of art, either by cutting part of the graphic off from view or by changing its size to fit the space available. You can position art anywhere on a page or in relation to a paragraph, column, or margin. And all of the art objects can be set up to have brochure text flow around them in various ways. The next few sections describe these formatting techniques.

Adding a Border

After you insert a graphic into your document, you can add a border to it, like framing a picture.

To add a border to a graphic, take these steps:

1 Click the graphic to select it. When you select the graphic, a box with sizing handles (small squares) appears around the graphic.

2 Choose the Format Borders And Shading command. The Format Picture dialog box appears with the Colors and Lines tab selected.

3 Select a line color and a line style, and click OK.

Word adds a box around the graphic.

III

Publications

Sizing—Scaling and Cropping

 SEE ALSO

For an example of exploding detail of a graphic, see the file XLPDART.DOC on the CD in this book.

When you insert a graphic, it appears at its full size. Sometimes the size is too large to blend elegantly into the surrounding subject matter. Other times, the size is too small to be seen clearly. Sometimes you might want only part of the graphic. At other times, you might want lots of space around a graphic. To change the size of the image, you scale the graphic. To change the amount of the graphic that appears, or to add space around a graphic, you crop it. To enlarge part of a graphic, crop it to show only that part, and then scale it to the larger size.

To scale or crop a graphic, you can use either the mouse or the Format Picture command. Use the mouse when you want to see the picture in relation to its surroundings. Use the Format Picture command when you want precise measurements.

Scaling and Cropping with the Mouse

Here's how to use the mouse to scale and crop a graphic:

■ To scale a graphic, drag any one of the sizing handles. Dragging the sizing handle toward the center of the graphic scales it down (decreases the size of the image). Dragging the sizing handle away from the center of the graphic scales it up (increases the size of the image).

 TIP

Drag one of the corner sizing handles if you want to maintain the proportion between the graphic's height and width. If you drag using a sizing handle that's not on one of the corners, you'll distort the picture as you resize it—which can be fun, too.

■ To crop a graphic, click the Crop button on the Picture toolbar, drag a sizing handle, and then, when you're done cropping, click the Crop button again. When you drag toward the center of the graphic, you cut off part of the image. When you drag away from the center of the graphic, you add white space along that edge of the image.

TIP

> To return a picture that you've scaled or cropped to its original size with no cropping, hold down the Ctrl key and double-click the picture. The picture returns to its original size in an Edit Picture window.

Scaling and Cropping with the Format Command

You can also change the sizing and scale with the Format WordArt and Format Picture commands. To do so, take these steps:

1 Click the picture or WordArt.

2 Click the Format WordArt button on the WordArt toolbar (or the Format Picture button on the Picture toolbar), or choose the Format WordArt command (or the Format Picture command).

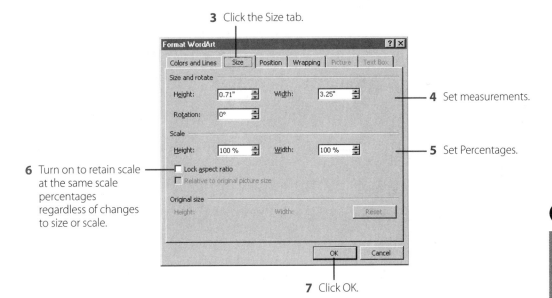

3 Click the Size tab.

4 Set measurements.

5 Set Percentages.

6 Turn on to retain scale at the same scale percentages regardless of changes to size or scale.

7 Click OK.

■ To scale a graphic in the Picture dialog box, change the percentages in the Width and Height boxes of the Scale section. A number less than 100 shrinks the image size; a number greater than 100 enlarges the image size.

As an alternative, you can enter the actual measurements for the picture in the Width and Height boxes of the Size and Rotate section. Word sets the scaling percentages to match.

III

Publications

■ To crop a graphic in the Picture dialog box, change the measurements in the Left, Right, Top, and/or Bottom box(es) in the Crop From section on the Picture tab. A positive measurement cuts off part of the image. A negative measurement adds empty space along that edge of the image.

SEE ALSO

For information about formatting drawings with Word's drawing tools, see "Drawing Pictures," page 458.

No matter what changes you make in the Picture dialog box, Word always displays the graphic's original dimensions at the bottom of the dialog box.

■ To return a graphic to its original size with no cropping, click the Reset button.

Positioning

When you put an object in your brochure, it's located at the insertion point you set before you choose the Insert command. After the object is in place, you can change its position with either the mouse or with the Format (Object) command.

To move an object with the mouse, take these steps:

1 Click the object.

2 Position the mouse pointer inside the object.

3 Drag it to a new position on the page.

To move an object with the Format (Object) command, take these steps:

1 Click the object.

2 Choose the Format (Object) command.

NOTE

The name of the button, toolbar, or command changes depending on the selected object.

3 Click the Position tab.

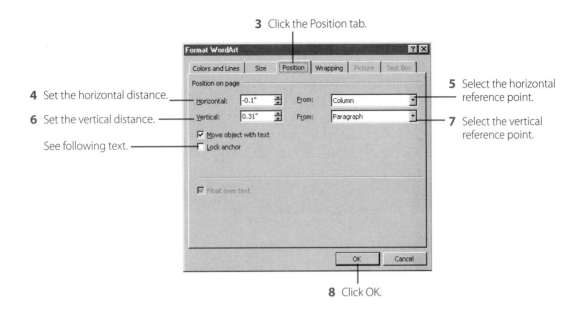

4 Set the horizontal distance.

6 Set the vertical distance.

See following text.

5 Select the horizontal reference point.

7 Select the vertical reference point.

8 Click OK.

Position On Page

In the Horizontal and Vertical boxes, set the distance from the reference points. The reference points are the choices you select in the two From boxes.

A negative measurement in the Vertical box moves the object above the reference point in the Vertical From box. A negative measurement in the Horizontal box moves the object to the left of the reference point in the Horizontal From box.

Move Object With Text

Turn on the Move Object With Text check box to link the object's position measurements to the nearest brochure paragraph. With this box turned on, moving the linked brochure paragraph also moves the object to a new position at the same distance from the paragraph. When you turn on this check box, Word automatically switches the Vertical From box to Paragraph. If you select a different reference point in the Vertical From box, Word automatically turns off this check box.

Lock Anchor

Turn on the Lock Anchor check box to keep an object on its current page when you change its position by dragging it. With this check box turned off, you can drag the object from one page to another.

III

Publications

Wrapping Brochure Text Around Objects

When you insert an object, it is set up to float over the top of the brochure text. If you set up an object that is clear, you'll still be able to read the brochure text. If you set up an object with color or patterns, the object will probably obscure the brochure text.

You can change this so that the object separates the brochure text. To wrap the brochure text around the object, take these steps:

1 Click the object.

2 Click the Format (Object) button on the (Object) toolbar, or choose the Format (Object) command.

The name of the button, toolbar, or command changes depending on the selected object.

3 Click the Wrapping tab.

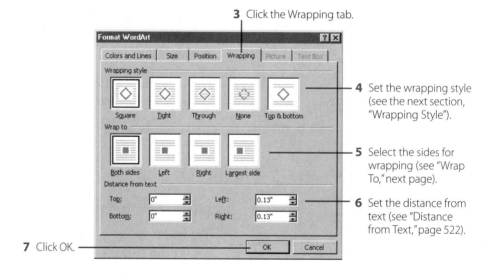

4 Set the wrapping style (see the next section, "Wrapping Style").

5 Select the sides for wrapping (see "Wrap To," next page).

6 Set the distance from text (see "Distance from Text," page 522).

7 Click OK.

Wrapping Style

- **Square**—Sets up the object in a box. The brochure text can wrap around all four sides of the object box. The Wrap To choice determines which sides of the object the brochure text appears on.

- **Tight**—Wraps the brochure text around the outside shape of the object rather than around the object box. The Top and Bottom wrapping measurements can't be changed. You can later adjust the wrapping fit—see "Adjusting the Wrap," next page.

- **Through**—Wraps the brochure text around the shape of the object text and through any open areas of the object text. The Top and Bottom wrapping measurements can't be changed. You can later adjust the wrapping fit—see "Adjusting the Wrap," next page.

- **None**—Floats the object over the brochure text. This setting can obscure brochure text. You can put the object behind the brochure text. To do so, take these steps:

  1 Turn on the Drawing toolbar.

  2 Click the Draw button, select Order, and then select Send Behind Text from the submenu.

- **Top & Bottom**—Wraps brochure text above and below the object but not on the sides. The Left and Right wrapping measurements can't be changed.

Wrap To

Wrap To choices are available only for the Square, Tight, and Through wrapping styles.

- **Both Sides**—Wraps brochure text along both sides of the object, if there is enough room (at least 0.6 inches).

- **Left**—Wraps brochure text only along the left side of the object, if there is enough room (at least 0.6 inches).

- **Right**—Wraps brochure text only along the right side of the object, if there is enough room (at least 0.6 inches).

- **Largest Side**—Wraps brochure text only along the wider side of the object, if there is enough room (at least 0.6 inches).

III

Publications

Distance From Text

The Distance From Text measurements set the amount of space between the edges of the object and the text that surrounds the object.

You can set all four distance measurements only for the Square wrapping style. For the Tight and Through wrapping styles, you can set only the Left and Right measurements. For the Top & Bottom wrapping style, you can set only the Top and Bottom measurements. You can't set any distance measurements for the None wrapping style.

Adjusting the Wrap

If you set wrapping for an object to Tight or Through, you can adjust the wrapping directly on the object in the brochure. To adjust wrapping, take these steps:

1 Click the object.

2 Display the Picture toolbar, if it isn't already displayed. (See "Using the Picture Toolbar.")

3 Click the Text Wrapping button, shown below.

4 Click one of the preset wrapping choices, or click the Edit Wrap Points command.

5 To adjust individual wrapping points, drag one of the black wrapping points to the new wrapping distance.

Click here to adjust individual wrapping points.

Using the Picture Toolbar

For more special tools for working on pictures, you can use the buttons on the Picture toolbar. To display the Picture toolbar (see Figure 10-11), either right-click a toolbar or choose the View Toolbars command. From the Toolbars shortcut menu or from the View Toolbars submenu, click Picture.

FIGURE 10-11.
The Picture toolbar.

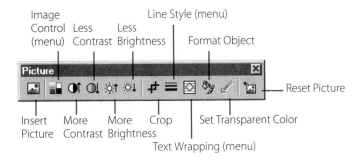

All of the buttons on the Picture toolbar are linked to choices and settings in the Format Picture dialog box, shown in Figure 10-12. Table 10-1 on the next page lists the submenu choices for the buttons that have them and the corresponding options in the Format Picture dialog box.

FIGURE 10-12.
The Picture tab of the Format Picture dialog box.

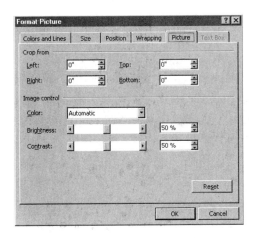

III

Publications

TABLE 10-1.   Picture Options from the Toolbar's Submenus and the Format Picture Dialog Box.

Picture Toolbar Button	Submenu Choices	Dialog Box Options
Image Control	Automatic (checked) Grayscale Black & White Watermark	Picture tab: Image Control section; Color box lists these same four choices
More Contrast Less Contrast		Picture tab: Image Control section; Contrast sliding bar and percentage box increase with each click of More Contrast and decrease with each click of Less Contrast
More Brightness Less Brightness		Picture tab: Image Control section; Brightness sliding bar and percentage box increase with each click of More Brightness and decrease with each click of Less Brightness
Crop		Picture tab: Crop From section; the four boxes record the distance you drag the crop tool (mouse pointer)
Line Style	¼ pt ½ pt ¾ pt 1 pt 1½ pt 2¼ pt 3 pt 4½ pt 6 pt 3 pt 4½ pt 4½ pt 6 pt More Lines…	Colors And Lines tab: Line section; Style and Weight boxes
Text Wrapping	Square Wrapping Tight Wrapping Through No Wrapping Top and Bottom Edit Wrap Points	Wrapping tab: Wrapping Style section lists these same five wrapping choices. Edit Wrap Points has no link to any dialog box.
Format Picture		Picture tab; can select any tab and set any picture formatting
Set Transparent Color		None
Reset Picture		Every Reset button on every tab

CHAPTER 11

Releasing a Press Release

Most organizations are media-conscious—they are aware that any information they can present as "news" might be printed or broadcast. These public "news" presentations represent free advertising. The major vehicle for whetting the interest of the world's newshounds is the press release. Word supplies three press release templates: an "elegant" press release, a "contemporary" press release, and a "professional" press release. Figures 11-1, 11-2, and 11-3 on the following pages give you a preview of each style of press release.

The press release templates contain two pages of samples and instructions for ways to use and customize the template. You need to customize templates because they are designed to be generic—suitable for use by a broad spectrum of people and groups. There are many ways you can customize the press release templates. You can refine certain parts to work better, plus you can add repeated text—for example, a descriptive statement about your organization and the names of people to contact for more information.

FIGURE 11-1.
Preview of the Contemporary Press Release template.

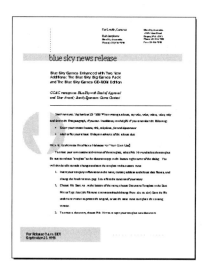

FIGURE 11-2.
Preview of the Elegant Press Release template.

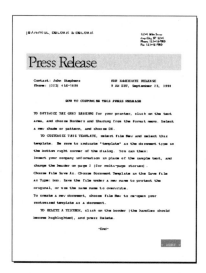

 TIP

Before you start customizing, print a copy of the press release template you're going to change. You can use the instructions in the press release template to transform the template.

This chapter shows you a number of ways you can customize the press release templates. First, however, you need to create a press release template that you can use as a basis.

FIGURE 11-3.

Preview of the Professional Press Release template.

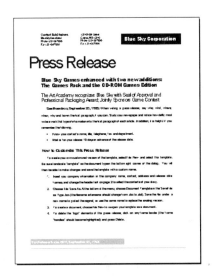

To create a press release template you can remodel, take these steps:

1 Choose the File New command.

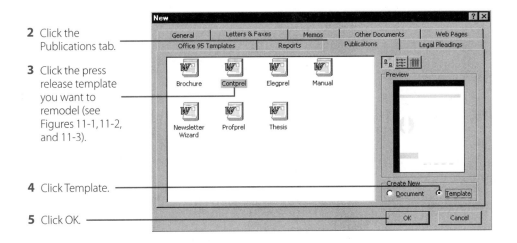

2 Click the Publications tab.

3 Click the press release template you want to remodel (see Figures 11-1, 11-2, and 11-3).

4 Click Template.

5 Click OK.

Viewing Options

For more information about the View tab of the Options dialog box, see "View Tab," page 960.

To help you see how a press release template is constructed and to see the parts as you read about them in this chapter, you should turn on a couple of viewing options; take these steps:

1 Switch to Page Layout view.

III

Publications

2 Choose the Tools Options command.

3 Click the View tab.

4 Turn on Object anchors.

5 Turn on Text boundaries.

6 Turn on All.

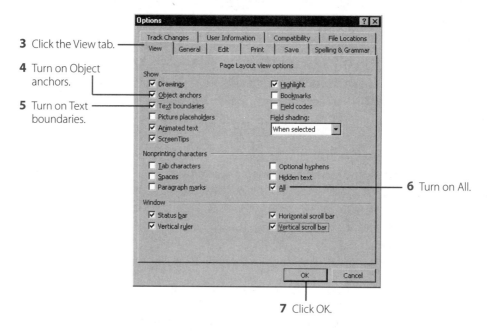

7 Click OK.

Figure 11-4 shows how the contemporary press release looks after you turn on these viewing options.

FIGURE 11-4.
The objects you can see in the contemporary press release with additional viewing options turned on.

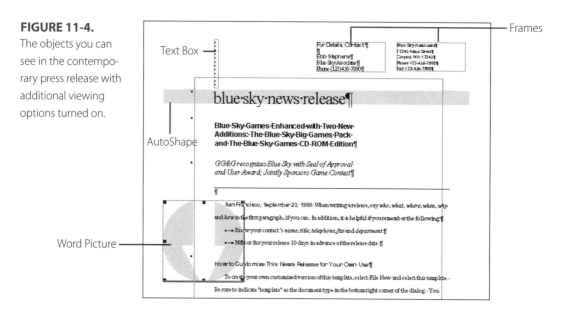

Stacking Layers of Reality

? SEE ALSO

For more information about text boxes, see "Wrapping Up Text Boxes," page 399, and "Formatting Art, Word-Art, and Other Objects," page 515. For more information about AutoShapes, see "Drawing Pictures," page 458.

As you can read elsewhere in this book, each page of a Word document has four layers (see the sidebar "The Drawing Layers on a Page," page 459). Each layer can hold multiple layers of drawing shapes, text boxes, and frames (see "The Nature of Drawing Programs," page 458). The objects can overlap so that you get a complete picture from the arrangement and layering of the pieces. In the Contemporary Press Release template, the designers have set up overlapping and stacked objects. Figure 11-5 identifies the objects and shows you where they overlap. This information should help you think of new ways you can decorate your press releases to draw attention to them.

FIGURE 11-5.

The layers of text boxes, AutoShapes, and frames in the Contemporary Press Release template.

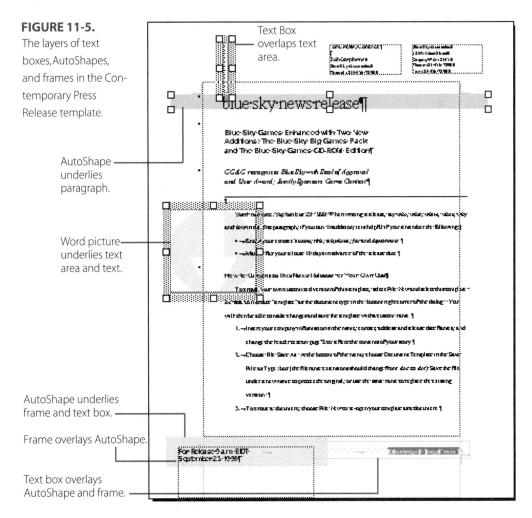

Text Box overlaps text area.

AutoShape underlies paragraph.

Word picture underlies text area and text.

AutoShape underlies frame and text box.

Frame overlays AutoShape.

Text box overlays AutoShape and frame.

III

Publications

You can move each object around the page (see "Positioning," page 518, and "Positioning Objects on a Page," page 409). You can also change the order of the layers by moving an object toward the back or toward the front (see "Ordering Drawing Layers," page 481, for instructions).

Changing the Picture

? SEE ALSO

For more information about pictures, see the sections about art in Chapter 8, "Filing Your Report," and Chapter 10, "Brocading a Brochure." In particular, see the sections "The Fill Color Button," page 491, "Drawing Pictures," page 458, and "Adding Art from Files," page 455.

In Figure 11-4, page 528, you see a box labeled as a Word picture. To get a good look at this picture (and to change it, if you want), double-click it. Word opens a picture window that displays only the picture, as shown here:

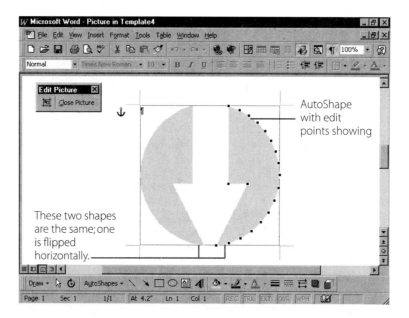

Frames

Word's frames are a carryover from earlier versions of Word. In Word 97, you'll most often prefer to use text boxes in place of frames. Word provides no direct way to convert a frame to a text box, though there is a direct way to convert a text box to a frame. To use a text box in place of an existing frame, you have to insert a text box, move the text to it, remove the frame, and then position the text box where the frame was. Clever, no?

To remove a frame, select it (click its border), choose the Format Frame command, and then click the Remove button in the Frame dialog box.

You can change the fill of the two shapes—using a different color, a texture, a pattern, or even a picture (see "The Fill Color Button," page 491). You can draw additional shapes in or around these two shapes. You can completely replace this picture with one of your own; for example, you can use your organization's logo.

Using Key Styles

Word's press release templates contain a number of special styles for you to use when you're creating and formatting a press release. Table 11-1 lists some of the key styles and their formatting uses.

Word in no way forces you to use these styles in the way their designers intended. You don't have to use these styles at all. I've listed them and their formatting uses here to show you how some of the key parts of the press release templates get their looks. If you prefer a different look for these elements, you can either change the definitions of the styles or apply different styles. For information about applying different styles, see "Using Different Styles," page 54. For information about changing these styles, see "Style Makeover," page 834.

TABLE 11-1. Key Styles in the Press Release Templates and Their Formatting Uses.

Style Name	Formatting Use
Contact	Name, company, and phone number of the person the reporter can contact for more information; the person sending the press release
Return Address	Name, address, phone number, and fax number of the organization sending the press release
Title	Title of press release; the headline
Subtitle	Subtitle, if any, of the press release; secondary headline
Date	Date and time when news can be published or broadcast
Lead-In Emphasis	City and date of news; at opening of first paragraph

III

Publications

Creating Headers for Page 2 and After

All three press release templates have a header set up for page 2 and after. The headers contain the title of the press release. This setup is a fine practice, but it's awkward for regular use. With this setup, you have to manually edit the header for page 2 and after for each new press release—bummer. With Word, you can automate the header for page 2 and after so that it always contains the title of the press release, but you do nothing more than type the title on the first page of the press release and apply a character style you create yourself (it's easy!). To set this up in your press release template, you'll perform these actions:

- Create a character style

- Insert a cross-reference in the header for page 2 and after that refers to the character style you applied

- Type the press release title

- Apply the character style you created to the part of the press release title you want to appear in the header for page 2 and after

Most of Word's press release templates are only one page long, but the template designers have set up a header for page 2 and after. You can't see it until the press release contains some text on page 2. To display the header on page 2, take these steps:

1 Position the insertion point at the beginning of a paragraph in the middle of page 1.

2 Press Ctrl+Enter to insert a page break.

You'll now see the header on page 2. For the Contemporary and Professional Press Release templates, the header contains only the first line of the press release title. When you have a long title, you'll want to shorten it a bit for the header on page 2 and after. That's why we're creating a character style—a style we can apply to part of the title (without affecting its formatting)—a style we can cross-reference from the header on page 2 and after. The next two sections explain how to create the character style and how to set up a cross-reference to it.

Creating a Character Style for Part of the Title

To create a character style for part of the press release title, take these steps:

1 Select a portion of the press release title. Do *not* include a paragraph mark!

2 Choose the Format Style command, and in the Style dialog box, click the New button.

3 Type a style name.

5 Click OK.

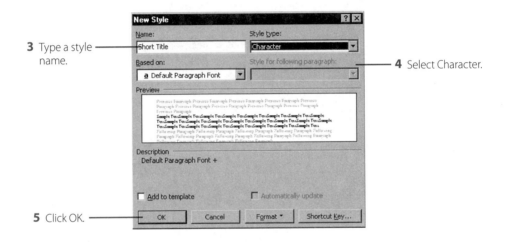

4 Select Character.

6 In the Style dialog box, click the Apply button.

SEE ALSO

For more about creating styles, see "Designing Your Own Character Style," page 832.

The text you selected in step 1 doesn't change its appearance because you neither added nor subtracted any font formatting. Your new character style simply uses the font formatting of the paragraph style (in this case, Title).

Now you're ready for the cross-reference from the header on page 2 and after.

Inserting a Style Cross-Reference in the Header for Page 2 and After

In the header for page 2 and after you can set up a cross-reference to the character style in the title by following the steps on the next page.

III

Publications

1 Be sure the press release has at least two pages. If not, insert a page break somewhere after the title on page 1. (You'll want to delete this page break later.)

2 Choose the View Header And Footer command.

Show
Next

3 If the header area label shows "First Page Header," click Show Next on the Header And Footer toolbar. If the header area label shows "Header" only, go to step 4.

4 Select the header text, and press Delete.

5 Choose the Insert Field command.

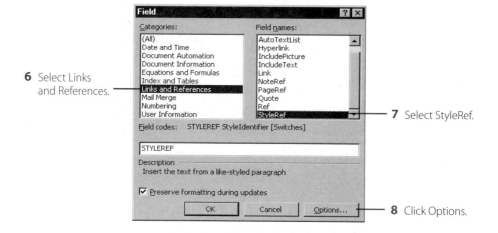

6 Select Links and References.

7 Select StyleRef.

8 Click Options.

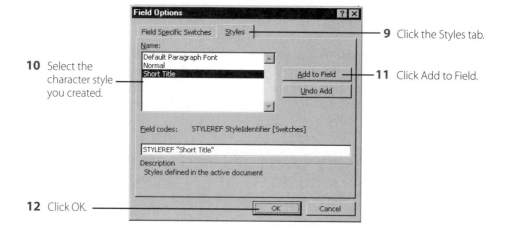

9 Click the Styles tab.

10 Select the character style you created.

11 Click Add to Field.

12 Click OK.

13 In the Field dialog box, click OK.

The header now shows the text from the title to which you applied your character style. Notice that the header text has the formatting of the Header style, not the formatting of the Title style.

Fashioning Footers That Help You

Most press releases I've seen have something like this printed at the bottom of the last page:

—End—

If the press release is longer than one page, the bottom of each page before the last page has something like this printed at the bottom:

MORE # #

You can set up your press release footers to automatically insert "End" on the last page and "More" on pages before the last page when there's more than one page. To set this up, take these steps:

1 Be sure the press release has at least two pages. If not, insert a page break somewhere after the title on page 1. (You'll want to delete this page break later.)

2 Choose the View Header And Footer command.

3 On the Header And Footer toolbar, click the Switch Between Header And Footer button.

Switch Between Header and Footer

4 Press the → key once to position the insertion point at the middle tab stop in the footer.

5 Press Ctrl+F9 to insert field characters with the insertion point between them: { | }.

6 Type *IF* and a space: { IF }.

7 Press Ctrl+F9 again, and then type *NUMPAGES* between the two new field characters: { IF { NUMPAGES } }.

8 Press the → key twice, type a space and >, another space, and then press Alt+Shift+P to insert a Page field ({ PAGE }), which shows the number of the page it's on—it will show 1 if you're on page 1 or 2 if you're on page 2; If you're on page 1, it shows the following: { IF { NUMPAGES } > { 1 } }.

III

Publications

9 Press the → key once, type a space and *"# # # MORE # # #"* *"—End—"* (press Alt+Ctrl+minus on the keypad to insert the em dashes; be sure to include the quotation marks): { IF { NUMPAGES } > { PAGE } *"# # # MORE # # #"* *"—End—"* }.

10 Press the → key once to position the insertion point to the right of the last field character, and then hold down the Shift key while you press the ← key to select all the fields and text you just inserted.

11 Press Ctrl+C to copy the selection to the Clipboard.

12 Click the Show Next button on the Header And Footer toolbar to jump to the footer for page 2 and after, if you are on page 1. If you're on page 2, click the Show Previous button.

13 Press the → key once to position the insertion point at the middle tab stop in the footer.

14 Press Ctrl+V to paste the fields into the footer for page 2 and after. You'll see the result of the field, not the field codes.

15 Click the Close button on the Header And Footer toolbar.

16 Switch to Normal view, and then switch back to Page Layout view. You should see *# # # MORE # # #* at the bottom of the first page and *—End—* at the bottom of the second page.

If you add another page (or several more pages), you should see *# # # MORE # # #* at the bottom of the pages before the last page and *—End—* at the bottom of the last page.

⭐ **TIP**

If you set up this footer for the elegant press release, delete the last paragraph of press release text, which contains *–End–*. Your new footer takes care of that now.

Adding a Standard Statement

Many organizations end their press releases with a statement of the nature and purpose of their organization. This statement is called boilerplate text: it's always the same every time. Word gives you several ways to add this boilerplate text:

■ Simply type the text into your template as the last paragraph—you must be sure that when you're typing your press release that you don't type over it, delete it, or accidentally add text after this standard statement.

■ You can type the text once and then save it as AutoText—when you need to insert it, you simply insert the AutoText at the proper place. For details about creating AutoText, see "AutoText," page 819.

■ You can type the text once, save it as AutoText, and then add a field to your footer fields to insert the standard statement from AutoText when the fields insert —*End*— on the last page. When you save the AutoText, be sure to select an empty paragraph mark before the statement, but not one at the end of it; you add the AutoText field inside the quotation marks around —*End*—: { IF { NUMPAGES } > { PAGE } "# # # MORE # # #" "—End—{ AUTOTEXT "Statement" }" }.

CHAPTER 12

Directing a Directory

Many organizations publish a directory of their members. Some organizations specialize in publishing directories of services, either for their staffs or for clients and customers. To help you set up a directory, Word supplies a Directory template. Figure 12-1 on the next page gives you a two-page preview of it.

The Directory template includes a sample cover page that you can customize to suit the needs of your organization. The template contains instructions telling you how to substitute your own text for the sample text provided.

But you can go one step further and remake the template so it reflects your personal style or that of your company or organization.

There are many ways you can do this. The next several sections present a variety of these ways.

FIGURE 12-1.
Preview of the
Directory template.

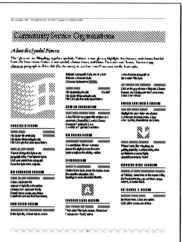

Before you start your remodeling project, it's a good idea to print a copy of the Directory template you're going to remodel. You can follow the instructions in the Directory template as the preliminary guide toward transforming the template.

The first thing you must do is create a new Directory template that you can alter to fit your special needs.

To create a Directory template you can alter, take these steps:

1 Choose the File New command.

2 Click the Publications tab.

3 Click the Directory icon.

4 Click Template.

5 Click OK.

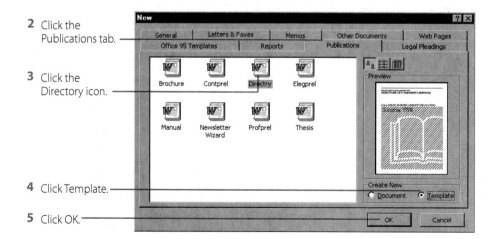

Clearing Out the Sample Text

Probably the first step you'll want to take to modify the Directory template is to clear out the sample text, while leaving the major parts of the structure. To help you see what you're doing here, click the Show/Hide ¶ button on the Standard toolbar to display all the paragraph marks, section breaks, and other structural details that don't print. Now take these steps:

1 Select the text of any paragraph you want to keep as a structure. Be sure you do not select the paragraph mark. Delete the text only.

2 Select duplicate paragraphs in the listings sections and delete them.

3 If you don't want the decorations on page 2 (the Windows logo and the down arrow), select them and delete them. If you want some decoration in these locations, double-click each one, and select the new decoration in the Symbol dialog box shown here.

4 Select the font. ───

5 Click a symbol. ───

6 Click Insert. ───

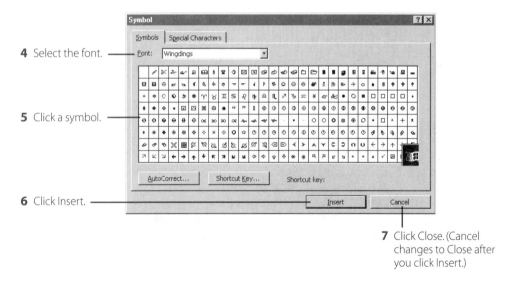

7 Click Close. (Cancel changes to Close after you click Insert.)

8 Click the Save button on the Standard toolbar, select the Publications folder (or any other folder you want to put your new template file in), type a name for your template, and then click the Save button.

You're now ready to make other alterations to your new Directory template.

Customizing Columns

The directory listings are set up in three columns. The columns are separated by a half-inch space but no line. You can change the number of columns, you can change the column widths, and you can add a vertical divider line between columns.

? SEE ALSO

For full details of columns, see "Dressing Up Columns," page 424.

If wider columns suit your directory entries better, you can decrease the number of columns. If you want to fit more columns on each page, you can increase the number of columns. If you need a little more width in each column (whether you increase or decrease the number of columns or keep the same number of columns), you can decrease the space between columns. Conversely, you can increase the width between columns to separate them more. If you decrease the space between columns, you might want to add a vertical divider line between columns.

To adjust the column setup in your directory template, take these steps:

1 Click a listing anywhere in a part of the directory that has three columns.

2 Choose the Format Columns command.

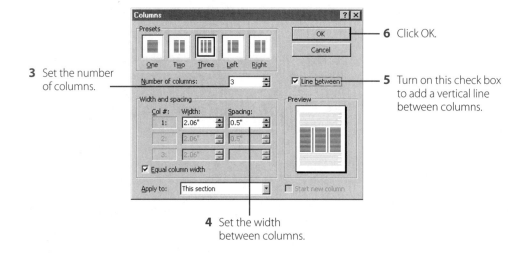

3 Set the number of columns.

4 Set the width between columns.

5 Turn on this check box to add a vertical line between columns.

6 Click OK.

TIP

Display Ads in Your Directory

Suppose you want to add larger entries or display ads to your directory (for a "small" fee, of course). Rather than trying to mangle the columns to fit in a display ad, insert a text box for the ad. After you insert the text box and position it, be sure you set it so that it does not float above the text and so that the regular listings wrap around it. For details of text boxes and wrapping text around them, see "Formatting Art, WordArt, and Other Objects," page 515, and "Wrapping Up Text Boxes," page 399.

Applying Wingdings Styles

As you can read in the original text of the Directory template, the following pictures (decorations) in the Directory template are characters chosen from the Wingdings character set: the book (on the cover page), the Windows logo, and the down arrow (on page 2). These three decorations are formatted with styles for each size, as shown in the following table.

Picture	Style	Wingdings Size
Book	Picture	525 points
Windows logo	Icon 1	160 points
Down arrow	Icon 2	44 points

All three of these styles set the font color to white to make the picture stand out against the background shading. (For more information about the background shading, see the next topic, "Using Paragraph Shading.") In each of these paragraphs, you can substitute any character you want from the Wingdings character set. If you want to use characters from the Wingdings 2, Wingdings 3, Symbol, or Monotype Sorts fonts, you have two choices (one for a specific situation, the other for wholesale change):

■ For a specific situation, you can double-click the Wingdings symbol to display the Symbol dialog box. In the Symbol dialog box, you can select the font that contains the symbol you want to use, click the symbol, and then click Close.

■ For wholesale change, you can change the font for the styles. To do this, select a paragraph with the style you want to change, choose the Format Style command, click the Modify button, click the Format button and select Font, select the font and click OK, click OK in the Modify Style dialog box, and then click Apply in the Style dialog box.

Using Paragraph Shading

? SEE ALSO

For details of changing paragraph styles, see "Changing a Paragraph Style," page xxx.

The cover page, the footers for page 2 and after (which contain the page number), and the heading letters for each alphabetical section of the directory have paragraph shading—a diagonal line pattern. This shading is part of the styles Date (for the date on the cover of the directory), Picture (for the cover page picture), Heading 1 (for the category of listing), Icon 1 (for pictures that span a column width), Icon 2 (for pictures that are narrower than the column), Section Title (for the section letters), and Footer (for the page number). Word provides four diagonal shading patterns; these styles use three of the four patterns, as shown in the following table.

Styles	Diagonal Shading Pattern
Picture, Date	Lt Up Diagonal
Heading 1, Icon 1, Footer	Lt Dwn Diagonal
Section Title, Icon 2	Dk Dwn Diagonal

The fact that the styles Picture and Date have the same diagonal shading pattern gives the impression that these two paragraphs share the same background. Notice that these two styles, which appear on the cover page only, are the only styles that have light, up-diagonal shading. All the other styles use a down-diagonal shading.

There are a number of different shadings available beyond the four diagonal choices. There are other patterns, and there are other colors. To change the shading of one of the styles that has shading (or any other style to which you want to add shading), take these steps:

1 Click a paragraph with the shading you want to change.

2 Choose the Format Style command.

3 In the Style dialog box, click the Modify button.

4 In the Modify Style dialog box, click the Format button and select Border.

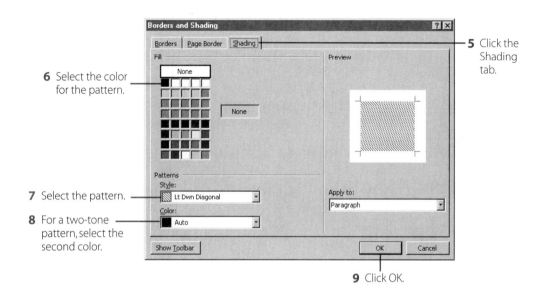

5 Click the Shading tab.

6 Select the color for the pattern.

7 Select the pattern.

8 For a two-tone pattern, select the second color.

9 Click OK.

10 In the Modify Style dialog box, click OK, and then click Apply in the Style dialog box.

Repeat these steps to change the shading for as many styles as you want.

 TIP

Changing the Font Color of the Footer

All the styles that have paragraph shading, except Footer, have the font color set to white. The white font color makes the characters stand out, as cutouts, from the shading. The Footer font color is black, which makes the page number hard to see against the light, down-diagonal shading pattern. The easiest way to make the page numbers stand out more is to change the Footer style font color to white. You could also change the Footer style shading to a different color, such as Turquoise, Bright Green, or one of the lighter gray shades.

III

Publications

Creating a Header for Page 2 and After

On page 2 of the Directory template, the header contains the text *Summer 1998* ■ *Directory of Community Services*. This text is the same as the text on the Directory cover page. *Summer 1998* on the cover is in a paragraph formatted with the Date style. *Directory of Community Services* is in a paragraph formatted with the Title Cover style. You can use these styles as the basis for a cross-reference from the header. That way, when you change the date of the directory or the title on the cover, the headers for page 2 and after will contain the correct text for the occasion without your having to edit the header yourself.

Also, the headers for the Directory template don't help you locate the entries. You're familiar with telephone directory, dictionary, and encyclopedia pages, which have headers that show the name of the first and last listing on a page. Using cross-references to styles, you can add the names of the first and last entries on each page of your directory.

Automating the Header Text

To automate the text in the directory headers on page 2 and after, take these steps:

1 Choose the View Header And Footer command.

Show Next

2 If the header area label shows *Header* only, go to step 3. If the header area label shows *First Page Header*, click Show Next on the Header And Footer toolbar.

3 Select the header text *Summer 1998*, press Delete, press Spacebar, and then press ←.

4 Choose the Insert Field command.

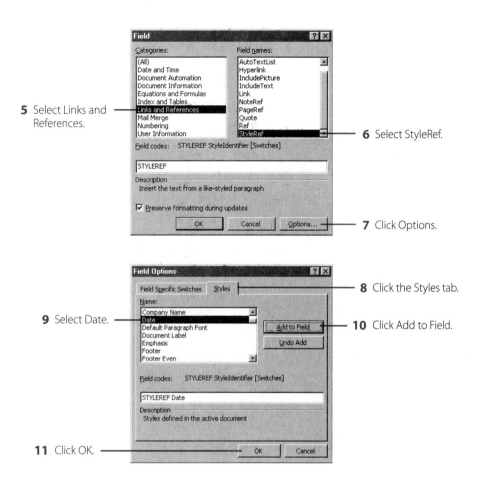

5 Select Links and References.

6 Select StyleRef.

7 Click Options.

8 Click the Styles tab.

9 Select Date.

10 Click Add to Field.

11 Click OK.

12 In the Field dialog box, click OK.

13 Select the header text *Directory of Community Services*, press Delete, and then press Spacebar.

14 Repeat steps 4 through 12, except in step 9 select the Title Cover style instead of the Date style.

15 Click the Close button on the Header And Footer toolbar.

The header now shows the same text as before. Notice that the header text has the formatting of the Header style, not the formatting of the Date and Title Cover styles.

Adding Directory Listings to Page Headers

To add the names of the first and last entries on each page of your directory to the headers on each page, take these steps:

1 Choose the View Header And Footer command.

2 If the header area label shows *Header* only, go to step 3. If the header area label shows *First Page Header*, click Show Next on the Header And Footer toolbar.

3 Press the End key to position the insertion point at the end of the header text *Directory of Community Services*, and then press Tab.

4 Choose the Insert Field command, select Links And References, select StyleRef, and then click Options.

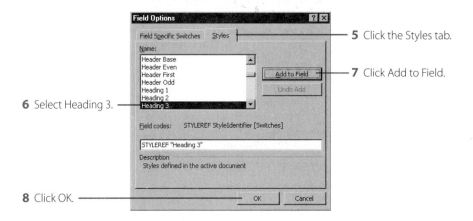

5 Click the Styles tab.

7 Click Add to Field.

6 Select Heading 3.

8 Click OK.

9 In the Field dialog box, click OK.

10 Press the End key, press Spacebar, insert an en dash (press Ctrl+minus on the keypad), and then press Spacebar again.

11 Choose the Insert Field command, select Links And References, select StyleRef, and then click Options.

12 Click the Styles tab.

13 Select the Heading 3 style.

14 Click the Add To Field button.

15 Click the Field Specific Switches tab.

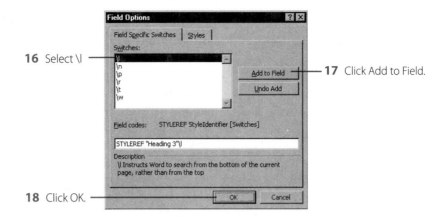

16 Select \l

17 Click Add to Field.

18 Click OK.

19 In the Field dialog box, click OK.

The header now shows the name of the first and last listings on the page, as shown here:

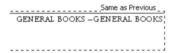

Placing Your Header Flush Right with the Margin

If you want the directory listing names in the headers to appear flush with the right margin, you need to change the tab stops set for the Header style. To do so, take these steps:

1 Choose the Format Style command, select Header in the Styles list, and then click Modify.

2 In the Modify Style dialog box, click the Format button and select Tabs.

3 In the Tabs dialog box, click the Clear All button.

4 In the Tab Stop Position box, type *7.17*.

5 Click the Right option in the Alignment group, click the Set button, and then click OK.

6 In the Modify Style dialog box, click OK, and then click Close in the Style dialog box.

III

Publications

Pulling Information from Information Files

Question: where do you get the listings for your directory? You can certainly type them in from paper records. But if you have the records stored on your computer, you might find it much more convenient to pull in the information from those files rather than retyping everything. You can certainly copy and paste the listings from another file, but this method is almost as tedious as typing the listings (though less error prone). Better still is to let Word do the work while you reap the kudos.

- Mail merge—You can set up a mail merge document from your modified Directory template, and then use that new document as a main document for collecting all the listings in proper arrangement for your directory. You'd then use the next method. See the next section, "Using Mail Merge to Build Your Directory Listings," for steps that use both methods.

- Insert file—You can simply insert a file that contains the listings into your directory document. This method works especially well for Word documents.

- Insert database—You can apply the steps for inserting databases to insert information from a file where you store the listings for other purposes. The other file can be a Microsoft Excel worksheet, an Access database, some other database, or even a simple information file.

For all three methods plus the copy-and-paste method and simply typing the listings, the Directory template contains four styles for you to apply to the various parts of each listing, as shown in the following table.

Style Name	Apply To
Heading 3	Listing Category.
Name	Name of the person, service, or organization and his or her telephone number; separate the name and number with a tab character.
List	All the other lines of each listing, except the last line.
List Last	The last line of each listing.

After you insert the information (or as you are typing it), you'll want to apply these styles to make the directory listings look correct and to set up the text for the cross-references in the headers. (You set up these cross-references in "Adding Directory Listings to Page Headers," page 548.)

Using Mail Merge to Build Your Directory Listings

? SEE ALSO

For details of mail merge, see Chapter 5, "Mass Mail Letters," and "Creating Mass Mail Address Labels," page 206. In particular, you need to use the Next Record merge field to add all the listings. For details about inserting information from a database, see "Pulling Data from Excel," page 367.

Mail merge can build lists of entries very quickly, but there is one problem with this approach—knowing how many entries there are. Because you don't want to count them and because you want Word to do most of the work, you have to take many steps, at least the first time you build a directory with mail merge. These steps can be summarized in the following stages:

- Open a new document with your Directory template file attached, and start the mail merge operation.

- Open a data source document, and set up a mailing label document as the main document for the merge operation.

- Apply styles from the Directory template to the main document's mailing label table.

- Convert the mailing label table to text.

- Perform the merge operation to create the document that will be inserted into the new directory document.

The sections that follow cover the steps for each stage of the process. Let's assume that you have a Word data document set up that contains the directory listings. While this data document might contain many kinds of information that won't go into a directory, for the purposes of the following steps, the data document contains information for the following merge fields: Name (name of organization), WorkPhone (business phone number), Address1 (street address), City, State, PostalCode, and Description (a short phrase that describes each entry's principal function). Under these conditions, take the steps in the following sections to create your directory from this data document.

Open a New Document and Start Mail Merge

1 Create a new document from your modified directory template.

2 Press Ctrl+End to jump to the end of the document.

3 Choose the Tools Mail Merge command.

4 Click the Create button and select Mailing Labels.

5 Click the New Main Document button when you see a message asking which document to use for a main document.

Open a Data Source
Document and Set Up a Main Document

1 Click the Get Data button, and then click Open Data Source.

2 In the Open Data Source dialog box, find and select the data document, and then click the Open button.

3 When Word asks whether you want to set up the main document, click the Set Up Main Document button.

4 When the Label Options dialog box appears, select 5160 - Address from the Product Number list, and then click OK.

5 When the Create Labels dialog box appears, set it up as shown in the following illustration.

6 Click here to select each merge field to insert.

7 Press Ctrl+Tab to insert tab character here.

9 When the label is set up, click OK.

8 Press Enter to start each new line.

10 Click the Edit button for the Main Document, and select the Labels document.

12 Delete these two columns.

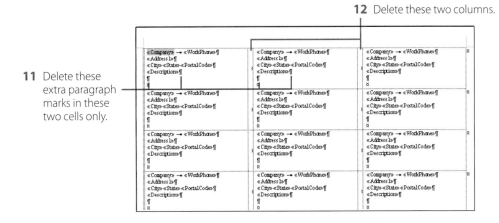

11 Delete these extra paragraph marks in these two cells only.

Attach Your Directory Template and Apply Styles to the Main Document

1 Choose the Tools Templates And Add-Ins command.

2 In the Templates And Add-Ins dialog box, turn on the Automatically Update Document Styles check box, and then click the Attach button.

3 In the Attach Template dialog box, find and select your modified directory template, and then click the Open button.

4 Click OK in the Templates And Add-Ins dialog box.

5 Press Ctrl+5 (on the number keypad) to select the entire table.

6 Apply the style named List Last to the entire table.

7 Apply the style named Name to the first paragraph in the first and second columns of the first row.

8 Apply the style named List to the second and third paragraphs in the first and second columns of the first row.

9 Position the insertion point in the first column in the first row, and then press the Tab key. This selects the entire contents of the second column in the first row.

10 Press Ctrl+C to copy the cell contents to the Clipboard.

III

Publications

11 Press the Tab key to move to the third column of the first row, and select its contents.

12 Press Ctrl+V to paste the Clipboard contents (a copy of the contents of the second column of the first row) into the third column of the first row.

13 Repeat step 11 and step 12 for each column of the second row.

14 Select the contents of the three columns of the second row by dragging from the first column to the third column. Do not select the row marker.

15 Press Ctrl+C to copy the cell contents to the Clipboard.

16 Press the Tab key as many times as is necessary to move to the first column of the next row, and select its contents.

17 Press Ctrl+V to paste the Clipboard contents (a copy of the contents of the three columns of the second row) into the row with the selection. Word replaces all the contents of the row with the contents of the Clipboard.

18 Repeat step 16 and step 17 until you have pasted the Clipboard contents into all the rows.

Convert the Table to Text and Save the Document

1 Select the entire table, and then choose the Table Convert Table To Text command. Select the table by highlighting the columns, but make sure you don't select the row markers—that is, *don't* press Ctrl+5 (on the number keypad) to select the table.

2 In the Convert Table To Text dialog box, click Paragraph Marks, and then click OK.

3 If, after the conversion, you see extra paragraph marks in the document, delete them. Also check the end of the document: delete the last empty paragraph mark and any section break characters you might find there.

4 Save this document. You can use it to build another directory from a mail merge data document. To do so, you simply perform the first two steps in this whole process: create a new document from your modified directory template, and press Ctrl+End to jump to the end of the document. Then complete the steps in the next section.

Complete the Mail Merge Operation

1 Click the Merge To New Document button on the Mail Merge toolbar.

2 When the merge is complete, save the resulting document. This document is the one you'll insert into your directory document.

3 Switch to the window that contains your new directory document.

4 Choose the Insert File command, find and select the merged document you just created and saved, and then click OK.

5 Add category labels if you want. Remember that your headers on page 2 and after are set up with cross-references to the style Heading 3. The Heading 3 style was designed to format categories. To insert a category label, simply insert a new paragraph where you want to add a category label, format the paragraph with the Heading 3 style (press Alt+Ctrl+3), and then type the category label.

6 Save your new directory.

Handling a Manual

A manual is often a group effort rather than the work of a single person. In Word, the foundation of group work is the master document—the document that contains and holds together the pieces of a project. From a master document, you open and work on pieces called subdocuments. When you save changes to a subdocument, those changes become part of the master document. In fact, a master document is mostly composed of subdocuments, but it can have its own special material in addition to the material that's contained in the subdocuments. The foundation of the master document is the outline. Outlining makes it possible for you to structure a document; it forces you to work out the logic of a comprehensive group project.

In this chapter, you'll learn about master documents, subdocuments, outlining, and a variety of ways you can build and control a large project that's ultimately put out as a single work.

Understanding Master Documents and Subdocuments

? SEE ALSO

You can find files on the CD in this book to help you create a book template and an article template. Consult BOOKDOT.DOC for directions on creating a book template.

When you work on a group project, such as a manual, you might find it beneficial to divide the work into parts that various authors, editors, artists, and compositors can work on individually toward the group goal of a complete work. A typical manual contains chapters. Chapters are good candidates for subdocuments. The master document collects the subdocuments into a whole work.

Before you can use master documents, you need to understand what a master document is. Part of understanding master documents is also understanding subdocuments—documents within a master document.

What Is a Master Document?

A master document is a Word document that contains one or more subdocuments. In a master document, you use the Master Document view (a special version of Outline view) to see parts of the master document—that is, to view the subdocuments in place.

In a master document, you can rearrange the order of subdocuments and make changes that affect all the subdocuments. These global changes include the following:

? SEE ALSO

A manual often contains artwork, tables, a table of contents, a table of figures, a list of tables, and an index. For information about adding artwork, see Chapter 8, "Filing Your Report," and Chapter 10, "Brocading a Brochure." For information about tables, see Chapter 8. For information about tables of contents, tables of figures, lists of tables, and indexes, see Chapter 14, Proving Your Thesis."

- Changing the section starts of the subdocuments

- Inserting cross-references

- Revising styles for the master document and all the subdocuments in the master document

- Adding material that belongs only in the master document and is not part of any of the subdocuments

- Changing material in a subdocument when you don't want to open the subdocument itself

What Is a Subdocument?

A subdocument is a part of a master document that is stored in a separate file from the master document. Because of this, you can hand out subdocument assignments to various team members. Word automatically adds all changes in a subdocument to the master document, so that you can be sure the master document always reflects the latest version of a subdocument.

Subdocuments can be new documents you create within the master document or existing documents that you add to the master document. When making changes to subdocuments, you can do all of the following:

- Convert into a separate subdocument any part of the master document that's not yet part of any subdocument

- Merge two subdocuments

- Split merged subdocuments back into separate subdocuments

- Convert a subdocument into master document material that's no longer part of any subdocument

Outlining Your Documents

Building master documents relies on outlining. In Word, outlining is integrated with the whole process of building any document that has headings. Some of you might remember outlining as a boring, pointless task that you had to perform for an English teacher. But here, outlining—besides structuring a document—can help you arrange your thoughts and organize the document, turn major ideas into document headings that you can collect into a table of contents, and provide a framework that lets you move quickly through your document. Time spent outlining is time spent building your document. This is especially true when you're building master documents.

Besides switching to Outline view to get to Master Document view (or switching to Master Document view to display your document in Outline view), you can use outlining to set up the topics that you'll convert to new subdocuments.

Here are a couple of facts about Outline view:

- If you have a new document and switch to Outline view, Word automatically sets up the single, empty paragraph as Heading 1. (Word applies the Heading 1 style.)

- In Outline view, when you start a new paragraph from the end of a paragraph, the new paragraph has the same style as the paragraph preceding it. This fact remains true regardless of which Style For Following Paragraph you have set up for the style.

With these facts in mind, type the headings you want for your document. When you want subheadings, demote the heading to the level you want it to have in the outline. When you want to return to a higher level, promote the heading. (Different ways of promoting and demoting are discussed in this section and the next.) You can also demote a paragraph to body text and type the body of your document.

When it's time to reorganize your outline, you move headings (and body text) up or down in the outline. You can move items by dragging the paragraph icons that appear beside every paragraph in Outline view, as shown here:

Indicates a heading that has no subheadings or body text

Paragraph icons —⌐ 🔲 **Proposed·Solution¶**
　　　　　　　└ ✛ **Schedule·for·Implementation¶**
　　　　　　　　🔲 ¶
Indicates body text
Indicates a heading that has either subheadings or body text or both

When you position the mouse pointer over a paragraph icon, the mouse pointer changes to this four-headed arrow:

Mouse pointer changes when it is over the icon.

✛ **Proposed·Solution¶**
✛ **Schedule·for·Implementation¶**

To move a paragraph by dragging, do one of the following:

- Drag the icon up or down (the mouse pointer changes to a two-headed arrow as you drag) until the gray horizontal line with an arrowhead that appears is positioned just above the paragraph where you want to move the heading, its subheadings, and all the associated body text.

- Drag the paragraph icon to the left to promote it or to the right to demote it.

TIP

If you want to promote or demote a heading without affecting its subheads, you cannot use the dragging technique. Instead, use either the Promote or Demote button on the Outlining toolbar, or use an outlining shortcut key.

You have nine levels of headings to play with. Each time you promote or demote a heading, Word assigns it a different style—Heading 1 through Heading 9. If you drag a heading to the farthest right position, you'll see the outline icon snap back under the heading just above. When the icon snaps back, the heading becomes body text, and Word gives the heading the Normal style.

 TIP

Manipulating Consecutive Headings

You'll need to use a slightly different mouse technique to move, promote, or demote multiple consecutive headings that are at the same level. First collapse the headings (see the next section, "Using the Outlining Toolbar"). Now select the headings. Then position the mouse pointer over the outline icon for any heading you've selected, hold down the Alt key, and drag the selection. If you don't use the Alt key, Word moves only the first heading.

Using the Outlining Toolbar

To manipulate the outline, you can click the buttons on the Outlining toolbar, shown in Figure 13-1. These buttons are especially handy when you want to move two or more consecutive paragraphs that are at the same heading level to a new location in your document, or when you want to promote or demote multiple headings to a different level. The list starting on the next page describes these buttons.

FIGURE 13-1.
The Outlining toolbar.

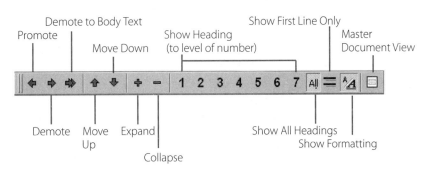

III

Publications

- To move the paragraphs upward and downward, select them, and then click the Move Up button or the Move Down button.

- To change the heading level of the selected paragraphs, click the Promote and Demote buttons on the Outlining toolbar to promote and demote the headings.

- To demote headings to body text, click the Demote To Body Text button. You can also apply a style that's not Heading 1–Heading 9.

- To expand a heading level to show its next level of subheadings, click the Expand button. Repeat this step to show the next lower level of subheadings. When all the subheadings are visible, clicking the Expand button displays the body text under the headings.

- To collapse a heading level to hide body text, click the Collapse button. When all the body text is hidden, clicking the Collapse button hides the lowest visible level of subheading under the selected heading. Repeat this step to hide the next higher level of subheadings.

- To expand the entire outline to a specific level of heading, click the Show Heading button with the number that corresponds to the number of heading levels you want to see.

- To see all headings and all body text, click the Show All Headings button. If you click the Show All Headings button again, Word hides the body text. This technique is one way to display headings at levels 8 and 9.

⭐ **TIP**

Selecting and Manipulating Headings and Their Subheadings

If you click the icon for a heading paragraph, Word selects the heading and all its subheadings and body text. When you click the toolbar buttons to move the heading, Word moves all the selected text at once. When you click the toolbar buttons to promote or demote the heading, Word promotes or demotes all the subheadings the same number of levels. For example, if you select a level 2 heading and its level 3 subheadings, and then click the Promote button, the level 2 heading becomes a level 1 heading, and the level 3 headings become level 2 headings.

TIP

> The paragraph icons for headings give you a quick way to expand or collapse all the subheadings and body text under a heading with just one stroke. Double-click the heading's paragraph icon to expand all the subheadings and body text under a heading; double-click the heading's paragraph icon again to collapse all the subheadings and body text under a heading.

- To show only the first line of body text paragraphs, click the Show First Line Only button. To see all lines of body text, click again on the Show First Line Only button. This button doesn't affect headings longer than one line. This button also doesn't affect the *display* of paragraphs in table cells. However, if you show only the first lines of body text, you can't select or position the insertion point in text beyond the first line in each cell. (For more about moving around and selecting in an outline, see "Moving Through Text and Selecting in Outline View," on page 565.)

- To see the outline in plain text (without font formatting), click the Show Formatting button. To see the font formatting of text in Outline view, click again on the Show Formatting button. This button does not show or affect paragraph formatting, which never appears in Outline view. To enforce this point, you cannot choose the Format Paragraph command in Outline view. The only paragraph formatting you can set is with the paragraph formatting keys (see Table 13-1 on the next page) and with styles.

- To switch to Master Document view, click the Master Document View button. To return to regular Outline view, click again on the Master Document View button. When you switch to Master Document view, Word displays the Master Document toolbar to the right of the Outlining toolbar. For details of the Master Document toolbar, see "Master Document View and Toolbar," page 576.

Most of the buttons on the Outlining toolbar have corresponding shortcut keys. See Table 13-2, page 565, for a list of outlining shortcut keys. Except as noted, the outlining shortcut keys work in Normal, Outline, Master Document, and Page Layout views.

III

Publications

⭐ **TIP**

To see keyboard shortcuts in ScreenTips, choose the Tools Customize command, click the Options tab, and click the Show Shortcut Keys In ScreenTips check box. Click Close to return to your document.

TABLE 13-1.   Shortcut Keys for Applying Paragraph Formatting.

Paragraph Formatting Shortcut Key	Action
Ctrl+L	Left-aligns the paragraph's lines.
Ctrl+E	Centers the paragraph's lines.
Ctrl+R	Right-aligns the paragraph's lines.
Ctrl+J	Justifies the paragraph's lines.
Ctrl+1 (above the letter keys)	Single-spaces the paragraph's lines.
Ctrl+2 (above the letter keys)	Double-spaces the paragraph's lines.
Ctrl+5 (above the letter keys)	Sets the paragraph's lines to one-and-a-half-line spacing.
Ctrl+0 (zero) (above the letter keys)	Adds or removes a line space above the paragraph (toggles).
Ctrl+M	Increases the left indent to the next tab stop (the default is 0.5 inch). The first-line indent moves by the same amount.
Ctrl+Shift+M	Decreases the left indent to the previous tab stop (the default is 0.5 inch). The first-line indent moves by the same amount.
Ctrl+T	Increases the left indent to the next tab stop (the default is 0.5 inch). The first-line indent remains at its current position (hanging indent).
Ctrl+Shift+T	Decreases the left indent to the previous tab stop (the default is 0.5 inch). The first-line indent remains at its current position.
Ctrl+Q	Removes any paragraph formatting, leaving only the look of the paragraph's style.

TABLE 13-2.   Shortcut Keys for Outlining.

Outlining Shortcut Key	Action
Alt+Shift+←	Promotes a heading; applies the next higher heading style
Alt+Shift+→	Demotes a heading; applies the next lower heading style
Alt+Ctrl+1	Applies the Heading 1 style
Alt+Ctrl+2	Applies the Heading 2 style
Alt+Ctrl+3	Applies the Heading 3 style
Ctrl+Shift+N	Demotes a paragraph to body text; applies the Normal style
Alt+Shift+↑	Moves a paragraph above the next visible paragraph
Alt+Shift+↓	Moves a paragraph below the next visible paragraph
Alt+Shift+1 through Alt+Shift+9	Shows headings up to the level specified (in Outline view only)
Alt+Shift+A, or * on the numeric keypad (without Alt+Shift)	Expands an outline to show all headings and body text or shows headings only (in Outline view only)
Alt+Shift+L	Shows full body text or shows the first line only (in Outline view only)
Alt+Shift+equal sign (=), or plus sign on the numeric keypad	Expands the selected headings to show the next level of subtext (in Outline view only)
Alt+Shift+hyphen, or minus sign on the numeric keypad	Collapses the selected headings to hide the next level of subtext (in Outline view only)

Moving Through Text and Selecting in Outline View

Moving through text in Outline view moves only through the visible text. When you have the outline fully expanded and all lines showing in Outline view, moving through the text with the mouse or cursor keys is the same as moving through text in Normal view. When you collapse body text or headings, moving with the cursor keys jumps over hidden body text and headings.

III

Publications

Because scrolling in Outline view is linked to scrolling in the other views, you can use Outline view to quickly scroll to a particular heading. If you scroll the heading to the top of the Outline view window and then switch to another view, that heading is visible in the window in that view. (See also the sidebar "Synchronized Scrolling" on the next page.)

When you show only the first lines of body text paragraphs, the → cursor key moves to the end of the visible portion of the line, and then jumps to the beginning of the next line. The ← cursor key moves from the beginning of a line to the end of the visible portion of a body text line in the preceding paragraph (or to the end of the heading text if the preceding paragraph is a heading). The Show First Line Only button does not affect the *display* of paragraphs in table cells. Note, however, that if you show only the first lines of body text, you can't select or position the insertion point in visible table text beyond the first line in each cell.

? SEE ALSO

Word has a special version of the outline, called the document map, which you use in Online Layout view. For details, see "Document Map," page 870.

In Outline view, you can select any amount of visible text within one paragraph. When your selection moves into a second paragraph, Word selects the entire paragraph where you started the selection and the entire second paragraph. Once you select an entire paragraph in Outline view, you can select only whole paragraphs.

- To quickly select a heading and all its subheadings and body text, click the paragraph icon for the heading.

- To select only one heading paragraph, click in the selection bar to the left of the paragraph's icon. When you select only a single paragraph, you can then manipulate that heading without affecting its subheadings or body text. This technique is handy when you want to promote or demote a heading without affecting the level of its subheadings.

- To select a body text paragraph, use the techniques you use for selecting paragraphs in Normal view.

? SEE ALSO

The techniques in this section also apply to tables of contents. For details, see "Setting Outline Levels for Other Paragraphs and Styles," page 568.

Selecting Styles in Outline View

Basically, you use Word's Outline view to organize your document. But as a side effect of setting up an outline, you are also using styles for the various headings in your document. In Outline view you can easily set and change these styles.

Synchronized Scrolling

Outline view is synchronized with the other views of a document. This synchronization gives you a special technique for scrolling a document with Outline view. To work this technique, take these steps:

1 Split the window for the document into two panes—drag the Resize bar from the top of the vertical scroll bar down the vertical scroll bar.

2 In one pane display the document in Outline view.

3 In the other pane, display the document in another view.

4 Scroll the outline.

As you scroll, the other pane scrolls automatically to keep the same portion of the document in view in both panes. You can also scroll the other view pane, which causes the outline to scroll as necessary.

Note that this technique doesn't apply when both panes show the outline or when both panes show views of the document other than Outline view.

Selecting Styles with the Outlining Toolbar

When you are in Outline view, the Outlining toolbar is visible. You can use this toolbar to select styles by doing the following:

1 Switch to Outline view either by choosing the View Outline command or by clicking the Outline View button at the left end of the horizontal scroll bar, shown here:

2 Select a paragraph in Outline view.

3 Use the Promote, Demote, and Demote To Body Text buttons on the Outlining toolbar (see Figure 13-1, page 561).

- Click the Promote button on the Outlining toolbar to apply the next higher heading style (Heading 1 through Heading 9 styles).

- Click the Demote button to apply the next lower heading style.

- Click the Demote To Body Text button to apply Normal style to body text.

You can use the Outlining toolbar to select paragraph styles for headings (Heading 1 through Heading 9) and Normal style for body text but not to select other styles, including character styles.

Selecting Styles with Outline Dragging

While you're in Outline view (and only in Outline view), you can also use the mouse to drag paragraphs to heading levels and to the body text level. When you drag the paragraph to a different level, Word automatically applies the style for that level. To drag paragraphs in an outline and select their styles, do the following:

1 Switch to Outline view.

2 Drag a paragraph icon to the left or to the right.

- Drag to the left to apply the next higher heading style (Heading 1 through Heading 9 styles).

- Drag to the right to apply the next lower heading style.

- Drag to the far right to apply Normal style for body text.

Setting Outline Levels for Other Paragraphs and Styles

Normally, a paragraph must have one of the heading styles (Heading 1– Heading 9) in order to appear as a heading in Outline view.

Now you can set up individual paragraphs and paragraph styles with the specific outline level you want without affecting the paragraph's appearance. This way, for example, you can display titles, subtitles, and chapter titles in Outline view as headings without using up heading level styles.

You can't set paragraph formatting in Outline view. If you're working in Outline view, switch to another view.

Viewing Style Names of All Paragraphs

In Outline view (and the other views), the Style box on the Formatting toolbar shows the style of the currently selected paragraph. If you have more than one paragraph selected and all the selected paragraphs have the same style, the Style box shows the style name. If the selected paragraphs have more than one style, the Style box is blank.

In addition, you can see only one style name at a time. To see the styles of all the paragraphs visible in the window, follow these steps:

1 Switch to Outline view. (You can also set up the view of styles in the following steps in Normal view.)

2 Choose the Tools Options command.

3 Click the View tab. ——

4 Set the width to 0.6". ——

5 Click OK. ——

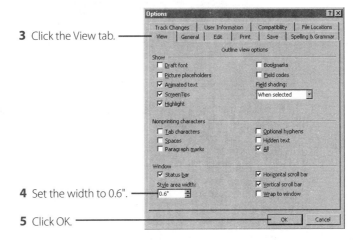

The style name appears in a column along the window's left edge, as shown here:

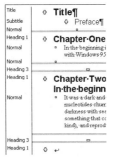

Anything other than "Heading" plus a number indicates body text.

III

Publications

To give a paragraph an outline level, take these steps:

1 Right-click the paragraph you want to give an outline level and choose Paragraph from the shortcut menu.

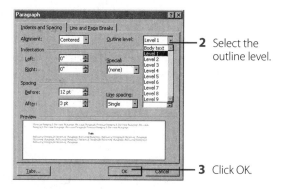

2 Select the outline level.

3 Click OK.

 NOTE

You can't change the outline level of a heading.

You can also set all the paragraphs with a particular style to a specific outline level. To do so, take these steps:

1 Select a paragraph with the style you want to give an outline level.

2 Choose the Format Style command.

3 In the Style dialog box, click the Modify button.

4 In the Modify Style dialog box, click the Format button and select Paragraph from the button's list.

5 In the Paragraph dialog box, select the outline level in the Outline box—see the illustration at the top of the page.

6 Click OK in the Paragraph dialog box.

7 Click OK in the Modify Style dialog box.

8 Click Apply in the Style dialog box.

A Quicker Way to Assign Outline Levels to Styles

If you want to give several styles an outline level without having to select a paragraph for each style, follow the previous steps, with these exceptions:

- Skip step 1.

- In step 3, select the style you want to give an outline level before you click the Modify button.

- Repeat modified step 3 through step 7 for each additional style you want to give an outline level.

- Only when you've modified all the styles, do you want to take step 8.

Numbering Your Outline

The style of your manual might require that you number every section; even every paragraph. In this case, you'll need to apply outline numbering to your manual.

To set up outline numbering, follow these steps:

1 In Normal View, type a list of items that you want to number or bullet at multiple levels. Do not type paragraphs you don't want numbered.

2 Select the items that you want to appear at the second level. If the second-level items are not all together in the list, you'll have to select the items separately and perform step 3 for each item.

3 Click the Increase Indent button on the Formatting toolbar *once*.

4 Select the items you want at the third level, and click the Increase Indent button *twice*.

5 For each additional level, select the items and click the Increase Indent button one less time than the number of the level needed. For example, click the Increase Indent button three times for the fourth level, four times for the fifth level, and so on.

6 Select the entire list.

7 Choose the Format Bullets And Numbering command.

III

Publications

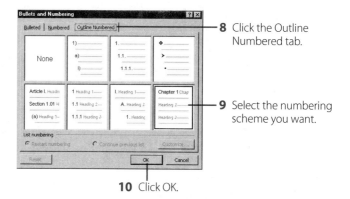

8 Click the Outline Numbered tab.

9 Select the numbering scheme you want.

10 Click OK.

⭐ **TIP**

When you start paragraphs from the numbered items, Word adds a number, even for Normal paragraphs. If you want to remove this number, simply press Backspace.

You can also change the scheme for each level. To do so, follow these steps:

1 Select the text with the line numbering scheme you want to change.

2 Choose the Format Bullets And Numbering command, select the Outline Numbered tab, and then click the Customize button.

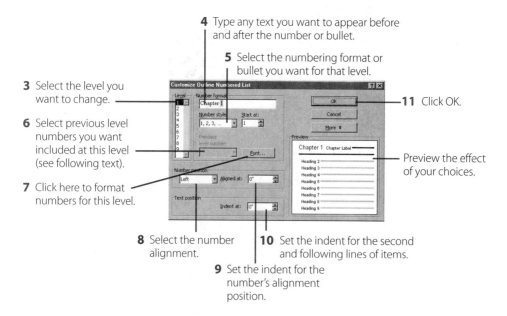

3 Select the level you want to change.

4 Type any text you want to appear before and after the number or bullet.

5 Select the numbering format or bullet you want for that level.

6 Select previous level numbers you want included at this level (see following text).

7 Click here to format numbers for this level.

8 Select the number alignment.

9 Set the indent for the number's alignment position.

10 Set the indent for the second and following lines of items.

11 Click OK.

Preview the effect of your choices.

Previous Level Number

In the Previous Level Number box, you select the level you want to add to the number of the current selection in the Level box. To add a previous number level for a level, follow these steps:

1 Select the level to which you want to add a previous level.

2 In the Number Format box, set the insertion point in the number format where you want the previous level's number to appear in the current level's numbering. You can insert any previous level's number anywhere in the number format.

3 In the Previous Level Number box, select the level you want to add. The list includes only the levels above the currently selected level in the Level box. For level 1, the list is empty.

4 Repeat step 2 and step 3 for each additional previous level number you want to add to the currently selected level.

5 Click OK.

6 Repeat step 1 through step 5 for each heading level that you want to add previous level numbers to.

To remove a previous level number, follow these steps:

1 Select the previous level number you want to remove in the Number Format box.

2 Press the Delete key.

 TIP

> **Removing a Previous Level Number with the Keyboard**
> If you set an insertion point to the right of the previous level number you want to delete in the Number Format box of the Customize Outline Numbered List dialog box and then press Backspace, Word selects the number. Press Backspace again to remove the number. If you set an insertion point to the left of the previous level number you want to delete and then press Delete, Word selects the number. Press Delete again to remove the number.

III

Publications

Advanced Outline Numbering Changes—The More Button

The More button in the Customize Outline Numbered List dialog box adds a lower section to the dialog box, as shown in Figure 13-2.

FIGURE 13-2.

The expanded Customize Outline Numbered List dialog box.

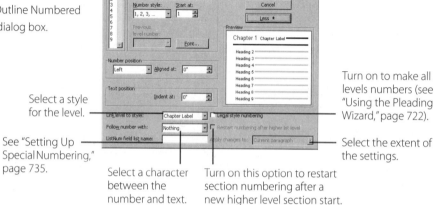

Select a style for the level.

See "Setting Up Special Numbering," page 735.

Select a character between the number and text.

Turn on this option to restart section numbering after a new higher level section start.

Turn on to make all levels numbers (see "Using the Pleading Wizard," page 722).

Select the extent of the settings.

Link Level To Style

In the Link Level To Style box, select a style that you want Word to give the numbering scheme for the currently selected level in the Level box. The style you select can be any style in the document. When you apply this style in the document, Word automatically gives that paragraph the numbering scheme you've set in this box.

You can also select (None) if you want no styles linked to this numbering level.

Restart Numbering After Higher List Level

SEE ALSO

Word also provides a special numbering feature that's specially designed for legal documents. If you have special numbering needs, see "Setting Up Special Numbering," page 735. This topic also touches on the ListNum Field List Name box.

Outline numbering is set up to restart numbering at 1 (or its equivalent in the Number Style you selected for the level) after you insert a higher level heading. This is the usual way outlines are numbered. If, however, you want all the headings at a particular level to number consecutively throughout the outline, turn off the Restart Numbering After Higher List Level check box.

One example of where you might use this in a manual is for chapters in a book that's divided into parts, as this book is. The parts have consecutive numbers throughout the book. The chapters, set at a lower outline level, are also numbered consecutively, regardless of which part they belong in. In this case, the part headings are Level 1, and the chapter titles are Level 2. For Level 2, you turn off the Restart Numbering After Higher List Level check box to keep chapter numbering consecutive rather than starting at 1 in each part.

Apply Changes To

Each change you make in the Customize Outline Numbered List dialog box can apply to the Current Paragraph or the Selected Text, to the Whole List, or to the selected items and the rest of similar items to the end of the document (the This Point Forward option). Select the choice that fits the extent to which you want the changes you made to affect outline numbering.

Creating a Master Document

To begin with, a master document is just like any other Word document—you set up, build, save, and print a master document in the same way that you create any other Word document. You can set up a master document from any Word template or wizard.

After you create a document to use as a master document, you switch to Master Document view. In Master Document view, you add subdocuments, either by starting a new document as a subdocument or by adding an existing document as a subdocument. As soon as you add a subdocument to a Word document, the resulting document becomes a master document.

To create a master document, follow these steps:

1 Set up a new document from any Word template or wizard, or open any existing Word document that you want to use as a master document.

2 Switch to Master Document view—either choose the View Master Document command or click the Master Document View button on the Outlining toolbar.

3 Add material that's part of the master document only, such as the title, author, headers, and footers.

4 Add subdocuments—see "Adding Subdocuments," page 578.

5 Build the subdocuments.

III

Publications

6 Add to the master document material built from subdocument material, such as a table of contents, index, or cross-references.

7 Save the master document. Word will also save all the sub-documents at the same time. If you create new subdocuments, Word creates new files for these subdocuments, using words from a subdocument's first paragraph for its filename.

Master Document View and Toolbar

In Master Document view, you see your document in outline form, as shown here:

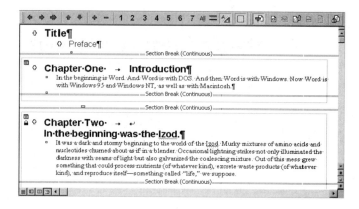

To switch to Master Document view, choose the View Master Document command. Or, on the lower scroll bar, click the Outline View button. In Outline view, click the Master Document View button on the Outlining toolbar. Or, in Outline view, choose the View Master Document command.

In Master Document view, the Master Document toolbar is displayed; use this for working with subdocuments. Each subdocument displays an icon that you double-click to open the subdocument in a separate window. Figure 13-3 shows the Master Document toolbar.

Why Not Just Use the Insert File Command?

As an alternative to using Word's master document, you can simply create a new document, and then add existing documents by using the Insert File command with the Link To File check box turned on in the Insert File dialog box. The new document functions as your main or "master" document, and the linked files that you add function as subdocuments. When you use this method, Word inserts IncludeText fields.

FIGURE 13-3.
The Master Document toolbar.

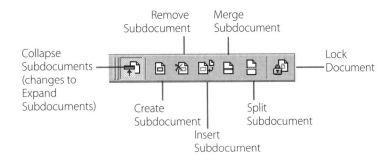

Remove Subdocument

Merge Subdocument

Collapse Subdocuments (changes to Expand Subdocuments)

Lock Document

Create Subdocument

Split Subdocument

Insert Subdocument

When you have an IncludeText field in your main document, you can change the result of the field—the contents of the linked file that has been inserted into the main document—and then send the changes back to the linked source file. So, for example, if you change the phrase "Gitcher Motor Runnin'" to "Starting Up" in the result of an IncludeText field in the main document, all you have to do is press the UpdateSource key (Ctrl+Shift+F7) to send the change to the source document.

Note, however, that unlike changes in a Word master document, where the changes automatically appear in the subdocument, changes made to the main document do not automatically appear in the source document. Also, you can't easily open a linked source document from an IncludeText field. In a true master document, you can simply double-click the subdocument icon to open the subdocument.

With the IncludeText field approach, you can still set up cross-references across linked documents, as you can in a true master document, and you can revise styles that affect all the contents of the main document as well as control sections.

Using the IncludeText field technique has one advantage that you don't have when using master documents. There is almost no limit to the number of documents you can add with IncludeText fields. In master documents, however, you are limited to 255 subdocuments, which might not be practical for some projects.

III

Publications

Another advantage of using IncludeText fields is that the source files are not opened as documents when you open the main document. If your computer is prone to running out of memory (or running low and therefore running slow), the IncludeText field approach might work better.

Adding Subdocuments

After you have set up a document that you want to use as a master document, you can add subdocuments. To add subdocuments you either convert an outline heading to a new subdocument or add an existing document as a subdocument.

Converting an Outline Heading to a New Subdocument

To convert an outline heading to a new subdocument, follow these steps:

1 Add a heading to the master document using a Heading style. You can add as many headings as you want, and you can add as many subheadings at any heading level and as much body text as you want.

2 Select the heading and subheadings you want as part of a single subdocument. The level of the first heading in the selection determines at what heading level Word breaks the selection into subdocuments. For example, if the first heading is Heading 2, and if there are no other Heading 2 paragraphs in the selection, the entire selection becomes one subdocument; if, however, there is another Heading 2 in the selection, a new subdocument will start at the second Heading 2.

3 Click the Create Subdocument button on the Master Document toolbar, shown in Figure 13-3, page 577. Word adds a subdocument icon next to the highest level of heading you've selected and inserts two continuous section breaks—one above and one below the selected headings, as shown here:

4 Repeat step 2 and step 3 to create other subdocuments.

5 Save the master document. Word sets up a file for the subdocuments, creates a filename from text at the beginning of the first paragraph, saves the subdocument, and then saves the master document.

Adding an Existing Document

To add an existing document as a subdocument, follow these steps:

1 Click the Insert Subdocument button on the Master Document toolbar.

2 If necessary, switch to a different disk and folder.

3 Select the document you want to add as a subdocument.

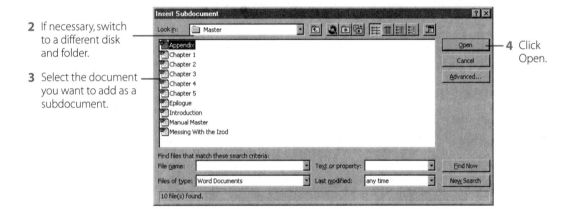

4 Click Open.

Which Window Do I Work From?

Because you can work on a subdocument either in the master document or in a separate window that displays only the subdocument, you need to decide when to work in the master document window and when to work in a subdocument window. Although individual situations might occasionally change your strategy, these two lists show changes that you'll usually make in the master document window and changes that you'll usually make in a subdocument window.

Changes made in a master document window include the following:

■ Adding, removing, merging, and splitting subdocuments

■ Reordering subdocuments

■ Moving or copying material from one subdocument to another

III

Publications

- Changing the template for the entire (master) document

- Changing section settings for the entire (master) document

- Adding a table of contents and an index

- Setting up headers and footers

- Adding and checking cross-references

- Numbering headings

- Changing styles

- Checking spelling

- Hyphenating

- Printing the entire (master) document

- Saving changes to the entire document (master document and subdocuments)

Changes made in a subdocument window include the following:

- Adding, removing, and changing material

- Adding footnotes and endnotes

- Checking spelling

- Printing part of a document

Perhaps the deciding factor is, however, none of these listed. The deciding factor may be this: if a team of authors, editors, illustrators, and typographers are working on the manual, you'll want each team member to be able to work on one piece (probably a chapter) at a time. In this case, you'll want the team members to work in subdocuments, which they open independently from the master document. In fact, in this case, you might wait to insert the subdocuments until the subdocuments-to-be are finished.

Using Templates

The template of the master document is the boss. When you set up a master document from a special template or change the template of the

SEE ALSO

For more information about changing style settings and applying the changes to a template, see "Format the Text with Styles," page 824.

master document, Word uses the styles in the master document's template for the paragraphs and text of the final document.

Master Document vs. Subdocument Styles

If you add an existing document as a subdocument, the subdocument might have a different template from the master document. In this case, Word displays the following message:

If a style with the same name exists in both the master document's template and in the subdocument's template, Word displays a message and gives you four choices, shown here:

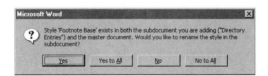

- Click Yes to keep the style as set up in the subdocument's template. In this case, Word sets up a new style with the same name but with a number added. For example, suppose you have a style named Author in both templates, but with different settings. If you click the Yes button, Word sets up a new style named Author1 in both documents. Word selects this new style for the paragraphs. (In the subdocument, both style names refer to the same style settings.) To use the style settings of the master document's template, select the original style name. To use the style settings of the subdocument's template, select the new style name. If there are other style conflicts, Word displays the message again.

- Click Yes To All to rename all styles in the subdocument's template with duplicate names.

- Click No to change this one style in the subdocument's template to match the style in the master document's template. If there are other style conflicts, Word displays the message again.

III

Publications

- Click No To All to change all the styles in the subdocument's template that have duplicate names to match the settings of the styles in the master document's template.

Master Document Templates

The special template you select to set up a new master document (or the special template you change to for the master document) controls the styles for the entire document. No matter how differently some styles are set up in a subdocument template, the styles in the master document's template apply when you're viewing and printing the master document. For this reason, you change style settings in the master document and apply them to the master document's template.

Subdocument Templates

If you add a new subdocument with the Create Subdocument button on the Master Document toolbar, Word always uses the Normal template for the subdocument. You can, of course, change the template of the subdocument to any other special template. My advice is to either leave Normal as the template of the subdocument (but remember that special templates override the Normal template) or change to the same template for a subdocument that you use for the master document. This way you avoid any style conflicts.

If you add an existing document to a master document as a subdocument, you can continue to use the style settings in the subdocument's template by clicking the Yes or Yes To All button when Word displays the conflict message. Clicking the No or No To All button synchronizes the styles in the two templates.

If you or a team member uses a different special template for a subdocument, you can override the subdocument's template by clicking the No To All button.

Reorganizing the Master Document

One of the great values of using master documents is that you have the ability to move the parts around easily. You can change the order of subdocuments, and you can move or copy part of a subdocument into another subdocument. All of this rearranging is easy because you are working in Word's Outline view. You move parts of a master document or subdocument around in the same way that you move parts of a document outline around.

Rearranging Subdocuments

To change the order of subdocuments in a master document, collapse the master document to its subdocument titles, and use one of the following methods:

- Drag the subdocument's icon to its new position. Be sure to move the subdocument between other subdocuments. If you drag the subdocument into another subdocument, it becomes a subdocument of the subdocument. You can, of course, use this fact to subordinate one subdocument to another.

- Select the subdocument, and then click the Move Up or the Move Down button on the Outlining toolbar.

- Select the subdocument and press the Move Up or the Move Down shortcut key (Alt+Shift+↑ or Alt+Shift+↓).

Rearranging Subdocument Content

At times you might end up with part of a subdocument out of place. You can easily move that part to a different place within the subdocument. At other times you might end up with a part of a subdocument in the wrong subdocument—that is, you might suddenly decide that you want part of a subdocument to appear in a different place in the master document, and that place happens to be part of a different subdocument.

WARNING

> When you're editing the master document, be careful not to delete any of the section marks that separate the subdocuments. If you do, you might inadvertently combine two subdocuments into one. Also, be sure to leave in place the paragraph mark at the end of a subdocument—the paragraph mark that follows the section mark at the end of a subdocument. You'll see this paragraph mark when you open a subdocument.

III

Publications

Moving Content Within a Subdocument

To change the order of the content within a subdocument, expand the subdocument outline, and then use one of the following methods:

- Drag the paragraph icon for the part to be moved to its new position in the subdocument.

- Select the part to be moved, and then click the Move Up or Move Down button on the Outlining toolbar.

- Select the section, and then press the Move Up or Move Down shortcut key (Alt+Shift+↑ or Alt+Shift+↓).

Moving Content Between Subdocuments

To move a part of a subdocument to a different subdocument, follow these steps:

1 Expand the outline for the subdocument that contains the part you want to move.

2 Expand the outline for the subdocument into which you want to move the contents.

3 Use one of the following methods to move the part:

- Drag the paragraph icon for the part to be moved to its new position in the new subdocument.

- Select the part to be moved, and then click the Move Up or Move Down button on the Outlining toolbar.

- Select the part to be moved, and then press the Move Up or Move Down shortcut key (Alt+Shift+↑ or Alt+Shift+↓).

Changing Subdocument Divisions

It can be difficult to get subdocuments set up exactly right. Sometimes the subdocument is too long or complicated for one person to finish on time. Sometimes the subdocument contains two distinct parts that should be worked on separately by people with different skills. Sometimes the subdocument is too short. Sometimes two subdocuments belong together as one piece so that one person can provide consistency and thoroughness. Master documents provide a remedy for all these situations. You can split a subdocument into two subdocuments, and you can merge two or more subdocuments into one.

Splitting a Subdocument

To split a subdocument, perform the following steps:

Split
Subdocument

1 Select the location where you want to split the subdocument into two separate subdocuments.

2 Click the Split Subdocument button on, the Master Document toolbar.

Word splits the subdocument in two by inserting a section break character. Use these same steps to split the new subdocument as many times as you wish.

Merging Subdocuments

To merge subdocuments, follow these steps:

1 Select all the subdocuments you want to merge. The subdocuments must be grouped together. If a subdocument you want to merge is separated from the others, move it next to the others before selecting.

Merge
Subdocument

2 Click the Merge Subdocument button on the Master Document toolbar.

Eliminating Subdocuments

As a project progresses, you might decide that you no longer need a subdocument, or that you need only part of it. After you move the part you want to keep into another subdocument, you'll want to remove the rest of the subdocument from the master document. At other times, you might decide that you want part of a subdocument (or all of it) to be part of the master document itself, rather than stuck in some obscure subdocument. Such a part might include common material that appears in all master documents you build—for example, title page material (author and organization name), author biography, or copyright material. Although you might store these items in subdocuments to make it easier to work on them, once the project starts, you don't want the material floating around in a subdocument, but safe and sound in the master document.

You can remove a subdocument entirely from the master document, and you can convert a subdocument to contents of the master document.

Removing a Subdocument

To remove a subdocument entirely, perform two steps:

1 Select the subdocument.

2 Press the Delete key.

Converting a Subdocument to the Contents of the Master Document

To convert a subdocument to master document contents, follow these steps:

1 Select the subdocument. To select a subdocument for conversion, you simply position the insertion point anywhere in the subdocument, or select some part of the subdocument.

Remove
Subdocument

2 Click the Remove Subdocument button on the Master Document toolbar.

> The Remove Subdocument button does not actually remove the subdocument from the master document, as its ScreenTip suggests. Rather, this button simply removes the "subdocumentness" from the selection—that is, the contents no longer exist in a separate file that can be opened as a document outside of the master document.

Opening Subdocuments

When you're ready to work on a subdocument, you open it. Although you can open a subdocument in the same way that you open any other Word document, Word gives you a way to open a subdocument from a master document.

Opening a Subdocument from the Master Document

To open a subdocument from a master document, follow these steps:

1 Switch to Master Document view.

2 Double-click the icon for the subdocument you want to open.

When you're done working on the subdocument, save it, and close the window. The changes appear in the master document.

Opening a Subdocument Independently

To open a subdocument independently, choose the File Open command or click the Open button on the Standard toolbar, select the subdocument in the Open dialog box, and click the Open button.

You'll note that this method is the same method you use to open any other existing Word document.

Creating Lists

A typical manual contains lots of lists: plain lists (without numbers or bullets), bulleted lists, and numbered lists. In some cases a bulleted list sits inside a numbered list. And in some cases a numbered list sits inside a bulleted list. You might even find occasions when you use bulleted lists inside bulleted lists and numbered lists inside numbered lists.

For the three basic types of lists (plain, bulleted, numbered), Word provides styles to format the list items. You can also just as easily set up plain lists with the Increase Indent button on the Formatting toolbar, numbered lists with the Numbering button on the Formatting toolbar, and bulleted lists with the Bullets button on the Formatting toolbar. Word also provides the Format Bullets And Numbering command to set up and to modify bulleted and numbered lists. In the Bullets And Numbering dialog box, you can also set up outline numbering.

List Styles

Word contains some built-in styles that you won't see in the Style box on the Formatting toolbar until you use them at least once.

TIP

To see all the built-in styles in the Style box on the Formatting toolbar, hold down the Shift key as you click the down arrow beside the Style box. You can also see all the built-in styles by choosing the Format Style command and selecting All Styles from the List box in the bottom left corner of the Style dialog box.

III

Publications

? SEE ALSO

To print a list of styles and their descriptions, see "Choosing What to Print," page 127.

Among the built-in styles in Word are styles for lists: plain lists (List, List 2–List 5), bulleted lists (List Bullet, List Bullet 2–List Bullet 5), numbered lists (List Number, List Number 2–List Number 5), and continued lists (List Continue, List Continue 2–List Continue 5). You can use these built-in list styles for setting up multilevel lists with as many as four sublists. The continued-list styles set up paragraphs under list items to keep the proper indention.

When you use the list styles to set up a multilevel list, you can then use the Format Bullets And Numbering command to adjust the multi-level numbering scheme and multilevel bullet characters.

Plain Lists

A plain list is a list of items that has neither bullets nor numbering. Usually, such a list is indented. The simplest way to set up a plain list is to take these steps:

1 Start a paragraph for the first list item.

2 Click the Increase Indent button on the Formatting toolbar.

Increase
Indent

3 Type the list of items.

4 When you finish the list and want to return to normal text, click the Decrease Indent button on the Formatting toolbar.

Decrease
Indent

You can also create a plain list by applying the List style to the list of items instead of clicking the Increase Indent button.

Bulleted Lists

Word can shoot bullets (small symbols that precede items in a list) into your document to create bulleted lists. You can shoot in standard bullets as well as custom bullets in different shapes, sizes, and colors.

Standard Bullets

To add bullets to a list, do the following:

1 Select the items you want bulleted.

2 Click the Bullets button on the Formatting toolbar.

Bullets

The Bullets button inserts the bullets you last selected in the Bullets And Numbering dialog box. If you want bullets of a different size or shape, do the following:

1 Select the list items you want bulleted.

2 Choose the Format Bullets And Numbering command.

3 Click the Bulleted tab.

4 Select the type of bullet you want Word to insert.

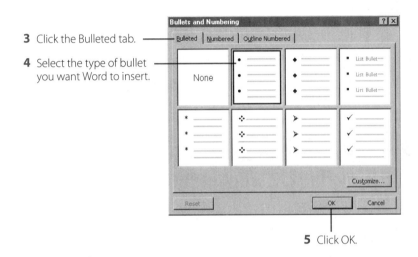

5 Click OK.

TIP

With the Automatic Bulleted Lists check box turned on, AutoFormat As You Type applies bulleted list formatting to paragraphs that start with a hyphen or an asterisk followed by a space or a tab or a lowercase letter *o*, or an uppercase letter *O* followed by a tab. Visit the AutoFormat As You Type tab in the Tools AutoCorrect dialog box.

The standard bullets take their color and other looks (font name, font style, font size, and other effects) from the default formatting of the paragraph, which is stored in the paragraph mark. You can change the bullets' looks in the Modify Bulleted List dialog box, as explained in the following sections.

NOTE

Word doesn't allow you to change bullets directly by selecting the bullet characters in the document. The only way you can change bullets is by using the Format Bullets And Numbering command.

III

Publications

Variations on Standard Bullets

Let's get out of the line of fire and look at some of the other bullet options. To check out other bullets, choose the Format Bullets And Numbering command. As you can see in the Bullets And Numbering dialog box, you can select from seven bullet characters. If you want to choose a different bullet character, or change the size or even the color of the bullet characters, you must select the Customize button.

To choose a bullet character that is different in size, color, or position from the bullet characters shown in the dialog box, do the following:

1 On the Bulleted tab of the Bullets And Numbering dialog box, select the type of bullet you want to replace, and then click the Customize button.

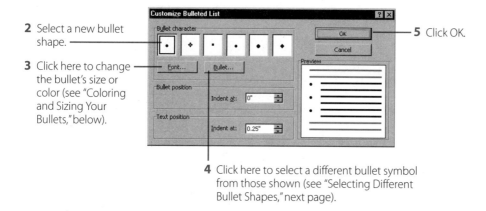

2 Select a new bullet shape.

3 Click here to change the bullet's size or color (see "Coloring and Sizing Your Bullets," below).

5 Click OK.

4 Click here to select a different bullet symbol from those shown (see "Selecting Different Bullet Shapes," next page).

Coloring and Sizing Your Bullets

You can also select one of 16 colors for your bullets or set your bullets at a different point size. To do so, follow these steps:

1 Select a bullet character in the Customize Bulleted List dialog box.

2 Click the Font button, which displays the standard Font dialog box.

3 Select a color from the Color list. The Auto setting in the Color box indicates the text color of the paragraph.

4 Set the point size for the bullet characters. You can set the size of a bullet from 1 point to 1,638 points.

5 Click OK.

 **TIP**

> To make the bullet the same point size as the text of bulleted items, delete any point size setting in the Size box.

Selecting Different Bullet Shapes

To choose a different bullet character, do the following:

1 In the Customize Bulleted List dialog box, select the bullet shape you want to replace from the shapes shown.

2 Click the Bullet button.

3 Select the font of the character you want to use.

4 Select the symbol you want to use as a bullet.

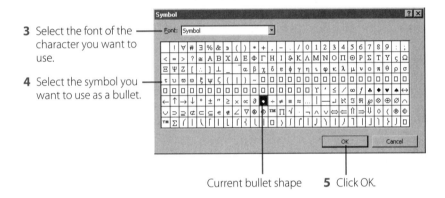

Current bullet shape   **5** Click OK.

The new symbol replaces the previously selected bullet and has the same size and color. You can use the steps in the previous section, "Coloring and Sizing Your Bullets," to change the color and size of the new bullet character. The new bullet remains selected until you select a different bullet.

Indenting Bulleted Lists

In the Customize Bulleted List dialog box, you'll see the Bullet Position Indent At box and the Text Position Indent At box. In these boxes, you set the indention for each bulleted list item.

The Bullet Position Indent At box sets the distance the bullet characters move away from the left margin. Typically, you'll set a distance in this box to indent the bulleted list from the text above the list.

The Text Position Indent At box sets the distance between the left edge of the bulleted text and the bullet. If the distance you set is less than

III

Publications

the distance Word uses between the bullet and the beginning of the first line of the item, the second and following lists wrap back under the bullet character. Word's standard distance between the bullet character and the beginning of the first line is 0.25–0.3 inch.

Removing Bullets

Word offers three ways to remove bullets from a bulleted list. To remove bullets, first select the items that will no longer have bullets. (To remove bullets from an entire list, select the whole list.) Then do one of the following:

- Click the Bullets button on the Formatting toolbar.

- Choose the Format Bullets And Numbering command, select None, and then click OK.

- Press the Reset Paragraph shortcut key (Ctrl+Q). The selected items switch to regular text formatting, unless you applied one of the List Bullet styles to the paragraph (List Bullet, List Bullet 2–List Bullet 5).

Numbered Lists

You can create numbered lists in Word. The numbers Word uses for lists change automatically as you move, insert, or delete items from the numbered list.

Standard Numbers

To add numbers to a list, do the following:

1 Select the items you want numbered.

Numbering

2 Click the Numbering button on the Formatting toolbar.

The Numbering button sets the style of numbering that you last selected in the Bullets And Numbering dialog box.

With the Automatic Numbered Lists check box turned on, AutoFormat As You Type applies numbered list formatting to paragraphs that start with a number, a period, and a space or a tab; it also replaces numbers that are manually typed with automatic numbers. Visit the AutoFormat As You Type tab in the Tools AutoCorrect dialog box.

Variations on Standard Numbers

To insert a different numbering scheme, do the following:

1 Select the list items.

2 Choose the Format Bullets And Numbering command.

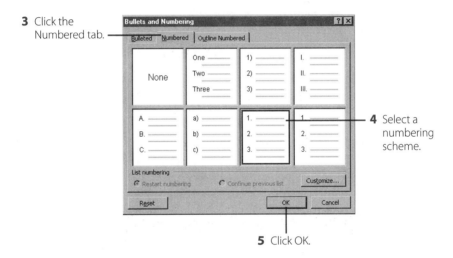

3 Click the Numbered tab.

4 Select a numbering scheme.

5 Click OK.

Word doesn't allow you to directly select the numbers of a numbered list in a document. (Word behaves as if the numbers aren't part of the document text.) You modify the numbers of a numbered list by using the Format Bullets And Numbering command. See "Using Different Numbers," page 594.

Skipping Numbers

Numbered lists can be funny things. You don't always want every paragraph in a list to have a number. You might want a second paragraph that explains an item more fully under the numbered item. Or you might want to start the numbering over again at 1 or at some other number. For these situations, Word gives you the tools both to skip numbering and to stop numbering.

It's easier to understand what happens if you try it rather than just read about it. To skip numbering, try the following steps:

1 Select list items somewhere in a numbered list.

2 Click the Numbering button on the Formatting toolbar to turn off numbering.

You see the effect shown in Figure 13-4.

FIGURE 13-4.
A numbered list with an unnumbered (skipped) line.

1. Registration
2. Breakfast
Get Acquainted
3. First Session
4. Break
5. Second Session
6. Lunch

? SEE ALSO

For information on removing numbers from list items or on removing all the numbers from a list, see "Removing Numbers," page 598. To start a list at a number higher or lower than 1, see "Starting with a Number Other Than 1," page 596.

To indent the unnumbered items so they line up with the text of the numbered items, click the Increase Indent button on the Formatting toolbar.

Using Different Numbers

The Numbered tab of the Bullets And Numbering dialog box displays several formats (Arabic, Roman, and so forth) for numbers. If none of the numbering formats appeals to you, you can set up an entirely different numbering system.

To create your own numbering form and format or to have a list start with a number other than 1, do the following:

1 Select the items you want to number.

2 Choose the Format Bullets And Numbering command, and click the Numbered tab.

3 Select the number format that most closely resembles the one you want to create. (You can actually choose any of the options, but your modification will go faster if you choose the scheme closest to what you want.)

4 Click the Customize button to display the Customize Numbered List dialog box.

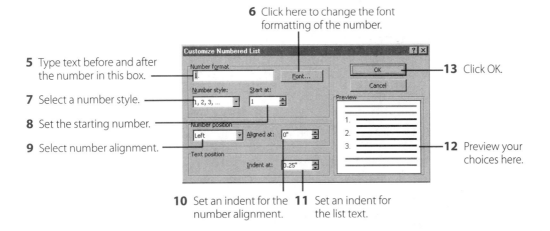

6 Click here to change the font formatting of the number.

5 Type text before and after the number in this box.

7 Select a number style.

8 Set the starting number.

9 Select number alignment.

13 Click OK.

12 Preview your choices here.

10 Set an indent for the number alignment.

11 Set an indent for the list text.

The following sections explain your choices more fully.

Number Format

List numbering can include any kind of text, symbols, or punctuation before and after the number. The standard punctuation following a number is a period. To change the separators, type new ones in the Number Format box. The separators can be up to 32 characters long. Delete all the text in the Number Format box if you want no separator character at all—not even a period following the number.

If you want blank spaces between the leading and following text and the numbers, be sure to type the spaces on both sides of the number in the Number Format box. For example, if you want numbers like this:— 1 —, type an em dash (press Alt+Ctrl+minus on the numeric keypad), a space to the left of the number, and a space and an em dash after the number in the Number Format box.

Number Fonts

If you want to use a special font, font style, font size, color, or other format for the numbers, click the Font button in the Customize Numbered List dialog box to display the Font dialog box, where you can make your formatting choices.

III

Publications

⭐ TIP

> To make the number the same point size as the text of numbered items, delete any point size setting in the Size box.

Number Style

In the Number Format section of the Customize Numbered List dialog box, you can select the numbering format from the Number Style list: (None); Arabic; Roman (uppercase or lowercase); alphabetic (upper-case or lowercase); ordinal (1st, 2nd, …); cardinal text (One, Two, …); ordinal text (First, Second, …); or leading-zero (01, 02, …).

Starting with a Number Other Than 1

If your list continues from earlier in the document and you do not want it to begin with 1, you set the starting number in the Start At box in the Customize Numbered List dialog box. You can type an Arabic number regardless of the number format you select, or you can type the starting number in the selected format for Roman and alphabetic forms. You must use an Arabic number if you are using ordinal, cardi-nal, ordinal text, or leading-zero formats. For example, you can type either *4* or *d* for the starting number of a list numbered with uppercase or lowercase letters, but you can use only *4* (not *fourth*) for the starting number if the list uses ordinal text.

Number Alignment

The Number Position box in the Customize Numbered List dialog box gives you three choices for number alignment: Left, Center, and Right. These positions refer to the numbers' alignment vertically down the numbered list. The alignment is relative to the setting in the Number Position Aligned At box. In the Number Position Aligned At box, set the distance from the left margin (or column edge) that you want the numbers to align around.

Most times, you'll probably use Left alignment. If, however, you have a list that contains more than nine items, you might prefer Right align-ment. The following table explains each choice and shows you an example.

Alignment	Description	Example
Left	The left edges of all numbers in the list are left aligned at the Number Position Aligned At setting. The example list here is left aligned at 0".	1. Registration 2. Breakfast 3. Get Acquainted 4. First Session 5. Break 6. Second Session 7. Lunch
Centered	The numbers in the list are centered between the left edge of the text and the Number Position Aligned At setting. The example list here is centered at .2".	6. Second Session 7. Lunch 8. Third Session 9. Break 10. Fourth Session 11. Happy Hour 12. Banquet 13. Entertainment 14. Dancing 15. Nightcap
Right	The right edges (or decimal points) of all numbers in the list are right aligned at the Number Position Aligned At setting. The example list here is right aligned at .2".	6. Second Session 7. Lunch 8. Third Session 9. Break 10. Fourth Session 11. Happy Hour 12. Banquet 13. Entertainment 14. Dancing 15. Nightcap

> **NOTE**
>
> With the number alignment set to Left in the Number Position box and the Number Position Aligned At box set to 0" (these are the default settings), if you then change the Number Position setting to Centered or Right, Word automatically increases the Number Position Aligned At setting to 0.2" to allow for the width of the numbers. If, on the other hand, you start with the Number Position Aligned At set to 0.2" or more, changing the Number Position setting has no effect on the Number Position Aligned At setting.

Text Indention

In the Customize Numbered List dialog box, the Text Position Indent At box sets the distance between the left edge of the numbered text and the number. If the distance you set is less than the distance Word uses between the number and the beginning of the first line of the item, the second and following lines wrap back under the number. Word's standard distance between the number and the beginning of the first line is 0.25–0.3 inch.

Removing Numbers

Word offers three ways to remove numbers from a list. First select the items that will no longer have numbers. (To remove numbers from an entire list, select the whole list.) Then do one of the following:

- Click the Numbering button on the Formatting toolbar. Any numbered items below the numbered items from which you just removed the numbers continue the numbering. The unnumbered items are skipped.

- Choose Format Bullets And Numbering, select None, and then click OK—see the next section, "More About None."

- Press the Reset Paragraph shortcut key (Ctrl+Q). The selected items switch to regular text formatting, unless you applied one of the List Bullet styles to the paragraph (List Bullet, List Bullet 2–List Bullet 5).

Emphasizing the Beginning of Each List Item

You've probably seen lists, either numbered or bulleted or even plain lists, where the beginning of each list item has some special formatting—bold, italic, underlining, or some combination of these. In Word 97, when you start the first list item in a numbered or bulleted list this way, Word automatically gives the beginning of the next list item the same special formatting. Here are a few clues to make this work right for you:

- Set up the font formatting you want for the beginning of each list item.

- Type a number or an asterisk or hyphen and press the spacebar or Tab key.

- Type the beginning words, type a period, a semicolon, or a colon, and type a space.

- Turn off the special formatting (press Ctrl+Spacebar).

- Type the rest of the text of the first list item, and then press Enter.

- Type the rest of the list items.

After you set up the first list item, Word turns on your special formatting at the beginning of each list item, and then turns it off when you type the punctuation mark you used in the first list item.

More About None

The None choice on the Numbered tab in the Bullets And Numbering dialog box performs two different actions, depending on the items you've selected for number removal:

- If you simply select the items and select None, Word removes the numbers and restarts the numbering of the remaining list items below the selected items.

- If you select the items, click the Increase Indent button on the Formatting toolbar, and then select None, Word removes the numbers but continues the numbering of the remaining list items below the selected items. This case is the same as skipping numbering, as described in "Skipping Numbers," page 593.

Lists Within Lists

You can easily set up sublists for bulleted and numbered list items. For example, you can create a list like the one shown in Figure 13-5.

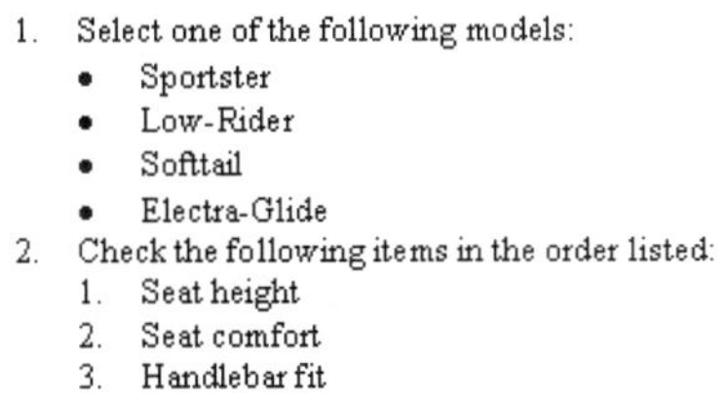

FIGURE 13-5.

An example of lists within a list.

1. Select one of the following models:
    - Sportster
    - Low-Rider
    - Softtail
    - Electra-Glide
2. Check the following items in the order listed:
    1. Seat height
    2. Seat comfort
    3. Handlebar fit

To create this list, follow these steps:

1 Type *1. Select one of the following models:*

2 Press Enter. AutoFormat As You Type converts the line you typed to a numbered item and numbers the current line.

3 Press Backspace to remove the numbering from the current line.

4 Click the Increase Indent button.

5 Type ** Sportster* and press Enter.

6 Type *Low-Rider* and press Enter.

7 Type *Softtail* and press Enter.

III

Publications

8 Type *Electra-Glide* and press Enter.

9 Press Backspace.

10 Click the Decrease Indent button.

11 Type *2. Check the following items in the order listed:* and press Enter.

12 Press Backspace.

13 Click the Increase Indent button.

14 Type *1. Seat height* and press Enter.

15 Type *Seat comfort* and press Enter.

16 Type *Handlebar fit* and press Enter.

17 Press Backspace.

18 Click the Decrease Indent button.

As an alternative to these steps, you could apply the styles for the various levels of bullets or numbering. In this case, you wouldn't type the numbers or the asterisk; you would simply type the text of each item. In the example list, you'd apply the List Number style to the two main numbered items, the List Number 2 style to the numbered sublist, and List Bullet 2 to the bulleted sublist. For more about using styles for lists, see "List Styles," page 587.

Using Sections

For many documents, setting the looks of pages is a "nonissue." That is, you build a new document from a template, add text, format it, save it, and print it. But in other documents, you'll want to work with the looks of the pages to achieve the best presentation possible.

In these documents, there might be whole parts in which you want to use different numbers of text columns, a different header and footer, a sideways table or two, and so forth. In order for you to set up different looks for different parts of the document, Microsoft Word gives you the option of dividing your document into sections. You can then set unique looks for each section of the document.

? SEE ALSO

For descriptions of the page elements you can control by section, see "Set Up Pages in the Page Setup Dialog Box," page 788. For information about setting columns, see "Dressing Up Columns," page 424. For information about vertical alignment, see "Controlling Brochure Text Vertically on the Page," page 453.

Just as a paragraph in Word is all the text between paragraph marks, a section in Word is all the text between section breaks. Every Word document initially contains one section. In this chapter, you'll learn how to add sections by inserting section breaks into your document. When you insert a section break, Word marks it with a section break character, which looks like a row of colons across the screen with a label *Section Break* followed by the type of section start in the middle. A Continuous section break is shown here:

Section Break (Continuous)

You can insert a section anywhere on a page. A section can be any length you need it to be—as short as one line (without even containing a paragraph) or as long as an entire document.

Once you have a section set up, you can control the text in the section by adjusting the page elements in that section. Page elements are the parts of a page—margins, headers and footers, page size, and so forth—that you can control and adjust to change the looks of the page.

Breaking a Document into Sections

? SEE ALSO

For details about how changes to sections apply, see the sidebar What Does All This Apply To?" page 789.

Breaking a document into sections is a simple matter of inserting section breaks where you want new sections to begin. Word provides one direct way to insert section breaks—the Insert Break command. Word also provides three indirect ways to insert section breaks—the Columns button on the Standard toolbar, the Format Columns command for setting up multiple columns, and the File Page Setup command for controlling the setup of the page.

> NOTE

If you set up a master document with subdocuments, Word inserts the subdocuments within their own sections. To maintain the integrity of the master document and subdocument structure, you *must* leave these section breaks in place. Within each section, however, you can adjust any part of the setup as described in this chapter.

III

Publications

Copying, Deleting, and Moving Section Breaks

You can copy section breaks just as you can copy any other character in a document. When you copy a section break, you copy all the page element settings for the section as well. When you paste the section break into the document, all the text from the preceding section break to the new section break takes on the page element settings of the section break you copied. The same thing happens when you use the drag-and-drop method to copy a section break.

If you delete a section break, the text preceding the deleted section break takes on the page element settings of the next section break following the location of the section break you just deleted.

When you use the drag-and-drop method to move a section break, the text preceding the section break has the page element settings you assigned to the section break, and the text following the section break has the page element settings of the next section break.

What this button and these commands do to your document depends on whether you select text first and then click the button or choose a command, or set an insertion point and then click the button or choose a command. The following table describes these actions.

What's Selected	Action
Insertion point	Changes the page elements for the current section; no new section marks are inserted
Selection entirely within one section; does not include section break	Inserts two section marks (above and below selection) and changes the page elements for the new section
Selection includes at least one section break	Changes the page elements for the current section; no new section marks are inserted

Remember that every document has at least one section, even though you don't see a section break—the break is hidden at the end of the document.

The Insert Break Command

The direct way to insert section breaks is with the Insert Break command. Not only can you insert section breaks, but you can select the section start for the following section at the same time.

To insert a section break, follow these steps:

1 Position the insertion point where you want the new section to begin.

2 Choose the Insert Break command.

3 Select the type of section start you want for the following section.

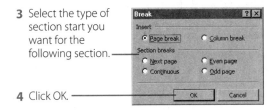

4 Click OK.

Inserting Cross-References

In a report or a book, you might want to refer your readers to other topics or to illustrations, tables, charts, or notes. To do this, you insert a cross-reference. Cross-references can be textual references (to the title of a topic or to the caption of an illustration or table); references to a page number (where the topic starts or where the illustration or table appears); or references to an item number (the label number of an illustration, table, paragraph, or heading). You can also simply type the cross-reference yourself. Cross-reference fields, however, make it easy to insert cross-references and keep them accurate.

For example, you can insert a cross-reference to a picture on a particular page. If the picture later appears on a different page because of text editing or changes to the document's looks, you can direct Word to track the change and show the correct page number for the picture in the cross-reference.

III

Publications

To insert a cross-reference, follow these steps:

1 Choose the Insert Cross-Reference command.

2 Select the type of item to be cross-referenced.

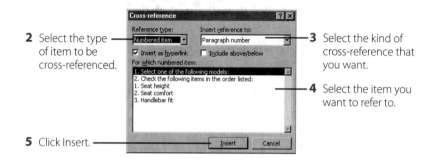

3 Select the kind of cross-reference that you want.

4 Select the item you want to refer to.

5 Click Insert.

Notice that the Cross-Reference dialog box remains open. This way you can insert any number of cross-references. To insert another cross-reference while the dialog box is still open, take these steps:

1 Click in the document.

2 Click where you want to insert the next cross-reference (scroll as much as you need to).

3 Click the Cross-Reference dialog box.

4 Follow step 2 through step 5 in the preceding procedure.

5 Repeat these steps for each additional cross-reference you want to insert while the Cross-Reference dialog box is open.

6 Click Close to return to your document.

Including Self-References

For more information about document properties, see "Setting Document Properties," opposite.

Within a document, you can print many kinds of information about the document. For example, you can print the document's title, author, number of pages, number of words, and filename. All this information comes from the Properties dialog box. To review the summary information, choose the File Properties command and select the Summary tab or the Statistics tab. You'll commonly use this self-referencing feature when your document is in the draft stage, but you can also include this information for the final printed document.

SEE ALSO

On the CD in this book, you'll find files that show you how to automatically put the manual's title into the header on the second and following pages (see HDRTITLE.DOC); how to automatically add the author's name to a manual (see ADAUTHOR.DOC); how to add a page count to a document (see PGCOUNT.DOC); how to add the filename of the document (see FILENAME.DOC); and how to create and add a unique serial number to a document (see SERIALNO.DOC).

You can also use fields to automatically spawn text that adds a special touch to your work. Table 13-3 lists the most common types of self-references you might use.

TABLE 13-3.   Common Types of Self-References and Their Associated Field Names.

Self-Reference	Field Name
Document title	Title
Author's name	Author
Filename	FileName
Number of Pages	NumPages
Number of Words	NumWords
Date document created	CreateDate
Date document last saved	SaveDate
Date document last printed	PrintDate

Setting Document Properties

With the release of Word version 7 (Word for Windows 95), Word documents gained a larger set of document properties. Document properties include all the information that was part of the File Summary Info command dialog box and the Statistics dialog box of earlier versions, plus the display of some additional properties. The Summary Info dialog box was replaced with the Properties dialog box, which has five tabs—General, Summary, Statistics, Notes, and Custom. The following sections describe each tab, what you find there, and what you can do on the tab.

General Tab

The General tab displays file properties you usually view in an Explorer or My Computer window on the file system, as shown on the next page.

You can make no changes on the General tab to the properties shown. To change these properties, you have to save the file or move it.

III

Publications

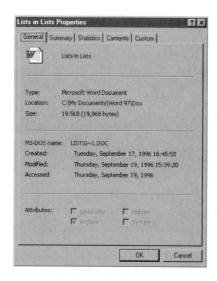

Summary Tab

The Summary tab provides spaces for you to type a variety of information about a document. The Summary tab is the replacement for the Summary Info dialog box in previous versions of Word for Windows.

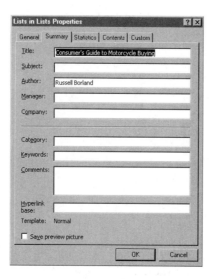

The following sections describe each box on the Summary tab. Three of the boxes are additions to the Summary Info dialog box in version 6 and earlier—Manager, Company, and Category.

Title

Type or edit the title of the document. If you haven't filled in this box when you save a document for the first time, Word inserts the first sentence of the document into the Title box as the document title. You can, of course, edit or replace this title at any time. The Title box is associated with the Title field.

Subject

Type the subject of the document. You can, of course, edit or replace this text at any time. For documents with a subtitle, the Subject box provides a logical place to record the subtitle as a document property. The Subject box is associated with the Subject field.

Author

Type or edit the author's name. When you create a new document, Word inserts the author's name from the Name box on the User Information tab of the Tools Options dialog box. You can edit or replace this name at any time. The Author box is associated with the Author field.

Manager

Type the name of the author's manager. You can, of course, edit or replace this name at any time. For documents that are part of a project, the Manager box provides a logical place to record the name of the project manager. The Manager box is associated with the DocProperty "Manager" field.

Company

Type the name of the author's company or a name that is identified with the document. You can, of course, edit or replace this name at any time. For documents that are part of a project for a client, the Company box provides a logical place to record the name of the client. The Company box is associated with the DocProperty "Company" field.

Category

Type a category name for the document. You can, of course, edit or replace this name at any time. The Category box is associated with the DocProperty "Category" field.

Keywords

Type a list of keywords to facilitate cataloging and locating the document later. You can, of course, edit or replace this list at any time. The Keywords box is associated with the Keywords field.

Comments

Type any comments you want to record about the document. You can edit or replace these comments at any time. The Comments box is associated with the Comments field.

Hyperlink Base

 SEE ALSO

For more information about hyperlinks and the hyperlink base, see Chapter 21, "Creating Online Documents."

Type the base address for all relative hyperlinks in the document. (A relative hyperlink contains only the name of the file that the link opens; for example, Gorgeous.doc or Glorious.html). The base address can be a Web site (URL, such as http://www.microsoft.com/mspress); a folder on your hard disk (for example, c:\My Documents\WebPage Documents); or a path to a folder on a network server (for example, \\Myserve\public\WebPages). The Hyperlink Base box is associated with the DocProperty "HyperlinkBase" field.

Save Preview Picture

When you save a document template, you can have Word save a preview of the first page of the template. Word displays this preview in the New dialog box when you click the icon for the template. If you leave this check box turned off when you save a template, Word cannot give you a preview in the New dialog box. Note, however, that once a preview has been saved, it doesn't go away, even if you later turn off this check box. Also, you must turn on this check box to display a list of headings on the Contents tab. For more information, see "Contents Tab," page 610.

Statistics Tab

The Statistics tab of the Properties dialog box lists statistical information about a document. The Statistics tab is the replacement for the Statistics dialog box in previous versions of Word for Windows.

You can make no changes on the Statistics tab to the properties shown. To change these properties, you have to save the file, move it, change the template attached to the document, open the file for viewing or editing, print the document, change the number of words, paragraphs, and pages in the document, or make some other change, such as formatting, that changes the size of the file of the document.

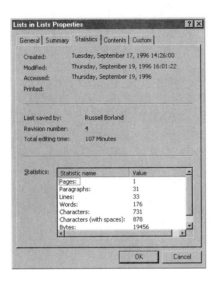

The values displayed on the Statistics tab are associated with fields with similar names, as shown in Table 13-4.

TABLE 13-4.   The Statistics Categories and Their Associated Fields.

Statistics Category	Associated Field Name
Created	CreateDate DocProperty "CreateTime"
Modified	DocProperty "LastSavedTime"
Accessed	(None)
Printed	PrintDate DocProperty "LastPrinted"
Last Saved By	LastSavedBy DocProperty "LastSavedBy"
Revision Number	RevNum DocProperty "RevisionNumber"
Total Editing Time	EditTime DocProperty "TotalEditingTime"

(continued)

III

Publications

TABLE 13-4. *continued*

Statistics Category	Associated Field Name
Pages	NumPages DocProperty "Pages"
Paragraphs	DocProperty "Paragraphs"
Lines	DocProperty "Lines"
Words	NumWords DocProperty "Words"
Characters	NumChars DocProperty "Characters" DocProperty "CharactersWithSpaces"
Bytes	FileSize DocProperty "Bytes"

Contents Tab

Contents lists the title of the document as set up in the Title box on the Summary tab. In addition, this tab will list all the headings in the document, but only if you turn on the Save Preview Picture check box on the Summary tab.

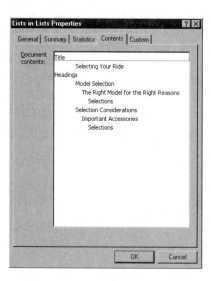

You can make no changes on the Contents tab to the properties shown. To change a property, change the title in the Title box on the Summary tab or change one of the headings in the document.

Custom Tab

Custom is the most important addition to the Properties dialog box. With this tab, you can set up properties you want to add to the document's list of properties. You can also link the custom properties you add to specific document contents.

To set up custom properties, take these steps:

1   Choose the File Properties command.

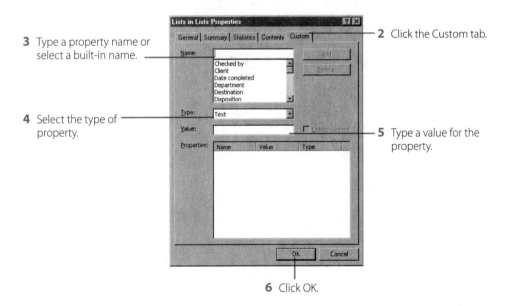

3 Type a property name or select a built-in name.

2 Click the Custom tab.

4 Select the type of property.

5 Type a value for the property.

6 Click OK.

7   Repeat steps 3 through 6 for the other custom properties you want to set up.

8   When you're done, click OK.

SEE ALSO

On the CD in this book, you'll find the file CONPROPS.DOC, which gives you an example of setting up custom properties for a contract form.

You can also set up custom properties that are linked to specific document content. Here are the steps:

1 Select text in the document you want to link to a custom document property.

2 Choose the Insert Bookmark command, type a bookmark name, and then click the Add button.

3 Repeat steps 1 and 2 for additional custom document properties you want to set up.

4 Choose the File Properties command.

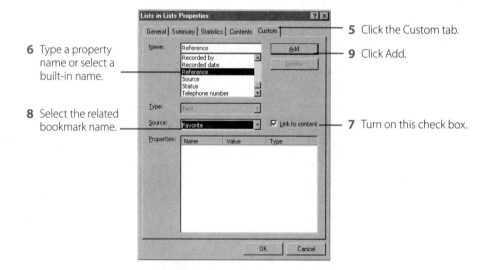

6 Type a property name or select a built-in name.

8 Select the related bookmark name.

5 Click the Custom tab.

9 Click Add.

7 Turn on this check box.

10 Repeat steps 5 through 9 for the other custom, linked properties you want to set up.

11 When you're done, click OK.

You'll see a list of properties with the link icon to the left of each custom property, as shown on the next page.

In the Type box, you select the type of information that the document property represents. The property value you type in the Value box must correspond to the selection you make in the Type box, as shown in Table 13-5.

TABLE 13-5.   Values That Correspond to Types of Document Information.

Type	Value	Example		
		Name	**Type**	**Value**
Text	Any typed text, including numbers and dates you want presented as text	Company	Text	reVisionary Partners
		Sales	Text	$1,234.56
		Serial Number	Text	S/N 987-654-BZ
Number	Any numeric value; the value cannot contain any letters or other characters that aren't numbers, except a decimal point; if you include commas, Word strips them out	Quantity	Number	1234567
Date	A date in the short date format set up in the Windows Control Panel	Due Date	Date	7/9/97
Yes Or No	One of the two buttons for Yes and No	Current Customer	Yes or No	Yes

 **NOTE**

> If you type a value for a number or date value that Word doesn't accept as a number or date, you see a message that tells you Word will set up the property as a Text property. Click OK to set up the property as Text type. Click Cancel to give yourself a chance to retype the value in the proper format.

Modifying a Custom Property

If you want to change the value of a custom property, take these steps to modify it:

1   Choose the File Properties command, and click the Custom tab.

2   Click the property name in the Properties list.

3   Type or select a new value in the Value box. If the property is linked to document content, you can only select a bookmark name (the box's label changes to Source); you can't type a new value. For a Yes or No type property, you can only click the Yes or the No option.

4   Click the Modify button.

5   Click OK.

Seeing the Properties List More Fully

When you first display the Custom tab of the Properties dialog box, the columns for Name, Type, and Value in the Properties list might be too narrow to show the full name or value. You can widen a column by positioning the mouse pointer on a column divider in the label bar of the Properties list and dragging the divider to the right.

When the width of the three columns exceeds the width of the Properties list box, the box acquires a horizontal scroll bar so that you can scroll to see the part of a property entry that's out of view.

You can also narrow a column by dragging the column divider to the left.

Removing a Custom Property

If you no longer want a custom property recorded, take these steps to remove it:

1 Choose the File Properties command, and click the Custom tab.

2 Click the property name in the Properties list.

3 Click the Delete button.

4 Click OK.

Tracking Changes

② SEE ALSO

You can also insert written and voice comments into a document so you can communicate ideas to other reviewers without changing the content of the document itself For more information, see "Making Comments," page 620.

Word can track changes to a document so that you can see what material was added, what material was deleted, and who did what to the document. You can choose what kinds of marking you want displayed when reviewers make changes to a document.

Track Changes On, Track Changes Off

To track changes, double-click the TRK button on the status bar. Word turns on change tracking, using the choices already set up in the Highlight Changes dialog box and on the Track Changes tab of the Tools Options dialog box. To stop change tracking, double-click the TRK button on the status bar again.

If you want to change the way Word tracks changes, you take these steps:

1 Choose the Tools Track Changes command, and then click Highlight Changes on the submenu.

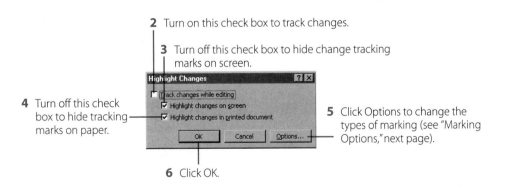

2 Turn on this check box to track changes.

3 Turn off this check box to hide change tracking marks on screen.

4 Turn off this check box to hide tracking marks on paper.

5 Click Options to change the types of marking (see "Marking Options," next page).

6 Click OK.

III

Publications

With change tracking turned on, the change tracking marks show where changes have been made to your document. When you position the mouse pointer over a tracked change, a tag appears that shows you who made the change and when the change was made, as well as the nature of the change, as shown here:

and·entertainment.·And,·Of·cou| **Russell Borland, 1/16/97 9:17 AM:** |·y·charity,·is·
                                   | Deleted |
building·ways·to·charge·fees·for·the·information·and·entertainment,·as·WELL·as·

⚠ WARNING

> Word does not track changes to paragraph formatting, except to mark bullets and numbers added to a paragraph. Word does track text formatting changes you make with the formatting commands, Formatting toolbar, and formatting shortcut keys.

Marking Options

Word has several options you can choose for tracking changes. You can select the type of marking you want for insertions and for deletions. You can select the type of marking you want for formatting changes (see the preceding Warning). You can also select the margin in which you want marks for changed lines to appear. You can turn off any of the four types of marking. For all four types of marking—insertions, deletions, formatting changes, and marks for changed lines—you can select the colors you want Word to use on the screen.

★ TIP

> To jump directly to the Track Changes tab of the Tools Options dialog box, choose the Tools Options command, and then click the Track Changes tab.

To change the marking options, use these steps:

1 Choose the Tools Track Changes command, click the Highlight Changes command on the submenu, and then click the Options button in the Highlight Changes dialog box.

2 Select the types of marks and colors you want.

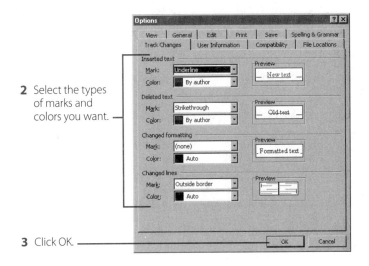

3 Click OK.

4 Click OK in the Highlight Changes dialog box.

If you choose the Tools Options command instead of the Tools Track Changes command and Highlight Changes subcommand, you skip step 4.

The following sections give you more details about these options.

Inserted Text

Word is set up to mark inserted text with an underline and to color-code inserted text with a different color for each author who revises a document. You can change both of these settings on the Track Changes tab in the Tools Options dialog box.

For marks indicating inserted text, your choices in the Mark box are (None), Bold, Italic, Underline, or Double Underline. If you select (None), Word doesn't mark inserted text, but does still apply a color.

If you want to be able to see at a glance the changes different authors have made in a document, your best choice in the Color box is By

III

Publications

Author. By Author uses eight different colors, in this order: Blue, Green, Red, Dk Cyan, Dk Magenta, Dk Blue, Dk Red, and Magenta. If more than eight authors make changes, Word repeats the colors in the same order for authors 9 through 16, 17 through 24, and so on. At this point, the color coding isn't much help. In this case, and in cases where you want all the inserted text marked with the same color, you can make a specific color choice for all inserted text.

For a specific, single-color choice, you have 16 colors to choose from. ("Auto" indicates the text color you set in the Display dialog box of the Windows Control Panel, which is one of the 16 basic Windows colors.) Whichever color you choose, all change marks appear in that color, even if various authors or reviewers inserted text while the color choice was set to By Author.

> If you set the Mark box to (None) and you don't want the inserted text marked with a color, select the color that you're using for the text in the document. For example, if your document text is black (or Auto), select Black (or Auto) in the Color box.

Deleted Text

Word is set up to mark deleted text with a strikethrough line and to color-code deleted text with a different color for each author who revises a document. You can change both of these settings on the Track Changes tab in the Tools Options dialog box.

For marks that indicate deletions, your choices are Hidden, Strikethrough, a caret (^), and a pound sign (#). If you select Hidden, Word hides deleted text but still applies a color. Hidden deleted text is not displayed in the same way as text with Hidden character formatting is displayed. The only way to see hidden deleted text is to review the changes (see "Reviewing Revised Documents," page 634). When reviewing changes, you see the color, and you also see the deleted text with a strikethrough.

The color choices and workings are the same for Deleted Text as for Inserted Text. For details, see the previous section on Inserted Text.

Changed Formatting

Word is set up to neither mark nor color-code changed formatting. The Mark box is set to (None), and the Color box is set to Auto, which is usually the color of the text. You can change both of these settings on the Track Changes tab in the Tools Options dialog box.

For marks indicating changed formatting, your choices in the Mark box are (None), Bold, Italic, Underline, or Double Underline.

The color choices and workings are the same for Changed Formatting as for Inserted Text. For details, see "Inserted Text," page 617.

> If you decide to color-code both inserted text and formatting changes by author, both kinds of changes will use the same color. To distinguish between a pure formatting change and inserted text, either leave the Changed Formatting Mark set to (None) or choose a different marking scheme from that set for Inserted Text.

Changed Lines

When a reviewer makes changes to a document with change tracking turned on, Word places Changed Lines marks in the outside margins of the pages next to each line that contains a change. You can change the position of the Changed Lines marks or turn them off. You can also select the color for the Changed Lines marks.

For Changed Line marks, your choices are (None), Left Border, Right Border, and Outside Border. If you select (None), no Changed Lines marks will appear on the pages.

Outside Border places the Changed Lines marks in the outside margin of the pages. What does "Outside Border" mean? Your first clue is the Preview picture on the Track Changes tab in the Tools Options dialog box. The effect of the Outside Border choice depends on the setting in the Mirror Margins check box on the Margins tab in the Page Setup dialog box. If you turn on the Mirror Margins check box, Outside Border means the Changed Lines marks will appear in the right margin of odd-numbered pages and the left margin of even-numbered pages. If you turn off the Mirror Margins check box, Outside Border means the Changed Lines marks will appear in the left margin of all pages. The

Left Border option positions the Changed Lines marks in the left margin of all pages, and Right Border positions the Changed Lines marks in the right margin of all pages.

Word is originally set up with Changed Lines marks in the Auto color—that's the text color you set in the Display dialog box of the Windows Control Panel. You can change the color to one of 16 colors.

Making Comments

Sometimes marking additions and deletions is simply not enough. You may want to add notes to your document before it goes out for review, or the reviewers may want to include comments when they return their changes. To include comments—either written comments or spoken ones—you use the Insert Comment command.

Comments are similar to footnotes in that a reference mark is placed in the document where you want to comment, and you enter your comment in a special pane. Unlike footnotes, however, comments are not normally printed with your document and are usually removed in the final form of the document.

The following sections show you how to insert comments in a document, review comments added to a document, print comments, and work from comments to revise the document.

Inserting Typed Comments

A comment can consist of any material that you can put in a document, including graphics. To insert a comment, do this:

1 Position the insertion point where you want to add a comment.

2 Choose the Insert Comment command. Word inserts a comment mark at the insertion point. The comment mark consists of the reviewer's initials (as set up on the User Information tab in the Options dialog box) and a number (see Figure 13-6 for an example). Word numbers comments consecutively for each reviewer. Word then opens the Comments pane, inserts the same comment mark in the Comments pane, and positions the insertion point at the end of the comment mark.

3 Add the material you want for your comment. A sample comment is shown in Figure 13-6.

To add another comment, repeat these three steps.

To close the Comments pane, click the Close button on the Comments toolbar, or double-click a comment mark in the Comments pane.

FIGURE 13-6.
A document with a comment reference mark and a Comments pane.

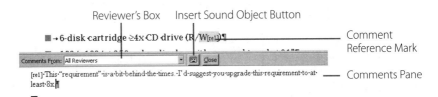

Inserting Voice Comments

? SEE ALSO

For information on setting reviewers' initials on the User Information tab in the Options dialog box, see "User InformationTab," page 982.

Instead of typing your comments, you might want to voice your opinions and ideas. In this case, you can add voice comments, either by themselves or in the midst of a typed comment. In order to play back spoken comments, you need a sound board installed in your computer, and in order to record spoken comments, you need a sound board with a microphone.

To insert a voice comment, follow these steps:

1 Choose the Insert Comment command.

Insert Sound
Object

2 On the Comments toolbar, click the Insert Sound Object button.

3 Click the Record button.

4 Speak your piece into the microphone.

5 When you're done speaking, click the Stop button.

6 Choose the File Exit & Return command. You see the speaker icon, shown at the left, in the Comments pane.

SEE ALSO

If you need more information about Sound Recorder and its tools, look in the Help file or consult your sound system's user manual.

 SEE ALSO

When you send out a document for review, you can protect it so that reviewers can only insert comments; they can't make other changes. For details, see "Protect for Comments," page 629.

While Sound Recorder is running, you can insert sounds from sound files. You do this with the Edit Insert File command. The sounds can be spoken words or music or other noises, such as "Ahhhhhh!" or "Ta-Da!" You can insert several sounds back-to-back to make longer sound bites. Sound Recorder also lets you mix sounds or even add an echo.

Reviewing Comments

When reviewers return a document with their comments, you can review comments from all reviewers at the same time, or you can focus on the comments from a particular reviewer. You can print the comments so that you can review them on paper. You can also take several actions with each comment. You can ignore a comment, but leave it in place; delete a comment you don't want to keep; or copy material from a comment and paste it in place of problem material in the document.

Viewing Comments

To view comments, you open the Comments pane, and then choose to display comments from all reviewers or from one specific reviewer. To view comments, follow these steps:

1 Open the Comments pane in one of the following ways:

- Choose the View Comments command. Word searches for the closest comment following the insertion point. The Comments pane opens, and the insertion point appears next to the closest comment.

- Double-click any comment mark. (Because comment marks are formatted as hidden text, they will not be visible unless hidden text is displayed.) Word opens the Comments pane, and the insertion point appears next to the related comment.

2 Select All Reviewers or the specific reviewer's name in the Reviewers box on the Comments toolbar (see Figure 13-6 on page 621).

3 If the comment includes a spoken comment, double-click the speaker icon to play the comment. (You need a sound board and speaker to play back a spoken comment.)

To return to where the insertion point was located in the document before you opened the Comments pane, do any of the following:

- Click the Close button on the Comments toolbar. The Comments pane closes.

- Double-click a comment mark in the Comments pane. The Comments pane closes.

- Click anywhere in the document pane. The Comments pane remains open.

- Choose the View Comments command. The Comments pane closes.

 TIP

To jump to a comment mark in a document, choose the Edit Go To command, select Comment in the Go To What box, select the individual reviewer or select Any Reviewer in the Enter Reviewer's Name box, and then click the Next or Previous button. You can also click the Browse By Object button, and then click the Browse By Comment button to jump to the next comment after the insertion point.

Printing Comments

If you want to review all the comments at once, you might find it handy to print them and review them on paper. You can print comments separately from the document, or you can print comments and the document together.

Here are the steps to print comments separately from the document:

1 Choose the File Print command.

2 Select Comments in the Print What box, and then click OK.

Here are the steps to print comments together with the document:

1 Choose the File Print command.

2 Choose Document in the Print What box.

3 Click the Options button.

4 Turn on the Comments check box in the Include With Document section in the Options dialog box. Word turns on the Hidden Text

box in order to print the comment marks, which are hidden text. Click OK.

5 Click OK in the Print dialog box.

Working from Comments

After you review the comments (or possibly as you review them), you'll want to do something about them. That is, you'll probably want to make some changes to your reviewed document. Before you can work with the comments, you need to remove protection for the document. (See "Removing Protection," page 630.) After you remove protection, you can change your document in response to the comments.

You can delete comments you don't want to keep, ignore comments but keep them in the document, and copy material from a comment and paste the material in your document.

To delete a comment, select the comment mark and press the Delete key.

To copy material from a comment, do the following:

1 Open the Comments pane.

2 Copy the material to the Clipboard.

3 Switch to the document pane and paste the material.

> You can also use drag-and-drop copying or moving to add comment material in the document.

Spotlighting Your Concerns with Word's Highlight Feature

Before you send out your document for review, you might want to take one final step to guide your reviewers to places where you want them to pay special attention. You can use Word's Highlight feature like one of those highlighting pens. You know the type: they have a felt-tip, are available in various bright colors, and you can read the text through the ink after you highlight words on the page. Well, Word's

Highlight is the electronic equivalent of the highlighting pen, and you can use it to spotlight text in a document for your reviewers.

The Highlight button shows the current color choice. If the current color on the Highlight button is the color you want to use, highlight text by following these steps:

Highlight

1 Click the Highlight button on the Formatting toolbar to turn on the button.

2 Drag the highlight-shaped mouse pointer over the text you want to highlight. You see an effect something like the following:

The Highlight button stays on until you click it again to turn it off. With this feature you can highlight lots of different pieces of text throughout the document without having to turn on the Highlight button for each piece.

TIP

You can also apply highlighting to text that is already selected—just click the Highlight button, and the selected text will be highlighted.

To spotlight text with a new color, follow these steps:

1 Click the arrow at the right side of the Highlight button on the Formatting toolbar to drop down the color list, shown here:

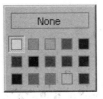

2 Select a color from the color list. (Select None to remove the Highlight color from text.) Word turns on the Highlight button.

3 Drag the highlight-shaped mouse pointer over the text you want to highlight.

III

Publications

Reviewing Highlighted Text

You might want to review any highlighted text in your document in case some reviewers might have added some highlighting or others might have responded to your highlighting. You can quickly search your document for highlighted text with the Edit Find command and add, delete, or change the color of the highlighting using the Edit Replace command.

To find highlighted text, follow these steps:

1. Choose the Edit Find command. Delete any text in the Find What box and clear any formatting.

2. Click the More button.

3. Click the More button if necessary, click the Format button, and select Highlight from its list.

4. Click the Find Next button. Word finds the next piece of text that is highlighted, regardless of the color used to highlight it.

To change the color of the highlighting in a document to the currently selected highlight color, do the following:

1. Choose the highlight color you want to use from the Highlight button list.

2. Click the More button.

3. Choose the Edit Replace command, and delete any text and formatting in the Find What box.

4. Click the Format button, and select Highlight from the list.

5. Click in the Replace With box, and delete any text and formatting.

6. Click the Format button, and select Highlight from the list.

7. Click the Replace button or click the Replace All button to change the highlight color.

You can also use the Find command to find specific highlighted text by typing the text in the Find What box. To find specific text and add highlighting to it, use the Replace command. For example, you could use the Replace command to find all instances of the copyright symbol (©)

in your document and add green highlighting so that later you could easily find any copyrighted text in the document.

Hiding Highlights

If you want to keep the highlighting in the document, but you don't want it distracting you (or someone else) for the time being, you can direct Word to hide the highlights. To do this, take these steps:

1 Choose the Tools Options command.

2 Click the View tab.

3 Turn off the Highlight check box in the Show section of the View tab.

4 Click OK.

To see highlights again, turn the Highlight check box back on.

Protecting a Document for Review

Now that the document is finished and you've set up tracked change marks, added comments, and highlighted your concerns, you want to send it to others for their review. But you want to be sure that the reviewers can't simply open your document and start adding, moving, and deleting material. To protect your document from hidden changes, you can ensure that any changes reviewers make are marked with the change marks you've set up. Or you can protect your document so that reviewers can add comments only. Both methods start the same way: with the Tools Protect Document command.

 TIP

If you store your document on a disk that people besides your team members use, you might want to further protect your document file. For this situation, you can choose from three different kinds of protection when you save your document. See "Safeguarding Your Masterpiece," page 139, for more information.

III

Publications

To protect your document for review, do the following:

1 Choose the Tools Protect Document command.

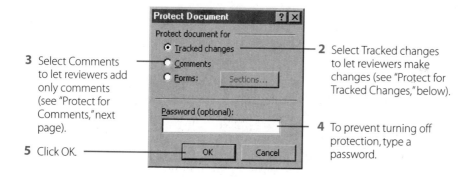

3 Select Comments to let reviewers add only comments (see "Protect for Comments," next page).

5 Click OK.

2 Select Tracked changes to let reviewers make changes (see "Protect for Tracked Changes," below).

4 To prevent turning off protection, type a password.

If you typed a password in step 4, the Confirm Password dialog box appears.

6 Type the password again exactly the same.

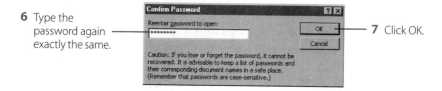

7 Click OK.

8 Save the document.

Now you can send the document to your reviewers, who can open the document but can work only within the protective restrictions you placed on the document.

Protect for Tracked Changes

When you turn on the Tracked Changes option in the Protect Document dialog box, reviewers can make any changes to the document they like. If a reviewer inserts or deletes text, Word marks the changes. If you have set the changes to be marked in color by author (set on the Track Changes tab in the Tools Options dialog box), each reviewer's changes appear in a different color. For more information about tracked change marks, see "Marking Options," page 616.

Word doesn't mark changes to paragraph formatting. Reviewers can make any changes they want to a document's paragraph formatting, and Word won't mark that text as changed.

Protect for Comments

When you turn on the Comments option in the Protect Document dialog box, reviewers can insert only comments into the document. This means that the only remarks or additions that go into the document are comment marks. A comment mark consists of a reviewer's initials (as set on the User Information tab in the Options dialog box) and a number. The comment text itself appears in a separate window pane, much like footnotes and endnotes do. For more information about comments, see "Making Comments," page 620.

If You Don't Know the Reviewer's Name

Word shows only a reviewer's initials and a number in comment marks. How do you find out the reviewer's name? Easily. Position the mouse pointer over the comment reference mark. Word displays the commentator's name and the text of the comment.

Protection and Master Documents

When a master document has protection for tracked changes or comments, the subdocuments are not individually protected. Anyone can open a subdocument, either from the master document or from outside the master document, and make changes.

When a subdocument has protection for tracked changes or comments, a reviewer must open the subdocument from outside the master document to make changes or add comments. If the reviewer opens a protected subdocument from the master document, Word opens the subdocument with read-only protection. The reviewer can't make any changes to the original subdocument. If the reviewer makes changes or adds comments, the subdocument must be saved with a different name. In effect, this defeats the purpose of setting up master documents and subdocuments for group work.

III

Publications

Here's the way to protect master documents for review:

- Protect the subdocuments and have reviewers open the subdocuments from outside the master document …

- … unless you are sending the entire master document for review as one piece. In that case, protect the master document and each subdocument individually.

Removing Protection

When it's time for you to review the reviewers' changes or comments and take action on them, you might want to remove the protection so that you aren't limited to tracked change marking or commenting only.

To remove document protection, do the following:

1 Choose the Tools Unprotect Document command. If you used a password to assure that no one else could remove the protection, Word displays the Unprotect Document dialog box.

2 If necessary, type the password for the document in the Password box, and click OK.

When you're working on a document as part of a team project, you'll want to be able to make the document available to all team members. Depending on your setup, you can do this in several ways, including copying the document on a floppy disk to be passed among team members, placing the document in a shared folder on your hard drive, distributing the document as an e-mail attachment, or routing the document with a routing slip (see "Sending a Manual for Review," page 633).

Tracking Versions of Your Document

As you're developing a manual or any lengthy document, you'll probably work through various drafts of the text. Each draft is a version of the final work. Most authors and editors find it useful to identify each version and keep a record of it for reference as newer versions evolve.

In Word 97 you can keep a record of versions of a document. Word still keeps a revision count on the Statistics tab of the Properties dialog box. That revision number is, however, simply a count of the number of times you saved the document. If, like me, you save often to assure that you don't lose very much work at any one time, the revision number can grow quite large, even though you're really working on the first draft (or version 1).

To start tracking of versions of a document, follow these steps:

1 Choose the File Versions command.

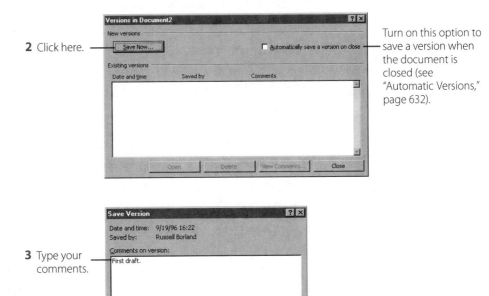

2 Click here.

Turn on this option to save a version when the document is closed (see "Automatic Versions," page 632).

3 Type your comments.

4 Click OK.

5 Click Close in the Versions dialog box.

At any time, you can save another version by following these five steps.

III

Publications

To review previous versions, follow these steps:

1 Choose the File Versions command.

2 Review the list of Existing Versions.

3 To see a comment that is too long to display in the Versions dialog box, select the version, and then click the View Comments button. You can't edit the comments.

4 To review a version, select it, and then click the Open button. Word opens the document in a separate window. The Title bar of the window shows the date and time the version was saved.

5 To delete versions, select them in the Existing Versions list, and then click Delete. Word asks if you're sure you want to delete the versions. Click Yes to delete the versions. Click No to keep them. Notice that once you delete a version, you can't get it back.

Automatic Versions

Turn on the Automatically Save A Version On Close check box to save an automatic version when you close the document. The only comment for an automatic version is *Automatic version*. And remember that you can't edit comments.

The action this check box directs may be useful if you open and close a document only once or twice a day. Do this more often, and the number of versions grows large and less useful because of the small differences between versions. In most cases, you're better off reminding yourself to save a version yourself. Not only will you be sure to save a meaningful version, but you can also add your own comments, such as a summary of the changes you made since the previous version.

If you often forget to save a version, you can turn on this check box to save the versions for you. You can still save a version yourself. And, of course, you can always delete automatic versions and any other version you don't want to keep.

Sending a Manual for Review

While the most common practice is probably to print a manual and then send out copies, Word's File menu contains commands for sending a manual through your computer. The File Send To command has a submenu with the Routing Recipient command. The Routing Recipient command lets you send your manual to a list of people who can then review it and make comments or changes. The Routing Recipient command can also give you reports on the status of the routing process.

To send your manual electronically, follow these steps:

1 Open the manual file (or the file for a portion of the manual).

2 Choose the File Send To command, and select Routing Recipient from the submenu. If a Choose Profile dialog box appears, select a profile name and click OK.

3 Click Address to add names to the To box.

4 Change the Subject if you want.

5 Type a cover message if you want.

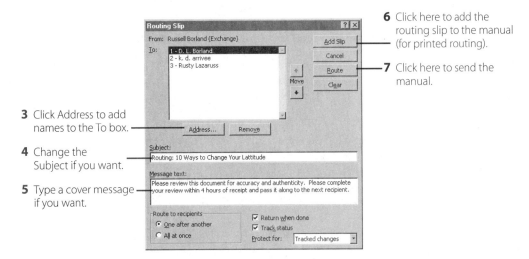

6 Click here to add the routing slip to the manual (for printed routing).

7 Click here to send the manual.

The bottom portion of this dialog box contains the following options:

- **Route To Recipients**—Click One After Another to send the message to the first name in the To box. After the first recipient reviews your memo, that recipient chooses the File Send To command and selects the Next Routing Recipient command from the submenu to send the memo to the next name in the To list.

Publications

(A reviewer can also choose the Add Routing Recipient command to add other names to the routing slip. This command works the same as choosing the Routing Recipient command.)

Click All At Once to send your memo to all the recipients at the same time. Reviewers must then send a reply message with their comments. You can collate the replies with the Tools Merge Document command. (Note that when you select All At Once, Word automatically turns off the Track Status option.)

■ **Return When Done**—Turn on this check box to have your mail system send you a message after the last reviewer closes the message that contains your memo. If you chose One After Another for Route To Recipients, you get the memo back after the person listed last in the To list closes it. If you chose All At Once for Route To Recipients, you get the memo back after the last person closes it, no matter what that person's position is in the To list.

■ **Track Status**—Turn on this check box to receive a mail message when a recipient forwards your memo to the next person in the To list. These messages keep you informed about the progress of your memo through the routing process.

■ **Protect For**—Choose the option that gives you the best information for this memo. Choose Tracked Changes to turn on marking of changes. With this choice, Word marks changes the reviewers make to your memo. Choose Comments when you want your reviewers to insert comments but not change your original memo. Choose (None) if you want to let reviewers change your memo, but you don't care how.

Reviewing Revised Documents

You've got your document back from your reviewers—now you need to look through the document yourself and decide whether to accept or reject tracked changes. The following sections tell you how.

To review tracked changes, do the following:

1 Open the document in which you want to review the tracked changes.

2 Choose the Tools Track Changes command, and then click the Accept Or Reject Changes command on the submenu.

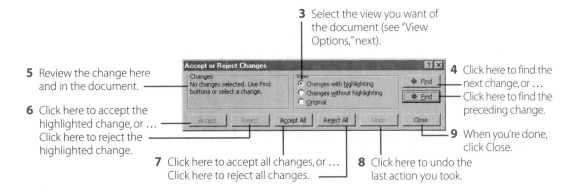

3 Select the view you want of the document (see "View Options," next).

5 Review the change here and in the document.

6 Click here to accept the highlighted change, or ...
Click here to reject the highlighted change.

4 Click here to find the next change, or ...
Click here to find the preceding change.

9 When you're done, click Close.

7 Click here to accept all changes, or ...
Click here to reject all changes.

8 Click here to undo the last action you took.

View Options

The Accept Or Reject Changes dialog box gives you three ways to view a document that contains tracked changes.

Changes With Highlighting

Word is set up with this choice turned on so that you can see the tracked changes marks. After you choose Changes Without Highlighting, click this choice to see the marks again.

Changes Without Highlighting

If you want to see the document without all the tracked changes marks (that is, if you just want to see what the text looks like with all the changes in place), click this choice. Word hides the marks for inserted text, hides deleted text, and hides all tracked changes marks and lines.

You can click Changes Without Highlighting at any point to see the current results of accepted and rejected changes. Word treats unreviewed changes as if you had accepted them. If you click Changes Without Highlighting before you accept or reject any changes, you will see what the document would look like if you accepted all the changes.

Original

If you want to see the document without all the tracked changes (that is, if you just want to see what the text looked like *before* all the changes were made), click this choice. Word hides inserted text, reverses formatting changes, and hides all tracked changes marks and lines. If you click Original before you accept or reject any changes, you will see what the document would look like if you rejected all the changes.

Merging Tracked Changes

If your document went out to several reviewers, you'll probably find that, although all your reviewers tracked their changes, they each made some very different changes. Now you've got to put them together and try to make sense of them. One way to do this is to merge the tracked changes. Then you can review all the changes and accept or reject them as you see fit.

To merge tracked changes, do the following:

1 Open the most recently saved document that contains tracked changes.

2 Choose the Tools Merge Documents command, which displays the Open dialog box, labeled Select File To Merge Into Current Document.

3 Select one of the documents you want to merge and click the Open button.

Word adds (merges) any text that was marked as being added or deleted in the second document to the first document. The first document now contains two sets of tracked changes—those from the first document and those from the second document. By merging the combined tracked changes with those in a third document, and so on, you can compile all the changes in one document.

If either document you are merging contains differences that aren't marked ("unmarked changes"), you see the following message:

If you click OK, Word merges only up to the first unmarked change and highlights it (selects it). Word doesn't add new material that isn't marked as Inserted Text. This means that if the merging document (the one you are opening) contains less material than the document in which you started the merge, you might see no changes. In this case, it's better to compare versions rather than merge changes. If you click Cancel, Word cancels merging.

Comparing Versions: Oops! I Forgot

If you sent out a document for review but forgot to turn on Track Changes, all may not be lost. If you saved your original document and the document returned from review with different filenames (or you stored a returned document that has the same name as the original in a different folder), you can compare the two documents to see where they differ. This also works when you yourself have changed an older document (but saved the changed document with a different name) and you just want to see how much you changed the newer document from the older one.

III

Publications

To compare two documents, do the following:

1 Open the document in which you want to see the changes. For example, if you want to see how much an old document changed, open the old document.

2 Choose the Tools Compare Versions command.

3 Select the document you want to use for comparison.

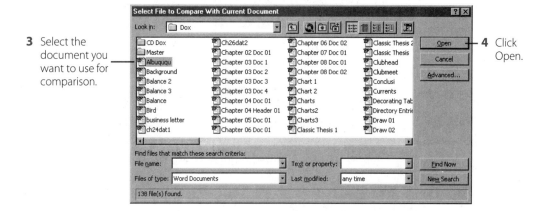

4 Click Open.

Word marks text that was added to the old document and text that was deleted from the old document. Word also places change lines in the margin with the marks and colors you set on the Track Changes tab in the Tools Options dialog box (see "Marking Options," page 616).

If you start with a newer document and compare it with an older document, you see all the newer text shown as deletions. If you start with an older document and compare it with a newer document, you see all the newer text shown as insertions.

If the first document contains changes, Word displays this message:

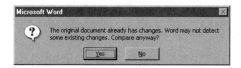

Click Yes to compare. Click No to cancel the comparison.

Printing Part or All of Your Document

When it's time to print your work, you can choose to print either a "chapter" (a subdocument) or the entire book (the master document).

Printing Chapters

To print a chapter (a subdocument), perform these two steps:

1 Open the subdocument, either from the master document or independently.

Print

2 Click the Print button on the Standard toolbar.

> If you want to set print options before you print a subdocument, choose the File Print command instead to display the Print dialog box. For information about printing options and other aspects of printing, see "Station 7: Print," page 124.

Printing the Outline

Word prints the outline as you see it in Outline view. If you want to print only an outline of your document, do the following:

1 Click the Outline View button at the lower left corner of the window to switch the document to Outline view. (You can instead choose the View Outline or the View Master Document command.)

2 Click the Show Heading 8 button on the Outlining toolbar to hide body text and leave only the outline headings showing. If you want to print only a certain number of levels of the outline (for example, only the first three levels), click the Number button on the Outlining toolbar for the lowest level of head you want to print.

Show
Formatting

3 If you want to print the outline in a draft font, on the Outlining toolbar turn off the Show Formatting button. (With the Show Formatting button turned on, Word prints all the text formatting.)

III

Publications

4 Print the document as you do in Normal or Page Layout view. Word prints only the paragraphs that you see in Outline view, nothing more.

Printing the Entire Book

To print the entire book (the master document), follow these steps:

1 Open the master document.

2 Click the Print button on the Standard toolbar.

> **NOTE**
>
> Any manual page breaks that are placed immediately before headings cause page breaks in the printed outline. Word ignores page breaks in hidden body text or hidden headings during printing.

> **TIP**
>
> If you want to print a part of the body text from the document, click the All button to display all paragraphs. You can then use the Collapse button on the Outlining toolbar to collapse the headings for sections whose body text you don't want to print.

Proving Your Thesis

A thesis for a master's or doctoral degree is a formal document that must be presented in a very specific format. Perhaps the most commonly followed format for theses is the one developed at the University of Chicago by Kate Turabian. Word supplies a Thesis template that follows the University of Chicago format.

As with many of Word's templates, the Thesis template is a point-and-shoot template. That means the template contains fields in which you click and then start typing. Certainly this is the approach you'd take if you were using a typewriter. But you're using Word, and you can have Word collect a table of contents, a list of figures, a glossary, and an index so that you don't have to type them yourself.

The Thesis template contains a cover page and pages for the abstract, table of contents, list of figures, acknowledgments, glossary, opening of the first chapter, bibliography, and index. It's unlikely that you'll write more than one or two theses of your own in your life, although you could become a typist for scholars who need someone to type their theses for submission.

Because the elements of the Thesis template in Word are intended to serve many different purposes, you might need to tweak them to better suit your needs and the style of your academic institution. Also, you might want to use the Thesis template as the basis for creating a term paper template. The sections in this chapter present a variety of ways to add material to a thesis and to convert the Thesis template to a theme paper template or essay.

Setting Up a Thesis Document

Before you can fill in a document based on the Thesis template, you need to create a thesis document. To create a thesis document you can fill in, follow these steps:

1 Choose the File New command.

2 Click the
Publications tab.

3 Click the Thesis icon.

4 Click OK.

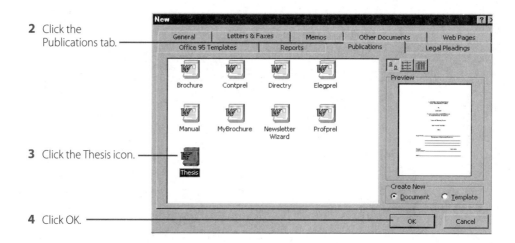

Most of the rest of this chapter describes how to fill in the thesis document. First you'll find descriptions of the pages where you simply type information. Then you'll find instructions on adding chapters, using Word's Thesaurus (to help you find the right words), and adding footnotes and endnotes. Once your thesis text is in place, you can add the table of contents, list of figures, and the index.

At the end of the chapter, you'll find instructions for turning Word's Thesis template into a term paper template.

Filling in the Blanks

You fill in the cover, abstract, acknowledgments, and bibliography pages by typing.

Cover Page Blanks

The cover page contains five "clicking fields," as shown in Figure 14-1. It also contains blank lines, which your supervisor fills in after you print the page.

FIGURE 14-1.
Preview of the cover page from Word's Thesis template.

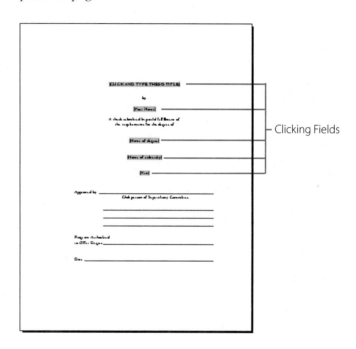

To fill out the cover page, click each clicking field and type the proper information.

 NOTE

To view the clicking fields with shading, set the Field shading box on the View tab of the Tools Options dialog box to Always.

III

Publications

To fill in the date, you can use one of the following methods:

- Type the date—use this method when the date is not today's date.

- Press Alt+Shift+D—this shortcut key inserts today's date in short format; for example, 8/13/97. If you want Word to insert a long format date (August 13, 1997), use the next method.

Choose the Insert Date And Time command, select the date format you want, and then click OK. This method also inserts today's date.

Fine-Tuning the Date

The long underscore after *Date* is set by a tab character with an underscore leader character. The underscore leader shrinks when you type or insert the date. To remove the underscore, press Delete at the end of the date. If you want the date centered, press Ctrl+E.

Abstract Page Blanks

The abstract page contains six "clicking fields," as shown in Figure 14-2.

FIGURE 14-2.
Preview of the abstract page from Word's Thesis template.

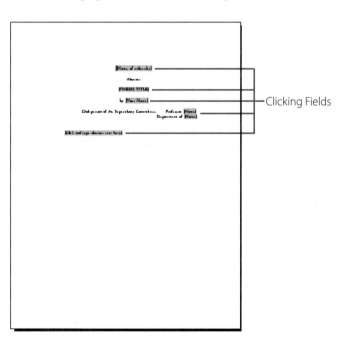

To fill out the abstract page, click each clicking field and type the proper information.

> While you could easily type the abstract yourself, you might find Word's new AutoSummarize command useful for creating an abstract. If you'd like to try this (I don't guarantee you'll like the results even one little bit), see "Automatic Summary."

Automatic Summary

Word 97 provides a tool to automatically generate a summary of a document—the Tools AutoSummarize command. This tool seems to be aimed primarily at generating an executive summary, which is usually associated with a corporate report. Because theses have abstracts, you might wish to try out this tool for generating an abstract. At the very least, it might give you seed text from which you can grow a proper abstract.

To have Word summarize a document, follow these steps:

1 After you complete the text of the document, choose the Tools AutoSummarize command. The AutoSummarize dialog box appears, as shown in Figure 14-3.

FIGURE 14-3.
The AutoSummarize dialog box.

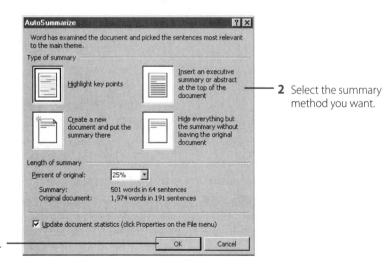

2 Select the summary method you want.

3 Click OK.

Selecting a Summary Method

As you can see in the AutoSummarize dialog box (Figure 14-3), you have four choices for the summary method. Two of the methods—Insert At Top (upper right) and Create A New Document (lower left)—actually collect text to copy it. The other two choices—Highlight (upper left) and Hide (lower right) simply add Word's Highlight color to key points. For these latter two choices, Word sets up a special view of the document. Here are the main points about this special view:

- After you click OK in the AutoSummarize dialog box, Word displays the AutoSummarize toolbar, shown here:

Highlight/Show Only Summary

Percent of Original

- The Highlight/Show Only Summary button switches between the two choices you had in the AutoSummarize dialog box. You could say the Highlight and the Hide choices are two sides of the same coin.

- The Percent Of Original box lets you set a different percentage from the one you set in the AutoSummarize dialog box. You can set from 0%—nothing showing—to 100%—everything showing. Neither of these two choices is meaningful. You'll probably set a percentage in the 5% to 30% range in most cases.

Because the abstract appear on page 2 of the Thesis template, you'll want to use either the Insert At Top or Create A Document choice. If you insert your summary at the top of your thesis, you can then select the summary and move it to the abstract page—using cut and paste. If you summarize your thesis in a separate document, you can use cut and paste, or you can insert the abstract file in the clicking field on the abstract page. For instructions on inserting a file into a document, see "Adding Chapters from Separate Files," page 652.

Selecting a Summary Percentage

As you'll see when you drop down the Summary Percentage box, you have eight choices for the size of the summary—10%, 25%, 50%, 75%, 10 Sentences, 20 Sentences, 100 Words Or Less, and 500 Words Or

Less. For a thesis, you'll probably want to choose 500 Words Or Less, but this will depend on the standards for your university.

For an executive summary of a 10-page report, the standard 25% setting is probably just about right. For very lengthy reports, you'll want to use the 10% setting or one of the sentence settings.

Acknowledgments Page Blanks

The acknowledgment page contains one "clicking field," as shown in Figure 14-4.

FIGURE 14-4.
Preview of the acknowledgments page from Word's Thesis template.

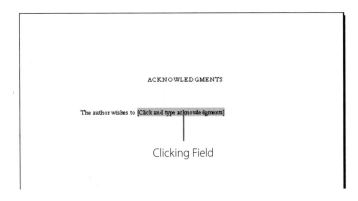

To fill out the acknowledgments page, click the clicking field and type the proper information.

If you prefer to start out your acknowledgments with text different from *The author wishes to*, simply delete that text and type the text you want.

Glossary Page

The glossary page contains one bold label, **Word.**, and one "clicking field," as shown in Figure 14-5.

To fill out the glossary page, follow these steps:

1 Select the paragraph that contains the text, and then press Ctrl+C to put the paragraph on the Clipboard.

2 Double-click **Word.**, and type a word you want to appear in the glossary.

III

Publications

FIGURE 14-5.
Preview of the glossary page from Word's Thesis template.

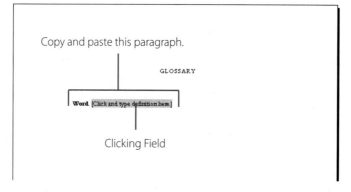

Copy and paste this paragraph.

GLOSSARY

Word. [Click and type definition here.]

Clicking Field

3 Click the clicking field, type the definition for the word, and then press Enter.

4 Press Ctrl+V to paste the paragraph you copied.

5 Repeat step 2 through step 4 for each word you want in the glossary.

TIP

Alphabetizing Glossary Entries
It can be difficult to keep the glossary entries in alphabetical order. It's probably easier simply to add them all to the list, and then let Word alphabetize the list when you're done. To alphabetize the list, select the list only, choose the Table Sort command, and then click OK.

Bibliography Page

The bibliography page contains two sample bibliographic entries. These entries show you how typical entries are formatted and show you that the bibliographic page is set up in two columns, as shown in Figure 14-6.

To add bibliographic entries, take these steps:

1 Select both sample bibliographic entries, and press Delete.

2 Type each bibliographic entry with the proper type styles, and then press Enter.

FIGURE 14-6.
Preview of the bibliography page from Word's Thesis template.

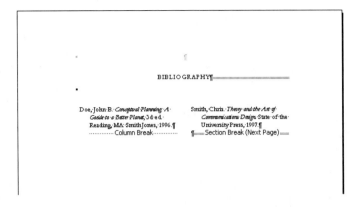

Adding the Chapters

The Thesis template comes with the chapter label *Chapter 1* already in place. Below this chapter label, you see a "clicking field" where you type in the text for the chapter's title, as shown in Figure 14-7.

FIGURE 14-7.
Preview of the Chapter 1 page from Word's Thesis template.

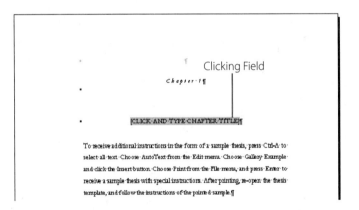

To fill out the chapter, click the clicking field and type the chapter's title.

When you're ready to start a new chapter, follow these steps:

1 In an empty paragraph after the end of Chapter 1, apply the Chapter Label style—click the Style box on the Formatting toolbar, and then click Chapter Label.

2 Type *Chapter 2* (or whatever the correct number of the chapter is), and then press Enter.

III

Publications

3 In the empty new paragraph, apply the Chapter Title style, type the chapter title, and press Enter.

4 If your chapter has a subtitle, type it now. If not, simply press Enter to start a Body Text paragraph.

5 Delete the empty chapter subtitle paragraph, and then type the text for this new chapter.

There's an easier way to start a new chapter, as explained in "Fixing Up the Chapter Numbers" (next). You might find the techniques in "Adding Chapters from Separate Files," page 652, useful as well.

Fixing Up the Chapter Numbers

In the Thesis template, the chapter numbers are simply typed in. Chapter numbers use the style named Chapter Label. This setup has a couple of problems:

- The numbers are not automatic. If you move a chapter, you have to renumber it yourself. There's a better way.

- The Chapter Label style doesn't set up the next paragraph with the Chapter Title style (the style the template uses for chapter titles). We can fix that, too.

To make the chapter labels (*Chapter 1, Chapter 2,* and so on) use automatic numbers, follow these steps:

1 Hold down the Ctrl key as you click the chapter label *Chapter 1,* and then press Delete. Be sure not to delete the paragraph mark.

2 Choose the Format Bullets And Numbering command.

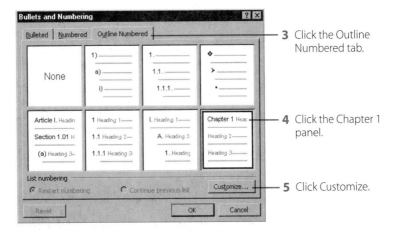

3 Click the Outline Numbered tab.

4 Click the Chapter 1 panel.

5 Click Customize.

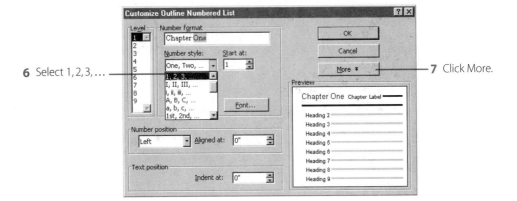

6 Select 1, 2, 3, …

7 Click More.

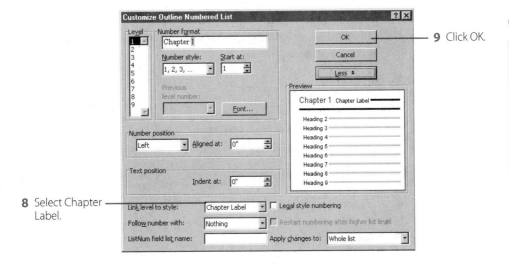

8 Select Chapter Label.

9 Click OK.

At this point, save the document so that you don't lose this work.

Now when you're ready to start a new chapter, simply apply the Chapter Label style to an empty new paragraph. Word automatically numbers it with the label *Chapter* and the correct number. If you later move the chapter, Word automatically renumbers it and all the chapters following its new position in the order of chapters.

To make the Chapter Label style set up the Chapter Title style when you press Enter at the end of the chapter label, follow these steps:

1 Select a Chapter Label paragraph.

2 Choose the Format Style command, and click the Modify button.

3 In the Modify Style dialog box, select Chapter Title in the Style For Following Paragraph box, and then click OK.

4 Click Apply in the Style dialog box.

At this point, save the document again so you don't lose this work.

Now when you set up a chapter label (chapter number) and then press Enter at the end of that paragraph to start a new paragraph, Word gives the new paragraph the Chapter Title style. All you do then is type the chapter title.

The Chapter Title style is set up to spawn the Chapter Subtitle style. If you don't use chapter subtitles, use the preceding steps that you used to set Chapter Title as the following paragraph style for the Chapter Label style, with one change— in step 3, select Body Text in the Style For Following Paragraph box.

Adding Chapters from Separate Files

If you write your thesis chapters separately and submit them for review before you submit the final version for approval, you might find it very convenient to write the chapters as separate files. When you're done writing and you're ready to assemble the chapters into the final document, you can insert the chapters into the thesis document. That way, you can easily generate the table of contents, the list of figures, and the index.

To create a separate thesis chapter document, follow these steps:

 SEE ALSO

A thesis is a candidate for Word's master document tool. Master documents are an attempt to semi-automate the process described in this section. If you want to check out this tool for handling large documents, especially documents in chapters, see "Understanding Master Documents and Subdocuments," page 558.

1 Open the thesis document you've been working on.

2 Select the title text on the *Chapter 1* page—the chapter label *Chapter 1* and the paragraph that contains *[CLICK AND TYPE CHAPTER TITLE]*.

3 Press Ctrl+C to copy the selected text to the Clipboard.

4 Create a new document from the Thesis template.

5 Select all the text from the beginning of the document up to, but not including, the Section Break (Next Page) character that precedes the *Chapter 1* label, and press Delete.

6 Select the title text on the *Chapter 1* page—the chapter label *Chapter 1* and the paragraph that contains *[CLICK AND TYPE CHAPTER TITLE]*.

7 Press Ctrl+V to paste the text in the Clipboard.

8 Select and delete all the text that follows the sample paragraph on the *Chapter 1* page to the end of the document.

9 Save this document as a chapter template.

10 Create a new chapter document from this new chapter template.

11 Click the sentence *[CLICK HERE AND TYPE]*, type the chapter, and save it.

12 Repeat step 7 and step 8 for each chapter.

TIP

For help with word choices as you write, see "Finding the Right Word: Thesaurus," page 654.

To add finished chapters to the thesis document, take these steps:

1 Open the thesis document.

2 Select the text on the *Chapter 1* page—the chapter label *Chapter 1*, the paragraph that contains *[CLICK AND TYPE CHAPTER TITLE]*, and the sample paragraph.

III

Publications

3 Choose the Insert File command.

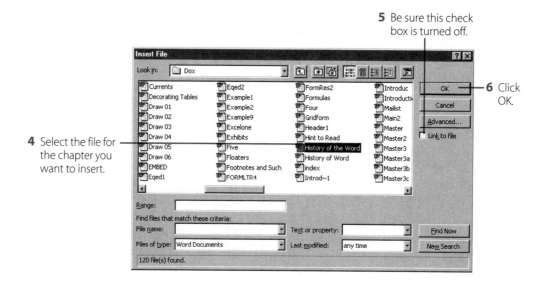

5 Be sure this check box is turned off.

4 Select the file for the chapter you want to insert.

6 Click OK.

7 Save the thesis document.

8 Repeat step 3 through step 7 for each chapter.

Finding the Right Word: Thesaurus

Using precise language in writing is always hard work, which is why many people turn to a thesaurus for help. You can use Word's thesaurus to look up a word or a phrase that's already in a document or one that you type or select in the Thesaurus dialog box.

To use the thesaurus, follow these steps:

1 Type a word or phrase, and select it. If you type a phrase, you must select it. If you type a single word, you can simply position the insertion point at the end of the word.

2 Choose the Tools Language command, and then select Thesaurus from the submenu, or press Shift+F7.

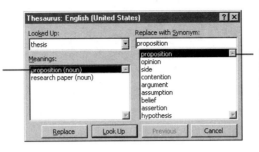

3 To see a list of synonyms for another meaning, select the meaning and notice the changed list of synonyms.

Word lists synonyms based on the meaning that is highlighted in the Meanings list.

Suppose that the synonyms list doesn't show a word you want to use. To search for another word, try following these steps:

1 Select a word or phrase from the Meanings list. This word now appears in the Replace With Synonym box.

2 Move the pointer to the Replace With Synonym box, and change the word to another closely related word. For example, change *proposition* to *proposal*.

3 Click the Look Up button.

4 From the new Meanings list, select a word or phrase that has the approximate meaning you want. Word displays a list of synonyms for the word or phrase you select. Repeat steps 2 through 4 until you're satisfied with the list of synonyms.

5 Select the word or phrase you want to use from the Replace With Synonym list.

6 Click the Replace button. The new word or phrase replaces the word or phrase selected in your document.

NOTE

You can use the thesaurus to look up words and phrases even if you haven't selected any words in your document. In this case, you must type the word or phrase you want to look up in the Replace With Synonym box, and then click the Look Up button. When you click the Replace button, Word inserts the selected synonym at the insertion point in the document.

III

Publications

Noting Your Smarts: Footnotes and Endnotes

Word provides both footnotes and endnotes. Footnotes appear on the page where you insert the footnote reference mark—either at the bottom of the page or just below the end of the text on a page. Endnotes appear either at the end of a section or at the end of the document. Word gives you the means to number or mark footnotes and endnotes differently.

Inserting a Footnote or Endnote

To insert a footnote or endnote, follow these steps:

1 Position the insertion point where you want to insert the footnote or endnote.

2 Choose the Insert Footnote command.

3 Select the type of note you want to insert.

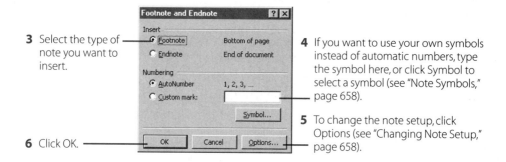

4 If you want to use your own symbols instead of automatic numbers, type the symbol here, or click Symbol to select a symbol (see "Note Symbols," page 658).

5 To change the note setup, click Options (see "Changing Note Setup," page 658).

6 Click OK.

Word inserts the footnote or endnote reference mark at the insertion point and puts the insertion point in the footnote or endnote area. What "the footnote or endnote area" means depends on the view you're working in.

If you're working in Page Layout view or in Online Layout view, you see the note reference mark in the place where Word will print the note, as shown on the next page.

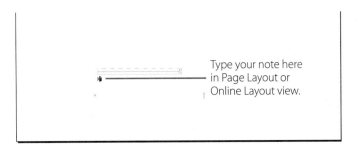

Type your note here
in Page Layout or
Online Layout view.

To return to the document text, you can use one of these techniques:

■ Double-click the note reference mark at the beginning of the note text.

■ Click in the document text.

If you're working in Normal view or Outline view, you see the Footnotes or Endnotes pane, as shown here:

Type your note here.

To return to the document text, you can use one of these techniques:

■ Click the Close button.

■ Double-click the note reference mark at the beginning of the note text. This technique also closes the note pane.

■ Click in the document text.

Here's what note references look like in document text:

special·instructions.··After·printing,·
thesis⌐·template,·and·follow·the·ins   Footnote reference
the·printed·sample.⌐¶   Endnote reference

III

Publications

Note Symbols

In the Footnote And Endnote dialog box, you can set up your own system of note references.

Using Automatic Numbering Schemes

Both footnotes and endnotes can use separately one of six automatic numbering schemes—Arabic numerals, uppercase or lowercase alphabetic, uppercase or lowercase Roman numerals, and a sequence of symbols. Before you decide to strike off on your own, you might check out the list of symbols Word uses for automatic numbering. For the steps you take to check this out, see "Changing Note Setup," below. Note that you can't set up your own sequence of automatic reference mark symbols.

You can either type a unique symbol for each note reference, or you can select a symbol. To select a symbol, take these steps:

1 In the Footnote And Endnote dialog box, click the Symbol button.

2 If you want to use a different font, select it here.

3 Select the symbol you want to use.

4 Click OK.

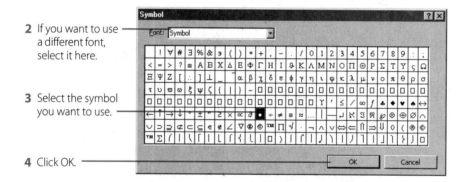

As long as you insert notes with automatic numbering, Word automatically updates the note numbers when you insert or delete a note earlier in the document.

Changing Note Setup

Initially, footnotes and endnotes are set up to number continuously through a document. For some documents—such as books or long theses—you might need to restart footnote or endnote numbering for each section (topic, chapter, or article). Footnotes are set up to number

To master the trick of putting endnotes, which would otherwise be printed at the end of a document, in front of the index, see the file named INXAFTEN.DOC on the CD in this book.

with Arabic numerals, and endnotes are set up to number with lowercase Roman numerals. Other number schemes are available for both types of notes—Arabic numerals, uppercase or lowercase alphabetic, uppercase or lowercase Roman numerals, and a sequence of symbols. Footnotes are set up to print at the bottom of the page. Endnotes are set up to print at the end of the document. You can change the print location.

To change footnote or endnote setup, use these steps:

1 Choose the Insert Footnote command.

2 In the Footnote And Endnote dialog box, click the Options button.

3 Click the tab for the note options you want to adjust.

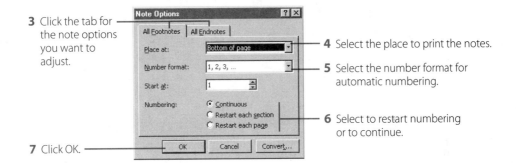

4 Select the place to print the notes.

5 Select the number format for automatic numbering.

6 Select to restart numbering or to continue.

7 Click OK.

Viewing Note Text

While it's possible to view footnote and endnote text either in the note pane (in Normal and Outline views) or in place (in Page Layout and Online Layout views), you'll find there's a better way to view note text—the note tip.

To view the note text for a note reference mark, position the mouse pointer over the reference mark. The mouse pointer changes to a note-paper shape, and then the text of the note appears in a tip box, as shown here:

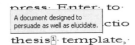

> You can't edit or perform any other action on the note text in the tip box, and tip boxes don't scroll. To see the tip, the Show Screen Tips check box option must be turned on (Tools Options View tab).

This quick and easy method of seeing note text might be inconvenient if the note text is very long. Word truncates (cuts off the end of) the note text in the tip box and shows an ellipsis (…) to indicate that the note text is longer than the text that's showing. In that case, you'll want to see the note text in its editable form. For the steps to do that, see "Editing Note Text," next.

Editing Note Text

When you need to edit a footnote or endnote, take these steps:

1 Locate the footnote or endnote reference mark using one of the following techniques:

- Click the Select Browse Object button, and then click the Browse By Footnote or Browse By Endnote button. Repeat this technique until you locate the proper note reference mark.

- Choose the Edit Go To command (or press Ctrl+G, press F5, or double-click the left one-third of the status bar). Select Footnote or select Endnote in the Go To What list, click Next or Previous until you locate the proper note reference mark (or if you know the note number, type it in the Enter Number box), and then click Close.

> Both techniques search in only one direction. Once you reach the last footnote or endnote reference in a document, clicking the Browse button or the Next button does nothing. Once you reach the first footnote or endnote reference in a document, clicking the Previous button does nothing.

2 Double-click the reference mark, or choose the View Footnotes command. Word displays the note text, either in the note pane (in Normal and Outline views) or in place (in Page Layout and Online Layout views).

3 Edit and format the note text as you wish. You can also edit and format the text of any other notes.

4 When you're done working on the note text, return to the document text, using one of these techniques:

- Click the Close button.

- Double-click the note reference mark at the beginning of the note text. This technique also closes the note pane, if it's open.

- Click in the document text.

The Facts of Life as a Note Pane

A note pane is a split window similar to a second pane on a document. You can adjust the height of the note pane to display more notes at once or all the text of a long note. The entire top border of the note pane above the toolbar acts as a split bar (see Figure 14-8).

To change the height of a note pane, drag the split bar up or down.

Besides showing you footnote or endnote text when you're in Normal view or Outline view, the note pane lets you make adjustments to the way footnotes print.

FIGURE 14-8.
The Footnotes pane.

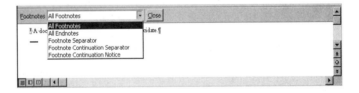

The choices in the drop-down list box are essentially the same for footnotes and for endnotes; only the labels change slightly. The choices are as follows:

- All Footnotes—displays all the footnotes in the document and changes the labels of the last three choices to *Footnote*.

- All Endnotes—displays all the endnotes in the document and changes the labels of the last three choices to *Endnote*.

Publications

III

- Footnote/Endnote Separator—displays the footnote or endnote separator character in the note pane.

- Footnote/Endnote Continuation Separator—displays the footnote or endnote continuation separator character in the note pane.

- Footnote/Endnote Continuation Notice—displays the footnote or endnote continuation text in the note pane.

The separator comes into play when your documents contain footnotes or endnotes. Word prints the separator above the first footnote or endnote on the page.

The last two choices in the notes box come into play in these circumstances:

- **Footnote Continuation Separator and Notice**—Appears when

  - a footnote is too long to fit at the bottom of the page on which its reference mark appears. A footnote is "too long" if the amount of text is longer than the space between the reference mark and the bottom margin.

  - there are too many footnotes on a page for all their text to fit at the bottom of the page.

- **Endnote Continuation Separator and Notice**—Appears when your document contains endnotes that continue beyond the page on which Word prints the first endnote.

Word has default separators but not continuation notices. The next three sections give you more details.

TIP

If you change the separator, continuation separator, or continuation notice, you can click the Reset button to restore the separator and continuation separator Word had set up originally. The continuation notice resets to empty.

Separator

As you can see in Figure 14-9, the standard footnote separator is a solid line, a couple of inches long. This line is a single character.

FIGURE 14-9.
The Footnotes pane displaying a footnote separator.

You can insert any text or art you wish for the separator. Word uses the separator between document text and notes. Word is originally set up with the same separator for both footnotes and endnotes.

Continuation Separator

As you can see in Figure 14-10, the standard continuation separator is a solid line that extends from the left to the right margin. This line is a single character.

FIGURE 14-10.
The Footnotes pane showing a footnote continuation separator.

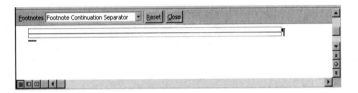

You can insert any text or art you wish for the continuation separator. Word uses your continuation separator every time notes continue on another page. Word is originally set up with the same continuation separator for both footnotes and endnotes.

 NOTE

> There is no separation character at the end of endnotes printed at the ends of sections and followed by sections that have a continuous section start. In this case, it can be difficult to distinguish where endnotes end and the new section begins. For more information about section starts, see "Section Starts," page 808.

Continuation Notice

Neither the endnote nor the footnote continuation notice contains any text. You can insert any text or art you wish for the continuation notice. A typical notice might read like the one on the following page.

III

Publications

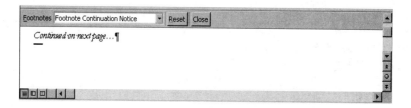

Word uses your continuation notice every time notes continue on another page.

Moving a Note

After you've inserted a footnote or endnote, you might edit the document text and find that the reference mark is not where you want it. Moving a note is the same as moving any text; take these steps:

1 Locate the footnote or endnote reference mark using one of the techniques described in "Editing Note Text," page 660.

2 Select the entire reference mark.

3 Drag the reference mark to the new location. If the new location is far away from its current position, you might use cut and paste to move it instead of dragging.

After you move the note reference mark with automatic numbering, Word updates its number and the numbers of all the footnotes or endnotes between the original position and the new position. If you type your own reference mark symbol or select a symbol, Word doesn't change the numbers of reference marks with automatic numbering.

Copying a Note

After you've inserted a footnote or endnote, you might want to repeat it from another location in the document. Copying a note is the same as copying any text; take these steps:

1 Locate the footnote or endnote reference mark with one of the techniques described in "Editing Note Text," page 660.

2 Select the entire reference mark.

3 Hold down the Ctrl key while you drag a copy of the reference mark to the new location. If the new location is far away from its

current position, you might use copy and paste to move it instead of dragging.

After you copy the note reference mark with automatic numbering, Word updates its number and the numbers of all the footnotes or endnotes between the original position and the new position. If you type your own reference mark symbol or select a symbol, Word doesn't change the numbers of reference marks with automatic numbering.

Copying a note reference mark also copies the note text. Instead of copying a reference mark, you can refer to it, as you can read about next.

Referring to a Note

For footnotes, a copy is convenient for your readers—they see the footnote text on the page they're reading. For endnotes that you print at the end of each section, a copy is convenient for your readers if the copies appear in different sections. For endnotes that you print at the end of a document, duplicating the entire text is unnecessary because the endnotes are printed together. In this latter case, you might prefer simply to refer to another endnote. If you want to mark more than one spot on a single page for the same footnote text, you can refer to another footnote. A reference to a footnote or endnote inserts the same number or symbol; that is, if the note you're referring to has the reference mark *5,* the reference shows 5 as its reference mark, too.

To refer to a footnote or endnote, take these steps:

1 Position the insertion point where you want to insert the reference to a footnote or endnote.

2 Choose the Insert Cross-Reference command.

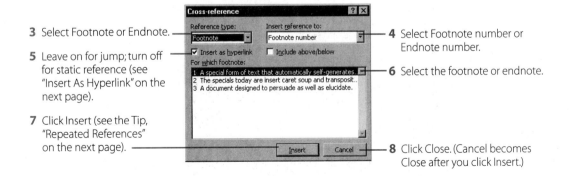

3 Select Footnote or Endnote.

4 Select Footnote number or Endnote number.

5 Leave on for jump; turn off for static reference (see "Insert As Hyperlink" on the next page).

6 Select the footnote or endnote.

7 Click Insert (see the Tip, "Repeated References" on the next page).

8 Click Close. (Cancel becomes Close after you click Insert.)

When you insert a reference to a note, Word doesn't change the numbers of any reference marks with automatic numbering.

Insert As Hyperlink

You can insert references to footnotes and endnotes as hyperlinks or static references.

? **SEE ALSO**

For more information about cross-references, see "Inserting Cross-References," page 603, and "Including Self-References," page 604. For more information about hyperlinks, see "Inserting Hyperlinks," page 878.

- A hyperlink reference sets up a link to the original note reference mark. When you position the mouse pointer over a hyperlink reference to another note, the mouse pointer becomes a hand. When you click the hyperlink reference, Word jumps to the original note reference mark.

- A static reference simply inserts the same reference mark as the original. There is no jumping link to either the original note reference mark or to the note text.

In both cases, if you add or delete footnotes or endnotes earlier in the document, Word renumbers the cross-references to notes, either when you print the document or when you select the cross-reference and press the Update Fields key (F9).

★ **TIP**

Repeated References

You can insert multiple references to notes at the same time. To add another reference to a note, follow these steps:

1 Click in the document. The Cross-Reference dialog box remains open.

2 Click where you want to insert the reference to a note.

3 Click the Cross-Reference dialog box to reactivate it.

4 Repeat step 3 through step 7 in "Referring to a Note," page 665.

Deleting a Note

If you no longer want a footnote or endnote in a document, take these steps to delete it:

1 Locate the footnote or endnote reference mark with one of the techniques described in "Editing Note Text," page 660.

2 Select the entire reference mark.

3 Press the Delete key.

Converting Footnotes and Endnotes

Sometimes you just get it backwards, like Wrong-Way Corrigan and Alan Page, formerly of the Minnesota Vikings football team. Sometimes you insert footnotes and then decide (or your editor or publisher does) that you should use endnotes instead, or vice versa. Sometimes a single footnote or endnote should be the other type. Sometimes you actually get them both backwards—footnotes that should be endnotes and endnotes that should be footnotes. And a host of other considerations may prompt you to make such a switch. Don't panic! Word provides the tools to fix up all these gaffes.

To convert a single footnote to an endnote or a single endnote to a footnote, take these steps:

1 Display the footnote or endnote text. Use any of the methods described in preceding sections to display the text.

2 Right-click the note you want to convert to display the Note shortcut menu.

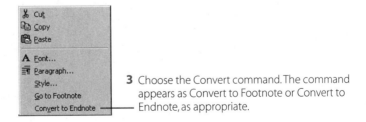

3 Choose the Convert command. The command appears as Convert to Footnote or Convert to Endnote, as appropriate.

To convert all footnotes and endnotes, take these steps:

1 Choose the Insert Footnote command.

2 Click the Options button.

3 Click the Convert button.

4 Select the type of conversion you want.

5 Click OK.

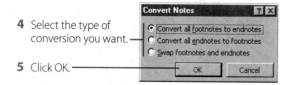

6 Click Cancel in the Note Options dialog box.

7 Click Cancel in the Footnote And Endnote dialog box.

Inserting a Table of Contents

After you finish adding text to your document and spiffing it up, you might want to collect lists of contents, figures, tables, and other items that appear in your document. These lists contain the names and page numbers of items. Because both the names and page numbers can change as you change the document, you might need to run your collection campaign a second or third time to keep the lists accurate. To do this, you just update the field for each list—click the list, press the Update Fields key (F9), select the type of update you want (entire list or just page numbers), and then click OK.

To collect these lists, you choose the Insert Index And Tables command. When you do, Word inserts a field, which makes getting a new, accurate list easy. The following sections describe how to create a table of contents, a table of figures, and other special lists of items.

As you know, a table of contents is a list of topics and their page numbers. Collecting a table of contents is an easy process, but you need to set up your document before you can begin.

Setting Up a Document for a Table of Contents

The easiest way to set up your document for a table of contents is to apply Heading styles. The setup process goes like this:

1 Apply Heading styles to the topics that you want to appear in the table of contents. (For an alternative, see "Setting Outline Levels for Other Paragraphs and Styles," page 675.)

2 Position the insertion point where you want the table of contents to appear. In a thesis created from Word's Thesis template, click the *Click and insert Table of Contents* sentence on the Table of Contents page, as shown here:

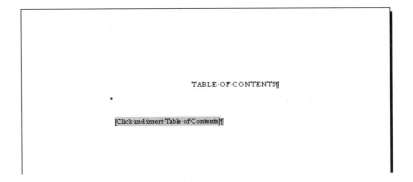

3 Choose the Insert Index And Tables command.

4 Click the Table Of Contents tab. The Index And Tables dialog box is shown in Figure 14-11.

FIGURE 14-11.
The Table Of Contents tab in the Index And Tables dialog box.

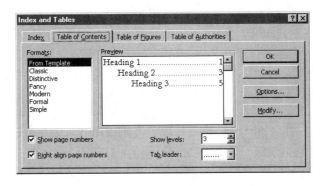

5 Click OK.

In documents in which you use Heading styles for your topic titles, Word collects copies of each instance of heading text and its page number and inserts them in the table of contents. But in a document based on the Thesis template, you see something quite unwanted, as shown here:

Error! No table of contents entries found.¶

You see this error message because the Thesis template doesn't use Heading styles for section or chapter titles. In documents based on this template, you need to use the instructions in "Table of Contents Options," page 673. When you do, you'll get a proper table of contents.

Updating a Table of Contents

If you change the document in ways that might affect the table of contents—for example, by adding or deleting text or changing the formatting—you can get a revised table of contents quickly with these steps:

1 Click anywhere within the table of contents.

2 Press the Update Field key (F9). Word displays the Update Table Of Contents dialog box, shown here:

3 Select the option you want.

4 Click OK.

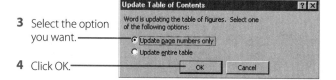

Word collects either just the new page numbers or an entirely new table of contents and positions the updated table of contents in the same place it was before.

If you insert a table of contents when your document already contains one, Word asks whether you want to replace the existing table of contents. Click Yes when you want Word to insert a new one at the same place. Click No when you want Word to insert another table of contents at a new position. (This allows you to insert a partial table of contents at the beginning of each section of a document.) Click Cancel to cancel the command.

Choices for a Table of Contents

In the preceding section, you saw how to collect a table of contents based on Heading styles. That's the easiest and fastest way to get a table of contents, but you have a lot more choices, as explained in the next sections.

Selecting a TOC Look

The Formats list on the Table Of Contents tab in the Index And Tables dialog box contains six preset looks for the table of contents, plus one look you can fiddle with. Note that for some of the looks in the Formats list, Word changes the settings in the bottom of the dialog box. You can see the effect of the format choices in the Preview box.

Table of Contents Page Numbers

You have three choices in the Index And Tables dialog box for the appearance of page numbers in a table of contents.

SEE ALSO

For information about an advanced way to separate TOC entries and their page numbers, see SEPGNUMS.DOC on the CD in this book.

If you want a table of contents without page numbers, turn off the Show Page Numbers check box. When you turn off this check box, Word deactivates the Right Align Page Numbers check box and Tab Leader box. You can use a table of contents without page numbers as an outline.

Usually, Word puts the page numbers at the right margin. If you want Word to put the page numbers after a space at the end of the entry in the table of contents, turn off the Right Align Page Numbers check box. When you turn off this check box, Word deactivates the Tab Leader box.

Using the TOC to Find Topics

When you insert a table of contents by using the Insert Index And Tables command, Word creates some magic. Word sets up the page numbers in the table of contents as hyperlinks. When you click a page number in a table of contents, Word jumps to the related topic heading in the document. In this way, you can use the table of contents as a quick way to "turn" to the page of a topic you want to find. Of course, this magic works only on the computer, not on paper.

For more information about hyperlinks, see "Inserting Hyperlinks," page 878.

For some of the looks in the Formats list, Word inserts a tab between the end of an entry and its page number. Word also selects the tab leader that fits the look. A tab leader is a series of characters that fills the space taken by the tab. You can select a different tab leader in the Tab Leader box. Table 14-1 lists your choices and identifies the leader character.

TABLE 14-1.   Tab Leaders for Tables of Contents.

Tab Leader	Name
(None)	Blank space
....	Periods
-----------	Hyphens
_____	Underscores

Adjusting Heading Levels

You can change the number of heading levels that appear in a table of contents. In the Index And Tables dialog box, shown in Figure 14-11 on page 669, you set the number of levels in the Show Levels box. If, for example, you want to collect only headings at levels 1 and 2, set the Show Levels box to 2.

Adjusting the Table of Contents Styles

In the Index And Tables dialog box, the Formats list on the Table Of Contents tab contains the item From Template. When you select From Template, Word uses the TOC styles as set up in the document template of the document you are working on. From Template is the only choice that gives you a way to change TOC styles directly from the Index And Tables dialog box.

When you select From Template from the Formats list, Word activates the Modify button. When you click the Modify button, Word displays the Style dialog box with only the TOC 1 through TOC 9 styles in the Styles list, as shown in Figure 14-12.

FIGURE 14-12.

The Style dialog box for a From Template table of contents.

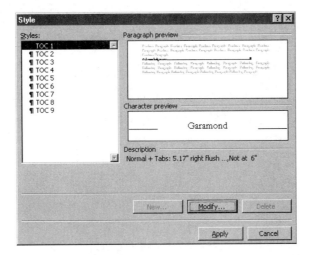

To set up a custom table of contents, perform these steps:

1 Choose the Insert Index And Tables command, and click the Table Of Contents tab.

2 Select From Template from the Formats list, and then click the Modify button.

3 Select any style you want to change.

4 Click Modify.

5 In the Modify Style dialog box, make changes to the style, and click OK.

6 Repeat step 3 through step 5 for each TOC style you want to change, and then click either Apply or Close in the Style dialog box.

7 Make any other changes you want in the Index And Tables dialog box, and then click OK to insert your custom table of contents.

Table of Contents Options

Most of the time, you probably won't need to change the way Word collects the table of contents entries from heading paragraphs. If, however, you do need to include paragraphs with other styles in a TOC—as you do in a document based on the Thesis template—click the Options button on the Table Of Contents tab in the Index And Tables

III

Publications

dialog box. When you do, you see the Table Of Contents Options dialog box shown in Figure 14-13.

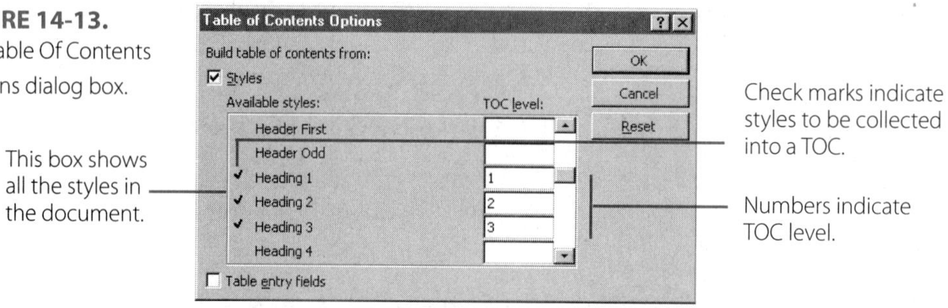

FIGURE 14-13.

The Table Of Contents Options dialog box.

This box shows all the styles in the document.

Check marks indicate styles to be collected into a TOC.

Numbers indicate TOC level.

When you look down the list of available styles, you'll typically see check marks beside the styles Heading 1, Heading 2, and Heading 3. In the boxes under the TOC Level label (to the right of the style names), you'll see 1, 2, and 3. These numbers tell Word which style to use as the first, second, and third level in the table of contents. You can type any level number (1 through 9) in any of the TOC Level boxes. When you type a number in a TOC Level box, Word displays a check mark beside the style name.

So what's the point? Because the Thesis template uses the Section Label and Chapter Title styles rather than the Heading 1 through Heading 9 styles for paragraphs that you want to appear in your table of contents, you should tell Word that the Section Label style fits level 1 and that the Chapter Title style fits level 2. (If you skip a heading style and want a different heading style to appear in your table of contents at a level different from its number, you set the level in the TOC Level box.) Here's what you do:

1. Choose the Insert Index And Tables command, click the Table Of Contents tab, and click the Options button.

2. In the Table Of Contents Options dialog box, delete the numbers in the TOC Level boxes beside Heading 1, Heading 2, and Heading 3.

3. In the TOC Level box beside Section Label, type *1*.

4. In the TOC Level box beside Chapter Title, type *2*, and then click OK.

5 In the Index And Tables dialog box, click OK.

Word collects the first-level and second-level topic titles (the titles that use Section Label and Chapter Title styles) in a table of contents. Titles with Section Label style appear at level 1 in your table of contents (and use style TOC 1). Titles with Chapter Title style appear at level 2 in your table of contents (and use style TOC 2), as shown in Figure 14-14.

FIGURE 14-14.
The Thesis template's table of contents page.

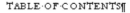

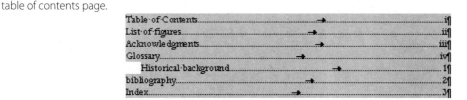

> At the bottom of the Table Of Contents Options dialog box, shown in Figure 14-13, you see the Table Entry Fields check box. You turn on this check box when you want to use table entry fields to identify entries for a table of contents. Inserting table entry fields in your document is an extremely tedious way to collect a table of contents, and I truly believe there's no good reason to use table entry fields instead of styles. If you like to make your work harder, however, look in Word's Help file for information about the table entry field.

Setting Outline Levels for Other Paragraphs and Styles

SEE ALSO
The techniques in this section also apply to Outline view. For details, see "Outlining Your Documents," page 559.

Normally, a paragraph must have one of the heading styles (Heading 1– Heading 9) in order to appear in a table of contents. The technique just described in "Table of Contents Options" is one way to put paragraphs with other styles into a table of contents. But that method has one drawback—it collects all the paragraphs with a given style into the table of contents at the same outline level.

You might want to set up individual paragraphs with the specific outline level you want without affecting other paragraphs with the same style.

III

Publications

Getting Around a Word Limitation

Word won't let you collect into a table of contents paragraphs that have any built-in style applied to them. But you can get around this limitation. First, apply a style you created to the paragraph. If you like the formatting of a built-in style, take these simple steps:

1 Apply the built-in style you like to the paragraph.

2 Press Ctrl+Shift+S.

3 Type a new style name (not one of the built-in style names), and then press Enter.

The new style looks like the original, but because it has a user-defined name, you can now give it an outline level that will appear in the table of contents.

To designate a paragraph with a style other than one of Word's built-in styles as part of the table of contents (give it an outline level), follow these steps:

1 Right-click the paragraph you want to give an outline level and choose Paragraph from the shortcut menu.

> **NOTE**

You can't set paragraph formatting in Outline view. If you're working in Outline view, switch to another view.

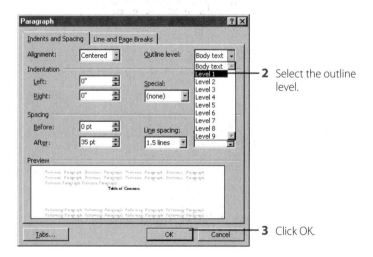

2 Select the outline level.

3 Click OK.

You can't change the outline level of a heading.

You can also set all the paragraphs with a particular style to a specific outline level. To do so, take these steps:

1. Select a paragraph with the style you want to give an outline level. (Remember: this technique doesn't work for built-in styles. The paragraph has to have a user-defined style.)

2. Choose the Format Style command.

3. In the Style dialog box, click the Modify button.

4. In the Modify Style dialog box, click the Format button, and select Paragraph from the button's list.

5. In the Paragraph dialog box, select the outline level in the Outline Level box.

6. Click OK in the Paragraph dialog box.

7. Click OK in the Modify Style dialog box.

8. Click Apply in the Style dialog box.

If you want to give several user-defined styles an outline level without having to select a paragraph for each style, follow the preceding steps, with these exceptions:

- Skip step 1.

- In step 3, select User-Defined Styles in the List box, and then select the style you want to give an outline level before you click the Modify button.

- Repeat modified step 3 through step 7 for each additional user-defined style you want to give an outline level.

- Only when you've modified all the user-defined styles should you take step 8.

III

Publications

Inserting a List of Figures

Using a method that's similar to adding a table of contents to a document, you can add a list of figures. A list of figures lists the captions of all the figures in your document, with their page numbers. "Captions" is an important word to notice in the preceding sentence. Without captions of some kind for your figures, you'll have real difficulty collecting a list of figures. The next section explains how to set up your document so that you can collect a list of figures.

Setting Up a Document for Collecting a List of Figures

To set up a list of figures, perform these steps:

1 Insert the figures in your document.

2 Select a figure and choose the Insert Caption command. For more information about captions, see "Adding Captions," page 396.

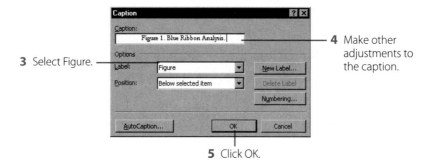

3 Select Figure.

4 Make other adjustments to the caption.

5 Click OK.

6 Repeat step 2 through step 5 for each figure.

7 Position the insertion point where you want the list of figures to appear. In a thesis created from Word's Thesis template, click the *Click and insert List of Figures* sentence on the List of Figures page, as shown on the next page.

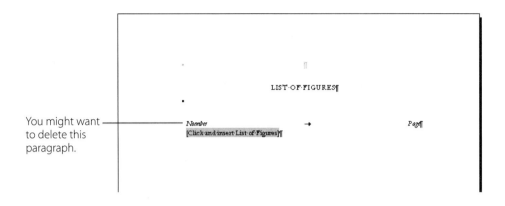

You might want
to delete this
paragraph.

8 Choose the Insert Index And Tables command.

9 Click the Table of Figures tab.

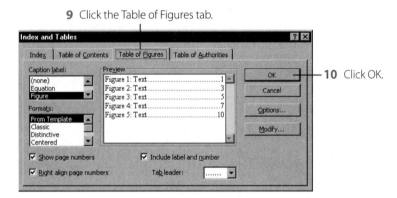

10 Click OK.

Word inserts a standard list of figures that looks something like the one
shown in Figure 14-15.

FIGURE 14-15.
A list of figures.

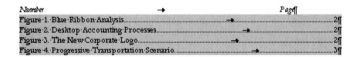

This is just one style for a list of figures, and it might suit you. You
have, however, several choices for setting up a list of figures with different looks, as explained in the following sections.

III

Publications

Choices for a List of Figures

In the preceding section, you saw how to collect a standard (Classic) list of figures. That's the easiest and fastest way to get a list of figures, but, as when you create a table of contents, you also have other choices. The next sections fill you in.

> **NOTE**
>
> For information about the Caption Label box on the Table Of Figures tab, see "Inserting a List of Tables or a List of Equations," page 683.

Selecting a List of Figures Look

The Formats list on the Table Of Figures tab contains five preset looks for a list of figures, plus one look you can fiddle with. As you select each look in the Formats list, the Preview box shows you what the list of figures will look like. Note that for some of the looks in the Formats list, Word changes settings in the bottom of the dialog box.

Inserting List of Figures Page Numbers

You have three choices for the way page numbers appear in a list of figures. If you want a list of figures without page numbers, turn off the Show Page Numbers check box. When you turn off this check box, Word deactivates the Right Align Page Numbers check box and Tab Leader box.

Usually, Word puts the page numbers at the right margin. If you want Word to put the page numbers after a space at the end of the entry in the list of figures, turn off the Right Align Page Numbers check box. When you turn off this check box, Word deactivates the Tab Leader box.

SEE ALSO

For information about an advanced way to separate the entries for a list of figures and their page numbers, see the file SEPGNUMS.DOC on the CD in this book.

For some of the looks in the Formats list, Word inserts a tab between the end of an entry and its page number. Word also selects the tab leader that fits the look. A tab leader is a series of characters that fills the space taken by the tab. You can select a different tab leader in the Tab Leader box. Table 14-1 on page 672, lists your choices and identifies the leader character.

Stripping Out Labels and Numbers

Normally, Word includes the label and number of each figure in the list of figures, as shown in Figure 14-15 on page 679. You can, however, collect a list of figures that omits the label and number. The list of figures then contains only the caption text, as shown here:

To strip labels and numbers from your list of figures, turn off the Include Label And Number check box on the Table Of Figures tab.

Adjusting the List of Figures Style

The Formats list on the Table Of Figures tab contains the item From Template. When you select From Template, Word uses the Table Of Figures style as set up in the document template of the document you are working on. From Template is the only choice that gives you a way to change the Table Of Figures style directly from the Index And Tables dialog box.

When you select From Template from the Formats list, Word activates the Modify button. When you click the Modify button, Word displays the Style dialog box with only the Table Of Figures style in the Styles list, as shown in Figure 14-16.

FIGURE 14-16.

The Style dialog box for a From Template list of figures.

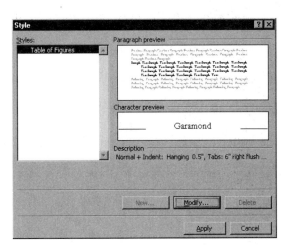

To set up a custom list of figures, perform these steps:

1 Choose the Insert Index And Tables command, and click the Table Of Figures tab.

2 Select From Template in the Formats list, and then click the Modify button.

3 Click the Modify button in the Style dialog box.

4 In the Modify Style dialog box, make changes to the style, and click OK.

5 Click either Apply or Close in the Style dialog box.

6 Make any other changes you want in the Index And Tables dialog box, and then click OK to insert your custom list of contents.

List of Figures Options

If you use the Caption style to identify your figures, most of the time you won't need to change the way Word collects the table of figures entries, but if you use a different style for figure captions, click the Options button on the Table Of Figures tab in the Index And Tables dialog box. When you do, you see the Table Of Figures Options dialog box, shown in Figure 14-17.

FIGURE 14-17.

The Table Of Figures Options dialog box.

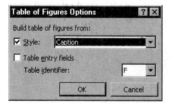

If you used a style other than Caption to identify your figures, select that style in the box to the right of the Style box. Word will build your list of figures from the paragraphs in your document that use the style you select here.

List of Figures Fields

At the bottom of the Table Of Figures Options dialog box, you see the Table Entry Fields check box and the Table Identifier box. You turn on the Table Entry Fields check box when you want to use table entry fields to identify entries for a table of figures.

The table entry fields include a letter to indicate the type of table you are identifying. In the Table Of Figures Options dialog box, you identify which table entry fields are used by specifying the letter in the Table Identifier box. Inserting Table Entry fields in your document is an extremely tedious way to collect a list of figures, and there's not much point in pursuing this difficult course. If you do want to pursue it, look in Word's Help file for information about the Table Entry field.

Inserting Other Special Lists

While you might not often find a need for types of lists other than a table of contents and a list of figures, the Insert Index And Tables command gives you a way to collect lists of tables and equations. And, with a little sleight of hand, you can collect just about any type of list.

Collecting lists of tables or lists of equations is easy—as easy as collecting a list of figures. Collecting lists of items other than tables or equations is almost as easy; it just takes one or two more (fairly) simple steps. You'll learn about these other lists after the following section on tables and equations.

Inserting a List of Tables or a List of Equations

Collecting lists of tables or lists of equations is about the same as collecting lists of figures. You really have to make only one change to tell Word to collect a different type of list. Follow these steps:

1 Insert the tables or equations in your document.

2 Select a table or an equation, and choose the Insert Caption command. For more information about captions, see "Adding Captions," page 396.

3 Be sure the label reads *Table* or *Equation*, make any other adjustments to the caption you want, and then click OK.

4 Repeat steps 2 and 3 for each table or equation.

5 Position the insertion point where you want the table of tables or the table of equations to appear, and then choose the Insert Index And Tables command.

6 Select the Table Of Figures tab, and select the appropriate label from the Caption Label list.

III

Publications

7 Make any other changes you want on the Table Of Figures tab, and then click OK.

The list of tables or the list of equations will look just like the list of figures in Figure 14-15, page 679.

Collecting a Graphical List of Figures

More and more, books and reports use a graphical list rather than a text list to guide readers to information. With very little trickery, you can build a graphical list of figures. Here's how:

1 Use a unique style for the paragraphs that contain the figures. Use the unique style only for the figures. The paragraphs should contain only the figures.

2 Choose the Insert Index And Tables command, click the Table Of Figures tab, and click the Options button.

3 Select the style you used for the figures from the list to the right of the Style box, and then click OK.

4 Set up your list of figures in the Index And Tables dialog box, and then click OK.

Word collects the figures and their page numbers and puts them into a list of figures something like this:

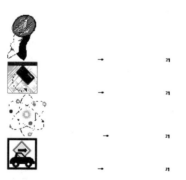

You can collect a graphical table of contents, too. For that, you simply insert your figures in the paragraphs that use Heading styles (or select the styles for the table of contents levels as directed in "Table of Contents Options," page 673; or give the user-defined styles you use for TOC entries the appropriate outline level as directed in "Setting Outline Levels for Other Paragraphs and Styles," page 675).

Inserting a List of Tips, a List of Notes, or a List of Sidebars

You might also want to make a list of tips, notes, and sidebars (or anything else in a document, really). Setting up lists of these other types of items is similar to setting up lists of tables and equations. Here's the major difference: you must create your own caption label for these items in order for Word to collect them into a list. In "Creating a Special Caption Label," page 397, you can find out how to create your own caption. To make a list of sidebars, for example, you must first make a new caption, *Sidebar*, in the Insert Caption dialog box. The following steps tell you how to create a list of sidebars. For other types of lists, just substitute the name of that type—say, "note" or "tip"—for "sidebar."

1 Set up a sidebar in your document and select it.

2 Choose the Insert Caption command.

3 Click the New Label button in the Caption dialog box.

4 Type *Sidebar* in the Label box of the New Label dialog box, and click OK.

5 Set up the caption that you want for the sidebar, and then click OK in the Caption dialog box.

6 Select each sidebar in the document, and add a Sidebar caption to it.

7 Choose the Insert Index And Tables command, and select the Table Of Figures tab.

8 Select Sidebar from the Caption Label list, make any other changes you want on the Table Of Figures tab, and then click OK.

The list of sidebars will look just like the list of figures in Figure 14-15, page 679, as will any other list of special items you set up.

Collecting a List of All Captioned Items

When you want to create a list that includes every captioned item in your document—that is, every figure, table, equation, and so forth—choose the Insert Index And Tables command, and then select the Table Of Figures tab. The Caption Label list on the Table Of Figures tab includes the item (None). When you select (None), Word dims the

III

Publications

OK button. The OK button remains dim until you tell Word which style to use for the list. So here's what you do:

1 Insert all the items into your document, and then use the Insert Caption command to give each of them a fitting caption. For more information regarding captions, see "Adding Captions," page 396.

2 Position the insertion point where you want the list of all captioned items to appear in your document, choose the Insert Index And Tables command, and then select the Table Of Figures tab.

3 Select (None) from the Caption Label list, and then click the Options button.

4 Turn on the Style box, select Caption from the Style list, and then click OK. The OK button on the Table Of Figures tab is now active.

5 Make any other changes you want on the Table Of Figures tab, and then click OK.

Word collects every captioned item in the document into a single list. The items won't be grouped by type; they'll appear in the list in the order Word finds them in the document, as shown here:

Figure 1. Blue Ribbon Analysis...1
Table 1. Balance Sheet for Q1 1998..1
Worksheet 1. P & L for Q2 1998..1
Equation 1. Formula for Success...1
Logo 1. Current Logo..1

Word uses the Table Of Figures style for the list.

Building an Index

When reading longer documents, about half of all readers prefer to look up topics in an index rather than in a table of contents. Whether a particular reader prefers to use a table of contents or an index, most readers expect a long document to have an index. Like a table of contents, an index can be hard to keep accurate because page breaks can change each time you change anything in a document. Letting Word spawn an index, however, makes it easy to get an accurate index at any time.

In Word, the steps for building an index are as follows:

1 Create index entries.

2 Insert an index.

These two steps seem quite simple, but there are a couple of quirks, plus a couple of tricks, that you will want to know about. The following sections explain how to perform these two basic steps.

One more note before you jump into the sea of indexing: both the index entries and the index itself use fields. Word hides index entries in special fields so that they don't affect page breaks. You can see index entry fields (which have XE as their field name) only if you direct Word to display hidden text. The index is spawned by the Index field, which collects information from the index entry fields to build the index.

Marking Index Entries

Before you can collect an index, you have to give Word clues to what you want included. The way to provide these clues is to mark index entries. The Insert Index And Tables command provides an easy way to insert the index entries. You just tell Word what you want for an entry, and Word inserts the index entry without further bother to you.

You have two choices when you insert an index entry: you can use text that's already in the document, or you can enter your own text, which may or may not match the document text word for word.

Using Existing Text for Index Entries

To insert an index entry from text that's already in the document, follow these steps:

1 Select the text that you want as an index entry.

2 Choose the Insert Index And Tables command.

III

Publications

3 Click the
Index tab.

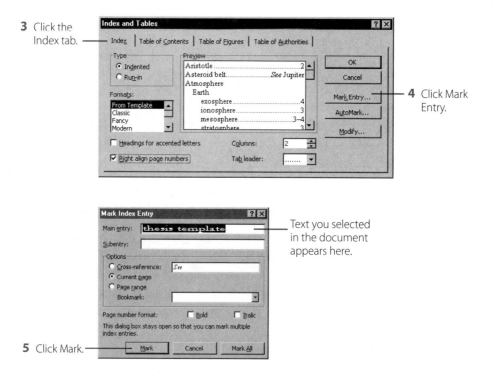

4 Click Mark
Entry.

Text you selected
in the document
appears here.

5 Click Mark.

Notice that the Mark Index Entry dialog box stays open so that
you can insert more index entries without having to choose the
Insert Index And Tables command over and over again.

6 Click in the document, select the next piece of text you want to
mark as an index entry, and click the Mark button.

7 Repeat step 6 for all the index entries you want to insert, and
then click the Close button.

For each index entry you mark, Word inserts an index entry field like
this one:

{ XE "Harley-Davidson" }

The dotted underline shows that this field has the Hidden Text font.
The text in quotation marks is what appears in the index.

When you have finished inserting index entries, you can collect an
index. To do so, follow the steps in "Collecting the Index," page 693.
But first, you might want to add index entries that contain text that's

not in the document word for word. The next section explains how to add such entries.

Other Types of Index Entries

Most professional indexers I know don't like indexing programs (or indexing commands in word processing programs). Why? Because most index commands can only use text that's already in the document. A professional indexer usually creates index entries that don't match document text word for word. For example, instead of the index entry "Harley-Davidson motorcycles," a professional indexer is more likely to insert "Motorcycles, Harley-Davidson" in an index. Also, a professional indexer is likely to insert index entries like "Harley-Davidson, *See* Motorcycles." For these types of index entries, you follow steps slightly different from those in the preceding section:

1 Position the insertion point next to the text you want included in the index.

2 Choose the Insert Index And Tables command, click the Index tab, and click the Mark Entry button.

3 In the Main Entry box of the Mark Index Entry dialog box, type the index entry as you want it to appear in the index. For example, if you want "Motorcycles, Harley-Davidson" to appear in the index, that's what you type.

4 Click the Mark button. Word inserts an index entry field like this:

{ XE "Motorcycles, Harley-Davidson" }

The Mark Index Entry dialog box stays open so you can mark additional index entries.

5 To continue marking index entries, click in the document, position the insertion point next to the text you want to index, click in the Mark Index Entry dialog box, type the index entry in the Main Entry box, and click the Mark button.

6 Repeat step 5 for all the index entries you want to insert, and then click the Close button.

III

Publications

Options for Index Entries

All the indexing methods you've seen so far insert standard index entries using only the Main Entry box in the Mark Index Entry dialog box. But as you can see, the Mark Index Entry dialog box has a bunch of options that insert a variety of index entries. The following sections explain these other options for index entries.

Subentry

Most indexes contain subentries, as shown in Figure 14-18.

FIGURE 14-18.

An index with subentries.

To create these types of entries, follow these steps:

1 Select text in the document, or position the insertion point. If you select text, it appears in the Main Entry box of the Mark Index Entry dialog box. If you position the insertion point, the Main Entry box stays empty; you must type the main index entry in the Main Entry box.

 NOTE

> If the text you select contains a colon (:), Word inserts a backslash (\) in front of the colon. The backslash tells the Index field to keep the colon as a colon in the index. Without the backslash, the Index field uses the colon to separate entry levels in the index; see the next step.

2 In the Subentry box, type the subentry text. For example, the index entry for European motorcycles, shown in Figure 14-18, was created by typing *Motorcycles* in the Main Entry box and *European* in the Subentry box. If the entry is a subentry of a subentry, separate the entries in the Subentry box with a colon. The entry for touring motorcycles in Figure 14-18 was created by typing *Motorcycles* in the Main Entry box and *American:Harley-Davidson:Touring* in the Subentry box. When you click the Mark button with this setup, Word inserts an index entry field like this:

{ XE "Motorcycles:American:Harley-Davidson:Touring" }

3 Repeat step 1 and step 2 for other index entries that you want to have as subentries.

Cross-Reference

Sometimes you might want to include index entries that don't have any direct relation to the document text. For example, you might use terms in your document that are peculiar to you or your organization. Your readers might have very different terms for the same thing. To help out your readers, you can add index entries that list the terms your readers might use and then direct them to look for the terms that you use. For example, you might use the term "common thrush," while your readers are used to the term "robin redbreast." For cases like this, you can insert a See entry in your index by following these steps:

1 Position the insertion point next to the text to which you want to assign a See entry, choose the Insert Index And Tables command, click the Index tab, and click the Mark Entry button.

2 In the Main Entry box, type the entry to which you want to assign a See reference. For example, type *Robin redbreast*. You can, of course, also type subentries.

3 Turn on the Cross-Reference option, and in the space after the word *See,* type the cross-reference. For example, type *Common thrush*.

4 Click the Mark button. Word inserts the following index entry field:

{ XE "Robin redbreast" \t "See Common thrush" }

The \t *"See Common thrush"* part of the field instructions directs Word to replace the page number with the text in quotation marks following the \t.

Current Page

This standard option tells Word to insert the number of the page on which the index entry field appears in the document. You'll need to select this option only if you selected a different option and then decide to use the page number instead.

Page Range and Bookmark

If you've ever looked at a variety of indexes, you probably noticed that some entries show a range of pages—for example, Harley-Davidson, 21–26. You can set up this kind of index entry in Word. Doing so requires another preliminary step—adding a bookmark to your document. To add a bookmark to your document, follow these steps:

1　Select all the text that you want to appear in the page range of the index entry.

2　Choose the Insert Bookmark command, and in the Bookmark dialog box, type a bookmark name, and then click the Add button.

3　Select the text, or position the insertion point where you want to insert the index entry field. You can insert the index entry field anywhere in the document.

4　Choose the Insert Index And Tables command, click the Index tab, and click the Mark Entry button.

5　In the Main Entry box, type the text of the index entry. You can, of course, add subentries.

6　Turn on the Page Range box, and then select the bookmark name in the Bookmark box.

7　Make any other changes you want in the Mark Index Entry dialog box, and then click the Mark button. Word inserts an index entry field similar to the following:

　　　{ XE "Wolves" \r "wolves" }

The \r *"wolves"* part of the field instructions tells Word to use the bookmark name "wolves" to insert the number of the first page and the last page of the bookmark in the index.

TIP

One of the major reasons for providing a page-range entry in the index is to indicate where the major portion of the information about a topic appears. When you set up a page-range entry, you might also want to set a font look for the page numbers—boldface, for example. See "Page Number Format," next, for directions.

Page Number Format

The page numbers that appear in the index can have one of four font attributes—plain, boldface, italic, and boldface italic. To select these font attributes, turn on or off the Bold and Italic boxes at the bottom of the Mark Index Entry dialog box.

Mark All Button

If you know that you want every occurrence of a word or phrase in a document listed in the index, you can quickly insert an index entry field next to every occurrence of the word or phrase. To do so, follow these steps:

1 Select the word or phrase you want for an index entry.

2 Choose the Insert Index And Tables command, click the Index tab, and click the Mark Entry button.

3 Make any changes you want in the Mark Index Entry dialog box, and then click the Mark All button.

Collecting the Index

After you've done all the hard work of inserting index entry fields (marking entries), collecting the index is really simple. Here's what to do:

1 Position the insertion point where you want the index to appear. In a thesis created from Word's Thesis template, select the sample entries, as shown on the next page.

III

Publications

2 Select these
two paragraphs.

3 Choose the Insert Index And Tables command, click the Index tab, select Classic from the Formats list, and then click OK. Word inserts a Classic index.

Besides this Classic index, you have a number of other choices for the look of an index, as explained in the following sections.

Making the Index Look Prettier

In the preceding section, you learned how to collect a standard (Classic) index. That's the easiest and fastest way to create an index, but you have a lot more choices. The next sections explain your other choices.

TIP

> An index usually appears at the end of a document. If you positioned the insertion point in an empty paragraph at the end of your document before collecting the index, the only time the index won't be the last part of the document is when you have endnotes that Word prints at the end. The endnotes will appear after the index. But you can change this. To find out how, see INXAFTEN.DOC on the CD in this book.

Selecting an Index Look

There are two major changes you can make to the look of an index, and you can make either or both types of changes, as you prefer. First, you have a choice of an indented index or a run-in index. (You'll read about this next.) You also have six preset ways to beautify an index, plus a free-form way to make your own changes to the Index styles.

Run-In Indexes

Most indexes are set up in the indented style. This means that sub-entries are indented under their superior entries, like this:

    Main entry 1
            Subentry 1
                    Subentry A, 3
    Main entry 2, 9

This is the setup that Word usually uses, unless you turn on the Run-In option on the Index tab. When you turn on the Run-In option, Word sets up the index like this:

    Main entry 1: Subentry 1; Subentry A, 3;
    Main entry 2, 9

One look at this mess shows you the problems with it. If you have more than one level of subentry, it becomes very difficult to tell where one subentry level ends and the next begins. Here's another example:

    Owl: Hoot; Eastern; Brown; Giant, 6; Pygmy, 6; Green, 6; Western, 6

Here's what the same index entries look like in indented form:

    Owl
            Hoot
                    Eastern
                            Brown
                                    Giant, 6
                                            Pygmy, 6

Run-in indexes can save space, as the two examples show. Be aware, however, that you might be slaughter readability on the altar of economy.

Options for Index Looks

The Formats box on the Index tab of the Index And Tables dialog box lists six preset looks for the index, plus one look you can fiddle with. Note that for some of the looks in the Formats list, Word changes settings in the bottom of the dialog box. You can see the effect of these changes in the Preview box.

Index Page Numbers

You have two choices for the way page numbers appear in an index. Usually, Word puts the page numbers at the end of the index entry, with a space between them. If you want Word to put the page numbers after a tab character at the end of the index entry, turn on the Right

Align Page Numbers check box in the Index And Tables dialog box. When you turn on this check box, Word activates the Tab Leader boxes.

For the Formal look in the Formats list, Word inserts a tab between the end of an entry and its page number. Word also selects the period tab leader. A tab leader is a series of characters that fills the space taken by the tab. You can select a different tab leader in the Tab Leader box whenever the Right Align Page Numbers check box is turned on. Table 14-1, page 672, lists your choices and identifies the leader character.

Formatting Indexes in Columns

Word is set up to print the index in two columns, but you have four other choices. On the Index tab you see the Columns box. You can set the number of columns from 1 through 4. The box also contains the choice named Auto. If you set the Columns box to one of the numbers (1 through 4), Word prints the index in that number of columns.

If you set the Columns box to Auto, Word prints the index in the number of columns you have set for the document (or for the section that contains the index—for information about sections, see "Using Sections," page 600). For example, if your document is set up in three columns, Word prints the index in three columns.

NOTE

With the Columns box set to Auto, Word attempts to print the index in the same number of columns as the document (or the section the index appears in). The index might not appear in the same number of columns, however. Why? Word fills one column before it starts to fill the next. If the index doesn't contain enough entries to fill the number of columns you've set for the document (or for the section the index appears in), you might see fewer columns in the index than in the document. The width of the columns in the index will, however, be the same as the width of the columns in the document.

Adjusting Index Styles

In the Index And Tables dialog box, the Formats box on the Index tab lists the item From Template. When you select From Template, Word uses the Index styles as set up in the document template of the document you are working on. From Template is the only choice that gives you a way to change the Index styles directly from the Index And Tables dialog box.

When you select From Template from the Formats list, Word activates the Modify button. When you click the Modify button, Word displays the Style dialog box with only the Index 1 through Index 9 styles in the Styles list, as shown in Figure 14-19.

FIGURE 14-19.

The Style dialog box for a From Template index.

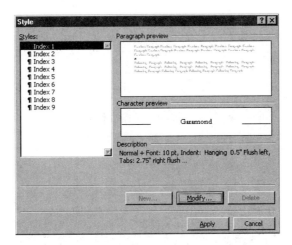

To set up a custom index, perform these steps:

1 Choose the Insert Index And Tables command, and click the Index tab.

2 Select From Template from the Formats list, and then click the Modify button.

3 In the Style dialog box, select the style you want to change and click the Modify button.

4 In the Modify Style dialog box, make changes to the style and click OK.

5 Repeat step 3 and step 4 for each index style you want to change, and then click Apply in the Style dialog box.

6 Make any other changes you want to make in the Index And Tables dialog box, and then click OK to insert your custom index.

III

Publications

Turning a Silk Purse into a Sow's Ear: Converting the Thesis Template into a Term Paper Template

The Thesis template could also be remodeled to become a term paper or essay template for yourself (and others). In your own term papers or essays, you'll use your name again and again. If you regularly type papers for others, you'll use their names again and again. You could easily add the names to a term paper template for each client. Also, the page numbers in the Thesis template appear at the bottom center of the pages. You might prefer to move them to the top right of the page.

Before you get into remodeling the Thesis template, however, you need to take some important preliminary steps: You need to create a template that you can remodel. Take these steps:

1 Choose the File New command.

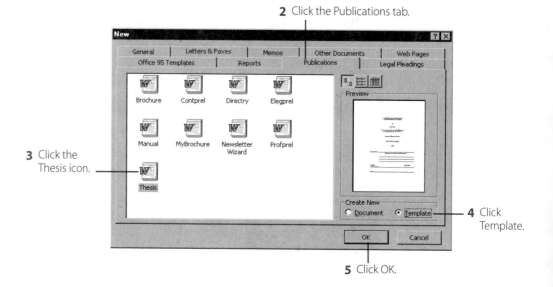

2 Click the Publications tab.

3 Click the Thesis icon.

4 Click Template.

5 Click OK.

Now take these steps to transform this copy of the Thesis template into a term paper template.

1 On the cover page, delete all the thesis verbiage. Leave only these items:

- *[TYPE THESIS TITLE HERE]*—we'll alter this sentence in step 2.

- *by*

- *[Your Name]*

- *[Year]*—this is optional; you can delete the date if you don't use it.

2 Select *[TYPE THESIS TITLE HERE]*, press Shift+F9 to see the field codes, delete only the word *THESIS*, and then press Shift+F9 again. You should see *[TYPE TITLE HERE]*.

3 Choose the File Page Setup command, click the Layout tab, turn on the Different First Page check box, and then click OK. This step omits page numbering from the cover page.

You're now done with the cover page. It's time to decide: do you want to keep any of the other parts of the Thesis template? Most term papers don't have an abstract, acknowledgments, a table of contents, a list of figures, chapters, or an index. Some term papers have a bibliography—let's assume that sometimes you include a bibliography. To convert the rest of this copy of the Thesis template to a term paper template, follow these steps:

1 Switch to Normal view.

2 Select the first paragraph on the Abstract page (page 2)—*[Name of university]*.

3 Scroll down until you see *BIBLIOGRAPHY* on the screen.

4 Hold down the Shift key and select the last line of the last paragraph before *BIBLIOGRAPHY*, and then press Shift+← to deselect the last paragraph mark.

5 Press Delete.

III

Publications

6 Choose the File Page Setup command, click the Layout tab, turn off the Different First Page box, and then click OK.

7 Choose the Insert Page Numbers command, select Top Of Page in the Position box, select Right in the Alignment box, and then click OK.

8 Select the two paragraphs of bibliographic entries but not the empty paragraph, and then press Delete.

9 Click the Section Break (Next Page) character between the empty paragraph following *BIBLIOGRAPHY* and the *INDEX* paragraph.

10 Press Ctrl+Shift+End, and then press Delete.

11 Choose the File Properties command, click the Summary tab, type a new title in the Title box, turn on the Save Preview Picture check box, and then click OK.

12 Choose the File Save As command, select the template folder where you want to store your term paper template, type a name for the template, and then click Save.

PART IV

Forms

Doing Business: Word's Other Documents

In your day-to-day business work, you may have need for a variety of business documents. Among the business documents that Word can help you create are meeting agendas, invoices, purchase orders, and time sheets. Using Word to create these documents is the subject of this chapter.

Setting an Agenda

Word provides an Agenda Wizard that helps you create an organized agenda for meetings. When Word runs the Agenda Wizard, you see several panels, on which you make choices and provide information for setting up an agenda that suits you. You can run the Agenda Wizard for each new agenda you create, but you can save yourself some time and effort if you create an agenda template for regular meetings for which you set the agenda. Then you can use the Agenda Wizard for setting up an agenda for a special meeting.

> **NOTE**
>
> When you create a template for a regular meeting, the agenda items (if you leave any in) will always be the same items, the time will always be the same time, and so will the meeting place. That is, an agenda template will freeze elements of the agenda that the Agenda Wizard sets up from the information you supply. You'll have to add, substitute, and remove agenda items; add, edit, and remove note spaces; and add or remove roles and the names of their players. For these reasons, you'll want to create an agenda template only for a very regular meeting that covers the same agenda items meeting after meeting without much change. This works best when the agenda items are general, such as Old Business, New Business, and so on.

To create an agenda template with the Agenda Wizard, take these steps:

1 Choose the File New command.

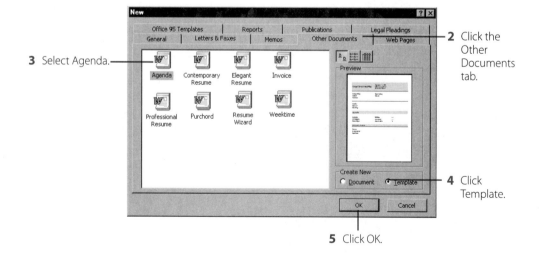

3 Select Agenda.

2 Click the Other Documents tab.

4 Click Template.

5 Click OK.

The Agenda Wizard's first panel appears, as shown in Figure 15-1. You can use the Next button to move from panel to panel to select settings that will help the wizard set up your agenda template. The Back button allows you to return to panels you've already seen. You can also use the map on the left, which remains displayed for each panel, to jump to any panel you want. After you've selected all the settings you want, you can then click the Finish button to have Word set up and display your agenda template in a document window.

FIGURE 15-1.
The first panel of the Agenda Wizard.

The Agenda Wizard has seven panels in addition to the Start panel you see in Figure 15-1. The panels allow you to select the following options for your agenda template or document:

- The Box, Modern, or Standard style on the Style panel
- The date, time, title, and location for the meeting on the Details panel
- Four possible headings on the Headings panel
- Seven possible name categories on the Names panel
- A list of topics on the Topics panel
- Whether you want a form for recording the meeting's minutes on the Minutes panel

Word sets up the agenda with the agenda items you typed on the wizard's panels and sets up the time slot for each item. (Word starts from the starting time you typed and then adds the minutes you allocated to each item to derive the time slots.) If you told the wizard you want notes pages with the agenda, Word sets up notes pages with spaces for Discussion, Conclusions, Action Items, and Person Responsible for each agenda item.

Even after you create an agenda document, you can make many adjustments to the agenda before you print it or send it.

Making Adjustments to an Agenda Template

As with any Word document or template, no matter how it was created, you can change anything and everything in the document at any time. In an agenda, there are probably three adjustments you'll want to make:

■ Add or remove agenda items

■ Change the picture in the agenda header

■ Add your department's name to the page footers

Adding and Removing Agenda Items

Despite your conscientiousness about listing and arranging all the agenda items while using the Agenda Wizard, you might find as the meeting approaches that you need to add or remove items. The best laid plans of mice and men ...

Adding an Agenda Item in the Middle of the List

To add an agenda item between other items, take these steps:

1 Select the table row that contains the agenda item *below* which you want to add a new item. If you want to add more than one item, select the same number of rows as the number of items you want to add.

2 Choose the Table Insert Rows command.

3 Type in the new agenda item, the name or role of the person responsible for leading the discussion, and the time slot for the item.

4 Adjust the times of the remaining items in the agenda *below* the item you just added.

Adding an Agenda Item to the End of the List

To add an item to the end of the agenda, take these steps:

1 Select the table row that contains the last agenda item.

2 Choose the Table Insert Rows command.

3 Press Alt+Shift+↓ to move the new row below the current last item.

4 Type in the new agenda item, the name or role of the person responsible for leading the discussion, and the time slot for the item.

Removing an Agenda Item

To remove an agenda item, take these steps:

1 Select the table row that contains the agenda item you want to remove.

2 Choose the Table Delete Rows command.

3 Adjust the times of the remaining items in the agenda *below* the item you just removed.

Working with Pictures and WordArt in the Agenda Header

On the Boxes style agenda, each page of the agenda contains a check mark graphic. On the Modern style agenda, the first page contains a piece of WordArt. (The Standard format agenda contains no artwork.)

You can easily substitute your own graphic, picture, logo, or WordArt for the check mark graphic on the Boxes style agenda or for the Word-Art on the Modern style agenda. You can also add graphic touches to the Standard format agenda.

To substitute another picture for the check mark graphic, follow these steps:

1 Click the check box graphic to select it.

2 Choose the Insert Picture command, and select Clip Art or From File from the submenu.

3 In the Microsoft Clip Gallery, select the category of art you want to use; or in the Insert Picture dialog box, locate the art file you want to use.

4 In the Microsoft Clip Gallery, click the picture you want; or in the Insert Picture dialog box, select the file that contains the art you want to use.

5 Click Insert.

6 Repeat these steps for the check mark graphic on the agenda's second page.

Of course, you can edit the check mark graphic by double-clicking it and then altering it with Word's drawing tools. You can also replace the check mark graphic with a drawing you create yourself with Word's drawing tools.

(?) SEE ALSO

For descriptions of dealing in art, see "Adding Art from Files," page 455, "Drawing Pictures," page 458, and "Bending Text—WordArt," page 507.

To substitute your own piece of WordArt for the WordArt on the Modern format agenda, follow these steps:

1 Click the WordArt.

2 On the WordArt toolbar, click the WordArt Gallery button to select a new preset format from the WordArt Gallery, or click the WordArt Shape button to select only a new shape.

3 Click the Edit Text button to substitute your own text.

4 If you want to change the position, drag the WordArt to its new position.

5 If you want to change the size, drag the sizing handles to the new size.

6 If you want to adjust the shape, drag the yellow diamond to skew the shape.

7 When you're done, click in the agenda outside the WordArt.

8 Repeat these steps for the WordArt on the second page of the agenda.

Adding Your Department Name to a Footer (or Header)

One enhancement you can easily make to an agenda template is to add your department's name (or your organization's name, or both) to the footers on the agenda pages. (You can, instead, add these items to the page headers if you wish. Or you can put the organization's name in the header and the department's name in the footer, or vice versa.) To set this up, you can either type the names yourself, or you can insert fields that retrieve the names from the Summary tab of the File Properties dialog box. Because typing the information is straightforward (and I assume you've encountered adding headers and footers before you got to this chapter), let's concentrate on getting Word to automatically retrieve this information for you.

To set up the footers to automatically insert your company's name, take the following steps.

 NOTE

> In the following steps, substitute "Department" for "Company" if you want to add your department's name instead of your company's name to a footer. Also, if you prefer to put a name or both names in the headers instead of the footers, substitute "header" for "footer" in the following steps.

1 Choose the File Properties command.

2 Click the Summary tab.

3 Type your department's name, organization's name, or both.

4 Click OK.

Document2 Properties

General | Summary | Statistics | Contents | Custom

Title: Creates an agenda for any type of meeting
Subject:
Author: Russell Borland
Manager:
Company: Microsoft Press: Acquisitions Department
Category:
Keywords:
Comments:
Hyperlink base:
Template: Normal
☑ Save preview picture

OK   Cancel

5 Choose the View Header And Footer command.

6 Click the Switch Between Header And Footer button to jump to the page footer.

7 Choose the Insert Field command.

8 Select Document Information.

9 Select DocProperty.

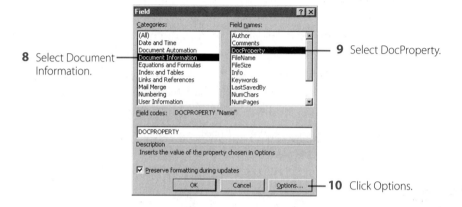

10 Click Options.

11 Select Company.

12 Click Add to Field.

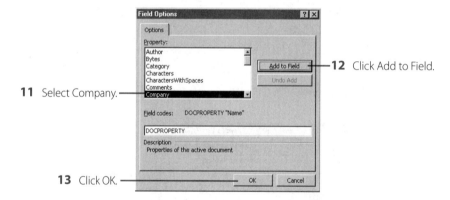

13 Click OK.

14 Click OK in the Field dialog box.

15 Click Close on the Header And Footer toolbar.

Creating an Agenda

After you build your agenda templates, you're ready to create an agenda for one of your meetings. To create an agenda, follow these steps:

1 Choose the File New command.

2 Click the Other Documents tab.

3 Select Agenda (for a special meeting) or one of the agenda templates you created.

4 Click Document.

5 Click OK.

Now fill in the blanks for the names, the reading material, materials to bring, and any special notes. Be aware that you can change any and all of the text in the agenda document after you create it.

Printing the Agenda

If you want to print all the agenda pages, simply click the Print button on the Standard toolbar. If, however, you want to print only certain pages, you need to tell Word this when you print.

To print only certain pages of your agenda, take these steps:

1 Choose the File Print command.

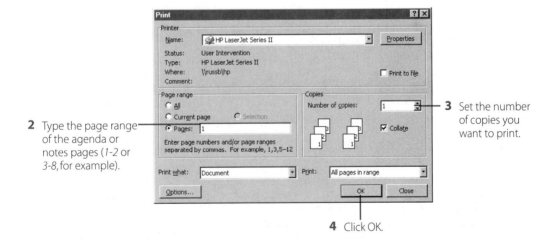

2 Type the page range of the agenda or notes pages (*1-2* or *3-8*, for example).

3 Set the number of copies you want to print.

4 Click OK.

Sending the Agenda Prior to the Meeting

When you want people to read materials beforehand or make other preparations for a meeting, they need the agenda in hand before the meeting. An easy way to get the agenda out is to send it by way of your e-mail system.

After you fill out the agenda form, take these steps to send the agenda to the people who need it:

1 Select the agenda pages.

2 Copy the agenda pages to the Clipboard.

3 Create a new document, and paste the agenda pages into it.

4 Choose the File Send To command, and select Mail Recipient from the submenu. If it's not already running, Word starts your e-mail program.

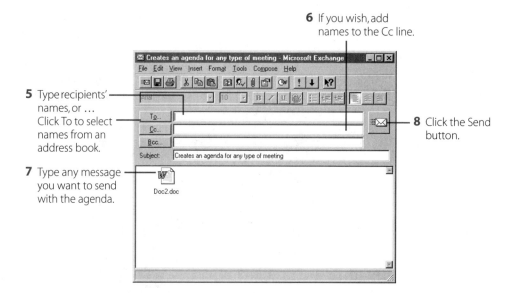

6 If you wish, add names to the Cc line.

5 Type recipients' names, or … Click To to select names from an address book.

8 Click the Send button.

7 Type any message you want to send with the agenda.

Billing Your Invoice, Cutting a Purchase Order, and Recording Your Time Sheet

For your organization to get paid for its products and services, you need to bill your customers and clients. The most common form of billing is an invoice, which shows who placed the order, where it was shipped, the terms of the sale, what was ordered, when it was ordered, how much was ordered, how much each unit costs, how much each item costs, the total bill, and several other pieces of pertinent information. To order goods and services from another organization, you'll often cut a purchase order that spells out what you want to buy, the agreed terms and prices, and delivery instructions.

Word provides an invoice template and a purchase order template, which are set up to show the usual information that appears on an invoice or purchase order. Word also provides a weekly time sheet template (named Weektime) on which hourly wage employees can fill in their hours. All three templates are set up with placeholders for your organization's name and address. You will, of course, want to identify your organization on the invoice, purchase order, and time sheet and save them as templates. Then you won't have to fill in this information each time you create an invoice, a purchase order, or time sheet.

NOTE

The following directions and sections focus on the invoice template. The purchase order template has almost the same setup as the invoice template. The weekly time sheet template also contains placeholders similar to those on the invoice and purchase order templates. You can apply the directions given here for the invoice template to the purchase order or weekly time sheet template. To do so, simply substitute "purchase order" or "weekly time sheet" (Weektime) for "invoice" in the steps and descriptions.

To create an invoice template for your organization, take these steps:

1 Choose the File New command.

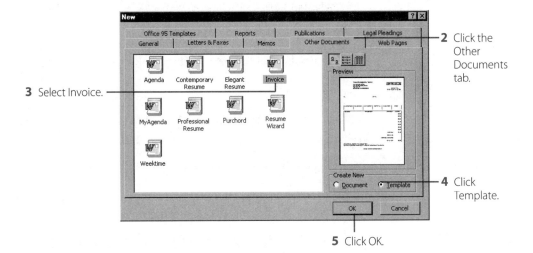

3 Select Invoice.

2 Click the Other Documents tab.

4 Click Template.

5 Click OK.

Word creates an invoice template that looks like this:

Substitute your
organization's
information for
these placeholders.

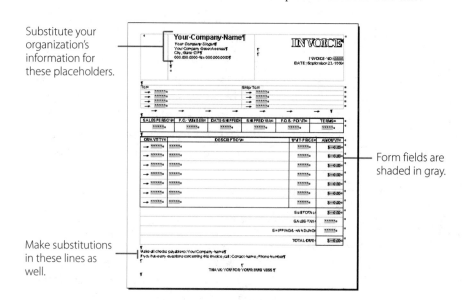

Form fields are
shaded in gray.

Make substitutions
in these lines as
well.

When you try to click the placeholders for organization information, you have no joy. Why? The invoice template is a protected form. That means you can only fill in the form fields until you remove form protection. After you remove form protection, you can customize the form in several ways. You'll find instructions in the upcoming sections for making the following changes:

- Substitute your organization's information for the placeholders

- Set up the Sales Tax field to calculate sales tax for you

- Set up the Shipping & Handling field to calculate shipping and handling charges for you

Customizing the Organization Information

To customize the invoice template, take these steps:

1 Choose the Tools Unprotect Document command.

2 Select the text for each part of the organization placeholder, and type the information for your organization.

3 If you want to change the *INVOICE* label in the upper right corner, double-click it, and use Word's drawing tools to edit it. You can also substitute other artwork—a logo picture, WordArt, text with special font formatting, or a picture you draw with Word's drawing tools. See Chapter 10, "Brocading a Brochure," for information about working with artwork.

4 At the bottom of the invoice form, substitute your organization's name, the name of the contact for questions about invoices, and the contact's telephone number.

Protecting and Saving Your New Invoice Template

1 Choose the Tools Protect Document command.

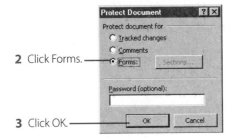

2 Click Forms.

3 Click OK.

4 Choose the File Save command.

5 Switch to the Other Documents folder.

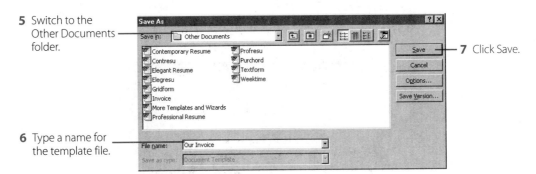

7 Click Save.

6 Type a name for the template file.

Automating Sales Tax and Shipping and Handling

The Sales Tax and the Shipping & Handling fields are simply fill-in blanks. You type the amounts in these fields, and Word recalculates the total. These fields are set up as entry fields because you might well ship goods and services to areas where the sales tax rate is different. Also, you probably have a fixed amount or fixed scale for shipping and handling charges, neither of which is routinely calculable.

> The weekly time sheet does not contain the fields and calculations described in the following three sections. For a time sheet, skip these three sections.

If, however, you always charge the same percentage for sales tax or you charge a percentage of the subtotal for shipping and handling, you can set up the fields for these two amounts to calculate the amounts for you. The next three sections tell you how to set this up.

Calculating the Sales Tax

If you always charge the same percentage for sales tax for every customer or client, take these steps to set up the Sales Tax field to calculate the sales tax for you:

1 Be sure the template form is not protected. If it is, choose the Tools Unprotect Document command.

2 Right-click the form field for Sales Tax, and select Properties from the shortcut menu.

4 Type *Subtotal** and the percentage with a percent sign.

3 Select Calculation.

5 Click OK.

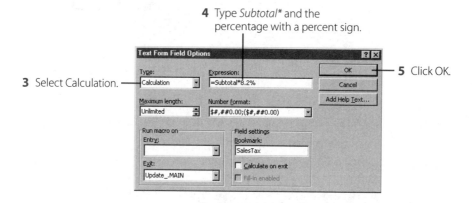

Calculating Shipping and Handling

If you always charge the same percentage of the subtotal for shipping and handling charges for every customer or client, take these steps to set up the Shipping & Handling field to calculate the shipping and handling charge for you:

1 Be sure the template form is not protected. If it is, choose the Tools Unprotect Document command.

2 Right-click the form field for Shipping & Handling, and select Properties from the shortcut menu.

4 Type *Subtotal** and the percentage with a percent sign.

3 Select Calculation.

5 Click OK.

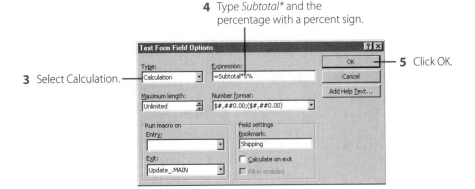

Making the Calculations Automatic

If you set up the Sales Tax and Shipping & Handling fields to calculate their amounts, you need to edit the macro attached to the template that calculates the Subtotal and Total amounts when you enter items in the invoice. To make the Sales Tax and Shipping & Handling calculations automatic, take the following steps to edit the macro.

> **NOTE**

This section is in no way an introduction to editing macros. This section provides only very specific steps for editing a specific macro in a specific way. For information about working on macros, you need to consult *Microsoft Word 97/VB Step-by-Step*, by Mike Halvorson and Chris Kinata (Redmond: Microsoft Press, 1997).

1 Be sure the template form is not protected. If it is, choose the Tools Unprotect Document command.

2 Choose the Tools Macro command, and then choose Macros from the submenu.

3 Select Update_.MAIN.

4 Click Edit.

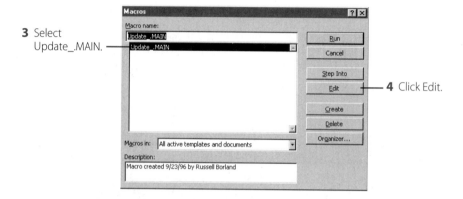

5 Insert apostrophes here.

6 Type these new lines here.

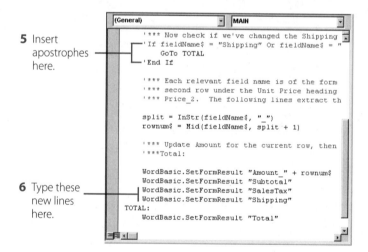

> **NOTE**
>
> This example assumes that you set up both the Sales Tax and Shipping & Handling fields to calculate their amounts.

7 Click Save.

8 If you haven't yet saved your new template, see "Protecting and Saving Your New Invoice Template," page 715.

9 Choose the File Close And Return To Microsoft Word command.

Issuing an Invoice

Now that you've created an invoice template for your organization, you're ready to start issuing invoices for goods and services you've supplied.

To create an invoice document, take these steps:

1 Choose the File New command.

2 Click the Other Documents tab.

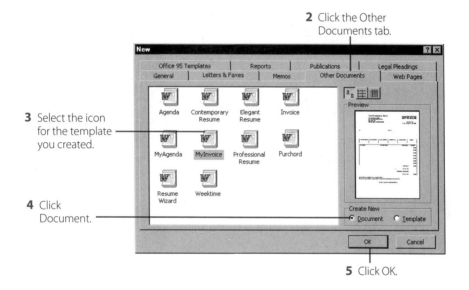

3 Select the icon for the template you created.

4 Click Document.

5 Click OK.

6 Type the invoice number, and press Tab.

If you aren't sure what field you're working on or what information you should enter, look at the status bar, where you'll see a message that describes what to enter in the current field.

7 Fill in the next field, and press Tab. Repeat this step until the invoice is filled out.

8 Save and print the invoice.

CHAPTER 16

Pleading Your Cause

Legal documents are very special animals. These documents have a special format and layout, and they contain features that you seldom find in any other kind of document. Among the unusual features you are likely to find in legal documents are special numbering schemes for the paragraphs, line numbering, citations of related cases, and a table of authorities, which collects all the citations into an organized list.

Using the Pleading Wizard

Word provides a Pleading Wizard to help you set up a legal document. And Word provides the tools you need to number paragraphs and lines, as well as to enter, control, and collect citations into a table of authorities.

To create a legal document, take these steps:

1 Choose the File New command.

2 Click the Legal Pleadings tab.

3 Click the Pleading Wizard icon.

4 Click Document.

5 Click OK.

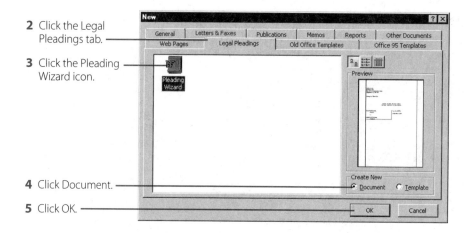

When the Pleading Wizard is ready for you to select your choices for task, court name, and other particulars, it displays the first panel, shown in Figure 16-1.

FIGURE 16-1.
The first panel of the Pleading Wizard.

Click these boxes to jump forward or backward through the Pleading Wizard.

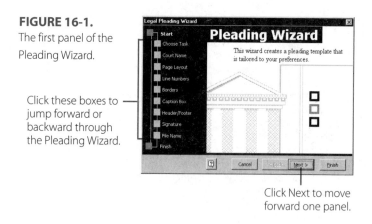

Click Next to move forward one panel.

As you work your way through the Pleading Wizard panels, you might decide that an earlier choice doesn't fit your needs. Click Back if you want to go back and choose a different style or different type or make other adjustments. The boxes along the left side of the Pleading Wizard show you which panels you have seen (dark gray), which panels you haven't yet seen (light gray), and the panel you're currently seeing (green square).

The following sections give you an overview of the types of decisions you face and the types of information you need to provide, as you work through the Pleading Wizard.

Choose Task

On the Choose Task panel of the Pleading Wizard, you use the steps shown here to select the task you want to perform.

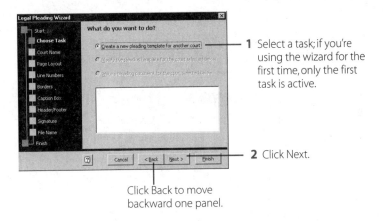

1 Select a task; if you're using the wizard for the first time, only the first task is active.

2 Click Next.

Click Back to move backward one panel.

The first time you use the Pleading Wizard, your only choice is Create A New Pleading Template For Another Court. After you create at least one pleading template, the other two choices become active the next time you run the Pleading Wizard—see "Preparing a Pleading," page 729.

Court Name

On the Court Name panel, you provide the name of the court for which this pleading template will be used to create court documents. You also select the alignment of the court name on court documents. Check existing court documents for the name and the alignment style.

TIP

If any text you type in the Pleading Wizard needs to appear as all uppercase letters on the pleading, be sure to type the text in all uppercase letters in the Pleading Wizard's boxes.

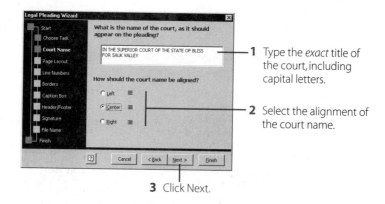

1 Type the *exact* title of the court, including capital letters.

2 Select the alignment of the court name.

3 Click Next.

The alignment of the court name is set relative to the margins of the document.

Page Layout

Many courts, especially higher courts such as courts of appeals and supreme courts, are very particular about the presentation of documents in cases heard before them. On the Page Layout panel, you select and set the style and measurements for page layout.

1 If the court requires or allows a different font, select it here.

2 Select the line spacing.

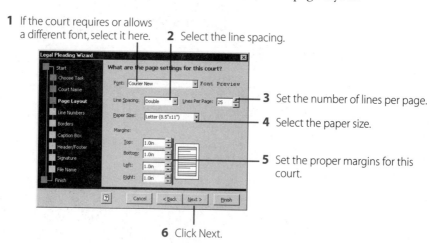

3 Set the number of lines per page.

4 Select the paper size.

5 Set the proper margins for this court.

6 Click Next.

Courier New is a standard font for court documents. It resembles typewriter print.

The Line Spacing and Lines Per Page boxes are connected. If you select Double line spacing, you can select between 25 and 40 lines per page. If you select 1.5 in the Line Spacing box, you can select between 30 and 50 lines per page. If you select Single, you can select between 50 and 70 lines per page. The choices for these settings are unaffected by the paper size you select or the margin settings.

The Pleading Wizard gives you three choices in the Paper Size box: 8.5" x 11" (standard letter paper), 8.5" x 14" (standard legal paper), and 8.27" x 11.69" (A4 paper).

Line Numbers

? SEE ALSO

For a complete rundown on line numbering, see "Numbering Lines," page 738.

The Pleading Wizard assumes that you want your legal document to have line numbers. On the Line Numbers panel, you decide whether to include or omit line numbers. If you decide to include line numbers, you select the line where you want the numbering to start and the starting number. You also select whether to increment the line numbers by 1 (every line is numbered—for single-spaced pleadings or double-spaced pleadings that require line numbers for the blanks between lines of text) or by 2 (every other line is numbered—for double-spaced pleadings that number only the lines of text).

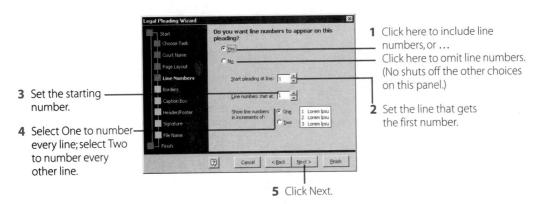

3 Set the starting number.

4 Select One to number every line; select Two to number every other line.

1 Click here to include line numbers, or …
Click here to omit line numbers. (No shuts off the other choices on this panel.)

2 Set the line that gets the first number.

5 Click Next.

If you want the body of the pleading to have line numbers but not the heading lines (court name, case, adjudicants, and so on), you'll want to start the line numbering at the first line of the pleading body.

Borders

Legal documents for different courts have different styles of borders along the edges of the pages. On the Borders panel, you select the border styles for the court.

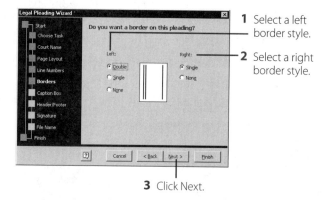

1 Select a left border style.

2 Select a right border style.

3 Click Next.

Caption Box

The caption box on a pleading lists the names of the adjudicants. On the Caption Box panel, you select a bordering style for the caption box.

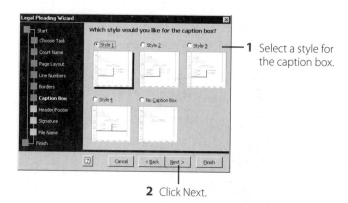

1 Select a style for the caption box.

2 Click Next.

The types of borders for each caption box option are as follows:

- Style 1 has a solid horizontal border under the left half of the caption box, with a centered vertical border made from right (or closing) parentheses.

- Style 2 has a solid horizontal border under the left half of the caption box, with a centered vertical border made from equal signs.

- Style 3 has a solid horizontal border under the left half of the caption box, with a centered solid vertical border.

- Style 4 has a solid horizontal border under both halves of the caption box, with a centered solid vertical border.

For some types of documents in some courts, you might not need a caption box. In this case, select No Caption Box.

Header/Footer

On the Header/Footer panel, you select the types of information you want in the headers and footers of the pages of the pleading document.

1 Turn on check boxes for information you want to include at the top of page 1; turn off check boxes to omit information.

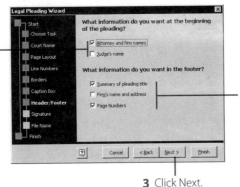

2 Turn on check boxes for information you want to include in the footers; turn off check boxes to omit information.

3 Click Next.

Signature

On the Signature panel you choose to include or omit a signature block. If you choose to include a signature block, you select a signature style and a position for the firm's name and address. You can also decide to include or omit the date in the signature block.

1 If you want a signature block, click Yes. If you don't, click No. (No shuts off the rest of the panel.)

3 Select a position for the firm's name and address.

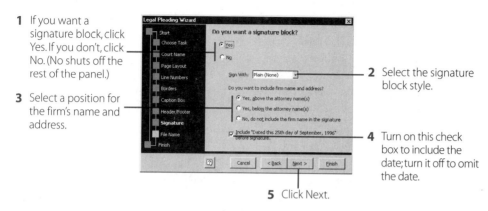

2 Select the signature block style.

4 Turn on this check box to include the date; turn it off to omit the date.

5 Click Next.

 NOTE

In the Sign With box, you can type text to be printed with the signature, such as Presented by.

File Name

You'll want to save the pleading template you've created here so that you can file pleadings with the court you named on the Court Name panel. The Pleading Wizard suggests the name of the court as the filename for the template. This can be a very long name. You can, of course, change the template name to any name that suits your purposes.

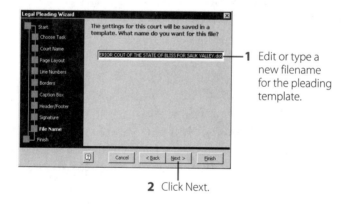

1 Edit or type a new filename for the pleading template.

2 Click Next.

At this point, you're at the Finish panel. Click Finish.

After you finish using the Pleading Wizard to set up a pleading template for a particular court, Word restarts the Pleading Wizard to help you set up a pleading document for that court. Its Start panel is shown in Figure 16-2. If you want to set up a pleading document later, click

IV

Forms

Cancel on the first panel of the Pleading Wizard. When you're ready to create a pleading document later, follow all the steps in the procedure in "Preparing a Pleading," below. If you want to set up a pleading document now, skip step 1 through step 5 and start with step 6.

FIGURE 16-2.
The Pleading Wizard's next Start panel. Notice the different panels in the box on the left.

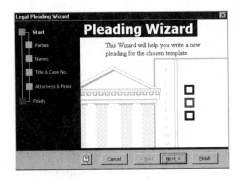

Preparing a Pleading

Once you have built a pleading template for a particular court, you are ready to create a court document. The Pleading Wizard can help you do that, too.

To create a court document, follow these steps:

1 Choose the File New command.

2 Click the Legal Pleadings tab.

3 Click the Pleading Wizard icon.

4 Click Document.

5 Click OK.

6 On the first panel of the Pleading Wizard, click Next.

 NOTE

If you're creating a pleading document directly after creating a pleading template, skip the rest of these steps and jump to the next section, "Parties."

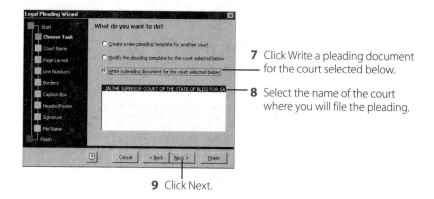

7 Click Write a pleading document for the court selected below.

8 Select the name of the court where you will file the pleading.

9 Click Next.

After step 9, the Pleading Wizard displays a new set of panels for creating a pleading document. These are discussed in the following sections. Note that if you create a document directly from one of the pleading templates (you select a pleading template instead of the Pleading Wizard in the File New dialog box), Word starts the Pleading Wizard for creating a pleading document.

Parties

On the Parties panel, you select the descriptions of the parties involved in the pleading.

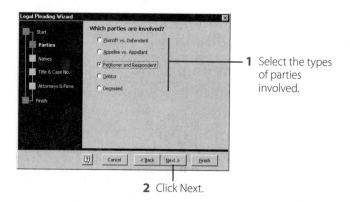

1 Select the types of parties involved.

2 Click Next.

Names

On the Names panel, you supply the names of the parties involved. The labels for the two boxes change to match the descriptions of the parties you selected on the Parties panel.

Forms

IV

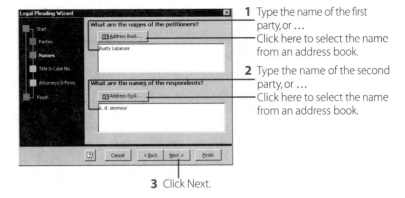

1 Type the name of the first party, or ...
Click here to select the name from an address book.

2 Type the name of the second party, or ...
Click here to select the name from an address book.

3 Click Next.

Title & Case No.

On the Title & Case No. panel, you enter the case number, the number of firms involved in filing this pleading, and the title and subtitle of the pleading.

1 Type case number if known; delete this number if the case number is not yet assigned.

4 Type the subtitle of the pleading, if any.

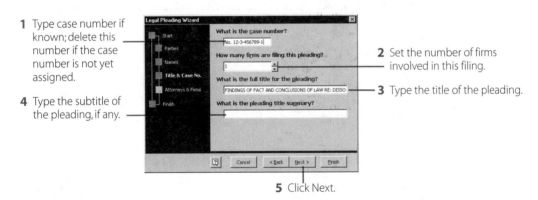

2 Set the number of firms involved in this filing.

3 Type the title of the pleading.

5 Click Next.

Attorneys & Firms

On the Attorneys & Firms panel, you type the names of the attorneys filing this pleading, and supply the firm's name and address. You can also add a line that reads "Attorneys for" and the description of the client—petitioner, plaintiff, defendant, respondent, and so on. You'll want to select the description that matches your choice on the Parties panel.

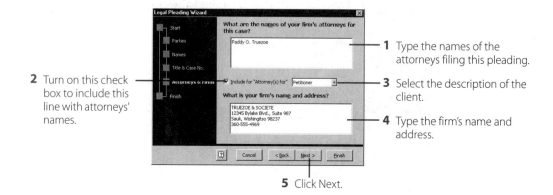

2 Turn on this check box to include this line with attorneys' names.

1 Type the names of the attorneys filing this pleading.

3 Select the description of the client.

4 Type the firm's name and address.

5 Click Next.

When you reach the Finish panel and click Finish, Word displays the pleading document, ready for you to add the text of the pleading. You also see the Legal Pleading toolbar.

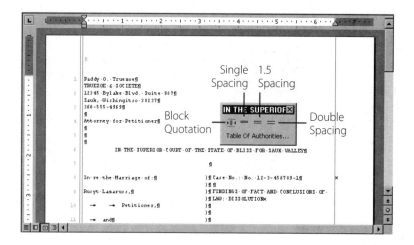

Setting Up Legal Numbering

Some legal documents have numbered sections. Some legal documents even have numbered paragraphs. In Word you can set up the legal numbering scheme you need for any particular legal document.

To set up a legal numbering scheme, follow these steps:

1 Choose the Format Bullets And Numbering command, and then click the Outline Numbered tab.

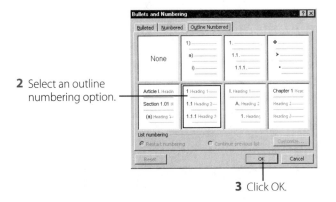

2 Select an outline numbering option.

3 Click OK.

After you use the Bullets And Numbering command, you'll find that the numbering schemes on the tabs might not contain the numbering scheme you want. If you don't see the Legal Style Numbering check box, take these additional steps:

1 On the Outline Numbered tab, select a numbering scheme that looks close to a legal numbering scheme, and then click the Customize button.

2 In the Customize Outlined Numbered List dialog box, click More.

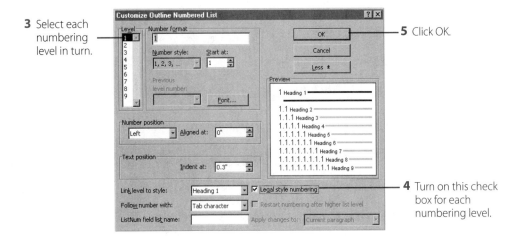

3 Select each numbering level in turn.

5 Click OK.

4 Turn on this check box for each numbering level.

When you turn on the Legal Style Numbering check box, Word makes all the numbers for every level appear as Arabic numerals, regardless of which numbering style was selected for that level. You'll notice that the Number Style box turns gray, indicating that you can't change the numbering style.

> NOTE

> In some cases, you might need an even more specialized numbering scheme for paragraphs or items within paragraphs. For these situations, see "Setting Up Special Numbering," opposite.

Numbering Paragraphs That Aren't Headings

If you want to number paragraphs that aren't headings with a level number, you can use the ListNum Field List Name box in the Customize Outline Numbered List dialog box. Suppose you want to number several paragraphs of text that share a style with paragraphs that you don't want to number. Take these steps:

1 Select the paragraphs you want to have the special numbers.

2 Choose the Format Bullets And Numbering command, and click the Outline Numbered tab.

3 Select any numbering scheme close to the one you want, and click the Customize button.

4 In the Customize Outline Numbered List dialog box, select the level of numbering you want in the Level box. Select the numbering style you want in the Number Style box.

5 In the Number Format box, add any characters you want before or after the number.

6 Click the More button.

7 In the ListNum Field List Name box, type a name.

8 Click OK.

Setting Up Special Numbering

In some cases, you might need a special numbering scheme for paragraphs or items within paragraphs. For these situations, you'll want to employ Word's ability to set up unusual numbering schemes. In one scheme, you can include multiple outline numbers on a single line. In another scheme, you can include numbered items in the middle of paragraphs. The next two sections explain how to set up these special schemes.

Using Multiple Outline Numbers on a Single Line

In an outline numbered list, you can include more than one numbering level on a single line. For example, if the list item is "A. 1)" or "Section 1.01 (a)," you can use the ListNum field for "1)" or "(a)" and any subsequent items on the same numbering level, as shown here:

Article·I. → Articles·want·to·be·free¶

Section·1.01·(a)·But·Writers·Want·to·be·Paid¶
(b)·And·editors·believe·they·deserve·all·the·credit¶

To create this type of numbering scheme, follow these steps:

1 Choose the Format Bullets And Numbering command, and then click the Outline Numbered tab.

2 Double-click the "Article I." list format.

3 Type the Article text you want, and press Enter.

4 To add "Section 1.01," select Heading 2 in the Style box (or press Alt+Ctrl+2).

5 To create the second outline level number on the same line—for example, (a)—choose the Insert Field command.

6 In the Categories box, click Numbering.

7 In the Field Names box, double-click ListNum.

8 Type the text for the list item, and then press Enter.

9 To insert the next number at the same level—for example, (b)—choose the Insert Field command, click Numbering in the Categories box, and then double-click ListNum in the Field Names box.

10 Click the Increase Indent button on the Formatting toolbar until the numbers are lined up vertically. If they don't line up vertically, slide the Left Indent marker on the ruler to line them up.

11 Type the text for the list item.

12 Repeat step 9 to continue numbering at this level.

 TIP

To change the number format—for example, from (a) to (i)—select the ListNum result, and then click the Increase Indent button or the Decrease Indent button.

Making ListNum Fields Handy

You can insert ListNum fields quickly by adding a button on the toolbar of your choice using these steps:

1 Choose the Tools Customize command, and click the Commands tab.

2 In the Categories box, click Insert.

3 In the Commands box, click Insert ListNum Field.

4 Drag the button to the toolbar you want to use.

For more information, see Appendix B, "Working with Toolbars."

Inserting Numbered Items in the Middle of Paragraphs

You've probably seen the style in which an author numbers sentences within paragraphs or numbers items within a sentence. Both styles are shown here:

Because·of·these·circumstances,·we·recommended·three·actions,·one·of·them·having·multiple·
steps.·1)·A·high-level·garden·mesh·should·be·installed·over·the·trees·to·lessen·the·impact·of·
untimely·heavy·rainfall.·2)·At·least·one·beehive·in·the·vicinity·of·(a)·the·yellow·plum,·(b)·the·
purple·plum,·and·(c)·the·yellow·Gravenstein.·3)·A·vertical·garden·mesh·should·be·set·up,·
possibly·tied·to·the·overhead·mesh,·to·reduce·the·brunt·of·the·prevailing·winds.¶

IV

Forms

Using a ListNum field, you can number these items automatically. That way, if you add or delete list items, Word automatically renumbers the list properly. To do this, you can use the steps listed in the previous section, "Using Multiple Outline Numbers on a Single Line," page 735. But if you want to number sentences with a particular format, or you want to number sentences with numbers and items with letters, you have to use the Seq field. The Seq field doesn't update its numbers automatically, but by pressing F9 you can get them to update properly.

To insert numbers in the middle of a paragraph, take these steps:

1 Position the insertion point where you want to insert the first number inside a paragraph.

2 Choose the Insert Field command.

3 Click Numbering.

5 Type a name for this sequence here.

4 Click Seq.

6 Click Options.

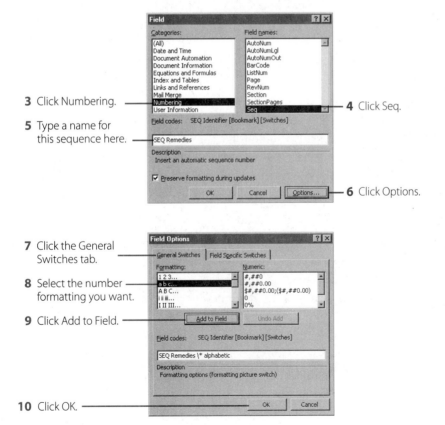

7 Click the General Switches tab.

8 Select the number formatting you want.

9 Click Add to Field.

10 Click OK.

11 Click OK in the Field dialog box.

12 If you want parentheses or brackets around the number to set it off from the text, type them.

13 Select the number and the characters you typed around it, if any, and then copy the selection to the Clipboard.

14 Type the text for the numbered item.

15 When you need another number in this sequence, paste it from the Clipboard.

16 Press Shift+F11 to select the field, and then press F9 to update the number.

17 Repeat step 14 through step 16 for additional items.

If you want to start another list that's not related, start over with these steps at step 1, but this time type a different name for the sequence in step 5.

Numbering Lines

For documents that require line numbers on some or all of the pages (such as contracts or legal documents), you can have Word automatically number lines. Word then prints a line number in the left margin beside each line or at an interval of lines that you select (such as every fifth line).

Because you can turn on and adjust line numbering for each section, you can also set up different line numbering schemes for different parts of a document. For example, you can number every line in one section and every fifth line in another section.

IV

Forms

To add line numbers to an entire document that has only one section, take these steps to turn on line numbering:

1 Choose the File Page Setup command.

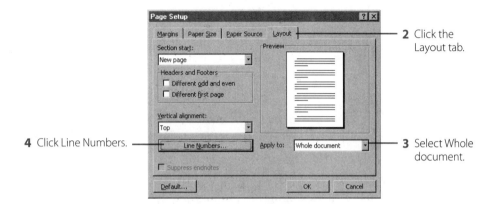

2 Click the Layout tab.

3 Select Whole document.

4 Click Line Numbers.

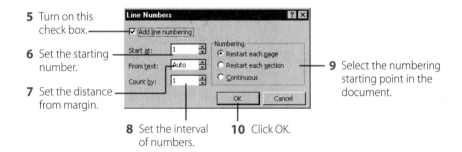

5 Turn on this check box.

6 Set the starting number.

7 Set the distance from margin.

8 Set the interval of numbers.

9 Select the numbering starting point in the document.

10 Click OK.

11 Click OK in the Page Setup dialog box.

To see the line numbers in a document, you must switch to Page Layout view or to Print Preview.

SEE ALSO

For more details of the choices in the Line Numbers dialog box, see "Setting Line Numbering Options," next page.

To print line numbers for only part of a document, you set that part aside in a separate section, and add line numbers to that section only. Here are the steps:

1 Select the part of the document you want to give line numbers.

2 Choose the File Page Setup command, and click the Layout tab.

3 In the Apply To box, select Selected Text.

4 Click Line Numbers.

5 In the Line Numbers dialog box, follow steps 5 through 11 in the previous procedure.

If your document has more than one section but you want line numbering for the entire document, first select Whole Document from the Apply To list on the Layout tab in the Page Setup dialog box, and then turn on line numbering.

> Line numbers appear beside lines of text, regardless of their line spacing or the space before or after a paragraph. Word displays a line number beside empty paragraphs, too.

Setting Line Numbering Options

When you click the Line Numbers button on the Layout tab in the Page Setup dialog box, the Line Numbers dialog box appears, as shown in Figure 16-3. Turn on the Add Line Numbering check box to activate the other options in the dialog box.

FIGURE 16-3.
The Line Numbers dialog box.

When you are numbering the lines of an entire document, the only option you need to set is the Add Line Numbering box. Making only this change in the Line Numbers dialog box sets numbers on every line and numbers the first line of every page as line number 1. Word gives you other choices.

Start At

In the Start At box, you select the starting line number for the starting point in the document you select in the Numbering section of the dialog box. The maximum starting number is 32,767. The minimum starting number is 1.

IV

Forms

From Text

In the From Text box, you indicate how far to the left of the left margin you want Word to print the line numbers. The standard setting, Auto, prints the line numbers about 0.25 inch left of the left margin. All the numbers are right aligned, so the From Text distance is to the right edge of the line numbers. You can select a distance as high as 22 inches, but for most situations, a distance more than 0.75 inch won't be practical. Printers need about 0.5 inch between the edge of the paper and the printed area, and a standard left margin of 1.25 inches leaves 0.75 inch (1.25 − 0.50 = 0.75).

 NOTE

> Word prints the numbers relative to the page margin, regardless of where the left paragraph indent places the subject matter. (The From Text box should probably be the From Margin box.) So what? If you set up a paragraph outdented into the left margin with line numbering turned on, Word prints the line number and the beginning of the first line on top of one another. If you simply must print a paragraph starting in the margin, you might want to turn off line numbering for that paragraph to avoid overprinting. See "Suppressing Enumeration," page 742, for details.

Count By

In the Count By box, you select the lines that will have numbers beside them. For example, if you want Word to number lines 5, 10, 15, ..., set the Count By box to 5. The highest Count By interval you can set is 100. Because most standard-size pages contain a maximum of about 70 lines (usually around 40–50 lines is more realistic), an interval higher than 5 or 10 is probably not useful to you.

Numbering

In the Numbering section of the Line Numbers dialog box, Word gives you three choices:

- You can start each page with the number set in the Start At box.

- You can start each section with the number in the Start At box.

- You can number the lines continuously and consecutively from the beginning of the document to the end, regardless of its length. If you select Continuous, Word will print the Start At number next to the first line of the document.

> **NOTE**

When you select a starting line number, you must also select one of two other compatible choices to get the effect you want. Assume, for example, that you want the second section of a document to begin with line number 35, even though the first section ends with line number 10. You set the Start At number to 35. Then you must either turn on the Restart Each Section option, or you must select a section start that starts on a new page. If the section start is Continuous and the Numbering option is Restart Each Page, the starting number of the section won't change. Likewise, regardless of the section start and the starting number, the Continuous Numbering option overrides the number you set in the Start At box, except when you select this choice for the first section of the document.

Suppressing Enumeration

So you have a document with line numbers. But wait just a minute! There is a paragraph here and another there that shouldn't have line numbers. How do you get rid of line numbers for the odd paragraph? Here's how:

1 Select the paragraph you don't want to have line numbers.

2 Choose the Format Paragraph command.

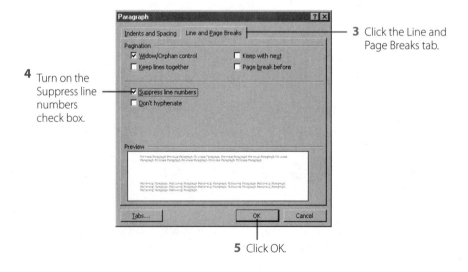

3 Click the Line and Page Breaks tab.

4 Turn on the Suppress line numbers check box.

5 Click OK.

IV

Forms

Word does not include the lines of paragraphs with suppressed line numbers in the line number count. The next line in the document with a line number has the next number in the sequence following the last line number before the paragraph with suppressed line numbers.

 **TIP**

> You can suppress line numbers, regardless of the paragraph style.

Inserting Citations

Many legal documents filed in plaintiff versus defendant cases include citations of precedent cases the attorneys deem relevant to the matters at hand. Word provides tools for inserting citations into a legal document and for later collecting these citations into a table of authorities. In Word, citations and a table of authorities are similar to index entries and an index. So it should not be surprising to you that the gateway to these tools is the Insert Index And Tables command.

To insert a citation, take these steps:

1 Position the insertion point where you want to insert a citation.

2 Type the citation into the document, and then select the citation.

3 Choose the Insert Index And Tables command.

4 Click the Table Of Authorities tab, and then click the Mark Citation button.

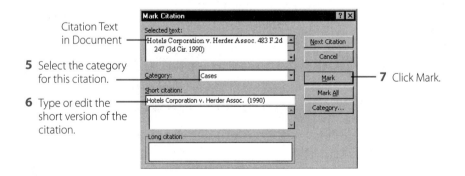

Citation Text in Document

5 Select the category for this citation.

6 Type or edit the short version of the citation.

7 Click Mark.

8 To mark any additional citation, click in the document, type and select the citation, click in the Mark Citation dialog box to reactivate it, and click the Mark button.

9 When you are through creating and marking citations, click the Close button in the Mark Citation dialog box.

Marking All Instances at Once

If a legal document repeats a citation at various places, you might want to mark all the citations at once. To do this, take these steps:

1 Insert a full citation at the first instance, and then insert a short citation at subsequent points.

2 Select the full citation.

3 Choose the Insert Index And Tables command.

4 Click the Table Of Authorities tab, and then click the Mark Citation button.

5 Select the category for this citation.

6 Type or edit the short version of the citation as it appears in the document.

7 Click Mark All.

Word marks the selected citation and all the short citations for inclusion in the table of authorities.

> **NOTE**
> The Mark All button finds and marks only short citations, not full citations.

Finding Citations: Next Citation Button

While the Mark Citation dialog box is open, you can jump from one citation to the next. To do so, take these steps:

1 Choose the Insert Index And Tables command.

2 Click the Table Of Authorities tab, and then click the Mark Citation button.

3 Select the category for this citation.

4 In the Short Citation box, select the short version of the citation as it appears in the document.

5 Click Next Citation. Repeat this step to see the next citation. At the end of the document, Word asks if you want to start at the beginning of the document. Click Yes to continue finding citations from the beginning of the document. Click No to stop searching.

 NOTE

Word uses the Edit Find command to find the citations, both for the Next Citation button and for the Mark All button. If you choose the Edit Find command, you'll see the short citation shown as the Find What text.

Setting Up New Categories

The Category box in the Mark Citation dialog box lists 16 categories for you to choose from. Categories 1–7 are named; categories 8–16 are numbers only. The named categories are listed here:

Category Number	Category Name
1	Cases
2	Statutes
3	Other Authorities
4	Rules
5	Treatises
6	Regulations
7	Constitutional Provisions

You can change these category names and give categories 8–16 names in place of their numbers. (You probably will want to limit changes of name to categories 8–16.)

To change a category name, take these steps:

1 If the Mark Citation dialog box is not open, press Alt+Shift+I to open it.

2 In the Mark Citation dialog box, click the Category button.

3 Select the category name or number you want to change.

4 Type the new name for the category.

5 Click Replace.

6 Repeat steps 3 through 5 for any other category you want to rename.

7 When you're done renaming categories, click OK.

8 If you want to mark a citation with this new category, do so now (use the steps in "Inserting Citations, page 743). If not, click Close in the Mark Citation dialog box.

Collecting a Table of Authorities

After you finish inserting all the citations that apply to the matters before the court in a case, you're ready to collect the citations into a table of authorities.

To collect a table of authorities, take these steps:

1 Place the insertion point where you want to insert the table of authorities.

2 Choose the Insert Index And Tables command, or click the Table of Authorities button on the Legal Pleading toolbar.

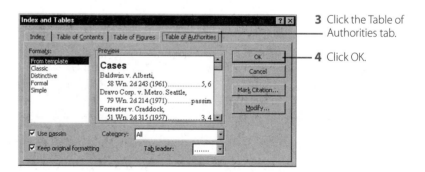

3 Click the Table of Authorities tab.

4 Click OK.

Word inserts a table of authorities.

You have a number of other choices for the look of a table of authorities, as explained in the following sections.

Selecting the Look of a Table of Authorities

The Formats box on the Table Of Authorities tab of the Index And Tables dialog box lists four preset looks for the table of authorities, plus one look you can fiddle with. Note that for some of the looks in the Formats list, Word changes settings in the bottom of the dialog box. You can see the effect of these changes in the Preview box.

Sort by Category

You can collect a single table of authorities that includes all the citations grouped into their categories. You can also collect a table of authorities that contains only one category of citation. In this way, you could insert a table of authorities for each category at different places in a document.

- To collect all citations into one list, select All in the Category box.

- To collect only one category of citations, select that category in the Category box.

If you changed the name of any category (see "Setting Up New Categories," page 745), the new name appears in the Category box. If, for example, you renamed category 8 as Public Records, Public Records appears in the Category box in place of 8.

Use Passim

Usually, Word puts the page numbers at the end of the table of authorities entry. If a citation appears more than five times in a document with the Use Passim check box turned on, Word substitutes *passim* for the page numbers. If you prefer to list all the page numbers instead of using *passim*, turn off the Use Passim check box.

Keep Original Formatting

Citations can have complex formatting, with some parts in italics and others underlined or in boldface. When Word collects a table of authorities, the formatting of the citation is kept intact in the citation that appears in the table of authorities. If you want to format the citations in the table of authorities differently or if you want to remove the special formatting from citations, turn off the Keep Original

Formatting check box. Leave it on to preserve the original formatting of the citations in the text.

Insert a Tab Leader

Word puts the page numbers at the end of the table of authorities entry, with a tab between the end of an entry and its page number. Word also selects the period tab leader. A tab leader is a series of characters that fills the space taken by the tab. You can select a different tab leader in the Tab Leader box. See Table 14-1, page 672, for a list of your choices and examples of the leader characters.

Adjusting Styles in a Table of Authorities

In the Index And Tables dialog box, the Formats box on the Table Of Authorities tab lists the item From Template. When you select From Template, Word uses the Table of Authorities and TOA Heading styles as set up in the document template of the document you are working on. From Template is the only choice that gives you a way to change these two styles directly from the Index And Tables dialog box.

When you select From Template in the Formats list, Word activates the Modify button. Click the Modify button to have Word display the Style dialog box with only the Table of Authorities and TOA Heading styles in the Styles list, as shown in Figure 16-4. Word uses the Table of Authorities style to format the citation entries in the table of authorities and the TOA Heading style to format the category names that appear in the table of authorities.

FIGURE 16-4.

The Style dialog box for a From Template table of authorities.

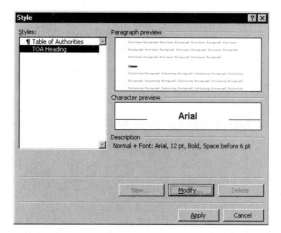

To set up a custom table of authorities, perform these steps:

1 Choose the Insert Index And Tables command, and click the Table Of Authorities tab.

2 Select From Template in the Formats list, and then click the Modify button.

3 Select the style you want to change.

4 Click Modify.

5 In the Modify Style dialog box, make changes to the style, and click OK.

6 Repeat steps 3 and 4 for the other table of authorities' styles you want to change, and then click Apply in the Style dialog box.

7 Make any other changes you want to make in the Index And Tables dialog box, and then click OK to insert your custom table of authorities.

CHAPTER 17

Submitting Résumés

Well, you've gone and done it. You've studied this book and become a Word guru. (You now know almost as much about Word as I do.) And now there's a job opportunity where you can put your Word skills to full use. To get that job, you need to submit a résumé. Word provides a Résumé Wizard, which you can use to set up a professional-looking résumé. Of course, you'll still have to supply the details, but making your résumé look good is an important first step.

Conjuring the Résumé Wizard

Because a résumé changes little over time and because you'll seldom create a résumé (at least one assumes so), creating a document template for a résumé is probably not the best approach. Conjuring Word's Résumé Wizard when you need to create a résumé is a much more flexible approach. Especially if you need to radically redesign it, you'll want the tools the Résumé Wizard can bring to the job.

To create a résumé document, take these steps:

1 Choose the File New command.

2 Click the Other Documents tab.

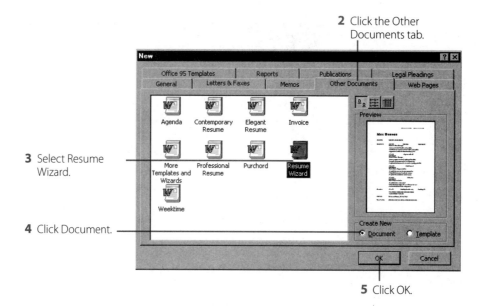

3 Select Resume Wizard.

4 Click Document.

5 Click OK.

When the Résumé Wizard is ready for you to select your choices for style, type, and particulars, you see the first panel, shown on the following page.

As you work your way through the Résumé Wizard panels, you might decide that an earlier choice doesn't fit your needs. You might want to go back and choose a different style or different type or make other adjustments. The boxes along the left side of the Résumé Wizard show you which panels you have seen (dark gray), which panels you haven't yet seen (light gray), and the panel you're currently seeing (green square).

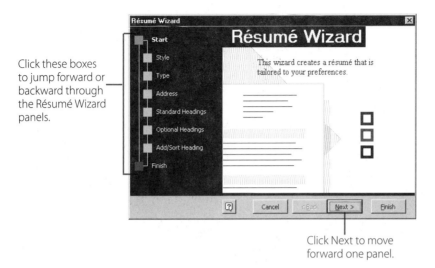

Click these boxes to jump forward or backward through the Résumé Wizard panels.

Click Next to move forward one panel.

The following sections give you an overview of the types of decisions you face and the types of information you need to provide.

Style

On the Style panel of the Résumé Wizard, you have your choice of three styles for a résumé: Professional, Contemporary, and Elegant, as shown here:

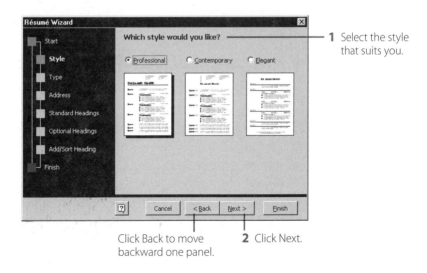

1 Select the style that suits you.

Click Back to move backward one panel.

2 Click Next.

The main differences are the positions of your name and address and the formatting of the headings.

If You Change Your Mind About the Style

You can change the style at any time while you're working your way through the Résumé Wizard panels. Simply click the Style box in the Résumé Wizard map, which appears along the left side of each panel. You can then quickly jump back to the next panel you need to work on by clicking its label in the Résumé Wizard map. You can also change the style after you finish with the Résumé Wizard by displaying the Office Assistant and clicking the Change Visual Style Of The Résumé button in the Office Assistant balloon.

Type

The Résumé Wizard gives you four choices for the type of résumé, as shown here:

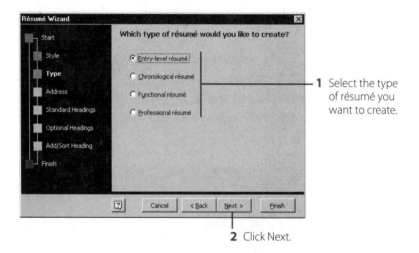

1 Select the type of résumé you want to create.

2 Click Next.

Your choice on this panel affects the choices Résumé Wizard shows you for the Standard Headings and Optional Headings panels. When you get to those panels, you'll see that the Résumé Wizard automatically selects only certain standard headings—the ones that typically fit the type of résumé you've chosen on the third panel. Your choice here also affects the order the Résumé Wizard proposes for the categories of information in the résumé document.

At this point in the Résumé Wizard, you have two choices of strategy:

- Don't worry about it; simply select one of the types and move on. You can later add categories and move them around on the Add/Sort Heading panel.

- Select one of the higher-level types (Chronological, Functional, or Professional). You can later remove categories and move them around on the Add/Sort Heading panel.

To help you decide which type to choose, consult Table 17-1, page 756, which lists the standard headings for each type of résumé. You can also consult Table 17-2, page 757, for the lists of optional headings the Résumé Wizard displays for each type of résumé.

Address

The Address panel in the Résumé Wizard displays boxes where you type your name, address, phone number, fax number, and e-mail address. Word fills in the Name and Address boxes from the User Information tab of the Tools Options dialog box. You can, of course, change any of the information as needed.

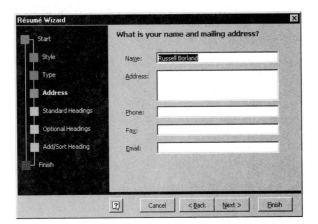

This panel is the same for every style and type of résumé you can select in the Résumé Wizard.

Standard Headings

On the Standard Headings panel of the Résumé Wizard, you see a list of what Microsoft designers consider the standard categories of information you'll most likely put in a résumé of the type you chose on the Type panel. For some types, the choices are similar but the order is changed slightly. Table 17-1 shows the lists and order for each type. Standard heading names in boldface in Table 17-1 are the ones the Résumé Wizard automatically selects for each type. You can turn off and turn on any of the headings listed.

Optional Headings

On the Optional Headings panel of the Résumé Wizard, you see a list of what Microsoft designers consider the optional categories of information you'll most likely put in a résumé of the type you chose on the Type panel. For some types, the choices are similar but the order is changed slightly. Table 17-2 shows the lists and order for each type. You can turn on any of the headings listed.

TABLE 17-1.   Standard Headings Lists for Each Type of Résumé.

Entry-Level	Chronological	Functional	Professional
Objective	**Objective**	**Objective**	Summary of Qualifications
Education	Summary of Qualifications	Functional Summary	**Education**
Awards Received	**Work Experience**	**Employ-ment**	**Professional Experience**
Interests and Activities	**Education**	**Education**	Patents and Publications
Languages	Extracurricular Activities	References	Additional Professional Activities
Work Experience	Accreditations		Professional Memberships
Volunteer Experience	Professional Memberships		Languages
Hobbies	Community Activities		Community Activities
References	References		References

TABLE 17-2.   Optional Headings Lists for Each Type of Résumé.

Entry-Level	Chronological	Functional	Professional
Extracurricular Activities	Interests and Activities	Summary of Qualifications	Objective
Summer Jobs	Volunteer Experience	Accreditations	Extracurricular Activities
Summary of Qualifications	Patents and Publications	Professional Memberships	Accreditations
Community Activities	Languages	Volunteer Experience	Hobbies
Professional Memberships	Security Clearance	Patents and Publications	Interests and Activities
Accreditations and Licenses	Civil Service Grades	Languages	Volunteer Experience
Patents and Publications	Awards Received	Security Clearance	Security Clearance
Civil Service Grades	Hobbies	Civil Service Grades	Civil Service Grades
Security Clearance		Awards Received	Awards Received

Add/Sort Heading

When you arrive at the Add/Sort Heading panel of the Résumé Wizard, you'll see a list of the standard and optional headings you selected on those two panels. On the Add/Sort Heading panel, you can add any heading that you think is missing, and you can rearrange the order of the headings to suit you. The order of the headings is the order in which the Résumé Wizard sets up the categories in the résumé document. A sample of the Add/Sort Heading panel for a Professional résumé with only the preselected standard headings is shown on the next page.

Type a new heading here, and then ...
Click here to add the new heading.

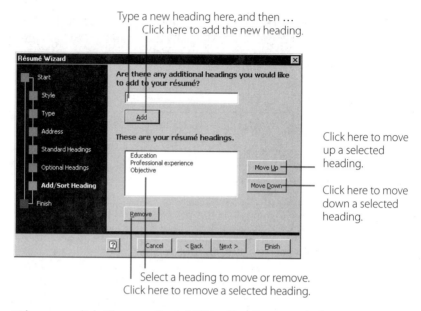

Click here to move up a selected heading.

Click here to move down a selected heading.

Select a heading to move or remove.
Click here to remove a selected heading.

When you click Next on the Add/Sort Heading panel, the Résumé Wizard displays the Finish panel. If you want to change any choices or information on any panel, click the panel's title in the Résumé Wizard map along the left side of the Finish panel, or click the Back button until you arrive at the panel you want to change.

Checking In with the Office Assistant

After you click the Finish button in the Résumé Wizard, Word sets up the résumé document according to your choices and information. Word also displays the Office Assistant, which gives you a list of topics that can help you with your résumé, as shown in Figure 17-1.

Two of these topics should be very useful to you: Add A Cover Letter and Send Résumé To Someone. You'll find a discussion of the cover letter next. You'll find a discussion of Send Résumé To Someone in "Sending Your Résumé to Someone," page 761.

Adding a Cover Letter

A cover letter for a résumé can help you present yourself better than a résumé alone. In a cover letter, you can highlight points you want to emphasize, you can tailor your presentation to the job requirements and advertisement, and you can include additional information or details that don't fit well into the résumé structure.

FIGURE 17-1.

A résumé document set up by the Résumé Wizard with the Office Assistant open.

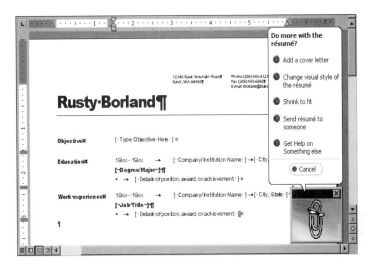

To add a cover letter to your résumé, follow these steps:

1 If the Office Assistant isn't open, click the Office Assistant button on the Standard toolbar.

Office Assistant

2 Click Add a cover letter.

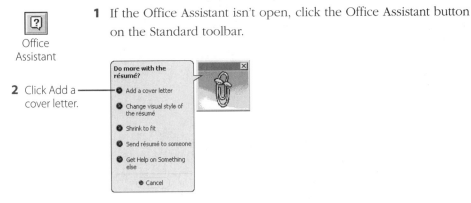

3 Word sets up a letter with sample content. The sample letter also contains your name and address, plus a complimentary closing and your name. You have several choices of what to do next:

- Fill in the name of the addressee and print or send the letter. This choice probably isn't the one you want unless the sample letter fits you to a *T*.

- Fill in the name of the addressee, edit the letter's contents, and print or send the letter.

- Close the cover letter window and don't save it. Then choose the Tools Letter Wizard command and create your own letter. See Chapter 3, "Enlisting the Letter Wizard," for information about the Letter Wizard.

- Close the cover letter window and don't save it. Then create a cover letter on your own.

If you're sending a printed copy of your résumé and cover letter through the mail, remember that after you finish the cover letter and résumé, you can choose the Tools Envelopes And Labels command to help you set up an envelope. See Chapter 4, "Setting Up and Printing Envelopes and Labels," for information about the Envelopes And Labels command.

Adding More Spaces for Education, Jobs, and Other Stuff

Show/Hide

The Résumé Wizard sets up a résumé in a table. To see this clearly, turn on the Show/Hide button on the Standard toolbar. Also turn on table gridlines by choosing the Table Show Gridlines command. With these two commands turned on, you'll see the table structure very clearly.

You'll have noticed by now that the Résumé Wizard sets up only one space (one table row) for each category of information. Unless you attended only one school, held only one job, or have only one reference to list, one space isn't enough.

To add more spaces for additional listings in any category, follow these steps:

1 Select the row *below* the category to which you want to add space.

2 Choose the Table Insert Rows command.

3 Repeat steps 1 and 2 for each additional space you want to add.

4 Position the insertion point in the first column of the category to which you just added rows, and then press Tab to jump into and select the contents of the second column. This second column contains a structure for each entry in the category.

5 Press Ctrl+C to copy the cell's contents to the Clipboard.

6 Press the ↓ key to move down to the next row in the second column, and then press Ctrl+V to paste the Clipboard contents into the cell. This cell now has the structure for the entry.

7 Repeat step 6 for each entry space in the category.

8 Repeat steps 4 through 7 for each category.

Adding Your Information to the Résumé

When you have the structure of the résumé set up, you're ready to add your information to it. To fill in the résumé entries, click each label and type the appropriate information.

The labels for the information are special fields that Word selects when you click them.

Sending Your Résumé to Someone

Because you're clued in to the electronic phenomena of networks, Web, and faxes, you have several ways to send your résumé:

- You can print the résumé, a cover letter, and an envelope, and send them through the mail.

- You can send your résumé and cover letter via fax. This method can be handy if you have a fax modem installed in your computer. This method depends on the addressee having a fax machine or fax-receptive computer.

- You can send your résumé and cover letter via e-mail. This method depends on the addressee having an e-mail account you can reach.

When you create a résumé with the Résumé Wizard, the Office Assistant provides a list of more things you can do with your résumé. If the Office Assistant isn't open, click the Office Assistant button on the

Standard toolbar. Now click Send Résumé To Someone, and you'll see the following dialog box:

1 Click the transport method you want to use. —————

2 Click OK. ————

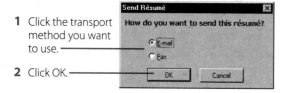

If you select E-mail, Word starts your mail program (if it's not running already), and sets up a new message with Résumé as the subject and your résumé document in the body of the message. You simply address the message and send it.

If you select Fax, Word starts the Fax Wizard, where you can set up and send a fax of your résumé. For information about the Fax Wizard and about sending faxes from Word, see Chapter 6, "Investigating the Fax."

CHAPTER 18

Creating Your Own Business Forms

F orms are an everyday part of business life, and they often crop up in personal life too. As you know, a form contains blank areas to be filled in. In a Microsoft Word document, you set up those areas with special fields so that you can easily fill in the form on your computer. Word has three kinds of form fields you can use for designing forms.

- Text form fields—blanks to be filled in

- Check box form fields—boxes to be marked

- Drop-down form fields—lists to choose from

You can set up a grid form, such as a registration form, by building a table that contains form fields. Or you can set up a text form, such as a contract, that has fill-in blanks, check boxes, and lists scattered throughout regular text.

After you design a form and save it, you can print the form so that you, or other people, can fill it out by hand or on a computer. When someone fills out a form on the computer, the completed form can be printed either on plain paper or on a pre-printed form. You can save a completed form, with or without the form structure, for use as a data document in mail merging or as a database file.

Designing a Form

Designing a form is fairly straightforward. To design a form, perform these steps:

1 Decide which type of form you want, and then build a document template (not a document!) that contains the form's structure.

2 Decide what types of form fields you need. For each form field, you can set the size, set standard values, determine the type of information a user will enter, create Help text, and assign macros that will run when the user enters or exits the field.

3 Protect the template and save it.

> **NOTE**
>
> Form *fields* are mainly for forms that someone will fill out on a computer. Form blanks are part of all printed forms. Both computer and printed forms have check boxes to mark. But no printed form has a drop-down list. In addition, all the form fields have some options that make sense only when someone is filling out the form on a computer. Keep this in mind as you read about each type of form field and its options.

SEE ALSO

You can find files on the CD included with this book to help you create a grid form and a text form, as well as files for the two types of forms. Consult GRIDFORM.DOC for directions on creating a grid form template. Consult GRID-FORM.DOT for a sample grid form template. Consult TEXTFORM.DOC for directions on creating a text form template. Consult TEXTFORM.-DOT for a sample text form template.

Designing the Form's Structure

The first step in designing your form is to build a new document template. To do so, perform these steps:

1 Choose the File New command, and click the General tab.

2 Select the Blank Document template, select the Template option, and click OK. This creates a new template based on the Normal template. You'll usually want the new template to be based on this blank template to avoid including the extra information and special formatting contained in other templates.

3 Choose the File Properties command, and click the Summary tab in the Template Properties dialog box.

4 Type a descriptive name for the form in the Title box, turn on the Save Preview Picture check box, and click OK.

By turning on the Save Preview Picture check box you make it possible to see a preview of the form in the New dialog box when you or other users of your form are picking a form to fill out.

You are now ready to lay out the form. Before you start your layout, turn on the Forms toolbar—right-click any toolbar or the menu, and then select Forms from the shortcut menu. The Forms toolbar is shown in Figure 18-1.

FIGURE 18-1.
The Forms toolbar.

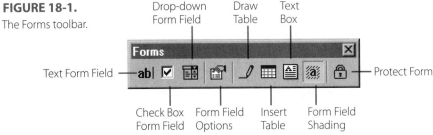

Putting a Text Form Field in Place

You plant a text form field where you want the user to fill in a blank. Use the following steps to plant a text form field:

1 Click the Text Form Field button on the Forms toolbar.

2 Click the Form Field Options button. The Text Form Field Options dialog box appears:

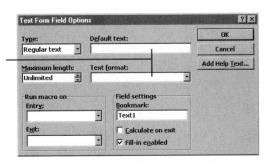

The names of these boxes change with the selected Type option.

3 Select the type of text form field. (See Table 18-1, next page.)

4 Type the default response that will appear in the field when someone uses the form.

TABLE 18-1. **Choices for the Type of Text Form Field.**

Type	Used For
Regular Text	General—all words, numbers, or symbols
Number	Numbers only
Date	Dates only
Current Date	Inserts the current date when you create a new form from the template
Current Time	Inserts the current time when you create a new form from the template
Calculation	Calculates a number from the formula you insert

5 Set the maximum number of characters you'll allow in a response, or select Unlimited.

6 Select the look (Text Format option) you want for the response. (See Table 18-2.)

7 Turn on the Fill-In Enabled check box to let people fill in the blank. Turn it off to prevent people from filling in a different response.

8 Click OK.

 NOTE

Someone filling in the form on a computer won't be able to fill in the blank until you protect your form template. See "Protecting Your Form," page 773.

Default Response

On the computer, default text, number, or date is not permanent; it can be changed or replaced. Set up the default entry when you know in advance what most people will usually type—a year or state, for example. This saves time and effort and ensures that the entry will be correct. If you select Calculation for the type, type a mathematical expression in the Expression box. (For information about mathematical expressions, see "Calculating Tables," page 353.) If you leave this box blank, the text form field appears as a blank in the form. You cannot enter anything in this box if you select Current Date or Current Time in the Type box.

TABLE 18-2. **Text Form Field Types and Their Looks.**

Type	Format	Example
Regular Text	Uppercase	MICROSOFT
	Lowercase	units
	First Capital	Fuzzy wuzzy
	Title Case	Over The Hill Gags
Number, Calculation	0	8
	0.00	8.58
	#,##0	5,858
	#,##0.00	5,858.58
	$#,##0.00; ($#,##0.00)	$5,858.58 or ($5,858.58)
	0%	58%
	0.00%	8.58%
Date, Current Date	M/d/yy	3/6/97
	dddd, MMMM dd, yyyy	Thursday, March 06, 1997
	MMMM d, yyyy	March 6, 1997
	M/d/yyyy	3/6/1997
	yyyy-MM-dd	1997-03-06
	d-MMM-yy	6-Mar-97
	M.d.yy	3.6.97
	MMM. d, yy	Mar. 6, 97
	d MMMM, yyyy	6 March, 1997
	MMMM, yy	March, 97
	MMM-yy	Mar-97
Current Time (also available for Date and Current Date)	M/d/yy h:mm am/pm	03/06/97 6:09 pm
	M/d/yy h:mm:ss am/pm	03/06/97 6:09:06 pm
	h:mm am/pm	6:09 pm
	h:mm:ss am/pm	6:09:06 pm
	HH:mm	18:09
	HH:mm:ss	18:09:06

Fill-In Enabled Box

If you select Current Date, Current Time, or Calculation in the Type box, you cannot turn on the Fill-In Enabled box.

Turning Check Boxes On or Off

You might want check boxes for "yes" or "no" answers in your form. For a form that people will fill out on a computer, you can decide whether the check box will be turned on or off when someone starts filling in the form. A turned-on check box in a form contains an X; a turned-off check box is a blank box. For forms that will be printed, you can use a check box form field as an empty box (turned off) that the user can mark with a pen or pencil.

To insert a check box form field, use these steps:

1 Display the Forms toolbar.

2 Click the Check Box Form Field button.

3 Click the Form Field Options button. Word displays the Check Box Form Field Options dialog box, shown in Figure 18-2.

FIGURE 18-2.
The Check Box
Form Field Options
dialog box.

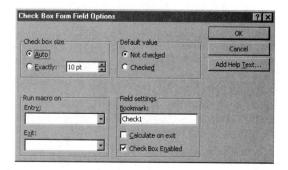

4 Set a size for the check box. Most often, you'll want the Auto option. This option sets a check box that is the same size as the text to the left of the check box form field (just as if you had inserted a character). If you prefer a check box that is larger or smaller than the text around it, turn on the Exactly option and set a size in the box to the right.

? SEE ALSO

For information about the Run Macro On boxes in any of the Form Field Options dialog boxes, see "Attaching Macros to a Form," page 772.

5 Select whether the check box will be checked (on) or not checked (off) when the form is first used. Turn on the Not Checked option for an empty box. Turn on the Checked option if you want the check box to show an X.

6 Turn on the Check Box Enabled box to let people turn the check box on or off. To keep the check box always turned on or always turned off, turn off the Check Box Enabled check box to prevent changes.

7 Click OK to insert the check box form field in the form.

TABLE 18-2. **Text Form Field Types and Their Looks.**

Type	Format	Example
Regular Text	Uppercase Lowercase First Capital Title Case	MICROSOFT units Fuzzy wuzzy Over The Hill Gags
Number, Calculation	0 0.00 #,##0 #,##0.00 $#,##0.00; ($#,##0.00) 0% 0.00%	8 8.58 5,858 5,858.58 $5,858.58 or ($5,858.58) 58% 8.58%
Date, Current Date	M/d/yy dddd, MMMM dd, yyyy MMMM d, yyyy M/d/yyyy yyyy-MM-dd d-MMM-yy M.d.yy MMM. d, yy d MMMM, yyyy MMMM, yy MMM-yy	3/6/97 Thursday, March 06, 1997 March 6, 1997 3/6/1997 1997-03-06 6-Mar-97 3.6.97 Mar. 6, 97 6 March, 1997 March, 97 Mar-97
Current Time (also available for Date and Current Date)	M/d/yy h:mm am/pm M/d/yy h:mm:ss am/pm h:mm am/pm h:mm:ss am/pm HH:mm HH:mm:ss	03/06/97 6:09 pm 03/06/97 6:09:06 pm 6:09 pm 6:09:06 pm 18:09 18:09:06

Fill-In Enabled Box

If you select Current Date, Current Time, or Calculation in the Type box, you cannot turn on the Fill-In Enabled box.

Turning Check Boxes On or Off

You might want check boxes for "yes" or "no" answers in your form. For a form that people will fill out on a computer, you can decide whether the check box will be turned on or off when someone starts filling in the form. A turned-on check box in a form contains an X; a turned-off check box is a blank box. For forms that will be printed, you can use a check box form field as an empty box (turned off) that the user can mark with a pen or pencil.

To insert a check box form field, use these steps:

1 Display the Forms toolbar.

2 Click the Check Box Form Field button.

3 Click the Form Field Options button. Word displays the Check Box Form Field Options dialog box, shown in Figure 18-2.

FIGURE 18-2.
The Check Box
Form Field Options
dialog box.

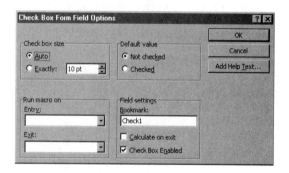

4 Set a size for the check box. Most often, you'll want the Auto option. This option sets a check box that is the same size as the text to the left of the check box form field (just as if you had inserted a character). If you prefer a check box that is larger or smaller than the text around it, turn on the Exactly option and set a size in the box to the right.

5 Select whether the check box will be checked (on) or not checked (off) when the form is first used. Turn on the Not Checked option for an empty box. Turn on the Checked option if you want the check box to show an X.

6 Turn on the Check Box Enabled box to let people turn the check box on or off. To keep the check box always turned on or always turned off, turn off the Check Box Enabled check box to prevent changes.

7 Click OK to insert the check box form field in the form.

? SEE ALSO

For information about the Run Macro On boxes in any of the Form Field Options dialog boxes, see "Attaching Macros to a Form," page 772.

> **NOTE**

Someone filling in the form on a computer won't be able to mark the check box until you protect your form template. See "Protecting Your Form," page 773.

Making Drop-Down Lists

A drop-down form field provides a list of choices to a person filling out the form on a computer. This field limits the choices only to those you put in the list. People can't type in a drop-down form field; they can only select from the list, which can contain up to 25 choices. The first choice in the list is the choice you see when you first see the form.

Here are the steps to insert a drop-down form field:

1   Display the Forms toolbar.

2   Click the Drop-Down Form Field button.

3   Click the Form Field Options button. The Drop-Down Form Field Options dialog box shown in Figure 18-3 appears.

FIGURE 18-3.
The Drop-Down Form Field Options dialog box.

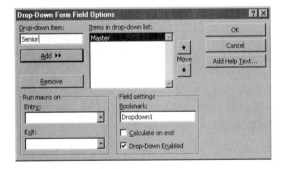

4   In the Drop-Down Item box, type a choice (up to 50 characters) that you want in the list, and then click the Add button below the box. Word adds the choice to the Items In Drop-Down List box. To add another choice, repeat this step. You can add up to 25 items to the list. To remove a choice from the list, select it in the Items In Drop-Down List box and click the Remove button.

5   If you prefer, rearrange the order of the choices. As you construct the list, you might add choices as you think of them rather than in the order you want them in the list. You can arrange the list in any order you like: alphabetic, chronological, most common

entries to least common, random, or any other order. To move a choice to a different place in the list, select the item. Click the up arrow above the Move label to move the selected choice one position higher in the list; click the down arrow below the Move label to move the selected choice down one position. Remember that the first choice in the list appears in the form when a user first sees the form.

6 Turn on the Drop-Down Enabled check box to let people choose from the list. To display only the first item from the list and prevent the user from displaying the full list, turn off the Drop-Down Enabled box.

7 Click OK to insert the drop-down form field into the form.

> Someone filling in the form on a computer can't use the list until you protect your form template. See "Protecting Your Form," page 773.

Setting Up Help for Form Users

To help people who are filling out forms, you can add Help for each form field. You can decide whether the Help should appear automatically in the status bar when a user enters the form field or whether it should appear only when the user presses the Help key (F1). Help that appears only when someone presses F1 appears in a message box rather than in the status bar.

> Help for a form field appears only after you protect your form template. See "Protecting Your Form," page 773.

To add Help to a form field, you must open the Options dialog box for the form field. To open the Options dialog box, do one of the following:

■ Click the Form Field Options button on the Forms toolbar after you insert a form field.

■ Double-click a form field in the document template.

IV

Forms

- Select a form field in the document template, click the right mouse button, and choose the Properties command from its shortcut menu.

- Select a form field in the document template, and click the Form Field Options button on the Forms toolbar.

To add Help to a form field, use these steps:

1 Choose the Add Help Text button in one of the three Form Field Options dialog boxes. The Form Field Help Text dialog box, shown in Figure 18-4, appears for all three types of fields, but the Help you add appears only for the selected form field.

FIGURE 18-4.
The Form Field Help Text dialog box.

2 Click the tab for the type of Help you want to add. To add Help in the status bar, click the Status Bar tab in the dialog box. To add Help to the F1 key, click the Help Key (F1) tab.

3 Select a source for Help text: None, AutoText Entry, or Type Your Own. For AutoText Entry, select the name of the AutoText entry that contains the Help you want to add to the form field. For Type Your Own, type the Help you want to add to the form field. For more details on these sources, see the following three sections.

4 Click OK in the Form Field Help Text dialog box, and then click OK in the Form Field Options dialog box.

None Option

Select the None option when you don't want to add Help or when you want to remove Help from a form field.

AutoText Entry Option

Select the AutoText Entry option when you want Help to come from AutoText. AutoText is especially helpful when several form fields can use the same Help or when you want to use Help for several form templates. (You can easily copy AutoText entries between templates with the Organizer dialog box. See "Sharing Elements Between Templates," page 862.)

After you select the AutoText Entry option in the Form Field Help Text dialog box, select the name of the AutoText in the box to the right of the label. The box lists all the AutoText names in the form template and any global AutoText names. If the AutoText entry doesn't exist yet, close the Form Field Help Text dialog box and the Form Field Options dialog box, set up the AutoText, and then return to the Form Field Help Text dialog box to select the AutoText. See "Creating an AutoText Entry," page 820.

TIP

Where to Place Help: Status Bar or F1 Key?

Help in the status bar can be up to 138 characters long but should be limited to 100 characters or fewer so that the text stays visible when the window isn't maximized. If you need longer Help, put it on the F1 key; the message box that appears can display up to 255 characters. Word automatically wraps Help for the F1 key to fit the width of the message box that appears. (You can't change the size of the message box.)

Type Your Own Option

If you prefer to type the Help text yourself, select the Type Your Own option, and then type your Help in the box. Remember, Word limits your text to 138 characters for the status bar and to 255 characters for the F1 key.

Attaching Macros to a Form

To every form field you fill out on a computer, you can hook up two macros: one to run when you enter the field and one to run when you leave the field. Entering a field means the insertion point jumps to the field—when you press the Tab key, click the field with the mouse, or a macro jumps to the field. Leaving a field means the insertion point jumps to another field—when you press the Tab key, click another field with the mouse, or a macro jumps to another field.

You attach macros in the Run Macro On Entry and Run Macro On Exit boxes in the Options dialog box for each type of form field. These boxes drop down to show you a list of the macros that are available to the form. If you see no macros in the list, it's because neither the form template nor any open general template contains a macro.

> **NOTE**

> You can record macros for some purposes, but in most cases, building useful macros for form fields requires knowledge of the Visual Basic for Applications programming language. For information about creating Word macros with Visual Basic, consult *Microsoft Word 97/Visual Basic Step by Step,* by Michael Halvorson and Chris Kinata (Redmond: Microsoft Press, 1997).

Protecting Your Form

After you set up a form, you should test it and then save it as a template. To test the form and to have documents based on your template work correctly, you must first protect the form. By protecting your form, you activate the fields so that they respond to actions (for example, when the user clicks on a drop-down form field, a list drops down) and you prevent anyone else from changing the form's structure. The only way the user can change a form you have protected is to fill it in.

Word provides two levels of protection: basic protection (without a password) and password protection. You can protect some sections of the form and leave others unprotected. (You'll want to leave unprotected only the portions that don't contain form fields.)

Basic Protection

You can give your form basic protection either with the Protect Form button on the Forms toolbar or with the Tools Protect Document command.

To protect your form template by using the toolbar, click the Protect Form button on the Forms toolbar. To protect your form template using a command, choose the Tools Protect Document command to display the Protect Document dialog box, and follow the steps you see shown here:

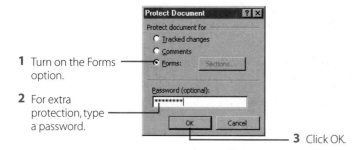

1 Turn on the Forms option.

2 For extra protection, type a password.

3 Click OK.

The entire form template is now protected except for the form fields that you enabled. (Recall that you can enable a form field by turning on the Enabled box in the form field's Options dialog box.)

Removing Basic Protection

To remove basic protection from a form, do one of the following:

- Click the Protect Form button on the Forms toolbar.

- Choose the Tools Unprotect Document command.

The Tools Unprotect Document command replaces the Tools Protect Document command after you turn on protection. After you choose Tools Unprotect Document, Word removes protection from the document and restores the Protect Document command to the Tools menu.

Password Protection

Form protection without a password allows any user to open the form and remove the protection. By adding a password to form protection, you ensure that only those who know the password can remove the protection and work on the form template.

To add a password, use these steps:

1 Choose the Tools Protect Document command.

2 Type a password in the Password box in the Protect Document dialog box. As you type, Word shows asterisks (*) instead of the characters you type. The asterisks ensure that no one can see the password as you type it.

3 Click OK. Word displays the Confirm Password dialog box.

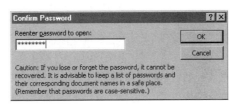

4 Type your password again, *exactly* the same, including uppercase and lowercase.

5 Click OK. The two passwords must match. If they don't, Word displays a message telling you so. Word again displays the Protect Document dialog box so that you can try again.

6 After you type the correct password in the Confirm Password dialog box, click OK to protect your document.

Removing Password Protection

Here's what you do to remove the password:

1 Open the template, which is still protected.

2 Choose the Tools Unprotect Document command. You can also click the Protect Form button on the Forms toolbar.

3 Type the password in the Unprotect Document dialog box, and click OK. If the password you type is wrong, you'll see a message. After you click OK in the Unprotect Document dialog box, the form template will still be protected.

Changing the Password

To change the password, follow these steps:

1 Remove the form protection. Use the steps in "Removing Password Protection," above.

2 Protect the form again with a new password. Use the steps in "Password Protection," opposite.

Section-by-Section Protection

Every Word document has at least one section, although it can have many more. A section is a portion of a document that can have a different page setup—in the margins, page orientation, or headers and footers, for example. For forms, you will seldom need more than one section. On occasion, however, especially in a text form, you might want to leave some passages unprotected so that people can make changes when filling in the form. You can protect a document section by section.

To protect only part of a form that has more than one section, use the following steps:

1 Choose the Tools Protect Document command. The Sections button in the Protect Document dialog box is active when the form has more than one section.

2 Click the Sections button to display the Section Protection dialog box, shown here:

Until you change the
settings, all the boxes
are turned on.

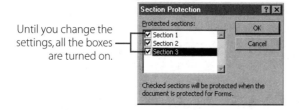

3 Turn off boxes to leave sections unprotected.

4 Click OK.

5 In the Protect Document dialog box, type a password, if you want one, and then click OK.

For information about
sections, see "Using
Sections," page 600.

A section that you protect shows the label "End of Protected Section" in its section mark (except, of course, the last section, which does not have a section mark), shown here:

....End of Protected Section..

Removing or Adding to Section Protection

To remove or add protection for any section, use these steps:

1 Remove the form protection.

2 Protect the form again, turning off boxes for sections you don't want to protect and turning on boxes for sections you do want to protect.

 NOTE

> Clicking the Protect Form button for a document in which some sections were protected but were later made unprotected will reinstate the protection for the previously protected sections only. You must use the Tools Protect Document command to change the status of the sections you want protected.

After you set up your form and protect it, you are ready to save the form as a document template.

Filling Out a Form

You'll often have reason to fill out a form, whether it's a form you created yourself or one created by someone else. Obviously, forms that contain drop-down lists are designed to be completed on a computer, but you can print any form and then fill it out manually. For information about printing forms for manual fill-in, see "Printing a Blank Form," page 781.

Filling Out a Form Online

To fill out a form on a computer, you create a new document based on the form template. Use these steps to create the new document:

1 Choose File New, and click the tab that contains your form template.

2 Select the appropriate form template from the Template list, and click OK.

When the form appears, only the form fields are accessible. If the person who designed the form included shading, you'll see light gray boxes for each form field. In addition, you might see Help for some or all of the form fields, either in the status bar or when you press F1 after moving to a field. If you don't see Help in the status bar, try pressing F1. If a Help message box appears, like the one shown in Figure 18-5, you're in luck. (And your form designer has done a good job!) If you see Word's Help file, no Help text exists for the form field.

FIGURE 18-5.
A sample Help message box that appears when you press F1.

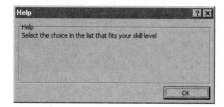

Restrictions on Filling Out a Form

As you fill out a form online, be aware of the following restrictions on the actions you can take:

- You can't alter any tables in the form.

- Word permits editing in form fields only.

- Because the document is protected, most commands on the menus, as well as many toolbar buttons and shortcut keys, are unavailable.

- Your movements in the form are restricted, as described in the next section.

Moving Around in a Form

When you create a form to fill out, you can use any one of several keys to move from one field to another in the form, as shown here:

Press One of These Keys	To Move To
Tab or →	The next field
Shift+Tab or ←	The previous field

If a text form field contains more than one character, the Right arrow and Left arrow keys move through the characters as they do in text in a regular document, until you reach the beginning or end of the text form field. The Right and Left arrow keys do not move to the next field from a text field. If a text form field contains more than one word, the Ctrl+Right arrow and Ctrl+Left arrow shortcut keys move through the words as they do in text in a regular document, until you reach the beginning or end of the text form field.

Filling Out the Various Types of Form Fields

Each type of form field requires a specific kind of response. If your response is not in the correct form, Word notifies you. (For details, see the sidebar "Data Matching," page 780.)

Text Form Fields

In Regular Text form fields, you simply type text. If the field has default text, you can change the text as you see fit.

In a Date text form field, you type a date in a recognizable date format, usually M/d/yy (*9/28/97*, for example). You can't type anything in a Current Date or Current Time form field; Word inserts the date or time for you. In a Number or Calculation text form field, you can type numbers only—no letters or other characters.

In text form fields whose maximum length is set to a number other than Unlimited, Word beeps when you try to type extra characters.

Check Box Form Fields

In a check box form field, you click the box or press the Spacebar to turn the check box on or off.

Drop-Down Form Fields

In a drop-down form field, click the down arrow beside the list or press Alt+↓ to display the list. When the list appears, click your selection, or press the ↑ or ↓ key to move to your selection, and press Enter. To make the list disappear without making a new selection, click outside the list or press Enter before you have selected a new choice.

Saving the Filled-Out Form

After you fill out a form, you'll probably want to save it. You can save the form (tables, labels, and other text) and the responses together, or you can save the responses only. How Word saves the form and responses depends on the Save Data Only For Forms check box on the Save tab of the Tools Options dialog box described below.

Saving the form and the responses together lets you print the filled-out form. Saving only the responses lets you use the information as data for mail merging or for use in a database program.

Data Matching

When you type information in a Date, Number, or Calculation text form field, the information must match the type of response the form field expects. For dates, the number must be in a recognizable date format. For numbers and calculations, you must type numbers only—do not type letters or other characters.

If your response does not match the type of response the form field expects and you then try to move to another field, Word displays a message telling you the type of response you must enter. Click OK in the message box. Word puts you back in the form field you were trying to fill out so that you can type a correct response.

NOTE

For each form you fill out, Word saves the responses, with or without the form, as a separate document. If you want all the responses from several forms in a single document, you can use the Insert File command to combine the responses into one document.

To save the responses with or without the form, do the following:

1 Choose the Tools Options command, and click the Save tab.

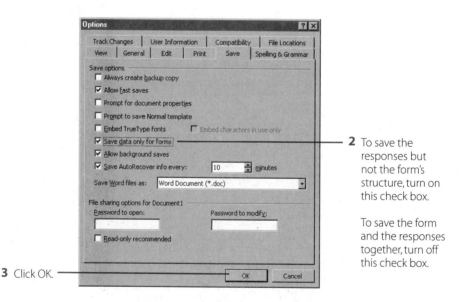

2 To save the responses but not the form's structure, turn on this check box.

To save the form and the responses together, turn off this check box.

3 Click OK.

Printing a Form

When you're ready to print a form, choose the File Print command. You can print a form for manual fill-in, you can print a form that was completed online, or you can print responses on a blank pre-printed form.

Printing a Blank Form

To print a form for manual fill-in, build the form with all the form fields empty. Because text form fields will be only as wide as the text you type into them, you should insert blank spaces in the Default Text box of the form field's Options dialog box. Experiment to find the number of spaces necessary to make the form field the correct width for the expected response.

 TIP

> Unless you plan to offer users the option of filling out the form either online or manually, you actually have little reason to insert form fields into a form that will be filled out by hand. If a form will be filled out only by hand, you can simply create the form in a table or use tab characters with underline leader characters to create blanks that can be filled in.

Printing a Completed Form

To print a completed form, follow these steps:

1 Choose the File Print command.

2 Check the print settings in the Print dialog box to be sure that Word will print what you want it to. Click the Options button in the Print dialog box to display the Print tab, shown on the next page.

3 If you want to print the form and its responses together, click the Print Data Only For Forms check box to turn it off. Turn it on to print the responses only for pre-printed forms.

4 Click OK.

5 Click OK in the Print dialog box shown on the next page.

Printing on Pre-printed Forms

You'll sometimes want to collect form responses online and then print them on pre-printed forms. Perhaps you have a large stock of pre-printed forms that you don't want to waste. Or perhaps your pre-printed forms have special artwork or colors that your printer can't reproduce.

To print on a pre-printed form, follow these steps:

② SEE ALSO

For information about positioning text on a page, see "Wrapping Up Text Boxes," page 399.

1 Set up the form template to match the pre-printed form exactly, taking measurements directly from the pre-printed form. For some form elements, you might need to insert a frame so that you can position the element precisely on the form.

2 Test print to confirm that the form responses print in the correct positions on the pre-printed form.

3 Collect the responses online.

4 Choose the File Print command, and click the Options button.

5 Turn on the Print Data Only For Forms box, and click OK.

6 Click OK in the Print dialog box to print the responses on a pre-printed form.

General Documents

Using Word's Blank Document Template

E ven though Microsoft supplies wizards and templates
for a wide variety of business and personal documents, chances are you'll want to create documents
that don't fit into the mold of any of those wizards and templates, even with extensive modifications. If you try modifying them, you might find you can do it, but spending all that
time fitting your star into a trapezoid isn't always worth it.

Instead, you're better off starting with a blank document that
has only a few fundamental pieces set up, setting up the document the way you want it and the way you need it, and
going on from there. It might seem like reinventing the
wheel, but remember, if no one had reinvented the wheel,
we'd still be rolling loads across logs laid in the path of travel.

In this chapter, you'll learn about a variety of ways you can
use Word's Blank Document template, Normal.dot, to build
templates that suit your document needs not met by Word's
wizards and templates.

Word bases all documents on the Blank Document template, named Normal. The Normal template stores Word's standard descriptions for the built-in styles and the standard setup for AutoText, AutoCorrect, the menus, keyboard, and toolbars. Initially, the Normal template includes no macros or text. Eventually, the Normal template supplies the styles, AutoText, macros, and the key, menu, and toolbar setups stored within it to every document you work on. Because the Normal template supplies every document, it is called a *global* template.

For this reason, you'll usually want to keep your global template very general in the kinds of content, formatting, and tools you add to it. Also for this reason, the Blank Document template makes a good starting point for creating any template that is unlike the special templates Microsoft supplies with Word.

In this chapter, you'll first read about setting up a new template from the Blank Document template. Then you'll get down to the business of creating your own templates—setting up the pages, fleshing out the text, adding special formatting, and setting up tools.

CHAPTER 19

Set Up a New Template from the Blank Document Template

When you create a special template from the Blank Document template Normal, you set up special features and elements so that you can reuse them. After you set up the features and elements, you simply base a new document on your special template.

To set up a new template from the Normal template, you need to perform the following tasks:

- Create a template file.

- Set up pages—select the paper size and source, set the margins, and decide on the layout.

- Flesh out the text—add text and art common to all the documents of this type, and add automatic corrections and AutoText entries.

- Format the text—build paragraph and character styles.

■ Set up tools—adjust the menus, change toolbars or set up new ones, remap the keyboard, and record macros.

■ Store your changes.

The sections in this chapter explain how to accomplish these tasks.

Create a Template File

While you can create a document based on the Normal template, set up pages, add text and formatting, and then save it as a template, you miss out on using AutoText entries and macros. AutoText entries and macros don't automatically transfer from a document to a template just because you save the document as a template. AutoText and macros stay with the template from which you created the document. So, to make all your work stick to the new template, create the template first.

 NOTE

If you want to make changes to the Blank Document template itself, you don't create a template, you simply open the Blank Document template, or you create a document based on the Blank Document template. Then you use the Default buttons in the dialog boxes that contain them or turn on the Add To Template boxes in the dialog boxes that contain them. As you work through this chapter, notes will point out these buttons and boxes.

To create a template, first choose the File New command to display the New dialog box. Then use the steps you see here:

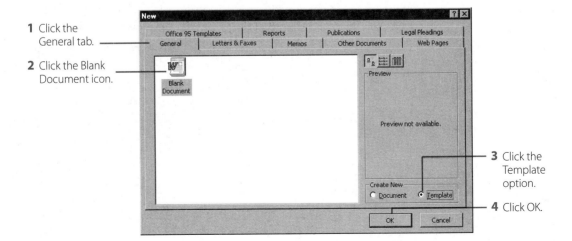

1 Click the General tab.

2 Click the Blank Document icon.

3 Click the Template option.

4 Click OK.

V

General Documents

Word creates a template and names it (temporarily) Template1. At this point, you should save the new template and give it a proper name. You might also want to save a preview picture of the template at some point. For details of saving a preview picture, see "Adding a Preview of the Template," page 854.

Set Up Pages in the Page Setup Dialog Box

When you want to make changes to page setup, choose the File Page Setup command to display the Page Setup dialog box, which has four tabs: Paper Size, shown in Figure 19-1 (page 791); Paper Source, shown in Figure 19-2 (page 793); Margins, shown in Figure 19-3 (page 795); and Layout, shown in Figure 19-7 (page 799). Two tabs—Paper Size and Paper Source—control the paper you'll use for the documents you create from this template. One tab—Margins—controls the margins. The other tab—Layout—controls the arrangement of headers and footers, vertical alignment, line numbers, and section starts.

> **NOTE**
>
> Each tab in the Page Setup dialog box contains a Default button. If you want to apply your changes to the Normal template, click the Default button. Word displays a message telling you that the Normal template will change. Click Yes to make the change. Click No if you don't want to make the change or if you don't want to change the Normal template.

Paper

Unless you're creating a template for online reading only, setting the paper choices is an important part of setting up pages in a template. It's possible, perhaps even likely, that you will need to make no paper setting changes. If you're using standard-size paper in portrait orientation (pages print down the length of the paper), and you're printing from only one paper source, you won't need to make any paper adjustments. If, however, you're setting up a template for odd-size paper or for printing landscape orientation ("sideways"—across the length of the paper) or you're using special paper feeding for printing, you'll need to make changes to the paper setup.

What Does All This Apply To?

Before you investigate the changes you can make with the File Page Setup command, you should understand how Word applies these changes to the template. When you choose the File Page Setup command, each tab of the Page Setup dialog box contains an Apply To box. All the Apply To boxes offer the same choices.

These choices depend on whether there is one, or more than one, section in your template and whether you have selected any part of the template. Table 19-1 lists the possible choices in the Apply To boxes. Table 19-2 shows the effects of each choice in the Apply To boxes.

TABLE 19-1.   Choices in the Apply To Boxes.

Number of Sections in Document	Selection in Document	Apply To Choices
One	Insertion point	Whole document This point forward
	Selection	Whole document Selected text
Two or more	Insertion point	This section This point forward Whole document
	Selection entirely within one section	Selected sections Selected text Whole document
	Selection includes two or more sections	Selected sections Whole document

TABLE 19-2.   Effects of Each Choice in the Apply To Boxes.

Apply To Choices	Effect of Changes
Whole document	Applies changes to the entire document
Selected text	Inserts section breaks at the beginning and end of the selection and then applies changes to the selection only
This section	Applies changes to the selected section only
This point forward	Applies changes to the selected section and all following sections
Selected sections	Applies changes to all the selected sections

On the Paper Size tab, you set up paper measurements and the printing orientation. On the Paper Source tab, you set up the feed arrangement for the first page and for the rest of the pages.

Changing the Paper Size

Word, like most word processing applications, lets you select various paper sizes. Many printers have different paper trays, allowing you to use them either one at a time or more than one at a time. Some printers also have a way for you to manually feed various sizes of paper. Some printers even have a means of feeding envelopes to the printer. For all of these cases, you need to be able to set the paper size. You do this on the Paper Size tab in the Page Setup dialog box.

> The Print dialog box contains a Properties button. You can click this button to set the paper size, orientation, and paper source for the entire document. You cannot set custom paper sizes in the Printer Properties dialog box. For custom paper sizes and to set paper size, orientation, and source for only part of a document, you must use the File Page Setup command. Page Setup affects sections of a document. Printer Properties affects the entire document.

Sometimes you want a particular page of a document to print on a different size paper. For example, if you write a letter and then use the Envelopes And Labels command on the Tools menu to set up an envelope, you can choose either to print the envelope directly or to add the envelope "page" to the document. The Envelopes And Labels command will direct Word to automatically set the paper size and margins for printing an envelope of the size you choose in the Envelopes And Labels dialog box.

When you add an envelope to the current document, Word also automatically sets up a section for the envelope. In this envelope section only, Word changes the paper size settings but leaves the page size settings for letter paper for the rest of the document.

You can also manually set up different paper sizes for different pages of a document. To do so, you set up a separate section and then adjust the paper size for that section only.

NOTE

When you set up a different paper size for a section, Word *requires* that the section print on a separate page. This seems obvious because a printer can't print on different sizes of paper on a single page. If you don't set the section to start on a new page, Word makes that change itself. If you want the section to print narrower than the paper size for a section in the middle of a page, change the margins for the section rather than the paper size.

When you select the Paper Size tab in the Page Setup dialog box, you see the tab shown in Figure 19-1.

The Paper Size list contains standard paper sizes for the country you specified in Windows, plus a Custom option.

FIGURE 19-1.
Page Setup dialog box with the Paper Size tab selected.

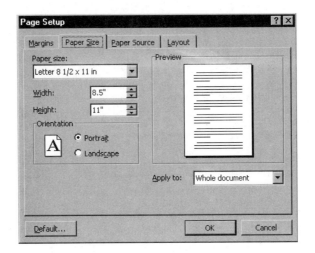

Setting a Custom Paper Size

The Custom option lets you set the paper size to any measurement from 0.1 inch to 22 inches. Note, however, that in practice, the minimum width is 0.5 inch because Word requires that columns be at least 0.5 inch wide. Also, if you set a very small paper size, Word will warn you that the margins, column spacing, or paragraph indents are too large. For example, if you set a paper width of less than 3 inches and leave the Left and Right margin settings at 1.25 inches, Word warns you that the column width cannot be less than 0.5 inch.

One more bugaboo: many printers cannot print closer to the edge of the paper than 0.5 inch because the printer needs the space to grab the paper and pull it through the printer. If your side margins are narrower than your printer's dead zone, Word displays the warning shown here:

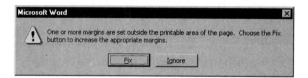

Click the Fix button to set the margins to the minimum required by the printer. Click the Ignore button if you want Word to ignore the minimum and set the margins the width you specified.

> Any time you change the Width or Height measurement to something other than one of the standard paper sizes on the Paper Size list, Word automatically selects the Custom Paper Size option.

Page Orientation

On occasion, you might have an extra-wide table or picture that fits better on a page if printed sideways. That is, instead of looking at the page with the shorter sides at the top and bottom, you look at the page with the longer sides at the top and bottom. Printers call such pages "turn pages" because you turn the page sideways to see its contents. In Word, a sideways page is called a "landscape page" because a photograph or painting of a landscape is typically set up to be wider than it is tall. (The other printing option is called "portrait" because a portrait of a person or object is typically taller than it is wide.)

The two Orientation choices in the Page Setup dialog box swap the measurements for Height and Width. For the standard U.S. letter paper size, the Landscape option sets Width to 11 inches and Height to 8.5 inches. Similarly, if you set a custom paper size that is taller than it is wide, the Landscape option swaps the Height measurement for the Width measurement.

NOTE

If you set up a paper size that is wider than it is tall, Word doesn't automatically turn on the Landscape option. Because of this, the first time you click the Landscape option, you see no change in the Preview box. If you then click the Portrait option, you see a change. Click the Landscape option again, and the Preview box returns to the paper size you set in the Width and Height boxes.

NOTE

When you set up a different page orientation for a section, Word requires that the section print on a separate page. If you don't set the section to start on a new page, Word makes that change itself. Word can't set up a page to print different directions on a single page. See "New Page," page 810. You can, however, use WordArt text boxes and tables to create text that prints with different orientations on the same page. See "Bending Text—WordArt," page 507.

Paper Source

The Paper Source tab in the Page Setup dialog box gives you a means of changing the paper feed on your printer. Select the Paper Source tab in the Page Setup dialog box, shown in Figure 19-2.

FIGURE 19-2.

Page Setup dialog box with the Paper Source tab selected.

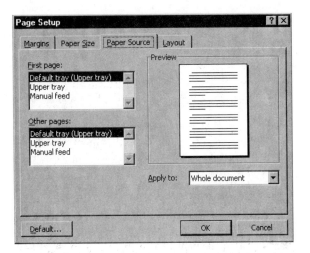

The Paper Source tab gives you two choices: the source of the first page and the source of all the other pages. When would you exercise these choices? Many organizations use a letterhead sheet for the first page of a letter and "second sheets" (sheets without letterhead) for all the other pages. In this case, you select the letterhead source for First Page and the second sheet source for Other Pages.

The exact list of sources depends on your printer. Some printers use only one paper tray at a time and have a slot for manual feeding. Some printers have two trays. In this case, the list will show two trays. For printers that have an envelope feeder, the Paper Source tab lists that option.

NOTE

You don't have to add sections to your document to print the first page on paper from a different source from the rest of the pages. But remember: if you set up a document with multiple sections, Word prints the first page of each section on paper from the First Page source. In this case, then, set a different paper source for the first page of the first section only. Change all the other sections to a single paper source.

Word gives you the benefit of the two paper sources automatically when you use the Tools Envelopes And Labels command. If you set up an envelope and ask Word to print the envelope, Word sets the First Page option to Manual Feed or Envelope Feeder, as appropriate. If you tell Word to add the envelope to your document, Word inserts the envelope in a separate section and sets the First Page source for that section to Manual Feed or Envelope Feeder, as appropriate.

Changing Margin Settings

As you probably know, margins leave blank space (also called white space) around the edges of a page. We've become quite used to this. The width of the blank space that frames a page is the width of the margins. In Word you can set the four margins—top, bottom, left, and right—separately, to the desired width or height.

To set a margin, you simply choose the File Page Setup command and enter a measurement for the width of that margin in the appropriate box on the Margins tab of the Page Setup dialog box.

The default margins for U.S. documents are 1 inch top and bottom and 1.25 inches left and right. These measurements give you a content area (the area of the page where text appears) 6 inches wide and 9 inches tall on standard U.S. letter paper. For help with figuring the width and height of the margins that you want to set, see the sidebar "Figuring Margin Settings," page 799.

When you select the Margins tab in the Page Setup dialog box, you see the dialog box shown in Figure 19-3.

FIGURE 19-3.

Margins tab in the Page Setup dialog box.

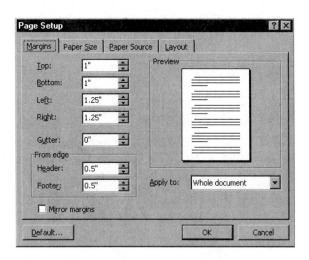

For each of the margins, you enter a measurement for the width or the height in the text boxes specifying each side of the page (Top, Bottom, Left, and Right). Figure 19-3 shows the standard margin settings in Word for U.S. letter paper.

The Gutter Margin

The term *gutter* is a printer's term for the part of a page next to the binding. As you look at this book, for instance, you'll notice that the pages arc down into the binding, creating a V shape at the binding. Imagine water (or wet ink!) flowing along this V, and you'll grasp why it's called a gutter.

When you bind pages together along one side, the binding takes up some of the margin along that side. If you print a document only on one side (face) of a page and bind it along the left edge of the page, the binding takes up some of the left margin. If you print a document on both sides of a page, the binding takes up part of the left side of the odd-numbered pages and the right side of the even-numbered pages (as with this book).

V

General Documents

For single-sided printing, you can simply add a little extra space to the left margin, say 0.25 inch to 0.5 inch, by adjusting the measurement in the Gutter box, as shown in Figure 19-4. By doing so, you move the usable space on the page to the right to allow for the unusable space in the gutter. For double-sided printing, you want to add the extra width to the left margin on odd-numbered pages and to the right margin on even-numbered pages, as shown in Figure 19-5.

FIGURE 19-4.
Single-sided printing with a gutter margin.

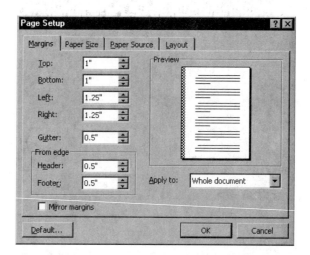

FIGURE 19-5.
Double-sided printing with a gutter margin.

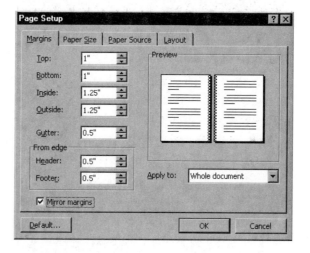

Setting a wider gutter margin manually, or even trying to explain how you would do it, is so tedious as to defy common sense. It is quite simple, however, to set a gutter margin on the Margins tab in the Page

Setup dialog box. When you do so, Word automatically adjusts the margin for binding.

To set a gutter margin for double-sided pages, you must also use mirror margins.

Mirror Margins

The term *mirror margins* means that the margins for the front of a page and for the back of the same page look like mirror opposites of each other. When you use mirror margins, Word flip-flops the left and right margins for each printed page. As noted earlier, the left margin measurement becomes the right margin measurement and vice versa for even-numbered pages. This flip-flopping makes a difference only in the following two cases:

- You set different widths for the side margins. For example, you could set the left margin to 2 inches and set the right margin to 1 inch.

- You set both left and right margins to the same width but also set a gutter margin. For example, you set the left and right margins to 1 inch and the gutter margin to 1 inch.

The point of making both examples perform the same work is that you can set up a gutter margin in two ways. Setting a gutter margin measurement is a simple way of adding width to the "inside" margin (the gutter). In fact, you'll notice when you turn on the Mirror Margins check box, the labels for the Left and Right margins change to Inside and Outside.

The major difference between using a gutter margin and using mirror margins is that the gutter margin is always on the inside—the left side of odd-numbered pages and the right side of even-numbered pages. With mirror margins, you can set either side. So, if you like pages that have an extra-wide margin on the outside edge (the side away from the binding edge), you can set up mirror margins to do this, as shown in Figure 19-6, next page.

V

General Documents

FIGURE 19-6.
Mirror margins wider on the outside edge of the page.

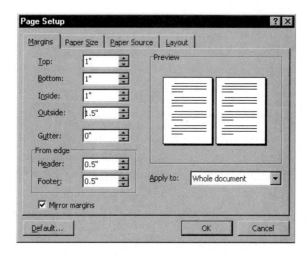

Staying Back from the Edge of the Paper

SEE ALSO

For vertical alignment, see "Controlling Brochure Text Vertically on the Page," page 453, which discusses vertical alignment in the context of creating a brochure.

The From Edge boxes on the Margins tab in the Page Setup dialog box show the distance from the edge of the paper where headers and footers start. The From Edge label gives you this clue: headers start at the distance shown from the top of the sheet; footers end (their lower edge) at the distance shown from the bottom of the sheet.

You'll probably find, as I do, that you seldom need to change the vertical position of headers and footers. But when you do need to change it, here are the steps:

1 Select the section in which you want to change the vertical positions of the headers and footers.

2 Choose the File Page Setup command, and select the Margins tab.

3 Set the new distance from the edge in the Header and Footer boxes, and then click OK.

Layout

SEE ALSO

For line numbering, see "Numbering Lines," page 738, which discusses line numbering in the context of a legal document.

For each section of a document, you have several choices for setting up headers and footers and for how to start the section, how to set the vertical alignment of the section, and whether you want lines numbered.

In a general template, you most likely want to change the headers and footers and set the section start. These topics are covered in the following sections.

To adjust the layout of pages, choose the File Page Setup command, and then click the Layout tab, shown in Figure 19-7.

FIGURE 19-7.

Layout tab in the Page Setup dialog box.

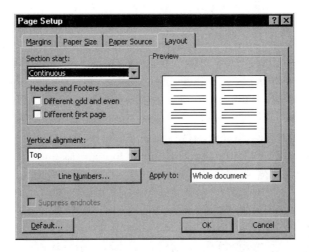

Figuring Margin Settings

To figure the width and the height of margins, you need to decide how high and how wide you want the text to be on the printed page. This figuring requires you to perform some basic math.

To figure the width of the side margins, decide on the width of the text on a page. If, for example, you want the text to span 5 inches horizontally, you subtract 5 inches from the paper width (8.5 inches for U.S. standard-size paper). Five inches from 8.5 inches leaves 3.5 inches. If you want both side margins to be the same width, make both the left and right margins 1.75 inches (3.5 divided by 2). If you want different-size margins, use part of the 3.5 inches for the left margin and part for the right margin—for example, 2 inches for the left margin and 1.5 inches for the right margin.

Figure the top and bottom margins in the same way as the side margins. If, for example, you want the page contents to be no more than 8 inches high, subtract 8 from the paper height (11 inches for U.S. standard-size paper). Eight inches from 11 inches leaves 3. If you want the top and bottom margins to be the same height, set both to 1.5 inches (3 divided by 2). Of course, as with the side margins, you can set the top margin height to be different from the bottom margin height. You could, for example, set the top margin to 1 inch and the bottom margin to 2 inches.

Calculating and using custom margin settings is especially useful if you plan on creating a document on smaller-size paper by trimming the paper after you have printed your document on it.

Changing Your Headers and Footers

One of the main reasons for using sections is to use different headers and footers for different parts of a document. If, for example, you have a document with three parts—Introduction, Recommendations, and Background—you might want the headers in each part to show the part title. By inserting section breaks between the three parts, you can set up a header containing the appropriate title in each part. You can also set different positions for the headers and footers in each section. On the Margins tab you can position headers and footers from the edge of the page. On the Layout tab you can select the types of headers and footers you want in your document. You can turn on or off either or both header and footer choices for each section.

Different Odd and Even Pages

You can set up a different header and footer for odd-numbered and even-numbered pages. In this case, Word checks the number printed on the page to determine whether the page number is odd or even. The only time the placement of odd and even headers and footers might be unusual is when you set the beginning page number of a section to an even number; that is, the first page appears on a left-hand page rather than a right-hand page. To print different headers or footers on odd and even pages of a section, use the following steps:

1 Select the section in which you want to change the headers and footers.

2 Choose the File Page Setup command, and click the Layout tab.

3 Turn on the Different Odd And Even check box, and then click OK.

Why Can't I Set Even-Page or Other-Page Headers and Footers?

If you try to set up odd-and-even headers and footers or a different first page header or footer in an empty document or template, you might run up against a difficult situation. When you choose the View Header And Footer command, you'll see the header space for the first page of the document. This header space has a label, either First Page Header or Odd Page Header. That's fine; it's a place to start inserting the contents of your headers and footers. But the only other space you can get to is the footer space for either the first page or the odd page. You cannot get to the header or footer space for other pages (with only Different First Page turned on), for even pages (with only Different Odd And Even turned on), or for odd or even pages (with both Different First Page and Different Odd And Even turned on). So what do you do to get to these other header and footer spaces?

To be able to set up headers and footers for pages other than the first page of a document when you have either or both Different First Page and Different Odd And Even turned on, follow these steps:

1   Close the header and footer view.

2   Press Ctrl+Enter to insert a page break. If you have both Different First Page and Different Odd And Even turned on, press Ctrl+Enter twice to insert two page breaks.

3   Choose the View Header And Footer command. You can now move to all of the header and footer spaces.

4   Set up all your headers and footers.

5   Close the header and footer view.

6   Delete the extra page breaks you inserted.

With the pages breaks removed, you can't see or get to the header and footer spaces beyond the first page. Note, however, that Word doesn't discard the contents you added to the other headers and footers. They're just invisible and inaccessible until you have enough pages in the template to require them for printing. To edit them, you'll have to reinsert the page breaks.

Different First Page

In the case of letters, memos, reports, and books, you might not want a header or footer on the first page of a section. Or you might want the header or footer on the first page to be different from those on the other pages of a section. For example, you might want the page number to appear at the bottom right margin on the first page but at the top right margin on the rest of the pages of a section. In this case, you create a different first page header and footer. Word sets up a header and footer, labeled First Page Header and First Page Footer.

To print a different header or footer on the first page of a section, follow these steps:

1 Select the section in which you want a different header and footer on the first page.

2 Choose the File Page Setup command, and click the Layout tab.

3 Turn on the Different First Page check box, and then click OK.

Changing the Contents of Headers and Footers

After you have created a document with headers and footers, you might want to change the contents of the headers and footers. Also, if you divide the document into different sections, you might want to change the contents of the headers and footers so they are unique to each section. To change the contents of a header or footer, use these steps:

1 Choose the View Header And Footer command.

2 Change the contents of the header or footer. See "The Header And Footer Toolbar," opposite, for help with switching between headers and footers.

3 Click the Close button on the Header And Footer toolbar to return to the document.

The Header And Footer toolbar is an essential and effective tool for working on your headers and footers, especially in a document broken into several sections. The next section explains how to use it.

The Header And Footer Toolbar

After you choose the View Header And Footer command to check and work on your headers and footers, the Header And Footer toolbar appears, as shown in Figure 19-8.

FIGURE 19-8.

Header And Footer toolbar.

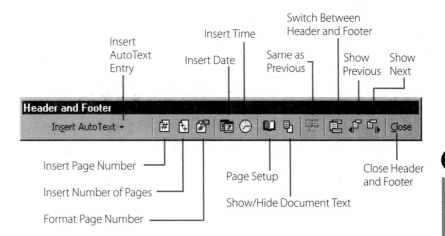

The following sections explain the function of each of the buttons on the Header And Footer toolbar. In general, to insert contents into a header or footer, use these steps:

1 Choose the View Header And Footer command.

2 Move to the header or footer you want to work on.

3 Position the insertion point where you want to insert contents.

4 Click the button that inserts the contents you want to add.

5 If you wish, repeat steps 2 through 4 until your headers and footers are completely set up.

6 When you're done, click the Close Header and Footer button.

Insert AutoText Button

Click the Insert AutoText button to see a list of AutoText categories that you can insert into a header or footer. The list includes categories for all the AutoText entries built into Word and AutoText entries you set up yourself under the normal category.

To select an AutoText entry, click on its category and then click on the name of the entry you want to insert.

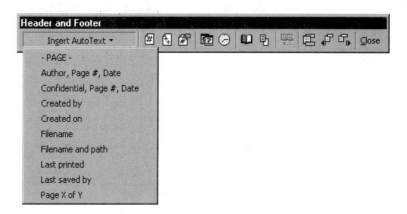

Insert Page Number Button

Click the Insert Page Number button to insert a Page Number field. This field adds the correct page number to each page of the document section that has the same type of header or footer (first page, odd page, even page, or all pages).

Insert Number Of Pages Button

Click the Insert Number Of Pages button to insert a Number of Pages field. This field adds the total number of pages to each page of the document section that has the same type of header or footer (first page, odd page, even page, or all pages). You use this button and field typically to set up a header with the text format: *Page X of Y*, where *X* represents the page number, and *Y* represents the total number of pages in the document. You type the words *Page* and *of,* plus the spaces. For the page number (*X*) in this header text format, you click the Insert Page Number button. For the number of pages (*Y*) in this header text format, you click the Insert Number Of Pages button. Of course, the inserted page number value changes for each page. The number of pages value appears on every page.

Format Page Number Button

To change the page number to Roman numerals or letters, to add a chapter number, or to set other formatting options, click the Format Page Number button. When you click this button, you see the Page Number Format dialog box, opposite.

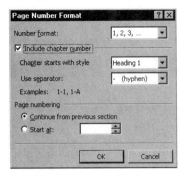

Insert Date Button

Click the Insert Date button to insert a Date field. This field adds the current date to each page of the document section that has the same type of header or footer (first page, odd page, even page, or all pages).

Insert Time Button

Click the Insert Time button to insert a Time field. This field adds the current time to each page of the document section that has the same type of header or footer (first page, odd page, even page, or all pages).

Page Setup Button

When you click the Page Setup button, the Page Setup dialog box opens to the Layout tab. (This same thing happens when you choose the File Page Setup command while viewing headers and footers.) You can, of course, change any or all of the section properties in the Page Setup dialog box.

Show/Hide Document Text Button

 SEE ALSO

For an example of using the Show/Hide Document Text button, see the file WATERMRK.DOC, which explains how to add a watermark to your pages.

When you view headers and footers, Word normally shows the document text dimmed, and the header or footer text is active so that you can see the relative positions of the headers and footers to the document text. For some of the work you'll perform in headers and footers—primarily adding art or text *behind* the document text—you need to hide the document text so that you have a clear view of the art or text you're adding. In these cases, click the Show/Hide Document Text button to hide the document text. To see a dim representation of the document text again, click this button again.

General Documents

Keeping the Date and Time Constant

The Insert Date and Insert Time buttons on the Header And Footer toolbar insert fields that put the current date and time into a header or footer. In some cases—for example, a draft document that will go through several revisions—you'll want the current date and time each time you print the document. In those cases, clicking these buttons works just fine.

If, however, you want the date and time to remain constant regardless of how many times you work on and print the document, you need to take these alternative steps instead of clicking on the Insert Date and Insert Time buttons:

1   Choose the Insert Field command.

2   In the Field dialog box, select Date And Time from the Categories list.

3   Select CreateDate from the Field Names list.

4   Click the Options button.

5   Select the date format you want.

6   Click the Add To Field button.

7   Click OK in both dialog boxes. The CreateDate field inserts the date when you create a document from the template.

8   Repeat these steps for the Time field, except in step 5 in the Options dialog box, select a time format instead of a date format. (Word can use either a Date field or a Time field to insert the date and time. The options you choose determine whether the field shows a date, a time, or both.)

Same As Previous Button

When you start editing headers and footers, Word turns on the Same As Previous button. When this button is on, all the headers and footers in all the sections are the same as the header and footer in the first section of the document. To change the header or footer from that of a preceding section, follow these steps:

1   Turn off the Same As Previous button.

2   Change the header or footer for the current section. All the sections following the current section now have the new header or footer.

To change headers or footers in later sections, follow these steps:

1 Click the Show Next button to jump to the header or footer for the next section.

2 Turn off the Same As Previous button.

3 Change the header or footer for the section.

When the Same As Previous button is turned on, the header and footer areas show the label "Same as Previous" on the right end of the top border of the area, as shown here:

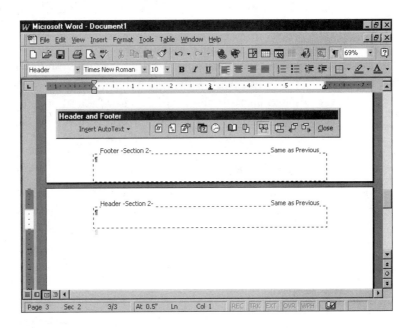

When you turn off the Same As Previous button, the label disappears from the top border of the header and footer areas.

Switch Between Header And Footer Button

Click the Switch Between Header And Footer button to jump from the header space to the footer space or to jump from the footer space to the header space.

Show Previous Button

Click the Show Previous button to jump to the header or footer on the first page of the previous section. If you have set up different headers or footers for the first page or for odd-numbered and even-numbered pages, this button jumps to the previous header or footer in either of these orders: odd header, even header, first page or even header, odd header, and first page. (The same progression applies to footers.)

> The Show Previous and Show Next buttons skip over pages as necessary to jump to the beginning of the section. If you want to see the header or footer on every page, click the Next Page and Previous Page buttons at the bottom of the vertical scroll bar.

Show Next Button

Click the Show Next button to jump to the header or footer on the first page of the next section. If you have set up different headers or footers for the first page or the odd-numbered and even-numbered pages, this button jumps to the next header or footer in either of these orders: first page, even header, odd header or first page, odd header, and even header. (The same progression applies to footers.)

Section Starts

Each section can have its own starting point. In a one-section document, the section starts at the top of a page—this is a Next Page section start. Word provides five different ways of starting a section, as shown in Table 19-3. Additional details about each type of section start follow the table.

> Word doesn't show what kind of section start a section break sets up. To find out, you move into the section, choose the File Page Setup command, click the Layout tab, and find the type of section start in the Section Start box.

Continuous

Using Continuous section starts, you can set up text in different combinations of multiple columns on the same page. You can also use the Continuous section start to balance columns at the end of a section. "Balancing columns" means ensuring that the bottoms of all the columns end at about the same depth on the page.

TABLE 19-3.   Different Ways to Start a Section and Their Effects on Page Layout.

Section Start	Effect on Page Layout
Continuous	Starts the new section immediately below the end of the previous section without starting a new page.
New Column	Starts the new section at the top of a new column, either on the same page of a multiple-column section or on a new page.
New Page	Starts the new section at the top of the next page of the document.
Even Page	Starts the new section at the top of the next even-numbered page. If the previous section ends on an even-numbered page, Word leaves a blank page between the sections.
Odd Page	Starts the new section at the top of the next odd-numbered page. If the previous section ends on an odd-numbered page, Word leaves a blank page between the sections.

Sometimes, because of paragraph spacing, line spacing, or paragraph Keep Lines Together or Keep With Next settings, columns won't balance very well, as shown in Figure 19-9. The upper section in this example has one column; the lower section has two. You can sometimes achieve better balance by inserting a column break (Ctrl+Shift+Enter) near the bottom of a column, as shown in Figure 19-10.

FIGURE 19-9.
Two continuous sections with "balanced columns." Note that the bottoms of the columns of the lower section are not very well balanced.

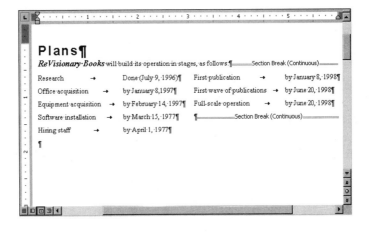

General Documents

FIGURE 19-10.

Two columns more evenly balanced by inserting a column break in front of the line starting with "Hiring staff."

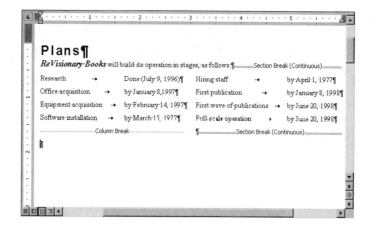

New Column

If your document contains only one column, a New Column section start begins the new section at the top of the next page. If the previous section is more than one column, the new section starts at the top of the next column. Of course, if the current column is the last (rightmost) column on the page, the next column is the first column (leftmost) on the next page. In essence, inserting a section break that has a New Column section start is similar to inserting a column break. Note, however, that a New Column section start also lets you change section properties, while a column break leaves you in the same section with the same section properties.

New Page

The New Page section start is one of the most commonly used section starts (along with Continuous). When you need to change or reset any page elements, a New Page section start fits the bill. For example, starting a section on a new page might coincide with the start of a new major part of a document. Inserting a New Page section break lets you change the headers and footers, if you want; collect endnotes; and restart the numbering of footnotes, line numbers, and endnotes. The only time you might choose a different section start when you want a new section to begin on a new page is when you want the new section to begin on either the left (even-numbered) page or right (odd-numbered) page. In those cases, you select either Even Page section start or Odd Page section start.

Even Page

An Even Page section start works the same as a New Page section start, except in one (and only one) case: when the previous section ends on an even page. If you want the new section to start at the top of the next even-numbered page, select Even Page section start. When the previous section ends on an even-numbered page, Word leaves a blank page (the odd-numbered page) between the two sections.

Odd Page

An Odd Page section start is the reverse of an Even Page section start. When the previous section ends on an odd page and you want the new section to start at the top of the next odd-numbered page, select Odd Page section start. Word leaves a blank page (the even-numbered page) between the two sections.

Flesh Out the Text: AutoText and AutoCorrect

As you're sure to have noticed, when you create a document from Word's Blank Document template, the new document is empty—blank. General templates are meant to be that way so you can create any kind of document without having first to remove a bunch of text. Take this, then, as your guiding principle: if you're creating another general template, you'll want to put very little, if any, text into the template. If you're creating a special template, you might want to put some text into the template—text you want to appear in every document you create from the template, that is, text common to every document of a particular type that you use the special template to create.

In addition, you might want to set up special AutoText and AutoCorrect entries for a template. When you store these entries in a template, they appear on the AutoText list, and Word uses the AutoCorrect entries only when you're working on a specific type of document—one created from this template.

Common Text

Text that is common to every document of a particular type—text you want to appear in every document you create from a particular template—can be part of the page contents and part of the headers and footers.

Common Text on Pages

Anything can be common text on pages. In earlier parts of this book, you'll find descriptions of a number of templates and wizards that set up common text for faxes, memos, reports, and other business documents. If you're creating a template for documents different from those found in other parts of this book, the common text you put on the pages will probably be totally different. If it's not, then you should consider changing one of Word's templates or using one of the wizards to create a template. That's a lot less effort.

Here are some questions to ponder when you're planning the common text for pages:

- Do you have common text you want to appear on various pages of a document? If so, you'll need to insert page breaks or section breaks. To insert a page break, press Ctrl+Enter. To insert a section break, choose the Insert Break command, select the type of section break you want to insert, and then click OK. (You can also use the Insert Break command to insert a page break or a column break.)

- What content is common to all the documents of the type for which you are creating a template? For example, does the document include the date, author's name, organization name, copyright notice, or a standard introduction or description?

- Can any content of a similar type be spawned by fields? For example, the date and author's name (if different people will use this template) are good candidates for fields.

Common Text in Headers and Footers

Headers and footers often contain the most similar information from document to document. The page number is very common, as are the date, author's name, and document title. You'll want to insert this common text into the headers and footers of a template so that you don't have to insert it into the document each time.

Headers and footers are most easily filled out if you insert fields. All of the items mentioned in the previous paragraph—page number, date, author's name, and document title—can be added to headers and footers by fields. To add the page number and date, you can click the

related buttons on the Header And Footer toolbar (see "The Header And Footer Toolbar," page 803). To add the author's name and document title, choose the Insert Field command, select Document Information from the Categories list, select either Author or Title from the Field Names list, and then click OK.

In the template, you might also want to set up different headers and footers for the first page of a document or different headers and footers for odd-numbered and even-numbered pages. For details about setting up these header and footer arrangements, see "Layout," page 798. Pay special attention to the sidebar "Why Can't I Set Even-Page or Other-Page Headers and Footers?" on page 801.

AutoCorrect

As you type, you might notice that Word automatically corrects some common typing mistakes. For example, if you capitalize the first two letters of the word at the beginning of a sentence instead of only the first letter, or if you type *teh* instead of *the*, Word corrects the mistake for you. Word calls this AutoCorrect. You can add to or customize the list of mistakes Word looks for by choosing the Tools AutoCorrect command and changing the settings in the AutoCorrect dialog box.

Setting Up Your Own Automatic Corrections

In the course of your work, when you come across a word that you repeatedly mistype or misspell, it's time to set up an automatic correction of your own. Use these steps to set up an automatic correction for mistyping or misspelling:

1 Select the word that you mistype or misspell.

2 Choose the Tools AutoCorrect command, and then click the AutoCorrect tab.

NOTE

To ensure that the misspelling you select appears in the Replace box of the AutoCorrect dialog box, the Check Spelling As You Type check box must be turned on and the Hide Spelling Errors In This Document check box must be turned off. To check these options, select the Tools Options command and click the Spelling & Grammar tab.

V

General Documents

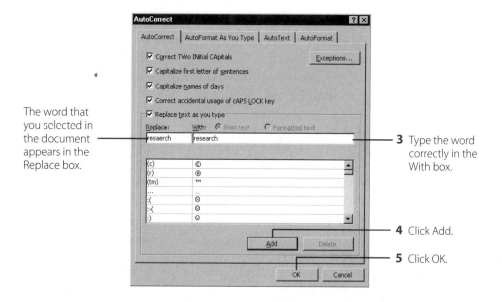

The word that you selected in the document appears in the Replace box.

3 Type the word correctly in the With box.

4 Click Add.

5 Click OK.

Adding Corrections from a Spelling Check

You can also add word corrections to AutoCorrect during a spelling check. When Word flags a misspelling, either correct it yourself in the Not In Dictionary box or select the correct spelling in the Suggestions box, and then click the AutoCorrect button. Word adds the entry to the AutoCorrect list and continues checking the document for misspellings.

You can also set up AutoCorrect to act as a quick way to insert long and formatted text while you type just a few letters. For example, it's a pain to type *Microsoft® Word 97 for Windows®*. In the first place, it's a lot of typing. In the second place, even though Word has a key combination for inserting the ® symbol, when you type it right after another letter or number, Word doesn't automatically set the symbol to 8-point size. Third, I set the 97 as small caps. Using AutoCorrect, I can type a short word, such as *w97,* and have Word insert *Microsoft® Word 97 for Windows®* for me, all properly formatted, whenever I type that word.

 **TIP**

If Word marks the word you select as misspelled, the selected word appears in the Replace box, as long as the Spell Checking While You Type feature is on and the Hide Spelling Errors In Document feature is off. If the word you select is spelled correctly (or marked as "ignore"), the word appears in the With box.

To set up a long or formatted word or phrase in AutoCorrect, use these steps:

1 Type the word or phrase, format it as you like, and select it.

2 Choose the Tools AutoCorrect command, and then click the AutoCorrect tab.

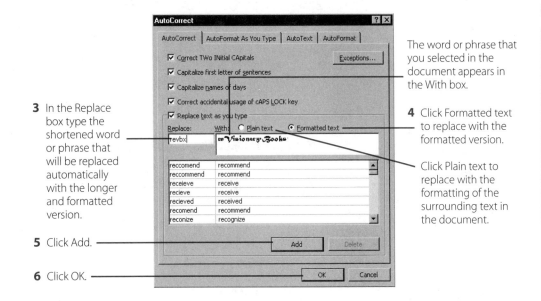

The word or phrase that you selected in the document appears in the With box.

3 In the Replace box type the shortened word or phrase that will be replaced automatically with the longer and formatted version.

4 Click Formatted text to replace with the formatted version.

Click Plain text to replace with the formatting of the surrounding text in the document.

5 Click Add.

6 Click OK.

 TIP

Adding Art to AutoCorrect
You can also add art and other objects to AutoCorrect. This way, all you have to do is type the "word" you've set up to represent the art, and Word automatically "corrects" the word with the artwork.

General Documents

Changing an Automatic Correction

Suppose that by mistake or on purpose you have set up an automatic correction (or Word has one built-in) that you don't like as is. You want an automatic correction for a particular typing or spelling mistake or a cumbersome formatted phrase, but the correction that's set up isn't the one you want. You can change it using these steps:

1 Choose the Tools AutoCorrect command, and then click the AutoCorrect tab.

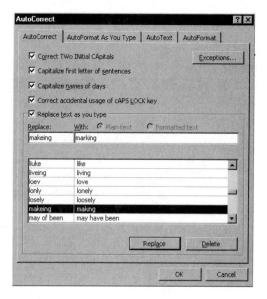

2 Select the automatic correction you want to change.

3 In the With box, type the correction you want in place of the existing correction.

4 Click Replace, and you see this message box:

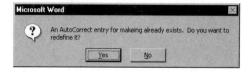

5 Click Yes to replace the current correction with your new one, or click No to keep the current correction.

6 Click OK.

Selecting AutoCorrect Options

The top part of the AutoCorrect dialog box lists five options that solve typical tough cases for typing.

Correct TWo INitial CApitals Option

Since the days of manual typewriters, typing two capital letters at the beginning of a sentence has been a bugaboo. We get to typing so fast that we don't lift our little fingers off the Shift key soon enough. For example, suppose the Correct TWo INitial CApitals check box is turned on, and you type *MAny's the time that I've wasted good riding weather.* Word corrects the mistake as follows: *Many's the time that I've wasted good riding weather.*

Capitalize First Letter Of Sentences Option

From time to time you might type a sentence that starts with a lower-case letter. Word fixes that for you. For example, suppose you type *if I have to tell you, you won't understand.* Word corrects your sentence to *If I have to tell you, you won't understand.*

> Word doesn't correct the first letter of the first sentence following a colon or a semicolon, even if the sentence following the colon or semicolon starts a new paragraph.

Capitalize Names Of Days Option

If you type *friday*, Word automatically corrects the word to *Friday*.

Correct Accidental Usage Of cAPS LOCK Key Option

You have a bunch of words to type in all capitals, so you press the Caps Lock key. Then you move the insertion point somewhere else and forget that you left the Caps Lock key on. When you start typing, this is what you get: *tHINGS ARE DIFFERENT ON A hARLEY.*

Arrgh! But no more! If you start typing with the Correct Accidental Usage Of cAPS LOCK Key check box turned on, Word corrects the letters and turns off the Caps Lock key for you. As soon as you type a space or tab character after the first word that has a lowercase first letter followed by all uppercase letters, Word fixes the mess. For example, if you type *tHINGS* because the Caps Lock key is on, Word turns off the Caps Lock key and changes *tHINGS* to *Things*.

Of course, there is a certain computer program on the market that has a lowercase first letter with the rest of the product name in uppercase. This is rare. If, however, you have lots of instances like this in a document, turn off the Correct Accidental Usage Of cAPS LOCK Key check box. If you have only one instance in a document, choose the Format Change Case command, select Toggle Case, and click OK. Toggle Case changes *Dbase* back to *dBASE*.

> **NOTE**
>
> When you press the quotation mark key, Word by default inserts curly quotes (" ", opening and closing quotation marks) instead of straight quotes (" ", also called inch marks). Word also inserts curly single quotes (' ', opening and closing single quotation marks) when you press the apostrophe key. These are called Smart Quotes because Word automatically determines whether the quotes you insert should be opening or closing marks.
>
> If you would rather use straight quote marks, choose the Tools Options command, and click the AutoFormat tab. Then turn off the Straight Quotes With Smart Quotes check box by clicking it.

Replace Text As You Type Option

With the Replace Text As You Type check box turned on, Word uses the typing correction list at the bottom of the AutoCorrect dialog box to correct your misspellings as you type. About the only time you might want to turn off this check box is when you want to avoid automatic correction and fix typing mistakes and misspellings yourself.

When Word corrects your typing, it replaces what you type (found in the left column of the correction list) with the contents of the right column. Word inserts either a plain text version or a formatted version of the replacement. You'll want to select the Formatted Text option when the replacement has special formatting, such as a special font. You'll want other replacements to look like the surrounding text. In these cases, set up the replacement with the Plain Text option. You select the Plain Text option or the Formatted Text option when you add new entries to AutoCorrect.

Displaying the AutoText Toolbar

Toolbars contain buttons, commands, and choices for actions you want to take in Word. Typically, a toolbar contains choices that you have previously found only in lists in dialog boxes.

You have two ways to turn toolbars on and off:

- Right-click a toolbar and then click the check box beside the toolbar you want to turn on or off.

- Choose the View Toolbars command, click the check boxes for the toolbars you want to turn on, click the check boxes for the toolbars you want to turn off, and then click OK.

You have one additional way to turn on the AutoText toolbar:

- Choose the Tools AutoCorrect command, click the AutoText tab, and then click the Show Toolbar button.

Also note that when you choose the View Header And Footer command, the Headers And Footers toolbar appears. This toolbar has an Insert AutoText button, which contains the same AutoText entries as the AutoText toolbar.

AutoText

AutoText stores entries so that you can reuse them easily. You can use AutoText to store bunches of words and lots of other things that you don't want to reconstruct every time you need them. When you store words as AutoText entries, you give them a simple name, even an abbreviation. Then when you want to add words from AutoText to your document, you simply type the AutoText name and ask Word to replace the name with the words from AutoText.

Of course, before you can use an AutoText entry, you have to create it. For information about using an AutoText entry after you create it, see "Putting an AutoText Entry in Your Document," page 822.

Using Built-In AutoText Entries

To assist you with typing, Word contains a fairly large number of built-in AutoText entries. To make using them easy, Word provides the AutoText toolbar.

Depending on what part of a document you are in, the AutoText toolbar contains AutoText names that apply to what you're currently working on. For example, if you're working on the greeting for a letter, the AutoText toolbar contains AutoText categories and each contains AutoText names for various salutations. If you're working in a header or footer, the AutoText toolbar contains names for elements you might find useful for a header or footer—for example, the date or page number field.

1 Click here to see the list of AutoText categories.

2 Click here to see AutoText names for the selected category.

3 Click a name to insert the AutoText entry in your document.

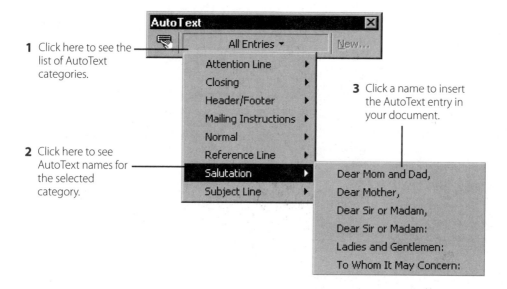

Creating an AutoText Entry

Before you can use an AutoText entry that isn't built into Word, you have to set it up yourself. This process is pretty easy; in fact, you have two ways to create an AutoText entry. You can click the New button on the AutoText toolbar, or you can use the AutoText tab in the Tools AutoCorrect dialog box.

To create an AutoText entry with the AutoText toolbar, use the following steps:

1 Type a word or phrase that you want to use for an AutoText entry.

2 Select the phrase you've just typed.

You can select any material in a document, including pictures, OLE objects, and nonprinting characters (such as paragraph marks, page breaks, section breaks, and tables).

To learn more about selecting, see "Selecting Text" page 85.

3 Click the New button on the AutoText toolbar. The Create AutoText dialog box will open.

4 Edit the name Word proposes, or type a new name for the AutoText entry.

5 Click OK.

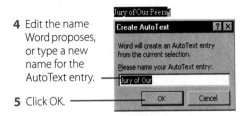

To jump to the AutoText tab of the AutoCorrect dialog box, click the AutoText button at the left end of the AutoText toolbar, as shown here:

Click here to jump to the AutoText tab.

Click here to create a new AutoText entry.

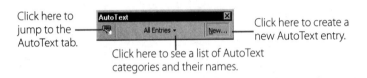

Click here to see a list of AutoText categories and their names.

Naming AutoText Entries

If the primary method you use to insert an AutoText entry is to type the Auto-Text name and then to press F3, type a short name for the AutoText entry. Also type a short name for the AutoText entry if you turn on the Show AutoComplete Tip For AutoText And Dates check box on the AutoText tab of the AutoCorrect dialog box. If, however, the primary method you use to insert an AutoText entry is the AutoText toolbar, you might find it more useful to accept the AutoText name Word suggests. This longer name makes it easier to identify the AutoText entry in the list on the AutoText toolbar.

To create an AutoText entry in the AutoText dialog box, use these steps:

1 Type a word or phrase you want to use for an AutoText entry.

2 Select the phrase you've just typed. You can select any material in a document, including pictures, objects, and nonprinting characters (such as paragraph marks, page breaks, section breaks, and tables).

3 After you select the phrase, choose the Tools AutoCorrect command, and then click the AutoText tab. Word uses part of the phrase you selected as the proposed name.

4 Edit the name Word proposes, or type a new name for the AutoText entry.

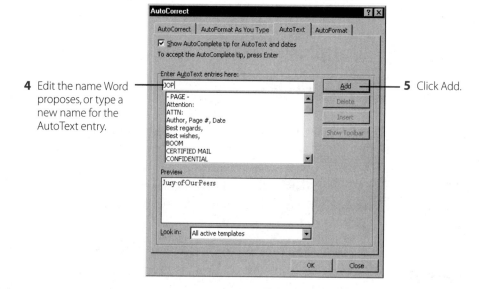

5 Click Add.

Putting an AutoText Entry in Your Document

To place an AutoText entry in your document, you can type its name in the document and direct Word to replace the name with the AutoText command on the Insert menu, or you can select the name from the AutoText toolbar.

Here are the steps to insert an AutoText entry by typing:

1 Type the AutoText name.

The AutoText name must be a separate word. This means the AutoText name must be preceded and followed by a space, a punctuation mark, or a nonprinting character (for example, a paragraph mark, a newline character, a tab character, a manual page break, or a section break). If it's not, Word reports on the status bar that the text is not a valid AutoText name. If this happens after you perform step 2, select the name, and then perform step 2 again.

2 Press F3.

To insert an AutoText entry by selecting it from the AutoText toolbar, use these steps:

1 Click the down arrow on the AutoText toolbar.

2 Select the AutoText name from the Name list.

Changing an AutoText Entry

At times, you might need to change an AutoText entry. For example, if you use an abbreviation for a company name and the company changes its name, you'll need to edit the AutoText entry to reflect the name change, if you want to keep using the same abbreviation as the AutoText name. Use the following steps to change an AutoText entry:

1 Select the new text or item for the AutoText entry.

2 Choose the Tools AutoCorrect command, and then click the AutoText tab.

3 From the Name list, select the name of the AutoText entry you want to change.

4 Click the Delete button.

5 In the Enter AutoText Entries Here box, type the name you just deleted.

6 Click the Add button.

Deleting AutoText

You'll probably find that you create some AutoText entries that you need for a while and then don't need anymore. You ought to throw out these leftovers for the sake of shortening the list of AutoText names, saving computer memory, and unburdening Word so that it can run as fast as possible. To delete an AutoText entry, take these steps:

1 Choose the Tools AutoCorrect command, and then click the AutoText tab.

2 From the Name list, select the name of the AutoText entry you want to delete.

3 Click the Delete button, and then click OK.

V

General Documents

Format the Text with Styles

Perhaps one of the most important tasks you can perform in a template to make it suitable for building a particular type of document is to set up styles that help you format the document as you create it. The following sections tell you about what styles are and how to set them up.

Style Foundations

Styles set the appearances of paragraphs and characters precisely because styles are built from text and paragraph formatting. A style offers all the character and paragraph looks listed in Table 19-4.

All it takes to make a style is a different name, even if two or more styles set all the same character and paragraph looks. All it takes to make a style *unique* is for any one of the character or paragraph looks to be different from the look in any other style.

You use a paragraph style to set the look of lines and the look of text for the entire paragraph. You use a character style to set the look of text within a paragraph. With a paragraph style you can set the look of a paragraph in any part of a document. You can apply a character style to any text anywhere in a document.

A paragraph style sets all the character and paragraph looks listed in Table 19-4. A character style, on the other hand, sets only the character looks shown in Table 19-4.

TABLE 19-4.   The Building Blocks of Styles.

Scope of Style	Formatting Choices
Character looks	Font name; font style; font size; underlining; color; effects (strikethrough, superscript, subscript, hidden, small caps, all caps); horizontal spacing; vertical position; kerning; and language
Paragraph looks	Indention (left, right, first, hanging); space before the paragraph; space after the paragraph; line spacing; alignment (left, center, right, justified); widow/orphan control; keep lines together; keep with next; page break before; line numbers; automatic hyphenation; tab stops (default and user-set); borders; numbering (numbers and bullets); and frame

Paragraph Styles

Word uses the Normal style for all your paragraphs and the Default Paragraph Font character style unless you tell Word to use a different style. Normal is the most basic style, usually used for most of the paragraphs in a document. The Normal style is also the basis for most of the other styles in Word.

Because you begin every document with the Normal style, any text or paragraph formatting you set actually changes the looks of the Normal style. For example, when you center a Normal paragraph, you overrule Normal's left alignment with centered alignment. In the same way, when you set text to boldface in a Normal paragraph, you overrule Normal's nonboldface look with boldface. If you give the whole bundle of changes and other original looks a new style name, you build a new style that you can apply to other paragraphs. If you give the whole bundle of changes and other original looks the same style name, you change the existing style, and the changes affect all the paragraphs in the document that use that style.

Each paragraph has its own style, which can be the same as or different from the styles of the paragraphs around it. The style name remains with each paragraph as long as you want. To change the look of the paragraph at any time, you use a different style. To change the look of all paragraphs with the same style, you change the building blocks (looks) of the style. When you change the looks of a style, Word uses the new looks for all the paragraphs that use that style.

Character Styles

In contrast to a paragraph style, which contains formatting settings for an entire paragraph, a character style sets a different look for selected text within a paragraph. The formatting of a character style overrules the text formatting of the paragraph style.

Word contains 10 built-in character styles: Comment Reference, Default Paragraph Font, Emphasis, Endnote Reference, FollowedHyperlink, Footnote Reference, Hyperlink, Line Number, Page Number, and Strong.

The Default Paragraph Font character style is basically a negative style. That means you use the Default Paragraph Font style to remove any special character formatting you added to text in a paragraph and to remove any other character style.

Character styles are useful for special text that needs a special format—for example, footnote reference marks, comment reference marks, page numbers, and line numbers. Other examples include book titles (in italics), dates and numbers (in a slightly smaller font size), or special terms (in boldface).

Designing Your Own Styles

Using styles to set the look of text gives you additional design power with a minimum amount of effort. Yet, even though Word contains 75 built-in styles, you'll find that these styles don't even begin to meet all your needs for the look of paragraphs and text. It's more than likely that you'll need to build your own styles.

You can build additional paragraph styles to set the look of special paragraphs—paragraphs you want to set apart from their surroundings, such as quotations, pictures, or sidebars.

? SEE ALSO

For more information on applying styles to documents, see "Using Different Styles," page 54.

You can also build additional character styles to set the look of special words and phrases within paragraphs. By building character styles, you make it easy to apply certain looks to special terms and phrases (and later change those looks). For instance, you can create character styles for technical terms, special names, or book titles.

You can build a style from the changes you make to paragraphs and text, or you can create a new style from scratch, that is, by setting the looks settings within the Style dialog box. The following sections explain how to use both methods for building both paragraph and character styles.

Designing Your Own Paragraph Style

To build your own styles, you can simply set paragraph looks—including the font—and then give the overall look a name.

You can practice creating a style with the following steps:

1 Set your line spacing to double by pressing Ctrl+2, and then type a sample paragraph.

2 Drag the left-indent marker (the square below the two triangles at the left end of the ruler) to the 1-inch marker.

3 Select the entire paragraph, and increase its point size by 1 by pressing Ctrl+].

4 With the paragraph still selected, click the Style box on the Formatting toolbar.

5 In the Style box, type a name for the new style—for example, *Essays*—and press Enter.

Style names can be as long as 255 characters and can include any character except a backslash (\), curly braces ({}), and a semicolon (;). Use commas only as special characters to separate multiple names for a style. The commas and the multiple names together cannot be longer than 255 characters.

After you have named the style, you have finished building it. You can click the down arrow beside the Style box to see that the new style has been added to the list. Word saves the style when you save the document.

 TIP

> **Check the Font Looks When Building Styles**
> When you build a style using paragraph formats, be sure that the insertion point or the selection is located in text that has the font you want the style to use. If a paragraph contains more than one font—for example, both regular text and boldface text—the new style will use the font at the beginning of the selection or at the insertion point.

Designing Styles from Scratch

To build a style, you can use the method explained in the preceding section: set up the paragraph the way you want it to look, apply character formats to its text, and then assign a style name. If you're new to styles and you need to build a style as you work on a document, this method is the quickest. It's quicker yet if you use shortcut keys to set the formatting so that you don't need to open any dialog boxes.

But you can also design a style from scratch—that is, set the style *?* *then* insert your text and apply the style to it. When you design *?*

from scratch, you choose the Format Style command only one time to design as many styles as you need, and then you close the dialog box when you finish your work.

This method takes more planning and an ability to visualize the look from abstract dialog box settings, but the benefits in speed and efficiency are great.

When you choose the Format Style command, the Style dialog box appears, as shown in Figure 19-11.

FIGURE 19-11.

Style dialog box.

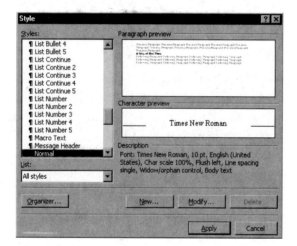

NOTE

You can copy styles from one template file to another. Click the Organizer button in the Style dialog box, open the two files to view their style lists in the Organizer dialog box, and select the styles you want to copy. The copy button displays an arrow that shows you which way the selected styles will be copied. See "Sharing Macros," page 848 for a similar procedure that applies to macros.

Understanding Style Descriptions

When you choose the Format Style command, the Style dialog box displays a description of the format settings the selected style gives a paragraph and its text, as shown here:

Description
Font: Times New Roman, 10 pt, English (United States), Char scale 100%, Flush left, Line spacing single, Widow/orphan control, Body text

The description shown in the next example begins with the style (Normal) that is the basis of the selected style, followed by a plus sign and any changes from the base style:

Description
Normal + Indent: Hanging 0.25"

In the description above, the text settings are the same as those in the base style, Normal. The second part of the description, however, includes a hanging indent that is not part of the Normal style. Notice the colon following the word "Indent." The colon gives you a visual clue about where a new part of the description begins. A style whose description simply reads "Normal +" is identical to Normal. In the following example, you see a description of a character style:

Description
Default Paragraph Font + Font: Haettenschweiler, No effect

All character styles are based on the Default Paragraph Font character style, which in turn is based on the font of the underlying paragraph style. (The exact description of the Default Paragraph Font may be different for paragraphs with different styles, depending on which font and font settings are defined for each paragraph style.) The rest of the description shows how the style differs from the Default Paragraph Font. In this case, the only change is the font.

V

General Documents

To design a new style from scratch, use the following steps:

1 Click the New button in the Style dialog box. The New Style dialog box will open.

2 Type the name for your new style.

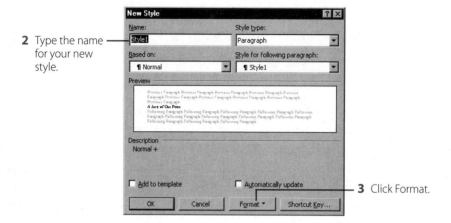

3 Click Format.

4 Choose one of the commands from the drop-down menu, shown here:

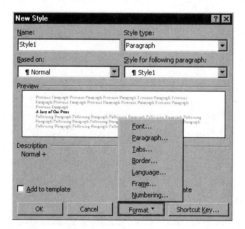

Each of these commands opens another dialog box in which you can set formats. The Style and New Style dialog boxes remain open underneath. When you select settings and close the dialog box, Word returns to the New Style dialog box so that you can set other settings for the style.

NOTE

The Based On list box in the New Style dialog box lets you select a base style to modify. For example, if you want to create your own heading style, you might want to start with the Heading 1 style. The Style For Following Paragraph box lets you specify what style will always be applied to the next paragraph after a paragraph that has the style you are creating. See "What's Next? Styles for Next Paragraphs," page 837, and "Building on the Past: Basing One Style on Another," page 837.

5 When you have finished setting all the necessary formatting for the style and you are back in the New Style dialog box, click OK. Word returns to the Style dialog box.

To design another style, click the New button again and repeat the steps you just completed. When you're all done designing styles, click Close in the Style dialog box.

Style Shortcut Keys

Instead of selecting a style from the Style box on the Formatting toolbar, you can assign shortcut keys to frequently used styles. (Word has already assigned shortcut keys for the Normal, Heading 1, Heading 2, and Heading 3 styles.) To assign a shortcut key when you create the style, follow these steps:

1 Click the Shortcut Key button in the New Style dialog box. Word opens the Customize Keyboard dialog box.

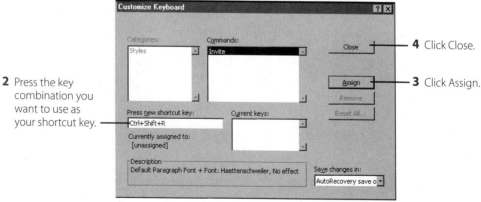

V

General Documents

> **> NOTE**
>
> If the shortcut key is already assigned, Word displays that assignment in the dialog box, and you should choose a new key combination. If you assign a key combination that is a shortcut key for another style, command, macro, AutoText, font, or symbol, you will cancel the shortcut key for that item, and the shortcut key will be assigned to your style.

To assign shortcut keys to your styles at any time, use the following steps:

1 Choose the Tools Customize command, and click the Keyboard button.

2 Click Styles in the Categories list.

3 Select a style in the Styles list.

4 Press the key combination for the shortcut key, verify that the shortcut key is not already assigned, and click the Assign button.

5 Repeat steps 3 and 4 to assign shortcut keys to all the styles you want, and then click the Close button.

For more information on assigning shortcut keys, see Appendix D, "Playing the Keyboard."

Designing Your Own Character Style

In addition to Word's built-in character styles mentioned earlier, you can also design character styles of your own. You might want character styles for special terms, or you might find a character style a convenient way to easily mark words that are in a different language for special proofing operations, rather than always having to choose the Tools Language command to mark the words.

To build a character style, use the following steps:

1 Insert some text, and then format it.

2 Select the formatted text, and then choose the Format Style command.

3 In the Style dialog box, click the New button to open the New Style dialog box.

4 Type a name for the character style. ────

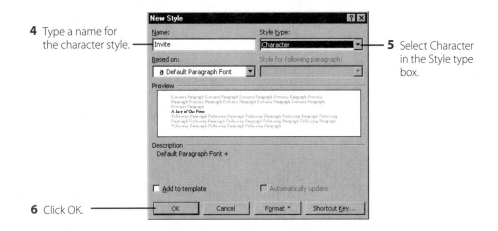

5 Select Character in the Style type box.

6 Click OK. ────

7 Click Apply in the Style dialog box.

If you click Close instead of Apply in the Style dialog box, Word doesn't apply the character style to the selected text. Rather, Word leaves the character style set to Default Paragraph Font and treats the formatting you've added as an addition to the paragraph style.

Choose the Format Style command again. In the Style dialog box, shown in Figure 19-12, you can observe the following points about character styles:

■ When the selected text in the document uses a character style, both the paragraph style and the character style show a right-pointing triangle (▶) next to their names in the Styles list. In fact, unless you select a different character style, the list shows Default Paragraph Font with a right-pointing triangle in addition to the name of the paragraph style you're using.

■ Paragraph styles appear with a ¶; character styles appear with a boldface underscored letter **a**.

■ When the selected text in the document uses a character style, the Character Preview box and the Description box show the effect and the description of the character style.

General Documents

V

FIGURE 19-12.
A character style in the Style dialog box.

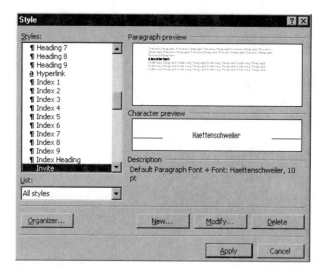

Style Makeover

For more information about sharing style changes among documents, see "Sharing Macros," page 848, and adapt the steps for styles.

The process of changing and refining a style is the same for all styles: you change a style by changing the font or paragraph formats of the text and then copying them to the style you want to change. The Formatting toolbar is the quickest way to change a style this way. You can also use the Format Style command to directly change the style's description. In the procedures that follow, you'll learn how to use these two different but equally effective methods to change the descriptions of built-in styles.

These procedures show you how to change styles within a single document only. To change a style for all documents, you must change the style's description in all the templates you use. In particular, you'll want to change the style's description in the Normal template, which will share the change with many documents.

You cannot change the names of Word's built-in styles, but you can create additional names; see "Renaming a Macro," page 850, and adapt the steps for styles.

Changing a Paragraph Style

After you design a style, you might want to change its settings. You can change a style by setting formats for the text and paragraphs and then adding those changes to the style's description. Here are the steps to change a paragraph style by example:

1 Select a paragraph with the style you want to change.

2 Set up the paragraph to look the way you want all paragraphs with this style to look.

To include font setting changes when you change a style by example, select an example of the new font before changing the style.

3 Click in the Style box on the Formatting toolbar, and then press Enter. This Modify Style dialog box appears:

Click here to change the style's formatting to the selected paragraph's formatting.

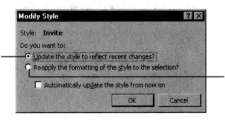

Click here to apply the style's existing formatting to the selected paragraph.

4 Select the Update The Style To Reflect Recent Changes option, and then click OK.

All paragraphs in your document with that style now change to match the example.

The other option in the Modify Style dialog box, Reapply The Formatting Of The Style To The Selection, removes the changes you made to the formatting. Clicking Cancel cancels the process of changing the style.

For information about how to add styles to templates, see "Sharing Macros," page 848, and adapt the steps for styles.

If you want a style change to appear in all new documents you create, add the style to your Normal template.

Changing a Character Style

Although the only way to create character styles is with the Format Style command, you can change them by using the Formatting toolbar,

V

General Documents

just as you do for paragraph styles. You change a character style with the Formatting toolbar as follows:

1 Select some text.

2 Select the character style from the Style box on the Formatting toolbar. If the character style doesn't appear in the Style box list, press Escape, hold down the Shift key, and then click the Style box. All styles, including the character style, should now appear in the list.

3 Add to the selected text the format settings you want to add to the style.

4 Press Ctrl+Shift+S, press Enter, and then choose OK in the Modify Style dialog box that appears.

You change a character style with the Format Style command as follows:

1 Choose the Format Style command, and select the character style.

2 Click the Modify button, click the Format button, and then select Font (or Language).

3 In the Font dialog box, select the format settings you want to change for the style, and then click OK. If you're changing the language, select the new language in the Language dialog box, and then click OK.

4 Click OK in the Modify dialog box, and then click Close in the Style dialog box.

Fine-Tuning Your Styles

As part of designing or changing a paragraph style, you have a couple more options that add power to a style. You can set up a style to automatically select a different paragraph style when you start a new paragraph from the end of a preceding paragraph. You can also create a new style based on any existing style.

Weaving Styles Together

There are two powerful ways to link styles—by setting the Style For Following Paragraph and by basing one style on another style. By linking a chain of paragraph styles, you can quickly set up special parts of your work to use the appropriate style automatically. Basing one style on another reduces the number of changes you need to make in order to build a new style. When a style is based on another style, changing a common setting in the base style makes that same change in all the styles that are based on it.

What's Next? Styles for Next Paragraphs

When you finish a paragraph, the paragraph style's Style For Following Paragraph setting sets the style for the next paragraph. If the setting is for a different style, the new paragraph automatically uses the different style. For example, after you insert a heading paragraph, you might want the next paragraph always to appear in the Normal style.

You change paragraph styles most often around headings, lists, and other such text. In many of these situations, the sequence of styles is predictable: a heading appears first, followed by some regular text; or a title appears first, then a subtitle, then the author's name, and then some regular text. When styles always—or almost always—appear in the same sequence, you can save yourself time and effort by setting up a style for the next paragraph to automatically select the next style.

Word takes advantage of this feature for some of its built-in styles. The styles Caption, Heading 1 through Heading 9, Index 1 through Index 9, Table of Authorities, Table of Figures, TOA Heading, and TOC 1 through TOC 9 all have Normal as their style for the following paragraph. The Index Heading style has Index 1 as its style for the following paragraph. All the other built-in styles simply use their own style for the following paragraph.

When you build a new paragraph style, Word uses that style for the following paragraph so that you can create a series of paragraphs with the same style. But when you know that the next paragraph should look different, you can set up a different style for the following paragraph.

Building on the Past: Basing One Style on Another

In the New Style dialog box and the Modify Style dialog box shown on page 839, you'll see a box called Based On. This box shows the base style for the style you're building or changing.

General Documents

> If the selected style is Normal, the Based On box in the Modify Style dialog box shows (no style)—and you can't change it.

Basing one style on another means starting with one style and then changing its description to build a new style. Remember that a style description includes the name of the base style, followed by a plus sign and a list of the changes. The name of the base style that appears in the style description also appears in the Based On box.

Basing one style on another offers an efficient way to build new styles that are variations of a common source style. It is possible to create groups of styles that are based on a single style or on a chain of styles, as shown in Figure 19-13.

FIGURE 19-13.

Relationship of styles based on other styles.

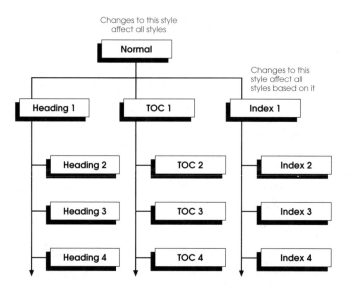

Three sets of Word styles in particular can work better if each group is based on a common style for the group: Heading 1 through Heading 9, TOC 1 through TOC 9, and Index 1 through Index 9. In any document that uses multiple heading levels, the similarities from one level to the next are strong. Basing the Heading 2 through Heading 9 styles on the Heading 1 style makes changing the common characteristics of the group easy. You need to change only the base style (Heading 1) in the group. Word then passes the new look to other styles in the group.

NOTE

When you change a base style, those changes pass to the styles that are based on it only if those styles have that part of their formats in common. If a style has a different text format or different paragraph settings from the part of the base style you change, the change does not pass to those parts of the styles that have a different setting. For example, if style 2 is based on style 1 and the difference is point size (say, style 1 uses 16 points and style 2 uses 12 points), changing style 1 to 18 points does not change style 2 to 18 points. If, however, both style 1 and style 2 use boldface and not italic, changing style 1 to boldface italic changes style 2 to boldface italic.

As an example of setting up a group of styles based on a common style, the following steps show you how to base styles Heading 2 through Heading 9 on Heading 1 instead of Normal:

1 Choose the Format Style command.

2 In the Style dialog box, select All Styles in the List box.

3 Select Heading 2 in the Styles list, and click the Modify button. The Modify Style dialog box opens.

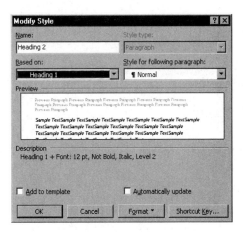

4 Select Heading 1 in the Based On box.

5 Change any parts of the description that are different from the Heading 1 description but that you want to match the Heading 1 description. For example, if the Heading 2 description shows Not Bold, click the Format button and choose Font, click the Font tab,

General Documents

select Bold from the Font Style list, and then click OK in the Font dialog box. Or, if the Heading style you are changing shows an indent different from Heading 1, click the Format button and choose Paragraph, click the Indents And Spacing tab, set the indent to the same as Heading 1, and then click OK in the Paragraph dialog box.

6 Click OK in the Modify Style dialog box.

7 For each of the Heading 3 through Heading 9 styles, repeat steps 2 through 6 (selecting the next Heading style in step 4).

8 When you finish changing the Based On styles, click the Close button in the Style dialog box.

Now, if you want to add a bottom border to all your heading styles, you need add it only to Heading 1.

The Font Dialog Box

When you set formatting for text, you can pass the format settings to the Normal style of the document's template. To do so, open the Font dialog box, shown in Figure 19-14, by choosing the Format Font command or by pressing Ctrl+D. This dialog box contains a Default button that is visible no matter which tab you make changes on.

FIGURE 19-14.
The Font dialog box.

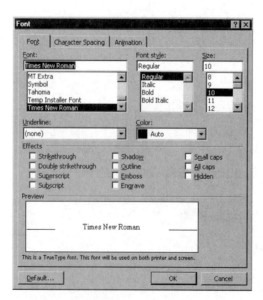

> ### What's the Root of All Styles?
>
> When you build a new style, you might use a style other than Normal as your base—but that base style, somewhere down the line, is also most likely based on Normal. A style can actually have as many as nine layers of styles between it and Normal; you can think of this arrangement as a tree, with the branches all connecting at the base to a single trunk. Figure 19-13, on page 838, provides an illustration of these links.
>
> All but one of the built-in paragraph styles in Word are based on the Normal style. All the character styles except Default Paragraph Font itself are based on the Default Paragraph Font character style. Most of the paragraph styles you build will probably also be based on Normal. And most of the character styles you create will probably be based on Default Paragraph Font.

To pass your changes on a tab to the Normal style in the document's template, click the Default button. Word displays a message that describes the change and the template that will change. Click Yes to make the change. Click No if you don't want to make the change or if you don't want to change the template named in the message.

The Set Language Dialog Box

When you select a language for a document, you can pass your language choice to the document's template at the same time. Open the Language dialog box, shown in Figure 19-15, by choosing the Tools Language command and then choosing Set Language from the submenu.

FIGURE 19-15.
The Set Language dialog box.

To pass your language choice to the document's template, click the Default button. Word displays a message that describes the change and the template that will change. Click Yes to make the change. Click No if you don't want to make the change described or if you don't want to change the template named in the message.

The New Style Dialog Box

When you build a new style using the Format Style command, you can store the style in the template as well as in the document. To store the new style in the template:

1 Choose the Format Style command, and then click the New button in the Style dialog box.

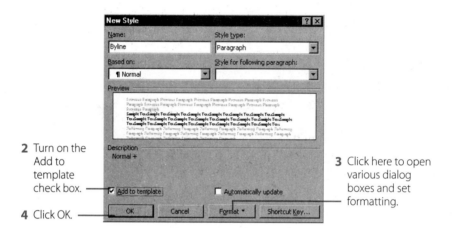

2 Turn on the Add to template check box.

3 Click here to open various dialog boxes and set formatting.

4 Click OK.

The Modify Style Dialog Box

When you change a style using the Format Style command, you can store the style changes in the template, as well as in the document:

1 Choose the Format Style command, and click the Modify button.

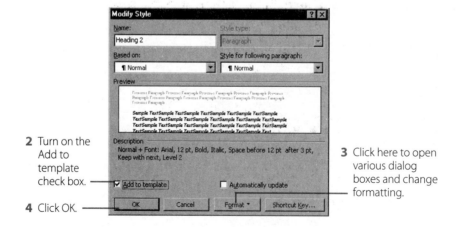

2 Turn on the Add to template check box.

3 Click here to open various dialog boxes and change formatting.

4 Click OK.

Set Up Tools: Recording and Running Macros

One of the most powerful ways to use a document template in Word, perhaps the most powerful, is using it to customize the working conditions in a document. A template can store changes to menus, toolbars, keyboard assignments, and macro projects. If the template you're creating needs special commands or interface changes, you'll want to set up these tools to enhance your powers with Word.

This section covers macros; you'll find directions for customizing menus, toolbars, and the keyboard in the appendixes.

 NOTE

> In Word 97, macros are built on Microsoft Visual Basic for Applications. While Word can convert and run macros built in earlier versions of Word, building a macro by hand now requires knowledge of programming in the Visual Basic for Applications Editor. This topic is far too extensive to be covered in this book. For information about programming macros by hand, see *Microsoft Word 97/Visual Basic Step by Step,* by Michael Halvorson and Chris Kinata (Redmond: Microsoft Press, 1997). You can, however, gain some limited use of macros by recording them.

General Documents

Building Robots: Recording a Macro

A macro is a miniature program of Word commands and actions that you can run simply by starting the macro. The easiest way to create a macro is to record a series of actions that you perform while you're processing a document. Here are the steps:

SEE ALSO

For information about changing toolbars, see Appendix B, "Working with Toolbars"; for changing menus, see Appendix C, "Establishing Your Menus"; for changing the keyboard assignments, see Appendix D, "Playing the Keyboard."

1 Start the macro recorder either by double-clicking the REC indicator on the status bar or by choosing the Tools Macro command and then the Record New Macro command from the submenu.

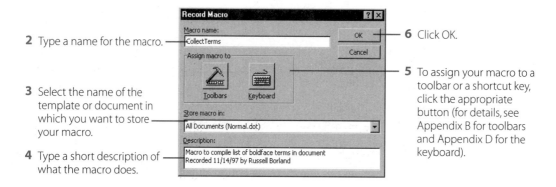

2 Type a name for the macro.

3 Select the name of the template or document in which you want to store your macro.

4 Type a short description of what the macro does.

6 Click OK.

5 To assign your macro to a toolbar or a shortcut key, click the appropriate button (for details, see Appendix B for toolbars and Appendix D for the keyboard).

> **NOTE**
>
> A template or document name appears in the Store Macro In list only if that template or document is open. You must either open the template or document or open a document that has the template attached to it. You can, however, use the Organizer dialog box to copy or move the macro to another template after you record the macro; see "Sharing Macros," page 848, for instructions.

Regardless of which method you use to start recording the macro, Word displays the REC button in the status bar to show that you're now recording. Word also displays the Macro Record toolbar and attaches a cassette tape icon to the mouse pointer, shown in Figure 19-16, when the pointer is in a document window.

FIGURE 19-16.
The Macro Record toolbar.

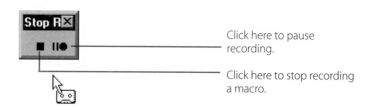

Click here to pause recording.

Click here to stop recording a macro.

? SEE ALSO
The three text files AUTOOPEN.DOC, LINETRIM.DOC, and MACBUTON.DOC give you instructions for recording three macro examples.

7 Perform all the actions you want to record as part of the macro. These actions affect the active document, so you can see the effects as you go.

If you need to pause during recording to set up your next step, click the Pause button, shown in Figure 19-16, on the Macro Record toolbar. When you are ready to resume recording, click the Pause button again.

> **NOTE**
>
> Be aware that Word does not record any mouse actions other than choosing a command from a menu and selecting options in a dialog box, on the ruler, or on a toolbar. In particular, Word does not record positioning the insertion point or selecting text with the mouse. In fact, Word doesn't even allow you to use the mouse in these capacities while you're recording; you must use the keyboard instead of the mouse. To let you know that mouse actions in the text area are not recorded, Word attaches the cassette tape icon to the mouse pointer on screen.

If you make an error as you record a macro, you can choose Edit Undo or click the Undo button on the Standard toolbar. Word records all actions, including those that you undo, but that's OK if the action is short and doing and then undoing an action won't affect the efficiency of the macro. If you open the wrong dialog box, simply press Escape; Word doesn't record the command when you cancel a dialog box.

If you find that your entire procedure is not going right, you should start over. To begin again, stop the recorder by clicking on the Stop button, shown in Figure 19-16, on the Macro Record toolbar. Then restart recording, and give the macro the same name you've been using. When Word asks whether you want to replace the existing macro, click Yes, and then begin to carry out the actions for creating the macro.

8 When you finish performing all the actions you want to record, click the Stop button on the Macro Record toolbar or double-click the REC button in the status bar. Word stops recording your actions and dims the REC button, hides the Macro Record toolbar, and removes the cassette icon from the mouse pointer.

The macro you recorded is now ready for you to run. You can also assign it to a toolbar, a menu, or a shortcut key (if you didn't assign it when you started recording).

Running a Macro

After you record a macro, it's ready to run. Use one of the following methods to run a macro.

- Choose the Tools Macro command, and then choose Macros from the submenu. (For information about using the Tools Macro command, see "Running a Macro with the Tools Macro Command," below.)

- Give the macro a toolbar button, and click that button.

- Give the macro a keyboard shortcut, and press those keys.

- Give the macro a command on a menu, and choose that menu command.

- Insert a MACROBUTTON field, and double-click that field. (For information about using a MACROBUTTON field, see "Launching Macros with the MACROBUTTON Field," next page.)

Shutting Down the Robot: Stopping a Macro

Before you run your macro, it's a good idea to know how to stop it in case it starts doing something not quite right. To stop a macro that's running, use these steps:

1 Press Escape. Word displays a message that the macro was interrupted.

2 Click OK.

Running a Macro with the Tools Macro Command

To run a macro with the Tools Macro command, use the following steps:

1 When a document is open, choose the Tools Macro command, and then choose Macros from the submenu. You'll see the Macro dialog box.

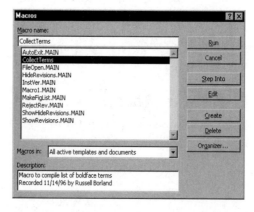

2   Select the macro you want to run.

3   Click the Run button. Word runs the macro in the active document window.

Launching Macros with the MACROBUTTON Field

The MACROBUTTON field runs a macro from within a document. When you double-click the MACROBUTTON field, Word runs the macro listed in the MACROBUTTON field's instructions. The instructions look like this:

```
{ MACROBUTTON FilePrint
Double-Click Here to Print This
Page}
```

TIP

> If you use the Insert Field command to insert a MACROBUTTON field, Word leaves a blank space in front of the right field character. Remove this space unless you want an extra space at the end of your result.

When you switch from the field's code to the result, the field looks like this:

```
Double-Click Here to Print This Page
```

The result of the MACROBUTTON field (what you see in your document) is always the text that you provide in the field's instructions. The result must fit on one line, regardless of the line's length. You can set any font settings you like for the result. By setting aside this field in a paragraph by itself, you can add to it any paragraph formatting and borders and shading you might want. If you don't add any special font settings to the result, it looks like regular text.

TIP

> Do not enclose the instructions for the field's result in quotation marks unless you want the quotation marks to appear in the result.

Because you can use graphics for the field's result, you can make the MacroButton look like anything you want. For example, you might want to use Windows Paint to create a custom button, save the button as a file, and then insert the graphic inside the MACROBUTTON field. The field can be surrounded with text explaining the options or placed in a table for alignment with other MacroButtons.

The MACROBUTTON field can run any macro or any built-in command, making it possible to create some exciting actions and results.

> In addition to double-clicking a MACROBUTTON field to run the macro, you can position the insertion point immediately in front of the field, or select the entire field, and then press the Run MACROBUTTON shortcut key (Alt+Shift+F9).

Macro Housekeeping

You can copy or move macros to different templates and documents to restrict or expand the macros' availability. You can also delete unneeded macros, and you can rename macros.

Sharing Macros

At times, you might record a macro in one template or document and then decide that you want to use the macro in all documents (globally). Or you might record a global macro that you really use in only one or two special templates. Perhaps you want to copy or move a macro from a template or document someone gives you into your Normal template, to one of your special templates, or to a document. Word makes it easy to copy or move a macro from one template to another.

Copying a Macro Between Templates and Documents

To copy a macro from one template or document to another, follow these steps:

1 Choose the Tools Macro command, and then choose the Macros command from the submenu.

2 Click the Organizer button, and click the Macro Project Items tab in the Organizer dialog box.

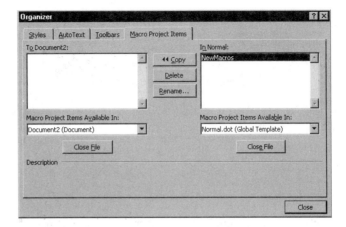

3 In the list on the left, open the template or document that contains the macro you want to copy. To open a different template or document in the Organizer dialog box, click the Close File button under the template you don't want to use. The button name changes to Open File; click it to display the Open dialog box. Select the template or document you want to open, and then click OK.

4 In the list on the right, open the template or document to which you want to copy the macro.

5 Select the macro you want to copy. (You can select more than one macro by holding down the Ctrl key as you click the names.)

6 Click the Copy button.

7 When you have finished, click the Close button to close the Organizer dialog box.

Moving a Macro Between Templates

To move a macro, you simply combine copying and deleting in the Organizer dialog box. First you copy the macro to the new template or document, as described in the preceding section. Then you delete the macro from its original template or document, as described in the next section.

Deleting a Macro

When you no longer need a macro, you should delete it to save computer memory, to save disk space, and to avoid confusion when you

V

General Documents

want to reuse a macro name. Here are the steps to delete a macro from an active template or document:

1 Choose the Tools Macro command, and then choose the Macros command from the submenu.

2 In the Macro Name box, select the macro you want to delete.

3 Click the Delete button.

4 Click Yes when Word asks you to confirm the deletion.

5 Click the Close button to close the Macro dialog box.

To delete a macro from a template that isn't currently active, follow these steps:

1 Choose the Tools Macro command, and then choose the Macros command from the submenu.

2 Click the Organizer button, and then click the Macro Project Items tab.

3 Click one of the Close File buttons. The button name changes to Open File; click it to display the Open dialog box. Select the template or document that contains the macro to be deleted, and then click OK.

4 Select the macro name, and then click the Delete button to delete the macro.

5 Click Yes when Word asks you to confirm the deletion.

6 Click the Close button to close the dialog box.

Renaming a Macro

Change the name of a macro with these steps:

1 Choose the Tools Macro command, and then choose the Macros command from the submenu.

2 Click the Organizer button, and then click the Macro Project Items tab.

3 If the macro you want to rename is not listed in one of the boxes, click one of the Close File buttons. The button name changes to

Open File; click it to display the Open dialog box. Select the template or document that contains the macro to be renamed, and then click OK.

4 Select the macro that you want to rename, and then click the Rename button to display the Rename dialog box, shown here:

5 Type a new name for the macro.

6 Click OK.

7 Click the Close button to close the dialog box.

Word's Automatic Macros

Word lets you record five automatic macros that Word runs when you perform certain actions. You can use these automatic macros to perform tasks for you when you start or quit Word and when you create, open, or close a document.

You record an automatic macro as you do any macro, but you give it one of the five special names that Word recognizes as automatic macros: AutoExec, AutoNew, AutoOpen, AutoClose, and AutoExit. The "Auto" part of each name indicates that Word runs these macros automatically. The second part of each name tells you when Word runs the macro, as follows:

- AutoExec runs when you start Word.

- AutoNew runs when you create a new document.

- AutoOpen runs when you open a document.

- AutoClose runs when you close a document.

- AutoExit runs when you quit Word.

Overriding AutoExec

To prevent AutoExec from running, hold down the Shift key when starting Word. Note that when you start Word with a different macro, Word does not run the AutoExec macro. For example, if you start Word from a shortcut and set the shortcut's Target property to something like *C:\winword.exe /mFile1*, Word runs the macro named "File1" but not AutoExec. To run AutoExec in this case, include it in the Target line of the shortcut's properties. For example, you would set the Target line to *C:\winword.exe /mFile1 /MAutoExec* to start Word and then run both the File 1 macro and the AutoExec macro.

The AutoNew, AutoOpen, AutoClose, and AutoExit macros are available for both global and special template macros. A global automatic macro runs every time you create, open, or close any document. An automatic macro in a special template runs when you create a document based on that template or when you open or close a document with that special template attached to it. The AutoExec macro runs only as a global macro.

Updating Fields with AutoNew and AutoOpen

A slick way to use the AutoNew macro is to have it update in each new document all the fields that are part of the template. For example, you can insert a field in the template that asks you for the name and address for a letter. The AutoNew macro can guide you through inserting specific text in a document and can place the text at the field's position. You can also set up an AutoOpen macro to update fields so that the document is up-to-date each time you work on it or print it. One example of this type of AutoOpen macro appears in the file AUTOOPEN.DOC on the CD in this book.

Store Your Changes

You can save the changes to the Blank Document template, or you can create a new template. If you save your changes to the Blank Document template, every document you work on will reflect the changes you made. If, however, you want to use the changed document for more specialized documents, you'll want to save the changes to a new document template, which keeps Word's Blank Document template unchanged.

To store changes to the Blank Document template as a new template, use the following steps:

1 Choose the File Save As command.

2 Double-click the folder in which you want to store the new template.

3 Give the template you've just remodeled a new name.

4 Select the Document Template option in the Save As Type box.

5 Click the Save button.

To store changes to the Blank Document template, quit Word. Word will, by default, automatically save changes to Normal.dot (the filename for the Blank Document template) when you quit Word. You do, however, have an option to control this saving process. You can direct Word to prompt you before saving Normal.dot, as follows:

1 Choose the Tools Options command, and then click the Save tab.

2 Turn on the Prompt To Save Normal Template check box, and then click OK.

3 Quit Word.

4 When Word asks if you want to save changes to the Normal template, click Yes.

WARNING

> You *must* save the Normal template the first time after you turn on the Prompt To Save Normal Template check box. If you click No when Word asks if you want to save changes, Word doesn't save the setting to prompt you.

5 Restart Word.

From now on, whenever you quit Word, you see the message that asks whether you want to save your changes to the Normal template. To end this prompting, turn off the Prompt To Save Normal Template check box.

Adding a Preview of the Template

When you're creating a new document using a template, it's handy to have a preview of the document the template is set up to create. If you save the template with a preview, you see a picture of the first page the template sets up when you select the template in the New dialog box.

To add a preview of the template, use the following steps:

1 Choose the File Properties command, and then click the Summary tab. You will see a Properties dialog box like this one:

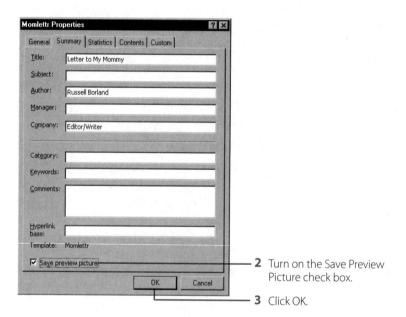

2 Turn on the Save Preview Picture check box.

3 Click OK.

4 Now save the template.

CHAPTER 20

Using Other Global Templates and Add-Ins

After you create a document, you can change the special template attached to it. This way you can use a different set of tools to help you finish the document. Alternatively, rather than swap templates, you can add the materials and tools of a special template as global materials and tools, which puts them at hand as backup.

When you change the special template attached to a document or open additional special templates as global templates, the AutoText and macros of the new templates become available, and the menus, shortcut keys, and toolbars might change. You can combine styles from the new template with styles already in the document. Or you can leave the document styles as they are. The text in the new template and other global templates doesn't merge into the document. This way Word protects the integrity of your document while giving you the new tools you want from another template.

Swapping a Template

You can attach a special template to a document created from the Blank Document template even after you've begun working on the document. You can then change the special template attached to a document. You'll do this to supply tools and materials that you want to use on the document but that the current special template does not contain. For example, if a memo grows too large, you might convert it to a report or a proposal and attach a different special report or proposal template you've set up to simplify finishing the document. If you change the special template to Normal, you in effect make no special template available for your work on the document.

Templates you use to create forms are protected. If you try to attach a form template to a document, Word tells you that it cannot attach a protected template. You can, however, use the Organizer when you want to copy elements from a protected template.

To attach a different special template to an open document, perform the following steps:

1 Choose the Tools Templates And Add-Ins command.

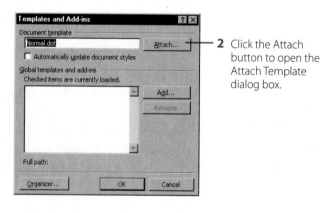

2 Click the Attach button to open the Attach Template dialog box.

5 Click Open.

3 Open the folder for the
type of template you
want to attach to the
current document.

4 Select the special
template you want to
attach.

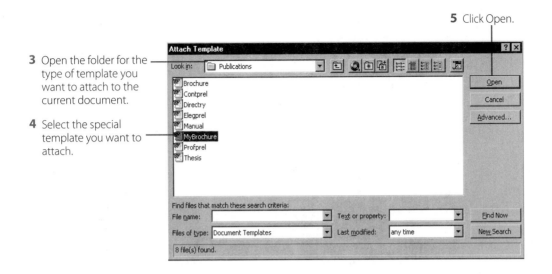

> **NOTE**

If you select the Normal template, the document will not have a special template.

If you want the styles of the new special template to join your current document styles, turn on the Automatically Update Document Styles check box. Turn this check box off if you don't want to use the styles from the attached template. Click OK in the Templates And Add-Ins dialog box to complete the switch to the new special template.

> **NOTE**

If you turn on the Automatically Update Document Styles check box, the descriptions of the template's styles replace the descriptions of the document's styles that have the same style names.

Substituting Your Own Template for Word's Blank Document Template

Whenever you start Word or whenever you click the New button on the Standard toolbar, Word creates a document from the Blank Document template named Normal.dot. If the setup of the Blank Document template doesn't suit you for most instances, you have two choices: you can modify the Blank Document template to suit you, or you can create a new template and substitute it for Normal.dot. In either case, the general template known as Blank Document must have the filename Normal.dot.

The steps to substitute your own template for Normal.dot are as follows:

1 Create a template that suits your needs, and save it in the Templates folder with a name other than Normal.dot.

2 Quit Word.

3 Open the Templates folder.

4 Rename the Normal.dot template supplied by Word—for example, you might call it Original.dot.

5 Rename your own template Normal.dot. (This can be any template that you want to serve as your general Blank Document template, no matter how specialized it is.)

6 Restart Word.

From now on, whenever you start Word or click the New button on the Standard toolbar, Word creates a document from your template (now named Normal.dot) rather than from the Normal.dot template supplied by Word. Also, any template changes you make that Word stores in the general Blank Document template will go into your template, which is now the general Blank Document template.

Using Several Templates at Once

The following steps allow you to make AutoText, macros, and other materials and tools of a special template globally available to all documents you're working on.

1 Choose the Tools Templates And Add-Ins command.

2 Click the Add button to display the Add Template dialog box.

3 Select the folder icon for the type of template you want to add, and then select the template you want to open. If necessary, switch to a different folder or disk. If you have trouble locating a template, use the Find Files That Match These Criteria list boxes.

4 Click the OK button to add the template to the Global Templates And Add-Ins list. Word turns on the check box beside the newly added template name in the Templates And Add-Ins dialog box.

You can add as many global templates as will fit into memory. To save memory, you can deactivate (close) or remove global templates in the Templates And Add-Ins dialog box. If you don't remove the template, it will be available (but not opened) the next time you start Word.

Deactivating Other Global Templates

While you might want to use the tools of additional global templates much of the time, there might be documents in which you don't want another global template muddying the waters. You can deactivate a general template during these times, yet still keep it handy for when you want to reactivate it quickly. Use the following steps to deactivate a global template.

1 Choose the Tools Templates And Add-Ins command.

2 In the Global Templates And Add-Ins list, turn off the check box beside the name of the template you want to deactivate.

3 Click OK.

Reactivating Other Global Templates

After you deactivate a general template, its name remains in the Global Templates And Add-Ins list in the Templates And Add-Ins dialog box. This arrangement makes it easy to reactivate a general template, as follows:

1 Turn on the check box beside the name of the template you want to reactivate.

2 Click OK.

Removing Other Global Templates

You can use the following steps to remove a global template, rather than simply deactivate it.

1 Choose the Tools Templates And Add-Ins command.

2 Select the template name you want to remove.

V

General Documents

3 Click the Remove button, and then click OK.

NOTE

If you set up Word to open an additional global template at startup (see the next topic), you have to use special steps to remove it. For the steps, see "Removing a Global Template Set Up to Open When Word Starts," page 861.

Having Word Open Global Templates at Startup

Use the following steps if you *always* want to start Word with specific global templates open.

1 Choose the Tools Options command, and then click the File Locations tab.

2 Select Startup in the File Types list, and then click the Modify button.

3 Switch to the Startup folder, if necessary.

TIP

If the Startup folder is not active, double-click the My Computer icon, the drive C icon, the Program Files folder, the Microsoft Office folder, the Winword folder, and then the Startup folder.

4 Click the OK button, and then click OK in the Options dialog box.

5 Quit Word.

6 Copy the templates you want Word to open as additional global templates to the Startup folder.

7 Restart Word. Word opens and activates all the templates stored in the Startup folder as global templates.

TIP

Copy templates to the Startup folder rather than move them. If you move template files, Word cannot include them in the Templates list in the New dialog box.

Removing a Global Template
Set Up to Open When Word Starts

Because you can't use the Templates And Add-Ins dialog box to remove global templates that are set up to open when Word starts, you have to use one of two special methods to remove them. You can either remove a template from the Startup folder or change the Startup setting on the File Locations tab in the Options dialog box. The first method removes only the templates you want to remove. The second method removes all the additional global templates you put in the Startup folder.

Use these steps to remove only a specific additional global template:

1 Quit Word.

2 Open the Startup folder.

3 Delete or move the template you no longer want Word to open at startup.

The Startup Folder or the Templates And Add-Ins Dialog Box?

You have two ways to open and use additional global templates: place them in the Startup folder or turn them on in the Templates And Add-Ins dialog box. Which one should you use?

If you copy a document template to the Startup folder, Word always loads it and always activates it, even if you deactivated it before you quit Word. (You can deactivate a template opened from the Startup folder during a Word session.) Also, if you set up a template in the Startup folder, you can't remove the global template in the Templates And Add-Ins dialog box.

If you add a global template in the Templates And Add-Ins dialog box, you control turning it off or on and removing it from one Word session to the next. If you deactivate a global template that you added in the Templates And Add-Ins dialog box, it will be inactive the next time you start Word. If you remove a global template that you added in the Templates And Add-Ins dialog box, Word doesn't open it the next time you start Word.

So here's a rule of thumb: if you *always* want another global template open and active and you don't want to remove it, copy that template to the Startup folder. If you want more control over when the template is active or you want the ability to remove it from use easily, add the template in the Templates And Add-Ins dialog box.

V

General Documents

 **NOTE**

You can, of course, use this method to remove all the additional global templates.

To remove all the additional global templates, use these steps:

1 Choose the Tools Options command, and then click the File Locations tab.

2 Select Startup in the File Types list, and then click the Modify button.

3 Delete the entire entry in the Folder Name box, and then click OK.

4 Click OK in the Options dialog box.

Sharing Elements Between Templates

When you set up styles, AutoText, custom toolbars, and macro project items, you might forget to select the special template instead of Normal. At other times, you might not realize that you want to create a special template until after you've set up elements in your Normal template while building a new type of document. With Word's Organizer, you can copy, rename, and delete styles, AutoText, custom toolbars, and macro project items. You can even perform these tasks on documents or templates that aren't currently open. The following steps show you how.

1 Choose the Tools Templates And Add-Ins command, and then click the Organizer button.

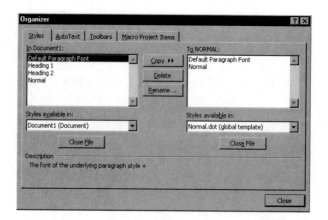

2 Click the tab for the type of pieces you want to work on. On the Styles tab, notice that the left-hand list shows elements in the current document or current template, and the right-hand list shows elements in the Normal template.

3 If necessary, close the file for one or both lists, and open different files—see "Opening a Different Template or Document," below, for the steps.

4 Select the element you want to work on.

5 Click the Copy, Rename, or Delete button—see Table 20-1 for descriptions of what each button does.

6 After you have worked on all the elements you want, click the Close button.

TABLE 20-1. Buttons in the Organizer Dialog Box.

Button	Action
Copy ▶▶	Copies selected elements from the list in which they're selected to the other list.
Delete	Deletes selected elements from the list in which they're selected.
Rename...	Renames a selected element in the list in which it's selected.

Opening a Different Template or Document

When you open the Organizer dialog box, you usually see the current document open in the left-hand list (or the current template for Auto-Text) and the Normal template open in the right-hand list. If the current document has a special template attached to it, you'll find its name listed in the Styles Available In box below the list of styles and elements on the left. If the document or template you want to work with is listed, simply select it to list its elements in the left-hand list. If, however, you want to work with different templates or documents in either list, you must open that document or template. You do this as follows:

1 On the tab currently displayed, click the Close File button below the list where you want to open a different file. The Close File button changes to Open File.

2 Click the Open File button.

3 Select the template or document you want to open, and then click the Open button.

Now you can work with the elements in the template or document you just opened.

 NOTE

> The template or document is only open as long as you keep the Organizer dialog box open. When you close the Organizer dialog box, Word closes the document or template. However, this action doesn't apply to documents or templates you have open in windows in Word.

Using Add-Ins

Add-ins are special programs that work closely with Word to enhance it and to make some tasks easier; in some cases, they make possible certain kinds of tasks that are not otherwise available in Word. Add-ins usually carry the filename extension WLL. You install add-ins either with a special Setup program supplied with the add-in or the same way you install additional global templates. Once an add-in is installed, you can then deactivate it, reactivate it, or remove it. You can also copy add-ins to the Startup folder. You accomplish all these tasks the same way you do with additional global templates.

Setting Up Template Tabs in the New Dialog Box

When you install Word, the New dialog box shows nine tabs, as you see here:

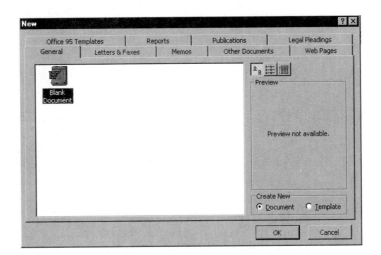

If you create or install templates that you don't think fit onto one of these tabs, you can set up a new tab in the New dialog box for a different category of document. To set up a new tab, take these steps:

1 Open the My Computer or Windows Explorer window.

2 Switch to the Templates folder inside the Microsoft Office folder inside the Program Files folder.

3 Choose the File New command, and then select Folder from the submenu.

4 Type the name that you want to appear on the new tab in the New dialog box.

5 Copy or move at least one document template into this new folder.

The next time you choose the File New command, you'll see a new tab for the folder you created inside the Templates folder, as shown in the illustration on the next page.

General Documents

NOTE

You don't have to quit and restart Word for the new tab to appear.

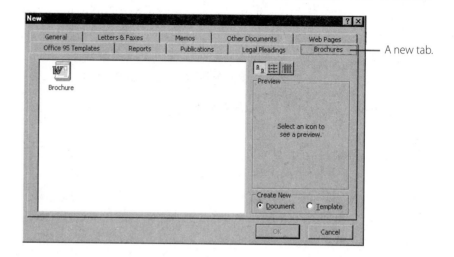

A new tab.

Renaming a Template Tab

Suppose you don't like the names Microsoft gave the template tabs in the New dialog box. Or, suppose you added a template tab and now you want to change its name. To change the name on a template tab in the New dialog box, change the name of the folder in the Templates folder.

 NOTE

If you rename the folder for a tab that Word sets up, it will appear to the right of the tabs Word sets up rather than in its original position, even if you later restore the original tab name.

Removing a Template Tab

If you want to remove a tab from the New dialog box, delete the folder for the tab or move it out of the Templates folder to another folder.

 NOTE

You can remove any of the template tabs, including the tabs Word sets up. Be aware, however, that if you later restore the folder for a tab that Word sets up, it will appear to the right of the tabs Word sets up rather than in its original position.

PART VI

Online Documents

CHAPTER 21

Creating Online Documents

Word 97 provides tools for creating online documents: hyperlinks, fonts that provide special looks on screen, the ability to enlarge fonts on the screen without affecting their size when you print the text, and a special Online Layout view, which shows you how your document looks when viewed on a computer screen. In this chapter, you'll learn how to use these and other Word tools to create online documents.

Using Tools for Online Documents

As an initial way to familiarize yourself with the tools Word provides for creating online documents, examine Table 21-1, which lists tools that work especially well for online documents and what you use them for. The sections following the table describe the tools.

 NOTE

> For online documents that your readers will view in Word, you can format the document and the text in any way you want. You can use all the tools, features, and skills you find in this book. Table 21-1 and the rest of the discussion in this chapter focus on tools that are especially useful for online documents.

Working in Online Layout View

As an aid to viewing online documents, Word 97 includes Online Layout view, which automatically wraps text to the width of the document window and enlarges small fonts up to a size you set. You have two ways to switch to Online Layout view:

- Online Layout button (see Figure 21-1)

- View Online Layout command

When you switch to Online Layout view, you see a document in a view like the one shown on page 872.

FIGURE 21-1.
The Online Layout View button and other buttons for viewing documents.

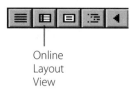

Online
Layout
View

Document Map

When you switch to Online Layout view, Word also turns on the document map. The document map is the outline of the document. You can quickly jump to a heading in the document by clicking the heading in the document map, and you can collapse and expand outline headings. (The document map works similarly to Outline view.) You can also turn on the document map in Normal view and in Page Layout view.

TABLE 21-1. Word's Tools for Working on Online Documents and What You Use Them For.

Command	Toolbar Button	Use
Edit Paste As Hyperlink		Paste a hyperlink from the Clipboard into a document.
View Online Layout	Online Layout View	Switch to Online Layout view to view a document as it will appear on a Web page.
View Document Map	Document Map	Turn on or off the document map, which shows the structure of the document.
Insert Hyperlink	Insert Hyperlink	Insert a new hyperlink.
Insert Object		Insert a variety of objects from other programs and files.
Format Font, Font tab		Set font formatting, including special font effects—Shadow, Outline, Emboss, and Engrave.
Format Font, Animation tab		Set animation properties for text.
Format Background		Set a background effect for a Web page.
Tools AutoCorrect, AutoFormat As You Type tab and AutoFormat tab		Automatically replace Internet and network paths with hyperlinks.
Tools Options, View tab: Show Animated Text check box		Turn on or off text animation.
Tools Options, View tab: Window Enlarge Fonts Less Than box		Enlarge the display of small fonts in online documents.
Tools Options, General tab: Provide Feedback With Sound check box		Turn on or off sounds for actions you take in Word.
Tools Options, General tab: Provide Feedback With Animation check box		Turn on or off animations for actions you take in Word.
Tools Options, Spelling & Grammar tab: Spelling Ignore Internet And File Addresses check box		Direct Word to ignore Internet and file addresses during spelling and grammar checking.

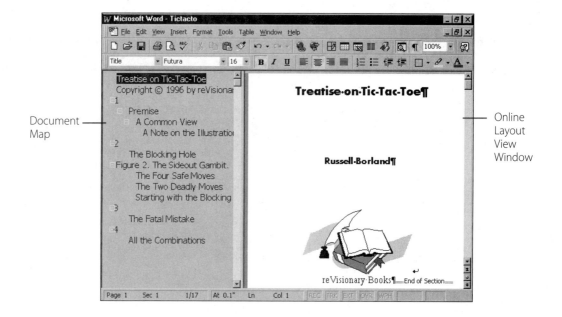

Document Map

Online Layout View Window

Word gives you two ways to manually turn on or turn off the document map:

■ Document Map button

■ View Document Map command

Enlarging Fonts

One of the tricks of the writing trade is to create a single document that can be read online and on paper. On paper, you can use a variety of font sizes that are quite legible to most readers (even though some, like me, need reading glasses), but which are very difficult to read off a computer screen. Rather than create two versions of a document with different font sizes for paper and screen, you can direct Word to use a minimum size for displaying fonts. This display doesn't affect the actual formatted size of the text and doesn't affect the size of the text for printing. You can think of it as Zoom mode exclusively for small fonts, rather than for the entire document, the way the View Zoom command works.

To enlarge the display of smaller fonts, take these steps:

1 Switch to Online Layout view.

2 Choose the Tools Options command.

3 Click the View tab. ——

4 Set the minimum —— font size.

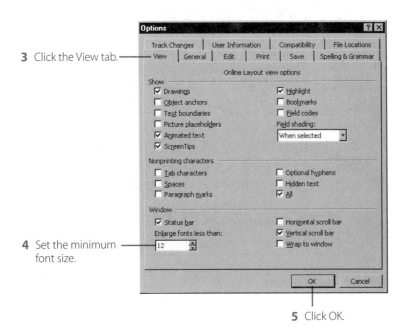

5 Click OK.

The minimum font size you set is the smallest size text appears on the screen. Any text smaller than this appears instead in the minimum point size. Text in sizes larger than the minimum size appears in the size you set it.

Setting the Background

 SEE ALSO

For information about custom colors, see "Checking Out More Colors," page 492. For information about fill effects, see "Tumbling to the Fill Effects," page 493.

In Online Layout view, you can set up a background for the text, art, and other objects. When you set a background for an online document, the background is the same for the entire document. The background can be a solid, built-in color, or a custom color or fill effect.

To set a background for an online document, take these steps:

1 Switch to Online Layout view.

2 Choose the Format Background command.

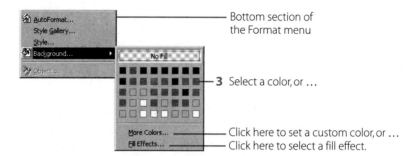

Bottom section of
the Format menu

3 Select a color, or …

Click here to set a custom color, or …
Click here to select a fill effect.

Applying Online Text Fonts

In online documents, you can set any font formatting for text, just as you do in a document you're going to print. But for online documents, Word provides four special font effects, plus animated text. These font effects are specifically designed for viewing on a computer screen. You can print the four special font effects, but they are less effective on paper; animated text doesn't print, of course, except as static text.

Combining Backgrounds with Text

Backgrounds can make documents more exciting to read online. Dark or bold colors or images, however, can interfere with dark text colors, making text difficult to read. To assure that your readers can read the text on your pages, observe the following guidelines when working in an online document with a background color.

- Set the text to a color that contrasts with the background colors.

- Avoid setting the text color to white because white text doesn't print on many printers. Also, Word displays backgrounds in Online Layout view only. If the reader switches to another view, such as Page Layout view, white text may not be visible.

- Keep in mind that some readers turn off the display of images—turn on the Picture Placeholders check box on the View tab of the Tools Options dialog box. When using a background image on a page, use a text color that's not so light that it's hard to read without the background.

Special Font Effects for Online Documents

The following table lists the four font effects that work especially well for online documents, shows you a sample, and gives you a description.

Font Effect	Sample	Description
Shadow	**Wild Ride**	Word adds a lighter color copy of the characters slightly below and to the right of the shadowed characters.
Outline	**Wild Ride**	Word fills the insides of the characters with white. If you choose White for the color, the characters disappear.
Emboss	Wild Ride	Word uses an outline along the right and bottom sides of the characters to imitate the effect of characters raised from the page. If the color is Auto when you select Emboss, Word changes the font color to white. If you have selected any other color already, Word uses a different color for the embossing outline.
Engrave	Wild Ride	Word uses an outline along the left and top sides of the characters to imitate the effect of characters pressed into the page. If the color is Auto when you select Engrave, Word changes the font color to white. If you have selected any other color already, Word uses a different color for the engraving outline.

To apply any of the font effects, take these steps:

1 Select the words to which you want to apply the font effect.

2 Choose the Format Font command, or right-click the selection and select Font from the shortcut menu. (You can also press Ctrl+D to display the Font dialog box.)

VI

Online Documents

3 Click the Font tab.

4 Click the check boxes for the font effects you want to apply.

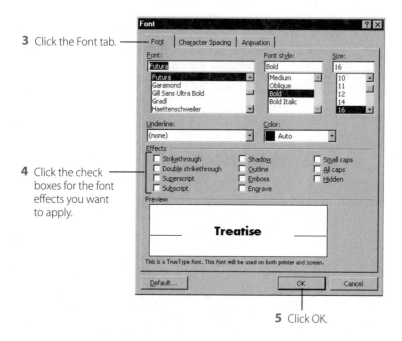

5 Click OK.

Choosing some font effects turns off others, as shown in the following table.

Choosing This Effect	Turns Off This Effect
Shadow	Emboss, Engrave
Outline	Emboss, Engrave
Emboss	Shadow, Outline, Engrave
Engrave	Shadow, Outline, Emboss

Dancing: Animated Text

In online documents, you can now apply animation to text. Animating words can help people read online documents by drawing attention to special text. Since we can't print animation, we'll have to settle here for descriptions of the animations (see Table 21-2 on the next page).

To apply an animation effect, take these steps:

1 Select the words you want to animate.

2 Choose the Format Font command.

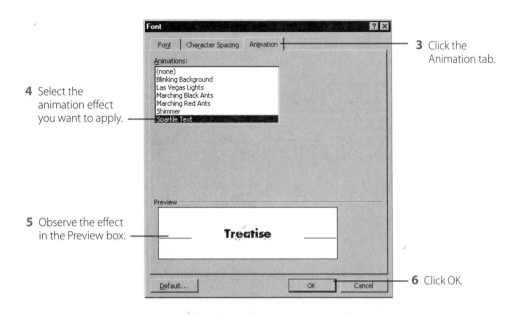

3 Click the Animation tab.

4 Select the animation effect you want to apply.

5 Observe the effect in the Preview box.

6 Click OK.

TABLE 21-2.   Animation Names and Their Effects on Text.

Animation Name	Animation Effect
(None)	Removes the animation effect currently applied to the selection.
Blinking Background	The background of the selection alternates between two colors. The selection itself (if necessary) alternates between the same two colors to stay visible.
Las Vegas Lights	A box of dots appears around the selected characters and changes to each of the available colors, except white.
Marching Black Ants	A box of black dashes appears around the selected characters and appears to move clockwise around the box.
Marching Red Ants	A box of red dashes appears around the selected characters and appears to move clockwise around the box.
Shimmer	The selected characters alternate between being partially visible and fully visible.
Sparkle Text	Various shapes of various colors appear in and around the selected characters. Each shape changes to each of the available colors, including white (which makes the shape seem to disappear for a moment).

VI

Online Documents

Using Hyperlinks

Perhaps the most distinctive feature of online documents is the hyperlink. Simplified from an idea developed by Theodore Nelson many years ago, a hyperlink is an active pathway to another online document. When you click a hyperlink, the computer displays the online document that the hyperlink points to (see the sidebar, "Following a Hyperlink," page 882).

? SEE ALSO

You can also create hyperlinks to Web pages (URLs). For details, see "Inserting Hyperlinks, page 928.

In previous versions of Word, you could simulate hyperlinks to an online document with a GoToButton field. (This method is still available, but why bother?) In Word 97, it's really quite simple to insert a hyperlink.

Inserting Hyperlinks

Word gives you three ways to insert a hyperlink into a document: (1) type the local disk drive path or network path, (2) choose the Insert Hyperlink command or click the Insert Hyperlink button on the Standard toolbar, or (3) choose the Edit Paste As Hyperlink command.

Typing Hyperlinks

If you know the local disk drive path or the network path to a file, you can simply type the hyperlink into your Word document.

A network path looks like this for an unmapped network drive (called a *share path*):

\\bigserve\public\reports\fy96_q1.doc

or like this for a mapped network drive:

x:\reports\fy96_q1.doc

A local disk drive path usually looks like this (the drive letter could be D, E, or even A):

C:\My Documents\Online Documents\fy96_q4.doc

Streamlining Spelling and Grammar Checking

With the large number of Web sites around the world and the many possible network paths you can use for hyperlinks, spelling and grammar checking of an online document with many hyperlinks would be a long, slow, laborious process of clicking on Ignore All to eliminate spelling and grammar sawtooth underlines from an online document.

Instead of wasting your time with this process, let Word direct the spelling and grammar checkers to ignore Internet and network paths during checking. This feature is turned on in Word. (The check box for this feature is on the Spelling & Grammar tab of the Tools Options dialog box.) You'll only want to turn this off if you're typing hyperlinks and you know the correct addresses and can change them after the check is finished.

If you elect to turn off the Ignore Internet And File Addresses check box and leave automatic spelling and grammar checking turned on, you might want to turn on the Hide Spelling Errors In This Document and the Hide Grammatical Errors In This Document check boxes on the Spelling & Grammar tab.

TIP

You'll want to use a mapped network drive path only if the drive mapping remains the same for all users all the time. In most cases, a share path is a far better solution. Be aware, however, that if you insert a hyperlink to a file on your hard disk, the hyperlink will most likely take the form C:\Folder\...\Folder\Filename.ext. The only way to set up a hyperlink to your hard disk with a share name is to share the folder first.

Using the Insert Hyperlink Command and Insert Hyperlink Button

Choosing the Insert Hyperlink command or clicking the Insert Hyperlink button displays the Insert Hyperlink dialog box (see Figure 21-2 on the next page), where you can type a local disk drive or network path. The dialog box also contains a Browse button you can click to locate the file to which you want to insert a hyperlink.

VI

Online Documents

FIGURE 21-2.

The Insert Hyperlink dialog box.

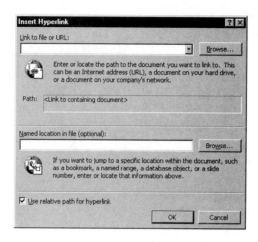

? **SEE ALSO**

For more information about bookmarks in Word documents, see "Bookmark Destinations," page 92.

In addition, if the document contains bookmarks (Word document) or named ranges (Microsoft Excel worksheet), you can specify the bookmark or name as the specific target for the hyperlink. The Insert Hyperlink dialog box also contains a Browse button for selecting the bookmark or name.

Finally, the Insert Hyperlink dialog box contains a box that specifies that the hyperlink use a relative pathname rather than the full pathname in the hyperlink that appears in your document.

Overall, the Insert Hyperlink dialog box gives you more choices for inserting a hyperlink than simply typing does.

To insert a hyperlink with the Insert Hyperlink dialog box, take these steps:

Insert
Hyperlink

1 Choose the Insert Hyperlink command, or click the Insert Hyperlink button on the Standard toolbar. (You can also press Ctrl+K to display the Insert Hyperlink dialog box.)

2 Type a local disk drive location or network path in the Link To File Or URL box, or click Browse (see Figure 21-3).

3 Type a bookmark or range name in the Named Location In File (Optional) box, or click Browse (see Figure 21-4).

4 Leave the Use Relative Path For Hyperlink check box turned on for a relative path, or turn it off for a full path—see the sidebar, "Relative Paths to Hyperlinks," next page.

5 Click OK.

FIGURE 21-3.
The Link to File
dialog box.

3 Select
the file.

1 Switch to the folder
that contains the file.

4 Click OK.

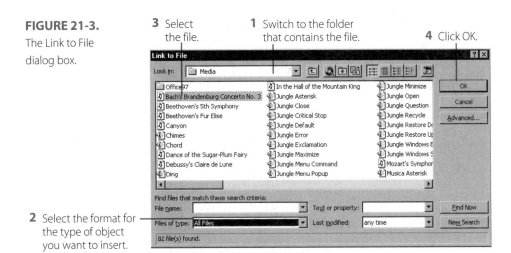

2 Select the format for
the type of object
you want to insert.

FIGURE 21-4.
The Bookmark
dialog box.

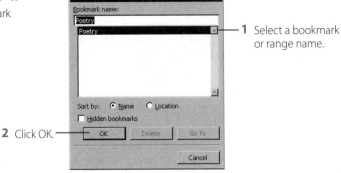

1 Select a bookmark
or range name.

2 Click OK.

Relative Paths to Hyperlinks

A hyperlink path can be relative to the location of the document that contains
the hyperlink or it can be an absolute path (full pathname).

When you turn on the Use Relative Path For Hyperlink check box in the Insert
Hyperlink dialog box, Word keeps track of the file the hyperlink points to, even if
you move it. So if you think that you might one day move the file, leave this
check box turned on.

When you turn off the Use Relative Path For Hyperlink check box, the
hyperlink shows the full path to the file. You'll want to turn off this check box
only if you're absolutely sure that you'll never move the file the hyperlink points
to from its current location.

VI

Online Documents

Using the Edit Paste As Hyperlink Command

If you have copied or cut the text of a hyperlink to the Clipboard, you can paste the Clipboard contents as a hyperlink. To do so, choose the Edit Paste As Hyperlink command.

Following a Hyperlink

When you see a hyperlink in a document, it most likely will appear in the formatting of the Hyperlink or Followed Hyperlink character style (see the next section, "Formatting Hyperlinks," for details).

When you position the mouse pointer over a hyperlink, the mouse pointer becomes a hand with a pointing index finger. To follow a hyperlink, click it.

This technique works every time, whether you have followed the hyperlink before or not.

Formatting Hyperlinks

To make hyperlinks stand out in a mass of text and to let readers know that the document contains a hyperlink to more information, Word applies automatically a special character style (named Hyperlink) to any hyperlinks. The next two sections describe this automatic process and the hyperlink styles built into Word.

Automatic Formatting of Hyperlinks

On the AutoFormat and AutoFormat As You Type tabs of the Tools AutoCorrect dialog box, you'll find a check box labeled Internet And Network Paths With Hyperlinks. When this check box is turned on, Word automatically converts a pathname to a hyperlink and applies the Hyperlink character style (described next). The AutoFormat tab works this magic when you choose the Format AutoFormat command. The AutoFormat As You Type tab works this magic soon after you type a path into a document.

Hyperlink Styles

Word has two built-in character styles designed specifically for hyperlinks: Hyperlink and Followed Hyperlink.

■ **Hyperlink**. This character style displays the hyperlink as blue, underlined text. This style is designed to show you and your readers that this link has not yet been followed from this page.

■ **Followed Hyperlink**. This character style displays the hyperlink as violet, underlined text. This style is designed to show you and your readers that this link has been followed from this page.

 **TIP**

If you want to restore a hyperlink to the look of a hyperlink that has not yet been followed, simply apply the Hyperlink style.

Mixing Other Objects into Your Online Document

? SEE ALSO

For details about adding pictures to an online document and the ways you can handle pictures and other objects, see "Adding Art from Files," page 455; "Drawing Pictures," page 458; "Bending Text—Word Art," page 507; "Adding a Border," page 515; "Positioning," page 518; and "Wrapping Brochure Text Around Objects," page 520.

More and more, documents include pictures, video clips, sound clips, as well as many other types of objects that you create with programs other than Word.

The Insert Object command gives you a long list of other objects you can insert into an online document (or any Word document, for that matter). You can either pull in one of these objects from a file, or if you have the programs to do it, you can create one of these objects and insert it.

VI

Online Documents

Selecting a Hyperlink

The methods you normally use to select text with the mouse don't work for hyperlinks. When you click the mouse on a hyperlink, Word tries to follow the hyperlink to its destination.

Instead of selecting a hyperlink with the mouse, you need to use one of the keyboard methods for selecting text. You can set the insertion point with the mouse at one end or the other of a hyperlink before you use the keyboard to select it. You can also use the mouse to drag a selection that starts outside a hyperlink and cross over it.

If the hyperlink is on a line by itself, you can click in the selection bar to select that line without activating the hyperlink.

Inserting Other Objects from Files

To insert an object from a file, take these steps:

1 Choose the Insert Object command.

2 Click the Create from File tab.

3 Type the filename, or ...
Click Browse (see Figure 21-3, page 881).

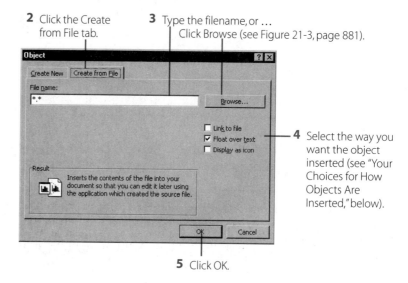

4 Select the way you want the object inserted (see "Your Choices for How Objects Are Inserted," below).

5 Click OK.

Your Choices for How Objects Are Inserted

You have three separate choices for how to insert an object file into your online document:

- **Link To File**. Turn on this check box if you want to set up a link to the original file. When you want to keep your online file as small as possible, use this check box. You also turn on this check box when you expect that you may change the source file in the future, and you want those changes to automatically appear in your online document. With this check box turned off, Word stores the contents of the source file in your online document. This method is handy if your online document won't have access to the source file from the location where readers view it.

- **Float Over Text**. With this check box turned on, the object floats over the text rather than being among the text of the page. A floating object is easy to reposition anywhere on a page. You can also wrap the text around a floating object. Turn off this check

? SEE ALSO

For information about wrapping text around an object, see "Wrapping Brochure Text Around Objects," page 520.

box if you want the object to appear as part of the text, as any text character does.

- **Display As Icon**. Turn on this check box if you want the object to appear as a file icon rather than as its contents. You'll use this check box most often for text and picture objects. For sound clips, there is no text or picture to display. For objects that have no visible display, you'll see an icon anyway.

Creating Other Objects

To create an object and insert it, take these steps:

1 Choose the Insert Object command.

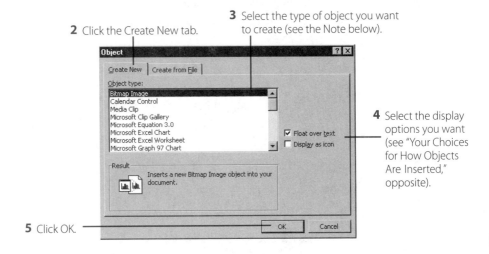

3 Select the type of object you want to create (see the Note below).

2 Click the Create New tab.

4 Select the display options you want (see "Your Choices for How Objects Are Inserted," opposite).

5 Click OK.

6 Create the object in the window of the program for the object.

7 When you're done, click in the Word document outside the object to return to Word.

The list of available object types depends on the programs you have installed. The more programs you have installed that can create OLE objects, the longer the list. Also note, however, that the list can contain items for which you don't have the necessary program. This is Windows trying to be helpful, if a bit deceptive. If you select an object type and don't have the necessary program, you see a message that Windows can't locate an associated program.

Sending Documents Online

 SEE ALSO

Word provides the File Send To command for sending documents through e-mail. For details about this command and its sub-commands, see "Sending a Memo Through Your Computer," page 273.

Passing around online documents actively (rather than, or in addition to, distributing them to a server where others can view them—*passive* passing around) is a popular and even strategically efficient way to share necessary information. Perhaps the most popular way to actively distribute online documents is "sneaker-net"—walk over to someone and hand him or her a floppy disk with the file on it. One of the newly popular ways to actively distribute an online document is through e-mail.

Word is "e-mail aware." That means Word knows how to work with an e-mail program that follows the MAPI standards. What this techno-gibberish means to you is that you can use Word to create, edit, format, and read e-mail messages. This feature is called WordMail. You gain access to it through your e-mail program.

The following sections introduce WordMail as it appears in Microsoft Exchange and Microsoft Outlook.

Turning On WordMail in Exchange

To set Word as the editor for e-mail messages in Microsoft Exchange, follow these steps:

1 Start Microsoft Exchange.

2 Choose the Compose WordMail Options command.

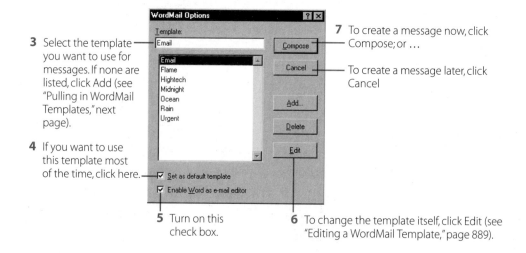

3 Select the template you want to use for messages. If none are listed, click Add (see "Pulling in WordMail Templates," next page).

4 If you want to use this template most of the time, click here.

5 Turn on this check box.

7 To create a message now, click Compose; or …

To create a message later, click Cancel

6 To change the template itself, click Edit (see "Editing a WordMail Template," page 889).

Turning On WordMail in Outlook

To set Word as the editor for e-mail messages in Microsoft Outlook, follow these steps:

1 Start Microsoft Outlook.

2 Choose the Tools Options command.

3 Click the E-mail tab.

4 Click here to turn on this check box, which sets Word for use as an e-mail editor.

5 Click the Template button to choose the e-mail template you want to use for your messages.

6 Click OK.

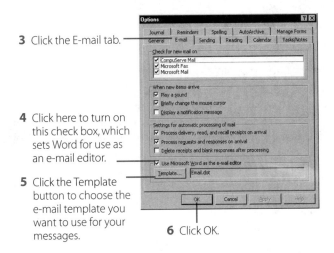

Pulling in WordMail Templates

Word has WordMail templates stored in the Office folder in the Msoffice folder. These templates help you build special electronic mail messages. Table 21-3 lists these additional templates for WordMail. The main features of the templates listed in Table 21-3 are that they have a special background set up, which you see only in Online Layout view—the appropriate view for editing a WordMail message. Most of them have standard settings for fonts, sizes, and colors of text that are different from the settings for Word's Normal template or the e-mail templates available in Exchange.

To use e-mail templates in Exchange, you need to add them to the Templates list in the WordMail Options dialog box. (The templates are automatically available in Outlook.) To do so, take these steps:

1 In the WordMail Options dialog box, click the Add button.

VI

Online Documents

2 Switch to the Office folder inside the Microsoft Office folder inside the Program Files folder.

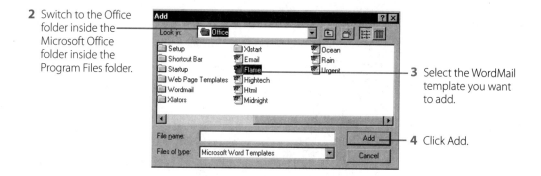

3 Select the WordMail template you want to add.

4 Click Add.

5 Repeat step 1 through step 4 to add another WordMail template.

TABLE 21-3. WordMail Templates and Descriptions.

Template	Background Image	Font
Email		Standard font is Arial 10-point Auto color.
Flame		Standard font is Arial 11-point Auto color.
Hightech		Standard font is Times New Roman 13-point Auto color.
Midnight		Standard font is Tahoma 11-point Dark Blue.
Ocean		Standard font is Tahoma 11-point Dark Blue.
Rain		Standard font is Arial 11-point Auto color.
Urgent		Standard font is Tahoma 10-point Auto color.

If you later want to remove a WordMail template from the list in the WordMail Options dialog box, select it, and then click Remove.

Editing a WordMail Template

You can change a WordMail template as you do any other Word document template. If you're running Microsoft Exchange, the easiest way to gain access for editing a WordMail template is through the WordMail Options dialog box.

To edit a WordMail template in Exchange, follow these steps:

1 In Microsoft Exchange, choose the Compose WordMail Options command.

2 In the WordMail Options dialog box, select the template you want to edit from the Templates list.

3 Click the Edit button.

4 Make the changes to the template, save it, and then close the template window.

5 Repeat step 2 through step 4 for each WordMail template you want to edit.

6 When you're done with the WordMail Options dialog box, click Compose to compose a new message now, or click Close to compose a message later.

If you're using Microsoft Outlook, open a template you want to edit using Windows Explorer. Then make the changes you want, save the template, and close the template window.

VI

Online Documents

Creating Web Pages

Word 97 provides tools for creating Web pages that you can publish on your organization's intranet or on the World Wide Web. You can also use Word to convert Word documents into Web pages.

In this chapter, you'll learn about how Word changes when you work on a Web page, how to build a Web page template, how to build a Web page and save it, and how to post your Web page for others to see and use.

⭐ **TIP**

Getting Help on Web-Related Topics

You'll find much of the information in this chapter in Word's Help files. It seems that the Office Assistant in Word is particularly keen on presenting topics about Web pages whenever you call on it for assistance. In addition, the Help menu in Word contains the command Help From Microsoft. The submenu for this command lists various topics for help you can get across the Web. For related information about this, see the sidebar, "Getting More Web Stuff from Microsoft," page 903.

Making Changes to Word During Web Authoring

When you open a Web page document or create a new document based on a Web page template or wizard, Word switches to the Web page authoring environment, in which some of the features, menus, and toolbars are different.

You can use many familiar Word features, such as spelling and grammar checking, AutoText, and tables, when you are using Word to author Web pages. Some commands, such as the Scrolling Text command on the Insert menu, are added for Web page authoring. Some features are customized to make Web authoring easier, such as graphic bullets and lines. Some Word features that aren't supported in the Web page authoring environment or by HTML, such as highlighting, are not available in the Web page authoring environment.

Table 22-1 lists features that change or are unavailable when you are authoring Web pages.

Menu Commands for Web Authoring

When you open a Web page document or create a new document based on a Web page template or wizard, you'll see a number of menu changes. These are summarized in Table 22-2, page 895.

TABLE 22-1.   Word Features That Are Different or Unavailable During Web Authoring.

Feature	Condition	Details
Columns	Changed	Newspaper columns aren't supported in HTML, but you can use tables to create a multicolumn effect.
Comments and change tracking	Changed	Word's comments and Track Changes features aren't supported in HTML. You can use strikethrough formatting to represent text that might be deleted. For comments, you can format text with the Comments style. Comments will not appear in Web browsers.
Highlighting	Unavailable	
Font sizes	Changed	Fonts are mapped to the closest HTML size available in the <FONT SIZE> tag, which ranges from size 1 to 7. These numbers are not point sizes but are used as instructions for font sizes by Web browsers. Word displays the fonts in sizes ranging from 9 to 36.
Bold, strikethrough, italic, and underline effects	Changed	Special underline effects, such as dotted underline, are not available.
Animated text effects (Format Font command, Animation tab)	Changed	Animations are not available. For an animated effect, insert scrolling text.
Emboss, shadow, engrave, small caps, all caps, double strikethrough, and outline effects (Format Font command, Font tab)	Unavailable	
Tabs	Unavailable	Tabs are not available because they are often displayed by Web browsers as spaces. To control the layout of your page, use a table.
Ruler	Changed	The ruler does not appear by default because margin settings, indents, and tabs differ in the Web page authoring environment. You can point to the gray area at the top of the document to display the ruler.

(continued)

VI

Online Documents

TABLE 22-1. *continued*

Feature	Condition	Details
Equations, charts, and other OLE objects	Changed	When you save charts, equations, organizational charts, and other OLE objects in HTML format, a graphic image is created. You can use these graphics on your Web pages, but you won't be able to update the data they represent. If you need to later update data in a chart or equation that you're displaying on a Web page, save a backup copy of your file as a Word document.
Drawing objects, such as AutoShapes, text effects, text boxes, and shadows	Changed	These items aren't available on the Drawing toolbar. They are available as Microsoft Word Picture objects—click Object on the Insert menu, and then click Microsoft Word Picture. Once you close your document, the graphic becomes a GIF image, and you will not be able to update it using the Drawing toolbar again.
Headers and footers	Unavailable	
Footnotes and endnotes	Unavailable	
Cross-references	Unavailable	
Master documents	Unavailable	Master documents aren't supported in Web page authoring. You can separate large amounts of text into unique Web pages, and then insert hyperlinks to these smaller documents on one Web page.
Mail merge	Unavailable	
Versions	Unavailable	
Styles	Changed	When you define your own styles, only the formatting that's supported in Web page authoring will be available.
Paragraph formatting	Changed	Some paragraph formats, such as settings to control how paragraphs flow and spacing before and after paragraphs, aren't available. To control the layout of your page, you can use a table.
Tables of contents, tables of authorities, and indexes	Unavailable	The Word tools for creating these items aren't available. You can simulate a table of contents by using hyperlinks.

(continued)

TABLE 22-1. *continued*

Feature	Condition	Details
Page borders	Unavailable	Borders around pages aren't supported in HTML. To make a page more interesting, you can add a background by using the Background command on the Format menu.
Page numbering	Unavailable	An HTML document is considered a single Web page, regardless of its length.
Margins	Unavailable	To control the layout of a page, you can use a table.

TABLE 22-2.   Commands for Working on Web Pages and What You Use Them For.

Command	Use
File New: Web Pages tab	Create an online document from a Web page template.
File Save As HTML File Save As: Save As Type: HTML Document	Save a document in HTML document format—this option is only available if you're viewing a Word document rather than a Web page.
File Save As Word Document	Save a Web page as a Word document—this option is only available if you're viewing a Web page rather than a Word document.
File Web Page Preview	Preview a Web document as you work on it; this option requires a Web browser on the computer.
File Properties	Except for the Title box, this dialog box is totally different for Web pages (see "Other Web Page Properties: Setting the URL and Language for a Web Page," page 923).
Edit Paste As Hyperlink	Paste a hyperlink from the Clipboard into a document.
View Online Layout	Switch to Online Layout view to view the document as it will appear on a Web page.
View Form Design Mode	Create a form as the structure of the Web page (see "Laying Out a Web Page as a Form," page 912).
View Toolbars: Web	Turn on or off the Web toolbar, which contains buttons for viewing Web pages.
View Document Map	Turn on or off the document map, which shows the document's structure.

(continued)

TABLE 22-2. *continued*

Command	Use
View HTML Source	View HTML code instead of the display of the Web page as it appears in a browser.
Insert Horizontal Line	Add a horizontal line to a Web page.
Insert Picture	Insert a picture; this command is slightly different from the Insert Picture command for a Word document (see "Inserting Graphics," page 933).
Insert Video	Insert a video.
Insert Background Sound	Add a background sound.
Insert Forms	Insert an existing form (for a new form, see View Form Design Mode, earlier in this table).
Insert Scrolling Text	Add scrolling text to a Web page.
Insert Object	Insert a variety of objects from other programs and files.
Insert Hyperlink	Insert a new hyperlink.
Format Text Colors	Set standard colors for text, hyperlinks, and followed hyperlinks. For accent colors on text, use the Format Font command or Font Color button on the Formatting toolbar.
Format Background	Set a background effect for a Web page.
Tools AutoCorrect, AutoFormat As You Type tab and AutoFormat tab	Automatically replace Internet and network paths with hyperlinks.
Tools Options, Save tab: Save Word Files As HTML Document (*.html; *.htm; *.htx)	Set HTML as the standard file format for saving documents.
Table Draw Table	Draw a table to serve as the structure of a Web page.
Table Table Properties	Set text wrapping, background, and space between columns.
Table Cell Properties	Set vertical alignment, background, and width and height of a table cell.
Table Borders	Set borders around all cells or remove them; set the width of borderlines.
Help Microsoft On The Web	Get help directly from Microsoft across the Web.

Toolbar Buttons for Web Authoring

After you save a document as a Web page or when you open a Web page, Word changes the buttons on the Standard and Formatting toolbars. Figure 22-1 and Figure 22-2 show these two toolbars with labels for the buttons that are particularly related to authoring Web pages. The Web toolbar, discussed next, also comes into play.

FIGURE 22-1.
The Standard toolbar for Web pages.

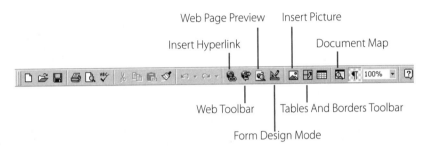

FIGURE 22-2.
The Formatting toolbar for Web pages.

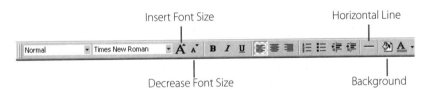

Using the Web Toolbar

When you're setting up hyperlinks on a Web page, it can be handy to have the tools you find on the Web toolbar in Microsoft Internet Explorer 3.0 readily available. The Web toolbar resembles the left half of the toolbar in Internet Explorer. The one button on this toolbar that's not in Internet Explorer is the Show Only Web Toolbar button.

Here's a look at the toolbar, with its buttons labeled. Following the picture, you'll find descriptions of the buttons.

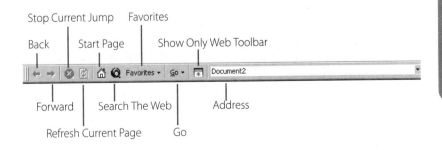

VI

Online Documents

Just the Web Toolbar, Jack

You can unclutter your screen while you're setting up hyperlinks on a Web page or trying to test the links by showing only the Web toolbar on the screen:

- Click the Show Only Web Toolbar button to hide all other visible toolbars.

- Click the Show Only Web Toolbar button again to redisplay all toolbars.

Pulling Up a Page

The Web toolbar has four buttons that help you get to other Web pages, either for review or to help you set up hyperlinks to them: Start Page, Favorites, Go, and Search The Web.

Start Page Button

Click the Start Page button to jump to the start page you set up for your browser. If you haven't yet set a start page or if you want to change it, use the Set Start Page command on the Go button menu—see the next topic. On the Go button menu, the Start Page command performs the same action as the Start Page button on the Web toolbar.

Setting the Start Page

To set a start page, take these steps:

1 Display the Web page you want to use as the browser's start page.

2 Click the Go button on the Web toolbar.

3 Select Set Start Page from the submenu.

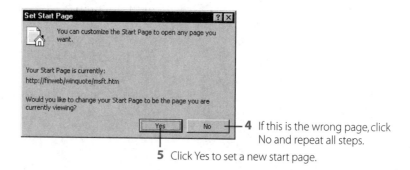

4 If this is the wrong page, click No and repeat all steps.

5 Click Yes to set a new start page.

NOTE

Setting the start page with the Web toolbar also sets the same start page for your Web browser.

Favorites Button

The Favorites button on the Web toolbar contains two commands and can contain a list of Web pages. The two commands are Add To Favorites and Open Favorites. The list of Web pages contains the names of Web pages you've added to your list of favorites with the Add To Favorites command.

To add a Web page to your favorites list, take these steps:

1 Open the Web page you want to add to your list of favorite pages.

2 Click the Favorites button on the Web toolbar, and select the Add To Favorites command.

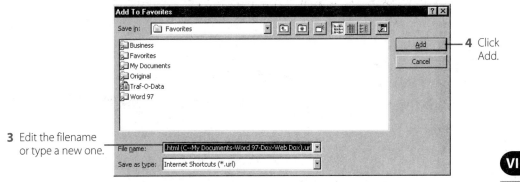

3 Edit the filename or type a new one.

4 Click Add.

The title of the Web page now appears on the Favorites button menu. Office also adds a button to the Favorites toolbar on the Microsoft Office shortcut bar.

If you want to delete a favorite, rename it, move it to another folder, or move a page into your Favorites folder, you want to open your Favorites folder. To do so, click the Favorites button and select the Open Favorites command.

VI

Online Documents

Go Button

The Go button on the Web toolbar displays a menu of commands for going to other pages. The commands other than Open are described in neighboring topics. Here, let's see about this Open command.

You use the Open command to go to any Web page anywhere (provided you have access to the "anywhere" you want to go). To open a different Web page, take these steps:

1 Click the Go button on the Web toolbar.

2 Choose the Open command.

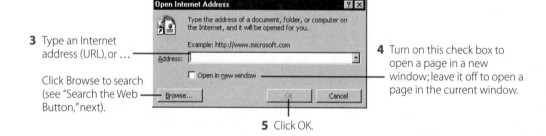

3 Type an Internet address (URL), or …

Click Browse to search (see "Search the Web Button," next).

4 Turn on this check box to open a page in a new window; leave it off to open a page in the current window.

5 Click OK.

Search The Web Button

When you want to search the Web for pages that fit your work or interests, click the Search The Web button. Word opens and displays your search page, from which you can search the Web for pages you want.

Besides the Web toolbar, the Search The Web button appears in all of these places:

- File Open dialog box

- Browse dialog box

- Insert File dialog box

- Insert Picture dialog box

 NOTE

On the Go button menu, the Search The Web command performs the same action as the Search The Web button.

Setting the Search Page

To set the search page, follow these steps:

1 Display the Web page you want to use as the search page for your browser.

2 Click the Go button on the Web toolbar.

3 Select Set Search Page from the submenu.

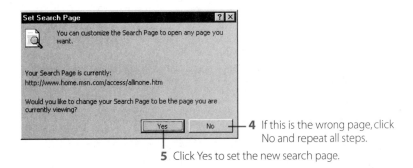

4 If this is the wrong page, click No and repeat all steps.

5 Click Yes to set the new search page.

Setting the search page with the Web toolbar also sets the same search page for your Web browser.

Moving Through Viewed Pages

After you view a second Web page, the Back and Forward buttons on the Web toolbar become active. Each time you click the Back button, your browser moves back to the Web page you saw before the one currently in view. You can back up all the way to the first page.

After you back up a page or more, you can click the Forward button to move forward again until you get to the last page you viewed.

The Address box at the right end of the Web toolbar contains a list of the Web pages you've visited recently. From this list, you can jump to another page—just click its name in the Address list. These Web page addresses are kept in your History folder. The number of pages depends on how many pages you view and how long you set up your browser to keep a page in the History file.

VI

Online Documents

> **NOTE**
>
> On the Go button menu, the Back and Forward commands perform the same actions as the Back and Forward buttons on the Web toolbar.

Getting the Latest Page

Web pages tend to be fluid; that is, their authors keep changing them all the time. Sometimes this is necessary, as on a Web page for traffic or weather conditions or for stock prices. Sometimes it's a warranted revision to correct a mistake or to add missing information. Sometimes it's just a redesign or some other bit of whimsy. Whatever the reason, Web pages change. If you believe that the Web page you're looking at has changed since you opened it, click the Refresh button to pull in the latest version of the Web page.

Stop! I'm Tired of Waiting

Sometimes you send your browser to fetch the wrong Web page but don't realize it until it starts pulling it in. Sometimes you mistype a Web page address and realize it after you set your browser to work. Sometimes a Web page is very large, or the Web server is very busy, or there are just lots of people pulling pages across the Web lines. All of these conditions lead to slow response. If you want to stop your browser from pursuing a particular Web page while it's working on pulling it in, click the Stop button. You can then pursue a different Web page or go offline altogether.

Using the Hyperlink Shortcut Menu

When you're working on a Web page and you click the right mouse button anywhere on the page, the shortcut menu that appears contains a Hyperlink command, a Picture command, and the Draw Table command. You can choose these commands for the same purposes that you would choose them from a menu or click the related buttons on a toolbar.

If you don't see hyperlink commands on the shortcut menu, you probably have a spelling or grammatical error in your text. The Hyperlink shortcut menu will not appear if the hyperlink display text contains a grammatical or spelling error and Word is automatically checking for proofing errors. Text with spelling errors contains a red wavy underline; text with grammatical errors contains a green wavy underline.

After you accept or reject the proofing error, Word can display the Hyperlink shortcut menu. To do this, right-click the text that contains the underline, and then accept the suggested correction, or click Ignore.

Getting More Web Stuff from Microsoft

Word provides additional Web-related tools and documents. You can download free additional Web Page Wizard content documents and visual styles from the Microsoft Word Web site.

As you'll see if you create a file from the template More Cool Stuff on the Web Pages tab of the File New dialog box, the Microsoft Office 97 CD-ROM contains four additional tools that can be very handy for working on Web pages. These tools are listed here:

Folder Name	Description
AXPlugin	A plug-in for Netscape that makes it possible to open Microsoft Office documents inside a Netscape browser.
WebPost	A wizard that takes you through the steps of posting a document to the Web.
PWebSrv	The Personal Web Server lets you run a Web server on your Windows 95 machine or Windows NT workstation.
IExplore	Internet Explorer 3.0.

To open these files, follow these steps:

1 Insert your Microsoft Office CD-ROM in your CD-ROM drive. (You may also need to have your Windows CD-ROM handy.)

2 In the My Computer or Explorer window, switch to the CD-ROM drive.

3 Open the ValuPack folder.

4 Double-click the name of the folder you want to open.

5 Double-click the file inside the folder.

Without going beyond your Word installation, you can find additional Web page documents and templates. For more about this, see "More Web Page Helpers," page 906.

VI

Online Documents

Firing Up the Web Page Authoring Tools

To use the Web authoring features in Word, you must use a Web page template or wizard, or convert an existing document to HTML, the format used for Web pages. When the Web authoring features are active, you'll notice that the toolbars and menus have been customized for working on Web pages.

The Web templates are on the Web Pages tab in the File New dialog box. To convert a document to HTML, click Save As HTML on the File menu.

Organizing Your Web Page

The first step in creating a well-structured Web page is knowing the message you want to convey. Do you want to sell a product, inform, or entertain? Structure the content and design around the purpose of your pages. For example, if your purpose is to sell, consider including information about pricing and availability.

If your Web site will contain several pages, plan how users will move to and from your pages. Sketching out how users will jump from one page to another may be helpful. When it's not clear how the pages relate to each other or how to move around your pages, users can become lost and frustrated.

Using similar graphics and layout ties your pages together and creates a professional look. Using common elements helps people who visit your site know they haven't followed a hyperlink to someone else's site.

The themes provided in the Web Page Wizard can help you create a consistent look. You can also download images from the Microsoft Web Art Page. There are also many libraries of images available on the World Wide Web. To locate them, use a Web search page, and type query terms such as *clip art* or *graphics*.

Building a Web Page

Word offers two easy ways for you to create Web pages. You can start a new page by using a wizard or template, or you can convert an existing Word document to HTML, the format used for Web pages.

Using the Web page authoring features to create your Web page will usually produce the best results. To assist you with creating Web pages, Word supplies the Web Page Wizard and a Blank Web Page template on the Web Pages tab of the File New dialog box. You can use the Web Page Wizard to start with sample content—such as a personal home page and registration form—and graphical themes—such as Festive and Community—to help you quickly create a Web page. If you prefer, you can start with the Blank Web Page template—in this case, create a new document from this template, and then jump to "Laying Out a Web Page," page 908, to build your Web page.

Use the HTML conversion method when you have existing Word content that you want to quickly convert to a Web page. Only the formatting and features that are supported by HTML will be converted. For more about this method, see "Saving a Document as a Web Page," page 947.

Creating the Web Page

If you've never created a Web page, probably the best place to start is with Word's Web Page Wizard. To create a Web page, take these steps:

1 Choose the File New command.

2 Select the Web Pages tab.

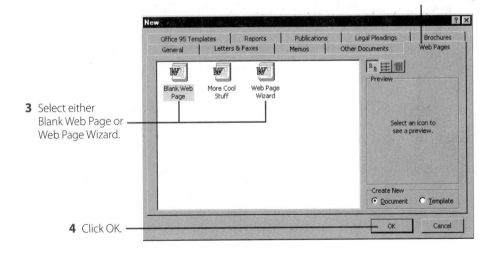

3 Select either Blank Web Page or Web Page Wizard.

4 Click OK.

If you choose the Web Page Wizard, you will see a sample Web page from which you can create your own. You will also see the Web Page

VI

Online Documents

Wizard dialog box with a list of 11 possible Web page types, including a blank Web page. The Simple Layout type is highlighted automatically, which represents the layout you see in the sample. Select another type, if you want, and then click the Next button to see a list of eight visual style choices for the Web page. Choose a visual style and then click the Finish button. Whether you choose the Web Page Wizard or the Blank Web Page template, proceed with the rest of this chapter as you need it.

More Web Page Helpers

? SEE ALSO

For more tools, templates, and information about creating Web pages in Word, see the sidebar, "Getting More Web Stuff from Microsoft," page 903.

The Office folder inside the Microsoft Office folder inside the Program Files folder contains the Web Page Templates folder. The Web Page Templates folder contains two folders: Content and Styles.

The Content folder contains sample Web pages. You might want to explore these sample Web pages for content that you can use. You could open a Web page that suits your purposes, modify it, and save it as your own Web page or Web page template. You can also look at these samples to get ideas for setting up your own Web page.

The Styles folder contains Web page templates, set up in various graphical styles. (The Web Page Wizard uses these templates when you select a graphical style on the second panel.) You might want to use or modify one of these templates to suit you.

To make these additional Web-pages templates readily available for creating Web pages without using the Web Page Wizard, use one of the following methods:

- You can set up a shortcut to the folder in the Web Pages folder.

- You can copy or move these templates into the Web Pages folder inside the Templates folder.

- You can add this folder as a separate tab in the File New dialog box. For instructions on how to do this, see "Setting Up Template Tabs in the New Dialog Box," page 865.

Accounting for Different Web Browsers

Web users view pages with different Web browsers, often on different operating systems. There are differences in the way that some Web browsers display Web pages. Although all browsers support HTML, the format for Web pages, your Web page may look different to others who view it, especially if it is viewed on the World Wide Web.

Some browsers support different versions of HTML and different HTML extensions. Custom options can be set in browsers, such as the default text and background colors and whether to display graphics. Graphics and text can wrap differently, depending on the video resolution—the size of the elements relative to the screen size.

You should design a layout that is readable in most or all circumstances. Here are points to consider:

- If you use advanced techniques, such as inline videos, make sure that no critical information is lost as a result of differences among browsers. In some cases, you can provide simple alternative text. For more information, see the sidebar "Alternatives to Graphics and Video," page 938.

- In some cases, the text of a special effect will appear if the browser doesn't support the effect. For example, the text in scrolling text will appear static in browsers that don't support scrolling behavior.

VI

Online Documents

■ Large images increase download time, especially for readers who gain access to Web pages by modem. Although graphics can make Web pages more interesting, you should use graphics strategically. For more information, see the sidebar, "Reducing the Size of Images and Video," page 940.

■ Consider testing your page in different Web browsers, some of which are available for downloading on the World Wide Web, to see if all your page elements successfully appear.

Previewing Your Web Page

In order to preview the Web page you're authoring, you must have a Web browser installed on your computer. (The Office 97 CD-ROM contains a copy of Internet Explorer. For more about this, see the sidebar "Getting More Web Stuff from Microsoft," page 903.)

■ Click the Web Page Preview button on the Standard toolbar.

■ To switch back to Word, click the Word icon in the taskbar, or close the browser.

Laying Out a Web Page

Before you put anything on a Web page, you should give it some structure, set the standard text colors and page background, and set up any horizontal lines you want as decorations or dividers on the page. These are all tasks that belong to laying out a Web page.

You could simply add text and graphics as you would in a Word document, but such "linear" approaches don't work well on a computer screen. Rather, your Web page will look much more enticing and readable if you give it a background structure that provides containers to hold various bits of information in various places on your page.

You have two tools available for laying out the structure of a Web page: tables and forms.

Drawing the Layout in a Table

You can use tables with or without borders to add graphical effects and manage the layout of your Web page. You can organize columns of graphics and text so that they will be aligned together in Web browsers. Without tables, it's difficult to keep graphics and text aligned in HTML.

You can insert a table either with the table drawing tool or with the Insert Table button or command. For directions on inserting and managing tables, see "Setting Tables in Your Report," page 295.

When you're working on a Web page, Word adds two new commands to the Table menu—Table Properties and Cell Properties. You use the Table Properties command to adjust text wrapping around a table and set the table background color—see "Setting Table Properties," below. You use the Cell Properties command to set the background color for a cell, to adjust its vertical alignment, or to adjust its width and height—see "Setting Cell Properties," next page.

When you insert a table, Word automatically adds a border around all the cells. If you don't want the border to appear on the finished Web page, you can remove it—see "Controlling Table Borders," page 911.

Even if the border is removed, gridlines may appear in your Word document to show the table boundaries. To control the display of gridlines, choose the Table Hide Gridlines or the Table Show Gridlines command. You can also click the Hide Gridlines or Show Gridlines button on the Tables And Borders toolbar. Gridlines do not appear on a Web page when viewed in a Web browser.

TIP

Most Web browsers now support tables, but some earlier versions do not. If you want a broad audience to view the content in a table, you may want to structure your information in text-only format as well, and then provide a hyperlink to the text-only version.

Setting Table Properties

The Table Properties command lets you adjust text wrapping around a table, set the background color for the entire table, and adjust the space between table columns.

VI

Online Documents

? SEE ALSO

When selecting table and cell background colors, be aware of the text colors you have set for text in the table. For more about this, see "Setting the Text Colors," page 918.

To change table properties, take these steps:

1 Position the insertion point in the table.

2 Choose the Table Table Properties command.

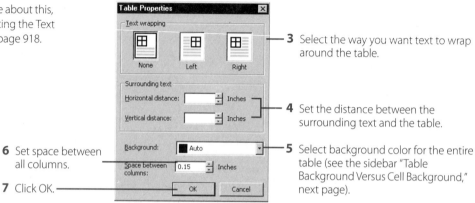

3 Select the way you want text to wrap around the table.

4 Set the distance between the surrounding text and the table.

6 Set space between all columns.

7 Click OK.

5 Select background color for the entire table (see the sidebar "Table Background Versus Cell Background," next page).

Setting Cell Properties

With the Cell Properties command you can set a cell's background color to be different from the background color of the table it's in, adjust the vertical alignment in a cell, or adjust the cell's width and height.

To change cell properties, take these steps:

1 Select the cells you want to change.

2 Choose the Table Cell Properties command.

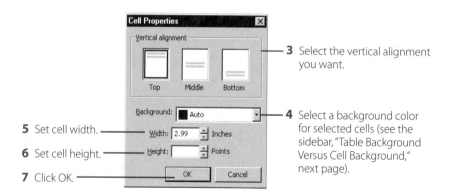

3 Select the vertical alignment you want.

4 Select a background color for selected cells (see the sidebar, "Table Background Versus Cell Background," next page).

5 Set cell width.

6 Set cell height.

7 Click OK.

TIP

The Tables And Borders toolbar contains buttons for setting vertical alignment in cells. You can click these buttons instead of choosing the Table Cell Properties command to set vertical alignment in cells.

Controlling Table Borders

For a table on a Web page, borders are an all-or-nothing proposition—all the table cells have borders around all sides, or there are no borders at all. You can, however, select the width of the borderlines.

To add borders and select a borderline width, follow these steps:

1 Position the insertion point in the table.

2 Choose the Table Borders command.

3 Click here to turn on cell borders, or …

4 Select the border's line width.

5 Click OK.

Click here to turn off borders.

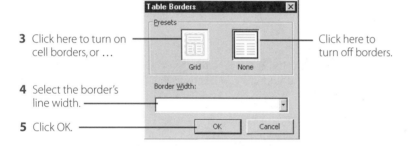

Table Background Versus Cell Background

The color you select in the Background box in the Table Properties dialog box affects the entire table. You can set individual cells to a different color with the Table Cell Properties command. If you set a cell to a background color different from the table background color and then choose the Table Table Properties command again, the Background box is empty to show you that at least one cell has a different color from the table background color. If you change the table background color, you'll have to reset the colors for individual cells you want to be a different color.

VI

Online Documents

Correcting Odd-Looking Tables

When you open a Web page that was authored in another program and that contains a nested table (a table within another table), the columns may not align or may seem very narrow. This problem occurs because Word converts nested tables to single tables with merged rows and columns. In Word, you can use the Draw Table tool to easily create complex table layouts. For more information about using the Draw Table tool in Word, see "Drawing a Table," page 297.

Laying Out a Web Page as a Form

Forms give Web pages the ability to collect and provide dynamic data. For example, forms can provide data from a database on request, they can be used to register for memberships or events, and they can help users send you comments about your site. Word has a Form Design mode for designing forms and setting the properties for the form's elements.

> Because forms require additional support files and, therefore, additional server support, it is recommended that you consult your network or Web administrator when planning the form.

Sample forms, such as feedback and survey forms, are available through the Web Page Wizard. You can use the wizard to create a basic form, and then modify it to fit your needs. Or if the wizard doesn't contain a form that suits your needs, you can create a form by inserting the controls you want.

To start a form, take these steps:

1 Choose the File New command, and click the Web Pages tab.

2 If the Web Page Wizard contains a form you want to use or modify, click Web Page Wizard, click OK, and choose the form you want. To create a form without using the wizard, click Blank Web Page, and then click OK.

Form Design Mode

When the Web page is ready to work on, you switch into Form Design mode and insert the form element. To switch to Form Design mode, choose the View Form Design Mode command, or click the Form Design Mode button on the Standard toolbar.

Word displays the Control toolbar and a floating Exit Design Mode button, shown here:

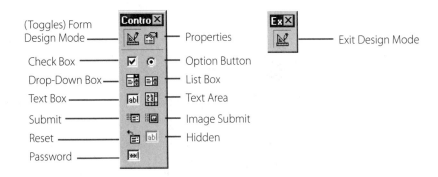

(Toggles) Form Design Mode — Properties

Check Box — Option Button

Drop-Down Box — List Box

Text Box — Text Area

Submit — Image Submit

Reset — Hidden

Password

Exit Design Mode

To exit Form Design mode, click the Design Mode button on the Control toolbar, or choose the View Form Design Mode command again.

When you exit Form Design mode, the Control toolbar remains visible. To hide it, click its Close button.

To lay out the form, follow these steps:

1 Click where you want to insert a form element.

When you insert the first form element, Word inserts a Top Of Form boundary above and a Bottom Of Form boundary below the element. To insert other controls in the same form, click within those boundaries. To add height to the form, insert paragraph marks. These boundaries appear only in design mode and don't appear when you view the page in a Web browser. Also note that you can set up more than one form on a single Web page.

2 Click the button on the Control toolbar for the form element you want to insert, or choose the Insert Forms command and select the form element you want to insert from the submenu.

VI

Online Documents

NOTE

If you click a button on the Control toolbar or choose a form element from the Insert Forms submenu after you exit Form Design mode, Word switches back to Form Design mode as it inserts the element.

3 Repeat step 1 and step 2 for each additional form element you want to insert. So that users can submit the form after filling it in, insert either a Submit or an Image Submit control somewhere in the form.

4 When you're done, exit Form Design mode and hide the Control toolbar by clicking its Close button.

 NOTE

The form elements available in Web page authoring are ActiveX controls that are based on standard form elements used on the World Wide Web. For more information about the form elements, see "Form Elements and Their Properties," next page.

To change the properties of a form element, follow these steps:

1 If necessary, switch to Form Design mode.

2 Double-click the form element you want to change, or select the form element and click the Properties button on the Control toolbar. The Properties dialog box that appears contains two tabs, Alphabetic and Categorized. Both tabs display the same information but are organized differently. The Alphabetic tab lists all the element's properties in alphabetical order, regardless of the category of the property; it looks like this:

The Categorized tab lists the element's properties organized into their categories; it looks like this:

3 Set or change the properties for the form element on either the Alphabetic or Categorized tab. For a little more information about the properties of each type of element, see Table 22-3, next page.

4 To close the Properties dialog box, click its Close button.

Form Elements and Their Properties

When you design a form for a Web page, you insert ActiveX controls as the form elements. ActiveX controls are standard form elements used on the World Wide Web to collect or display dynamic data.

Form elements appear on a Web page as pictures. While you're in Form Design mode, selecting a form element displays a picture frame around the element. Just like pictures, the form element's picture frame has sizing handles with which you can change its size and shape. The Web authoring environment also includes the Format Picture command and the Picture toolbar. For information about formatting pictures, see "Formatting Art, WordArt, and Other Objects," page 515.

> **NOTE**

Forms on a Web page are based on Visual Basic and ActiveX controls. To fully understand the inner workings of form elements, you need to understand Visual Basic and ActiveX. You can still create a form, but changing its properties will elude you until you understand the programming background of the elements. Table 22-3 lists the form elements and some of the properties you can set or change without extensive knowledge of Visual Basic and ActiveX controls.

VI

Online Documents

TABLE 22-3. A Little More Information About Form Elements and Their Properties.

Form Element	Use	Properties
Checkbox	Display a stand-alone choice that you turn on or off, or display each item in a group of choices of which you can select more than one.	**Checked:** Enter True if the check box is on by default; False if it's off by default.
Option button	Display each item in a group of two or more choices of which you can select only one. To place text beside this button, type it onto the form; this button doesn't have a caption property for this purpose.	**Checked:** Enter True if the option button is on by default; False if it's off by default.
Drop-down box	Display available choices in a drop-down list.	**DisplayValues:** Enter the items you want to appear in the list. Separate items with a semicolon; do not type spaces between two items. For example: Item1;Item2;Item3. **MultiSelect:** Defaults to False, which means the user can select only one item. If you change MultiSelect to True, the control becomes a list box. If you change MultiSelect settings, the setting for Selected is cleared. **Selected:** Defaults to True, which means the first item appears in the box and is selected by default; False means no item is selected by default. **Size:** The size of the font. Defaults to 1.
List box	Display available choices in a list format. If the list exceeds the box size, the user can scroll through the list to view additional choices.	**DisplayValues:** Enter the items you want to appear in the list. Separate items with a semicolon; do not type spaces between two items. For example: Item1;Item2;Item3. **MultiSelect**: Defaults to False, which means the user can select only one item. If you change MultiSelect to True, the control becomes a list box. If you change MultiSelect settings, the setting for Selected is cleared. **Selected:** Defaults to True, which means the first item appears in the box and is selected by default; False means no item is selected by default. **Size:** The number of items (lines) visible in the box at a time. Defaults to 3. A list box can be Size 1 if MultiSelect=True.

(continued)

TABLE 22-3. *continued*

Form Element	Use	Properties
Text box	Allow a user to enter one line of text.	**MaxLength:** The number of characters the user can enter. Defaults to 0, which doesn't restrict the length. **Value:** The default text to display in the text box (optional).
Text area	Allow a user to enter multiple lines of text.	**Columns:** The width of the text area in number of columns. **Rows:** The height of the text area in number of rows. **Value:** The text that appears by default (optional). **WordWrap:** Virtual, Physical, or Off. Text will wrap in the box if WordWrap is set to Virtual or Physical; if set to Off, text will not wrap as a line fills up with text. Not all Web browsers support word wrap.
Submit	Submit the data that the user has entered in other form elements. Every form must have one Submit or one Image Submit button.	**Action:** Enter the location of the file that opens when the user clicks Submit. The action becomes the URL of the <FORM> tag. Mailto operations are supported in this field: enter the Internet mail address after *mailto:*.
Image Submit	Display a graphic the user clicks to submit data. When you insert this element, the Picture dialog box appears; select the image you want. When you copy the Web page to the server, copy the button image also. For more information about managing files, see the sidebar "Relative Paths to Hyperlinks," page 931.	**Caption:** The text that appears on the button (Submit button only). **Method:** The method to be used for submitting the form: POST or GET.
Reset	Reset the form elements to their default settings and remove data the user has entered into the form.	**Caption:** The text that appears on the button.

(continued)

VI

Online Documents

TABLE 22-3. *continued*

Form Element	Use	Properties
Hidden	Pass information to the server—such as information about the user's environment—when the user submits the form. Outside of forms design mode, this control is visible when hidden text is showing in your document.	**Value:** The default text that is sent to the server. The Hidden control will always return its value.
Password	Collect a user's password; you can display asterisks (***) to mask text that the user types.	**MaxLength:** The number of characters the user can enter. Defaults to 0, which doesn't restrict the length. **Value:** Default text (displayed as asterisks) for this field (optional).

Setting the Text Colors

When laying out a Web page, you can set the standard color for text and hyperlinks on the Web page. This setting doesn't change the color of text you set in the Font dialog box or with the Font Color button on the Formatting toolbar.

To set the standard colors for text and hyperlinks, follow these steps:

1 Choose the Format Text Colors command.

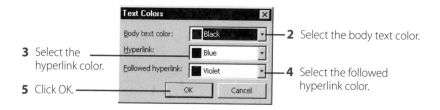

3 Select the hyperlink color.

5 Click OK.

2 Select the body text color.

4 Select the followed hyperlink color.

To set a different color for particular text, follow these steps:

1 Select the text you want to make a different color from the standard text color.

2 Click the Font Color button's drop-down arrow on the Formatting toolbar. Its floating toolbar appears, as you see on the facing page:

3 Click the color you want to apply.

Setting the Background

? SEE ALSO

For information about custom colors, see "Checking Out More Colors," page 492. For information about fill effects, see "Tumbling to the Fill Effects," page 493.

A Web page can have a background color. The color can be a solid color, a pattern, a texture, or a picture. Think of the Web page background color as colored paper on which the text and graphics appear.

To set a background for a Web page, follow these steps:

1 Choose the Format Background command, or click the Background button on the Formatting toolbar.

2 Select a color, or ...

... Click here to set a custom color, or ....

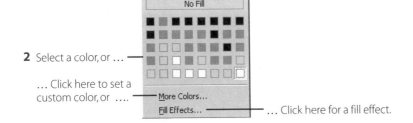

... Click here for a fill effect.

Where Have All the Colors Gone?

When creating Web pages, you can choose from 16 colors for fonts and table backgrounds. Colors other than the 16 are not supported for fonts and table backgrounds, but you can use a wider range of colors for the background of your Web page.

The colors you can use for fonts are available on the Font Color floating toolbar and the Format Text Colors dialog box. The colors you can use for table backgrounds are available in the Table Cell Properties and Table Table Properties dialog boxes.

The colors you can use for the page background are available in the Format Background dialog box. Choose one of the colors in the palette, or click More Colors to see more choices. When you save your Web page, Word converts the background colors to the RGB equivalent color in HTML.

Drawing Horizontal Lines on a Web Page

Horizontal lines are often used on Web pages to separate sections of the page.

1 Position the insertion point where you want to insert the line.

2 Choose the Insert Horizontal Line command.

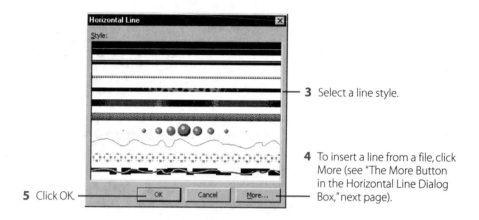

3 Select a line style.

4 To insert a line from a file, click More (see "The More Button in the Horizontal Line Dialog Box," next page).

5 Click OK.

Background Versus Text Colors

Backgrounds can make documents more exciting to read online. Dark or bold colors or images, however, can interfere with text colors, making text difficult to read. There are some steps you can take to ensure that users can read the text on your pages.

To make a document that contains a colored background easier to read, set the text in a contrasting color. For example, use a light text color on a dark background, and vice versa.

In Word documents, avoid formatting text as white, however, because white text doesn't print on many printers. Also, Word displays backgrounds in Online Layout view only. If the user switches to another view, such as Page Layout view, white text may not be visible.

To format the color of text and hyperlinks on a Web page, click Text Colors on the Format menu. Keep in mind that some people prefer to set their own text colors in their Web browser. Also, if you click Auto in the Body text color box, the color of the text will depend on the settings in the reader's Web browser.

Remember that some readers turn off the display of images. When using a background image on a Web page, therefore, use a text color that's not so light that it's hard to read without the background. The default background color in many Web browsers is light gray, but users can change this setting.

Horizontal
Line

To quickly insert another line with the same style, click the Horizontal Line button on the Formatting toolbar.

The first line in the Horizontal Line Style box will be drawn by a Web browser when someone opens the page. The other line styles are graphical images. When you save this Web page, the line will be saved as an image, such as Image.gif, Image1.gif, in the same location as the Web page. If you move the Web page—for instance, when publishing the page—you should also move the image of the line. For more information, see the sidebar "Relative Paths to Hyperlinks," page 931.

The More Button in the Horizontal Line Dialog Box

When you click the More button in the Horizontal Line dialog box, Word displays the Insert Picture dialog box. You can insert a picture from any picture file. If the picture is not a line, you can scale the picture to the width and height you want in order to make the image look like a line. Of course, the image will be very distorted after such scaling. For more information about scaling pictures, see "Sizing—Scaling and Cropping," page 516.

Pouring in Text

Even though Web pages have become more graphical in the last year, the majority of information on a Web page is still text. Because many Web surfers have slow connections (even 28.8 KBaud is pretty slow), waiting to download graphical elements can sometimes try the patience (and pocketbooks) of the people who connect to your Web pages. Text downloads much faster because it takes fewer bits to store and transmit. (For more about this, see the sidebar "Alternatives to Graphics and Video," page 938.)

Word gives you several ways to add text to a Web page:

- Type the text. To start a new paragraph, press Enter (as you do in a regular Word document). Paragraphs will automatically contain space before and after them. To set up paragraphs with no space between them, press Ctrl+Enter instead of Enter.

- Copy or cut and paste the text.

VI

Online Documents

- Insert a file—see "Adding Chapters from Separate Files," page 652.

- Insert AutoText—see "AutoText," page 819.

Text appears in the standard text color you set for a Web page—see "Setting the Text Colors," page 918—but you can also format text and paragraphs in many of the ways you format text and paragraphs in a regular Word document—see "Formatting Text on a Web Page," page 944.

Titling a Web Page

When someone opens your Web page, the title appears in the title bar of the Web browser. If someone stores a link to your Web page, the title appears in that person's history list and favorites list. You set the title in the File Properties dialog box.

If you don't specify a title, Word suggests a title based on the first few characters that appear on your Web page. So if you type the Web page title in the first paragraph on the Web page, Word will use that title in the Title box of the Document Properties dialog box when you save the Web page for the first time.

To set the title of your Web page, follow these steps:

1 Choose the File Properties command.

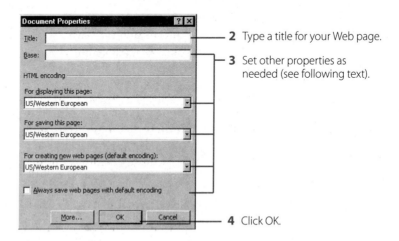

2 Type a title for your Web page.

3 Set other properties as needed (see following text).

4 Click OK.

Other Web Page Properties:
Setting the URL and Language for a Web Page

The following paragraphs give you some information about the rest of the boxes and buttons in the Document Properties dialog box for Web pages.

- **Base.** In this box, type the URL or base hyperlink for this document. When you do this, you can then insert relative hyperlinks, which are shorter than full hyperlink paths. If you leave this box blank or if the path is incorrect, a browser substitutes the URL it used to open this document.

- **HTML Encoding.** When you are authoring a Web page, you can specify the language of the font, or the encoding, that a Web browser will use to display the page. For instance, if you want the page to appear with Greek characters, set the language to Greek. You can also set a default language encoding for new pages that you create.

> **NOTE**
>
> Some languages have more than one encoding scheme. To view the available encodings, see the lists under HTML Encoding.

- **HTML Encoding For Displaying This Page.** To specify the language code that Word will use to display the page if the page is not already displayed with the correct language encoding, click the language you want in the For Displaying This Page list. This setting is also used when loading subsequent pages, if the language encoding cannot be determined.

- **HTML Encoding For Saving This Page.** To specify the language code for saving the page, click the language you want in the For Saving This Page list.

- **HTML Encoding For Creating New Web Pages (Default Encoding).** To specify a default encoding for new Web pages that you create, click the language you want in the For Creating New Web Pages (Default Encoding) list.

VI

Online Documents

- **Always Save Web Pages With Default Encoding.** To have Word always save your pages using a default language encoding, turn on the Always Save Web Pages With Default Encoding check box. This setting affects the current page and future pages that you save. This setting is useful if you reuse pages from other sources and want to store every page in one encoding.

- **More button.** Click this button to display the standard Properties dialog box for Word documents.

Shooting Bullets

You can create bulleted lists when authoring Web pages, similar to the way you create bulleted lists when creating Word documents. One main difference is that you can use graphical images in addition to bullet symbols.

To bullet paragraphs with a particular style of bullet, follow these steps:

1 Select the paragraphs you want to bullet.

2 Choose the Format Bullets And Numbering command.

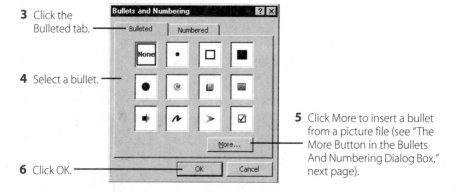

3 Click the Bulleted tab.

4 Select a bullet.

5 Click More to insert a bullet from a picture file (see "The More Button in the Bullets And Numbering Dialog Box," next page).

6 Click OK.

 **TIP**

Changing Bullet Images

When you use images as bullets, you can change the image by using the Bullets And Numbering command. Before changing a bullet image, however, you must delete the existing bullet images. If you inadvertently apply new bullet images without deleting the first images, just delete the first bullet images by selecting them and pressing Delete.

Bullets

To bullet a paragraph with the current bullet style, click the Bullets button on the Formatting toolbar.

Some settings for bullets and numbering that aren't supported by HTML aren't available when you author Web pages. For instance, it's not possible to change the distance between bullets or numbers and text in the Web authoring environment.

The More Button in the Bullets And Numbering Dialog Box

Text bullets that are supported by HTML are also available. In addition to using text bullets that are supported by HTML and the graphical bullets that appear on the Bulleted tab of the Bullets And Numbering dialog box, you can click the More button to use other images as bullets. When you click the More button in either the Bullets And Numbering dialog box or the Horizontal Line dialog box, Word displays the Insert Picture dialog box. You can insert a picture from any picture file. After choosing the image you want, click Insert.

When you use images as bullets, the images are saved as GIF images (unless you insert a JPEG image, which stays in JPEG format), and they are saved in the same location as your Web page or in a location relative to it. For more information about managing files and links, see "Posting a Web Page," page 954.

Numbering Your Points

Numbering on Web pages is similar to numbering in Word documents, except that automatic outline and heading numbering isn't available in the Web authoring environment. By applying different numbering styles and indents, however, you can create a list that appears to have multiple levels. For more information, refer to the related topic, "Lists Within Lists," page 599.

VI

Online Documents

To number paragraphs with a particular numbering scheme, follow these steps:

1 Select the paragraphs you want to number.

2 Choose the Format Bullets And Numbering command.

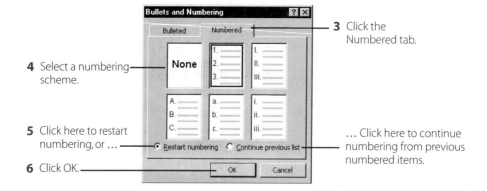

3 Click the Numbered tab.

4 Select a numbering scheme.

None

5 Click here to restart numbering, or …

… Click here to continue numbering from previous numbered items.

6 Click OK.

Numbering

To number a paragraph with the current numbering scheme, click the Numbering button on the Formatting toolbar.

Making Text Scroll

You can enhance your Web page with scrolling text, which moves across the page.

If you want to make text that's already on your Web page scroll, select it, and cut it to the Clipboard. Then in step 8 in the following procedure, paste the text instead of typing it.

To set up scrolling text, follow these steps:

1 Position the insertion point where you want to place the scrolling text.

2 Choose the Insert Scrolling Text command.

3 Select the type of scrolling—Scroll (one side to the other and repeat), Slide (one side to the other and stop), Alternate (slide back and forth).

4 Select the direction— Left or Right.

5 Select a background color.

6 Select the number of loops.

7 Set scrolling speed.

8 Type the text you want to scroll here.

Preview each setting here.

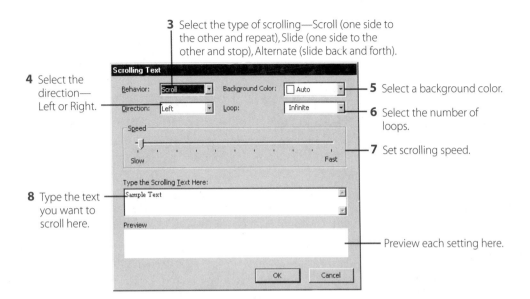

Scrolling text is supported in all versions of Microsoft Internet Explorer except version 1.0. Some other Web browsers don't support scrolling text. In those browsers, the text will appear but it won't scroll.

Inserting HTML Codes

Word provides features that help you create a Web page without writing HTML codes. You can, however, insert HTML codes onto a page by following these steps:

1 Type the HTML codes that you want.

2 Select the codes.

3 Hold down the Shift key as you click the Style box on the Formatting toolbar, and click HTML Markup style.

Here are a couple other points about entering HTML codes directly:

- You can also enter the HTML source directly when you are viewing the source of a Web page. View the source, and then type the HTML codes that you want. For more information about viewing the HTML source, see the sidebar "Viewing the HTML Source of a Web Page," next page.

VI

Online Documents

■ Applying the HTML Markup style will format text as hidden. If you need to view this text and hidden text is not showing, click the Show/Hide ¶ button on the Standard toolbar.

Inserting Hyperlinks

? SEE ALSO

For hyperlinks to online documents rather than to Web pages, see Chapter 21, "Creating Online Documents."

Perhaps the most distinctive feature of Web pages is the hyperlink. Simplified from an idea developed by Theodore Nelson many years ago, a hyperlink is an active pathway to another Web page. When you click a hyperlink, your Web browser displays the Web page that the hyperlink points to (see the sidebar "Following a Hyperlink," page 933).

Until recently, adding hyperlinks to a Web page was a programming process. In Word 97, it's really quite simple. Word gives you four ways to insert a hyperlink into a Web page: type the Internet or network path, choose the Insert Hyperlink command or click the Insert Hyperlink button on the Standard toolbar, use the right mouse button to drag a selection to another Web page, or choose the Edit Paste As Hyperlink command.

Viewing the HTML Source of a Web Page

When you save your Web page, Word works behind the scenes to create HTML tags, which Web browsers interpret to display your text, graphics, sounds, and videos. For example, when you press Enter to create a new line, Word converts the paragraph mark to a <P>, or paragraph tag, in the HTML source.

It's usually not necessary to view the HTML source as you author Web pages, but you can if you like. To view the HTML source, you should first save unsaved changes to the file.

1 Click the Save button on the Standard toolbar.

2 Choose the View HTML Source command.

3 To return to the Web page, click the Exit HTML Source button on the toolbar.

Typing Hyperlinks

If you know the Internet path (URL) to a Web page, the local disk drive path, or the network path to a file, you can simply type the hyperlink into your Word document.

An Internet path (URL) looks like this:

> http://www.microsoft.com

A network path looks like this for an unmapped network drive (called a *share path*):

> \\bigserve\public\reports\fy96_q1.doc

or like this for a mapped network drive:

> X:\reports\fy96_q1.doc

A local disk drive path usually looks like this (the drive letter could be D, E, or even A):

> C:\My Documents\Online Documents\ fy96_q4.doc

 TIP

More About Share Paths

You'll want to use a mapped network drive path only if the drive mapping remains the same for all users all the time. In most cases, a share path is a far better solution. Be aware, however, that if you insert a hyperlink to a file on your hard disk, the hyperlink will most likely take the form C:\folder\…\folder\filename.ext. The only way to set up a hyperlink to your hard disk with a share name is to share the folder first.

Can't Access the Internet

If you can't access the Internet, you're most likely experiencing Internet connection problems. You must have access to the Internet, either through a modem or through a network connection that provides Internet access.

- If you're using a modem to gain access to the Internet, check your modem connection. Most external modems have lights that show when they're sending or receiving signals. Consult your modem's documentation for more information.

- If you connect to the Internet through an Internet service provider, you may need to log on to the service again. You may also want to test other Internet connections from the same service provider.

- If you're gaining access to the Internet through your company's or organization's network, there could be network problems or Internet connection problems. If the problem persists, see your network administrator.

Insert Hyperlink Command and Insert Hyperlink Buttons

? SEE ALSO

For more information about bookmarks in Word documents, see "Bookmark Destinations," page 92.

The Insert Hyperlink command and the Insert Hyperlink button display the Insert Hyperlink dialog box (see Figure 22-3) where you can type an Internet path (URL), a local disk drive path, or network path. The dialog box also contains a Browse button you can click to locate the URL, local disk file, or network file you want to insert a hyperlink to.

In addition, if the document contains bookmarks (Word document) or named ranges (Microsoft Excel worksheet), you can specify the bookmark or name as the specific target for the hyperlink. Another Browse button lets you select the bookmark or name.

The Insert Hyperlink dialog box also contains a box that specifies that the hyperlink use a relative pathname rather than the full pathname in the hyperlink that appears in your document.

Overall, the Insert Hyperlink dialog box gives you more choices for inserting a hyperlink than simply typing does.

FIGURE 22-3.

The Insert Hyperlink dialog box.

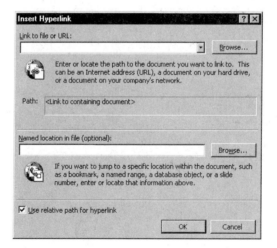

Can't Find Web Page Files

Once you have used the Web page authoring tools, your Web page files—those with HTML, HTM, ASP, or HTX extensions—appear by default in the File Open dialog box. Before you use the tools, you can get Web page files to appear in the list by clicking All Files in the Files Of Type box.

To insert a hyperlink using the dialog box, follow these steps:

Insert
Hyperlink

1 Choose the Insert Hyperlink command, or click the Insert Hyperlink button on the Standard toolbar. (You can also press Ctrl+K to display the Insert Hyperlink dialog box.)

2 Type a URL, a local disk drive location, or a network path in the Link To File Or URL box, or click the Browse button.

3 Type a bookmark or range name in the Named Location In File (Optional) box, or click the Browse button.

4 Leave the Use Relative Path For Hyperlink check box on for a relative path; turn it off for a full path—see the sidebar "Relative Paths to Hyperlinks," below.

5 Click OK.

Relative Paths to Hyperlinks

A hyperlink path can be relative to the location of the document that contains the hyperlink, or it can be an absolute path (full pathname).

When you turn on the Use Relative Path For Hyperlink check box in the Insert Hyperlink dialog box, Word keeps track of the file for the hyperlink, even if you move it. So if you think that you might one day move the file, leave this check box turned on.

When you turn off the Use Relative Path For Hyperlink check box, the hyperlink shows the full path to the file. You'll want to turn off this check box only if you're absolutely sure that you'll never move the file for the hyperlink from its current location.

Dragging Objects into Hyperspace

For information about formatting hyperlinks, see "Formatting Hyperlinks," page 946.

You can create a hyperlink by using the right mouse button to drag selected text or graphics from a Word document or PowerPoint slide, a selected range in Microsoft Excel, or a selected database object in Microsoft Access to your Word publication. When you drag text and graphics from an Office program to a Word document, Word recognizes the location of the information. Take the following steps.

VI

Online Documents

1 Display both files on the screen. If you are dragging text between two Word files, open both files, and then choose the Window Arrange All command. If you are dragging text between two programs, resize the windows of both programs so you can see them at the same time.

2 In the file that is the destination of the hyperlink, select the text, graphic, or other item you want to jump to.

3 Press the right mouse button and drag the selection to the position on the Web page where you want the hyperlink.

4 When the shortcut menu appears, select Create Hyperlink Here.

You don't need to create bookmarks in the destination document or name the range in the destination worksheet.

Edit Paste As Hyperlink Command

If you have copied or cut the text of a hyperlink to the Clipboard, you can paste the Clipboard contents as a hyperlink. To do so, choose the Edit Paste As Hyperlink command.

Changing the Face of a Hyperlink

When you insert a hyperlink, you see the Internet or file path on your Web page. There will probably be many times that you want this face on a hyperlink. But sometimes, the path to another Web page or document can be very long and even very complex. In these cases, you might want something a little more visually appealing. Some Web pages provide both a graphical and a text face for two hyperlinks that lead to the same Web page or document. What this means is that a hyperlink can have any text or any graphic as its face.

To change the face of a hyperlink, follow these steps:

1 Select the hyperlink text—see the sidebar "Selecting a Hyperlink," page 935.

2 Either type new text or insert any picture you want. To insert a picture, choose the Insert Picture command—more about this in "Inserting Graphics," next.

Following a Hyperlink

When you see a hyperlink in a document, it most likely will appear in the formatting of the Hyperlink or Followed Hyperlink character style (see "Formatting Hyperlinks," page 946, for details).

When you position the mouse pointer over a hyperlink, the mouse pointer becomes a hand with a pointing index finger.

- To follow a hyperlink, click it. This technique works every time, whether you have followed the hyperlink before or not.

If an error message appears when you click a hyperlink, look for these causes:

- The destination of the hyperlink may have been removed or renamed.

- The path to the destination of the hyperlink may have been created as a fixed file location, which identifies the destination by its full address, such as C:\My Documents\Sales.doc, and then the destination was moved to another location. To change the hyperlink and make the path to the destination a relative link, right-click the hyperlink, point to Hyperlink on the shortcut menu, and then click Edit Hyperlink. Clear the Use Fixed File Location check box.

- If the destination of the hyperlink is located on the Internet or the World Wide Web, you must have access to the Internet (for example, you may have access by using a modem and an Internet account through an Internet service provider, or through the network if you are in a corporation). If you have these things, the site may be too busy. Try to open the document later.

- If the destination of the hyperlink is located on the intranet, check your network connections to make sure the network server you use is running. See your administrator to make sure you have access to the location of the destination.

Inserting Graphics

? SEE ALSO

For more information about inserting pictures, see "Adding Art from Files," page 455.

Pictures and drawing objects (AutoShapes, text boxes, and WordArt effects) can be inserted onto Web pages.

When you save your Web page, Word converts these objects to GIF images, such as Image.gif, Image2.gif, and so on. Once you close your file, you won't be able to edit the image in Word again. If you will need to update a drawing later, save a copy of your file as a Word document.

VI

Online Documents

Inserting Pictures

Pictures are the easiest form of graphic to add to a Web page because the artwork exists and you simply insert it. To insert a picture on a Web page, follow these steps:

1 Position the insertion point where you want to insert the picture.

2 Choose the Insert Picture command.

3 Select the source of the picture.

4 Take one of the following actions:

- **Clip Art.** In the Microsoft Clip Gallery, click the tab for the type of item you want to insert, select the item, and click Insert.

- **From File.** In the Insert Picture dialog box, switch to the disk and folder of the picture you want, select it, and click Insert.

(?) SEE ALSO

For information about wrapping text around a picture and aligning a picture, see "Aligning Images on a Web Page," page 943.

You can scale all pictures and graphics on a Web page. All artwork on a Web page, anything except text and table structure, are saved as graphical images in GIF or JPEG format.

To scale a picture, follow these steps:

1 Click the picture.

2 Drag the sizing handles that appear at each corner and in the middle of each side to set the size and shape you want. Here's a list of how you can drag to scale a picture:

- Drag a side sizing handle away from the middle of a picture to increase size in that direction only.

- Drag a side sizing handle toward the middle of a picture to decrease size in that direction only.

- Drag a corner sizing handle away from the middle of a picture to increase size along the two sides connected to that corner and maintain the same proportions as the original picture.

- Drag a corner sizing handle toward the middle of a picture to decrease size along the two sides connected to that corner and maintain the same proportions as the original picture.

- Hold down the Ctrl key as you drag any sizing handle to move the opposite side or the opposite corner the same amount at the same time.

Selecting a Hyperlink

The methods you normally use to select text with the mouse don't work for hyperlinks. When you click the mouse on a hyperlink, Word tries to follow the hyperlink to its destination.

Instead of selecting a hyperlink with the mouse, you need to use any of the keyboard methods for selecting text. You can use the mouse to set the insertion point at one end or the other of a hyperlink before you use the keyboard to select it. You can also drag a selection that starts outside a hyperlink and crosses over it.

If the hyperlink is on a line by itself, you can use the mouse in the selection bar to select that line without activating the hyperlink.

Inserting Drawing Objects

Insert drawing objects onto Web pages by first creating a Microsoft Word Picture object and then using the options on the Drawing toolbar.

To insert a graphic, follow these steps:

1 Choose the Insert Object command and click the Create New tab.

2 Under Object Type, double-click Microsoft Word Picture.

3 Using the Drawing toolbar, insert and format the drawing objects you want.

4 When you are finished, click Close Picture on the Picture toolbar.

Here are some important points about working with drawing objects:

- The options for working with drawing objects are available only if you are working in a Microsoft Word Picture object.

- If you apply transparency to drawing objects—for instance, by selecting the Semitransparent check box for fills—these objects will not be retained in the GIF image. Microsoft Photo Editor, which is included with Microsoft Office, can help you create GIF images with transparent areas, and you can insert these images on your Web page as you would any picture or graphic. For more information about installing Microsoft Office components, see "Giving Graphics Transparent Areas," next.

Giving Graphics Transparent Areas

 SEE ALSO

For more information about using Photo Editor, search on the keywords *transparent areas* in the Online Help Index in Photo Editor.

You can use Microsoft Photo Editor, which comes with Microsoft Office, to create GIF images with transparent areas for Web pages. When an image contains a transparent area, the background of the Web page "shows through" the image.

From Word, you can insert a Photo Editor object, and then apply transparency to the background color.

To insert a Photo Editor object, follow these steps:

1 Choose the Insert Object command and click the Create New tab.

2 Under Object Type, double-click Microsoft Photo Editor 3.0 Photo.

3 In Photo Editor, open the graphic or photo you want to apply a transparent area to.

4 Use the Set Transparent Color tool to apply transparency to the image.

Inserting Video

You can add an inline video to your Web page, which means the video is downloaded when the user opens the page. You can determine whether the video will play when the page is opened or when the user points to the video with the mouse. Because not all Web browsers support inline video, you may want to provide alternative text and images or avoid presenting essential information in videos—see the sidebar "Alternatives to Graphics and Video," page 938.

Save your document before inserting videos.

To insert a video on a Web page, take these steps:

1 Position the insertion point where you want to insert the video.

2 Choose the Insert Video command. The Video Clip dialog box appears, as shown in Figure 22-4.

FIGURE 22-4.
The Video Clip
dialog box.

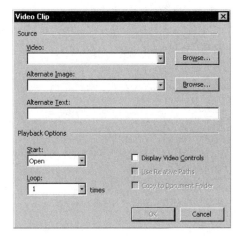

3 Type the file address or URL of the video in the Video box, or click the Browse button to search for it.

4 Type the file address or URL of an alternate image in the Alternate Image box, or click the Browse button to search for it.

5 Type text to substitute for a video or graphic in the Alternate Text box.

6 Select when the video will play in the Start box. You have the following choices:

- Open causes the video to play when the user downloads the Web page.

- Mouse-Over causes the video to play when the pointer moves over the video.

- Both causes the video to play in both cases.

VI

Online Documents

7 Set the number of repetitions in the Loop box.

8 Turn on the Display Video Controls check box to display video controls while authoring.

9 Turn on the Use Relative Paths check box for maintaining a relative path—see the sidebar "Relative Paths to Hyperlinks," page 931.

10 Turn on the Copy To Document Folder check box to copy the video file to the same folder as the Web page.

11 Click OK.

Alternatives to Graphics and Video

Some people who browse Web pages turn off the display of graphics and videos so they can browse the World Wide Web more quickly. Those with slow Internet connections may opt not to download large videos, and some Web browsers don't support all video formats. When your graphics or videos contain information you don't want others to miss, you can provide alternative text for images and videos and alternative images for videos.

You can specify alternative text for images in the Format Picture dialog box. To do so, take these steps:

1 Select the image.

2 Choose the Format Picture command.

3 Click the Settings tab.

4 Type the text you want in the Picture placeholder box.

Specify alternate text and an image for a video in the Video Clip dialog box when inserting a video—see Figure 22-4, page 937.

In some browsers, if the display of images and videos is turned on, alternative text may appear as the video or graphic is downloading.

Instead of inserting large graphics or videos on a Web page, you could insert hyperlinks to them. So the user can make an informed decision about whether to download the file, add the filename and file size near the hyperlink. Some Web page authors include *thumbnails*, or smaller versions of graphics, which the reader can click to obtain the larger versions. You could also create a text-only version of a page that contains complex graphical elements, and then provide a hyperlink to it.

Keep the following points in mind when working with videos:

- The video will play after you insert it. If you've selected the Mouse-Over option for video playback, the video will also play in your Web page document when your mouse moves over it.

- Video files can be very large and take a long time to download. For tips on reducing the size of images, see the sidebar "Reducing the Size of Images and Video," page 940.

- You can also insert a hyperlink to a video, which means the user can click the hyperlink to download the video and play it. For more information about inserting hyperlinks, see "Inserting Hyperlinks," page 928.

Inserting Audio

You can have a background sound play automatically when someone opens your Web page. To set up a background sound for a Web page, follow these steps:

1 Choose the Insert Background Sound command, and click Properties on the submenu.

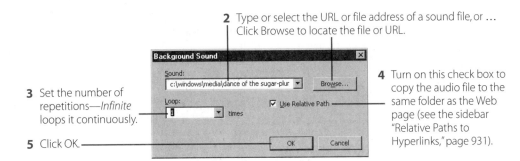

2 Type or select the URL or file address of a sound file, or ... Click Browse to locate the file or URL.

3 Set the number of repetitions—*Infinite* loops it continuously.

4 Turn on this check box to copy the audio file to the same folder as the Web page (see the sidebar "Relative Paths to Hyperlinks," page 931).

5 Click OK.

Here are some pointers about adding sound:

- To review the sound while you are authoring the Web page, choose the Insert Background Sound command and click Play on the submenu. To stop the sound, choose the Insert Background Sound command and click Stop on the submenu.

VI

Online Documents

■ For others to hear background sounds, they must have a sound system installed, and their Web browser must support the sound format of the file you inserted. You can insert sound files in WAV, MID, AU, AIF, RMI, SND, and MP2 (MPEG audio) formats.

■ The background sound plays automatically every time your page is opened or returned to. For frequently opened pages, such as home pages, this repetition could become annoying. You could add the background sound instead to a page that the user is likely to jump to less frequently. Or you could insert a hyperlink that the user can click to download a sound file. For more information about inserting hyperlinks, see "Inserting Hyperlinks," page 928.

■ You may want to use caution when selecting Infinite for a looping option, because the sound will play continually while the page is open.

Reducing the Size of Images and Video

Graphical images and videos can make Web pages more exciting. But because the file size of these elements can be large, they can also increase the amount of time it takes pages to download. Download time is especially critical on the World Wide Web, where some people pay an hourly rate for Internet connections. With planning, you can decrease the file size and download time for graphics and videos.

To decrease the file size of a graphic, use fewer colors, reduce the height and width or crop the graphic, and repeat images when you can. For instance, when you use the same image for a bullet throughout all your Web pages, the image is downloaded only once, even if it appears on several pages. You can use a graphics program—such as Microsoft Photo Editor, which is included with Microsoft Office—to edit the image file. For information about how to install a program or component, click Help on the Windows Start button menu.

A video that's a few seconds long can take several minutes to download on a slow system. To decrease the file size of videos, you can edit out unneeded frames, reduce the height or width of the video, use fewer panels, consider black and white instead of color, and use file compression.

Adding Other Objects to Your Web Page

 SEE ALSO

For information about wrapping text around an object, see "Wrapping Brochure Text Around Objects," page 520.

More and more, Web pages include pictures, video clips, sound clips, as well as many other types of objects that you create with programs other than Word.

The Insert Object command gives you a long list of other objects besides video and sound clips that you can insert in a Web page. You can either pull in one of these objects from a file, or if you have the programs to do it, you can create one of these objects and insert it.

You can add charts, equations, and other objects to a Web page, although once you close the Web page, you can't update the objects as you can OLE objects. The chart, equation, or other object becomes a GIF graphic that you can no longer update.

Insert a chart, equation, or other object by using the Object command on the Insert menu. Just keep in mind that you can't make changes to the object once you close the document. If you plan to work with a complex equation or chart that you want to continue to update, you can instead store it in a Word document and then paste it on your Web page when you're finished working on it.

Inserting Other Objects from Files

To insert an object from a file, follow these steps:

1 Choose the Insert Object command.

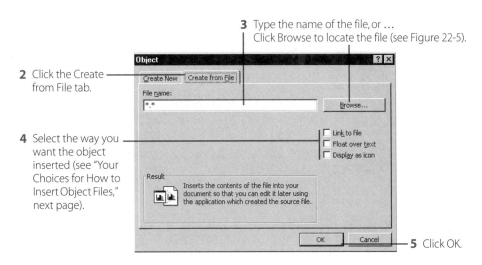

2 Click the Create from File tab.

3 Type the name of the file, or ...
Click Browse to locate the file (see Figure 22-5).

4 Select the way you want the object inserted (see "Your Choices for How to Insert Object Files," next page).

5 Click OK.

VI

Online Documents

FIGURE 22-5.

The Browse dialog box.

Switch to the disk and folder containing the file, or ...
Click the Search The Web button (see "Search The Web Button," page 900).

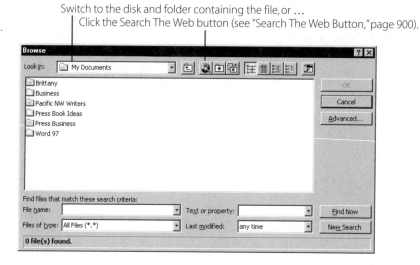

Your Choices for How to Insert Object Files

You have three choices for how to insert an object file into your online document:

- **Link To File.** Turn on this check box if you want to set up a link to the original file. Choose this when you want to keep your online file as small as possible and when you expect that you may change the source file in the future and you'll want those changes to automatically appear in your online document. With this check box turned off, Word stores the contents of the source file in your online document. This method is handy if your online document won't have access to the source file from the location where readers view it.

- **Float Over Text.** With this check box turned on, the object floats over the text rather than being among the text of the page. A floating object is easy to reposition anywhere on a page. You can also wrap the text around a floating object. Turn off this check box if you want the object to appear as part of the text, as any text character does.

- **Display As Icon.** Turn on this check box if you want the object to appear as a file icon rather than as its contents. You'll use this check box most often for text and picture objects. For sound clips, there is no text or picture to display. For objects that have no visible display, you'll see an icon anyway.

Creating Other Objects

To create an object and insert it, follow these steps:

1   Choose the Insert Object command.

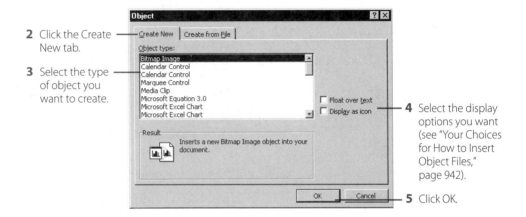

2 Click the Create New tab.

3 Select the type of object you want to create.

4 Select the display options you want (see "Your Choices for How to Insert Object Files," page 942).

5 Click OK.

6   Create the object in the window of the program for the object.

7   When you're done, click in the Word document outside the object to return to Word.

Aligning Images on a Web Page

When you insert a graphic, such as a picture, on a Web page, the graphic aligns with the left margin, and text does not wrap around it. To change the alignment and the way text wraps a graphic, take the following steps.

★ TIP

You can also use the buttons on the Picture toolbar to change the way text wraps around a graphic.

VI

Online Documents

1 Select the graphic.

2 Choose the Format Picture command.

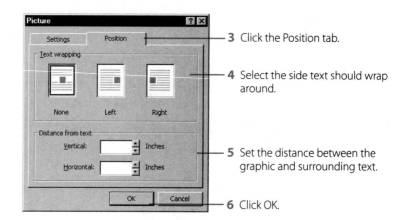

3 Click the Position tab.

4 Select the side text should wrap around.

5 Set the distance between the graphic and surrounding text.

6 Click OK.

Some points to keep in mind when aligning graphics:

- Left and right alignment aren't available for graphics set in table cells.

- Multiple images cannot appear in the same paragraph with the same alignment. For side-by-side graphics, set the graphics in table cells.

Formatting Text on a Web Page

SEE ALSO

You can set the colors for text, hyperlinks, and followed hyperlinks for the entire page with the Format Text Colors command—see "Setting the Text Colors," page 918.

When you create Web pages in Word, you can use many of the same text formatting tools you use for Word documents. For instance, you can apply bold formatting to text, or you can apply any style.

The HTML source that Word creates for the Web page doesn't contain formatting, but it contains codes that instruct a Web browser to format text. Word takes care of the HTML codes behind the scenes, though, so all you need to do is apply the formatting you want.

Formatting that isn't supported by HTML or some Web browsers isn't available in the Web authoring environment in Word—for a list, see Table 22-1, page 893.

To format text, follow these steps:

1 Select the text you want to format.

2 Choose the Format Font command.

3 Select a font. ——
4 Set point size.
5 Set color. ——
6 Select effects. ——
7 Click OK. ——

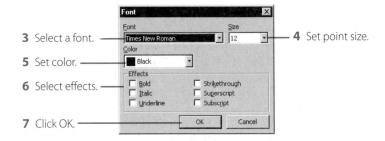

Instead of choosing the Format Font command, you can click buttons on the Formatting toolbar, shown in Figure 22-2, page 897. You can apply bold, italic, and underline to selected text with the Bold, Italic, and Underline buttons. You can increase or decrease the size of selected text with the Increase Font Size and Decrease Font Size buttons. You can also change the font in the Font box, but keep in mind that others viewing your Web pages may not have the same fonts on their systems. Also, some Web browsers display text in a default font only.

You can change the color of selected text—for instance, a word or a sentence—with the Font Color button. Setting the default text colors for the page doesn't change text color for text you've changed with the Font Color button.

To format paragraphs on a Web page, follow these steps:

1 Select the paragraphs you want to format.

2 Click the buttons on the Formatting toolbar for the formatting you want to set:

- You can indent text in .25-inch increments by clicking the Increase Indent button.

- You can reduce an indent in .25-inch increments by clicking the Decrease Indent button.

- You can change the alignment of text by clicking the Align Left, Center, or Align Right button.

VI

Online Documents

You can also give paragraphs bullets or numbers—see "Shooting Bullets," page 924, and "Numbering Your Points," page 925.

 TIP

> Paragraphs will automatically contain space before and after them. To create paragraphs with no white space between them, press Ctrl+Enter.

Formatting Hyperlinks

SEE ALSO

For another way to easily set the color of hyperlinks, see "Setting the Text Colors," page 918. For information about how to select a hyperlink without activating it, see the sidebar "Selecting a Hyperlink," page 935.

To make hyperlinks distinctive in a mass of text, Word is set up to automatically apply a special character style (named Hyperlink) to them. The next two sections describe this automatic process and the hyperlink styles built into Word.

Automatic Formatting of Hyperlinks

On the AutoFormat and AutoFormat As You Type tabs of the Tools AutoCorrect dialog box, you'll find a check box labeled Internet And Network Paths With Hyperlinks. When this box is turned on, Word automatically converts an Internet or network pathname to a hyperlink and applies the Hyperlink character style (described next). The AutoFormat tab works this magic when you choose the Format AutoFormat command. The AutoFormat As You Type tab works this magic after you type an Internet or network path into a document.

Hyperlink Styles

Word has two built-in character styles designed specifically for hyperlinks: Hyperlink and Followed Hyperlink.

- **Hyperlink.** This character style displays the hyperlink as blue, underlined text. This style is designed to show you and your Web page readers that this link has not yet been followed from this page.

- **Followed Hyperlink.** This character style displays the hyperlink as violet, underlined text. This style is designed to show you and your Web page readers that this link has been followed from this page.

 TIP

> If you want to restore a hyperlink to the look of a hyperlink that has not yet been followed, simply apply the Hyperlink style.

Applying Styles on a Web Page

You can apply built-in styles that correspond to formatting that's supported by HTML on Web pages. You apply styles to text on Web pages the same way you apply styles to Word documents, but there are some differences in how styles work.

When you are creating a Web page, Word adds the HTML styles to the Style box on the Formatting toolbar and to the Styles list in the Style dialog box. One character style, HTML Markup, should be used for HTML source codes that you want to enter manually.

The HTML-specific styles, such as Address and H2, correspond directly to HTML tags; any modifications you make to these styles will not be retained. If you modify one of Word's built-in styles, such as Heading 1, the formatting associated with the style will be exported to a corresponding HTML tag, provided the formatting is supported in HTML.

You can define and modify your own styles. When you save the page as HTML, only the HTML-supported formatting is converted—any other formatting is lost when you view the page in a Web browser.

Saving a Document as a Web Page

 SEE ALSO

For directions on saving a Web page as a Web page template, see "Making Your Own Web Page Templates," page 955.

Because Microsoft made Word to be a tool for creating Web pages, you'll find several ways to save a document in HTML file format.

- **Directly: File Save As HTML.** The File menu contains the command Save As HTML. When you want to save a document as a Web page, simply choose this command. As with any Word document, the first time you save a document, you'll need to supply a filename for the document. But Word takes care of the filename extension and the file format.

- **Indirectly: File Save As Command.** To cover all the bases, the Save As dialog box lists HTML Document as one of the choices in the Save File As box. To use the File Save As command to save an online document, simply select HTML Document in the Save As Type box before you click the Save button in the Save As dialog box.

> **NOTE**
>
> After you save a document in HTML file format the first time, the Save button on the Standard toolbar will save additional changes to the document in HTML file format.

What Saving a Document as a Web Page Does to the Document

When you save a Word document as a Web page, Word closes the document and then reopens it in HTML format. Word displays the Web page similar to the way it will appear in a Web browser. Formatting and other items that aren't supported by HTML or the Web page authoring environment are removed from the file. Table 22-4 shows the elements that Word changes or removes upon conversion.

TABLE 22-4. Elements That Word Changes or Removes Upon Conversion of a Document to a Web Page.

Element	Word to HTML	Notes
Comments	Changed	Comments inserted with the Comments command on the Insert menu are removed. After saving the document in HTML format, however, you can enter comments and apply the Comments style. The comments will not appear when the Web page is displayed by a Web browser.
Font sizes	Changed	Fonts are mapped to the closest HTML size available, which ranges from size 1 to 7. These numbers are not point sizes but are used as instructions for font sizes by Web browsers. Word displays the fonts in sizes ranging from 9 to 36.
Emboss, shadow, engrave, all caps, small caps, double strikethrough, and outline text effects (Format menu, Font command, Font tab)	Removed	These character formats are lost, but the text is retained.
Bold, strikethrough, italic, and underline effects	Retained	Some special underline effects, such as dotted underlines, are converted to a single underline, and some underline effects aren't converted.

(continued)

TABLE 22-4. *continued*

Element	Word to HTML	Notes
Animated text (Format menu, Font command, Animation tab)	Changed	Animations are lost, but the text is retained. For an animated effect, insert scrolling text into your page in the Web page authoring environment.
Graphics	Changed	Graphics, such as pictures and clip art, are converted to GIF format, unless the graphics are already in JPEG format. Drawing objects, such as text boxes and shapes, are not converted. Lines are converted to horizontal lines.
Tabs	Retained	Tabs are converted to the HTML tab character, represented in HTML source as &#9. Tabs may appear as spaces in some Web browsers, so you may want to use indents or a table instead.
Fields	Changed	Field results are converted to text; field codes are removed. For instance, if you insert a DATE field, the text of the date converts, but the date will not continue to update.
Tables of contents, tables of authorities, and indexes	Changed	The information is converted, but indexes and tables of contents, figures, and authorities can't be updated automatically after conversion because they are based on field codes. The table of contents displays asterisks in place of the page numbers; these asterisks are hyperlinks that the reader can click to navigate through the Web page. You can replace the asterisks with text that you want to have displayed for the hyperlinks.
Drop caps	Removed	In the Web page authoring environment, you can increase the size of one letter by selecting it and then clicking the Increase Font Size button. Or, if you have a graphic image of a letter, you can insert it in front of the text.
Drawing objects, such as AutoShapes, text effects, text boxes, and shadows	Removed	You can use drawing tools in the Web page authoring environment by inserting Word Picture Objects. The object is converted to GIF format.
Equations, charts, and other OLE objects	Changed	These items are converted to GIF images. The appearance is retained, but you won't be able to update these items.

VI

Online Documents

(continued)

TABLE 22-4. *continued*

Element	Word to HTML	Notes
Tables	Retained	Tables are converted, although settings that aren't supported in the Web page authoring environment are lost. Colored and variable width borders are not retained.
Table widths	Changed	By default, tables are converted with a fixed width. To convert a table with a percentage width (so that the table is sized relative to the browser window), consult the Microsoft Word file.
Highlighting	Removed	
Revision marks	Removed	Changes entered with the TrackChanges feature are retained, but the revision marks are removed.
Page numbering	Removed	An HTML document is considered a single Web page, regardless of its length.
Margins	Removed	To control the layout of your page, you can use a table.
Borders around para- graphs and words	Removed	You can place borders around a table, and you can use horizontal lines to help emphasize or separate parts of your Web page.
Page borders	Removed	There is no HTML equivalent for a page border. You can make your pages more attractive by adding a background using the Background command on the Format menu. You can also place borders around a table, and you can use horizontal lines to help emphasize or separate parts of your Web page.
Headers and footers	Removed	There are no equivalents for headers and footers in HTML.
Footnotes and endnotes	Removed	
Newspaper columns	Removed	For a multicolumn effect, use tables.
Styles	Changed	User-defined styles are converted to direct formatting, provided the formatting is supported in HTML. For instance, if you convert a style that includes bold and shadow formatting, the bold formatting is retained as a direct formatting, but the shadow formatting is lost.

Setting the Standard File Format to HTML

If your primary task with Word is to create online documents that you save in HTML file format, you might consider setting HTML as the standard file format for saving. Here are the steps:

1 Choose the Tools Options command.

2 Click the Save tab. The Save tab of the Options dialog box is shown in Figure 22-6.

3 Select HTML Document in the Save Word Files As drop-down list box.

4 Click OK.

FIGURE 22-6.
The Save Word Files As option on the Save tab of the Options dialog box.

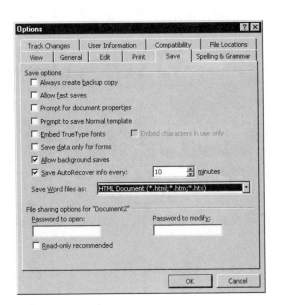

Some Problems You Might See When Reopening a Web Page

When you reopen a Web page, you might notice things that don't look right to you. The following topics discuss the more common problems you might see.

VI

Online Documents

Unreadable Text on Some Web Pages

If some or all of the text on a Web page is unreadable, here are two possible reasons:

■ The page is encoded for a different language, and Word cannot automatically determine the language. To correct this, choose the File Properties command. In the For Displaying This Page list under HTML Encoding, select the language you think the page is encoded in. Some languages have more than one encoding, so try each encoding until you can read the text. (For more information about the File Properties command and its dialog box, see "Other Web Page Properties: Setting the URL and Language for a Web Page," page 923.)

■ The page is encoded for a language your system doesn't support.

To add support for European languages in Windows 95, open the Control Panel, double-click Add/Remove Programs, click the Windows Setup tab, and select the Multilanguage Support check box. In Windows NT, multilanguage support is already included.

To add support for Asian languages in Windows 95 and Windows NT 2.51, install support for the appropriate language from the ValuPack on the Office 97 CD-ROM. If you are using Windows NT 4.0, install support for the appropriate language from the Windows NT 4.0 CD-ROM.

Brackets and Codes Appear Instead of Content

If you see brackets and codes, such as <HTML>, <HEAD>, or <P>, instead of the content of your Web page, one of the following may be true:

■ You may be viewing the HTML source code, the language used to create Web pages. You may have entered this view by choosing the View HTML Source command. If *Exit HTML Source* appears on the toolbar, you are viewing the HTML source. To return to the visual display of your Web page, click the Exit HTML Source button.

■ You may have opened a file that is in a format used for Web pages but doesn't have one of the following file name extensions: HTML, HTM, HTX, ASP, or OTM. You may be viewing HTML source for this file instead of the visual display of the content. To correct this problem, follow these steps:

1 Choose the Tools Options command, and then click the General tab.

2 Turn on the Confirm Conversion At Open check box, and then click OK.

3 Close the file, and then reopen it in Word.

4 In the Convert File dialog box, select HTML Document, and then click OK.

Tag Information Changes After Open and Save

If the HTML source of a Web page appears different after you open an HTML file and save it, here are two possible reasons:

- If the former HTML source in your file differed from standard HTML source—for instance, if the codes were placed in a non-standard order or used lowercase letters—Word may have changed the codes to fit HTML standards when you closed the file. These changes generally won't affect the way Word displays your Web page.

- Word retains most HTML source, even if the item is not available in the Web page authoring environment. For instance, the <BLINK> code is retained, even though the text does not blink when it's displayed in Word. One exception is HTML colors for text, table backgrounds, and hyperlinks that aren't the same as those available in Word. Those colors are converted to the closest color that's available in Word.

- When Word does not recognize an attribute of a tag that it converts, the attribute is lost.

A Web Page Looks Different After Closing and Reopening

When you save a document as a Web page, Word closes the file, reopens it, and then displays the page similar to the way it will appear in a Web browser. Word converts the content and formatting to HTML, the format used for Web pages. Formatting and other items that aren't

VI

Online Documents

supported by HTML are converted to the closest formatting or feature in HTML or removed from the file.

If you copy and paste text from another Word document or insert a file on your Web page, the content will look the same until you save your file again. Therefore, some content may not match the display in your browser until you close and reopen the file in Word. For more information about what happens when you convert a file to HTML format, see "What Saving a Document as a Web Page Does to the Document," page 948.

Posting a Web Page

The steps that you take to make your pages available to other people depend on how you want to share the pages. To make pages available to other people on your network, save your Web pages and related files, such as pictures, to a network location. If your company uses an intranet based on Internet protocols, you may need to copy your pages to a Web server. Contact your network or Web administrator for more information.

To make your Web pages available on the World Wide Web, either you need to locate an Internet service provider that allocates space for Web pages, or you need to install Web server software on your computer. Some factors to consider in setting up your computer as a Web server are your computer's speed and availability. If you don't want to leave your computer on most or all hours of the day, you may not want to set up your computer as a Web server.

If you are working with an Internet service provider or a Web administrator, you should ask how the Web pages, graphics files, and other files should be structured on the server. For instance, find out whether you need to create separate folders for bullets and pictures, or whether you need to store all the files in one location. If you plan to use forms or image maps, you should ask about any limitations on using these items because they require additional server support.

Setting up a Web server requires special software. You can use Personal Web Server, which is available in the ValuPack folder on the Office 97 CD-ROM, to set up a Web server—for more about this, see the sidebar "Getting More Web Stuff from Microsoft," page 903. You can also use Microsoft Internet Information Server to set up an advanced Web server. If you have access to the Web, you can learn more about Microsoft Internet Information Server.

Making Your Own Web Page Templates

You can create a custom template that you base Web pages on. To create a Web page template, use one of these three methods:

- Create a new template from the Blank Web Page template, and then set up the new template as you would any Word template.

- Create a new template with the Web Page Wizard, and then set up the new template as you would any Word template.

- Create a Web page from one of the Web page templates, set it up as you would set up a template, and then save the page as you would save any template from a document.

To create a new template from an existing template or the Web Page Wizard, follow these steps:

1 Choose the File New command.

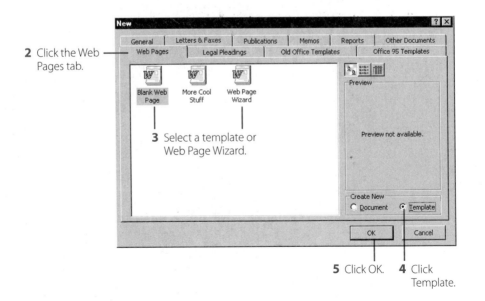

2 Click the Web Pages tab.

3 Select a template or Web Page Wizard.

5 Click OK.   4 Click Template.

6 If you select the Web Page Wizard, follow the instructions in the wizard. If you select a template, build the structure of the Web page as directed in "Laying Out a Web Page," page 908.

7 After you finish setting up the template, choose the File Save As command.

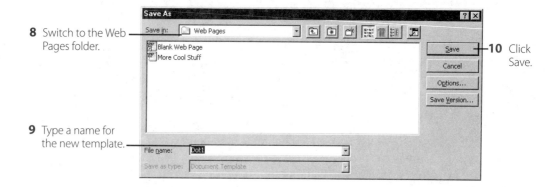

8 Switch to the Web Pages folder.

9 Type a name for the new template.

10 Click Save.

To create a template from an existing Web page, follow these steps:

1 Choose the File Save As command.

2 In the Save File As Type box, select Document Template (*.dot).

3 Switch to the Web Pages folder.

4 If you want to give the template a new name, edit the current name or type a new name in the File Name box.

5 Click the Save button.

Appendixes

Exercising Your Word Options

I f you've ever struggled with a word processor that was set up awkwardly, you'll be relieved to know that Microsoft Word lets you control many aspects of how the Word program operates with the options in the Tools Options command.

When you choose the Tools Options command, you see 10 tabs in the Options dialog box. You can jump directly to some of the tabs from other dialog boxes that control some of Word's operations—for example, you can jump directly to the Print tab from the Print dialog box. The following sections for each tab describe the ways you can customize the look and operation of Word, and they also discuss the dialog boxes you can open from the tabs. The sections follow the same order as the tabs in the Options dialog box.

Word also provides two sets of options for automatic formatting. You can see the tabs for the two sets of AutoFormat options by choosing the Tools AutoCorrect command. For details of the AutoFormat options, see "AutoFormat Options," page 987.

View Tab

Word provides a View tab for each of the four views: Normal, Page Layout, Outline (and Master Document), and Online Layout. The type of View tab Word displays depends on the view you are in when you open the Options dialog box. You'll notice that the Normal and Outline View tabs are similar.

Normal and Outline Views

The View tab you see when Normal or Outline view is active is the same except for the label that appears above the Show section: in Normal view, the label reads Normal View Options; in Outline and Master Document views, it reads Outline View Options. Note that the settings affect the specified view only. The View tab for Normal View Options is shown in Figure A-1. Following are the options on the View tab.

FIGURE A-1.
The Options dialog box with the View tab selected and Normal view options displayed. (Outline view options are the same.)

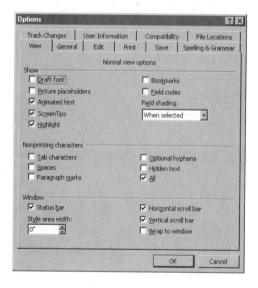

Draft Font check box. Displays text in a 12-point sans serif font.

Picture Placeholders check box. Displays an empty box for all pictures. This option is not available in Macro view.

Animated Text check box. Displays the animation on the screen. Turn off this box to see how animated text prints on the screen.

Screen Tips check box. Displays the name of the commenter and the comment when you place the mouse pointer over a comment reference mark. Also, the comment reference mark and the word before it appear marked with a yellow highlight.

Highlight check box. Turns the colored highlighting feature on or off. When it is on, colored highlighting can be applied to selected text by clicking the Highlight button on the Formatting toolbar.

Bookmarks check box. Shows square brackets around text marked with a bookmark. This option is not available in Macro view.

Field Codes check box. Displays field codes instead of field results. This option is not available in Macro view.

Field Shading drop-down list box. Sets shading for fields. The choices are Never, Always (fields are shaded whether selected or not), and When Selected (shading appears whenever the insertion point or selection is in a field). This option is not available in Macro view.

Tab Characters check box. Displays tab characters as arrows ($\rightarrow$).

Spaces check box. Displays spaces as dots.

Paragraph Marks check box. Displays paragraph marks as the paragraph symbol (¶).

Optional Hyphens check box. Displays optional hyphens as logical NOT symbols (¬).

Hidden Text check box. Displays hidden text, with dotted underlining.

All check box. Displays all nonprinting characters.

Status Bar check box. Displays or hides the status bar.

Style Area Width text box. Opens the style area and sets its width to up to half the window width. This option is not available in Macro view.

Horizontal Scroll Bar check box. Displays or hides the horizontal scroll bar.

Vertical Scroll Bar check box. Displays or hides the vertical scroll bar.

Wrap To Window check box. Wraps text lines at the right window border, regardless of paragraph width, making all text visible in the window.

Page Layout View

The following explanations include only the options that differ from those available in Normal and Outline views. The View tab for Page Layout view options is shown in Figure A-2.

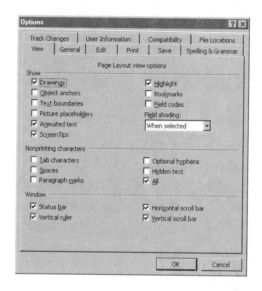

The Page Layout view options don't include the Draft Font and Wrap To Window options found on the Normal and Outline View tabs.

Drawings check box. Displays drawings when on; hides drawings when off. This option has no relation to the Picture Placeholders option. You create drawings using Word's drawing tools, without inserting a picture or a frame.

Object Anchors check box. Displays anchors for frames. You can drag an anchor to position a frame relative to a new anchor point.

Text Boundaries check box. Displays dotted boxes around the text areas of a page, main text, pictures, headers and footers, frames, footnote reference marks, and annotation reference marks.

Vertical Ruler option. Displays a ruler on the left edge of the window. This option replaces the Style Area Width option found on the Normal and Outline View tabs.

Online Layout View

The following explanation includes the only option that differs from Page Layout view. The View tab for Online Layout view options is shown in Figure A-3.

FIGURE A-3.
The Options dialog box with the View tab selected and Online Layout view options displayed.

Enlarge Fonts Less Than text box. Enlarges fonts that are smaller than the size you set up in the text box. For example, if you set this text box to 14, all fonts in the document smaller than 14 points appear in 14-point size on the screen. This setting does not affect the actual font size of the text for printing or viewing in other views.

General Tab

The General tab options let you set some overall operations of Word that apply to all documents in all views. Figure A-4 shows the General tab. Descriptions of the options follow.

Background Repagination check box. Repaginates the document as you work. (This option is unavailable in Page Layout and Online Layout views because pagination is necessary to properly display a document in these views.)

FIGURE A-4.
The Options dialog box with the General tab selected.

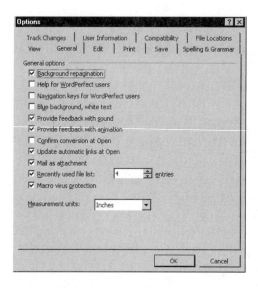

Help For WordPerfect Users check box. "Reads" WordPerfect keystrokes and displays a dialog box that tells you the Word commands and keystrokes that reproduce the WordPerfect actions.

Navigation Keys For WordPerfect Users check box. Sets the functions of the Page Up, Page Down, Home, End, and Escape keys to their WordPerfect equivalents.

Blue Background, White Text check box. Makes the window background blue and the text white; makes the window look like a Microsoft Word for MS-DOS window.

Provide Feedback With Sound check box. Turns on and off sounds for actions in Word—beeps for errors and completion of tasks. Most sounds require a sound card. If you have a sound card, you can change the sounds associated with various actions. To do so, double-click the Sounds icon in the Windows Control Panel.

Provide Feedback With Animation check box. Turns on and off animated mouse pointers and screen animations for other actions, such as background saving and printing.

Confirm Conversion At Open check box. Displays the Convert File dialog box when you open a file that is not a Word document.

VII

Appendixes

Update Automatic Links At Open check box. Automatically updates OLE links when you open a document that contains them.

Mail As Attachment check box. Inserts Word documents as attachments that appear as icons in a Mail message. Turn this option off to display Word documents as text in a message.

Recently Used File List check box. Displays at the bottom of the File menu a list of filenames of documents most recently used in Word.

Entries text box. Sets the number of filenames listed at the bottom of the File menu. The maximum is nine.

Macro Virus Protection check box. Turn on this check box to activate Word's built-in macro virus protection. When Word opens a template that contains macros, you see a warning message. Beware especially when someone sends you a document that has the DOT filename extension rather than the standard DOC filename extension.

Measurement Units drop-down list box. Sets the unit of measure for dialog boxes and the ruler (inches, centimeters, points, or picas).

Edit Tab

The Edit tab lets you set editing options that affect editing in all documents and in all views. The Edit tab is shown in Figure A-5. Following are the options on the Edit tab.

Typing Replaces Selection check box. When you turn on this option, typing deletes a selection when you type the first character. When you turn off this option, typing inserts characters in front of the selection.

Drag-And-Drop Text Editing check box. Turns on or off the ability to move or copy a selection by dragging it with the mouse. This option does not affect the moving or copying of drawings in Page Layout view.

When Selecting, Automatically Select Entire Word check box. When this option is on, if you extend a selection by dragging the mouse from the middle of a word to another word, both words are selected.

Use The INS Key For Paste check box. Switches the Insert key from overtype/insert mode toggle to Paste (the same as Ctrl+V).

FIGURE A-5.
The Options dialog box with the Edit tab selected.

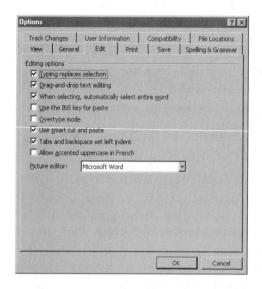

Overtype Mode check box. When this option is on, typing from an insertion point replaces one character at a time as you type. With text selected, the first character replaces the selection, and typing then replaces one character at a time.

Use Smart Cut And Paste check box. Corrects the spacing (adds or removes spaces) when you cut or paste.

Tabs And Backspace Set Left Indent check box. When this option is on, if the insertion point is at the beginning of a paragraph, pressing the Tab key once indents the first line to the first tab stop (first-line indent). Each subsequent time you press the Tab key, the first line is indented to the next tab stop and the remaining lines of the paragraph are indented one tab stop (left indent). When you press the Backspace key, the first line moves back to the preceding tab stop so the first-line indent is zero. Each subsequent press of the Backspace key moves the left indent back to the preceding tab stop until the left indent is zero.

If the insertion point is at the beginning of any line other than the first line, each time you press the Tab key, the left indent moves right one tab stop, and each time you press the Backspace key, the left indent moves back to the preceding tab stop until the indent is zero.

Allow Accented Uppercase In French check box. Enables Word to suggest adding accents to uppercase characters in French words when

VII

Appendixes

you proofread or use the Change Case command. This option requires that you have a French dictionary installed and that the words be formatted as French words.

Picture Editor drop-down list box. Sets the picture editor that Word starts when you double-click on a picture in a document. The choices are Microsoft Word (Word's picture editing window and drawing tools), Microsoft Imager 3.0 Picture, and any installed OLE picture editing programs.

Print Tab

> You can jump directly to the Print tab from the Print dialog box.

Using the Print tab options, you can control how a document is printed and what elements in the document are printed. To set other options relating to the printer, you can use the File Print command and the File Page Setup command. When you choose File Print, clicking the Options button in the Print dialog box opens the Options dialog box, and Word selects the Print tab, which is shown in Figure A-6. Following are the options on the print tab.

Draft Output check box. Prints your document as quickly as possible. The output varies depending on the printer. Your document might print without pictures, using a monospace font.

Update Fields check box. Updates fields in your document before printing.

Update Links check box. Updates links to OLE objects before printing.

Allow A4/Letter Paper Resizing check box. Turn off this check box if you want Word to automatically adjust the paper size of a document set up for the standard paper size in another country to your country's standard paper size. For example, if you, as a U.S. user, receive a document formatted in A4 paper size, turning off this check box automatically adjusts the paper size for printing to the U.S. standard letter size. This check box affects the paper size for printing only. It has no effect on the screen display of the document.

FIGURE A-6.

The Options dialog box with the Print tab selected.

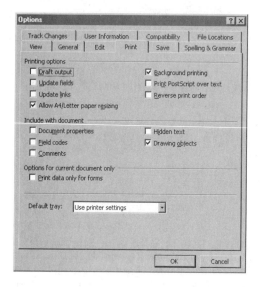

Background Printing check box. Sends pages to the print spooler while you continue working on your document. Printing is slower, but you regain control of Word more quickly.

Print PostScript Over Text check box. Turn on this check box if you have converted a document from Word for Macintosh and want the PostScript to print on top of the text inside or behind it. This check box has no effect if the converted document doesn't contain any Print fields (the fields that contain the PostScript instructions).

Reverse Print Order check box. Prints the document from last page to first. Turn this option on if pages are normally in reverse order in the printer output tray. This option makes printing extremely slow.

Document Properties check box. Prints a page of information about the document based on information in the Properties dialog box.

Field Codes check box. Prints field codes instead of field results.

Comments check box. Prints annotations on separate pages after printing the document and includes the annotation reference marks in the text. Turning on this check box also turns on the Hidden Text check box.

Hidden Text check box. Prints any hidden text in your document as regular text with a dotted underline.

Drawing Objects check box. When this option is turned off, Word "hides" (does not print) drawing objects. This option does not affect pictures; to avoid printing pictures, turn on the Draft Output check box.

Print Data Only For Forms check box. Prints only the data and not the structure or boilerplate text of a form.

Default Tray drop-down list box. Selects the paper tray for this document only. This setting overrides the Windows 95 setting on the Paper tab in the printer's Properties dialog box.

Save Tab

 TIP

You can jump directly to the Save tab from the Save As dialog box.

The Save tab lets you set the options for saving your documents (including automatic saving) and for saving the Normal template. When you choose the File Save As command, clicking the Options button in the Save As dialog box opens the Options dialog box with the Save tab selected. The Save tab is shown in Figure A-7. Following are the options on the Save tab.

Always Create Backup Copy check box. Word creates a backup copy of the document every time you save. Saving replaces the previous backup copy.

Allow Fast Saves check box. When this option is on, Word uses its fast save feature, which saves only the changes in the document. When this option is off, Word performs a full save every time. Full saves usually produce smaller files and make searching for files more accurate.

Prompt For Document Properties check box. Displays the Properties dialog box for the document when you first save a document or when you choose File Save As to save a document with a different name or location.

Prompt To Save Normal Template check box. When this option is on, Word asks whether you want to save changes to the Normal template. When this option is off, Word automatically saves all changes to the

FIGURE A-7.
The Options dialog box with the Save tab selected.

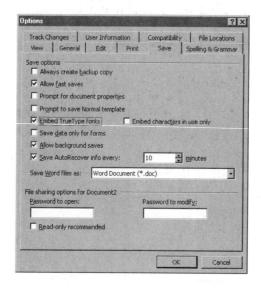

Normal template. Note that you must save the Normal template after turning off this option in order to make the option stick.

Embed TrueType Fonts check box. Embeds in the document when it is saved any TrueType fonts that were used in the document. Embedded fonts can be displayed in the document on another system even if the system does not have the fonts installed.

Embed Characters In Use Only check box. When you've turned on the Embed TrueType Fonts check box, you can turn on this check box to embed only the TrueType font styles that you've actually used. If you used 32 or fewer characters of a TrueType font in a document, turning on this check box directs Word to embed only those characters, which can significantly decrease the size of a document file. This check box is unavailable when you turn off the Embed TrueType Fonts check box.

Save Data Only For Forms check box. When this option is on, Word saves only the data that was filled in on a form. When this option is off, the form is saved with the data in place.

Allow Background Saves check box. Turn on this check box to save a document in the background while you continue to work. When you turn on this check box, you'll see a pulsating floppy disk icon in the status bar while Word performs the background save. A background save occurs when you choose the File Save or File Save As command.

Save AutoRecover Info Every check box. Turns on automatic saving. Word saves automatically saved documents in a special format and uses them to recover lost work if you end a Word session without exiting properly. This lets you recover work after a power failure or some other inadvertent shutdown of the computer.

Minutes text box. Sets the maximum time interval between saves. The maximum time available between automatic saves is 120 minutes; the minimum is 0 minutes. Setting the Minutes text box to zero is the same as turning off AutoRecover. Word might save more frequently than what you specify when you make many complex changes or when the document is extremely large.

WARNING

> AutoRecover does not replace saving. You must still save a document when you want it saved or when you close the document.

Save Word Files As drop-down list box. Lets you select the standard file format in which you want to save your documents. This list contains the same options as the Save File As Type list in the Save As dialog box. There you select a file format for the individual document. Here you select the file format you want to use most often.

Password To Open text box. Lets you specify a password to open the file for read only. When you try to open the file, Word requests the password with the following dialog box:

You can open the file for read only after you type the correct password. A read-only document can be edited and saved under a different name. The password can contain up to 15 letters, numbers, and symbol characters. Letters can be both uppercase and lowercase. When you use the password to open the file, you must type the letters in the correct case.

Password To Modify text box. Lets you specify a password to permit saving an edited version of the file. When you try to open the file, the following dialog box opens, in which you can either enter the password to open the file for editing or open the document as read only without the password.

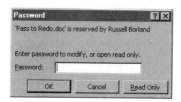

A read-only document can be edited and saved under a different name. The password can contain up to 15 letters, numbers, and symbol characters. Letters can be both uppercase and lowercase. When you use the password to open the file, you must type the letters in the correct case.

Read-Only Recommended check box. Specifies that Word display a message box when the document is opened, recommending that the document be opened as read-only unless changes need to be saved and asking whether the document should be opened as read-only. The message box looks like this:

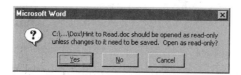

Clicking the Yes button opens the document as read-only; clicking the No button opens the document for editing.

Spelling & Grammar Tab

You can jump directly to the Spelling & Grammar tab from the Spelling and Grammar dialog box.

You set the options for proofreading a document in the Spelling & Grammar tab. The Tools Spelling And Grammar command controls spelling and grammar checking. Clicking the Options button in the Spelling dialog box opens the Options dialog box with the Spelling & Grammar tab selected. The Spelling & Grammar tab is shown in Figure A-8. Descriptions of the choices follow.

FIGURE A-8.
The Options dialog box with the Spelling & Grammar tab selected.

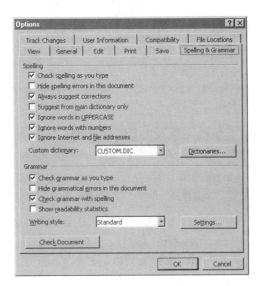

Check Spelling As You Type check box. Automatically checks your spelling as you type and underlines with a red sawtooth underline words not found in any active dictionaries.

Hide Spelling Errors In This Document check box. Hides the red sawtooth underlines Word uses to mark misspelled words. Turning on this check box doesn't affect automatic spelling checking, only the visibility of its markings in the document.

Always Suggest Corrections check box. When this option is on, Word always lists suggestions (if any) for correcting words it doesn't recognize. When this option is off, no suggestions appear in the Spelling dialog box.

Suggest From Main Dictionary Only check box. When this option is on, Word uses only the main dictionary to find suggestions. Turn this option off to use custom dictionaries in addition to the main dictionary.

Ignore Words In UPPERCASE check box. Prevents Word from checking the spelling of words you type in all uppercase. This option does not affect words typed in lowercase or mixed case that have Small Caps formatting.

Ignore Words With Numbers check box. Prevents Word from checking the spelling of words that contain numbers.

Ignore Internet And File Addresses check box. Turn on this check box to omit Internet addresses and file pathnames from proofreading. You'll probably only want to turn off this check box when you set up a custom dictionary for checking the correctness of Internet addresses and file pathnames.

Custom Dictionary drop-down list box. From the list, select the custom dictionary to which you want to add words during proofreading.

Dictionaries button. Displays the Custom Dictionaries dialog box with a list of your custom dictionaries; see "Custom Dictionaries Dialog Box," next page.

Check Grammar As You Type check box. Turn off this check box if you do not want to automatically check grammar during proofreading.

Hide Grammatical Errors In This Document check box. Turn on this check box to hide the green sawtooth underlines for grammatical errors. Turning on this check box does not suspend automatic grammar checking.

Check Grammar With Spelling check box. Tells Word to check the spelling in each sentence before checking the grammar to ensure that Word isn't trying to make grammatical and stylistic sense of a sentence that contains misspelled words.

Show Readability Statistics check box. Displays readability statistics after each grammar check.

Writing Style drop-down list box. Lists the names of the available sets of rules. The list contains the choices Casual, Standard, Formal, Technical, and Custom. You can customize any of these sets of rules in the Grammar Settings dialog box (click the Settings button). See "Grammar Settings Dialog Box," page 977.

Settings button. Displays the Grammar Settings dialog box, in which you can change specific rules used by the selected writing style.

Check/Recheck Document button. After you change spelling options, you can click this button to check the spelling in your document again. The button label is Check Document if you haven't yet checked the spelling. The button label is Recheck Document if you have already checked the spelling—this includes automatic checking.

Custom Dictionaries Dialog Box

The Custom Dictionaries dialog box, shown in Figure A-9, is displayed when you click the Dictionaries button on the Spelling & Grammar tab. You can use the dialog box to turn custom dictionaries on or off, create new custom dictionaries, edit a custom dictionary, add an existing custom dictionary to the list, or remove a custom dictionary. You can also set the language for a custom dictionary.

FIGURE A-9.
The Custom Dictionaries dialog box.

Custom Dictionaries list box. Lists Custom.dic and the custom dictionaries you have added. Turn on the check boxes beside the dictionary names you want to use during spelling checking.

Language drop-down list box. Sets the language for the selected custom dictionary. If you select any setting other than None, Word uses the dictionary only to check text formatted in the specified language. If you select (None), Word uses that dictionary for all text, regardless of its language.

If you create a custom dictionary and set it for a specific language, you can add words in that language to the dictionary. This process effectively creates a mini-dictionary for that language without your having to buy a spelling dictionary file for that language.

Full Path label. Shows you the full MS-DOS pathname to the dictionary file selected in the Custom Dictionaries list box.

New button. Displays the Create Custom Dictionary dialog box, shown here:

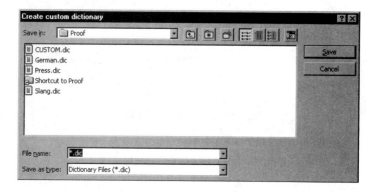

To create a new dictionary, type a name for the new custom dictionary in the File Name box, leave the Save As Type box set to Dictionary Files, and click OK.

Edit button. Opens the selected custom dictionary as a Word document so that you can add or remove words directly. When you add words, insert them in a separate paragraph in the correct alphabetic order. After editing the custom dictionary, be sure to save the document as Text Only.

Add button. Displays the Add Custom Dictionary dialog box. To add a custom dictionary to the list, select the dictionary file to be added and click OK. The dialog box looks almost exactly like the Create Custom Dictionary dialog box.

Remove button.   Removes the selected custom dictionary from the list but does not delete the custom dictionary file from the disk.

Store your custom dictionaries in the Proof folder inside the Microsoft Shared folder inside the Common Files folder inside the Program Files folder.

Grammar Settings Dialog Box

The Grammar Settings dialog box, shown in Figure A-10, is displayed when you click the Settings button on the Spelling & Grammar tab. You can use the dialog box to change specific rules in one of Word's established sets of grammar rules.

FIGURE A-10.
The Grammar Settings dialog box.

Writing Style drop-down list box. Lists the names of the available sets of rules. This box and its list is the same as the Writing Style box on the Spelling & Grammar tab.

TIP

To keep the four built-in sets of rules intact, customize the Custom setting.

Grammar And Style Options list box. Lists all the grammar or style rules Word uses. When a check box is turned on, that rule is in effect for the currently selected set.

Comma Before Last List Item drop-down list box. Lets you select the style you want to use for a series of items. Some writers prefer to put a comma before the last item in a series; for example, *I'm sending you a book, a disk, and a coupon.* Other writers prefer to omit the comma before the last item in a series; for example, *I'm sending you a book, a disk and a coupon.* Your choices in this box are Don't Check—you don't want Word to check for the presence or absence of a comma before the last item in a series; Always—you always want a comma before the last item in a series; and Never—you never want a comma before the last item in a series.

TIP

If you set series comma checking to Always, Word will mark the following series as missing a comma—*For breakfast this morning, I had orange juice, coffee, toast, and ham and eggs.* When a compound expression, such as *ham and eggs*, is an item in a series, placing the phrase anywhere but last in a series will ensure that Word doesn't incorrectly mark a missing comma.

Punctuation With Quotes drop-down list box. Some stylists want all punctuation inside the quotation marks for a sentence, clause, or phrase. British publishing practice and other stylists want all punctuation outside the quotation marks for a sentence, clause, or phrase. Many stylists use a mixture of inside and outside; for example, colons and semicolons are placed outside the quotation marks, as are question marks and exclamation points when they aren't part of the quotation.

And then there are books about computer software that contain text that the reader must type exactly. In these cases, the practice varies, but usually the punctuation appears either inside or outside the quotation marks when the quotation marks and the punctuation are part of what the reader must type.

Your choices for checking punctuation and quotation marks are Don't Check—you don't want Word to worry about it, a choice you'll want to use when you mix or vary the order of punctuation and quotation marks; Inside—you want the punctuation to always appear inside the quotation marks; Outside—you want the punctuation marks to always appear outside the quotation marks.

Spaces Between Sentences drop-down list box. In the days of typewriters, typists inserted two spaces between sentences as an additional visual cue to where sentences ended. When you're using a monospace font (typewriter-style font, such as Courier New), it's still a good practice to insert two spaces between sentences. With the rise in the use of proportional-space fonts, the common practice has become one space between sentences. And then again, sometimes when you're typing or pasting, you might end up with two spaces between sentences when you want only one.

Your choices for checking spaces between sentences are as follows: Don't Check—you don't want Word to check the number of spaces between sentences; 1—you want only one space between sentences, a choice you'll probably select when you're using only proportional-space fonts; and 2—you want two spaces between sentences, a choice you'll probably select when you're using only monospace fonts.

Reset All button. Resets the rules in the selected set to original settings.

Grammar Explanations

When you click the Assistant button in the Spelling And Grammar dialog box, grammar explanations appear in an Assistant balloon, like the one shown in Figure A-11. The Assistant explains the rule for the grammatical error in the highlighted part of the sentence in the Spelling And Grammar dialog box. To collapse the balloon, click its Close box.

FIGURE A-11.
The Assistant, display-ing an explanation for a grammatical error.

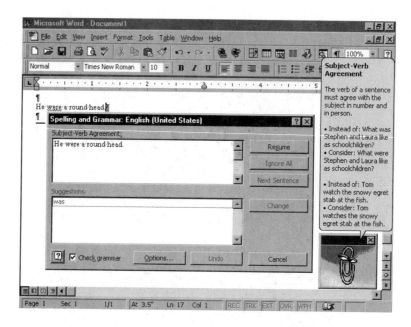

Track Changes Tab

You can jump directly to the Track Changes tab from the Highlight Changes dialog box.

The options on the Track Changes tab let you decide how Word marks changes to a document. The Tools Highlight Changes command con-trols tracking changes. The Track Changes tab is shown in Figure A-12. Descriptions of the options follow.

In previous versions of Word, Track Changes was called Revision Marking.

Inserted Text Section

Mark drop-down list box. Sets the type of marking for inserted text. The options are None, Bold, Italic, Underline, and Double Underline.

Color drop-down list box. Sets the color for marking inserted text. The default is By Author, which sets a unique color for each of the first eight authors who revise a document. Word repeats the series of colors if

FIGURE A-12.
The Options dialog box with the Track Changes tab selected.

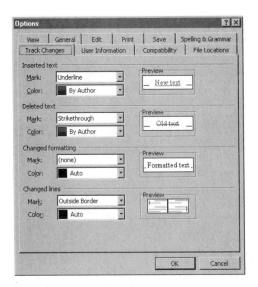

needed. The other choices are Auto and the 16 basic Windows colors. Auto is the text color you set on the Appearance tab in the Display Properties dialog box that you reach through the Windows Control Panel. Choosing one of the 16 basic Windows colors or Auto makes all the inserted text the same color, regardless of which author inserted the text.

Preview window. Displays the mark and color you have selected.

Deleted Text Section
Mark drop-down list box. Sets the type of marking for deleted text. The options are Strikethrough, Hidden, ∧ (a caret), and # (a pound sign). If you select either of the last two options (∧ or #), Word replaces deleted text with the character.

Color drop-down list box. Sets the color for marking deleted text. The color choices are the same as those in the Color drop-down list box in the Inserted Text section.

Preview window. Displays the mark and color you have selected.

Changed Formatting Section
Mark drop-down list box. Sets the type of marking for text with changed formatting. The options are (None), Bold, Italic, Underline, and Double Underline.

Color drop-down list box. Sets the color for marking text with changed formatting. The color choices are the same as those in the Color drop-down list box in the Inserted Text section.

Preview window. Displays the mark and color you have selected.

Changed Lines Section

> In previous versions of Word, Changed Lines was called Revision Bars.

Mark drop-down list box. Sets the position of revision bars for revised text. The options are (None), Left Border, Right Border, and Outside Border. The Outside Border option places a revision bar on the left side of even-numbered pages and on the right side of odd-numbered pages.

Color drop-down list box. Sets the color for revision bars. The default is Auto, the text color you set in the Color dialog box of the Windows Control Panel. The other choices are the 16 basic Windows colors.

Preview window. Displays the selected position and color.

User Information Tab

> You can change the name and address information on the User Information tab from the Return Address box in the Envelopes And Labels dialog box.

The User Information tab, shown in Figure A-13, displays information about the user, who is normally the person registered to use the software. Following are the options shown on the User Information tab.

Name text box. Displays the name of the user, usually the name of the person to whom the software is registered.

Initials text box. Displays the user's initials, which Word uses as an identifier in annotation reference marks. Word sets up the first letters of the name in the Name box, but you can change the initials to appear any way you want.

FIGURE A-13.

The Options dialog box with the User Information tab selected.

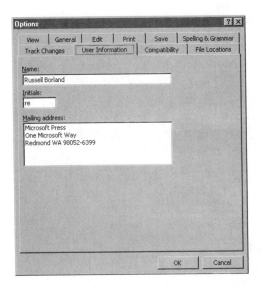

Mailing Address text box. Displays the user's name and address. Word uses the name and organization name you typed when you installed Word. This information is the standard return address on envelopes.

Compatibility Tab

On the Compatibility tab, you can set special conversion and display options for documents created in earlier versions of Word or in other word processing programs. These options fine-tune conversions so that Word interprets special characters in the document correctly and so that the converted documents more closely match the appearance and behavior of the original documents. The Compatibility tab is shown in Figure A-14. Following are the options on the Compatibility tab.

Font Substitution button. Displays the Font Substitution dialog box (see "Font Substitution Dialog Box," page 985). If all the fonts used in the document are available for the selected printer, Word displays a message that no substitutions are necessary.

Recommended Options For drop-down list box. Lets you select the file format to which the selected options will apply. Your selection also turns on a set of recommended options in the Options box. The program file formats listed are Microsoft Word 6.0–7.0, Word for Windows

FIGURE A-14.

The Options dialog box with the Compatibility tab selected.

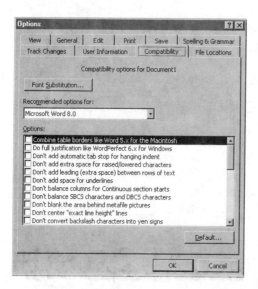

1.0, Word for Windows 2.0, Word for the Macintosh 5.x, Word for MS-DOS, WordPerfect 5.x, WordPerfect 6.x for Windows, WordPerfect 6.0 for DOS, and Custom. Use the Custom setting for file formats not on the list.

Options List Box

Compatibility options for the selected file format are listed in the Options list box. The following descriptions explain some of the compatibility settings you might find most useful. Turn on the option to produce the effect described here.

Don't Balance Columns For Continuous Section Starts. Prevents Word from balancing columns before the beginning of a new section if the section break is continuous. This option is recommended for Word-Perfect documents.

Print Colors As Black On Noncolor Printers. Prints all color items as black instead of using a gray scale when printing on a noncolor printer. This option is recommended for Word for Windows 1.0 and 2.0 documents. Turn it off to print colors as shades of gray.

Suppress Extra Line Spacing At Top Of Page. Prevents Word from increasing the top margin because of the line spacing in the first paragraph. Line spacing will be equivalent to the Auto setting. This option is recommended for Word for the Macintosh 5.x.

Suppress Space Before After A Hard Page Or Column Break. Prevents Word from adding extra line spacing before a hard page break or a column break by ignoring the Spacing Before setting in the paragraph immediately after the break. This option is recommended for Word for Windows 2.0 and Word for MS-DOS documents.

Treat \" As "" In Mail Merge Data Sources. Converts the backslash and quotation mark combination to two quotation marks in a data source file so that Word displays a quotation mark in the field that contained the combination. This option is recommended for Word for Windows 1.0 and 2.0 documents.

Font Substitution Dialog Box

If a document contains fonts that are not available to you, you can click the Font Substitution button to open the Font Substitution dialog box, shown in Figure A-15. You can then designate fonts to substitute for the unavailable fonts. If the document's fonts are all available, then Word displays a message telling you so when you check the Font Substitution button.

FIGURE A-15.

The Font Substitution dialog box.

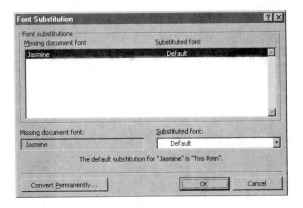

Missing Document Font column. Displays the names of fonts not available for the selected printer.

Substituted Font column. Displays the current font substitution choice. The Default setting allows Word to make the choice; Word picks a font from the same font family if possible.

Missing Document Font label. Specifies the font for which you want to make a substitution. Select a different font by choosing its name in the Font Substitutions section.

Substituted Font drop-down list box. Allows you to select a substitute font from those available for the selected printer.

Convert Permanently button. Sets a permanent substitution for the missing font in the document. If you do not click this button, the substitution applies only to the document in the current Word session.

File Locations Tab

Word needs to know where to find the files it needs and where to store saved files. The locations of files are initially established during Setup, when you install the Word program or add components. If you have moved the location of files that Word uses, or if you want files saved to a different default location, you should use the File Locations tab, shown in Figure A-16, to inform Word of the change. Following are the options on the File Locations tab.

FIGURE A-16.
The Options dialog box with the File Locations tab selected.

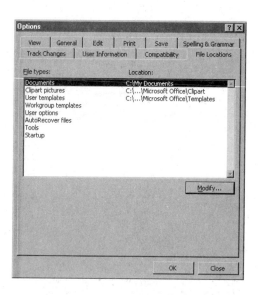

File Types column. Lists the types of files Word uses.

Location column. Specifies the pathname of the Folder where files for the selected file type are stored.

Modify button. Displays the Modify Location dialog box.

Modify Location Dialog Box

When you click the Modify button on the File Locations tab to change the path to a type of file, the Modify Location dialog box appears, as shown in Figure A-17. If you modify a location, be sure to move any necessary files to the new location before you restart Word.

FIGURE A-17.
The Modify Location dialog box.

AutoFormat Options

You can jump directly to the AutoFormat tab from the AutoFormat dialog box.

On the AutoFormat tab, you can set the options for automatic formatting of a document. You can format a document automatically either as you type or after typing by choosing the Format AutoFormat command. Word provides two sets of AutoFormat options: AutoFormat As You Type (see the tab shown in Figure A-18, next page) and AutoFormat (see the tab shown in Figure A-19, next page). Both sets of options are discussed in the following sections.

AutoFormat As You Type Options

Apply As You Type Section

Headings check box. Applies heading styles to paragraphs that appear to be headings.

Borders check box. Replaces three or more consecutive hyphens in a paragraph with a ¾-point borderline or rule as the bottom border of the preceding paragraph; replaces three or more consecutive underscores in a paragraph with a 1½-point borderline or rule as the bottom border of the preceding paragraph; and replaces three or more equal signs in a paragraph with a ¾-point double borderline or rule as the bottom border of the preceding paragraph.

FIGURE A-18.

The AutoCorrect dialog box with the AutoFormat As You Type tab selected.

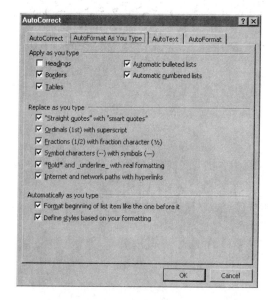

FIGURE A-19.

The AutoCorrect dialog box with the AutoFormat tab selected.

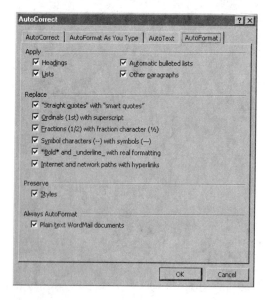

Tables check box. Converts a line composed of plus signs (+) and hyphens (-) into a table row. To insert an empty table by typing, begin a new line with a plus sign and then type one or more hyphens and another plus sign. Repeat this sequence on the same line for the number of columns you want in the table. The width of each cell (column) will depend on the number of hyphens you type between each plus sign. Type a plus sign for the last character on the line (the end of the paragraph). When you press Enter to start a new paragraph, Word coverts the line of plus signs and hyphens into a table row. If you want to add additional rows to the table, you can place the insertion point in the last cell and press Tab.

Automatic Bulleted Lists check box. Applies bulleted list formatting to paragraphs that start with a hyphen, an asterisk, a lowercase letter *o*, or uppercase letter *O* followed by a tab. Automatic bulleted list formatting is also applied when a space follows a hyphen or asterisk only. AutoFormat replaces manually typed bullets with bulleted characters.

Automatic Numbered Lists check box. Applies numbered list formatting to paragraphs that start with a number, a period, and a space or a tab. AutoFormat replaces numbers that are manually typed with automatic numbers.

Replace As You Type Section

"Straight Quotes" With "Smart Quotes" check box. Replaces straight quotation marks (" ") with curly quotation marks (" ") and replaces straight apostrophes or quotation marks (' ') with curly apostrophes or quotation marks (' ').

Ordinals (1st) With Superscript check box. Formats the ordinal abbreviations (*st*, *nd*, *rd*, and *th*) as superscript so that you see 1st instead of 1st.

Fractions (1/2) With Fraction Character (½) check box. Replaces the typed fractions (number, slash, number)—1/4, 1/2, and 3/4—with their fraction characters—¼, ½, and ¾. Word doesn't replace any other typed fractions, such as 3/8.

★ TIP

Outsmarting Smart Quotes

The "smart" part of Smart Quotes is that Word knows when you need opening quotation marks and apostrophes (" and ') and when you need closing quotation marks and apostrophes (" and ')—usually. But you'll have to work around some difficult situations. For example, try typing the information inside the second set of parentheses in the previous sentence. You'll get the same result as in the first set of parentheses—(" and ')—instead! The same thing happens after any punctuation mark—period, comma, semicolon, colon, hyphen, em-dash, en-dash, and so on. In these situations, you have a bother. Here's my solution: I type two quotation marks or apostrophes in a row, and then, after typing the rest of the text included in quotes, move back and delete the first quotation mark or apostrophe.

Symbol Characters (--) With Symbols (—) check box. Replaces typed characters that represent symbols with symbol characters. With this option turned on, if you type two hyphens (--) with no space before them, they are replaced by an em dash (—) automatically. If you type two hyphens with a space before them, Word inserts an en dash (–) automatically. Note that the AutoCorrect feature inserts the symbols ®, ©, and ™ when you type (r), (c), and (tm), respectively.

Bold And _Underline_ With Real Formatting check box. Turn on this check box to automatically replace text that you surround with asterisks (*) with boldface font formatting and text that you surround with underscores (_) with italic font formatting. Word applies the font formatting as soon as you type the second asterisk or underscore. To achieve this effect, Word applies the character style Strong to text for boldface and the character style Emphasis to text for underlining.

Internet And Network Paths With Hyperlinks check box. Turn on this check box to automatically create a hyperlink for an Internet location (such as a site on the World Wide Web) and for a path to a network server site. When you click a hyperlink, Windows jumps to the destination of the Internet or network location. As part of this formatting, Word applies the character style Hyperlink, which underlines the text and applies the color blue.

Automatically As You Type Section

Format Beginning Of List Item Like The One Before It check box. Many lists start with special font formatting at the beginning of each item, as in this example:

- **Monday.** Review sales from the previous week.

- **Tuesday.** Follow up on sales queries.

- **Wednesday.** Collect new orders.

- **Thursday.** Ship new orders.

- **Friday.** Order inventory.

Turn on the check box to automatically begin the next list item with the same font formatting as the previous item—in this example, bold-face. As soon as you type the space following the punctuation mark in the next paragraph, Word automatically resets the font formatting to the style of the rest of the list item. This automatic formatting works for bulleted lists, numbered lists, and indented lists that have neither numbers or bullets.

Define Styles Based On Your Formatting check box. When you turn on this check box, Word compares the formatting you apply to a paragraph to a built-in paragraph style. When Word finds a match, Word applies the matching paragraph style to the paragraph. Likewise, when you apply boldface or underlining to the beginning of a list item, Word applies the matching character style.

AutoFormat Command Options

The following explanations include only the options that differ from those available on the AutoFormat As You Type tab of the AutoCorrect dialog box.

Apply Section

Lists check box. Applies list styles to lists.

Other Paragraphs check box. Applies paragraph styles to paragraphs that are not headings, parts of a list, or other special types of paragraphs.

Preserve Section

Styles check box. When this option is on, AutoFormat ignores all paragraphs that are not Normal style. When this option is off, AutoFormat determines whether another style would better suit the paragraph.

Always AutoFormat Section

Plain Text WordMail Documents check box. Turn on this check box when you want Word to automatically format a WordMail message that was sent to you as plain (unformatted) text. This box only affects a WordMail message when you open it in Word. This box does not affect any other plain text document.

Working with Toolbars

Toolbars provide fast, easy ways to issue commands: simply click a button, and the job is done. You can decide which toolbars Word displays and how they are displayed. You control the display of toolbars by choosing the View Toolbars command and then selecting from the Toolbars submenu the name of the toolbar you want to display or hide. The Toolbars submenu lists the most commonly used toolbars (at least according to Microsoft). To see a list of all the toolbars, select Customize from the Toolbars submenu, and then click the Toolbars tab in the Customize dialog box, shown in Figure B-1. (You can also choose the Tools Customize command to open the Customize dialog box.)

FIGURE B-1.

The Customize dialog box with the Toolbars tab selected.

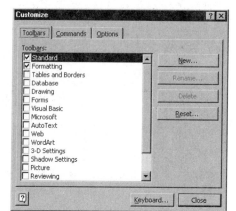

You might find that the commands you use most often are not present on the built-in toolbars. Or perhaps the commands are located on several toolbars. Instead of opening multiple toolbars and hunting for the correct button, you can customize or create a toolbar so that it contains all the buttons you need.

Word can store the changes you make to the toolbar in the Normal template or in any other open template. This lets you create custom toolbars for different types of documents. For information about changing the toolbar buttons, see "Modifying a Toolbar's Appearance," page 1000.

The Toolbars list shows the available toolbars. You can display a toolbar by turning on the check box next to the toolbar's name and clicking Close. To hide the toolbar, turn off its check box and click Close.

> NOTE

Even though Menu Bar appears in the Toolbars list, you can't turn it off.

The Options tab of the Customize dialog box, shown in Figure B-2, contains three check boxes that apply to all the displayed toolbars.

Turn on the Large Icons check box to increase the size of buttons on the screen, making them easier to see.

If you turn on the Show ScreenTips On Toolbars check box, Word displays a label with the name of the button when you point to and pause over a button on a toolbar. You turn on the Show Shortcut Keys In ScreenTips check box to see the shortcut key for a button along with its name.

FIGURE B-2.
The Customize dialog box with the Options tab selected.

Click here to turn on large toolbar button display.

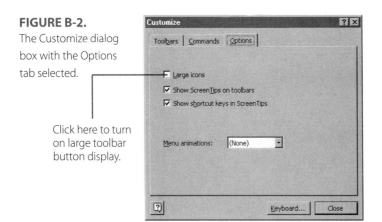

Floating Toolbars

When you click certain toolbar buttons (for example, the Font Color button) you will see a menu with a color stripe across the top. This is also true for some menu commands. When you position the mouse pointer on the color stripe, a tooltip appears, as shown here:

As the tooltip indicates, simply drag the submenu to another location in the Word window. This changes the submenu into a floating toolbar. Floating toolbars are useful for keeping options you use frequently at hand while you work. You can use, position, and customize floating toolbars in all the same ways you can with ordinary toolbars.

VII

Appendixes

To see the shortcut key for a toolbar button, you must turn on the Show ScreenTips On Toolbars check box for the Show Shortcut Keys In ScreenTips check box to have an effect.

Some of Word's toolbars appear only when you need them. For example, the Print Preview, Comments, and Macro Record toolbars appear only when you are performing the related tasks for which their buttons can be used.

The following sections show you how to customize Word's toolbars, including how to change buttons, change the action of the buttons, or even create your own toolbars.

Positioning Toolbars

The standard position for most toolbars is at the top of the Word window, just below the menu bar and above the ruler (if the ruler is turned on). But you can move a toolbar to the following other positions:

- The top of the window, even above the menu bar

- The right side of the window (with the toolbar displayed vertically)

- The left side of the window (with the toolbar displayed vertically)

- Floating (with the toolbar positioned anywhere on the screen, even outside the Word window)

- On top of another toolbar (See the sidebar "Stacking and Unstacking Toolbars," opposite.)

To move a toolbar, use these steps:

1 Position the mouse pointer on a seam between buttons or in a blank area of the toolbar (not on any button), as shown here:

VII

Appendixes

2 Drag the toolbar to the new position. When you drag the outline to a position along the side of the Word window, the toolbar "snaps" into position. The toolbar appears along the left side of the window, as shown below.

> **NOTE**

Word might slightly modify the appearance of the toolbar when you move it. As you can see in the following example, Word changes the Style, Font, and Font Size list boxes on the Formatting toolbar to buttons when you position the toolbar along the right or left side.

Formatting
toolbar's list boxes —
change to buttons.

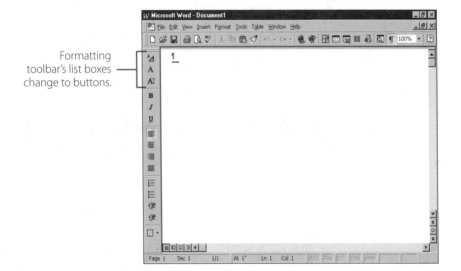

Stacking and Unstacking Toolbars

In Word 97 it's possible to stack toolbars at the "fixed" positions. You could do this intentionally, to save screen space, or it could happen inadvertently when you are dragging a toolbar back to one of the edges. Unless you release the mouse button at a precise position, the toolbar could end up on top of another toolbar.

When you want to unstack toolbars, drag the toolbar on top to a different position, either above or below the toolbar beneath it, or to another position entirely.

Altering Toolbar Order

Toolbars appear in the order in which you turn them on, but you can rearrange the order. Simply drag a toolbar to a new position.

Making a Toolbar Float

If you prefer to place a toolbar on the screen away from any of the window borders, you can float the toolbar (and even adjust its size and shape). You can also place a floating toolbar outside the Word window, if the Word window doesn't take up the entire screen.

To float a toolbar, double-click a seam between any two toolbar buttons, or use the following steps:

1 Drag the toolbar away from its window border position to a position anywhere on the screen.

2 Release the mouse button. You'll see a toolbar that looks like this:

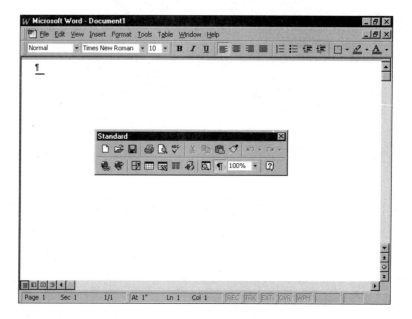

To hide a floating toolbar quickly, without using the View Toolbars command or the Toolbars shortcut menu, click the Close button that appears in the upper right corner of the floating toolbar.

Changing the Size and Shape of a Floating Toolbar

You can change the size and shape of a floating toolbar to give it a different number of rows or columns. To do so, drag the border of the floating toolbar. The resized floating toolbar must be wide enough to display at least the widest element on the toolbar—one button or the widest text box or list box, as shown here:

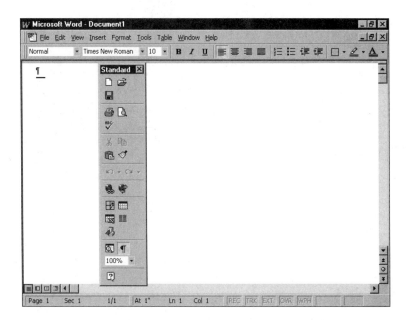

Moving a Floating Toolbar to a Fixed Position

To quickly return a floating toolbar to its most recent fixed position at the top or sides of the Word window, double-click its title bar. At its fixed position, you can double-click a seam between toolbar buttons to switch a fixed toolbar to a floating position. The floating toolbar appears in the size and position that you chose the last time you set it up as a floating toolbar.

Modifying a Toolbar's Appearance

You have lots of ways to change the appearance of a toolbar by manipulating its buttons. You can move a button to a different position on its toolbar, remove it from its toolbar, move or copy it to another toolbar, or change its appearance. You can also add new buttons to any toolbar, and if you want, you can reset a toolbar to its original condition.

Moving a Button

You can create your ideal toolbar in several ways. Perhaps one of the toolbars already includes all the tools you need, but the order in which the buttons appear is not convenient. You can adjust the position of the buttons on a toolbar simply by holding down the Alt key while dragging the buttons to their new positions.

Suppose you want to change the position of the Print Preview button on the Standard toolbar. Simply point to the Print Preview button, press and hold the Alt key, and drag the button to a different position on the Standard toolbar.

You can use the same method when you want to move a button from one toolbar to another. For example, you might want to move the Standard toolbar's Drawing button to another toolbar. Clicking the Drawing button on the Standard toolbar displays the Drawing toolbar at the bottom of the Word window, as shown here:

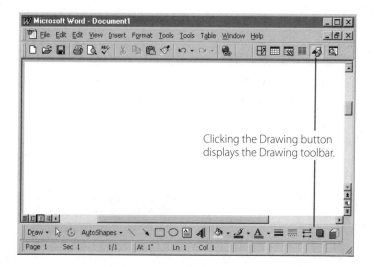

Clicking the Drawing button displays the Drawing toolbar.

If you frequently use the Drawing toolbar, you might want to move the Drawing button to the Formatting toolbar, next to the type style buttons (Bold, Italic, and Underline). To move the Drawing button, point to the button, hold down Alt, and drag the button from the Standard toolbar to a new location on the Formatting toolbar. When you release the mouse button, the other buttons move to the side, and the moved button is in its new position, as shown here:

The Drawing button
that was here …

… was moved to the
Formatting toolbar here.

Removing a Button from a Toolbar

You can further customize a toolbar by deleting buttons that you never use. To remove a button, hold down the Alt key and drag the button to an area of the screen where no toolbar is displayed. When you release the mouse button, the toolbar button disappears.

Copying a Button Between Toolbars

Just as you can move buttons to other toolbars, you can also copy a button from one toolbar to another. If you want to copy a button rather than move it, hold down both the Alt and Ctrl keys while dragging the button between the toolbars.

Adding a New Button to a Toolbar

Many of Word's commands have buttons assigned to them, although the buttons do not appear on a built-in toolbar. You can, however, place any of these buttons on a toolbar, as follows:

1 Display the toolbar to which you want to add a new button.

2 Choose the Tools Customize command, and select the Toolbars tab.

3 If the Customize dialog box is already visible and the toolbar you want to change is not yet visible, click the check box beside its name on the Toolbars tab. Word then displays the toolbar.

4 Select the Commands tab.

5 Select a category.

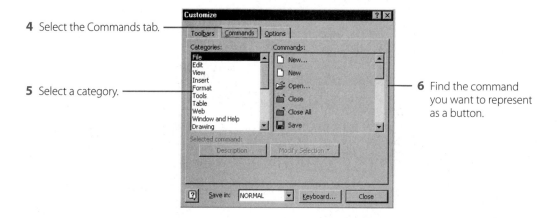

6 Find the command you want to represent as a button.

7 Drag the command onto the displayed toolbar at the position you want it.

Most commands have buttons already set up for them, but for those that don't, you can place your own buttons on toolbars. The new button will appear with a text label, but you can assign an image to it later. See "Changing the Appearances of Toolbar Buttons" below. To place one of these commands on a toolbar and assign it a button, use the following steps:

1 Display the Commands tab of the Customize dialog box.

2 Select the category that contains the command, and then select the command.

3 Drag the command from the Customize dialog box to the toolbar. You see a button with a text label.

Changing the Appearances of Toolbar Buttons

To further customize a toolbar, you can change the appearances of its buttons without changing the commands with which they are associated. To place a new image on a button, you can copy an image from

VII

Appendixes

another button, select one of the supplied button images, edit a button image, or create an image in a drawing program.

To use any of these techniques, you must have the Customize dialog box open, with the Commands tab selected—either choose the Tools Customize command and then click the Commands tab, or right-click a toolbar, and select Customize from the shortcut menu.

Using a Supplied Button Image

Word supplies a variety of button images. You can substitute one of these images for an existing button image, or you can assign a supplied button image to a new button with a text label that you created. Here are the steps to use one of these images:

1 Open the Customize dialog box, and select the Commands tab.

 TIP

> If the Customize dialog box is already visible and the toolbar you want to change is not yet visible, click the box beside its name on the Toolbars tab. Word then displays the toolbar.

2 Right-click the button (on the toolbar) that you want to change. As an alternative, click the toolbar button you want to change, and then click the Modify Selection button in the Customize dialog box.

3 Point to the Change Button Image command on the shortcut menu, and then click the image you want to use on the submenu, shown here:

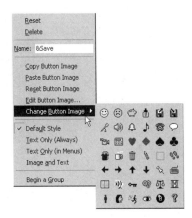

After you select a button image, you can edit it by right-clicking the button and then selecting the Edit Button Image command from the shortcut menu. Word displays the Button Editor, shown in Figure B-3, which lets you edit the individual dots of the button's graphic. When you are satisfied with the edited image, click OK to assign the image to the button.

FIGURE B-3.
Use the Button Editor to modify the image on a toolbar button.

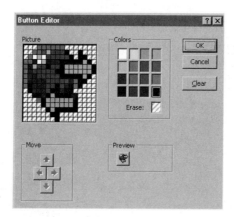

Removing a Text Label from a Button

When you select a supplied button image (or edit one) for a button that previously contained a text label, the text label remains on the button beside its newly assigned button image. You can remove the text label by following these steps:

1 Open the Customize dialog box, and select the Commands tab.

2 Right-click the button (on the toolbar) you want to change. As an alternative, click the toolbar button you want to change, and then click the Modify Selection button in the Customize dialog box.

3 On the shortcut menu, click the Text Only (In Menus) command to turn it on, which turns off the previously checked Text Only (Always) command.

The button's text label no longer appears.

Copying a Button Image

You can copy a button image from any button, as follows:

1 Open the Customize dialog box, and select the Commands tab.

2 Right-click the button (on the toolbar) you want to change. As an alternative, click the toolbar button you want to change, and then click the Modify Selection button in the Customize dialog box.

3 On the shortcut menu, click the Copy Button Image command.

Word copies the image on the button to the Clipboard, and the image is ready to paste on another button. Because you are using the Clipboard, you can copy only one image at a time and should immediately paste the image on a button.

Pasting a Button Image

Once a button image is in the Clipboard, you can paste it on another button. To paste an image on a button, use these steps:

1 Right-click the button you want to change. As an alternative, click the toolbar button you want to change, and then click the Modify Selection button in the Customize dialog box.

2 On the shortcut menu, click the Paste Button Image command.

Editing a Button Image

You can edit the image on a toolbar button with the Button Editor (see Figure B-3), using the following steps:

1 Open the Customize dialog box, and select the Commands tab.

2 Right-click the button you want to change. As an alternative, click the toolbar button you want to change, and then click the Modify Selection button in the Customize dialog box.

3 Click the Edit Button Image command from the shortcut menu. The Button Editor dialog box appears, displaying the image from the button to which you pointed.

4 Edit the image by adding dots of different colors and erasing other dots.

5 Click OK in the dialog box. The button on the toolbar now contains the edited image.

Creating a Button Image

You can also use other drawing programs to create button images. Make your drawing approximately the same size as the button to prevent distortion from scaling the drawing. Copy the drawing to the Clipboard, using a bitmap or picture format if possible. Then paste the Clipboard's contents on the toolbar button—for the steps, see "Pasting a Button Image," page 1005.

You can also create a button image from scratch with the Button Editor, as follows:

1 Open the Customize dialog box, and select the Commands tab.

2 Right-click the button whose image you want to change. As an alternative, click the toolbar button you want to change, and then click the Modify Selection button in the Customize dialog box.

3 Click the Edit Button Image command from the shortcut menu. The Button Editor dialog box appears, displaying the image from the button you pointed to.

4 Click the Clear button.

5 Create the image by adding dots of different colors.

6 Click OK in the dialog box. The button on the toolbar contains the new image.

Resizing a Text Button or a Box

You can change the width of any text button, text box, or list box on a toolbar. (You can't change the width of a regular button.) When you change the width of a list box, any associated drop-down list is also resized. For example, if you decrease the width of the Zoom Control box on the Standard toolbar, the width of the drop-down list also decreases.

To change the width of a text button, text box, or list box, do the following steps:

1 Open the Customize dialog box, and select the Commands tab.

2 Click the button (on the toolbar) you want to resize, and then move the mouse pointer onto the right border of the button until

the pointer turns into a vertical bar with two arrows, as shown here:

3 Drag the border of the button or box to the left to decrease the width or to the right to increase the width.

Restoring the Default Button Image

If you have modified a toolbar button but do not like the result, you can return the button to its default form, as follows:

1 Open the Customize dialog box, and select the Commands tab.

2 Right-click the button (on the toolbar) you want to restore to its original button image. As an alternative, click the toolbar button you want to change, and then click the Modify Selection button in the Customize dialog box.

3 Choose the Reset command from the shortcut menu.

The button returns to its default form, and any edits are lost. If the button was originally a blank one to which you added a picture, Word restores the blank when you choose the Reset Button Image command.

Resetting a Toolbar

After you customize Word's built-in toolbars and close the Customize dialog box, you might decide that you don't like the changes. Rather than trying to move everything back to its original position, you can simply reset the toolbars to their original settings by following these steps:

1 Open the Customize dialog box, and select the Toolbars tab.

2 In the Toolbars list, select the toolbar you want to reset.

3 Click the Reset button. The Reset Toolbar dialog box appears, as shown on the next page.

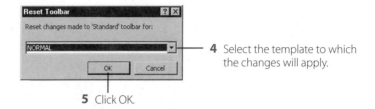

4 Select the template to which the changes will apply.

5 Click OK.

The toolbar you reset returns to Word's original setup.

Creating Your Own Toolbars

You can create your own custom toolbars. By creating different custom toolbars and storing them in different templates, you will have the tools that are specific to certain tasks or certain types of documents at your fingertips. Use the following steps to create your own toolbar.

1 Open the Customize dialog box to the Toolbars tab.

2 Click the New button. The New Toolbar dialog box opens, as shown:

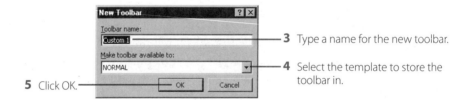

3 Type a name for the new toolbar.

4 Select the template to store the toolbar in.

5 Click OK.

Word displays a small floating toolbar, which is empty except for the toolbar's name. Now you can add the commands you want to appear on your new custom toolbar. For the steps, see "Adding a New Button to a Toolbar," page 1001.

A custom toolbar functions just like a built-in toolbar: it can be turned on or off, moved, reshaped, or positioned at the top, bottom, or sides of the window. You can assign any of the commands or other items listed in the Customize dialog box to a custom toolbar, and you can use any of the techniques discussed earlier for modifying or creating buttons on a custom toolbar. You can also copy or move buttons and boxes between a custom toolbar and other toolbars. Custom toolbars are listed in the Toolbars box on the Toolbars tab of the Customize dialog box and on the Toolbars shortcut menu.

One difference between built-in toolbars and custom toolbars is that you cannot use the Reset command in the Customize dialog box to return a custom toolbar to its original settings because Word has no default settings for custom toolbars. When you select a custom toolbar in the Customize dialog box, the Reset button becomes the Delete button. If you click the Delete button, Word deletes the custom toolbar.

Renaming a Custom Toolbar

The Toolbars tab of the Customize dialog box contains a Rename button. You can rename any toolbar you create; however, you cannot rename a built-in toolbar. To rename a custom toolbar, follow these steps:

1 Open the Customize dialog box, and then select the Toolbars tab.

2 Select the custom toolbar you want to rename.

3 Click the Rename button. The Rename Toolbar dialog box appears.

5 Click OK.

4 Type a new name for the custom toolbar here.

6 Click Close in the Customize dialog box.

 **TIP**

You can also use the Organizer dialog box to rename a custom toolbar. For details, see "Copying a Custom Toolbar," next.

Copying a Custom Toolbar

When you store a custom toolbar in a template other than Normal.dot, it is available only to documents based on that specialized template. If you want to use the toolbar in other documents, you can copy the toolbar to other templates by using the Organizer dialog box. You can also use this dialog box to rename a custom toolbar.

To copy a custom toolbar to the Normal template, which makes it available to all documents, follow these steps:

1 Open the special template that contains the custom toolbar. (You can either open the special template itself or open a document based on the special template.)

2 Choose the Tools Templates And Add-ins command to open the dialog box.

3 Click Organizer.

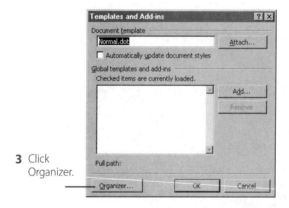

The Organizer dialog box appears, as shown here:

4 Click the Toolbars tab.

5 Select the custom toolbar you want to copy.

6 Click Copy. Word copies the toolbar to the Normal template, and the toolbar's name appears in the list at the right.

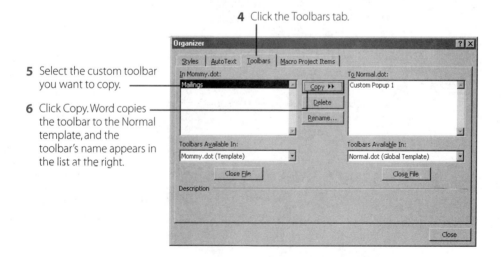

To rename a custom toolbar while the Organizer dialog box is open, use these steps:

1 Select the custom toolbar's name from the list for the template in which you want to rename it.

2 Click the Rename button.

3 Type the new name.

4 Click OK.

5 Click Close in the Organizer dialog box.

You now have two copies of the custom toolbar. One is stored in the special template; the other is stored in the Normal template. You can either delete the custom toolbar from the special template, because it's now available to all documents, or keep the custom toolbar in the special template so that you can further customize it for documents based on that template.

Deleting a Custom Toolbar

If you no longer want a custom toolbar, you can delete it from its template, as follows:

1 Right-click a toolbar and select Customize from the shortcut menu. As an alternative, choose the Tools Customize command, and then click the Toolbars tab.

2 In the Toolbars list, select the toolbar you want to delete.

3 Click the Delete button. Word asks if you want to delete the toolbar.

4 Click OK, and then click Close in the Customize dialog box.

Establishing Your Menus

Word gives you the power to customize menus by adding and deleting commands and other items from the default menus. You could, for example, place commonly used styles or fonts on the Format menu or replace some standard commands with customized macros. You can also change the name of any menu or command. And, if you want full customization, you can create and add your own menus.

Menu changes are stored in templates so that you can create different menu structures for different types of documents. For example, you might want to create a menu structure with an enhanced Edit menu and with other menus that are specific to special tasks, as shown here:

Commands added
to the Edit menu

To modify or create menus, use the Tools Customize command. In the Customize dialog box, click the Commands tab, shown in Figure C-1.

FIGURE C-1.
The Customize dialog box, with the Commands tab selected.

If you want the changes to be in effect for all documents, select Normal in the Save In box at the bottom left corner of the Customize dialog box. To restrict menu changes to a specific template, select that template in the Save In box. (A template appears in this box only when it is open or attached to your document.)

Adding a Command

You can add commands to any Word menu (including the shortcut menus), using the following steps:

1 Choose the Tools Customize command, and click the Commands tab.

2 Click the menu (on the menu bar) to which you want to add a command. It drops down and stays down until you click the menu name again (see step 6).

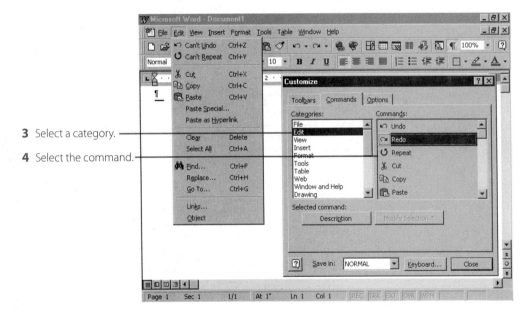

3 Select a category.

4 Select the command.

5 Drag the command to the position you want it on the menu. A thick horizontal line shows you the position.

6 Click the menu name to close the menu.

7 To add another command to a menu, repeat steps 2 through 6.

8 When you're done adding commands, click Close to close the Customize dialog box.

 **TIP**

If you're adding only one command to one menu, you can skip steps 6 and 7. When you close the customize dialog box, Word closes the menu for you.

Renaming a Command

If the name of a menu command is not useful or enjoyable for you, or if you simply find another name more familiar, you can change the name of the command without changing the action it performs. Use the following steps to change the name of a command:

1 Choose the Tools Customize command, and click the Commands tab.

2 Click the menu that contains the command you want to change.

3 Right-click the command whose name you want to change. As an alternative, you can click the Modify Selection button in the Customize dialog box. A menu appears, like the one shown here:

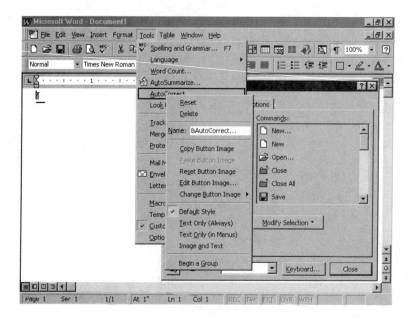

4 Type a new name. Include an ampersand to set the letter for selecting the command from its menu with the keyboard.

5 Click Close in the Customize dialog box.

Moving a Command

If you don't like the position of a command on its menu, or if you prefer to move a command to a different menu, use the following steps:

1 Choose the Tools Customize command, and click the Commands tab.

2 Click the menu that contains the command you want to move.

3 Drag the command to its new position. You can drag the command within its current menu, or you can drag the command to a new menu. To do so, drag to the new menu name, and then when the new menu drops down, drag the command to the position you want it on the new menu.

4 Click Close in the Customize dialog box.

Deleting a Command

You can also delete any item from a menu. You should use caution in doing so, however, because you might make it difficult to run certain commands. (See "Resetting a Menu," page 1020, for a simple way to restore deleted commands.) Here are the steps to delete an item from a menu:

1 Choose the Tools Customize command, and click the Commands tab.

2 Click the menu that contains the command you want to delete.

3 Right-click the command you want to delete. As an alternative, you can click the Modify Selection button in the Customize dialog box.

4 Click Delete on the menu.

TIP

A quick way to delete a command is to press Alt + Ctrl + hyphen. The mouse pointer turns into a boldface minus sign. Use the mouse to open the menu and click the command. Word immediately deletes the command you select. If you press Alt + Ctrl + hyphen and then decide you don't want to delete a command, simply press Esc, and the mouse pointer returns to normal.

Resetting a Command

If you no longer need the changes you have made to a command, you can reset the command to its original Word name with the following steps:

1 Choose the Tools Customize command, and click the Commands tab.

2 Click the menu that contains the command you want to reset.

3 Right-click the command you want to reset. As an alternative, you can click the Modify Selection button in the Customize dialog box.

4 Click Reset on the menu.

5 Click the Close button to close the Customize dialog box.

Renaming a Menu

To better reflect your style of work, you can change the name of any menu that appears on the menu bar. To change a menu name, use these steps:

1 Choose the Tools Customize command, and click the Commands tab.

2 Right-click the menu name you want to change on the menu bar. As an alternative, you can click the menu name you want to change on the menu bar, and then click the Modify Selection button in the Customize dialog box.

3 Type a new name for the menu in the Name box. To allow for using the keyboard to open the menu, include an ampersand before the letter to be used with the Alt key to select the menu.

4 Click the Close button in the Customize dialog box.

Moving a Menu

If you don't like the order of the menus on the menu bar, you can move them to a new position, as follows:

1 Choose the Tools Customize command, and click the Commands tab.

2 Drag the menu to its new position.

3 Click the Close button to close the Customize dialog box.

> The only way to restore a menu to its original Word position is to move it back, using the steps for moving a menu.

Creating a Menu

You can add as many new menus as you like; however, you cannot create new shortcut menus. To create a menu, use the following steps:

1 Choose the Tools Customize command, and click the Commands tab.

2 In the Categories box, select New Menu.

3 Drag New Menu from the Commands scroll box to the position on the menu bar where you want it.

4 Use the steps in "Renaming a Menu," page 1018, to name the menu.

5 Use the steps in "Adding a Command," page 1015, to add commands to the menu.

6 Click the Close button to close the Customize dialog box.

Removing a Menu

There are two ways you can remove an entire menu. If you want to remove all the menus you have added, as well as undo all other menu changes, you can reset the menus, as will be discussed in the next section. You can also remove any individual menu from the menu bar, whether or not you added it, but you cannot remove a shortcut menu. When you remove a menu, all items on the menu are deleted. Here are the steps to remove a menu:

1 Choose the Tools Customize command, and click the Commands tab.

2 Right-click the menu you want to remove. As an alternative, you can select the menu name you want to remove and click the Modify Selection button in the Customize dialog box.

3 Click Delete on the menu.

4 Click the Close button to close the Customize dialog box.

Resetting a Menu

If you have menu changes that you no longer need, you can reset a menu to its original Word setup, using the following steps:

1 Choose the Tools Customize command, and click the Commands tab.

2 Right-click the menu that you want to reset. As an alternative, you can select the menu you want to reset and click the Modify Selection button in the Customize dialog box.

3 Click Reset on the menu.

4 Click the Close button to close the Customize dialog box.

Restoring a Removed Menu

If you removed a menu and want it back, follow these steps:

1 Choose the Tools Customize command, and click the Commands tab.

2 In the Categories box, select Built-in Menus.

3 Drag the name of the menu you want to restore from the Commands scroll box to its position on the menu bar.

4 Click the Close button to close the Customize dialog box.

 TIP

Another Way to Open the Customize Dialog Box

If you delete the Tools menu, you cannot use the Tools Customize command to reset the menus. However, you can open the Customize dialog box another way. To open the Customize dialog box, right-click the menu bar or a toolbar, and then select Customize from the shortcut menu. The Customize dialog box appears, allowing you to make changes to the menus or to restore them.

VII

Appendixes

Playing the Keyboard

Assigning commands and other Word operations to particular shortcut keys can simplify and speed up your work. Knowing which shortcut keys are assigned to which functions is important in designing your Word work environment. Because word processing often involves extensive periods of typing, you might find certain shortcut keys inconvenient, or they might be difficult to remember. But when a keyboard is set up specifically for you, it feels natural, and special key combinations are then logical and easy to remember.

Word predefines many key combinations as shortcut keys for choosing menu commands, such as Ctrl+O as a shortcut for choosing the File Open command. Other shortcut keys are the only way certain commands can be run, for example Ctrl+F9, which inserts an empty field. And still other shortcut keys are assigned to insert special characters that are not on the keyboard, for example Alt+Ctrl+C, which inserts a copyright symbol (©). Word gives you the power to change the predefined shortcut keys and to assign new shortcut keys to different commands, as well as assign shortcut keys to macros, fonts, AutoText, styles, and common symbols.

The following keys and combinations are available for making your own combinations:

- Function keys (except F1)

- Shift+any function key (except F1)

- Ctrl+any letter, number, or function key

- Ctrl+Shift+any letter, number, or function key

- Alt+Shift+any letter, number, or function key

- Alt+Ctrl+any letter, number, or function key

- Alt+Ctrl+Shift+any letter, number, or function key

TIP

Word provides special help for WordPerfect users who have switched to Word. For details, see "Setting Keys for Former WordPerfect Users," page 1029.

You use the Customize Keyboard dialog box, as shown in Figure D-1, to assign shortcut keys.

Changes to key assignments are recorded in templates. To make the changes available to all documents, store the changes in the Normal template. To limit the key assignments to a particular group of documents, store the changes in the template for those documents. Use the Save Changes In box in the Customize Keyboard dialog box to specify where the changes will be stored. Only the Normal template appears in the Save Changes In box unless a separate template is open or attached to the active document.

FIGURE D-1.
The Customize Key-
board dialog box.

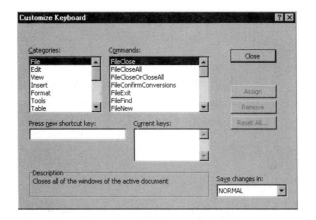

Change the Keyboard Layout in Windows

You cannot change the character assignment of individual standard keyboard keys in Word, but you can change the overall keyboard layout in Windows to another language or layout, such as British, Norwegian, or Dvorak. To change the layout, add a new language to those available, or change the properties for an available language, use the Language tab in the Keyboard Properties dialog box, which you access via the Control Panel.

Creating Key Assignments

You can assign a shortcut key to any Word command, macro, font, AutoText name, style, or common symbol. All assignments are made in the Customize Keyboard dialog box, where you select the command or other item and then press a unique key combination as the shortcut. If you assign a new command to a shortcut key that already has an assignment, the new assignment replaces the previous one.

You can use several methods to open the Customize Keyboard dialog box, and the content of the dialog box will differ depending on the method you use. If you choose the Tools Customize command and then click the Keyboard button, the dialog box will appear as shown in Figure D-1. You can then assign a shortcut key to any of the commands or other items that can be assigned a shortcut key. Other methods of opening the Customize Keyboard dialog box include those listed on the following page.

- Click the Keyboard button in the Record Macro dialog box. Word opens the Customize Keyboard dialog box and lists the current macro only.

- Click the Shortcut Key button in the New Style dialog box or the Modify Style dialog box. Word opens the Customize Keyboard dialog box and lists the style being defined only.

- Click the Shortcut Key button in the Symbol dialog box. Word opens the Customize Keyboard dialog box, lists only the category All Commands, and applies the key assignment only to the symbol you selected in the Symbol dialog box.

- Press Alt+Ctrl+plus sign (on the numeric keypad). Move the mouse pointer, which is now a command symbol (⌘), over a menu item or a toolbar button and click. Word opens the Customize Keyboard dialog box and lists only the command or item associated with the menu item or toolbar button you clicked.

Regardless of the method you use to open the Customize Keyboard dialog box, the method of assigning a shortcut key is basically the same (although in some cases the category or item is already selected by Word). To assign a shortcut key, begin by opening the Customize Keyboard dialog box, using one of the methods described previously. Then follow these steps:

1 Select a category.

2 Select the command (or other item).

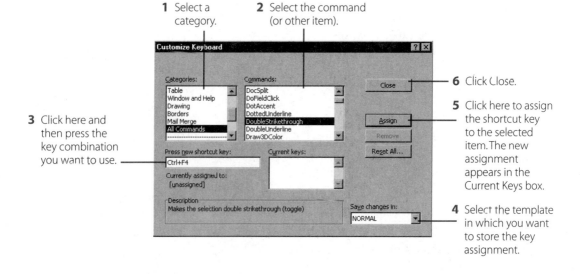

3 Click here and then press the key combination you want to use.

6 Click Close.

5 Click here to assign the shortcut key to the selected item. The new assignment appears in the Current Keys box.

4 Select the template in which you want to store the key assignment.

The new shortcut keys are immediately in effect and will be saved when the template is saved.

Customizing Keyboard Dialog Box Options

Take a closer look at the options available to you in the Customize Keyboard dialog box.

Categories Box

Similar to the parallel option for customizing toolbars, the Categories box lists groups of commands and items (with the addition of the Common Symbols category). See "Adding a New Button to a Toolbar," page 1001, for details. The Common Symbols category contains the symbols displayed on the Special Characters tab in the Symbol dialog box plus common non-English text characters.

Commands Box

The label on the Commands box changes depending on what is shown in the box. When you select other categories, the name of the category appears. Any shortcut keys currently assigned to the item appear in the Current Keys box.

Press New Shortcut Key Box

The shortcut key you type for the selected command or item appears in the Press New Shortcut Key box. You must click in this box to enter a shortcut key combination.

Current Keys Box

The current shortcut key assignment or assignments for the selected command or item, if there are any, appear in the Current Keys box. Shortcut key assignments can be removed by selecting them in this box and clicking the Remove button. (See "Removing Shortcut Keys," page 1028.)

Description Box

A message appears in the Description box to tell you the purpose of the selected command.

⚠ WARNING

When assigning shortcut keys, remember that Word has already assigned all the function keys and their variants, plus almost all Ctrl and Ctrl+Shift key combinations, as shortcut keys for performing Word actions and applying formatting. If you reassign one of these key combinations, you might be losing a very useful tool. Other than displaying the current assignment for a key combination in the Customize dialog box, Word does not warn you that you are wiping out the original shortcut key assignment.

Modifying Shortcut Key Assignments

From time to time you may find that you need to modify shortcut key assignments, depending on the types of documents or content you work with. In the Customize Keyboard dialog box, you can reassign shortcut keys, assign different shortcut keys to a command or item, or delete shortcut keys.

Reassigning Shortcut Keys

To reassign an existing shortcut key to another command or item, select the item, type the shortcut key in the Press New Shortcut Key box, and click the Assign button. The shortcut key is then assigned to the selected command or item, and the old assignment is canceled.

Removing Shortcut Keys

To remove a shortcut key without assigning it to another command or item, select the command or item, select the shortcut key in the Current Keys list, and click the Remove button.

Assigning Additional Shortcut Keys to a Single Action

To assign additional shortcut keys to a command or item, select the command or item, type the shortcut key in the Press New Shortcut Key box, and click the Assign button. The shortcut key is added to the Current Keys list. To replace the existing shortcut key instead of adding another, first delete the old shortcut key by selecting it in the Current Keys list, and then click the Remove button.

Using Multiple-Key Shortcut Combinations

Word has already assigned many of the available shortcut key combinations. To make more combinations available, and to enable you to group similar items with similar shortcut keys, Word allows you to use two key combinations in your key assignments. To group similar items, use the same initial key combination for all the items, with an additional letter key or key combination for specific items. For example, you might assign Alt+Ctrl+Shift+M as the initial key combination for all macros, and then assign an additional letter key to identify each specific macro. So the key combination Alt+Ctrl+Shift+M,A might be assigned to the macro AddTechnicalWords, and Alt+Ctrl+Shift+M,Q to the QuotationDesign macro.

To use the double-key combinations, hold down the modifying keys (the Alt, Ctrl, and Shift keys) and press the first key combination. Then release those keys and press the second key combination. For example, to use Alt+Ctrl+Shift+M,A, hold down Alt+Ctrl+Shift and press the M key, release those keys, and then press the A key. If you use a letter in the second key combination, you can make the second letter uppercase or lowercase; Word makes a distinction between the two. When you assign multiple-key shortcuts, be careful not to assign an initial key combination that is the same as a full-key combination used by another command or item, or you won't get the result you expect. The key assignment for the first item will be lost.

Resetting All Shortcut Key Assignments

If you no longer need any of the shortcut keys that you have assigned, you can reset all the key assignments by clicking the Reset All button. A dialog box appears that asks whether you're sure you want to remove all key assignments (those that were not preassigned by Word). Click Yes to reset or No to cancel. If you want the changes to apply only to a specific template, select that template in the Save Changes In box before clicking the Reset All button.

Setting Keys for Former WordPerfect Users

If you are a former WordPerfect user who has switched to Word, special help is available for you. Word provides changes to some keys so that they act the same in Word as they do in WordPerfect. In addition, Word provides special help or demonstrations for other WordPerfect for DOS key combinations.

To turn on the special features in Word for former WordPerfect users, choose the Tools Options command, click the General tab, and then follow these steps:

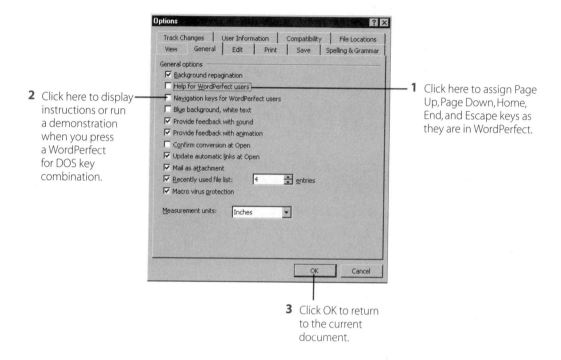

2 Click here to display instructions or run a demonstration when you press a WordPerfect for DOS key combination.

1 Click here to assign Page Up, Page Down, Home, End, and Escape keys as they are in WordPerfect.

3 Click OK to return to the current document.

When you turn on Navigation Keys For WordPerfect Users by itself (Help For WordPerfect Users is turned off), you will see WPN on the status bar when you return to the document. When you turn on Help For WordPerfect Users by itself (Navigation Keys For WordPerfect Users is turned off), you will see WPH on the status bar. When you turn on both boxes, you will see WP on the status bar. You can double-click any one of these labels on the status bar to see a Help for WordPerfect Users dialog box that shows you what key combinations in Word perform a function you used in WordPerfect.

Index

*Page numbers in italics refer
to tables, figures,
or illustrations.*

Colophon

The manuscript for this book was prepared and submitted to Microsoft Press in electronic form. Text files were prepared using Microsoft Word 95. Pages were composed using Corel Ventura 4.2 for Windows with text in Garamond and display type in Myriad. Composed pages were sent to the printer as electronic pre-press files.

Cover Art Direction
Gregory J. Erickson

Cover Graphic Design
Tim Girvin Design

Cover Illustration
Landor and Associates

Interior Graphic Design
designLab

Production Manager
Tory McLearn
   Labrecque Publishing Services

Layout Artist
Curtis Philips

Technical Editor
Terrence O'Donnell

Copy Editor
Judith Brown

Proofreader
Erin Milnes

Indexer
Rebecca Plunket

Keep things **running** smoothly around **the Office.**

These are *the* answer books for business users of Microsoft® Office 97 applications. They are packed with everything from quick, clear instructions for new users to comprehensive answers for power users. The Microsoft Press® *Running* series features authoritative handbooks you'll keep by your computer and use every day.

Running Microsoft® Excel 97
Mark Dodge, Chris Kinata, and Craig Stinson
U.S.A. $39.95   ($53.95 Canada)
ISBN 1-57231-321-8

Running Microsoft® Office 97
Michael Halvorson and Michael Young
U.S.A. $39.95   ($53.95 Canada)
ISBN 1-57231-322-6

Running Microsoft® Word 97
Russell Borland
U.S.A. $39.95   ($53.95 Canada)
ISBN 1-57231-320-X

Running Microsoft® PowerPoint® 97
Stephen W. Sagman
U.S.A. $29.95   ($39.95 Canada)
ISBN 1-57231-324-2

Running Microsoft® Access 97
John L. Viescas
U.S.A. $39.95   ($53.95 Canada)
ISBN 1-57231-323-4

Microsoft Press® products are available worldwide wherever quality computer books are sold. For more information, contact your book retailer, computer reseller, or local Microsoft Sales Office.

To locate your nearest source for Microsoft Press products, reach us at www.microsoft.com/mspress/, or call 1-800-MSPRESS in the U.S. (in Canada: 1-800-667-1115 or 416-293-8464).

To order Microsoft Press products, call 1-800-MSPRESS in the U.S. (in Canada: 1-800-667-1115 or 416-293-8464).

Prices and availability dates are subject to change.

Microsoft Press

Take productivity in stride.

Microsoft® Excel 97 Step by Step
U.S.A. $29.95   ($39.95 Canada)
ISBN 1-57231-314-5

Microsoft® Word 97 Step by Step
U.S.A. $29.95   ($39.95 Canada)
ISBN 1-57231-313-7

**Microsoft® PowerPoint® 97
  Step by Step**
U.S.A. $29.95   ($39.95 Canada)
ISBN 1-57231-315-3

Microsoft® Outlook™ 97 Step by Step
U.S.A. $29.99   ($39.99 Canada)
ISBN 1-57231-382-X

Microsoft® Access 97 Step by Step
U.S.A. $29.95   ($39.95 Canada)
ISBN 1-57231-316-1

**Microsoft® Office 97 Integration
  Step by Step**
U.S.A. $29.95   ($39.95 Canada)
ISBN 1-57231-317-X

Microsoft Press® *Step by Step* books provide quick and easy self-paced training that will help you learn to use the powerful word processor, spreadsheet, database, desktop information manager and presentation applications of Microsoft Office 97, both individually and together. Prepared by the professional trainers at Catapult, Inc., and Perspection, Inc., these books present easy-to-follow lessons with clear objectives, real-world business examples, and numerous screen shots and illustrations. Each book contains approximately eight hours of instruction. Put Microsoft's Office 97 applications to work today, *Step by Step.*

Microsoft Press® products are available worldwide wherever quality computer books are sold. For more information, contact your book retailer, computer reseller, or local Microsoft Sales Office.

To locate your nearest source for Microsoft Press products, reach us at www.microsoft.com/mspress/, or call 1-800-MSPRESS in the U.S. (in Canada: 1-800-667-1115 or 416-293-8464).

To order Microsoft Press products, call 1-800-MSPRESS in the U.S. (in Canada: 1-800-667-1115 or 416-293-8464).

Prices and availability dates are subject to change.

***Microsoft*Press**

Get quick, easy answers—anywhere!

Microsoft® Excel 97 Field Guide
Stephen L. Nelson
U.S.A.   **$9.95**   ($12.95 Canada)
ISBN: 1-57231-326-9

Microsoft® Word 97 Field Guide
Stephen L. Nelson
U.S.A.   **$9.95**   ($12.95 Canada)
ISBN: 1-57231-325-0

Microsoft® PowerPoint® 97 Field Guide
Stephen L. Nelson
U.S.A.   **$9.95**   ($12.95 Canada)
ISBN: 1-57231-327-7

Microsoft® Outlook™ 97 Field Guide
Stephen L. Nelson
U.S.A.   **$9.99**   ($12.99 Canada)
ISBN: 1-57231-383-8

Microsoft® Access 97 Field Guide
Stephen L. Nelson
U.S.A.   **$9.95**   ($12.95 Canada)
ISBN: 1-57231-328-5

Microsoft Press® Field Guides are a quick, accurate source of information about Microsoft® Office 97 applications. In no time, you'll have the lay of the land, identify toolbar buttons and commands, stay safely out of danger, and have all the tools you need for survival!

Microsoft Press® products are available worldwide wherever quality computer books a.e sold. For more information, contact your book retailer, computer reseller, or local Microsoft Sales Office.

To locate your nearest source for Microsoft Press products, reach us at www.microsoft.com/mspress/, or call 1-800-MSPRESS in the U.S. (in Canada: 1-800-667-1115 or 416-293-8464).

To order Microsoft Press products, call 1-800-MSPRESS in the U.S. (in Canada: 1-800-667-1115 or 416-293-8464).

Prices and availability dates are subject to change.

Microsoft·Press

Things are looking up!

Here's the remarkable, *visual* way to quickly find answers about the powerfully integrated features of the Microsoft® Office 97 applications. Microsoft Press® *At a Glance* books let you focus on particular tasks and show you with clear, numbered steps the easiest way to get them done right now.

Microsoft® Excel 97 At a Glance
Perspection, Inc.
U.S.A. **$16.95**   ($22.95 Canada)
ISBN: 1-57231-367-6

Microsoft® Word 97 At a Glance
Jerry Joyce and Marianne Moon
U.S.A. **$16.95**   ($22.95 Canada)
ISBN: 1-57231-366-8

Microsoft® PowerPoint® 97 At a Glance
Perspection, Inc.
U.S.A. **$16.95**   ($22.95 Canada)
ISBN: 1-57231-368-4

Microsoft® Access 97 At a Glance
Perspection, Inc.
U.S.A. **$16.95**   ($22.95 Canada)
ISBN: 1-57231-369-2

Microsoft® Office 97 At a Glance
Perspection, Inc.
U.S.A. **$16.95**   ($22.95 Canada)
ISBN: 1-57231-365-X

Microsoft® Windows® 95 At a Glance
Jerry Joyce and Marianne Moon
U.S.A. **$16.95**   ($22.95 Canada)
ISBN: 1-57231-370-6

Microsoft Press® products are available worldwide wherever quality computer books are sold. For more information, contact your book retailer, computer reseller, or local Microsoft Sales Office.

To locate your nearest source for Microsoft Press products, reach us at www.microsoft.com/mspress/, or call 1-800-MSPRESS in the U.S. (in Canada: 1-800-667-1115 or 416-293-8464).

To order Microsoft Press products, call 1-800-MSPRESS in the U.S. (in Canada: 1-800-667-1115 or 416-293-8464).

Prices and availability dates are subject to change.

Microsoft Press

Register Today!

Return this
Running Microsoft® Word 97
registration card for
a Microsoft Press® catalog

U.S. and Canada addresses only. Fill in information below and mail postage-free. Please mail only the bottom half of this page.

1-57231-320-XA   *RUNNING MICROSOFT® WORD 97*   *Owner Registration Card*

_____

NAME

_____

INSTITUTION OR COMPANY NAME

_____

ADDRESS

_____

_____

CITY   STATE   ZIP

Microsoft®*Press*
Quality Computer Books

For a free catalog of
Microsoft Press® products, call
1-800-MSPRESS

BUSINESS REPLY MAIL
FIRST-CLASS MAIL   PERMIT NO. 53   BOTHELL, WA

POSTAGE WILL BE PAID BY ADDRESSEE

MICROSOFT PRESS REGISTRATION
RUNNING MICROSOFT® WORD 97
PO BOX 3019
BOTHELL   WA   98041-9946